MEMOIRS OF WILLIAM HICKEY

William Hickey in middle life, by Thomas Hickey: originally thought
to be a portrait of the elder Joseph Hickey.

By courtesy of the National Gallery of Ireland

MEMOIRS

of

WILLIAM HICKEY

Edited by
PETER QUENNELL

HUTCHINSONS OF LONDON

HUTCHINSON & CO (*Publishers*) LTD
178–202 Great Portland Street, London W.1

London Melbourne Sydney
Auckland Bombay Toronto
Johannesburg New York

★

First published 1960

*This book has been set in Linotype Caledonia. It has
been printed in Great Britain by William Clowes and
Sons Ltd, London and Beccles, on smooth wove paper
and bound by them*

CONTENTS

ILLUSTRATIONS

PREFACE

D URING the winter of the year 1808, a new inhabitant appeared
in the little Buckinghamshire town of Beaconsfield—a retired
lawyer named William Hickey, who, having long practised his
profession with considerable advantage at the Indian bar, had recently,
much against his will, been obliged to give up his practice and return
to England, when the iron constitution on which he prided himself at
length showed signs of breaking down. No doubt, like most of his fellow
nabobs, Hickey had a yellow ravaged face. Otherwise, considering his
age—he had been born in 1749—he must have presented, to judge
from his last portrait, an energetic and commanding figure, with his
smooth dark wig, his brass-buttoned coat, his buckskin breeches and
his top boots. The new arrival's immediate household consisted of a
pair of elderly unmarried sisters, his favourite Indian servant Munnoo
and a large parti-coloured English dog.

Originally, he had taken a house in the town. Then, at Michaelmas
1809, he moved to a "pretty cottage called Little Hall Barn . . . the
property of Edmund Waller, Esquire, a lineal descendant of the celebrated poet . . . which premises were adjoining to and part of his own
magnificent seat of Hall Barn." Here he passed his time pleasantly
enough, "going in rotation (he tells us) to the houses of different
friends, and usually running up to London once in six weeks or there-
abouts. . . ." At home, he cultivated his garden or walked and rode
around the country; and, despite gloomy prognostications as to the
effect of the English climate upon his "shattered and debilitated
frame," he found that, even in the coldest weather, it was seldom
necessary to wear an overcoat. He still suffered, however, from the
agonizing headaches that had begun to trouble him before he left the
East, and, now and then, from "comparatively slight attacks of my old
disagreeable nervous sensations, that are not easily described, but
exceedingly distressing to those afflicted with them." Luckily, there
was an intelligent doctor at hand, who rendered "the most affectionate
assistance. . . ."

A sensible, apparently harmonious life; yet after a while he grew
dissatisfied and melancholic. At Beaconsfield, Hickey explains, a
"trifling" place "with a very limited society," he soon "experienced the
truth of an observation I had frequently heard—viz. that want of
employment is one of the greatest miseries that can be attached to a

mind not altogether inactive." From the tedium of the present day his thoughts turned towards the adventures of the past—his "strange and variegated" career and the "extraordinary scenes" that he had gone through; and it occurred to him tha the might "fill a painful vacuum and beguile a few hours on those days when confined to the house either from bad weather, or indisposition," by setting his memories in order and writing down his life-story. The writer's hopes were extremely modest. Such a record, he imagined, could not be "in any way interesting to those unacquainted with me, and indeed, not very much so even to my most attached friends." He was writing, he assures us, solely for his own amusement. But, as his hand travelled across the paper, this casual pastime seems to have become an all-engrossing occupation. Before he abruptly abandoned his narrative, having carried it on to the year 1810, he had produced a gigantic manuscript volume, which contains over seven hundred and forty closely written folio pages. Neat coloured sketches were inserted here and there—drawings of a native boat and of two of the author's houses, together with an elegantly designed map.

The *Memoirs of William Hickey* is one of the most remarkable books of its kind ever published in the English language; for not only does Hickey draw an incomparably vivid self-portrait—at least as vivid and entertaining as that designed by James Boswell—but he gives us a brilliant panoramic impression of English society during the reign of George III, against a background both of England itself and our national outposts overseas. The hero of the story is a Prodigal Son, who redeems his character and makes good. More than once, as a boy and a young man, Hickey's outrageous conduct had nearly broken his indulgent father's heart. Thus, at the age of seventeen, while employed in the family law firm, he had raised money by cooking the office ledgers; and not long afterwards, having been entrusted with a substantial banker's draft, he had realized the proceeds, fallen into bad company, got helplessly drunk and had his pocket picked. His first lapse had involved the elder Hickey in a loss of "near five hundred pounds," which his son had purloined during the course of seven months and immediately squandered upon fast living. "Disgrace deservedly followed: my father declared himself at a loss how to act, or what to do with me." But not until he had made his second mis-step did Joseph Hickey reach the limits of his patience and decide that William must be shipped abroad, to seek his fortune, as so many others had done, in the service of the rich East India Company. At the age of nineteen, therefore, leaving behind him his devoted mistress Fanny Hartford—an expensive *demi-mondaine*, who had been doing her best to keep him away from worse companions—Hickey set sail in the *Plassey* and, after an adventurous five months' voyage, reached

Madras, where he was expected to serve, early in May 1769. But his new position failed to please him; as a cadet, he was intended to become an officer in the East India Company's armed forces; and he now discovered that the pay he would receive was "too contemptible to afford the common necessaries of life"; while prospects of early promotion seemed at the moment to be unusually poor. He thereupon decided to return home, again upon the friendly *Plassey*, although the captain's next destination was the port of Canton. Hickey enjoyed his visit to China, from which he finally set sail in December 1769. By the end of April 1770, he had once more crossed his father's threshold and was listening to a painful homily; "my father addressed me very gravely and truly, representing the enormous expense incurred in equipping me for the East Indies, the whole of which was wantonly thrown away. . . ."

Another effort to dispose of the Prodigal was made during the autumn of 1775, Hickey having relapsed into his old courses, and appropriated and squandered large sums of his father's money; and he was sent off to practise the law in Jamaica, where he much enjoyed the social pleasures of the island, but very soon managed to convince himself that he could never hope to earn a decent income. . . . From this point the reformed rake may be allowed to tell his own tale, which he does without a touch of false shame, despite many expressions of remorse and sorrow; and we must turn to Hickey's character and to the circumstances that helped to shape his life. Joseph Hickey was of Irish descent, and had been educated at the University of Dublin. But he had quitted Ireland at an early age—"in consequence (William explains) of throwing a leaden inkstand at his master's head"—and had applied for advice to a family friend, the respectable Mr. Bourke, father of Edmund Burke, with whose assistance, five years later, he was "admitted as an Attorney of the Court of King's Bench, and a Solicitor of the Court of Chancery." Henceforward he steadily improved his position; and by the time William was born—he was his parents' eighth child—Joseph Hickey had achieved a high degree of affluence. In St. Albans Street, just off Pall Mall, he possessed a large and comfortable London house; and at Twickenham, we are told, he had lately "built and completed a handsome spacious mansion . . . upon the margin of the Thames . . . commanding a charming prospect, particularly of Richmond Hill and Park." Servants and equipages were numerous; and, like his son after him, Joseph Hickey was fond of entertaining. Among his closest friends were the Burkes, through whom he had been introduced into Samuel Johnson's private circle. Sir Joshua Reynolds painted his portrait and produced delightful pictures of two of the Misses Hickey; and Oliver Goldsmith, in *The Retaliation*, portrays him as an habitué of a well-known literary club—a "most blunt, pleasant creature," who cherished his friends and relished his wine, though his bluntness and outspokenness seem sometimes to have annoyed the poet. In a supplement to *The Retaliation*, published in 1778, Richard Cumberland adds that the good-natured lawyer had a generous appetite for whiskey-punch.

Such was the parent from whom William Hickey inherited his gusto and abounding physical vigour. But he was also a typical product of his age, so far as any gifted man can be considered typical of the period that gives him birth, and belonged to a section of society that played an important part in eighteenth-century England. The world William Hickey describes is that of the rising upper middle class, sophisticated, rich, extravagant, devoted to social life and the pleasures of the table, yet distinguished by its love of elegance and by a deep regard for art and learning—a world that Zoffany portrays in his unequalled conversation pieces. True, Hickey himself was neither a scholar nor a dilettante. But, granted his limitations, he had some of the characteristics of an eighteenth-century Man of Taste. At least, wherever he found it, he valued quality and appreciated style, enjoyed colour, admired neatness of design and liked everything about him to be substantial, trim and ship-shape—the craft he sailed, the carriages he used, the equipment of the beautifully appointed rooms where he and his friends sat down to dinner, if possible with the noblest clarets and the most expensive and expertly prepared dishes. Among his favourite epithets of praise are "magnificent," "capital," "choice" and "fine"; and, although he was never averse from sharing the frolics of the London mob—in the brothels, taverns and "night cellars" that flourished around Covent Garden—he also prided himself, at soberer times, of moving in the "best company," not so much because he was a social climber as because it gratified his sense of fitness, and accorded with his private conception of how an English gentleman ought to pass his days. That he was a gentleman, by temperament and breeding, at no juncture did he feel the smallest doubt.

Here perhaps he may have been unduly sanguine: Joseph Hickey was a self-made man, and William exhibits some of the failings of a rich careerist's spoiled and dissipated son. Thus he had a passion for gaudy clothes, which now and then he lacked the courage to exhibit; and, despite the fact that he was not a little proud of his aristocratic boon companions, it is obvious that he usually met them in public and seldom encountered them beneath their own roofs. Charles James Fox was a close contemporary; but, notwithstanding the similarity of their tastes, they did not frequent the same houses or get drunk at the same London clubs. Yet Hickey seems to have felt no desire to rise in the contemporary social scale. He enjoyed the world into which he had been born, and was greatly attached to the metropolitan underworld.

At an early age he had begun to cut a dash in the higher circles of the *demi-monde*, where, even as a boy, he was petted and indulged by some of the more celebrated kept women of the age. Never once did he court a fashionable beauty; and only on one occasion do we hear of him engaged in the pursuit of a respectable girl—the offspring of Thomas Malton, a worthy drawing-master, who detected Hickey's subversive intentions and presently drove the young man from his home.

For Hickey was an unscrupulous amorist. Yet unquestionably he was also a Man of Feeling. Although he hoodwinked his friend Mordaunt, profiting by Mordaunt's folly to seduce the mistress he adored, and did not scruple during her protector's absence to sleep with Bob Pott's beloved Emily—regardless of his romantic affection for Pott, the dearest friend he ever made—it is evident that he had a genuinely affectionate nature, and that he was "sentimental" in the eighteenth-century meaning of that nowadays much mis-used adjective. He loved the parent he cheated; and to hurt his father caused him acute pain. He was glad, he tells us—and we may take his word for it—that at the last moment his intrigue had miscarried and that he failed to get his way with Ann Malton. Finally, after years of dissipation, his heart came to rest upon a single object. Charlotte Barry, whom he had stolen from Mordaunt, a *demi-mondaine* "then in high vogue," became the greatest passion of his whole existence. She refused to accept his offer of marriage but consented to assume his name; and in 1782, when Hickey was thirty-two, the happily united pair embarked for India. There she died in 1783. "Safely may I say (the elderly author writes) I truly, fondly loved her, loved her with an affection that every new day, if possible, strengthened." The loss of Charlotte cut short his youth; her place in his emotions was never to be filled.

So far we have considered William Hickey as a not unrepresentative product of his social period. But just as interesting are some of the problems raised by an examination of his remarkable literary talent. How did this boisterous, hard-living attorney, who, during his youth, had paid little attention to books, succeed himself in writing a book that deserves to be ranked among the most memorable efforts of its kind? Where did he acquire the skill to breathe life into the accumulated records of his past? If there is such a thing as a born storyteller, Hickey must have been one. He does not, of course, write well in the sense that he writes correct English: the same syntactical mistakes are repeated again and again; and he has a repertory of hackneyed turns of phrase, which regularly recur as his narrative rolls along. Nevertheless, in a somewhat different sense, he is a master of his literary medium. He peoples his stage with men and women whom the reader finds that he can never quite forget—Bob Pott, the handsome "pickle boy," a showy, arrogant, facetious young man, though in Hickey he seems to have inspired a devotion that was half-romantic: Henry Mordaunt, Pott's antithesis, coarse, sullen, cantankerous as Bob was gay, generous and easy-going: William Cane, a faithful ally, whose good-natured prodigality was afterwards to prove his downfall: Emily Warren, lovely and volatile but frigid: the exquisite Charlotte Barry, who sacrificed wealth and health to follow her lover into eastern exile, where she died calling down blessings on Hickey for the happiness that he had brought her. All are brilliantly characterized; all, as Hickey describes them, address us in their own words.

Hickey has a masterly gift both of unfolding a story and of equipping it with realistic detail. What could be more expressive, for example, than his account of the plight in which he discovered himself when he had got drunk, fallen among thieves and awoken with almost empty pockets:

> "My first return of sense or recollection was upon waking in a strange, dismal-looking room, my head aching horridly, pains of a violent nature in every limb, and deadly sickness at the stomach. . . . Getting out of bed, I looked out of the only window in the room, but saw nothing but the backs of old houses, from which various miserable emblems of poverty were displayed, such as ragged shifts, petticoats, and other parts of female wardrobes hanging to dry. . . . I rung a bell I found in the room for the purpose of ascertaining where I had got to. . . . No one answered until I had three or four times repeated my application to the bell rope, when at last a yawning man, who seemed half asleep, made his appearance, immediately exclaiming, 'Good God, how drunk and riotous you was, Sir! I never saw anything to equal it.'"

No less conspicuous is Hickey's gift of remembering and reporting dialogue. Mordaunt's blackguard outbursts are wonderfully well conveyed; and just as convincing are the utterances of sailors, landlords, smugglers, constables, sharpers, strumpets, bullies. The language he puts into their mouths possesses a Shakespearian breadth and freedom; but it is interesting to note that, in his more sentimental passages, he employs the diction of the high-flown contemporary novel, and that Joseph Hickey, if particularly shocked and offended, always uses the style of an injured parent in one of the popular romances of the day:

> "William, I lament that you should once more have deceived and disappointed me. . . . But I have observed that plans fondly laid by parents for their children very early in life are seldom or never made effectual. It has pleased an all-wise providence to heap upon me accumulated afflictions; but God's will be done; it is as much my

duty as my inclination humbly to bow to these visitations. . . . And now leave me; I feel too weak and exhausted to say more."

This, presumably, is how Hickey thought that he recollected his father speaking, or how he felt he should have spoken; but one suspects that Joseph Hickey's reproof was delivered in a much more forthright manner. Yet occasional literary touches do not detract from the general air of verisimilitude. Hickey's picture of eighteenth-century society can stand comparison with those drawn by Boswell and Walpole; and then, having fixed his impressions of the rowdy, vigorous England he had known—its festivities, its resplendent clothes, its rich domestic interiors, its middle-class splendour and its infamous proletarian squalor—he goes on to depict the eastern territories, to which England was then indebted for a large proportion of her national wealth. Hickey gives us many unflattering glimpses of English adventurers in the Indian promised land—that receptacle of "undone heroes," where the spendthrift son, the ruined gambler, the broken rake and the impoverished dandy gathered to recoup their fortunes, often dying of fever or dysentery, but sometimes surviving to reap prodigious rewards. Unlike their immediate predecessors, they made no concessions to the Indian climate—they wore heavy laced uniforms, curled and powdered wigs, skin-tight breeches and tight polished boots. Nor did they often trouble to acquire the usage of a native tongue. Bob Pott, it is true, had some knowledge of the Indian dialects; but Hickey seems to have learned no more than was sufficient to give his host of menials their appropriate orders.

These are the pictures he evokes with unassuming, unself-conscious art. But now we have to decide just what his original sources were: how far he relied on memory, and whether, now and then, he may not have been assisted by imagination. According to his own preface, he had "few documents" to guide him, and "scarcely any memorandum whatever. . . ." Elsewhere, having described the terrific hurricane of 1782, in which, on their way out to India, he and Charlotte, now "Mrs. Hickey," very nearly lost their lives, he remarks that the whole contents of his escritoire was "completely destroyed" apart from three letters that he had put into a leather pocket-book, and that "what I lamented above everything else . . . was the loss of a large book in which I had copied the journals of every voyage I had made. . . ." Yet a comparison between Hickey's narrative and the log book of the *Plassey* for December 1768, now preserved in the Library of the India Office, shows that, although Hickey made mistakes, they were not, at least from a modern reader's point of view, particularly serious errors. He frequently mis-dates a landfall by a week or ten days; a wind is described as blowing from the wrong quarter; Anthony King, the ship's carpenter, who died of a violent cramp, is mis-named Peter King, in Hickey's tale. But both series of entries evidently deal with the same voyage; and the errors are of the kind that we might any of us commit while casually keeping up a diary, often several days after the events recorded.

Similarly, the text of the petition to the House of Commons that Hickey brought home in 1780, on behalf of "British Subjects residing in the Provinces of Bengal, Bahar and Orissa, and their several Dependencies," can still be examined among the "House of Commons Journals," and corroborates, as do independent historians, Hickey's version of his friends' dispute with the tyrannical Lord Chief Justice, Sir Elijah Impey. There can be no doubt, I think, that William Hickey was, in the main, a conscientious reporter of fact. It is, none the less, difficult to understand how, if all his written records had been destroyed in 1782, he should have been able to recollect so clearly, and with so many vivid supplementary details, the experiences that he had enjoyed thirty or forty years earlier. Such a feat of memory has rarely been equalled; and yet, in some mysterious fashion, Hickey seems to have accomplished it. One concludes that he must have possessed phenomenal powers of recollection, and that they were further strengthened by the effect of the somewhat lonely life he led at Beaconsfield, where, inactive and sick of the present day, his mind was driven back upon its own resources.

* * *

Hickey's *Memoirs*, in their manuscript form, cover seven hundred and forty-two pages, with seldom less than seventy lines to the page. From this impressive total of words, the substance of four volumes was extracted between 1913, when the first volume appeared under the editorship of Mr. Alfred Spencer, and 1925, when the last was published under the same editorship. It has now been determined to present his autobiography in a single volume; and for that purpose we have thought it best to break off the narrative with Charlotte's death at the year 1783—a crucial point in the story of Hickey's career, after which he gradually discarded some of the traits of his impulsive youth. Never again would he love so passionately; henceforward, indeed, he seems to have avoided violent passions. Charlotte's loss temporarily deadened his senses; and, once he had begun to regain vitality, he was content with more prosaic loves—an Indian favourite, whom he was forced to dismiss, having caught her in flagrant delight with one of his own native servants, and her successor, the devoted Jemdanee, an amusing and good-tempered companion, known as "Fatty" to his masculine friends. But Jemdanee, "as gentle and affectionately attached a girl as ever man was blessed with," died in 1796; and the son she had borne him, "a lovely child," followed her some nine months later. Meanwhile his professional existence went on profitably from year to year. He received various lucrative employments, including the posts of Under-Sheriff and Clerk to the Chief Justice, moved in the best company, gave successful parties and drank as hard as his shaken health permitted. By the time Hickey said good-bye to Bengal he was keeping a household of sixty-three servants, had five horses to dispose of, besides "furniture, plate, jewellery, paintings and engravings, books, a billiards table, chamber organ, a stock of the best liqueurs," a buggy "finished in the first style" and a "very elegant chair palankeen," and had accumulated a personal fortune that amounted to one hundred and forty-nine thousand, one hundred and eighty-nine sicca rupees, the sicca rupee then being valued at the rate of two and sixpence.

It was not an enormous fortune by Anglo-Indian standards, but enough to keep him in moderate comfort for the remainder of his days. Exactly how he spent them we do not know, after he had completed the composition of his *Memoirs*; but it would appear that he presently moved to London, where his sisters, Sarah and Ann, died in 1824 and 1826 respectively. The date of his own death is uncertain; but a William Hickey died at Little King Street on 31st May 1830, and was buried in St. Pancras Churchyard. As for the huge manuscript he had been carrying around with him, it came—possibly by the author's gift —into the possession of a Captain Montagu Montagu of the Royal Navy, who bequeathed the book to his nephew, Colonel Horace Montagu of the 8th Hussars; from whom, when he died in 1910, it was inherited by the later Major Robert Poore, whose descendants today preserve it among the archives of their family. An inscription records that the huge vellum-bound volume was presented to Major Poore by Colonel Montagu's sister in remembrance of an "old old friend. . . ."

The manuscript, finely and, for the most part, neatly written, contains astonishingly few corrections, has no chapter-headings and is divided into very long paragraphs. Here the text has been re-paragraphed and the spelling modernized; and many extensive passages have necessarily been omitted. Not, however, in the interests of propriety. The original editor considered that numerous episodes were entirely unfit for publication; and, in addition to removing lengthy sections, he occasionally toned down a too explicit phrase. The modern reading public is undoubtedly less prudish than that of 1913 or even of 1925; and, despite Hickey's school-boyish predilection for offensive scatological jokes, in his treatment of sexual subjects he is remarkably frank but not deliberately salacious. Boswell's detailed descriptions of his love-affairs are generally very much more coarse; for Boswell, a confirmed neurotic, was always doubtful of his amatory gifts, whereas Hickey felt no doubt that he was an uncommonly virile and attractive man, and knew that the pleasure he gave was in proportion to the pleasure he received.

The author of *Abinger Harvest* has provided Hickey with a carefully balanced epitaph. First, he praises his dispassionate candour and freedom from any sort of conventional humbug: Hickey was never "pretentious or insincere . . . never regretted or repented or said 'I have lived' or 'I have served England in my little way.' . . . How pleasant it would be to have met him. . . ." And yet, Mr. Forster goes on, "how strange it is to realize that one has often met him and fled from him. For he must be reincarnate today in many a smoking room, many an overseas club. . . ." With the final sentences of this summing-up I feel obliged to disagree. Although in certain respects he may represent the type of the *homme moyen sensuel*, although his view of the world was somewhat limited and his personal ambitions were by no means exalted, he possessed one outstanding characteristic that lifted him high above his kind—a gift not only of attracting adventures but of turning them to intellectual profit. He did not merely take refuge amid dreams of the past as other elderly adventurers have done; he re-lived his youth so vividly and intensely that the act of recollection absorbed his whole being. Hence the peculiar quality of his work. Hickey's *Memoirs* may bear some resemblance to a brilliant picaresque novel; but their fascination is far more lasting since they produce a much deeper sense of life. Hickey, we understand, was a man who had always loved life; his autobiography is an extraordinarily vital production, even in the latter pages when his gusto at length begins to flag; and it is the sense of life it evokes, rather than the story it tells, that gives a book its permanent literary value.

PETER QUENNELL

I

BIRTH AND CHILDHOOD

RETURNING from a very busy and laborious life, in India, to comparatively absolute idleness, in England, and having fixed my abode in a country village, with a very limited society, I there experienced the truth of an observation I had frequently heard —viz. that want of employment is one of the greatest miseries that can be attached to a mind not altogether inactive. Feeling the full force of the foregoing remark, my thoughts turned to the strange and variegated life I had passed, and the extraordinary scenes I had gone through in different quarters of the world; in contemplating which it occurred to me that I might in some measure fill up a painful vacuum and beguile a few hours on those days when confined to the house either from bad weather, or indisposition, by committing to writing the different events that had happened to me during a period of nearly sixty years.

True it is I had few documents to guide me, and scarcely any memorandum whatever to assist in the execution of such a plan, at least for the early and greater part of my life; yet, trusting to memory alone, I felt convinced I could trace back the most material circumstances that had happened respecting myself; and I can safely aver, there is not a single fact recorded in the following sheets, that is not, to the best of my knowledge and belief, most truly and correctly stated. Equally true it is, and I am perfectly aware of it, that such a production cannot be in any way interesting to those unacquainted with me, and indeed, not very much so even to my most attached friends. Besides, there are many low and indelicate anecdotes related, and many gross and filthy expressions used, by no means suited to meet the eye of any chaste person, and, of course, not at all adapted for critical disquisition. Should, however, those pages at any time fall into the hands of strangers, be it remembered, that I retraced the following circumstances of my life, solely for my own amusement, and to fill up some tedious hours that would otherwise have hung heavy upon my hands.

I was born in St. Albans Street, Pall Mall, in the Parish of St. James, Westminster, on 30th June 1749, being the seventh child my parents had.* My father was the youngest son of a numerous family, all Irish sprung from a very ancient and honourable stock, being of Milesian descent; the original name was O'Hickey, at what period the "O" was dropped I never heard, nor is it of any importance.

My mother, whose maiden name was Boulton, was of a very old and highly respectable family, who for several centuries resided in Yorkshire, where they possessed considerable landed property. My father and mother's was a love match, against the consent of her relations, as he ran away from his friends in Ireland at the early age of seventeen, being then an articled clerk to an attorney in Cashell, in consequence of throwing a leaden inkstand at his master's head, the said master having, as my father conceived, wantonly and grossly insulted him. He was not overburdened with cash at the time he reached the capital of Great Britain, but he had received the best of education, having been brought up in the University of Dublin, where he had the character of being an uncommonly good classical scholar. The gentleman he had been articled to was an eminent attorney practising in the City of Cashell, the town in which my father was born. Upon his arrival in London he applied to, and was most kindly received by a Mr. Bourke, then residing at Plaistow, in Essex, where he carried on business as an attorney and solicitor, with much credit and advantage to himself. This respectable gentleman was the father of Mr. William Burke, an intimate friend of my family's who subsequently made a conspicuous figure in public life.

With Mr. Bourke, of Plaistow, who chose to retain the "o" in his name, as being the original way of spelling it, my father served a regular clerkship, and at the expiration of his five years was admitted as attorney of the Court of King's Bench, and a solicitor of the Court of Chancery. My father's abilities and respectable connection soon procured him abundant business; but, being naturally of a convivial and expensive turn, he was sometimes hard pressed in pecuniary matters, and I have often heard him say that when he married, which took place after but a short courtship, he had no more than five guineas in his possession, and was obliged to furnish a house, and procure all the requisite establishment of a family man, upon credit; of course he felt all the inconveniences and embarrassments arising from such a situation, but never lost his spirits, nor was he ever, even at that early period, nor through the whole course of a very long life driven to commit a dishonourable or ungentlemanlike action.

When married only a few months, he dined with a large party at

* Hickey had evidently forgotten the brother "that lived only a few hours": see below.

the King's Arms tavern in Pall Mall, where, after the whole party had drank freely, it was, at a late hour, proposed to adjourn to the Ridotto, at the opera house, where it was then the custom to have public hazard tables. When the going to the Ridotto was first mentioned, my father observed to his friend Colonel Mathews, of the Guards, who sat next to him, that he could not be of the party, as after paying his proportion of the dinner bill, he should have only a few shillings left, whereupon Colonel Mathews took out his purse, and counted the amount therein, which was twenty-four guineas; of these he gave twelve to my father saying, they would play in partnership, and if fortune was kind, whatever both, or either won should be deemed joint stock, and be equally divided between them. Upon these terms they proceeded to the opera house, where my father having in a few minutes lost his twelve guineas, went and stood at the back of Colonel Mathews's chair, who threw so successfully that by four o'clock in the morning he had collected nearly the whole amount of cash at the table, upon which they adjourned to my father's house in Gerard Street, Soho, and there actually divided upwards of three thousand two hundred guineas, each having sixteen hundred and odd to his share. This sum laid the foundation of my father's fortune. He immediately paid everyone to whom he was indebted; and after having so done a surplus of several hundred pounds remained.

Soon after this circumstance had occurred, my eldest sister, Mary, was born, being the first child. In due time another came forth who died in early infancy. Next my brother Joseph, who in eleven months was followed by a boy that lived only a few hours; next, my brother Henry; and within the two next years, two others, who both died young. Then I made my appearance, that is to say, on 30th June 1749.

My god-fathers were the above-named Colonel Mathews and Mr. Ryan, proprietor of the King's Arms tavern in Pall Mall, then a very fashionable house, in which he (Ryan) acquired a very large fortune. I was soon pronounced a most lovely child. My mother had suckled the first three infants herself, but this being deemed prejudicial to her health, she was forbid continuing it, and I was therefore sent to be nursed at Hampstead, at a clean and neat cottage, the property of a respectable old woman named Page, from the breast of whose daughter, Ann Page, (for she had married a person of her own name) I drew my first nourishment. Ann Page was an uncommonly beautiful creature, who almost adored me. I have a faint recollection when between three and four years of age, of my brother Joseph's being highly offended by her kissing a certain substantial part of my body, at the same time telling him, that she had much rather kiss my posterior than his face.

At Hampstead I remained until nearly four years old, when my first breeches were put on, and I was then taken away from my dearly loved, "sweet Ann Page," the separation from whom wrung my little heart with the first sorrow it ever felt; nor did I ever forget her extreme affection for me. At the time I thus quitted the arms of my darling nurse, I was reckoned an uncommonly beautiful boy, and I presume not without reason, for I perfectly well remember being frequently stopped in the park, and in the streets, by females of all sorts, who rapturously kissed me, with exclamations of surprise at my extraordinary beauty. I may now without vanity speak of my infantine perfections as to features, all such having long since passed away, for since reaching my fourteenth year I became as ugly a fellow as need be.

My god-fathers were both greatly attached to me, especially Mr. Ryan, who, as well as his wife, would willingly have had me constantly with them; and, as my father, previous to my birth had removed into St. Albans Street, I was frequently at the King's Arms, sometimes with consent, often without; for although peremptorily forbid ever to go out alone, least any accident should befall me, I nevertheless used to watch my opportunity of finding the street door open, and away I darted fast as my little legs would carry me to Pall Mall, where I knew I should be permitted to do whatever I pleased, and where I was a pet of every individual in the house, besides which, I was often noticed and caressed by the first people of the kingdom. It was not however at my god-father Ryan's only that I was too much indulged, for I was a universal favourite; and it is therefore not to be wondered at that I became in some measure a spoiled child. My father at the time of my coming into the world had got into immense practice in his profession, having the honour of being consulted and employed by many of the nobility, and persons of the most exalted rank in society. He lived expensively, seeing much company, keeping a carriage and several saddle horses, and having a handsome country house at Twickenham.

With all my father's friends and acquaintances I was a great favourite; his military friends declaring I must be a soldier, while those of the navy insisted upon that line being the best adapted to such a volatile and high-spirited boy as I was. By the time I was five years of age, I got the nickname of *Pickle*, a name I fear I have through life proved to have been but too well applied. My father's own wish respecting me was that I should be brought up to the Law, to qualify me for which profession, he intended to give me the best of education, and in due time have me called to the Bar, where he was pleased to say from the quickness of my parts, and excellent talents, he was convinced I should make a conspicuous figure. But, alas, through life it has been my misfortune, or more properly speaking, my fault, to mar and disappoint all his views, his kind and generous intentions respecting me.

This tendency first betrayed itself when I was only seven years old, by my then attaching myself to an intimate friend of my family's, Captain Gambier, (father, I believe, of the present Lord Gambier) who was at that time a post-captain in the Royal navy, and with whom I declared my positive determination to go, no matter where his destination might be. This greatly pleased Captain Gambier, but sadly distressed both my father and mother, who, as long as possible opposed my going to sea, but at length yielded to the captain's earnest solicitations that they would comply with my inclination and wish, to which I obstinately adhered; and in consequence I was forthwith entered upon the books of the *Burford*, a 74-gun ship, just put into commission and in the course of a few months to go to the West Indies, under Captain Gambier's command.

Not having had the smallpox, it was considered necessary previous to my embarking in my new way of life, to have me inoculated, for which purpose I was taken to Twickenham, where my father had just built and completed a handsome spacious mansion, situated close to our celebrated poet, Pope's, upon the margin of the Thames at the part called cross deep, and commanding a charming prospect, particularly of Richmond Hill and Park. Here I was put under a regimen and course of medicine, according to the custom of those days, preparatory to inoculation; after being dosed for three weeks, a day was fixed for performing the operation. At the appointed hour, Mr. Scott, the surgeon and apothecary of the place, attended, when lo! the little patient was nowhere to be found. After searching every hole and corner in and about the house, the garden, and all my usual haunts, not forgetting the boat, in vain, the utmost alarm prevailed. Servants were dispatched in every direction round the neighbourhood, but with no better success; no tidings could be obtained of little Pickle, until it occurred to the gardener to take a peep into the wooden habitation of Caesar, an immense-sized house dog of the mastiff breed, who though uncommonly fierce I could do anything with; and sure enough there I was found, snug in the kennel with my trusty friend, and where for above half an hour before, whilst making a pillow of Caesar's shaggy hide, as he slept, I had been laughing at, and enjoying the uproar and confusion arising from my supposed loss.

Being thus discovered, I was dragged forth, and after some upbraidings from my mother for the fright I had given her, was taken to my bed chamber, where an incision was made in each arm, as if the operator intended to cut me up, the wound being at least two inches in length, and nearly to the bone, in depth, the scars of which remain very visible at the present day. Yet all this butchery (which was the mode then universally pursued) was of no avail, for owing to the matter being too old, or from some other unknown cause, I did not take the infection. This was in the summer of 1756. In the month of July of that year a large party dined with my father, at Twickenham, at which were present Lord Cholmondeley, and his brother, the general, Sir Charles Sheffield, the owner of the Queen's Palace in St. James's Park, then called Buckingham house, Sir William Stanhope, to whom Pope's place belonged, Mr. Simon Luttrell, afterwards Earl of Carhampton, my god-father Colonel Mathews, and others. As I was setting upon the knee of the latter, after dinner, having just swallowed a bumper of claret which he had given me, I, with a deep sigh said to him, "I wish I was a man."

"Aye," observed the Colonel, "and pray why so, William?"

To which I quickly replied, "That I might drink two bottles of wine every day."

This wish, and the reason, being communicated to the company made a hearty laugh; and Mr. Luttrell, who was a famous hard liver, pronounced that I should live to be a damned drunken dog, the rest agreeing, that I should undoubtedly be a very jolly fellow! I believe, with no more than justice to myself, I may say, the latter prediction, as the milder of the two, proved nearest the truth; I certainly have at different periods drank very freely, sometimes to excess, but it never arose from the sheer love of wine; society—cheerful companions, and lovely seducing women—always delighted and frequently proved my bane; but intoxication for itself I detested, and invariably suffered grievously from. Spirits of every kind I greatly disliked and never touched: generous wine, in the way above mentioned, I had no objection to, preferring claret, yet enjoying a bottle of port.

My coat and all the other paraphernalia of a midshipman were now prepared, and a day appointed upon which I was to leave London for Portsmouth, with my commander, who was to eat his last dinner at my father's, and carry me off with him in a post-chaise. He accordingly came, and found his young midshipman properly equipped; but a circumstance occurred at the dinner that totally altered my mind, and put a stop to my intended naval career. It was this: I had a natural, and unconquerable antipathy to fat of every kind, and never could swallow a morsel. This my mother, imagining to arise merely from caprice, did all in her power to make me get the better of, and mentioning the circumstance to Captain Gambier, he instantly said, and in a tone of voice and manner that I did not approve of:

"Oh! never fear, Madam, when once William and I are fairly out at sea, he will forget all his absurd prejudices, and I daresay will be glad to have a bit of fat with his brother midshipmen."

From that moment I had done with Captain Gambier, and directly exclaimed that I did not like him, and would not go to his ship. He was astonished, appearing really disappointed and vexed. He said and did everything in his power to make me change my determination, but I resolutely adhered to it, protesting he never should have it in his power to force me to eat what I abhorred. My father and mother too by no means seconding him in endeavouring to prevail on me to proceed, he was obliged to depart without me. Notwithstanding this capriciousness in me, he continued my name as a midshipman upon the *Burford*'s books the whole time that ship remained in commission, which was for a period of six years, and whenever he afterwards saw me, used, very good humouredly, to call me his little fickle midshipman, adding, that as my rank was still going on, he yet hoped he should live to see me in the road to becoming an admiral. It has since been my lot to be very much at sea, but I have never in the whole course of my life been able to eat fat, not even that of venison or turtle.

2

EARLY ADVENTURES

I N the autumn of this year there came to live with my mother a pretty, smart little girl named Nanny Harris, who was strongly recommended by the Duchess of Manchester. Her situation in our family was between that of a companion and servant, in the latter capacity being chiefly to attend to two young sisters of mine, twins, the last children my mother had. The whole of the mornings she worked at her needle in the same room with my mother, and dined in the nursery, where she also slept, my bed being in an adjoining closet. Nanny Harris at once became my delight, and I was no less so hers. Every night when the servant had taken away the candle, she used to take me to her bed, there fondle and lay me upon her bosom; nor shall I forget my sensations, infant as I was, at awaking one morning and finding myself snugly stowed between her legs, with one of my hands upon the seat of Love, where I have no doubt she had placed it, for she was as wanton a little baggage as ever existed, and it was some years afterwards discovered that the Duchess of Manchester had discarded her for debauching Master Montagu (her only son) when thirteen years old, which circumstance her Grace most improperly omitted to mention, when recommending the girl, as a confidential servant in a private family. Upon such conduct I shall make no comment, nor should I have noticed it at all, but that the early intercourse I had with Nanny Harris strongly influenced me through several years of my life, and materially operated in fixing my attachment to women of loose and abandoned principles. This infatuating jade did not continue much above a year in our family. Her amours were too numerous, and too undisguisedly carried on not to be seen by my mother. She was consequently discarded with ignomiy, and immediately after went into keeping with a young gentleman of fortune, who had seen and admired her whilst living with us. I shall have occasion to make further mention of this unfortunate girl hereafter.

My father now resumed his hopes that I should fulfil his wishes, and that he might possibly live to see me a Chief Justice or Lord Chancellor of England, for which purpose he exerted his utmost endeavours to lead my young mind to look up to, and aspire to those dignified and elevated situations.

The famous poet, Charles Churchill, had just at this period published proposals for receiving into his house, and educating for the universities, six youths of good connections; and my father had it in contemplation to send me as one of the number. But upon consulting some friends thereon, particularly Mr. Edmund Burke, with whom, and all his family, he lived upon the most familiar terms, that gentleman was on opinion that the profligacy and immorality to Churchill's private character rendered him a most unfit person to undertake the education of, and training young people; and it should seem the same sentiment generally prevailed respecting him, as not even a single pupil was offered to him. It was then determined that I should be sent to Westminster School, preparatory to which I was placed at a day school in Charles Street, St. James's Square, for the purpose of learning to read and write, as well as to acquire the rudiments of the Westminster Grammar. At Christmas my brothers were taken from Harrow where they had been upwards of two years, and in January 1757, we all three went to Westminster; they, having made some proficiency in Latin, were stationed in the upper second, whilst I took my seat in what was denominated, "the idle class," that is, as the very bottom of the school, where all those who have not received some previous instructions in Latin are placed.

I, however, soon got out of that disgraceful and ignorant form, passed with rapidity and éclat the under and upper petty, and entered into the upper first, where most unluckily for me the famous Bob Lloyd, the elegant poet and scholar, but dissipated friend and companion of the above-mentioned Charles Churchill, presided as usher. He was an only son of the worthy and truly respectable Dr. Lloyd, then, and for many subsequent years, the Under-Master, the equally respectable and esteemed Dr. Markham, afterwards Archbishop of York, (who lately closed a long and honourable life) being the Head Master. From some boyish, but mischievous pranks of mine, this reverend gentleman, Mr. Robert Lloyd, though himself far from a saint, took a strong and rooted dislike to me, which he had many opportunities of betraying; and in consequence of his prejudice he let no occasion pass of what is there termed "showing me up," that is, conducting me to his father the doctor, to procure me a flogging, the ushers having no authority to use the birch; that tremendous instrument to schoolboys, the rod, being within the peculiar province of the two Masters only. The culprit thus "shown up" is never heard in the way of defence, the charge, as exhibited by the usher, is conclusive, and the posteriors of the unhappy delinquent undergo a castigation.

This is a ceremony the frequency of its recurrence in no degree reconciled me to; and, as I imagined I was often unjustly punished, I took a violent dislike to the school, and everything appertaining to it, with the exception of a few of the boys, to whom I was greatly and sincerely attached.

Amongst these, my chief favourites were Sir Watkin Williams Wynne, the father of the present Baronet, and Robert Henley, who afterwards succeeded to the title of Earl of Northington; the latter and myself were sworn brothers, and many a scrape we mutually got each other into. The disgust at the harsh treatment I met with produced an indifference as to all the school exercises. I falsely argued that, as I was to be flogged, it had better be for some offence, than without cause; instead, therefore, of preparing my theme, verses, or construing Virgil, I loitered away my time in Tothill Fields, and St. James's Park, or if I could muster cash, hired a boat to cruise about Chelsea reach; in most of which excursions my friend Henley accompanied me, and consequently came in for his share of stripes. One of our chief amusements was going to the parade at the Horse Guards, to look at the soldiers exercising, and at nine o'clock accompanying the daily relief in their march to Kensington, where His Majesty then resided.

My mother had, I think, five children within the eight years after my birth, who all died in early infancy. In 1758 she was delivered of the twins before mentioned, both girls, who were born within ten minutes of each other, and so alike that a ribbon was put round the arm of the eldest, to distinguish her from her sister. These twins were christened Ann and Sarah, and are both still living. The likeness however did not continue long; Ann became an erect, slim, and beautiful figure, whilst Sarah remained a fat fubsy—as she still is.

On 22nd October 1760, I had intended to skip school, and take the usual march with the Guards to Kensington; but, knowing that I was too early for the parade, I was sauntering about the Abbey between seven and eight o'clock in the morning, when I heard an elderly gentleman address an acquaintance of his who was looking at the monuments, and after the common salutation, ask him if he had heard the news; to which being answered in the negative, he added, "The King is dead, I saw a messenger who brought the intelligence to Whitehall just now. His Majesty was seized with an apoplectic fit at six o'clock this morning, and died in half an hour." Upon hearing this I instantly ran into school, where Mr. Hinchliff, (afterwards Bishop of Peterborough) was the only usher then present, and I roared out, "The King's dead"; whereupon Mr. Hinchliff came up to me, and taking hold of my ear, said, "What's that you say, young man? Do you know you are liable to be hanged for treason?" Whilst I was explaining the manner in which I had gained the information, Doctors Markham and Lloyd entered the school, announcing the melancholy event; and as certain official situations which they respectively held made their personal attendance requisite, an immediate adjournment of school took place, when the boys, unmindly of the sad event that had occasioned the unexpected "early play," set up a loud huzza, according to custom when a holiday out of the common course was obtained, the technical term for which was "an early play."

Early in the year 1761, Mr. Thomas Hicky, an old acquaintance of my father's, came over from Ireland. This gentleman was an opulent merchant of Dublin. After being a fortnight with us in St. Albans Street, he took a great liking to my brother Henry, and proposed to my father to bring him up to his business, for which purpose he would receive him as an apprentice, and at the expiration of his clerkship would admit him a partner. This offer was too advantageous not to be readily accepted of; and, Henry being much pleased with it, he in another month took his departure for Dublin with his new master. During four years they agreed wonderfully well, at the end of which period Henry, getting into bad company, often stayed out all night, which occasioned remonstrances, without effect; whereupon Mr. Hicky told him that, if he persisted in such evil courses, they must part. A temporary reform then took place and all went on smoothly. The time of servitude (five years) being nearly out, Mr. Hicky, who was a bigoted papist, proposed to my brother to become a Roman Catholic, observing, that upon his doing so, he would give him his niece in marriage, take him into partnership, and at his death would leave him his heir. This advantageous offer Henry, upon principle, rejected, not thinking it correct to abandon the religious tenets in which he had been brought up; and he had the more merit in this from the greatness of the temptation, for, besides the pecuniary consideration, the proposed bride was everything a man could wish for.

The old zealot was enraged at Henry's refusal, and desired he would instantly quit his house for ever, which he accordingly did, and forthwith launched out into every species of extravagance and dissipation the City of Dublin admitted of. Within a twelvemonth the young lady died, and her uncle survived only a few months, leaving nearly two hundred thousand pounds sterling to different public charities. Upon Henry's return to England, after the above failure in the Irish scheme, my father, through the interest of the Earl of Egmont, procured him a situation of two hundred and fifty pounds per annum, in the victualling office; but such an income as that proved very inadequate to the style of living Henry had engaged in. He had connected himself with many of the gay adventurers of London, men who lived by their wits; that is, nobody knew how, though some of them kept carriages, race horses, and establishments of the most expensive kind. Amongst the most conspicuous of these gentry was Major Walter Nugent, of His Majesty's Corps of Marines, whose fate it had been to fight several duels, although there never existed a milder or better tempered person than he was. Henry's other chief companions were, Tethrington, the notorious Dick England, Gilly Mahon, Swords, Wall, and many more of the same description; with all of whom I, as a fine forward youth, was in high favour, and many a bumper of champagne and claret have I drank in the society of this set, at taverns and brothels, accompanied by the most lovely women of the metropolis, and this before I had completed my fourteenth year.

After such an account of the males of the party, I scarcely need add that their resources arose from gambling; but it is no more than common justice to say, all and each of them invariably discouraged me by every means and every argument in their power from ever playing; and, whenever they were about to commence hazard, I was always sent away. The consequence was, and has been through life, that I have never felt the least inclination to gamble, and have at least escaped the evils attending that vice. Would it were in my power to say the same of many other vices, especially those of women and wine; but truth will not admit of it; in those two excesses I have too freely indulged.

My brother Henry's follies cost him many a painful, many a melancholy day, and ultimately were the cause of his death. He continued the style of life, and in the society above mentioned until the year 1770, when, in a drunken riot, he being one of a party that sallied forth from Mrs. Harrington's Bagnio at Charing Cross, brimful of burgundy, and at a late hour of the night, an affray suddenly arose in the street in which a man was unfortunately killed, being as it was imagined, run through the body by England. The consequence was the whole set immediately secreted themselves; and my brother Henry receiving information the following morning, that he was particularly named to the magistrate before whom an account of the transaction had been officially laid, he thought it prudent to leave the country and set off for Paris; though he afterwards often assured me by letter and parolly, in the most solemn manner, that he neither drew his sword, or struck a single blow, and had nothing at all to do with the unlucky accident further than being one of the company. After spending a few months at Paris, he went and settled with a respectable Abbé, at Caen, in Normandy, in which retirement he made himself a proficient in the French language, and passed the only three quiet, inoffensive, and happy years of his life.

The widow of the unfortunate man who lost his life having, long after the circumstance occurred, accepted a pecuniary compensation from some of the party, engaged never to prosecute any of them on account of her husband's death; which being communicated to my brother Henry, he and the others who had fled returned to England; when my father, being at a loss what to do with his said son Henry, at last obtained a cadetship for him in the East India Company's army at Madras, and at the end of the year 1773 he embarked for Fort St. George, on board the *Colebrooke*, which ship struck on a sunken rock going into False Bay, at the Cape of Good Hope, and was totally lost, the passengers and crew being all saved by the boats of the fleet in company. My brother, after a long and disastrous voyage, reached his destined port of Madras; but, though in the prime of life with respect to years, he was, owing to the excesses already alluded to, very old in constitution, his whole system being so shaken and enervated that he could not stand the sudden and violent change of climate. In six months after his arrival, a fever proved fatal to him.

In detailing these latter circumstances relative to my brother Henry, I have carried my narrative to its conclusion with some anticipation as to the order of time, as I have also done in some other instances herein-after. To return therefore to the year 1761. In the month of January of which year my elder brother (Joseph) left Westminster School, and was articled to my father as an attorney, I continued at the school, but as well might I have been anywhere else, for I never attended to the books I read, further than barely to enable myself to pass through the daily examination, which was in fact a mere ceremony, the master seldom observing whether the book was open or shut. I, however, not-withstanding all my idleness and inattention, reached the upper fourth, and of course had commenced Greek, the whole of which, as also the Latin I acquired, has long since so far escaped my memory that I should find it difficult to translate a single sentence of either Horace or Virgil.

Whenever I was at Twickenham I passed much of my time upon the water, rowing about in a boat of my father's and, when I could get a companion, as I could not alone manage, sailing. In one of these excursions, having a Mr. William Cane, (of whom I shall hereafter have occasion to speak much) and a first cousin of mine, John Edwards, then a lieutenant of infantry, with me, we were running up against the stream at a quick rate, when the boat, from a sudden gust of wind, taking a deep heel, I tumbled overboard and down I went; but, as I had the sheet of the sail in my hand at the time, on my quitting it upon falling into the water, the sail blew about loose, which kept the boat nearly stationary. Edwards, who swam tolerably well, jumped over to endeavour to recover me. I rose twice, as Cane said, and was just again sinking when my cousin caught hold of me by the hair and, with Mr. Cane's assistance, got me into the boat when nearly exhausted. In consequence of this accident I was forbid going upon the water; but, never very obedient to orders that I did not approve or considered tyrannical, I found frequent opportunities of taking a cruise; to put an end to which my father's next measure was securing the boat with an iron chain and padlock.

This unjust step, as I pronounced it, only set my wits to work. I recollected that Mr. Hindley, who possessed a house, late the property of Lord Radnor, a short distance from ours, had a small canoe, which was kept in a narrow channel, or creek of the Thames, opposite his house, merely as a pretty object for the eye. This I conceived would answer my purpose; and I prevailed on the gardener not only to let me have the use of it, but to make me a double-feathered paddle to work it with, which, when ready I began my manoeuvres, taking special care until I became used to my ticklish vessel, not to venture into deep water. This canoe was just my own length, only fifteen inches wide, and of so tottering a nature that bending my body to the right or to the left would endanger the upsetting it. During my practice I got many a ducking; but in a few weeks I became so expert in the management of it that I with confidence ventured into deep water. Both ends were exactly of the same form, so that I could go either way without turning; it had no seat, I therefore placed myself as nearly in the centre as I could, and working the feathers of the paddle alternately, went on at a quick rate. Having thus accomplished the perfect management of my little vessel, the next object I had in view was unexpectedly to exhibit myself in it, and thereby dreadfully to alarm my fond mother for the safety of her darling boy; to effect which cruel and ungrateful purpose, I fixed upon a day when company were to dine at our house, who being assembled and walking upon the lawn previous to dinner, I embarked at Lord Radnor's and going round an island suddenly made my appearance in the middle of the Thames, opposite my father's, to the infinite terror and alarm of my dear mother. But even this did not satisfy me, for laying myself flat along in the canoe, the whole party concluded the bottom had given way and that I was gone, never more to appear.

A loud and general scream ensued from the party; servants were dispatched in all directions to procure assistance; our own boat, Mr. Hindley's, Sir William Stanhope's, Mr. Hudson's, and two fishermen's punts were in a few minutes all in motion, pulling away to endeavour to recover my little carcase. When I heard their oars near my canoe, to the utter astonishment of those on board them, up I rose on my breech. My father was excessively angry at this prank; but my mother's joy was so great at seeing me safe that she proved a successful advocate in obtaining my pardon. My friend Mr. Hudson* took that opportunity of once more remarking there was not the least danger of my being drowned, fate having decreed me a very different end. Very soon after the above-mentioned trick, I had another very narrow escape from a watery grave; I was paddling away close to the island I have already spoken of, when sticking the end of the paddle into the bank to shove the canoe forward, the soil, being a stiff clay, made such a resistance as instantly to upset my tottering vehicle, and I was immersed in at least eight feet of water, under a perpendicular bank; and here my career would have ended had it not been for a fisherman named Rogers, who happened to be near the spot at the time in his punt, arranging baskets for catching eels, and seeing me in the water he instantly came to my assistance and picked me up.

I had other escapes from perilous situations I got into with my canoe, which made my father think it would be better to indulge me with a boat of a safer kind. He accordingly ordered a small wherry to be built expressly for my use, in which I used to row myself up and down, to and from Twickenham and London, a distance from the windings of the river of at least eighteen miles. Sculling this boat up in the spring of the year, when the freshes prevailed, was an arduous and fatiguing task; I have often been tugging with all my might for five hours between Kew and my father's house.

The coronation of His present Majesty being fixed for the month of September, my father determined that all his family should be present at the ceremony. He therefore engaged one of the nunneries, as they are called, in Westminster Abbey, for which he paid fifty guineas. They are situated at the head of the great columns that support the roof, and command an admirable view of the whole interior of the building. Upon this occasion they were divided off by wooden partitions, each having a separate entrance with lock and key to the door, with ease holding a dozen persons. Provisions, consisting of cold fowls, ham, tongues, different meat pies, wines, and liquors of various sorts were sent in to the apartment the day before, and two servants were allowed to attend. Our party consisted of my father, mother, brother Joseph, sister Mary, myself, Mr. and Miss Isaacs, Miss Thomas, her brother (all Irish), my uncle and aunt Boulton, and their eldest daughter. We all supped together in St. Albans Street on 21st September, and at midnight set off in my father's coach and my uncle's, and Miss Thomas's chariot. At the end of Pall Mall the different lines of carriages, nearly filling the street, our progress was consequently tedious; yet the time was beguiled by the grandeur of the scene; such

* Thomas Hudson, the portrait painter, Joseph Hickey's next-door neighbour beside the Thames, a "remarkably good-tempered" man and one of William's "first-rate favourites."

2+

a multitude of carriages, with servants behind carrying flambeauxs, made a blaze of light equal to day, and had a fine effect.

Opposite the Horse Guards we were stopped exactly an hour without moving onward a single inch. As we approached near the Abbey, the difficulties increased, from mistakes of the coachmen, some of whom were going to the Hall, others to the Abbey, and getting into the wrong ranks. This created much confusion and running against each other, whereby glasses and panels were demolished without number, the noise of which, accompanied by the screeches of the terrified ladies, was at times truly terrific. It was past seven in the morning before we reached the Abbey, which having once entered, we proceeded to our box without further impediment, Dr. Markham having given us tickets which allowed our passing by a private staircase, and avoiding the immense crowd that was within. We found a hot and comfortable breakfast ready, which I enjoyed, and proved highly refreshing to us all; after which some of our party determined to take a nap in their chairs, whilst I, who was well acquainted with every creek and corner of the Abbey, amused myself running about the long gallery until noon, when notice being given that the procession had began to move, I resumed my seat.

Exactly at one they entered the Abbey, and we had a capital view of the whole ceremony. Their Majesties, (the King having previously married), being crowned, the Archbishop of Canterbury mounted the pulpit to deliver the sermon; and, as many thousands were out of the possibility of hearing a single syllable, they took that opportunity to eat their meal when the general clattering of knives, forks, plates, and glasses that ensued, produced a most ridiculous effect, and a universal burst of laughter followed. The sermon being concluded, the anthem was sung by a numerous band of the first performers in the kingdom, and certainly was the finest thing I had ever heard.

The procession then began to move towards Westminster Hall, at which moment, my father received a paper from Lord Egmont, enclosing four Hall tickets, two of which he gave to Mr. Thomas and me, desiring us to make the best of our way. We descended, and attempted to follow the procession, but were stopped by the soldiers, and told no one could be allowed to pass that way, and that we must go round to the Palace Yard Gate. Whilst endeavouring to prevail on the men to let us proceed, I spied my friend Colonel Salter, of the Guards, who was upon duty, and applying to him for assistance, he directly took us with him, and we reached the Hall, which we otherwise never should have accomplished. Upon getting into the raised gallery, it was so crammed that I could not see an inch before me, until some gentlemen kindly made way to let me forward, and then some ladies, who were in a part that was railed off, seeing a fine-looking boy (which at that time I was) in distress, they with the utmost good humour let me in, making room in the front row.

Thus I found myself in the very best place in the Hall, and within a few yards of their Majesties. I afterwards learnt that this situation belonged to the Duke of Queensbury, in right of some official post he held, they who occupied it being relations and friends of the Duchess. We were supplied abundantly with every kind of refreshment. Setting perfectly at my ease, I saw the dinner, the ceremony of the champion, and every particular, and was at a loss to decide which I thought the most magnificent, the Abbey scene, or that of the Hall. About ten at night the whole was over, and I got home as fast as the crowd would permit, highly delighted at all I had seen, but excessively fatigued, not having had any sleep the preceding night, and having been so actively employed the entire day.

In the winter of this year I accidentally met in the park, Mr. Murrough O'Brien, afterwards Earl of Inchiquin, and finally Marquis of Thomond. After questioning me about the school, he gave me a guinea, the first I believe I ever had possessed. Having just then discovered the residence of my wanton little bedfellow, Nanny Harris, I directly went to her lodgings which were in a court that run out of Bow Street, Covent Garden. I told her the strength of my purse, and proposed going to the play, which she consenting to, there was I a hopeful sprig of thirteen, stuck up in a green box, with a blazing whore. From the theatre she took me home to supper, giving me lobster and oysters, both of which she knew I was very fond of, and plenty of rum punch; with my head full of which, at a late hour I went home, and as I would not tell where I had been, I received a smart flogging from the arm of my old operator, Doctor Lloyd.

In the summer of 1762, just as I was embarking in my wherry, at Dicky Roberts's at Lambeth, intending to proceed to Twickenham, one of the City Companies' barges went by, on their annual excursion of pleasure, having a band of music with them. This was an irresistible attraction to me. I accompanied them up the river, keeping upon their quarter, except that now and then I exerted myself and dashed ahead as if they had been at an anchor. Vanity induced me to do this, in order to show my superior skill and adroitness, in which my object was fully answered, the gentlemen appearing delighted at the dexterity with which I manoeuvred my boat. They presented me with cakes and wine from their windows. At the end of the terrace at Kew they stopped, in order to let the men who rowed rest a little and take some refreshment. Upon again moving from Kew, they invited me to come on board their barge, which I immediately did, and upon finding that I was going to Twickenham, they insisted upon my remaining with them, and directed my wherry to be made fast astern of the barge.

By the time they had reached Richmond I had made myself of so much importance by my spirits and fun that one and all protested I must stay and eat turtle with them. I, who at no period of my life could resist a convivial party, very readily consented. By this time I had discovered that it was the Fishmonger's Company, going to a turtle and venison feast at the Castle Tavern at Richmond. The party in general were very civil and attentive to me, but more especially an elderly gentleman of the name of Grubb, an eminent attorney in the City, and Clerk to the Company. He desired me to set down next to him at table, and he would take care of me. At two o'clock we landed at the Castle, and by three the party, consisting of upwards of one hundred, set down to a magnificent dinner, consisting of three courses, in which every luxury in the eating way appeared. This was followed by a dessert equally splendid and costly with every hothouse fruit procurable. My new friend Mr. Grubb, who seemed to have taken a prodigious liking to me, observing that I poured down champagne at a great rate, with much good nature cautioned me, observing that as I could not be in the habit of drinking such potent wine, it would soon affect and make me ill; to which I replied that I could drink as much as the best of them; and, thanks to my friend Henley, and other Westminsters with whom I frequently took of large potations, though not of champagne certainly, but port, strong ales, and punch, and when our funds were low as sometimes happened, hot flip, I had, for such a youngster, a tolerable strong head.

As the evening advanced, my spirits were exhilarated, and I sung several songs with which the company were highly pleased, though some of them expressed no little surprise at my selection, which undoubtedly was not of the modestest sort. The party sat to a late hour; but I held out until they broke up, when I was so drunk that on rising from my chair I fell flat on the floor where I was given in charge of the master of the house who knew me well. He had me put to bed, where I slept as if dead until ten the next morning, at which time I awoke with an excruciating headache, and found myself and the bedclothes in woeful plight, having whilst I lay like a beast, quite senseless, disgorged from my overcharged stomach all the good things I had put into it. Upon going downstairs I found considerable relief from drinking strong coffee which the landlord's wife had very considerately prepared for me. I was then told that the company had departed about one in the morning; some of them in full as bad a state as myself, having been carried bodily to the barge, wholly incapable of walking or using their limbs. At noon I got into my boat, and rowed up to my father's, but did not recover from this debauch for several days, and was in sad disgrace at home on account of it.

I have already mentioned my extraordinary sensations upon discovering the situation in which Nanny Harris had one night placed me whilst in bed with her at Twickenham. I then had no idea of the spot on which I found my hand, or the delicious pleasures I was shortly to derive from it. My first venereal attempt was made on a dark night in St. James's Park, upon the grass, about Christmas of the year 1762, in company with Bob Henley, and grievously disappointed I was. I cannot easily describe my feelings upon the occasion; but undoubtedly they were not altogether pleasant. The same evening that this happened I was to go home and sleep there, my mother having some friends to sup with her, one of whom was desirous of seeing me. From the park therefore I went to St. Albans Street, where in the drawing-room several ladies were assembled, and amongst them Mrs. Cholmondeley, wife of the Honourable and Reverend Mr. Cholmondeley, son of Lord Malpas, and grandson of Lord Cholmondeley. Upon my entering the apartment, Mrs. Cholmondeley immediately laid hold of my arm and drawing me towards her began questioning me about Westminster and what books I was reading; after which, with peculiar archness in her manner, she asked,

"And what is the school paved with, stones or brick?" to which I replied:

"Neither, Madam, it has a boarded floor."

"Aye, indeed (rejoined she) I should have thought, from your knees, it was of grass."

This naturally attracted my eyes to the knees of my breeches, which unfortunately were of leather and new, when to my confusion, I saw them both strongly marked with green. I knew not what to say, but most cordially wished my interrogator at the Devil. After some very lame attempts to account for the appearance of my breeches, I made a precipitate retreat for the kitchen, where I was always sure of finding friends. We had at that time a man-servant named Samuel Campion, who was very musical, and had an admirable voice. With him I used to sing duets, and he taught me a variety of songs, also to imitate the French horn, which we did together and so inimitably well that it was often thought to be a pair of that instrument performing. To Campion, who was my confidant upon all occasions, I related what had just passed in the drawing-room. He was surprised at my unusual dullness and asked me why I had not instantly said that, in my haste and eagerness to get home, running through the park I had fallen down and stained my knees. I wondered at my own stupidity; but I was taken by surprise, and probably Mrs. Cholmondeley, conjecturing I had been at some mischief, resolved to distress me; in general I was sharp and ready enough.

Notwithstanding my first connection with the fair sex did not answer my expectation, it in no way discouraged me from making further attempts. Whilst at Westminster I had a weekly allowance of half a crown from my father, for pocket money. This was usually expended in boating by day and attending puppet shows at night, of which latter amusement I was particularly fond, the conflicts between Master Punch and his Satanic Majesty affording me the highest gratification. There were half a dozen of my father's friends who were always generous in their donations to me; and I took especial care, when in want of a supply, to put myself in the way of some or one of them, by which I secured a handsome tip, the Westminster phrase for a present of cash. From one of those gentlemen I got half a guinea, and therefore determined to renew my acquaintance with my old Twickenham bedfellow, Nanny Harris, for which purpose I called at her lodgings, where I heard she was gone to Ireland. Returning melancholy and dejected at the absence of my favourite, towards my boarding house at Westminster, under the Piazza of Covent Garden, a very pretty little girl, apparently not much older than myself in years, joined me, took hold of my arm, and, looking earnestly in my face, said,

"You are a fine handsome boy and too young to be walking in such a place as this alone, and I'll take your maidenhead."

Pleased with her manner, I accepted her challenge, and accompanied her to a very indifferent-looking apartment up three pairs of stairs in a dark, narrow court out of Drury Lane. There we took off our clothes and got into a dirty, miserable bed. This was my first exhibition under a roof. My companion gave me great credit for my vigour, saying I was a famous little fellow, and should prove an invaluable acquisition to whatever girl was lucky enough to fix me. In this den of wretchedness I passed three truly happy hours; and very different indeed were my feelings from what I experienced in the St. James's Park scene. Upon getting out of bed, however, I was dreadfully alarmed at perceiving the tail of my shirt covered with blood, and screamed out. The poor girl seemed to be in great agitation and distress, which increased my fright; whereupon she eagerly endeavoured to assuage my fears, assuring me no sort of injury would arise, that what I saw proceeded from a natural cause, though she had not been aware of it coming on. She added that to avoid discovery she would wash the linen; and, making me again go into the bed, she pulled off my shirt, which she carried downstairs, and in a little more than half an hour returned with it quite clean and dry. I then produced my half-guinea, which I offered to her. She enquired whether I had any more, from which question I imagined she did not consider it sufficient.

I therefore assured her I had no more, but that I would bring her a further supply the first opportunity. In supposition, however, I did this generous girl great injustice and she immediately replied: "If that is all you have, I will not touch it."

In liberal feelings my spirit was equal to her own, and a smart contest ensued between us relative to the said half-guinea, which ended in a compromise, she consenting to retain five shillings. She therefore went out to get it changed, and not a penny more could I prevail on her to take. This was more disinterested as I afterwards learned as she had not at that time a single sixpence in her possession. This kind and generous creature I occasionally visited for several years after, and sometimes met her accidentally in the streets, when she always addressed me as "her dear little maidenhead." I ever found in her the most sincere and affectionate attachment, and received from her the best advice relative to my future intercourse with her sex.

My propensity to women and to the frequenting of public places of entertainment increased monthly, and, if possible, I became more idle and inattentive in the prosecution of my school duties than ever. This my father easily discovered from my inability to answer the questions he put to me on the subject of the authors I ought to have been reading. Upon finding me altogether ignorant of what I should have been perfect in, he remonstrated, upbraided, coaxed, threatened, in short did everything that a fond parent could, to induce more attention to what, as he truly observed, was intended solely for my own advantage, and although I felt the force of his remarks, it was all in vain. He then stopped my weekly allowance, hoping that might have some effect; instead of which it only set my wits to work in what manner to raise cash. At last, my idleness, dissipation, and neglect of the school exercises drew upon me the censure of Dr. Markham, who finding his repeated lectures and repeated floggings equally unavailing, he told my father, whose intentions relative to me he was well acquainted with, that it was in vain to think of making me a classical scholar, and that he had better adopt some other line than that of a learned one. Whatever cause I may have to regret this determined inattention and idleness, whereby the plan suggested by my fond and indulgent parent was entirely frustrated, clearly I have been the author of my own misfortune, and can blame no other than myself. My father, upon Dr. Markham's representation, reluctantly abandoned all hopes of seeing me shine as a lawyer, and at the end of the year 1763 I was therefore taken from Westminster School, most deservedly in high disgrace.

Some weeks after my leaving Westminster in the manner above related, my father one day gravely addressed me, observing that I had then been at home near two months, during which, notwithstanding former misconduct, he had flattered himself with the daily hope that my spirit would have induced me to propose some line of life for myself, and not indolently continue to eat, drink, and sleep away my time, labouring too, as I must feel I deserved, under his and my mother's displeasure; but, as he had been again disappointed in his hopes, he would no longer support me in idleness. (Upon this subject I had long wished to speak and was only deterred from a consciousness of my ill behaviour, and how little I deserved to be believed as to any assurances I might make. I therefore put it off from day to day until my poor father's patience was quite exhausted.) He then asked me whether I would be an attorney, there being still time enough left for me, if diligent, to acquire a knowledge of that profession: that he did not approve of having two sons in the same line of business, but my misconduct had left him without alternative. I readily consented to become an attorney, promising the most indefatigable attention, a promise I certainly meant to keep.

It was thereupon determined that I should be instructed in the common acquirements of a gentleman, for at Westminster nothing is taught but the classics. My father, anxious to keep me as much as possible out of temptation, made enquiries as to where I might be likely to receive the best education out of the capital; and an academy, then of considerable repute, at Streatham in Surrey, five miles from London, was fixed upon. It was kept by a widow lady of great respectability, a Mrs. Keighley, the Reverend Mr. Jackson, a pious and very learned man, officiating as master. I went to Streatham in March 1764, and with the utmost zeal commenced arithmetic, writing, French, drawing, and dancing. I also resumed Latin and Greek, to the whole of which I bestowed unremitted attention for five months, when I was taken very ill with a fever, which soon showed itself the forerunner of smallpox. It therefore became necessary, on account of the other boys, to remove me, and my situation being announced to my father by special messenger, he immediately sent his coach wth two trusty servants to convey me home, and wrapped up in blankets I safely reached St. Albans Street.

Whether this removal in the height of the fever tended to increase the malignancy of the disease or not, I cannot tell; but I had it very severely. Dr. Nugent, an able physician, father-in-law of Mr. Edmund Burke, and a very intimate friend of my family's attended me with unremitting kindness. I was equally fortunate in the apothecary, Mr. Hernon, an eminent practitioner of Suffolk Street. These two gentlemen at once pronounced the pock to be of a good sort, but that, as I should be very full, I should consequently undergo considerable pain and uneasiness. This was completely verified, my face being so swelled and inflamed that for many days I could not see at all. The violent

itching almost made me frantic; and, if I had not been closely watched day and night, I should probably have made a dismal figure of myself, and in spite of all the watching, I was so perpetually clawing at my nose, (always a prominent feature,) as materially to increase its size.

At the proper stage of the disease, my sisters, Ann and Sarah, were brought into my room for the purpose of receiving the infection, which they both did, and had it very favourably. Although naturally good tempered, I was exceedingly irritable and impatient under my confinement. Upon recovering, and looking at myself in a glass, I discovered that there was an end of all my beauty, which was, as I emphatically observed, "for ever gone," and I became quite as plain as my neighbours. An old servant, named Mary Jones, who had lived in our family prior to the time of my birth, endeavoured to console me by saying I still had a pair of bewitching eyes, which thereafter would make many a poor girl's heart ache.

3

SCHOOLING AND DISSIPATIONS

I N January 1765 I returned to Streatham, when my conduct became very different from what it had before been. No longer diligent or attentive, I, on the contrary, neglected every duty, except drawing, because of that I was very fond. My chief business was running after the maidservants, particularly one named Nancy Dye, a fine luscious little jade who allowed me to take every liberty with her person, except the last grand one; and thus she continued tantalizing me for six months, when I accomplished all I wished, but had reason to think I was not the first nor only one that partook of her favours, a circumstance that I was quite indifferent about as I knew that, whenever I wished for half an hour's entertainment, I had only to enter the dairy at a certain hour, where I was sure to find the wanton Nancy Dye ready to meet my embraces.

She also frequently visited me at night; for, as one of the privileges of a parlour boarder, I had a small bed chamber to myself, to get to which, however, I was obliged to pass through a room where seven or eight of the boys slept, amongst whom was one named Blackall, of nearly the same age as I was and having the same amorous propensities, but being a sulky, ill-tempered fellow he was equally disliked by the scholars and servants. This lad discovered my amour by happening to be awake two or three times when she passed by his bed. Having clearly ascertained that I was the object of these nocturnal visitations, he, without saying a syllable to me of his discovery, proposed himself to become a partaker, which ·Nancy very contemptuously rejected, nor would she ever submit to the most trifling familiarity from him. This hauteur of the cherry-cheeked dairymaid raised Blackall's indignation, and he threatened if she persisted in refusing to him what she had so freely granted to me, he would inform Mrs. Keighley of her behaviour. Of this threat Nancy informed me, whereupon I remonstrated with Blackall; but instead of attending thereto he was insolent, and I gave him a sound drubbing, which had he possessed a grain of spirit could not have happened, he being in

form and strength must superior to me. Upon receiving this chastisement, he ran blubbering away to Mr. Jackson to make his complaint,
and state the circumstance of the girl's nightly visits to me, which,
being of course communicated to Mrs. Keighley, a terrible uproar
ensued.

I was threatened with expulsion, about which I was wholly indifferent; but I was greatly distressed at the evils that might arise to
the partner of my guilt, who, after being glossly abused and called by
all sorts of approbrious names, was ordered instantly to leave the
house; whereupon I ventured, notwithstanding I was in such high
disgrace, to plead for her, attaching to myself the additional crime of
seduction. But Nancy, on hearing this, with great spirit assured her
mistress it was no such thing, nor was there any seduction in the case,
and, turning to me, desired that I would not make myself unhappy on
her account, and that, as to being turned away, the place was no such
catch and thank her stars she could get a better any day in the week.
"Indeed," added she, "I fully intended leaving it at the end of the
month, for I am going to be married." (I had soon afterwards the
pleasure to hear that she did marry a confidential servant of Sir
Charles Blount's, who lived in the neighbourhood, and that she was
very happy.) I was severely lectured on all quarters for my libertinism
at so early an age, and my future misery and ruin predicted should I
continue the same bad courses.

Every individual of the family frowned upon me, except a daughter
of Mrs. Keighley's, an elegant young woman of about two-and-twenty,
who, in spite of the grievous offence I had committed, spoke to me at
meals as usual and frequently gave me an arch leer, as if she did not
like me the worse for my gallantry. Being by the departure of Nancy
Dye deprived of a bed fellow in the house, I was obliged to seek
abroad for object to satisfy my sensuality. The distance from London
being only five miles, I used upon half holidays, on leaving the dining-
room about two o'clock, under pretence of taking a walk, to set off as
fast as I could run to town, there visit my little maidenhead, or some
other frail sister, and then post back to my school, a practice I pursued
for many months without discovery or suspicion.

I had made the acquaintance at Streatham with Mr. Rose Fuller, a
banker, and man of large fortune, who had a handsome house near
the academy, where he lived in a splendid style. This gentleman became very partial to me, and generally once a week, at least, sent a
servant to Mr. Jackson to request I might be permitted to spend the
day with him, which, from his rank in life, and respectability of
character never was refused. He was a widower, with one son just of
age. To Mr. Fuller, upon his questioning me on the subject of pocket
money, I did not hesitate to say that what my father allowed me was

very inadequate to my wants, upon which representation he furnished me with a supply, and desired whenever I had occasion for a little cash that I would consider him as my banker, a liberal permission that I did not presume upon, nor ever availed myself of, but upon real emergency. In this manner passed away the summer of 1765.

Towards autumn, two fine West India lads, named Harrison and Lewis, who were wards of Mr. Fuller's, came from Eton School to pass some weeks with him, previous to embarking on their return to their parents in Jamaica. They had therefore as great a range in point of amusements as they chose, and an abundant supply of cash. These young men, who were my seniors by eighteen months, were my constant companions; and, as they knew the state of my finances, one or other of them always insisted upon paying during the frequent excursions we made either on horseback or in post-chaises. In December of the same year (1765) we three went, as we had often done before, to London, where I had introduced them to two females, with whom they were delighted. Having effected the object of this jaunt, we were preparing to return to Streatham when one of the girls said there was to be a new play performed that night at Covent Garden, and proposed our going to it. Though at all times prone to mischief, the boldness of such a proposal nevertheless staggered me, and I strongly objected; but I was laughed at for my prudence, my objection overruled, and to the theatre we proceeded. The performance being finished, the ladies suggested the propriety of a little supper, to which Harrison entered his caveat, whereupon I observed, " 'In for a penny in for a pound,' we shall be no worse off by arriving at three o'clock than at one." My logic prevailing, we went to the Shakespear, and after eating heartily, qualifying the victuals with a sufficient quantity of punch, we took a hackney coach to Westminster Bridge, where we mounted our nags and rode off for Streatham, which we reached a quarter before three, and found the whole village in an uproar.

The person to whom the horses belonged told us that Mr. Fuller, Senior and Junior, also Mr. Jackson and Hodgson (the head usher) had been there several times, and made such minute enquiries he had been obliged to declare the truth, and that we were gone to London; at which they all appeared greatly shocked. My friends then took leave and I gently rung the gate bell, and being let in, was received by an old maiden sister of Mrs. Keighley's, who said they had been under the greatest terror about me, that her sister and Mr. Jackson had only just retired to their chambers, the latter from extreme agitation, very ill. Whilst stating these facts, Mrs. Keighley made her appearance, assuring me I should the following morning be conducted to St. Albans Street, for that she would not have the character of her academy injured, if not entirely ruined, by such a profligate boy as I was.

With this denunciation I was dismissed, and went to my room. Agitation at the serious scrape I had involved myself in prevented sleep; a severe headache came on; and before the customary hour of rising I was seized with so violent a vomiting, with considerable fever, as to be thought actually dying. The apothecary being summoned pronounced me alarmingly ill, and that I must be kept as quiet as possible. I remained the whole day in bed; at night the fever increased with a delirium, in consequence of which Mrs. Keighley determined to send to my father to let him know the state I was in; but on the second morning the medical man pronounced me better, and it was therefore deemed unnecessary to alarm my family. I kept my room a week, and was wonderfully pulled down by the severity of the attack. The first day I appeared in the parlour I had a very serious lecture from Mr. Jackson, who said he should recommend my father to send me to sea in order to preserve me from absolute destruction: that as the school was to break up in a few days for the Christmas holidays, I might remain until then, but return I never should.

In a week after I went home, when my father observed to Mr. Jackson that I was now arrived at an age that made it right to establish me in a profession, and therefore I should not return to Streatham. He then thanked him for his attention during my stay at Streatham, which he trusted had not been ill-bestowed. The reverend gentleman very kindly and considerately made no complaint, merely saying he hoped my future conduct would be such as to merit his (my father's) approbation. Then shaking me with great cordiality by the hand, he wished me well and departed; and this was the last time I ever saw him; in the following spring he was during the night seized with a fit of apoplexy, and in the morning was found a corpse.

A most important change in my life was now about to occur; from a mere schoolboy I was to become in a great measure my own master, at least for some hours in the day, and, unfortunately for myself, I was more forward and manly than youths of my age usually were. Of this my father was perfectly aware, and in consequence somewhat alarmed. He knew how volatile I was, and my tendency to dissipation and conviviality. He therefore, upon my coming home, addressed me very gravely, slightly touched upon former errors, and observed that I must now have done with all such follies; that I was arrived at an age when boyish tricks no longer became me, and I ought to begin not only to think but to act like a man endued at least with common understanding; that I must turn to, heart and hand, to improve myself, which could only be accomplished by intense application to my studies; that a good inclination was all that was necessary, for being (as he was pleased to say) blessed by nature with no ordinary talents, I had it in my power to do anything I pleased. This paternal anxiety

and excellent advice I duly felt, and determined to act, in every respect, with diligence and propriety, which I was conscious must be for my own benefit and advantage. How long I adhered to these good resolutions will soon appear.

In the year 1765 my father had taken my brother Joseph (then admitted an attorney) into partnership, also Mr. Nathaniel Bayley, who had practised several years, and was considered an uncommonly clever solicitor. This gentleman had inherited, and run through a fortune of twenty-five thousand pounds in less than ten years, pursuing for that period, with avidity, all the follies of the times, thereby sacrificing both his property and his health, bringing on a premature old age. This brought him to his recollection. With the wreck of his fortune he quitted his debauched companions, went to reside in chambers, and attended as closely as his health would permit to the law, for which profession he had originally been intended; and at the time of his connecting himself with my father he was in every respect regularity itself.

To this Mr. Bayley, in the month of January 1766, I was articled as a clerk, for five years, my father conceiving he, as a stranger, would have more control over me than himself. As an encouragement to me to be diligent and attentive, I had an allowance of half a guinea a week for pocket money, also a guinea on the first day of each term, besides which I was told that I should frequently receive presents of from two to five guineas, upon attending the execution, and becoming a witness to deeds of various descriptions drawn in the office. All this I thought augured well, and I was much pleased at the prospect before me. I was further gratified by having my hair tied, turned over my forehead, powdered, pomatumed, and three curls on each side, with a thick false tail, my operator being Nerot, a fashionable French hair-dresser and peruke-maker justly considered the best in his line, in London. And thus equipped, I came forth a smart and dashing clerk to an attorney.

For eight months my conduct was irreproachable, my attention to the business such as to gain the highest approbation of my father and of my master, Mr. Bayley. I soon became a favourite with most of the then leading men at the Bar. These were, the Attorney-General, Mr. Yorke, and Mr. Willes, Solicitor-General, Mr. De Grey, Sir Fletcher Norton, Mr. Wedderburn, Mr. Dunning, Mr. Maddocks, Mr. Perryn, and others, who used to compliment me upon my quickness; and they frequently congratulated my father and Mr. Bayley upon their having so promising a youth for a son and clerk. Amongst those most kind upon all occasions, it would be ungrateful in me did I not particularize the late Lord Thurlow, who was my fast friend. He, however, not-withstanding his favourable opinion of me, used sometimes to express

his doubts whether I was calculated to make an attorney, having from his observation upon my habits and manner conceived that I never should bring myself to submit to the dull and irksome drudgery of that laborious profession, but should be disgusted with it as soon as the novelty of the employment ceased.

Mr. Thurlow was at that time just rising into eminence as a lawyer. My father, who considered him as possessing abilities greatly superior to any of his contemporaries, was anxious as far as lay in his power, to bring him forward. Mr. Thurlow, though indefatigable in his attentions to whatever he once undertook, was by no means a laborious man in general, especially during the early part of his life, when he avowed his disinclination to going to his desk, or looking into a book in an evening. Consequently, he never, except on particular occasions, was to be found at his chambers after five o'clock in the afternoon; and in order to avoid being interrupted in his hours of recreation by attorneys or their clerks, it was a rule with him never to dine two following days at the same house, but to use various taverns and coffee houses (in the neighbourhood of the Temple, where he lived,) indiscriminately; and, wherever he went, the waiters had a general and positive order, if enquired for, to deny his being there, and this usually succeeded.

A business was transacting in our office, whereon my father was extremely desirous of consulting Mr. Thurlow. The matter pressed in point of time, not an hour was to be lost; and as two of the clerks who were sent in search of him had failed in their object, my father bid me try what I could do, and if I succeeded he would give me a guinea. Out I set; and, as I had at the commencement of my clerkship made friends with most of the head waiters in the taverns and coffee houses in Chancery Lane, Fleet Street, and that part of the town, I felt confident I should obtain the promised reward, and did so, though after more difficulty than I expected. After going the usual round in vain, I called upon the barmaid at Nando's, with whom I was a favourite, and entreated her to tell me where Mr. Thurlow was. At first she protested she knew not, but by a little coaxing I got the secret, and proceeded to the Rolls Tavern, where I had already been; but there happening to be two new waiters who were of course unacquainted with me, they were faithful to their orders, and denied his being there. Upon my second visit I went into the bar, where addressing the landlord, I told him I had ascertained Mr. Thurlow was in the house, and see him I must. The host was inflexible, and would not peach, but in a few minutes after I entered, he called out:

"Charles, carry up half a dozen of red sealed port into No. 3."

It instantly struck me that must be the apartment my man was in; and, as the waiter passed with the basket of wine, I pushed by him,

ran up to No. 3, boldly opened the door, and there sat Mr. Thurlow
and four other gentlemen at a table with bottles and glasses before
them. Upon seeing me he exclaimed:

"Well, you young rascal, damn your blood, what do you want? How
the devil did you find me out? Take away your papers, for I'll be
damned if I look at one of them. Come, come, you scoundrel, I know
what you came for; you take after your father and are a damned
drunken dog; so here, drink of this," filling a tumbler of wine which
I had not the smallest objection to, and drank to the health of the
company. "But how did you find me out?" asked Mr. Thurlow.

"Why, Sir," answered I, "I heard the master of the house order six
bottles of port for number three, and I was certain there you must be,
so up I ran and entered without ceremony."

This made a great laugh, putting Mr. Thurlow into high good
humour, who swore I was a damned clever fellow, and should do,
and turning to his companions he said:

"This is a wicked dog, who does with me as he pleases, a son of Joe
Hickey's."

I was thereupon particularly noticed by them all, and pulling out
my papers Mr. Thurlow looked them over and immediately wrote a
note to my father upon the subject, which I carried home, thereby
gaining not only the promised guinea, but credit for the manner in
which I had effected the business. (The barmaid at Nando's was the
chère amie of Mr. Thurlow, with whom she continued all her life, and
was by many supposed to have been his wife. She bore him two
daughters, both now women and well married, he having left them
large fortunes.)

I had the same sort of influence over Sir Fletcher Norton, who by
nature, was a rough, violent man. He wrote a vile hand, yet nothing
offended him so much as any of it being referred back to him for
explanation; and, when such a circumstance did occur, he was not
sparing of abuse to the messenger, in consequence of which all the
attorney's clerks had a great dislike to going near him; but I heeded
him not. He had once answered a case of importance for my father,
relative to a plantation appeal, where the opinion was so execrably
written that neither my father, who could in general decipher his
scrawl, nor anyone else could make it out. I was therefore dispatched
to his chambers in Lincoln's Inn, where his clerk told me he was so
busy he could not be broken upon. I declared I must and would see
him, but the clerk would not go in to tell him; so down I sat in the
outer room, his carriage being at the door to take him to the House
of Commons. In about half an hour he was passing through in a great
hurry when I arrested his progress, with my case. He would not touch
it, endeavouring to put me aside, saying,

Covent Garden Piazza in 1768, by Edward Rooker after T. Sandby.

Robert Pott, by George Romney, now at Greystones, Somerset.

By courtesy of Lady Pott

"My dear boy, I am already too late. It is impossible for me to stop one moment, I am going to the House, and then to a consultation. Come tomorrow," and on he pushed downstairs. I nevertheless stuck close, and to his utter astonishment followed him into the carriage. At first, he seemed offended, but soon observed I had done wisely, adding, "And now, my man, tell me what's your business."

I presented my case telling him the predicament his opinion stood in.

"What," said he, "cannot your father read it?"

"No, Sir."

"Nor Bayley?"

"No, Sir."

"Nor you, or anyone in the office?"

"No, Sir."

Then looking over it himself he exclaimed:

"By God, nor I either. I must answer it again: come to me at nine this evening."

Taking out a pencil and bit of paper, I made him write "admit."

"And pray what is that for?" asked he.

"Oh Sir," replied I, "my going to your chambers would otherwise avail nothing, I should not be admitted."

"Well thought of, my man," said he.

By nine I was at Lincoln's Inn, the clerk peremptorily refusing me admittance; and even after producing the written word, he made many objections. At last I prevailed and got in, and at half-past eleven marched off with my opinion in legible characters. Sir Fletcher, besides writing so execrably, was sadly dilatory in business, and had a particular dislike to answering cases, so that it was extremely difficult to get one from him.

There was at this period an old Irish woman, named Judy White, daily at our office, having come to England on behalf of a near female relation who was involved in an Equity suit, and for whom Mrs. White acted as agent, supplying such information as my father, who was her solicitor, called for. She had formerly been considered the handsomest girl in Dublin, where she was long the reigning toast with the men. The remains of beauty, though she was now upwards of sixty, were still very visible. Prolixity was one of her grand foibles, and at times worried my father (not the most patient of men) exceedingly. When more than ordinarily out of humour, he would let fly a volley of oaths, swearing he neither could nor would waste his time by listening to the damned infernal nonsense of such chattering stupid old gossips and bidding her get out of his office. These ebullitions of passion sadly annoyed Mrs. White, who used to come into the clerks' office and declare that Mr. Hickey's violence and brutality was such that he

would not allow her to state her relation's case, or say half that was necessary relative to it. As my father's warmth was always of short duration, he, upon recollecting himself, felt sorry at hurting the old lady, and generally apologized, though not often with effect. A fracas of this nature had occurred one morning that I was to accompany her into the City to witness the execution of some deeds. On our way to Lombard Street, in her carriage, she suddenly exclaimed:

"What an abominable brute that man is, sir; he is an absolute devil in human shape." (The old lady imagined me to be a common articled clerk, no way related.) As I seemed rather to agree in opinion with her, she continued abusing him vehemently. At length, she asked, "Pray, young gentleman, is the wretch married?"

"Yes, ma'am."

"No child, I sincerely hope."

"Yes, ma'am, several."

"God Almighty help them," said she. "How can they exist with such a horrid monster?"

"Oh ma'am," replied I, "he is only a little passionate, which those used to do not mind, and it is soon over."

"Soon over indeed," retorted she. "The Devil confound him, he frightens me out of my wits."

With this conversation we arrived at the place of destination, where, after Mrs. White had executed the deeds, I signed my name as a witness; whreeupon she with a great brogue, screeched out:

"Oh holy Jesus, and so, you little imp, I have been abusing your father to you all the way. Why did you not stop me by letting me know you was one of the race?" Observing me grin, she continued, "Aye, aye, I see you are a true Hickey—all devils alike."

Upon our return to St. Albans Street, she said to my father:

"Faith and troth but I have made a pretty mistake here, in giving a very free opinion of you to your own flesh and blood, and that saucy whipper-snapper monkey, let me go on deeper and deeper. However, I don't care, I said nothing but the truth, and what I still think."

My father laughed heartily, and enjoyed the old lady's anxiety. Soon after this she became so habituated to his manner that it ceased to terrify her; and, when he flew into a rage, she, with the utmost composure, said:

"Be quiet, Hickey; none of your abominable cursing and swearing; I know you now, and don't value you a fig. I will have my own way, and say all I have to say, too"; which conduct completely answered, always restoring my father instantly to good humour.

Except during term time, or that there was any cause of consequence coming on, my father rarely slept in London during the summer months. It was customary for my mother and family to remove to

Twickenham shortly before Easter, and there to remain until the middle of November, at which season they returned to London, my father's principal object in receiving Mr. Bayley as a partner having been to take the burden of the business from himself, thereby enabling him to live more at his ease and amongst his friends. During the vacations between the terms I usually went to Twickenham and stayed until Monday morning, often sculling myself up and down, as I still possessed my little wherry. Everything went on smoothly until August 1766, at which time my father and mother set out for France, taking the twins Ann and Sarah with them for the purpose of placing them in a convent for education. About the same time my brother Henry returned from Ireland, accompanied by Tethrington, whom I have already mentioned. He (Tethrington) did not look more than seventeen, though he was full four-and-twenty, and had already passed some winters in all the profligacy and dissipation of Dublin.

There was nothing remarkably attractive either in his face or person; yet altogether he was a smart little man, had the most intelligent and piercing eyes, sung an admirable song, a proficient at tennis, fives, billiards and all fashionable games, was an uncommonly elegant dancer, and blessed with so strong a head that he could put the stoutest fellows under the table at fair drinking. Besides all these qualifications, he was a prodigious admirer of the fair sex, and a universal favourite of theirs; I have heard many lovely girls declare him irresistible and assert that he fascinated every female he addressed. He was a younger son of an Irish gentleman who had a large family and limited fortune. Like myself, his father had intended him for the Bar; and, like myself, Jack disappointed his parent's views. Whilst in the College of Dublin he associated with his superiors, by whom he was led into an expense he could not afford, which first drove him to gaming tables, where proving fortunate he obtained frequent and ample supplies. Such a life was inconsistent with study, his books were neglected and Coke lay upon his table unopened.

The ultimate consequence may be easily seen; he became embarrassed, for good luck could not last for ever; and being threatened with a gaol, the horrors thereof induced him to decamp, and he embarked for England in the same vessel with my brother Henry, with whom he had previously associated in Dublin. There is an old English vulgarism, "Birds of a feather flock together," which was completely verified in Tetherington and myself; and at our first meeting we became friends, for several years after which he showed the utmost regard for me; and, although he no doubt led me into some extravagances I might otherwise have avoided, yet he always gave me excellent advice and never would allow me to gamble, to which in fact I never had an inclination. His purse was ever at my service; when in

parties together at taverns and brothels, without a shilling in my pocket, as was sometimes the case, I had only to give him the slightest hint and my reckoning was discharged. Moreover, whenever I required a couple of guineas, or more, I had only to send to his lodgings and my wants were supplied.

In short, it was my peculiar good fortune to meet with uncommonly generous and disinterested whores and rogues. With my introduction to Tethrington ended all my good resolutions, and former follies were resumed in an increased degree. I had seen him play at billiards in a style of execution that delighted me; and I became so fond of the game that morning, noon and night was I looking on at the players, and at length took up a cue myself, instead of attending to my business, passing my time at some public table; and this continued for a couple of years. Let me, however, again observe it was not from a wish to win money at it, but a real liking to the game; nor did I ever lose anything material. The old sharks, of which there was a certain number that frequented each house, knew me very well, and the state of my finances.

Aware that if I lost a sum that vexed me, I should probably cease to play, they conducted themselves accordingly. At first they challenged me to play simply for the charge of the table, but after a week or so declared me wonderfully improved, and proposed sixpence a game, at which rate they would entertain me as long as I chose, taking care never to leave off winners of more than half a crown, that is, five games at one time; and they would often permit me to be even, or loser of an odd game, although had they used the superiority they possessed, I should not have got a single game in a month; yet they always appeared to wish to make the match even, by giving such odds as they pretended to deem equal. These poor devils also taught me to guard against the various tricks and stratagems practised by sharpers to deceive and cheat the young and unwary. Having no other mode of subsistence than what they cursorily picked up from novices and strangers, I proved a fine subject for supplying funds for a daily meal, with which they were satisfied, and so was I. The tables I usually frequented were Windmill Street, Whitehall, the Admiralty, The Angel, at the back of St. Clements, and Chancery Lane, at one or other of which I usually spent at least a couple of hours daily, and sometimes much longer; and I was as well known at all those places as at any of the public offices about Lincoln's Inn or the Temple.

In September, my favourite, Nanny Harris, returned from Ireland, where she had resided for some time, and called several times in St. Albans Street before I knew anything of the matter, as the servants had been cautioned respecting her. But a new one, who had recently come from Dublin with my cousin John Edwards, upon my coming

home one evening told me that a smart young lady had the instant before been enquiring for me, and could not then be many yards from the door. Having ascertained the way she went, I pursued, soon overtook, and recognized my early bed-fellow. She appeared greatly rejoiced at the meeting, telling me she had been in Ireland with a man of large fortune, with whom she continued until his marriage, when they separated, he presenting her with a couple of hundred pounds, with which sum in bank-notes as well as a handsome and plentiful wardrobe, she sailed for England, and had been in London one week, during which she had every day in person, enquired for me in St. Albans Street, and twice sent chairmen with notes for me; but the cursed servants, faithful to the charge they had received from my mother, returned the notes and never told me a word of the visits. This I afterwards learnt was entirely owing to the zeal of my friend, Molly Jones, all the other maids being desirous of telling me, from doing which she dissuaded them, stating Nancy Harris to be a wicked, artful hussy, whose object was to ruin me.

"And now, my dear Billy," said Nancy, "we are once more together, let's see who shall part us."

She was highly pleased at hearing my father and mother were abroad, and conducted me to a very comfortable, neat and well-furnished lodging in Berwick Street, Soho, where I passed the night. Upon going to office the following morning, my brother Joseph thought proper to call me to account for staying out all night, and interrogated as to where I had been. But not feeling that his having come into the world a few years sooner than myself gave him any authority over me, I pertinaciously declined response, receiving his lecture and admonitions with contemptuous silence. When he ceased to speak, I, in peremptory tone, desired his right to question or censure me, and refused to satisfy what I pronounced his impertinent curiosity.

He then threatened to complain to my master, Mr. Bayley, which only excited my mirth; for I cared as little for that gentleman as I did for himself; and for the next three nights my abode was the first floor in Berwick Street, to which place my brother having traced me, Mr. Bayley thereupon called upon my fair companion, whom he successfully alarmed by assuring her that, if she persisted in receiving me, he would cause her to be committed to hard labour in Bridewell, which she was liable to for inveigling away and harbouring an apprentice. Quite in terror, she informed me, who, though greatly vexed, was as much frightened as herself at the threat. I instantly went to Mr. Bayley; and, upon his agreeing not to molest her, I faithfully promised never to stay out another night, or go again to Berwick Street. The first condition I adhered to for some time at least; but the latter was quite out of the question and I made my visits by daylight, when

Nancy said she would save my word as to not going to Berwick Street, by changing her lodging, which she accordingly did, and took a first floor in Cecil Street in the Strand, a convenient situation for me, being in my road to the Temple, etc.

In November my father and mother returned from Paris; and, as neither Mr. Bayley nor my brother said anything of my misconduct during their absence, I received from my father approbation and congratulations for my good behaviour, which I felt I was as undeserving of as any young gentleman within His Majesty's dominions. My father further said he was sure the utmost confidence might now be placed in my future well-doing. Conscience certainly reproached me on receiving these unmerited encomiums and compliments; and I made in my own mind many fair promises, every one of which proved transitory as before, and I yielded to the first temptation that offered.

My brother Joseph had been instructed in every gentlemanlike qualification, amongst which he was a very tolerable swordsman, having been taught by Mr. Telligori, an Italian then in high repute. My father, as an encouragement to me to continue in the right line, sent for this person to attend and give me the requisite number of lessons. Upon his first visit, my father being in the room, I took up the foil with my left hand, having always been what is termed "left-handed." My father instantly exclaimed:

"Look at the awkward boy. Change hands, sir; surely you cannot suppose Mr. Telligori will attempt to instruct a left-handed fellow."

But the Italian directly replied:

"Oh yes, I will, sir, and recommend you by all means to let him be so taught; for, as a manly exercise and accomplishment, the effect will be precisely the same, and should he ever be obliged to use his sword in serious attack or defence of himself, the advantage from his so doing with the left hand will be great and manifest."

With the left therefore I learnt to fence; in fact, I used my left hand playing at all games, cricket, billiards, tennis, etc., etc.

My father had all his life been a remarkably early riser; I, on the contrary, was a sluggard and, if allowed to pursue my own inclination, never left my bed before nine o'clock. It was therefore much against the grain that I was now compelled to rise every morning by five, sometimes earlier, my father calling me himself, and directing me to go to my books, using every argument in his power to persuade me to read hard. Over and over again would he say: "Now is your time, my dear William, for studying to advantage; read hard, read day and night. Until you are forty it will all prove beneficial, and you will retain it; but after that age reading becomes a mere amusement for the time, as the memory then begins to flag." For two or three months I did obey my father's injunctions, and read a good deal, doubtless with con-

siderable advantage to myself. Had I through life continued the same course, I should at this day have been a very different sort of creature to what I am.

From the end of the year 1766, I was in a great measure deprived of my respected monitor, my father being very little in London; and, except when he was at my elbow urging me to what was correct, I thought of nothing but dissipation and folly; my books were entirely neglected, and I became idleness personified.

In February 1767 my father went to spend a month at Bath. Previous to leaving town he recommended Mr. Bayley to make me "the out-of-door clerk," that is, executing all business at the different law offices, issuing writs, and every other process in the progress of a cause, delivering briefs, and all other documents to counsel, and paying the fees; and this he advised as the most effectual mode of making me master of the practical part of the profession. My brother, who acted as cashier, was directed to furnish me with money for those purposes, and kept a book in which I was ordered to enter all receipts and disbursements. My father likewise made it his particular request that either Mr. Bayley or my brother would every Saturday night examine and check my account, receiving back all my vouchers.

Had they done as desired by my father, probably much of the subsequent evil that accrued to me and themselves would have been avoided; but unfortunately they wholly neglected the use of such precaution. Mr. Bayley being satisfied by once in three of four months in looking at the totals and, finding the debtor and creditor sides corresponded, made no further scrutiny or examination of the items. My error commencde in not keeping my pocket money distinct and separate from that belonging to the office. The consequence of not doing so was that I had unconsciously trespassed upon the latter before I was aware, and at the first discovery thereof was greatly alarmed.

This proper feeling, however, soon subsided; and, like all those that once commenced upon bad habits, I became by regular gradations, first uneasy, next indifferent, and by continued practice callous. Finding the balance every week considerably increasing against me, I endeavoured to counteract it by introducing sums I had never disbursed, entering others higher than I actually paid. True it is, the old and faithful monitor conscience frequently reminded me that such means were as dishonourable as unjustifiable, and upon discovery, which I knew must in the end take place, would bring me to disgrace and shame. Still, these internal upbraidings grew less and less, and I reconciled myself making false entries by feeling that the cash I was thus purloining belonged to my father, and that plundering him was different thing entirely to robbing a stranger.

I now became a constant frequenter of the Bedford and Piazza coffee houses; but my chief place for eating was young Slaughters, in St. Martin's Lane, where I supped every night with a set of extravagant young men of my own stamp. After some time we were displeased with the noise, and the promiscuous company that frequented the coffee room, chiefly to read the newspapers, especially half a dozen respectable old men, whom we impertinently pronounced a set of stupid, formal, ancient prigs, horrid periwig bores, every way unfit to herd with such bloods as us. It was therefore resolved that we should have private rooms, and we were transferred to the two-pairs-of-stairs front room, where we established ourselves into a roaring club, supped at eleven, after which we usually adjourned to Bow Street, Covent Garden, in which street there were then three most notorious bawdy houses, all which we took in rotation. The first was kept by a woman whose name I have forgotten; it was at the corner of a passage that led to the theatre. The second was at the top of the street in a little corner or nook, and was kept by an old Irish woman, named Hamilton, with whom I was upon remarkable good terms, of which she gave me most convincing proof in many times offering me money, saying, "My dear boy I always have plenty of loose cash about me, and it will do my heart good to furnish your pocket when in want of lining." Though I felt the kindness, I never availed myself of the offer, I believe to her great surprise.

I, however, did not scruple turning her partiality towards me to use in another way, by enjoying any particularly smart or handsome new piece, upon their becoming inmates with her; and she never failed giving me due notice when such was to be the case, besides a favourable introduction to the girls themselves; and certainly, low and infamous as these houses were, I have at times met with very beautiful women in them. The third brothel was kept by Mother Cocksedge, for all the Lady Abbesses were dignified with the respectable title of Mother. In these days of wonderful propriety and general morality, it will scarcely be credited that Mother Cocksedge's house was actually next, of course under the very nose of that vigilant and upright magistrate, Sir John Fielding, who, from the riotous proceedings I have been a witness to at his worthy neighbour's must have been deaf as well as blind, or at least, well paid for affecting to be so.

In these houses we usually spent from three to four hours, drinking arrack punch, or, as far as I was concerned pretending to do so; for being a composition I had an uncommon dislike to, I never did more than put the bowl to my lips, without swallowing a drop, and romping and playing all sorts of tricks with the girls. At a late, or rather early hour in the morning, we separated, retiring to the private respective

lodgings of some of the girls, there being only two that resided in the house, or to our homes, as fancy led, or according to the state of finances. My pocket being generally well stocked, I often went to Nancy Harris's, or to some fresher and therefore more attractive female.

THE PLEASURES OF LONDON

IN the summer we had another club, which met at the Red House in Battersea fields, nearly opposite Ranelagh, a retired and pretty spot. It was kept by an aged pair named Burt, having one daughter called Sally, about nineteen, and very pretty, with whom I speedily ingratiated myself; and, as she, soon after I began to frequent the house, married a young man, who from his avocations could only go to her occasionally, our amour continued without apprehensions of any kind. This club consisted of some very respectable persons, amongst them were Mr. Powell, of the Pay Office; Mr. Jupp, the East India Company's architect; Mr. Whitehead, a gentleman of independent fortune; King, the celebrated actor; Major Sturt of the Engineers; and others. The game we played was an invention of our own and called field tennis, which afforded noble exercise.

The situation of the house, which was close upon the edge of the river, and no public carriage road near it on the land side, rendered it as private as if it had been exclusively our own. Our regular meetings were two days in each week, when we assembled at one o'clock, at two sat down to dinner, consisting of capital stewed grigs,* a dish Mrs. Burt was famous for dressing, a large joint of roast or boiled meat, with proper vegetables and a good-sized pudding or pie; our drink consisting of malt liquors, cider, port wine, and punch. At four our sport commenced, continuing until dark; during the exercise we refreshed ourselves with draughts of cool tankard, and other pleasant beverage. The field, which was of sixteen acres in extent, was kept in as high order, and smooth as a bowling green. When we could no longer see, we returned to the house and drank tea or coffee; after which the bill was called for and, each paying his quota, the party broke up. I generally remained to pass an agreeable hour or two with my fair Sally; and fair she literally was, her hair being the lightest in colour I ever saw. She was generally distinguished by the wits of the Thames, with the name of Sally "Silver Tail."

* Small eels.

Our club consisted of twenty, and was always well attended; any member who absented himself, no matter from what cause, on a club day forfeited half a crown, which was put through a hole made in the lid of a box, kept under lock and key, and opened only once a year, when the amount of forfeits was laid out in an extra dinner at the Red House, generally about 20th December, and consisting of venison and of all sorts of dainties, the liquors being claret and madeira, purchased for the occasion. Besides our regular days, some of the members met every evening during the summer months to have a little field tennis. It was just a mile from Buckingham Gate to the Chelsea waterworks, from whence Burt's boat immediately conveyed us across the water, being rowed by an extraordinary man, who, though born deaf and dumb, was the quickest and most intelligent creature, and could make us perfectly understand who were already arrived, having a particular sign by which he distinguished each member. This person went daily to Clare Market, where he would execute punctually every order, purchasing all that was wanted as correctly as if he had not been deprived of the faculties of speech and hearing. At the time I am now speaking of, he was a stout well-looking fellow of about two- or three-and-twenty, and as we all saw, a laborious and useful servant.

The annual dinner I have above alluded to, took place this year (1767) on 19th December, on which day I rowed myself up to the Red House, got abominably drunk, as did most of the party, and in spite of the remonstrances of Burt and his wife, backed by Sally too, I, at two o'clock in the morning, staggered to my boat, which I literally tumbled into, and, without recollecting one word of the matter, obstinately refused to let anyone accompany me, and pushed off. Whether, intoxicated as I was, it came into my head everybody would be in bed at Roberts's at Lambeth, where my boat was kept, or not, I cannot tell, or what guided my proceedings; but it seems I ran her ashore at Milbank, there got out, and endeavoured to walk home. Unfortunately for me they were then paving anew the lower parts of Westminster, and I in consequence encountered various holes, and various heaps of stone and rubbish, into and over which I tumbled and scrambled, God only knows how, or how I contrived to get so far on my way as Parliament Street; but a little after seven in the morning, a party who had supped, and afterwards played whist all night, at a Mr. James's, were just sallying forth to get into a hackney coach, waiting to convey them to their respective homes. Mr. Smith, one of the company, who was a riding master of His Majesty's, stepping to the rear of the coach to make water, descried a human figure laying in the kennel, whereupon he called to his companions, who, upon examination, found it was poor pilgarlic in woeful plight.

Being thus recognized, though I was utterly incapable of giving any account of myself, or of even articulating, they lifted me into their coach, Mr. Smith and another attending to support me; and thus I was conveyed to my father's and there put to bed, having no more recollection of a single circumstance that had occurred for the preceding twelve hours, than if I had been dead. My boat, which was known to all the watermen above bridge, was found at daylight laying aground at Milbank, having only one scull in her. Upon enquiry, a watchman said he had observed a young gentleman, who appeared very tipsy, land from her, and seeing how incapable he was of walking, and that he fell every yard, offered to assist him, which was violently rejected; and he therefore went to his watch-house, it being near break of day.

I awoke the following day in my own bed, as from a horrible dream, unable to move hand or foot, being most miserably bruised, cut and maimed in every part of my body. The three first days, my old friend Dr. Nugent, and Mr. Samuel Hayes, an eminent surgeon, were much alarmed, telling my father I was in imminent danger, a strong fever having come on, and from some symptoms they apprehended serious internal injury. Youth, however, and a naturally good constitution, befriended me. I got better in a week, and on the tenth day was allowed to rise for an hour; but more than three weeks elapsed ere I left my chamber.

At the Red House I became acquainted with Mr. Symonds, as worthy and truly honest a man as ever lived. He was a great politician and patriot, not according to the modern acceptation of that term, but from sheer principle. He was a Liveryman of London, in executing the duties of which station his sole object was the advantage and well-doing of his native land; nor was he ever known to give his aid or influence to mere party measures, or to censure or find fault with ministers, only because they were in office. This truly respectable gentleman continued to carry on the business of a wholesale stationer in which he had succeeded his father, in a large mansion close to the East India house in Leadenhall Street, serving that Company, the Bank of England, and other public bodies; and this notwithstanding he possessed an ample fortune, which fortune, shortly after my acquaintance with him commenced, was materially increased by the death of a relation, who left him an estate of upwards of two thousand pounds per annum, in consequence of which he took the name of Smith.

He had a noble house upon the border of the river, a little above the town of Battersea, where he lived in the true style of old English hospitality, in the midst of a happy family consisting of a wife, one son, and one daughter, entertaining his numerous friends with a warmth and cordiality that never was exceeded, seldom equalled. After a liberal quantity of the best port and madeira, which followed an excellent dinner, himself and guest adjourned to the billiard table or bowling green, according to weather or season of the year. From either of those amusements they went to the drawing-room, where tea and coffee being served, music filled up the space till ten, at which hour supper was served; and at eleven everybody retired to their homes, or if his guests for the night, to their chambers, where every comfort awaited them. And here did I, who in London passed my evenings and nights in theatres, taverns, and brothels, amidst abandoned profligates of both sexes, and in every species of folly and intemperance, at least once in every month, and sometimes oftener, quietly and soberly, as well as rationally, spend Saturday and Sunday in the society of this worthy and respectable family; with the utmost complacency, and actual satisfaction to myself, complying with all the customary and decent forms of the house, regularly attending the whole family on Sunday, both morning and evening, (of such force is example, whether good or bad,) to the meeting house, their place of worship, Mr. Smith being a Dissenter, and rigid observer of all the forms adopted by that sect.

On the Sabbath, therefore, we never had the billiard room opened, nor any amusement except admirable sacred music. Mr. Smith was very fond of sailing, and had a fast-going little vessel, built from a Dutch model, in which I took many a cruise with him, he constantly standing at the helm, with a pipe in his mouth, being a great smoker. My father, who was by this time but too well acquainted with my vicious habits, would not give me credit for passing two days a week in so respectable a family and so sedate a manner as I described, and upon my often assuring him on my honour that I had been there, and nowhere else, would feelingly exclaim how depraved and lost to all sense of shame I must be to pledge so solemn an affirmation to what I must be conscious was utterly false. Really mortified at this doubt of my veracity, though certainly I had given too much reason to bring it into question, I pettishly answered:

"If, sir, no reliance is to be placed on my word, why do you not call at Mr. Smith's and ascertain the truth or falsehood of what I say?"

"And so perhaps I may, and sooner than you will like," replied my father.

Shortly after this had passed, I was surprised at a sudden alteration in my father's manner towards me. From an angry and offended countenance, with the coldest behaviour at all times when we met, he resumed his natural character respecting me by becoming kind and affectionate as ever, and everything I said or did seemed to please him. For this change I could in no way account, knowing that I had done nothing to entitle me to it. Upon my mother's coming to town for a day on some business, I asked her if she knew what had occa-

sioned this favourable change as to me; when she told me that he had
a few mornings before rode over to Mr. Smith's, where upon enquiry
he found that I had said what was true; that Mr. Smith spoke of me
in the most affectionate language, and terms of the highest panegyric,
saying that, so far from my betraying any symptoms of profligacy or
immorality during the many times I had been his guest, I showed
myself the most correct and best principled young man he ever knew;
that my lively and cheerful disposition deservedly made me a favourite
with everyone acquainted with me, so much so that not only himself,
but every individual of his family felt gratified when they saw me
enter the house.

A eulogium so unexpected and so flattering to me had delighted my
poor father. The same morning on which I received this information,
my father learnt from my mother that it had been so communicated.
He then sent for me to his office, when, putting five guineas into my
hand, he burst into tears, tears that cut me to the soul, and drew from
my eyes a gush of exquisite anguish. After a silence of some minutes,
he pressed me close, kissed my cheek, and adding, "Persevere, my
dearest boy, in the right line and you will be an honour to yourself
and me," dismissed me. I can safely aver that these five guineas were
the only ones I in my life ever received without feeling a particle of
satisfaction or pleasure in the possession of them; but such is the fact.
The same silent but powerful monitor, that had often before, spoke
within, again told me how very undeserving I was of my father's
affectionate attentions, and that the same were bestowed upon a repro-
bate and an ingrate. The drawing tears, though in part tears of satisfaction, from such a parent hurt me more than I can express. I formed
a thousand good resolutions, but alas, as usual, to end in nothing.

In January 1768, my father by way of recreation, took me with him
to Bath. Whilst there, we made excursions to the seats of different
friends of his who resided at Bristol, Gloucester, and other places in
that part of England; and after an absence of five weeks spent in the
pleasantest manner, we returned to London.

In consequence of the good resolutions I made upon receiving the
undeserved five guineas from my father, more than two months had
elapsed without once going to any of my old haunts; and I had during
that period conducted myself with the utmost propriety and decorum,
so that I began to congratulate myself upon a complete reformation.
My vanity even carried me so far as to suppose I now possessed fortitude sufficient to resist temptation, and that I might venture occasionally to visit the club of Slaughters without renewing my former
vicious habits. Full of this erroneous idea, I, one evening in March,
called in at Slaughters, where some of my quondam associates immediately gathered round me, with warm congratulations upon my return

to them protesting that they would have a gala night to celebrate the restoration of so worthy a member. Up I went to the club-room, down went the wine and punch, and away went all my plans of reformation. Society, as usual, proved my bane; for, although I at first attempted to flinch, pleading ill-health and being forbid spirituous liquors, I was only laughed at and ridiculed. In short, my resistance was of no avail; I yielded, and drank deep as the rest.

I was informed with vast glee by these wild young men that, during my secession, they had discovered two new houses of infinite merit, with which they were sure I should be wonderfully pleased, and to both of which they would introduce me before we parted. At the customary hour, being brimful of wine, we sallied forth, went the old Bow Street rounds, from whence I was led into an absolute hell upon earth. The first impression on my mind upon entering those diabolical regions never will be effaced from my memory. This den was distinguished by the name of Wetherby's, situate in the narrowest part of Little Russell Street, Drury Lane. Upon ringing at a door, strongly secured with knobs of iron, a cut-throat-looking rascal opened a small wicket, which was also secured with narrow iron bars, who in a hoarse and ferocious voice asked, "Who's there?" Being answered "Friends," we were cautiously admitted one at a time, and when the last had entered, the door was instantly closed and secured, not only by an immense lock and key, but a massy iron bolt and chain.

I had then never been within the walls of a prison; yet this struck me like entering one of the most horrible kind. My companions conducted me into a room where such a scene was exhibiting that I involuntarily shrunk back with disgust and dismay, and would have retreated from the apartment, but that I found my surprise and alarm were so visible in my countenance as to have attracted the attention of several persons who came up, and good-naturedly enough encouraged me, observing that I was a young hand but should soon be familiarized and enjoy the fun. At this time the whole room was in an uproar, men and women promiscuously mounted upon chairs, tables, and benches, in order to see a sort of general conflict carrying on upon the floor. Two she-devils, for they scarce had a human appearance, were engaged in a scratching and boxing match, their faces entirely covered with blood, bosoms bare, and the clothes nearly torn from their bodies. For several minutes not a creature interfered between them, or seemed to care a straw what mischief they might do each other, and the contest went on with unabated fury.

In another corner of the same room, an uncommonly athletic young man of about twenty-five seemed to be the object of universal attack. No less than three Amazonian tigresses were pummelling him with all their might, and it appeared to me that some of the males at times dealt him blows with their sticks. He, however, made a capital defence, not sparing the women a bit more than the men, but knocking each down as opportunity occurred. As fresh hands continued pouring in upon him, he must at last have been miserably beaten, had not two of the gentlemen who went with me, (both very stout fellows) offended at the shameful odds used against a single person, interfered, and after a few knock-me-down arguments, succeeded in putting an end to the unequal conflict. This, to me, unusual riot, had a similar effect with Othello's sudden and unexpected appearance before his inebriated officer, Michael Cassio, for it produced an immediate restoration of my senses, the effect of which was an eager wish to get away; for which purpose I, in the confusion, slunk out of the room into the passage, and had just began fumbling at the street door, hoping to be able to liberate myself, when the same fierce and brutal Cerberus that had admitted my party coming up, roughly seized me by the collar exclaiming: "Hulloa, what the devil have you been about here?"

To which I answered meekly: "Nothing, but not being well I am desirous of going home."

"Oh you are, are you! I think you came in not long since, and with a party. What! Do you want to tip us a bilk? Have you paid your reckoning, eh? No, no, youngster, no tricks upon travellers. No exit here until you have passed muster, my chick."

More shocked than ever, I was compelled to return to the infuriate monsters, the ferocious door-keeper following me and addressing one of my companions whom he knew, said:

"So the young'un there wanted to be off, but I said as how I knew a trick worth two of that, too much experience to be taken in by such a sucker, told him not to expect to catch old birds with chaff, didn't I, young'un, hey?"

In this dreadful hole I was therefore obliged to stay until my friends chose to depart; and truly rejoiced did I feel at once more finding myself safe in the street. I expressed in strong terms my disgust at which I had just witnessed, declaring my determination never to subject myself to the like again. This only excited the laughter of my companions, who, notwithstanding all my remonstrances and resistance, dragged me with them to another scene of nocturnal dissoluteness, situate in the same street, but on the opposite side. This was called "Murphy's," where, although there was no actual personal hostilities going on when we entered, the war of words raged to the utmost extent; and such outré phrases never before encountered my ears, though certainly until that night I had considered myself a tolerable proficient in blackguardism. I found that it was the custom at Wetherby's never to serve any liquor after the clock struck three, so that those jolly blades whose bottles or bowls were empty when that hour arrived then adjourned to Murphy's, which at the end of that year changed its name to "Marjoram's"; and here also the time for serving liquors was limited, the hour being five in the morning.

From this latter nest of pickpockets, and lowest description of prostitutes, we got away about half-past four, I inwardly wishing every mishap might attend me if ever I again crossed the threshold of either of the Russell Street houses during the remainder of my life. I continued to frequent the club as Slaughters, but rigidly adhered to my resolution not to accompany them to Wetherby's. In the early part of May, however, having dined with my brother Henry, and a party of his convivial associates, at the Shakespear, someone at a late hour proposed a visit to Wetherby's, when I instantly entered my negative. The company, surprised, asked the reason, and I related what had occurred to me, which excited much mirth. They, however, told me that I had been unlucky in necountering such a riot. Tethrington and my brother then said they would escort me, and I should find it a very different thing. Thus encouraged and being fortified with an ample dose of claret, I made no further objection, and was agreeably disappointed.

At the sound of Tethrington's voice, the door was opened wide, Upon entering the former place of action, all was not perfect peace, where three or four small parties of both sexes were drinking in high mirth and good humour. The women jumped up and ran to us, vociferously enquiring of my brother and Tethrington what they had been doing with themselves for an gae past; then directing their attention towards me, they asked, "And who is this nice youth, pray?" Being informed I was a brother fo Henry's, half a dozen of them assailed me, and I thought would have stifled me with their endearments. One of them was particularly lavish of her kindnesses, in whom to my utter astonishment, I recognized one of the ferocious combatants of the former night, whose name I now learnt was Burgess.

Our party adjourned from the public room to a private one in the rear of the house, where I at once discovered my brother and Tethrington to be quite at home. Burgess sung a number of admirable songs, and was very entertaining, as was another sad profligate girl, who had justly acquired the name of Blasted Bet Wilkinson. Burgess and I became very sociable, and I asked her how it happened that she could have been a principal in such a horrid broil as I have witnessed; to which she replied, that both herself and her antagonist were exceedingly intoxicated, having drank an unusual quantity of spirits, and in their cups had quarrelled; that the other battle royal, of which I was also a spectator, arose from the man (who was a notorious woman's bully) having basely robbed the two who attacked him; that the rest concerned were the friends of one party or the other, and acted

3+

accordingly. This Miss Burgess lived for several years afterwards with Dibdin, the actor, who had just at the above period commenced his theatrical career, in the character of Hodge in the comic opera of *The Maid of the Mill*.

After spending a couple of hours with great glee at Wetherby's, we all crossed the street to Marjoram's, which we found well stowed, a large crowd being collected round the famous and popular Ned Shuter, who, although immoderately drunk, was entertaining the circle of bystanders, with all sorts of buffoonery and tricks. Here, too, my companions seemed to be as well known and in as high favour as at Wetherby's; for, upon our approach, an opening was voluntarily made and chairs placed for us close to the facetious comedian, who, for above an hour, by his drollery kept us in a continued roar of laughter, when he suddenly fell from his seat as if he had been shot, and I really feared was dead; until those better acquainted than myself observed, if he was, it was only dead drunk, a finale nightly repeated. He was then lifted up and carried off like a hog to his lodgings, which were in the neighbourhood, and we departed to our beds, I being as much pleased with the night's amusement, as I had on the former been disgusted.

The following day I asked my brother Henry how it happened that I, who had been above a twelvemonth ranging about the jelly shops, and all the bawdy houses of Covent Garden, had never met with Burgess, or any of the women I saw at Wetherby's and Marjoram's; when he told me the females that frequented those two houses, scarcely ever went anywhere else, unless it were to the Dog and Duck in St. George's Fields, or to Bagnige Wells and White Conduit house, near Islington, at both which places I had been once or twice; but as I never was partial to those kind of entertainments, nothing took me to them but company.

My Battersea friend, Mr. Smith, had now purchased from a Mr. Clark of Christchurch, in Hampshire, a beautiful yacht, about fifty tons burden, a heavy dull sailer, but with capital accommodations, having a spacious cabin aft her whole width with sash windows astern. This was used as the sitting and eating apartment from thenceforward; on each side were three comfortable cabins with fixed bed-places, so that a party of six or eight might be well lodged on board. Mr. Smith told me he had thoughts of collecting a few friends and making an excursion of a week or ten days, and if I was so inclined and could obtain my father's permission, he should be happy that I made one. The next time I visited Battersea, he said, Major Sturt, Mr. Pritzler and Captain Cecil had arranged the tour, and they proposed embarking in the *Lovely Mary*, the yacht's name, the ensuing Monday. I promised to apply to my father, and having his leave, to join them at the appointed time. But, as I felt certain my father would object to my absenting myself for so long a period, when there was much business in the office, I thought I had better dispense with the application, and accordingly putting up some linen and other necessaries in a portmanteau, I privately sent them off on Saturday, and on Sunday went myself to Mr. Smith's.

After supper, instead of retiring to our chambers we went on board to sleep, that we might drop down in the night close to London Bridge, so as to pass through at high water, and thereby secure an entire ebb to start with and carry us clear of all the shipping in the Pool. We commenced our voyage on 20th April, with charming clear and open weather, having a fine breeze of wind from the westward, which in five hours carried us to Gravesend, at which place we anchored, all hands going on shore to call upon Mr. Pendock Neale, an intimate friend of Mr. Smith's, and acquainted with all the party. He held an appointment under the East India Company, which made it necessary he should reside at Gravesend. He insisted upon our staying the remainder of the day with him. At dinner was one of the largest and finest-flavoured turbots I ever tasted. After being most hospitably entertained, at eleven at night we returned to our vessel, proceeding downward.

The following day it blew fresh at south-west, which rattled us on at such a rate that by dusk we reached Margate, landed, and went to Michiner's, where we got an excellent supper, and then re-embarked. On the 23rd we left the pier, steering direct for the Nore, at which we turned off by Sheerness, entered the Medway, passing Chatham and Rochester, and after a delightful sail up that romantic and picturesque river, early in the morning of the 25th arrived at Maidstone; and here we spent five days very agreeably, our headquarters being Mr. Watman's, a great paper manufacturer, who entertained us in a princely style. His mills and extensive works were a source of amusement to us several hours in each day, every one of our party making (awkwardly enough) a sheet of paper. In the evenings, little dances and parties of the most select kind filled up the time to the hour of bed, never later than twelve. Early in the morning of the 30th we once more went on board the *Lovely Mary*, leaving the good-humoured and unostentatious hospitality of Maidstone with much regret.

As we approached home, I began to feel some unpleasant doubts respecting the reception I should meet with. We arrived at Battersea on 2nd May, in the evening, where Mr. Smith found a letter from my father, written in a very severe and reproachful terms respecting me. He had learnt from the family in Battersea that I was gone down the river. In this letter he did Mr. Smith the justice to conclude that I had made him believe I had my master's permission to be absent; instead of which consent, my father stated the clandestine manner in which I had left the house without saying a word to anyone, leaving business of importance which it was my duty to have attended to totally neglected. He concluded by entreating of Mr. Smith never more to admit me within his doors, for I should only bring disgrace upon everyone who showed me kindness, repaying them with black ingratitude, if not worse, if worse could be.

This address gave Mr. Smith real concern, and certainly both vexed and mortified me from tending to lower me in the opinions of my friends. I was, however, too firmly established with Mr. Smith and his family to lose their esteem without a struggle. A consultation was held by them and Major Sturt, unknown to me, what steps should be taken most likely to soften my father's anger; when, as I subsequently found, Mr. Smith determined to call upon him in person and plead for me; which he did, and so successfully, that instead of upbraidings and reproaches which I felt I so richly deserved, my father upon my going home only shook his head, observing that I had a most zealous and powerful advocate in Mr. Smith, and ill merited the affectionate regards of such respectable and worthy people. "I have," continued my father, "given my word once more to pass over this new transgression, and I hope by future diligence and attention you will make up for lost time."

Thus easily did I escape from a serious scrape, and vowed to myself to follow my father's advice and fulfil his hopes; but alas, I never possessed a single grain of self-command or control over my passions; one short week ended all my good resolves, and I sunk deeper than ever in error. Not a night but I passed a considerable portion of in every degree of dissipation and debauchery, mixing with the most abandoned of both sexes. In addition to Wetherby's and Marjoram's, I had now discovered two other receptacles of the same stamp or, if the degrees of depravity and infamy would admit, even worse. The one was facetiously called, "The Soup Shop," a dirty vile ale-house in Bridges Street, Drury Lane, where it was the custom to take a basin of ox-cheek broth at six o'clock in the morning, a villainous compound of filth I took special care not a drop of should ever pass my lips. The other new discovery was significantly named, "The Finish." This was a shed in Covent Garden Market, thentofore dignified by the title of "Carpenter's Coffee House," and where they still continued to dole out a Spartan mixture, difficult to ascertain the ingredients of, but which was served as coffee. Returning home from these intemperate scenes, if my father was out of town, as he generally was, I went to bed for four or five hours, but, if in town, I went directly to my desk, where, laying my head down upon it, I soon fell asleep, in which state Mr. Bayley would often find me; when, awaking me, he with a solemn face would say, "Indeed, William, these are sad doings, and God only knows to what a life of such excess will lead you."

Unfortunately for me, who required no encouragement, or any persons to show me bad example, my own evil propensities being quite sufficient, there was at this time in the office a young man, employed as a hackney writer, whose name was Daniel Weir. He was Irish, a smart well-made fellow, and a great admirer of the fair sex, with whom he was a universal favourite, and I believe from the same reason as Tethrington. This person sometimes accompanied me in my nocturnal rambles, which he found both pleasant and convenient, not being overburdened with cash, and wherever we went I being paymaster. In return, however, for my money he at different times introduced me to women of a very superior sort to any I had thentofore been acquainted with. There were mostly in keeping, and as I suspect is almost always the case, were unfaithful to their immediate patrons, always having one or more gallants for their own private gratification. Indeed, my brother Henry and Tethrington had both often told me, that with my qualifications and companionable talents, my amours never ought to cost me a guinea, unless by paying for admission to the theatres and other public places.

One of Weir's fair friends to whom he had introduced me, called herself Fanny Temple, and afterwards changed it to Hartford. A finer woman in every respect could not be. With her I became so great a favourite that she never was happy unless I was with her. Unlike the generality of women in that line of life, her manners were perfectly correct; nor did I ever once hear a vulgarism of coarse expression pass her lips. She was mistress of music, had an enchanting voice, which she managed with the utmost skill, danced elegantly and spoke French, *assez bien.* She inhabited an excellent house in Queen Anne Street, and had besides neat lodgings in the country, pleasantly situated near the waterside just above Hammersmith, and kept her own chariot, with suitable establishment of servants, the whole being paid for, as well as her domestic expenses, which were liberally allowed for, by a gentleman of rank and fashion, possessed of a splendid fortune, whom she told me my family was well acquainted with. Yet, notwithstanding I frequently entreated her to tell me his name, she never would, though urged even in the moments of greatest endearment, observing that she had made a solemn promise never to divulge it to anybody whatsoever; and being a most liberal and worthy man, she considered herself bound in honour and conscience never to betray him.

This being a line of conduct every man of sentiment must approve, I ceased to importune her on the subject. In a few weeks, however, I discovered the person without the smallest blame attaching to her. Thus, she and I had been one evening to Ranelagh, from whence I had accompanied her to Queen Anne Street, there to pass the night. Having supped, we were undressed, and just stepping into bed, when we heard someone running quickly upstairs, and a great bustle in the passage, whereupon she exclaimed, "My God! I am undone, there is Mr. ——." I darted into a closet, the door of which was scarce closed, when in he walked, and to my inexpressible astonishment I recognized the voice of a gentleman I was perfectly well acquainted with, whom I knew was married to an amiable and accomplished woman, who had borne him eight children, all then living, with which wife he was upon the best terms; and they were by the world considered as a rare instance of conjugal felicity in high life. He was, too, at this time considerably above sixty years old.

Fanny, with a readiness that seldom fails the sex, called the maid to take out and air clean sheets, leading her friend by the hand into the dining-room. The servant instantly locked the door, and gathering up my clothes, carried them down to the parlour, to which I softly descended, there dressed myself, and made good my retreat. The following day I received a note from Fanny, desiring me to come and dine with her. I accordingly went, when after a warm embrace she observed what a narrow escape we had had, where one minute more must have been fatal. It seems the coachman had just stepped across the street to order some porter for himself and kitchen companions, leaving the door ajar in the interim. The old gentleman arriving, he, of course, entered unannounced, and was marching upstairs when the cook hearing him, and fearing what might be the case, ran up screeching, crying thieves, in order to prepare us.

The result is already known. Fanny informed me everything passed off without the lease suspicion on his part. Luckily he entered the room at the contrary side to where my clothes lay, or he must inevitably have seen them on the couch. He asked what ailed her, for she seemed uneasy and flurried, which she ascribed partly to headache, and partly to the unexpected happiness at seeing him! And all went off admirably. He had been out of town for some time, when being suddenly summoned to London to be present at a wedding of a relation, he availed himself of that opportunity to enjoy himself in the arms of his Dulcinea. This critical escape taught us to be more upon our guard in future. From that night I never undressed in the bed chamber, but upon another floor; and, when in bed, we always bolted and locked the doors, which never had before been done.

5

FOLLY AND PENITENCE

ARLY in this month, May [1768], the famous riots occurred, on
account of Mr. Wilkes, then confined in the King's Bench prison
under a sentence of the Court of King's Bench. A prodigious
mob assembled for several days successively, in front of the prison;
but no violence was committed until the 9th, when a large body of
sailors made their appearance, some of whom like monkeys scrambling
up the wall, were in a minute at the window of Mr. Wilkes's apartment, whom they offered directly to liberate, declaring if he gave the
word they would soon have the prison level with the ground. Mr.
Wilkes very prudently begged them to desist, expressed his thanks
for their personal regard to him, adding he had no doubt the laws of
his country would ultimately d ohim justice. He therefore besought
them to do as he should, that was patiently to wait the result, and that
they would return peaceably to their own homes. Upon which they
gave three cheers and dispersed, saying they would come again the
next day, in case he (Wilkes) should change his mind and wish to
come out.

Upon their arrival at the prison, Mr. Thomas, the Marshal, being
much alarmed, sent off for a party of the Guards. These soldiers very
imprudently on reaching the prison, where not one of the sailors then
remained, began beating and maltreating the lookers-on, which irritated the mob, some of whom threw stones at the guards; but nothing
serious happened that day. As I had been present the whole of the 9th
and concluded there would be a renewal of the disturbance on the
following day, I was stationed close to the prison gates by nine in the
morning of the 10th, where I found already assembled a large party
of the Third Regiment of Guards, which consisted principally of
Scotsmen, a circumstance that tended to increase the mischief. Several
justices of the peace, and an immense body of constables were also in
attendance.

At ten o'clock, full a thousand seamen made their promised visit,
again mounting to Mr. Wilkes's window, offering him liberty if he

chose it, notwithstanding the presence of the "lobsters" (as they called the soldiers), Wilkes renewing his entreaties that they would depart quietly. They as before, cheered, and did so, a mere gaping inoffensive mob remaining. A stupid, over-zealous justice, however, thought proper to read the Riot Act, which not one-hundredth part of the crowd knew had been done; after which the same blockhead of a magistrate (Mr. Gillam) ordered the constables to disperse the mob, which they attempted by seizing several inoffensive persons and delivering them into charge of the military. This ill-timed and unnecessary violence at last raised a general indignation amongst the spectators; loud hisses commenced and abuse of the Scotch soldiers, and some few stones were thrown, one of which hit Gillam, whereupon the magistrates ordered the Guards to fire, which the infernal scoundrels instantly did, with ball, whereby several persons lost their lives, some of them not being in the mob at all; for the vile assassins fired in all directions, and even across the public high road. One poor woman was killed seated upon a cartload of hay going by at the time.

At the time the firing commenced, I was leaning upon the railing that separated the fields from the road, talking to a gentleman who stood near me; and we were mutually reprobating the infamous conduct of the soldiers and magistrates when we observed several of the Guards running towards us; and soon they were in pursuit of a man in a scarlet waistcoat, who jumped over the rail within a foot of us, four soldiers being about fifty yards behind him in chase. My new acquaintance and I followed. The pursued man ran round a windmill; when finding himself in danger of being overtaken, he made for an inn near the Borough, kept by a Mr. Allen, the yard of which he entered, darting through a barn used as a cow-house, having a door at each end, two of the Guards being then close at his heels.

At the very instant he passed the second door, the son of Mr. Allen entered by the opposite one, and unluckily having a red waistcoat on, one of the soldiers, upon seeing him, presented his firelock and the young man in a fright dropped on his knees; when the soldier fired, killing him upon the spot. All this was the work of a minute, my companion and myself being witnesses of the whole bloody transaction. The mob, now justly irritated at the brutality of the soldiers, became outrageous, and volleys of stones flew in every direction. The soldiers loaded and fired again and again, by which many lives were wantonly sacrificed. It struck both me and my companion as wonderful that the soldier who shot Allen and his comrades were suffered to return unmolested, except by hooting and hissing, to the main body; but the uproar then increasing, it was thought a proper precaution to withdraw him from duty, and he was lodged within the prison.

The fellow pretended that it was not his intention to have fired, and that his musket went off upon half cock. A very large body of Horse Guards having now joined the Foot, galloping round the ground, striking everyone they met violently with their broad swords, made the remaining there any longer a service of danger. I therefore proposed leaving the spot, to which my new acquaintance acceded, and we agreed to dine together, during which meal I learnt that his name was Baker, that he resided at Deal, in which town he had a large estate in houses. With this gentleman I afterwards became intimate.

A coroner's inquest being held upon the mangled corpse of young Allen, after a full investigation of the circumstances, returned a verdict of "Wilful murder by certain persons whose names they could not discover, but whom they had ascertained to be private soldiers in His Majesty's 3rd Regiment of Foot Guards." A monument was erected over the grave, with an inscription stating that the deceased had been barbarously murdered by a party of Scotsmen belonging to the Third Regiment of Guards.

In the month of June 1768, my early favourite, Nanny Harris, whom I have already so often mentioned, died, a martyr to a life of excess and to venereal taints. The death of this young creature caused me real and unfeigned sorrow. I was at this period no more than nineteen years old. A strong instance I was of how prone youths of that age are to be fickle. For, although I had the entrée whenever I pleased, not only to Fanny Temple's, but to others of the finest women then upon the Town, amongst whom were Madame La Tour—kept in the most extravagant manner by Sir Peniston Lamb, now Lord Melbourne— Mrs. Sturgess, Miss Larkin, etc., etc., and with any or either of these I never need have expended a shilling, yet, probably from that very reason, and a natural perverseness of disposition, I frequently preferred going to a bagnio with the most hackneyed and common woman, which not only ran away with my money, but injured my health. Of the latter, however, I never thought, nor much, indeed, of the former. There was an extravagant and common little harlot, named Brent, to whom I was strongly attached. She was not at all pretty, being much pitted with the smallpox, mercenary in the highest degree, and addicted to drinking. Yet, notwithstanding all these failings, there was a something about her which fascinated me; and often did I prefer taking her to Malby's, under the Piazza of Covent Garden, and there passing the night at a considerable expense, to partaking, as I might have done gratis, every species of elegance and luxury, at the accomplished Fanny Temple's, or others I have alluded to.

Great part of the day I generally passed at tennis, billiards, the Red House, with Silver Tail, and in every sort of dissipation; my nights, as already mentioned. Sometimes I went with parties upon the water, and I still continued an uncommonly expert and skilful rower. I was

3*

one of the eight proprietors of a rowing cutter, in which we made excursions upon the Thames and wore very smart uniforms, having a waterman in a rich livery to steer us. In the end of June 1768, we performed what was, by all the Thames people and those conversant in such matters, deemed a very extraordinary feat, nothing equal to which had ever been done before. We started from Roberts's, at Lambeth, at high water, being then four o'clock in the morning; reached Gravesend, a distance of forty miles, by half-past seven; at nine, left it on our return, passed Lambeth a little after twelve, and got to the Castle at Richmond by three, where we dined and remained near four hours; at seven got again on board our cutter, and by half-past ten at night landed at Lambeth, having thus rowed ourselves full one hundred and thirty miles in thirteen hours.

In July of the same year, we exhibited ourselves in a very superior style. The Earl of Lincoln, who had a beautiful house at Weybridge, near Walton Bridge, having with him a large party of the nobility, male and female, upon a visit, adopted various modes of amusing them. Amongst others he planned what was termed a Regatta, to which all the gentlemen of the neighbourhood who kept boats were invited. The whole were to assemble at the foot of his lordship's terrace, from thence in procession (the order of moving being previously arranged) drop gently down with the stream to Hampton Court, in the garden of which an elegant collation was prepared in tents put up for the occasion. After remaining there till towards sunset, they were to pull up again to his seat, where a magnificent dinner awaited them, with fireworks and superb illuminations, the night to conclude with a ball.

This entertainment we determined to partake of, as far as with propriety and civility we could; and, having heard and seen the costly preparations the noble host had made for the reception of his party, we agreed at least not to disgrace the cavalcade we intended to accompany. We accordingly had our cutter entirely new dressed and fitted up. She was painted of a bright azure blue, with gold mouldings and ornaments, the oars and every article finished in the same way, richly embellished with aquatic devices. The awning was of the same colour, in silk, as were the dresses of the eight rowers, the packets and trousers being trimmed with an uncommonly neat spangle and foil lace, and made easy, so that we could row perfectly well in them. We wore black round hats with very broad gold bands and small bright blue cockades in front. The ensign was of richest silks; under the awning we had capital french horns and clarinets, the performers being dressed exactly like the rowers.

We sent the cutter, covered with matting, by West Country barge to Walton, where we assembled in the morning of the day of the entertainment; and having equipped ourselves at the inn close to the bridge, we started from thence to attend the Regatta. The novelty, as well as the splendour of our appearance, drew every eye upon us; and we undoubtedly made a very showy and brilliant figure, far surpassing any one of the boats in the procession. We pulled what is called the man-of-war's stroke, that is, only four in each minute. The rapid manner in which we moved in all directions and our masterly manoeuvres, surprised, and seemed highly to gratify the ladies of the party, so much so that nothing but our boat was attended to. Thus we accompanied the noble party to Hampton Court, at times rowing ahead, and then again dropping astern of the fleet.

Upon bringing to, Lord Lincoln sent a servant to our helmsman to enquire who we were; and having ascertained that we were gentlemen, he very politely came in person to our boat, returned his own and his party's thanks for the great addition we had made to their entertainment, and requested our company, to partake as well of their cold collation as of the dinner in the evening. This we as civilly declined; but our band continued playing alternately with their own while they remained at Hampton Court, his Lordship sending us an abundant supply of refreshments, with ices and iced wines of all sorts. The repast being over, we attended the procession back to Weybridge, our band playing martial tunes whilst the company were landing. Being all on shore, we arose, and took leave with three cheers, which was most cordially returned by the gentlemen and ladies waving their handkerchiefs, and Lord Lincoln again very politely thanked us for our company.

It is scarcely necessary to add that such a life as I led must unavoidably have been attended with a much greater expenditure than my funds admitted of. In July my father proposed taking a journey to Paris, with my mother, sister Mary, and brother Joseph, to see the twins then in the Convent of Panthemont. When preparing for this excursion, he was more in London than usual, and soon discovered the irregularity of my conduct; aware that my allowances could not enable me either to dress as I did, or to be so much from home, he desired Mr. Bayley immediately and accurately to investigate my office accounts. This being done accordingly, a deficiency of near five hundred pounds appeared within the last seven months. Disgrace deservedly followed: my father declared himself at a loss how to act, or what to do with me. In a most disagreeable state of suspense I continued a week, during which I never made my appearance before the family.

At the end of that time, I thought of applying to my mother to intercede in my favour, and I did so. At first she peremptorily refused, observing that I had behaved so uncommonly ill, and that, too, after such repeated forgiveness, that she had not a word to say in my behalf; nor dared she entertain a serious hope that I should ever forsake the evil courses I had so unfortunately fallen into, and, she was sorry to be obliged to add, against which I did not seem to make the slightest struggle. At this period, however, I possessed the power of persuasion in a considerable degree, especially with those fond and partial as my mother was, and finally I prevailed. My mother kindly undertook to make the application, and, having made it, succeeded. Another tender, and to me, truly distressing scene took place between my father and me, at which I made a thousand protestations of altering my habits of life; and I can truly say I once more resolved rigidly to keep my word, and become a new man.

My father assured me that everything that had passed should be buried in oblivion, and that no one should ever upbraid me respecting my late irregularities. As a proof of the reliance he placed in me, and the confidence he had in my honour, he said he should leave me sole master of both Twickenham and St. Albans Street houses, with the keys of the cellars, etc., etc., the use of his saddle horses, and, in short, everything appertaining to town or country; his carriage and pair of horses he intended taking with him to Paris. On 6th August, the family departed for Dover, to which place my father had previously written to hire a vessel to conduct them all across the Channel. On his leaving London he gave me a draft upon his bankers, Messrs. Drummonds, for seventy-odd pounds, also a letter to Mr. Motteux, desiring him to settle an account then subsisting between them, and in case of my calling for it to pay to me whatever the balance in his favour might be.

They left St. Albans Street before five o'clock in the morning; and, as I had got up to see them depart, I then returned to my bed to finish my sleep. At ten I arose fully determined to act correctly, and in no way betray the confidence my father had so generously placed in me. It being the long vacation, and circuit time, there was little to do in the office. I therefore resolved to pass a couple of days at Twickenham, principally with a view to avoid encountering any of my dissolute companions, and keeping myself out of the way of temptation. At noon I mounted a beautiful blood mare of my father's, and rode to Twickenham, where I dined and passed the rest of the day with our neighbour, Mr. Hindley. The next morning I went over to Hampton, to enquire about a cricket match, which had been made more than a month before by the Duke of Dorset, between eleven gentlemen who had been educated at Westminster, and eleven of Eton, in which I was nominated as one of the former, being considered a famous stop behind wicket.

At the inn I was informed that great enquiries had been made after me, and much surprise expressed at my not attending the days of practice, of which due notice had been sent, and I certainly received; but, this happening during my disgrace, I could not leave home. I further learnt that it was to be played the following Wednesday on Moulsey Hurst, for twenty guineas each person, the amount to be given to the poor of the two parishes of Moulsey and Hampton, any one of either side neglecting to attend on the day was to forfeit twenty guineas. The hour of pitching the wickets was eleven.

The next day I returned to Town and immediately went to Queen Anne Street, not having seen my fair friend Fanny Hartford for a fortnight, though I had written her a particular account of all that had occurred in my family. She most heartily congratulated me upon the good resolutions I had made; and no bishop could have penned a better lecture upon morality than she did, strenuously advising me to show myself deserving of the good opinion my father entertained of me, and worthy of the implicit confidence he had placed in me. Above all things she recommended me to persevere in my determination of keeping out of the way of temptation, by avoiding all my gay associates, fairly confessing she had no other reliance upon any of my good resolutions than that of my avoiding evil example. "If," said she, "you will put yourself under my care, I will engage to save your honour, so seriously given in deposit to your father. Come to my house as often as your requisite attention to business will permit. We will go together to the public places that are open, and I shall at least have the merit of keeping you out of harm's way."

For two days I did so; when, mentioning the cricket match, she exerted all her persuasive powers to prevent my going to it, saying she would cheerfully pay double the forfeit rather than have me there; and she did everything she could devise to deter me from making one of the set. I argued that I could be in no danger from going; the party consisting of none but young men of the best connections, several of fashion and large fortune, the head of it being His Grace of Dorset— also Lord Francis Osborne, Lords Bulkeley and Molesworth, my old friend Bob Henley, Sir Watkin Williams Wynne, Mr. Colquhoun, Ramus Pinnock, etc., not one of my London acquaintances being likely to be present. She at last, though very unwillingly, consented to my going, exacting a faithful promise that I would avoid excess in wine at the dinner, which I had told her was to be at the Toy after the match was over.

The next morning, being Tuesday, I went to Drummonds and received the amount of my father's draft, which was paid in the Portuguese coin of half Joes, or six-and-thirty shilling pieces, at that time made current in Great Britain. I then called to say adieu to Hartford, who renewed her endeavours to prevent my going; but, finding me inflexible, she contented herself with very gravely requesting me to bear in mind my sacred promises to my father and mother, I again assuring her, as the fact was, that I ran no risk whatever from the cricket party. I then went home, put on my boots, and by way of lounging away an hour walked into the Park, intending to pass through it up Constitution Hill and to Hall's stables, near Hyde Park Corner, where my father's horses then stood.

Unhappily for me, in the Mall, I met two young men to whom I was very partial, brothers, of the name of Williams, both born in the West Indies, from whence they had been sent to England for education by their guardians, and had been in England about five years when I first became acquainted with them. They were lively, pleasing lads, according to fame living at a rate greatly beyond their means. They expressed much joy at meeting me, saying I must join a nice snug little party at the Shakespear that day.

This I pronounced impossible, telling them I was then on my way to Twickenham, and that the following day I was to play in a great cricket match upon Moulsey Hurst. They continued walking by my side, soliciting me to join their gay set, which need not interfere at all with the cricket; that Vincent and Newton (two remarkably pleasant women) were to be present, and that it was a choice party, one after my own heart. I resisted long, but finally agreed to attend, determining, however, within myself to avoid excess and to leave them early. Alas!—I never could depend upon myself when once embarked in convivial society. The consequences of that, to me fatal, night gave an extraordinary turn to the whole tenor of my future life. Instead, therefore, of proceeding to Twickenham, I merely took a ride in Hyde Park, returned to Hall's and desired the mare might be saddled and ready for me at nine o'clock in the evening, by which hour I should be there again.

Booted and spurred as I was, I then went to the Shakespear, where I found the two Williamses, a man of the name of Jennings, a great sportsman, who kept several racers, and lived in a most dashing style, though no one knew from whence his resources came, a Captain Taylor, who commanded the *Hampshire* East Indiaman, Lowry, an eminent banker's son, Clapereau, a remarkably handsome youth, who was afterwards for some years a companion of the Prince of Wales's, the above-mentioned Misses Vincent and Newton, with two other equally jovial damsels. The whole party, male and female, were of the description yclept "hard goers." This did not alarm me, for in those days I could keep way with the best of them at fair drinking. After my spirits were exhilarated by a liberal dose of champagne (still keeping in mind my determination to go to Twickenham that night) one of the waiters came in and said a gentleman wished to speak with me. I went out and found Tomkins, the Master of the House, who directly said:

"I sent for you, Mr. Hickey, to put you on your guard. You are in bad company such as you should avoid; above all things, avoid getting drunk. Take my advice as a well-wisher; I promised Tethrington and your brother, if ever I saw you in danger, to protect you. You are so now. So take care."

I felt all he said, and assured him I would be on my guard and leave the party immediately. Upon my return into the room, Newton was singing one of her best and most convivial songs, in the progress of which at least half a dozen bumpers were toped down. Her example was followed by Vincent in a song of the same kind. I was next called upon, and sang "Let poor priggish parsons, etc." By the time I had finished, so much wine was in my head that prudence and all my good intentions were drowned; none then so vociferous for more champagne as myself; and, as was always the case with me when at a certain pitch of intoxication, I became desperate, drank past all recollection; and of what ensued during several subsequent hours I was wholly insensible, but collected the various circumstances at subsequent periods, and from different persons.

Between eight and nine o'clock, it seems, the women, tired of drinking, proposed going to tea at the Pack Horse, Turnham Green, and there have a swing. Carriages were ordered and away we went, I being drunk as a beast. After tea, Jennings proposed a supper at Stacey's, the Bedford Arms in Covent Garden, which was vehemently opposed by Captain Taylor, and Clapereau, who from shirking the wine had kept tolerably sober; I was decidedly for the supper, which was therefore determined on, and to Stacey's we went, Clapereau accompanying, solely with the humane intention of rescuing me from the fangs of the harpies he saw I was the object of. He therefore begged and entreated me to let him carry me home, which only excited my anger and indignation. After submitting to the grossest abuse from me for a long time, he at last got up, told the triumvirate that he knew I had a considerable sum of money about me and was too stupidly drunk to take care of myself, that they were therefore bound in honour to protect and take care of me; and with this hint to them that he suspected their intentions, he left me to my fate.

The three worthies, Jennings and the Williamses, having thus succeeded in getting me to themselves, *picked* my pocket!—*literally* so, as I have every reason to believe. My first return of sense or recollection was upon waking in a strange, dismal-looking room, my head aching horridly, pains of a violent nature in every limb, and deadly sickness at the stomach. From the latter I was in some degree relieved by a very copious vomiting. Getting out of bed, I looked out of the only window in the room, but saw nothing but the backs of old houses, from which various miserable emblems of poverty were displayed, such as ragged shifts, petticoats, and other parts of female wardrobes hanging to dry. I next took up my breeches to examine the pockets; well stored as they had been the preceding day, not a sixpence remained. My gold watch and appendages were likewise gone. To describe my feelings, mental and bodily, upon this occasion would require a much abler pen than mine. At that moment I do not believe in the world there existed a more wretched creature than myself. I passed some minutes in a state little short of despair; I rung a bell I found in the room for the purpose of ascertaining where I had got to, and other particulars.

No one answered until I had three or four times repeated my application to the bell rope, when at last a yawning man, who seemed half asleep, made his appearance, immediately exclaiming, "Good God, how drunk and riotous you was, Sir! I never saw anything to equal it." I enquired where I was, observing that the night before I had a considerable sum of money, of which nothing was left, my watch, chain, and seals being also gone. The man replied that I was at the Cross Keys Bagnio, in Little Russell Street, Drury Lane, having been brought there by the watchmen at five o'clock in the morning, in woeful plight; that the watchman said I had been turned out of Wetherby's, which they were not surprised at, for so noisy and ungovernable a young gentleman they never before met with; that they were obliged to summon a number ere they could secure me, which having effected, they had determined to convey me to Covent Garden watch-house, there to wait the rising of a magistrate. But two of those respectable guardians of the night stood my friends, saying they knew me well from frequenting the houses in that neighbourhood, and that I had given them many a shilling to drink; one of the waiters also, coming out from Wetherby's, became a zealous advocate for me; and, assuring the watchmen I was a generous fellow who would amply reward them, he recommended their carrying me to the Cross Keys, in the same street, which they accordingly did. I resisted as long as I was able; that, upon giving me into the hands of the waiters, the watchmen pointed out that I had lost one of my silver spurs, they knew not where, but supposed whilst I was struggling with them, but that my watch was safe, the waiter pulling it from his fob.

He further said he had searched my breeches pockets in presence of the watchmen, and found them quite empty. The recovery of my watch, which was a valuable one, was some consolation. I found it was then just nine o'clock. Whilst putting on my clothes, the waiter assisting me, he observed on taking up my coat there was something sounded like money. Whereupon, feeling in the pocket, I, to my inexpressible joy, found seven half-Joes, or six-and-thirtys, and from the other pocket I took a letter which proved to be my father's to Mr.

Motteux enclosing the draft for balance of an account. This was like a reprieve to a man under sentence of death; I liberally rewarded the waiter and watchmen, two of whom I was informed were waiting at the door for me; and, although so ill that I could scarcely hold up my head, I got into a hackney coach, directing to be driven to St. Albans Street. I vomited out of the coach window the whole way, to the great entertainment of the foot passengers.

On my arrival at home, the servants were shocked to see the condition I was in, looking pale as a corpse. They strenuously recommended my going to bed, but that I declared absolutely impossible, as I must be at Moulsey in little more than an hour. The clearing my stomach of the vile stuff it contained had in some measure relieved me, though I still had an excruciating headache. Whilst changing my clothes, the servants prepared some very strong coffee, which proved of infinite benefit. Having washed, put on clean linen, and had my hair dressed, I again stepped into the same coach that brought me home, and drove to Hall's stables, stopping on the way to purchase a new pair of spurs, and a whip, for that was also lost. By the time I mounted the mare it was a quarter-past ten, so that I had only three-quarters of an hour to go twelve miles in. I made the noble animal (always willing enough to dash on) put her best leg foremost, and notwithstanding a horrible headache, and at times sickness, I went at speed the whole distance, the clock striking eleven just as I entered Hampton.

I found the contending parties then in the act of crossing the Thames, having got a volunteer to supply my place as they had given me up. I instantly followed, and thus saved my credit and my money. Our party proved successful, after a hard match. As the Westminsters insisted, we should have won easier had I played as usual; but I was so ill all the time that I let several balls pass me that ought not to have done so, by which our adversaries gained a number of notches. We then adjourned to the Toy, where a magnificent dinner was prepared, no part of which could I relish, the loss of my money the night before, and the early forfeiture of my promises to my parents, weighing heavy on my spirits. Even champagne failed to cheer me; I could not rally. The moment, therefore, the bill was called for, and our proportions adjusted and paid, I mounted my mare, and in sober sadness gently rode to my father's at Twickenham, a distance of between two and three miles.

I never could account for the seven pieces of gold and the draft upon Motteux being in my coat pockets, nor how they came there, unless, with the degree of cunning that lunatics generally show, the same sentiment operating with me drunk as I was, I secreted them by shifting them from my breeches to my coat with the idea of saving something. Clear it is, I think, that my scoundrel companions would not have let even that small proportion of the booty escape them, had they known I possessed it. Possibly my father's draft upon Motteux they might have left as useless, from not having my endorsement upon it. Whilst upon the subject, I may as well conclude the account of this transaction, and the history of the three plunderers. The way I discovered the robbery was this. Walking in St. James's Park, near three months after the circumstance above related had happened, one of the Williamses joined me, and, after the customary salutations were exchanged, he began to speak of the Shakespear and Bedford Arms party, observing how much concerned he had been at my obstinately persevering in my determination to play, notwithstanding the rest opposed it, whereby I had been a sufferer. Conscious, and certain as I was, that in the whole course of my life I never was the person to propose gambling, nor ever played at any games but tennis and billiards, and that for amusement, but at the same time anxious to gain all the information I could relative to that night, I appeared to acquiesce in all he said, observing that it arose from my being so abominably drunk. I added that I had paid dearly for my folly, having lost near seventy pounds. Whereupon Williams, with great quickness, replied:

"Oh no! Not near so much; you did not lose more than fifty pounds, at most."

I then said: "Why really, my head was so full of wine that I have a very imperfect recollection about the matter, and do not even remember what we played at."

"Dear," answered Williams, "I wonder you forget that, because it was you that named the game of Brag, declaring you would play at nothing else."

"And pray," asked I, "how did I perform? Like a novice, I suspect."

"Oh no, very well, and sharp enough I assure you."

"That's not a little extraordinary," said I, "for it so happens that I never played, or even saw the game of Brag played in the course of my life; nor do I at this moment know a single card at it."

The rascal looked quite confounded, began to hem and haw, to talk of the weather, horse-racing, and other matters in quick succession; when, finding I made no answer to any of the subjects he thus broached, he affected to see a person he wanted to speak to upon business of importance, and suddenly darted off. Having learnt the above circumstances from one of the party concerned, I immediately went to Stacey, to ask some further particulars. He made no difficulty in telling me that Jennings was the person who called for cards, and that two packs were taken up, neither of which were opened; and he was positive no cards were played at all. "Indeed," added he, "you was so drunk as to be utterly incapable of knowing what you was about, and I recommended that a chair should be called for to convey you home; to which the gentlemen acceded, and I ordered a waiter to call one." Thus it is beyond all doubt that they actually picked my pocket! The fate of these three men was extraordinary. The elder Williams shortly afterwards was thrown from his horse at Guildford races and broke his neck; the younger brother, having run out everything, was thrown into the Fleet prison by his creditors, where, being in want of the common necessaries of life, he finished his career by putting a pistol to his head. Jennings was taken up for a highway robbery, tried, and, but for the leniency of his prosecutor, must have suffered at Tyburn. He was transported for life. So much for my three precious friends.

I remained at Twickenham the following day, being far from recovered from my debauch of two days before. In the evening, feeling better, I went to Kew Gardens to see some fireworks, which were to be exhibited in honour of the Prince of Wales's Birthday, at which the King of Denmark, then just arrived in England, was present. From Kew I returned to sleep at Twickenham. On the morning of the 14th I mounted my horse and rode to town. I found Mr. Bayley at his post; but, as I had requested his permission to be absent a few days on account of the cricket match, nothing was said to me on that subject, except his remarking that I looked very ill. After staying a few hours in the office, I walked up to Fanny Hartford's; but she had left town that morning for a short time. On my return I casually met my brother Henry, who told me Tethrington and three other jolly dogs were to meet him at Mrs. Harrington's, at Charing Cross, that day, and there dine; and he asked me to join them, which I consented to, and accordingly went; but an unaccountable depression of spirits so harrassed me I could not get on. The party rallied me and plied champagne and burgundy. It was in vain; and finding this, Tethrington kindly advised me to go home to bed, and he had no doubt I should be perfectly well the next day and able to enjoy the society of the same set with some girls who were to meet and dine together at the Rose Tavern.

I did as recommended and had a tolerable night's rest. Still, I rose sadly dejected; and after taking a long ride, feeling myself unequal to encounter the gaiety of the Rose party, I took a solitary meal at Slaughters at an early hour. In the afternoon I walked towards Chelsea, intending to cross over to the Red House; but at Pimlico I was overtaken by some acquaintances who said they were going to see Balloni played, an Italian game then just come into fashion and played at a public house at Pimlico. As I had never seen it, I joined them and looked at until dusk, when we went into the house to which the Balloni ground was attached, and drank coffee. It was then proposed to spend the rest of the evening at Vauxhall, whither we all went; but, the same lowness of spirits oppressing me, I left the party, and taking a boat I landed at Westminster Bridge, from whence I walked to Queen Ann Street, hoping to revive in the society of my fair friend; but she not being returned to town, I resolved to go quietly home.

Upon reaching St. Albans Street, about eleven at night, I knocked with, I knew not why, a tremulous hand and an uneasy sensation I could not account for, which was increased by seeing the street door opened by a manservant who had attended the family to France; at the same moment I observed trunks in the passage. This servant looked melancholy and distressed, but uttered not a word. My first idea was that some fatal accident had occurred, and I eagerly enquired for my father. The servant replied, "My master, Sir, is above in his bed chamber, extremely ill." I then concluded this illness had occasioned their sudden return; until, asking after my mother, the same servant, bursting into tears, said, "My poor mistress is dead."

This event so sudden, so entirely unexpected, gave me the severest shock I ever felt. It instantly came across my mind that, in those moments I was spending in riot, drunkenness and excess, my revered parent was breathing her last. Conscience smote me severely; I had nothing to palliate my conduct; and I retired to my room grievously oppressed in mind, looking forward with terror to a meeting with my father, a meeting I was every way so ill-prepared for, but which I every moment expected to be summoned to, feeling too utterly at a loss what to say for having so shamefully forfeited my honour. My grief for the death of a fond and partial mother was ardent and sincere. I, however, derived a melancholy consolation from feeling that she had left the world unacquainted with my last folly, and scandalous breach of promise. I sat myself down upon my bed without taking off my clothes. During the night I closed not my eyes, and heard a constant bustle and running up and down stairs until five in the morning, when worn out by anxiety and want of rest, I sunk into a disturbed, unrefreshing slumber for a couple of hours, when I rose and, softly opening my door, I looked out.

Everything being quiet, I descended to the kitchen, where one of the maids was sitting, who to my utter astonishment informed me that my father and sister had set off in a post-chaise for Twickenham before six o'clock. This I own was a relief, as it afforded me time to prepare for the meeting I so much dreaded with my father. She further told me that, upon my father's leaving town, my elder brother retired to his chamber, desiring not to be disturbed until he rung his bell, as he had been several nights with scarce any sleep. This servant was ignorant whether my father had made enquiries about me or not.

Upon my brother's coming down, he informed me that they had embarked on board a commodious vessel that had been hired for my father on the morning of 8th August, with a strong wind from the northward. My poor mother, who always had a great dread of the sea, was extremely sick, as were the whole family. For two hours she remained up on deck, when being quite exhausted and faint from excessive vomiting, she took the captain's advice by going down to the cabin, to which she was assisted by him and the cabin boy, neither of the servants being able to move. In a few minutes the boy returned up on deck, telling my father the lady had laid down upon the bed, and was better, appearing to be in a doze. In little more than half an hour afterwards they entered Calais pier, where, all motion ceasing, every-one became instantly well, and Molly Jones, descending to inform my mother, screamed out that her mistress was dead.

My father and everyone else thereupon rushed towards the cabin. It was, alas, too true; the vital spark had for ever fled, though she looked as if in a tranquil sleep; and she, who only three hours before was in the full vigour of health and spirits, now lay an inanimate, breathless corpse. My father's distress and agony was beyond descrip-tion. Naturally of uncommonly strong passions, and possessed of extra-ordinary sensibility, the blow so unlooked for, so awfully sudden, nearly overwhelmed him. Fortunate it was that my brother Joseph was of the party. Though equally feeling the irreparable loss he had sustained, he had more command over himself than my father; and, sensible the peculiarity of their situation required the most active exertions, the first step he took was to procure the best medical aid that Calais afforded.

Two French physicians and a surgeon went on board the vessel, who, upon inspection and examination of the body, were all of opinion that life was irrecoverably gone, and the cause, apoplexy, probably brought on from extreme terror. These important points being thus ascertained, my brother then applied to the master, or captain of the vessel, forth-with to convey the family and my mother's corpse back to Dover. But this he said was not in his power to do, being engaged to transport part of the Danish monarch's suite across the Channel, as was the case with every other vessel then at Calais; nor, indeed, could anything possibly get out of the pier, the wind blowing hard and directly into the har-bour. In this truly distressing situation, my father and family were not only obliged to quit the sloop, but to have the corpse landed also, which the very hour it took place, the police and clergy interfered, claiming all the property of the deceased from being an heretic.

With much trouble and at a considerable expense, my brother at last got all matters arranged. Two days elapsed before the King of Den-mark's people were embarked, and two more ere my brother could procure a vessel to convey himself and our family to Dover. In the interim my mother's corpse had been enclosed in a leaden coffin; and on the 18th was put on board a small fishing vessel in which the family also embarked, except the coachman who was left in charge of the carriage and horses, which the boat was not large enough to receive. At ten the next morning they landed at Dover, and immediately set off post for London, Molly Jones and another female servant remaining to attend the corpse, which Messrs. Minet and Factor of Dover, had undertaken to forward in a proper manner to town. My brother also told me that my father, upon his arrival, had made particular enquiries about me, but had declined seeing Mr. Bayley, from being too ill and too much agitated. He had, however, requested him to go down to Twickenham the next day.

6

LEAVE-TAKING

THE same evening (17th August) the hearse containing my mother's body, and a mourning coach with the servants, reached St. Albans Street. The following morning before eight o'clock, Mr. Bayley, who also resided in St. Albans Street, sent for me to tell me he had the preceding day been to my father at Twickenham, who he found in a most pitiable state and so dreadfully affected by the misfortune that had happened, that he really apprehended it would break his heart. "I was so shocked at finding him so ill" (added Mr. Bayley) "that I dared not venture to say how ill you had behaved, and how little I had seen of you at the office during the ten days of his absence. But, William, the hour of reckoning is at hand; your father will require your presence the moment he acquires strength enough to bear the interview. Prepare therefore for it, and if you can, to account for your conduct since he had been away. Let me also have a statement of the cash he left with you, which ought to be entire, as I see by the book you have not disbursed a shilling for the office."

I then briefly and candidly represented to Mr. Bayley every circumstance that had occurred, and the consequences to me, returning to him the draft upon Motteux, which was all that remained. He was sadly shocked; yet, seeing my contrition and how much I was distressed, he humanely forebore all reproaches, merely observing he could not but dread the effect a discovery of my misconduct would have upon my poor father. In three days after my interview with Mr. Bayley, I attended my mother's funeral. She was buried in a vault constructed for the purpose in Twickenham churchyard, the service being performed with great solemnity by Mr. Duval, the then rector. Previous to this last sad ceremony, my father removed from his own house at Twickenham to my Uncle Boulton's at Coleherne, near Kensington, where he was informed of every particular relative to me; and I was desired to attend in person at Coleherne the following Sunday morning. Could the meeting by any means have been avoided, I know not what sacrifice I would not have made in preference to encountering it; but, as I knew it was unavoidable and must take place, I began to consider how I should act.

At one time I thought it would be most prudent to plead guilty and throw myself upon my father's mercy; but then conscience told me I had so frequently done the same that I could neither flatter myself with the hope of forgiveness, nor of having the smallest reliance placed in anything I should say or any promises I might make. I then thought of declaring myself incapable of fixing steadily to anything, and that I must submit to be forsaken and left to my fate. In short, I planned twenty different ways for conducting myself when before my father, every one of which was forgotten and abandoned upon seeing the grief-worn countenance, the deadly, yet strongly speaking, melancholy impressed upon his sorrowful and expressive features. I was struck dumb with grief at beholding my much loved, indulgent and honoured parent in such a lamentable state, and at my having, instead of being, as I ought to have been, a comforter, and a soother of his calamity, been an additional thorn in his side, an aggravator of his misery.

Upon entering the chamber he was in, I burst into a passion of tears, bordering upon convulsion. The source of my father's were dried up, quite exhausted; he uttered not a syllable, but looked so agonized that my uncle, who was present, alarmed for his life, eagerly and instantly taking hold of my arm, led me out of the room. For ten days I saw no more of my father. At the end of that time I was again summoned to his room, he being still at Coleherne.

I found him composed, but looking dreadfully ill, thin and pale. He languidly said: "William, I lament that you should once more have deceived and disappointed me." Then, pausing and covering his face with both hands for some moments, he continued: "But I have observed that plans fondly laid by parents for their children very early in life are seldom or never made effectual. It has pleased an all-wise providence to heap upon me accumulated afflictions; but God's will be done; it is as much my duty as my inclination humbly to bow to these visitations. As I find you cannot settle yourself to anything in your native land, we must try another line and another country for you; and may the Almighty in his unbounded goodness vouchsafe to turn your heart. I still believe, notwithstanding all that has passed, that your wish is to do right, and that you are not void of sensibility and generosity; but resolution, or control over your passions, you have none. Through life, young as you are, you have hitherto suffered them heedlessly to run away with you, even without a struggle." After another pause, he added: "Since I saw you last I have procured for you the situation of a cadet in the East India Company's service; and God grant you may do better in future than you have hitherto. And now leave me; I feel too weak and exhausted to say more."

In my way back to London, I reflected very seriously upon recent events, and the important change about to take place respecting myself; but, as novelty is everything to a youthful mind, more cheerful ideas soon predominated, and I looked forward with something like pleasure.

In the middle of September, several friends having recommended my father to go some place at a distance, in order to try to get rid of a nervous affection that preyed upon his spirits, he resolved to visit Bath and to take me with him. In three days after, we accordingly set off in my father's post-chaise, attended by one manservant. After remaining one week at Bath, we went to Bristol, and from thence crossed the water into Wales, which we traversed until we reached Flint, at which town resided Mr. Chetwood and family, consisting of a wife, and three grown-up, fine young women daughters, Ann, Hessy, and Elizabeth, with all of whom I was acquainted, they having spent some time with us at Twickenham. During our sojourn with this worthy family, my father's health and spirits materially improved. He would not, however, stay any longer, being anxious to get to London in order to prepare for my departure to the East. On 6th October, therefore, we took leave of the Chetwoods, and on the 9th arrived in St. Albans Street. During this excursion my father often, although with great moderation and temper, touched upon my follies and irregularities, earnestly beseeching me to learn to check my passions, and not, as thentofore had been the case, to yield to every temptation that presented itself. He then gave me permission to get what clothes I pleased made up, adding that he would accompany me into the City to learn what things were proper and necessary for me, and that with all such I should be supplied. A few days after our return to town he took me to visit Sir George Colebrooke, the director who had nominated me a cadet. The baronet received us with great politeness, telling my father it afforded him pleasure to have had it in his power to comply with his request. He said he had appointed me for Madras in preference to Bengal, which was by many considered the most advantageous for a military man, because the Coast of Coromandel was then the seat of an active war with Hyder Ally, and consequently more likely to give promotion to a young soldier; and that, instead of remaining a cadet two, three, or four years, as would probably happen to those who went the ensuing season to Bengal, I should obtain a commission in the Madras army upon landing.

From Sir George Colebrooke's, we went to Mr. Laurence Sullivan's, then a man of great influence and a leading director. He likewise was very kind, and promised to give letters that would be of essential service to me. He recommended my father to lose no time in securing a passage for me, as the ships would all be much crowded. From Mr.

Sullivan's we went to the India House, where I was introduced to Mr. Coggan, one of the Company's principal officers, who, being then very busy, desired I would call the following morning and he would put me in the way of doing what was requisite.

I accordingly did so, when he gave me a printed list of necessaries for a writer, observing that most of the articles therein specified would be equally useful to a military man; only I must recollect, in addition, to take a few yards of scarlet, blue, green, and yellow cloths, in order to make up regimentals according to the corps to which I should be attached, the infantry wearing scarlet, but with different facings of blue, yellow, or green, the artillery, like His Majesty's, blue with scarlet facings, and the engineers scarlet faced with black velvet. He advised me to try for a passage to Madras in the *Plassey*, and gave me a letter of introduction to Captain Waddell, who commanded her and who was a particular friend of his.

This letter I delivered the same day to Captain Waddell at his house in Golden Square. He received me with much civility, saying that, although he had determined not to take any more passengers than he had already got, he could not refuse his friend Mr. Coggan, and room must therefore be made for me. He told me he expected to sail early in December, and that I, as well as everybody else, must be on board prior to the ship's leaving Gravesend. I next ascertained what was to be paid, and found it to be fifty guineas for a seat at the captain's table. I then went to my father's tailor, Anthony Marcelis, of Suffolk Street, Charing Cross, to order regimentals; but, not knowing to what corps I should be appointed, I conceived the best thing I could do would be to have a suit of each description, which I directed accordingly. Upon my way from Marcelis, I met in the street a dashing fellow in a scarlet frock, with black waistcoat, breeches, and stockings, which in my eyes appeared remarkably smart. I therefore returned instantly to the tailor to bespeak a similar dress, as I was then in mourning for my mother. Marcelis suggested an improvement; which was to have the coat lined with black silk, and black buttons and button-holes, which not only looked better than the plain red but was more appropriate as military mourning.

Mr. Walter Taylor, a very old friend of my father's, presented me with a beautiful cut-and-thrust steel sword, desiring me to cut off half a dozen rich fellow's heads with it, and so return a nabob myself to England. In three days after I received this sword, my clothes being sent home, I burst forth a martial buck of the first stamp; and not a little vain was I of the figure I made. I seldom appeared two successive days in the same dress; my intimates beheld me with astonishment, observing I was going abroad in a splendid style; some of my brother Joseph's acquaintances enquired what the devil regiment I had got into, for that they met me in half a dozen different uniforms in as many days.

I was now a gentleman at large, thinking myself at perfect liberty to make the most of the short time I had to remain in London. About this period, my brother Henry proposed introducing me to a society he said he was sure I should like, and in the evening took me to the Globe tavern in Craven Street, when I was directly initiated as a Buck and, as Henry had predicted, was much pleased, all being laugh and pleasantry. I found a set of young men accoutred in splendid ornaments, arranged in great form, one who presided being elevated about three feet above the rest. In about an hour after my admission, all the business of the meeting being finished, the lodge was closed, when every person did as he pleased. Some ordered supper in detached parties of from three to six, others only drank wine, or punch, as fancy led. The eating being over, the best singing I ever heard commenced. There I first had the pleasure to hear Dodd, the player, sing his famous song of "Cease rude Boreas," and a charming performance he made it. He was followed by Hook, Champnes, Banister, Dibdin, and many other celebrated voices, who were all Members of the Lodge, which was distinguished by the name of "The Euphrates." There I spent a night of infinite gratification. In the midst of dissipation my poor mother's recent death was, I am ashamed to say, almost forgotten. Yet, in my minutes of reflection which would sometimes occur, I upbraided myself for thus soon nearly forgetting a fond and affectionate parent, as she had ever proved to me.

My attached Fanny Hartford was much pleased with my appearance *en militaire*, but grieved at thinking she was so soon to lose me. As she, like myself, had never seen the inside of a ship, I early in November proposed taking her to Gravesend, where the *Plassey* then lay taking in cargo. To this she consented; and we went down, and were received with the utmost attention by the commanding officer, Mr. Peter Douglas, the third mate, who conducted us through every part of the ship, explaining the uses of the different articles. He made a thousand apologies for the dirty state of the ship, which he said was unavoidable whilst receiving the cargo, but that, if he had previously known we were coming, things should have been in somewhat less disorder, and he would have prepared refreshment, whereas he now had nothing better to offer than a beef steak. We thanked him for his politeness, observing we had ordered dinner at the inn, and should be happy if he would favour us with his company, which he promised he would.

The ship certainly was in a sad dirty plight; but Mr. Douglas's cabin was an exception to the general filth, being neatness itself, and most elegantly fitted up. It was painted of a light pea green, with gold beading, the bed and curtains of the richest Madras chintz, one of the most complete dressing tables I ever saw, having every useful article in it; a beautiful bureau and book-case, stored with the best books, and three neat mahogany chairs, formed the furniture. In all my subsequent voyages I never saw so handsome an apartment in a ship. He said, if we would wait until he changed his dress, he would attend us on shore. This we willingly agreed to, and found abundant entertainment in looking about the round house, where everything was quite new to us.

At three in the afternoon we landed, and sat down in half an hour afterwards to as good a dinner as the cook of the Falcon Inn could furnish. We luckily found the champagne very passable, and gave our guest as much as he chose of it. He stayed with us till past midnight, when he returned on board the *Plassey*, promising to spend the following day with us. Upon taking leave of me that night, he expressed himself as being delighted with the beauty and elegant manners of Hartford, and often since has declared to me that the two days he passed with her and me were amongst the pleasantest of his life.

Towards the end of the month (November) by desire of Mr. Coggan, I attended before a Committee of Directors to undergo the usual examination as a cadet. Being called into the committee room after waiting of near two hours in the lobby, at which my pride was greatly offended, I saw three old dons sitting close to the fire, having by them a large table, with pens, ink, paper, and a number of books laying upon it. Having surveyed me, as I conceived, rather contemptuously, one of them in such a snivelling strange tone that I could scarcely understand him, said:

"Well, young gentleman, what is your age?"

I having answered "Nineteen," he continued:

"Have you ever served, I mean been in the army? Though I presume from your age and appearance you cannot."

I replied, I had not.

"Can you go through the manual exercise?"

"No, sir."

"Then you must take care and learn it."

I bowed.

"You know the terms upon which you enter our service?"

"Yes, sir."

"Are you satisfied therewith?"

"Yes, sir."

A clerk, who was writing at the table, then told me I might withdraw; whereupon I made my congé and retired. From the committee room I went to Mr. Coggan's office, who, after making me sit down for near an hour, presented me with my appointment as a cadet, also an order for me to be received and accommodated with a passage to Madras on board the *Plassey*. But another document, wholly unexpected on my part, pleased me much more than either of the others. This was a cheque upon the paymaster for twenty guineas. Mr. Coggan, seeing my surprise, and that I did not know the meaning of this draft, observed that, as it did not fall to the lot of every lad that went to India as a cadet to have friends that could fit him out for the voyage, the Company always supplied them with twenty guineas to purchase bedding and other necessaries. As these articles were already provided, I thought I could not dispose of the Honourable Company's donation better than in the society of a few unfortunate females. I therefore called upon Brent, and told her I was desirous of getting half a dozen poor girls together, and giving them a good meal, with their skins full of wine, at the Shakespear the next day, asking her if she was acquainted with any damsels to whom a dinner would be acceptable.

"Oh, that I am," replied she, "with many who, I am afraid, fast from not having the means of purchasing food"; and she undertook to collect the party and order the dinner in my name. At four o'clock the following day, I marched to the Shakespear, expecting to be the only male of the party; when lo, I was ushered into a room where I found my brother Henry, Tethrington, Major Nugent, Gilly Mahon, and others, with a parcel of women, several of whom I did not know. Upon my entrance there was a shout, the men calling me "A Grand Turk," that I wanted a seraglio to myself; and much wit at my expense was sported. The women, however, defended me and my good-natured plan for the benefit of the distressed sisterhood. I now learnt that Brent had betrayed me, by communicating my intention to her male friends. They relished my scheme exceedingly and resolved to carry it into effect upon a more enlarged scale, and not at my sole charge. Dinner being announced, I was, much against my inclination, voted into the chair, and Pris Vincent became my vice; and a more competent one to the situation never sat at a table. Indeed, we both did justice to our stations; nought but harmony and good humour prevailed.

We sat to a late hour; but, as I wished to avoid making a Dutch feast of it, I acted with caution and kept tolerably sober. I felt that the expense must far exceed the strength of my purse; and, not then being in the secret as to the determination of my male friends, I slipped out of the room to tell Tomkins I had not cash enough to pay his bill, but, if he would let me know the amount, the next day I would discharge it. Whereupon he desired me not to give myself any trouble on that account, for that he had cash in his hands more than adequate to the payment of his bill, even were the company to continue drinking for four-and-twenty hours longer. He said he was glad to see me in so different a party to that I had last been there with, alluding to

Williams's. Rejoining the company, I observed to them that as I had been forestalled in my object, I must at least apply a part of my little fund for the relief of some unfortunate female.

Tomkins, being summoned, was asked whether he knew of anyone in distress; to which he answered he had that very day received a letter from Lucy Cooper, who had long been a prisoner for debt in the King's Bench, stating that she was almost naked and starving, without a penny in her pocket to purchase food, raiment, or a coal to warm herself. I instantly put down ten guineas; and, the gentlemen present also subscribing liberally, fifty pounds were raised. This sum afterwards was put into Tomkins's hands to forward to her. I had afterwards the satisfaction of hearing that this seasonable aid had probably saved the life of a deserving woman, who, in her prosperity, had done a thousand generous actions. At a late hour our party separated, Tethrington and his set being engaged to a hazard table. I therefore strolled to my old haunt, Wetherby's, where I had not been since my lamentable Brag scene.

Upon my entrance the whole room attacked me, expressing their surprise at that night's exhibition, enquiring what I had done to myself; for that I was absolutely mad, and not one of my favourites had the least influence over me; that they were all astonished at seeing me, who had always been perfectly good humoured in my cups, so entirely the reverse, and actually quite savage. Of course, I had nothing to say in my defence, not having the least recollection of any one circumstance that passed, nor even that I had been in the house; but it has often struck me as very extraordinary that I, who was remarkable for my jocularity and good temper when drunk, should that night alone have been in the other extreme; and I have therefore been induced firmly to believe that the infamous scoundrels who plundered me of my money had also introduced some poisonous drug or ingredient into the liquor I drank, that caused a temporary insanity.

My brother Joseph wishing to see the ship I was to go in, we took a post-chaise and ran down to Gravesend. When at the foot of Shooter's Hill, my brother, by the shadow upon the ground, saw some person had mounted behind, which, from the hill being very steep, he did not approve of. He, therefore, leaned out of the window, desiring a stout ferocious-looking fellow that was seated there to get down. The man, instead of doing so, replied, "Damn and blast your bloody eyes, you b——r, if you don't keep your head in, I'll cut your eye out." My brother's indignation being raised at this coarse speech, he hastily called to the postboy to open the door and let him out, intending to thrash the fellow for his insolence, as he (my brother) piqued himself upon his skill in pugilism. The man, notwithstanding his bulk and apparent strength, directly leaped down, at the same time hailing some

of his companions who were a little way astern, with, "I say, messmates, heave a head. Damn my eyes if here is not a lousy landlubber
who wants to bring us to action."

My brother, although very angry, did not think it prudent to encounter half a dozen. He, however, expressed an earnest desire to
discover who the fellow was, that he might cause him to be punished
for his insolence. In vain I argued that Jack (for he was evidently a
seaman) had done nothing but what was natural, and should be
laughed at. We proceeded on our journey, hearing no more of the men
in our rear. As it was too late to go off to the ship that afternoon, we
proceeded on board the next morning, when the very first man I saw
upon deck was our Shooter's Hill friend, who I was rejoiced to
find my brother did not recognize. I found he was one of the quarter-
masters. He was afterwards of great use to me upon various occasions,
slinging my cot, and doing any job I wanted effected. I invariably
found him to be a quiet, civil, and obliging fellow. After we had been
some weeks at sea, I one day asked him if he recollected getting up
behind a post-chaise on Shooter's Hill ."Oh, yes" (said he), "that I do,
and that an ill-natured b——r, in the inside would not let me ride a
bit."

In the beginning of December, a set of noblemen and gentlemen of
the Scavoir Vivre club proposed giving an entertainment to His Danish
Majesty and suite; and a masquerade was determined on as likely to
afford the greatest novelty. The Opera House, being engaged upon
the occasion, was magnificently fitted up. My father, having procured
tickets, gave me one, and my sister Mary supplied me with a domino,
and other requisites. At ten at night my brother Joseph and I got into
sedan chairs and were conveyed to the Opera House, where we found
an immense company already assembled. The *coup d'œil* upon the
first entrance was the grandest and most sublime thing I had ever
beheld. This being the only masquerade that had taken place for many
years, everybody was anxious to see it, and even fifty guineas was
offered by advertisement in the public papers for a ticket.

In a few minutes after us, the King of Denmark and his party entered
the theatre. He had nothing dignified or majestic in his figure, but
seemed affable and good humoured. The crowd being very great, it
became difficult to move. His Majesty, however, bustled about, getting
on by dint of elbowing. I had during the night more than once the
superlative honour of being jostled and having my toes trod upon by
a crowned head. His royal elbows not appearing to me a bit less
pointed or rough in their application to my sides than would have been
those of the vilest plebeian. The buffets, which were numerous, were
abundantly supplied with refreshments of every kind, amongst them
ices, and the choicest fruits. At one o'clock the doors of the supper

rooms were thrown open, the tables of which were fancifully decorated with emblematical figures complimentary to the royal guest; and the whole supper was worthy of the noble donors. A little before the hour of supper, finding the heat very oppressive, and seeing several persons had unmasked, I did the same, soon after which I was laid hold of by a Minerva, whom I at once discovered to be Fanny Hartford. She had by the arm a gentleman in a rich old English dress, to whom she immediately said, "This is a young friend of mine that I must take care of." The gentleman looking at me answered, "By all means." She then whispered me that her companion was the Duke of Grafton, one of the principal managers and conductors of the entertainment, and she desired me to stick close to her. This I did, and was led into a private passage which went to an apartment at the head of about a dozen steps, in which was a table set out for the duke's friends, and from the front of which we had an admirable view of the table at which the King was seated.

His Majesty ate as if he was hungry, looked with much complacency around, and seemed highly gratified with the whole scene. After supper dancing was resumed. Between three and four o'clock some of the indefatigable votaries to Bacchus, who had sacrificed too freely at the jolly god's shrine, became very noisy and troublesome. Bottles and glasses flew about in various directions, and some of the most turbulent heroes came to fisticuffs. At four, the King departed, and the house began to thin. I continued till near eight in the morning, when I went home much pleased with all I had seen. Going to my bed I slept soundly for five hours, when I rose, dressed and drove in a hackney coach to Hartford's, with whom I dined, and at night accompanied her to Covent Garden playhouse.

The following morning she took me in her carriage to the India house, and Jerusalem coffee house. At the latter I met Captain Waddell, who told me he had just taken leave of the Court of Directors, and that I ought to send my chest down to the ship as soon as possible, and be on board myself by that day week. Upon my return home, therefore, I had my clothes all packed, and two days after despatched the same, together with a case of foreign liqueurs which I had bought at an Italian warehouse in the Haymarket at the price of sixteen guineas, by a Gravesend boy down to the *Plassey*. I then wrote to inform my father what Captain Waddell had said, in consequence of which he came to town, and we again visited Mr. Sullivan, who gave me letters to his Asiatic friends, as did Colonel Maclean, Sir Charles Sheffield, Admirals Sir Samuel Cornish and Sir George Pocock, also the Burke family, and others of my father's acquaintances.

I now heard, and with much pleasure, that a young London friend, Richard Bourchier, a nephew of the Governor of Madras, was going

out a cadet on board the *Plassey*, a circumstance we were mutually
glad of. He was a smart fellow, about a year older than myself, and
like me had been somewhat profuse and dissipated, which made his
family think it prudent to send him out of England, for a short time
at least, in order to get quit of a set of dissolute companions to whom
he had attached himself. He had been educated in the surgical line,
and was a pupil of the famous Gataker. Bourchier and I agreed to
depart for Gravesend on the 18th. Having therefore only four days left,
my time was fully occupied in bidding adieus to friends of all description, male and female. My parting with Fanny Hartford was a distressing scene and caused many tears from each of us. She presented me
with an elegant tooth-pick case, having an admirable miniature likeness of her on the inside of the lid, as a keep-sake.

On the 17th in the morning, I went to take leave of my Uncle
Boulton at Coleherne, and of his family. I certainly expected a present
of at least fifty guineas, as he was very rich, and in all probability
would never see me more. He was liberal enough in his advice. After
touching pretty forcibly upon the evil courses I had long pursued, and
the consequent distress of mind to my father, he reminded me that, as
I was now going into the world, it behoved me to act very differently
to what I had done, and constantly to bear in recollection what an
indulgent father I had and how handsomely and expensively he had
equipped me. He ended his lecture by putting into my hand *five
guineas!* which I felt a great inclination to return to him; but, curbing
my indignation, I coolly turned from him, saluted my aunt and cousins,
and left the house. In passing the outer gate, which a manservant
opened for me, I put the five guineas into his hand, saying I was sure
my uncle had intended that amount for him. The man looked surprised,
but bowed low, wishing me health and happiness. Upon my return
home I fairly related to my father all that had passed, and how I had
disposed of the paltry present, of which he highly approved, calling
my said uncle a mean and contemptible scoundrel.

That day, being our last in London, Dick Bourchier and I agreed to
dine together. He collected three other jovial bucks and had a pleasant
party at the Shakespear. At night we went the rounds of Covent
Garden and Drury Lane, and did not retire to our beds until after
daylight the following morning. Bourchier came to breakfast in St.
Albans Street, a post-chaise having previously been ordered to be at
the door by noon to convey us to Dartford on our way to the ship.
Breakfast being over, my father took me into his study, where after
fervently recommending me to the care of a protecting providence, he
gave me a beautiful Fusee,* which cost him forty guineas, a pair of
pistols of exquisite workmanship, and a purse containing fifty guineas

---

* A light musket or firelock.

4+

in cash and a twenty-five pounds bank-note. About half-past twelve we took our seats in the chaise, both sadly dejected at thus leaving all that was dear behind us, and in all likelihood taking a last adieu of our native city.

For the first ten miles we exchanged not a word, each being deeply wrapped in thought; but by the time we reached Dartford, where we changed horses, we became more reconciled to our fate, and began to converse a little. Between four and five we arrived at Gravesend, and drove to the Falcon, which, being crowded with guests, they crammed us into a miserable little hole of a room so enveloped in smoke we could scarce see the candles they placed upon a table. In a couple of hours they brought an abominable ill-dressed dinner. In short, everything was so disgustingly bad that I proposed to Bourchier going back to Dartford to sleep, which a waiter hearing, who had recognized me from having been there twice before, he very civilly said the house had been unusually full all day, but that a party would in a few minutes leave one of the best rooms which, although already promised, he would secure for us. He kept his word, soon showing us into the room Fanny and I had occupied, where, putting wax candles upon the table, and bringing a magnum bonum of very palatable claret which I ordered, we became reconciled to the house.

Having finished our wine, we went to the public billiard table, where we found a motley collection of people. After looking at the players for an hour, we returned to our inn, ate a few oysters, and went to bed. The next day being the 19th, we hired a boat and went on board the *Plassey* to ascertain where our cots were to be hung. We found Captain Waddell in the cuddy, who said the ship would not move for a couple of days. He pressed us to stay for dinner, which we declined, having ordered one on shore. Mr. Douglas was very attentive and showed us our berth, which was spacious and airy, being two-thirds of the great cabin. He, however, told us that another young gentleman, named Chapman, who was going out as a cadet, would have his cot also in the same place, to which no possible objection could be made, there being abundant room. The ship was in so lumbered a state we could scarcely crawl into the great cabin, and the quarterdeck was covered with packages; but all these Douglas assured me would be cleared away prior to leaving Gravesend.

On the 20th Mr. Jacob Rider came down, and introduced himself upon hearing we were going out in the *Plassey*, which ship he said he should likewise embark on, returning to Bengal as a factor. He dined with us, and we were much pleased with his manners. In the evening he ordered a chaise-and-four to convey him the first stage towards London, at which I observed we were to sail the following, or at farthest, the second day, as Captain Waddell had informed me.

Mr. Rider replied that he was to have charge of the Company's final dispatches, and should travel by land with them to Deal, from which place he should go on board.

The next day Captain Waddell sent to desire we would come off, as the pilot intended to break ground at high water. We accordingly took, as I thought it would be, our last leave of British ground and proceeded to the ship, where we found an excellent dinner just set upon the table, clean, neat, and looking remarkably well cooked; and we were agreeably surprised by being told we should have as good a dinner as we then saw before us every day during our voyage, which certainly was the case. Our party in the cuddy then consisted of Captain Waddell, Samuel Rogers, chief officer, Charles Chisholme, second, Peter Douglas, third, Walter Gowdy, surgeon, Richard Jones, purser, James Grant, a writer for Bengal, Mr. Forbes, an assistant surgeon for the same place, Mr. Denil Court, also a surgeon, . . . Chapman, a cadet for Madras, Dick Bourchier and myself. The fourth mate's name was Williams, the fifth, Thompson, and the sixth, Lane. At the mates' mess there was a Madras cadet, named Ross, a man at least forty years of age, who had been a captain in the King's service, but reduced to such distress as to be obliged to sell his commission and accept a cadetship in the Company's service. With the midshipmen there messed another cadet, a tall, raw-boned, lank Scotch lad of seventeen, named Smith; and these, with Mr. Rider, were the whole of the passengers.

In the afternoon we unmoored; but, a fresh easterly wind blowing, we only kedged down to the bottom of Gravesend reach. The 22nd the wind continuing in the east we made little progress; the 23rd we got below the Nore, when, the ship beginning to pitch, I became desperately sick, could neither eat, drink or sleep, and continued in that horrid state, expecting every hour would be my last, until the 25th (Christmas Day) when Mr. Douglas came into the cabin to tell me we were at an anchor in Margate roads; it blowing strong from the eastward, which, as long as it continued, would keep us there; that there was a boat coming off by which, if I chose it, I might go on shore, and proceed to Deal by land. The instant I heard this, I jumped out of my cot, ill as I was, dressed myself and went upon deck. This was the first view I had ever had of a boisterous ocean, and dreadful did it appear. The ship was in violent motion, and a large Margate boat that had just come alongside, was by the swell thrown up level with the gunwale and the next moment sunk into the abyss below. It was horrible to behold. The boatmen asking if anyone wanted to go on shore, I eagerly answered, "Yes, I did very much." Whereupon Captain Waddell, who was upon deck, advised me to stay where I was and get the sea-sickness over, which it probably would be in another day, whereas if I landed it would be renewed when I again came on board.

I was, however, so wretchedly ill that I resolved to land, although I knew not how I should possibly contrive to get into the boat from the high sea that was running. Bourchier and Grant, who were nearly as bad as myself, also agreed to go on shore; so getting a few shirts, etc., in a trunk, we by the kind assistance of the officers and sailors, managed to seat ourselves in the boat where I had not been a minute ere the sickness entirely left me, notwithstanding the quick and violent motion. Not so my companions, with whom the evil increased. Leaving the *Plassey*, we darted on at a prodigious rate, and in about an hour stepped ashore within the pier, and in five minutes were placed by a clear fire in a comfortable room at the inn then kept by Michiner. Here we ate our Christmas dinner, took a moderate share of port, and at an early hour went to our beds, in order to make up for two sleepless nights we had passed on board.

In the morning we found that the wind had veered round to the north-west and the ships were weighing their anchors to go round the North Foreland into the Downs. Having breakfasted, we ordered a post-chaise in which we drove to the Three Kings at Deal. The *Plassey* came to in the Downs in the afternoon, immediately after which it began to blow strong from the westward. We amused ourselves running about the country to different places. On the 28th Bourchier proposed our accompanying him to Dover to visit a relation of his, Captain Pritty, who commanded one of the government packets that sailed between Calais and Dover. This gentleman's house we accordingly drove to; he insisted upon our staying for dinner, entertaining us most hospitably. Upon our going away at night, he made us promise to eat our New Year's dinner with him, which we were all three willing enough to do, provided we remained till then on shore. He then assured us we should have a westerly wind for a week longer, when the moon changed; and, should the fleet sail during our absence, he would himself put us on board in a cutter of his own.

The 31st Mr. Rider came down with the Company's after packet, bringing with him a smart girl, and his brother, John Rider. In the morning of 1st January 1769, the latter gentleman came into the room in which we were setting to ask if either of us was disposed to take a trip to France; that there was a nice little smuggler just about to run over to Boulogne, the master of which engaged to convey him over and bring him back to Deal within thirty hours. Finding no one disposed to join him, he went alone, whilst we got into a chaise to attend our engagement to Dover. The former visit had been unexpected; yet we were well pleased with our reception and fare. But this time the entertainment was capital, an admirable dinner, and the best wines of all sorts. Captain Pritty had got some of his marine friends to join us, who proving jolly fellows, we had by nine o'clock swallowed a considerable quantity, and prudence whispered me it was time to think of moving, which I soon after proposed; whereupon, our host, who was tolerably drunk, called me, "a slip slop, moll dawdling boy. Damn me," (continued he) "if ever I saw such milk sop poor devils as ye are. What's got into the present race! There is not an ounce of proper spirit about them. Gad so, when I was of your age, I'd as soon have hung myself as lost a week in that sink, Deal. No, damn me, I'd have run up to Lunnun, and at least had a night on't; but you wishy-washy soft masters, fresh from mammy's apron strongs, have no nounce. Damn me, there's nothing in ye; no, nothing in ye."

He then called for a fresh batch of champagne; whilst drinking which I was considering what he had said, and thought the London trip a monstrous good idea, declaring myself ready to adopt it. Bourchier said the same; but Grant professed his fears, and that he dare not venture, which excited Captain Pritty's wrath, who called him, "A shiddle-come-shite, kiss my a——e wary Sawnie," and that his cousin (Bourchier) and me were of the right kidney. Ringing the bell, I desired the servant to order a chaise-and-four for Canterbury; but to that one of the tars present objected with, "Avast heaving upon that rope, my tight one—it is a cruel dark night, and you'll not be able to carry sail—mount a couple of nags, take a pilot to run ahead and steer the proper course, and you'll be at Canterbury in no time."

This morsel of eloquence receiving the approbation of our host, horses and a guide were ordered. At eleven we mounted, Captain Pritty desiring us to keep a good look out (though it was dark at pitch) and if the wind shifted to bear away for his port with all the sail we could crowd, and he'd ship us. With this caution, off we set as hard as we could pelt, leaving Grant to return to Deal alone. Our guide led the way in great style; we got on famously, and with only one little stoppage occasioned by my poor Rozinante coming down heels over head, and away I flew like a shot, my greatest danger arising from Bourchier, who was close behind, riding over me as I lay extended in the mud. This fortunately did not happen; and, my quiet beast standing stock still where he recovered his legs, I remounted without the slightest injury, the whole performance not having occupied five minutes.

7

A PASSAGE TO INDIA

WE reached Canterbury at half-past twelve, where, dismissing our Dover guide, we took a post-chaise-and-four, and thus dashed on towards London, which we reached before nine in the morning, driving straight to Malby's, where we ate a hearty breakfast, the exercise having carried off the fumes of Captain Pritty's dose of wine. We then went to bed, intending to sleep two or three hours; but, as I found my mind too much employed to expect sleep, I almost immediately arose, dispatching a porter for Brent, who was soon with me, all astonishment at my return. Getting into a hackney coach with her, after ordering dinner, I sallied forth, calling upon Tethrington, and two or three other friends, all of whom quite alarmed me by their grave remarks upon this ill-judged journey, and the risk I ran of losing my passage. This deterred me from visiting Queen Anne Street, as I intended, for I knew how much Fanny would have blamed me, and I did not choose to make her uneasy.

At two Brent and I returned to Malby's; Bourchier was out, but returned half an hour after us, and we three sat down to dinner. In the evening we went to one of the most retired upper boxes of Covent Garden Theatre; but the anxiety Bourchier and myself were under did away every idea of pleasure, and before the play was over we left the house, took some hot jellies and retired to bed, having previously ordered a chaise to be at the door precisely at eight in the morning. I had a wretched night; and, not having had any sleep the night before, I became feverish, and Brent very uneasy about me. Towards morning I fell asleep, and she would not allow me to be disturbed when the chaise came, until Bourchier, half crazy with alarm, at eleven waked me. I then rose much refreshed, and we got into the chaise a little before twelve. By paying the post boys well we went on rapidly to Sittingbourne, where we were detained near two hours for want of horses, so that it was past ten when we reached Canterbury, where we intended to sup, not having had any refreshment since we left London. Upon entering the Fountain Inn, I asked the landlord how the wind was, to which he answered, "I suspect from the clearness of the sky, easterly." Whereupon Bourchier instantly cried out, "Zounds! then give us a chaise instantly for Dover." Our host then said, "I am not certain about the wind, but will ascertain it in two minutes, having a weather-cock at the top of the house." He accordingly ascended, and soon came back with the comfortable tidings that there was very little wind, but what there was, was westerly. We therefore ordered supper, and after eating it went to bed.

The moment daylight appeared we proceeded to Deal, having a fine bright sunshine. When at the top of a hill about five miles from Deal, commanding a prospect of the Downs, we saw the ships, as we supposed, under full sail, and dreadfully frightened thereat, directed the postilions to go to Dover instead of Deal, as the ships were going away; when one of the boys, conversant in maritime matters, said, "The fleet are fast at anchor, and must remain so while the wind continues as it now is, south-west. They have only loosed their sails to dry after the rain of yesterday." This was very consolatory, and we went on our way to Deal. Arriving at the Three Kings we received the congratulations of Mr. Rider upon our return; for, having heard from Grant that we were gone to London, he thought we must inevitably lose our passage.

Upon entering the sitting-room, the first object that met my eyes was Mr. John Rider, so metamorphosed that, until he spoke, I knew him not. He had returned from his French excursion about an hour before we arrived. Instead of the plain brown cloth suit we had last seen him in, with unpowdered hair and a single curl, we now beheld a furiously powdered and pomatumed head with six curls on each side, a little skimming dish of a hat, the brim not four inches deep—two of which was covered with silver lace—and immensely wide in front. His coat was of a thick silk, the colour sky blue, and lined with crimson satin, the waistcoat and breeches also of crimson satin, coat and waistcoat being bedizened with a tawdry spangle lace. The cut, too, was entirely different from anything we had seen, having a remarkable long waist to the coat with scarce any skirts. He was a little fat squab of a man, which made his appearance the more extraordinary. Altogether, so grotesque a figure I never beheld, and we had a hearty laugh at him. This suit he assured us was the latest and veritable Parisian fashion; he had it made up during the few hours he remained at Boulogne. The hat he purchased at Calais where they put in, and where his head was made à la regle. The hat was said to have been introduced by the Duc de Nivernois, French Ambassador at the British Court, and was therefore distinguished by the name of "Chapeau Nivernois." I thought his habiliments preposterous and ugly, except the hat, which appeared becoming, and I gave that as my opinion;

whereupon he (John Rider) told me the master of the vessel had purchased some of them upon speculation, and if I chose it he would
purchase one for me. This I requested him to do, and I thus obtained
a *"Nivernois"* even more *outré* than Rider's, and which was afterwards
the cause of great mirth at Madras. Mr. Jacob Rider was quite delighted with the whole of the French dress, telling his brother that he
must let him have it to make the people stare in Bengal; and he
actually made John strip, and had the suit put into his own trunk, the
height and form of the two brothers being exactly similar.

We had passed a very merry day, and were just talking of going to
bed when we heard a gun fired, and soon after several others from
different ships in the Downs. A Deal man coming in told us the wind
had suddenly gone to the north-east, and the fleet were getting under
weigh. Instead, therefore, of retiring to our comfortable beds, we were
obliged to prepare for embarking. In a few minutes the house was all
hurry and confusion—paying bills, packing trunks, etc., etc. I had
luckily a week before engaged with a boatman for one guinea to put
me on board the *Plassey* whenever a signal for sailing was made, be
the weather what it might; for which some of my shipmates laughed
at me as being more than was necessary, a crown being the usual price.
I now found that I had acted wisely; for as it was a bleak night, blowing smartly, with snow, the boat people would not receive a soul under
three guineas each, and some even paid five. The man I had engaged
with behaved honourably, coming to show me to his boat, taking
Bourchier with me. At half-past one in the morning of 4th January
1769, we got into the boat, and reached the *Plassey* in perfect safety.
Giving the people three guineas for myself and Bourchier, they were
well satisfied. I immediately got into my cot; the sea being smooth and
the wind right aft, I slept tolerably well till eight o'clock in the morning, when I awoke rather qualmish; but, dressing and going upon deck,
the sharp air recovered me.

I heard upon enquiry that we were below Dungeness, and that the
East Indiamen in company were the *Pigot*, Captain Richardson;
Triton, Honourable Captain Elphinstone; *Hector*, Captain Williams;
Nottingham, Captain Stokes; *Ashburnham*, Captain Pearce; *Earl of
Lincoln*, Captain Hardwicke; *Hampshire*, Captain Smith; *Cruttenden*,
Captain Baker; *Osterley*, Captain Welch; *Speaker*, Captain Todd;
Royal Charlotte, Captain Clements; *Glatton*, Captain Doveton; and
the *Speke*, Captain Jackson; besides a great number of vessels bound
to the West Indies, America, and different parts of the world, the
whole fleet forming to me, who had never before beheld anything of
the kind, a grand and interesting spectacle.

Being summoned to the cuddy to breakfast, I had not been there
five minutes when I turned deadly sick, was obliged to retire to my

cot, from whence I scarcely stirred for ten days, during which I was in a very lamentable condition, straining so violently, from having nothing in my stomach to throw up, that I often thought I must, like my poor mother, die upon the ocean. Mr. Gowdie, the surgeon, afterwards told me he for several days had been under serious alarm about me, considering me in imminent danger of bursting a blood vessel. We had tempestuous weather through the Bay of Biscay, with a prodigious sea; but the wind being fair, our progress was rapid, of which the officers frequently told me by way of comfort; but so ill was I that it was actually indifferent to me what became of the ship, and I should, I verily believe, have heard with composure that she was sinking. This continued until we reached the Canaries, when Mr. Rogers, the chief mate, came into my cabin one morning soon after day broke, desiring I would get up and go upon deck to see the land; to which I replied, as I really thought was the case, that I had not strength left to enable me to do so. Whereupon Rogers, (a rough, vulgar, swearing seaman, but as good a creature as ever lived) said, "Pooh! pooh! Damn my eyes! (a common phrase of his upon all occasions) what blasted stuff and nonsense is this! Do you want to lay there and die? Come, come, get up, I say, and draw a mouthful of fresh air, which will cure you."

Finding I did not seem disposed to take his advice, he without further ceremony cast off the lanyards of my cot, and down it came. I, therefore, had nothing left but to try and put on my clothes, Rogers sending his servant to assist me, and returning himself to help me upon deck, where, on my arrival, a sublime scene presented itself to my sight. We were close inshore, under the Island of Teneriffe. The sun, which had not risen to us, was shining upon the upper part of the peak, giving the most luxuriant tints to the snow-capped summit of that stupendous mountain, and varying the colours as its light descended downwards, until the glorious orb appeared above our horizon, when a thousand new beauties of nature were displayed. The sea was serene and smooth as a looking-glass. This I believe I may pronounce the first time I ever saw the sun rise except over the tops of houses in the smoky atmosphere of London. I continued upon deck, looking at the land as we gradually glided on until dinner was announced, when I entered the cuddy, eat near half of a boiled fowl, drank a pint of wine, and felt quite renovated. From that hour my sickness ceased, and I began to enjoy myself; I entered into all the fun and joined in all the tricks that went forward in the ship.

Captain Waddell, then about forty years of age, naturally grave, with an appearance of shyness or reserve, possessed one of the mildest and most equal tempers that ever man was blessed with; nor did J, during a voyage out and home which I made in his ship, ever once see him angry, or hear him utter a single oath or hasty expression. He

4*

loved to set the young people at some gambol or other, and was constantly promoting it. He was himself wonderfully active and strong, amongst various proofs of which, he did one feat that amazed the whole ship's company, and which I never knew any other person come at all near. It was this—standing upon the quarter-deck, under the main shroud, he laid hold of the first ratline with his right hand, then sprung to the second, with his left, and so on alternately, right and left, up to the last, close to the futtock shrouds. The exertion in accomplishing this must have been prodigious; nor was there another man in the ship—and we had many fine, active fellows on board—that could get beyond the third ratline, and only two that reached even the third.

Having recovered my health, I mixed with all my shipmates. I have already spoken generally of the commander, and the chief mate, the latter of whom from some peculiarities was called "Black Sam" and "Blackguard Sam," the first owing to his complexion, being very dark. He was by birth an American; the second title he certainly merited, being uncommonly rough. He never uttered a sentence without embellishing it with oaths, "Damn my eyes" always uppermost, and he chewed tobacco in large quantities; yet, as before observed, there never existed a better-hearted man, or a more zealous friend. In his profession he could not be surpassed. The second officer, Chisholme, a proud Scotsman, was a handsome fellow, upwards of six feet high, and a perfect seaman. His family were proprietors of a valuable estate in the West Indies, in the marine trade of which he had learnt his business. He had received an excellent education prior to going to sea; he was fond of argument, in which he often showed great positiveness, and even insolence; yet he had candour enough to admit that such a mode of supporting an opinion was unbecoming and improper, adding, he had always been a spoilt child. This was only his second voyage to the East, and he used to boast that his interest would procure him the command of one of the Company's ships upon his return.

Douglas, whom I have also mentioned as third officer, was remarkably dressy, so much so, as to be distinguished in the service by the title of "Count Douglas"; but although he laid out more money upon his person than was usual with men in his station, no one kept a stricter look out after the main chance than he did, well knowing how to make the most of every shilling and let pass no opportunity of doing so. His cabin, as I before observed, was elegance itself. His person was pretty good, but his features hideous, so ugly it would have been no easy matter to caricature it. In fact, it was more the face of a baboon than a human creature, notwithstanding which, so unacquainted was he with his own countenance, or so eat up with vanity, that he thought every woman that beheld him must unavoidably fall in love with him. His address was certainly that of a gentleman, and man of the world.

He was from the first very attentive and civil to me, desiring whenever I wanted to write, or wished to be alone, that I would make use of his cabin; he also gave me the key of his bookcase that I might supply myself with any books I pleased. He likewise was a Scotsman, as was Mr. Gowdie, our surgeon, a plain, unaffected, good-natured man, considered skilful in his line, and had been several voyages surgeon of an East Indiaman.

Jones, the purser, was one of those common characters one meets with every day. Mr. Jacob Rider, with whom I formed a friendship that continued uninterrupted through life, had been sent out a writer to Bengal in the year 1763. His family were connected by marriage with a branch of Lord Clive's, which nobleman, upon going to Bengal as Governor in 1764, made Rider's interest one of his first objects, giving him the appointment of Paymaster General to the army, a situation that in those days would have yielded him an overgrown fortune in a few years; but, unfortunately for Rider, in about six months after he filled that advantageous post a dispute arose between Lord Clive and the officers of the army, occasioned by a measure of his Lordship's which they deemed unjust and tyrannical, in which however Lord Clive persisting, the officers drew up a remonstrance, couched in terms not only disrespectful, but little short of the language of mutiny. Aware of the consequences likely to ensue thereon, they adopted a practice then used in the Navy, signing their names in a circle, or what sailors called "a round Robin," to avoid any individuals being singled out for punishment.

In this instance, the scheme did not succeed, for Lord Clive could give a tolerable guess who were the ringleaders, and accordingly dismissed a number of officers from the service, amongst whom were Mr. Rumbold, afterwards Governor of Madras, and Mr. Stables, a Supreme Counsellor in Bengal, at that time both captains in the Army. In looking over the names subscribed to the remonstrance, Lord Clive noticed that of "Jacob Rider" and immediately said to his Secretary, "Who is this Rider? I don't recollect an officer of that name." The Secretary, who had ascertained the fact, replied, "My Lord, it is the Paymaster General." "The Paymaster General," (exclaimed his Lordship), "what can have induced the blockhead to lend his name to such an inflammatory, unjustifiable paper, with the subject-matter of which he could not in any manner be affected? However, let him abide the consequences of such absurd conduct"; and he gave orders forthwith to recall Rider, appointing another person in his stead, and upon his arrival at the Presidency, sent him on board a ship bound for England, declaring he never should be restored to the service.

Thus dearly did Rider pay for ridiculously engaging in a controversy with which he ought not to have had anything to do. When

Lord Clive returned to Europe, he was applied to on behalf of the *ci-devant* Paymaster, but refused to see him or have anything to say to him. He, however, after some time, so far relented as to say that, though he never would befriend Mr. Rider again, he would not oppose his restoration to the service. Rider had personal influence enough to get that point carried, and was returning with his rank (a Factor) when I met him in the *Plassey*, on board which ship he had a third of the great cabin, in which apartment, or in Douglas's, I passed most of the mornings. Rider had with him an enormous dog of the Newfoundland breed, who soon attached himself so much to me that I could not stir without his being close after me. His name was Beau, and a noble animal he was. Of poor Beau more hereafter.

The *Plassey* was a remarkably fast sailer, from which she had acquired the name of "The Flying Plassey." In running down the British Channel, we beat all the fleet; and, as I was informed, by the time we were abreast the Land's End, the whole of them were out of sight astern.

Passing the Canary Islands, the next land we saw was the Cape De Verds,* through the cluster of which, forming a very pleasant sight, we ran in smooth water and fine weather. When drawing near the Line, we had for several days and nights successively tremendous thunder and lightning, such as we landsmen had never before beheld, and, when little wind, a number of sharks following close to the ship. These fish being near a ship, seamen, who are generally superstitious, deem a bad sign, and to portend death on board. Whether this idea be well founded or not, I cannot take upon me to say; but certain it is that, during the attendance of at least a dozen sharks, we lost a man, and one of no small consequence, being no less a personage that the captain's cook, who being seized with a fever, was carried off by it within thirty hours. His death, however, did not prove so serious a loss as we were at first apprehensive it would, Mr. Chisholme having a Caffre servant who had been taught to dress turtle in the West Indies, and afterwards attended the kitchens of some of the most celebrated taverns in London, which had cost his master upwards of fifty guineas. He undoubtedly was an admirable cook.

Upon crossing the Line, all those who had never done so before paid the customary forfeit of a gallon of rum to the ship's crew, except Mr. Smith the Scotch cadet, who not being overstocked with money to purchase the spirits, preferred submitting to the ceremony of ducking and shaving, which he went through to our infinite amusement.

There was nothing I felt the want of so much as bread; for in those days it was not customary to make that article on board East Indiamen, and it unluckily happened that the biscuit was uncommonly bad and

* The modern Cape Verde.

flinty, so that it was with difficulty I could penetrate it with my teeth. This being the subject of conversation one day at table, a question arose as to the time in which a person might eat one of these biscuits, which ended in a wager of five guineas between Rider and Grant, the former laying the latter that he did not get rid of one by his teeth in four minutes. He was to have no liquid to aid him. A bag of biscuits being brought to table, the doctor by mutual consent put his hand in and brought out one, which was to be that of trial. Chance here operated against Grant, for it proved an uncommonly hard one, and he had difficulty in breaking it in two. A watch being laid upon the table, at it he went with a set of remarkably strong teeth; but, strong as they were, we all thought he must lose his bet, and he was twice in extreme danger of choking, by which he lost several seconds. Notwithstanding this, however, he, to our great surprise, accomplished his object, and won the wager, being six seconds within the given time.

In March, we approached the Cape of Good Hope, where Captain Waddell had given us hopes of stopping; and we landsmen were delighted with the expectation of soon setting our feet once more upon terra firma; when the Captain one morning, whilst we were at breakfast, observed that there was a glorious breeze, fair as it could blow, which would speedily take us round the tremendous promontory of Africa, a circumstance of far more importance than eating grapes at the Cape Town, and lengthening our voyage perhaps a month. The "glorious breeze," however, in no way consoled us for our disappointment; and we were rather sulky during a couple of days, at the end of which time we were reconciled to passing our favourite port, and good humour was restored.

Having completely rounded the Cape and coast of Africa, we bore up for the Mosambique Channel, or inner passage. Passing the southern point of Madagascar, the weather became moderate clear, and a smooth sea. I was one morning walking the deck, when Rogers, whose watch it was, sitting upon the quarter, called to me in his usual style, "Come here, Bill." I accordingly stepped upon one of the quarter-deck guns, and observing him to point downwards, I looked into the sea, where to my great terror and surprise I beheld the rocks, as they appeared to me, close to the ship's bottom; but Rogers assured me they were at least forty fathoms below us. In a few minutes after, however, he exclaimed, "Damn my eyes if I like this," and instantly ran into the round house. Captain Waddell, returning with him upon deck, ordered the course to be altered three points, and the lead to be cast; which being done, they found only four fathoms, so that if there had been any sea the ship would have struck. These rocks it seems were not properly laid down in the charts, at the time we were over them, not being in sight of land and the charts making them within five leagues of Madagascar, whereas we were upwards of twenty offshore. By standing off an hour we lost sight of the rocks, and were once more in deep water. Ten days after this occurrence, a strange sail was discovered upon our beam, standing as we did, which upon nearing us hoisted English colours. In the afternoon she joined company, proving to me the *Hampshire*, Captain Smith, one of the fleet that left the Downs with us. The commanders agreed to continue together, and put into Johanna for supplies of water and fresh provisions. In four days we made the land.

The Island of Johanna* in approaching it affords one of the most luxuriant and picturesque scenes it is possible to conceive, and doubtless it abounds with natural beauties—a most elegant and poetical description of it is given by Sir William Jones, that eminent and learned man who stopped there on his way to India. It is not considered healthy, especially at night, and Captain Waddell advised us by no means to sleep on shore, but to go early and amuse ourselves during the day, returning on board before dark, which advice we followed. Upon coming to an anchor, the ship was immediately surrounded by canoes, crowded with people (who in appearance much resemble Caffres) bringing with them poultry, eggs, fish, fruits of various kinds, for sale, of which latter we enjoyed the pineapples, oranges, guavas and bananas exceedingly. They spoke a strange jargon, intended as English, frequently repeating these words, "Johanna man, Englishman, all a one brother come. Englishman man very good man, drinkee de punch, fire de gun, beatee de French, very good fun." Their canoes are formed out of the trunk of a single tree, long and very narrow, consequently so unsteady it would be scarcely possible to use them but for the outriggers. These are strong and straight poles, one laid across at the head, another at the stern of the canoe. From the extremity of each end a flat plank is laid, and securely tied, of about ten inches in width, so that when the canoe heels either way these planks coming flat upon the surface of the sea, naturally make a resistance sufficient in common cases to prevent her oversetting, which without such a contrivance she certainly would do.

Upon going ashore at the watering place, we walked from thence to the town, distant about a mile. The streets, if such they may be called, not being above four feet wide, are long and straight, the habitations constructed of clay and wicker-work, and from their regularity and cleanliness make a pretty and very neat appearance. Here we got abundance of eggs, good fowls, but a very small breed, plenty of excellent fish, well-tasted beef, the cattle also remarkably small, and many

* Now known as Anjuan Island, one of the Comoro Islands which lie to the north of Madagascar. East Indiamen, on the outward voyage. took in water and provisions there.

kinds of vegetables quite new to us. The natives amuse themselves with their bulls, which are fierce little animals. Turning one of these loose, four or five men, wholly unarmed, encounter him, each person carrying in his hands a piece of cloth about six feet in length and three in width, which they spread out, dancing before the bull, who becomes enraged thereat and with vast fury assails the person nearest to him, who with much activity and dexterity entangles the horns of the beast with his cloth, thus preventing any injury to himself. While the animal is endeavouring to disencumber himself of the cloth, they continue singing and dancing around him. Having accomplished the destruction of the cloth, chiefly by means of his forefeet, he attacks another of his opponents, and so on until the beast is so fatigued as to fall down, or that the men themselves are sufficiently tired. They told us that accidents sometimes, though not frequently, did happen, and the men got severely gored.

Having spent the day very agreeably, we returned to the ship. Beau, Mr. Rider's Newfoundland dog, was our constant companion in our rambles, and we had no small difficulty in preventing him from attacking the bulls, which, in fact, were not much larger than himself. The second day we again landed early, wandering about the country and going to see a stupendous natural cascade, where an immense body of water poured down a declivity nearly perpendicular, of at least five hundred feet. It was in a most romantic part of the island, about three miles inland. Within sight of this noble fall of water we sat down to dinner, having carried provender with us, under one of the largest and most spreading trees I ever beheld, the branches of which were covered with a species of bats, which Europeans call flying foxes, having a head greatly resembling that animal, with beautiful white and strong teeth, their bite being very severe. My companions, who had guns with them, shot several.

The third morning we prepared for another excursion, Captain Waddell desiring us to be on board again by sunset, as Captain Smith and he had settled to leave the island soon after, with the breeze that generally came off the land. While a boat was getting ready for us, we heard an amazing outcry in the steerage, which upon enquiry we found proceeded from His Royal Highness the Prince of Wales!, who upon being told that was the title given to the King of England's eldest son, insisted upon his having it also, as he was the King of Johanna's only son. His Highness, however, forgetting his elevated rank, had stolen a silver teaspoon while visiting Mr. Chisholme in his cabin, and his Prime Minister, not to be behindhand with his royal master, purloined a blanket. Both culprits being caught in the act, Chisholme was administering summary justice by horse-whipping those great men, which occasioned the uproar. The unfortunate prince and his officer of state, after a smart chastisement, were turned out of the ship with ignominy, and orders given that they neither of them should ever more be permitted to come on board.

Having landed and amused ourselves as on the preceding days, about five o'clock we left the town, walking towards the watering place in search of the pinnace which daily attended near that part, to carry us off. In our road we met the surgeon of the *Hampshire*, who said, if we would follow him we should see some sport. Two foolish lads, passengers of theirs at the third mate's table, going out cadets to Bombay, had gambled during the voyage, and upon settling their card account that morning, differed materially as to the balance, which produced a violent quarrel. After abusing each other in the most scurrilous and blackguard language, they boxed, whereupon the officers interfered, observing that, if upon their arrival in India the Commander-in-Chief should hear of such ungentlemanlike conduct, they certainly would be dismissed the service; and they persuaded them that the only way to avoid such a fate would be to meet as officers should, and settle their dispute in the field. So serious a measure neither of the disputants seemed willing to adopt, until assured if they did not they would be sent to Coventry by their mess-frightened at the thoughts of such a step. The fourth mate consented to a meeting; but it would have been difficult to decide which was most frgihtened at the thoughts of such a step. The fourth mate consented to be second to one of the combatants, the doctor's assistant to the other, these seconds having privately agreed not to put any ball in the pistols. Having been made acquainted with these particulars, we accompanied the doctor to the spot where the dire conflict was to take place, the two heroes having arrived there just before us and in a sad tremor.

The ceremony of loading the pistols by the seconds being finished, they next spoke of distance, the doctor proposing six paces! upon which both violently protested against being so near, one of them saying he understood thirty yards was the usual space. The seconds told them the pistols would not carry much further. After much argument and discussion, it was resolved that twelve paces should be the distance. This the parties concerned pronounced absolute butchery. They, nevertheless, were obliged to yield, and finding that to be the case, insisted that the fourth mate, who had much longer legs than the deputy surgeon, should measure the space; and he accordingly did so. The antagonists were then desired to take their stations, there being no time to spare. The object the principals appeared to have in view was to squabble and dispute until it really became too late to fight; but the seconds, seeing that, insisted upon their presenting and discharging their pistols at each other upon the word being given. Unwillingly they took their respective stations, when one of them turned to his second, saying his antagonist owed him forty dollars, and it was very hard that he should be obliged to risk his money as well as his life. This created another pause, but was settled by the seconds engaging, in the event of the debtor being slain, that he would pay to the survivor the amount due, gravely adding, he conceived he was not in much danger of being called upon, as in all probability two such desperate champions would both end their lives upon the spot. The poor devils, not being able to devise any further mode of delay, and the signal being given to fire, they did so in the same moment, when to our surprise and alarm down dropped one of them, apparently dead.

This led us to apprehend that the seconds had not kept the private agreement, or at least that one of them had loaded with ball. We all ran up to the prostrate youth, and had the satisfaction to find him unhurt, having fallen through sheer terror. A glass of brandy from the pocket flask of one of the company soon restored him, when he positively declared he heard the ball whizz by close to his ear, which he thought it had hit. The combatants were then congratulated upon the gallantry they had both shown and were assured that they had done all that was required of men of honour and gentlemen, upon which they shook hands, mutually rejoiced at having got so well out of a dangerous scrape. This comedy had nearly proved tragic to some of us; for we had bestowed so much time upon it that the sun had sunk below the horizon near an hour when we arrived at the watering place.

A beautiful full moon, however, had risen with a cloudless sky. We were told that the coxwain of the pinnace, supposing we should not come there, had taken the boat to the town to look for us. Seeing both ships with all their sails set, though there was scarcely a breath of wind, we grew uneasy, and applied to the people of a large canoe that was going a fishing, to take us off to the ships, who consented to do so for five dollars, which we paid and embarked, our party consisting of Messrs. Rider and Grant, the surgeon of the *Hampshire* and myself, besides poor Beau and the boat people, two men and a boy, this cargo being more than the boat with propriety ought to have held in her at once, as we sunk the outriggers quite to the surface of the water, thereby destroying much of their effect. Just as we were pushing from the shore, our ship's gunner came to the waterside requesting a cast on board. I observed we were already too deep, asking the gunner whether he could swim, to which he answered:

"No, sir, not a stroke."

Then added I:

"You shall not come in here; we are enough to be drowned at once."

The gunner said:

"Very well, gentlemen, then I'll get another conveyance," and we proceeded, the two natives paddling and the boy steering.

Soon after we had so put off, the doctor, thinking he could work harder than the man that sat directly before him, took his paddle out of his hand, and laboured at it several minutes until about mid-way, that is, a mile from the shore and the same distance from the ship; when, turning his head to look towards the ship, he thereby missed his stroke, lost his balance and, falling on one side, his weight overset the canoe, and we were all submerged in the ocean. As I immediately sank, I gave myself up for lost, as I reasonably might, for I could not swim and had a heavy laced, regimental coat on, with boots; but, soon finding my head above water, I splashed and dashed at a great rate. On my first rising, the Johanna boy was close to me, holding out Rider's famous Nivernois hat as if he expected me to take it; at the same time Rider, who was close to me, and I grappled, and down we went together; but, when under water, an immense thick, false club of hair which I had lashed on—having been advised to cut my own hair off previous to going to sea—and which he unfortunately had seized hold of, came off in his hand and we got clear of each other, when I again found my head above water, and Grant, who was an uncommon fine swimmer, came to my assistance.

The instant he did so, I seized him round the neck, and under water we went together, where from his superior skill, by a sudden dart downward he got rid of me, and considered me then as irrecoverably gone; but, to his great surprise, I once more made my appearance on the surface, and notwithstanding my former fastening upon him, he again swam towards me, calling out that he wished to assist me and take me to the canoe, which he would try to do if I would let him and not attempt violently to grasp hold of him; for, if I did, it could tend to the destruction of both. Exhausted and terrified as I was, I had still recollection enough to feel the force of what he said, and I therefore let him take my arm round his neck without any violence on my part; and he thus conducted me to the canoe which lay bottom upwards, and I hung by one of the outriggers, the doctor of the *Hampshire*, who was seated astride upon her, lending his aid to keep me up. Grant then went to assist Rider, who, besides swimming a little, was, from his form, much more buoyant than me, and he helped him also to the upset canoe. Grant had no doubt made me his first object, induced thereto from knowing that I could not swim at all; but this Rider never would give him credit for, often afterwards angrily saying, "Nonsense, it is no such thing. He had a more substantial and selfish reason. He knew well that by the death of a Madras cadet he could be no gainer, whereas by mine, he got a step in the service, and therefore he passed me to go to the assistance of Hickey."

Captain Waddell, after repeatedly hearing this illiberal declaration of Rider's one day mildly said, "he thought he (Rider) did Grant injustice, for had he been capable of such reasoning and motives at such an awful crisis, he would probably have left us both to perish, instead of risking his own life to preserve ours, as he certainly had done; and in doing which he had shown a most extraordinary degree of personal bravery and perseverance."

After Grant had thus conveyed Rider and me to the overset canoe, and we had been clinging to her several minutes, every one of which appeared an age, we were suddenly from an unaccountable motion of the canoe, again under water and again relieved by our preserver Grant, soon after which we had the supreme felicity to see another canoe paddling towards us; but, on coming near, the natives in her stopped, crying out, "Too much man, too much man," and were actually turning about to pull away, when the gunner who was in her, and had been attracted by our cries, partly by threat and partly by bribes, made the people approach us; but, having accomplished that, it was found impossible to receive us, the canoe being a very small one. After some consultation, the gunner made the men belonging to her jump overboard, and with their assistance I was got into the canoe, which having effected they righted the upset one, Rider and the rest getting into it. The doctor had never once let go his hold, sticking constantly to some part of the canoe and scrambling up till he seated himself upon her bottom. As I was nearly senseless and full of the water I had swallowed, the doctor directed the canoes to return to the shore, there to use means to restore me. This was accordingly done; the moment we reached the shore they got me out and dispatched the smallest canoe to the ship for assistance; but, in five minutes after we landed, three boats belonging to the *Hampshire*, with Captain Smith himself in one of them, came, in consequence of one of the canoe men having swam on board her, and told them all the gentlemen were drowned.

On their way from the ship they observed something white floating upon the water, which they rowed to, supposing it to be one of us, when it was found to be the dog Beau, quite dead. The only way so singular a circumstance could be accounted for, the animal being almost amphibious, was that being asleep when the canoe overset, he naturally endeavoured to strike upwards, which was, of course, in vain, being the canoe's bottom, and that thus the noble creature was suffocated before he cleared himself. It was also conjectured that the dip under water we experienced whilst hanging by the outriggers was owing to his last and expiring struggle. It certainly was a wonderful thing that four persons, three of whom could not swim, should be in the sea such a time as we were, so often under water too, and yet all be preserved, whilst so powerful a water dog as Beau should lose his life in that element; yet so it was.

Captain Smith, seeing how nearly gone I was, and how extremely ill

I continued, made the people lay me in his cutter, being the swiftest boat of the three, and himself with his doctor attended me to the *Plassey*, on our way to which we met the latter's boats going in search of us. Being hoistered in by a chair, I was put to bed in the captain's apartment, the round house, as the quietest part of the ship, and there fumigated with a succession of flannels steeped in hot brandy mixed wth laudanum, the flannels being laid on my breast and stomach hot as could be borne. Doctor Gowdie sat up with me all night, having little hope of my surviving till morning as I was in great agony, and with extreme difficulty respired. Captains Waddell and Smith—the latter either coming in person, or sending daily to enquire after me—were unremitting in their kindness and attention, as indeed was everybody about me, and it was very flattering to find myself so much the object of anxiety to both ships. I continued in a dangerous and precarious state during eight days, at the end of which time I recovered rapidly. Rider had been a good deal hurt, too, by the quantity of salt water he had swallowed. He never cordially forgave Grant for passing him and swimming to my relief. The first time we conversed together after I was out of danger, instead of expressing gratitude to a benevolent providence for his marvellous escape, he began a bitter lamentation upon the loss of his darling dog, saying he wished he had been drowned himself rather than poor Beau. This improper language caused him a severe rebuke from Captain Waddell for his impiety and ingratitude.

We had light winds for a fortnight after leaving Johanna, being so long in company with the *Hampshire*; but her course then differing from ours, she being bound to Bombay, we separated, each ship's crew giving three cheers on parting.

8

LIFE IN MADRAS

O N 1st May we made the coast of Coromandel, a few miles to the southward of Pondicherry, running along the land until evening, when falling calm, we came to an anchor, to wait the land breeze, which would carry us into Madras roads by daylight of the following morning. At the usual hour I went to my cot; but the thoughts of being so near the place of our destination entirely banished sleep, and finding all my efforts were in vain, I put on my clothes and went upon deck. Just as I got my head above the companion ladder, I felt an indescribably unpleasant sensation, suddenly, as it were, losing the power of breathing, which alarmed me much; for I supposed it to be the forerunner of one of those horrid Indian fevers of which I had heard so much during our voyage.

Whilst worried by this idea, my friend Rogers, whose watch it was, said to me, "Well, Bill, what do you think of this? How do you like the delightful breeze you are doomed to spend your life in?" Enquiring what he meant, I found that what had so surprised and alarmed me was nothing more than the common land wind blowing as usual at that hour directly offshore, and so intensely hot that I could compare it only to standing within the oppressive influence of the steam of a furnace. At daybreak we weighed anchor, standing for Madras, which we had scarcely reached when we heard that Mr. Peter King, the ship's carpenter, a strong-made, vigorous man, was taken suddenly and violently ill with universal cramp in his limbs and stomach. He was put into a warm bath as soo nas water could be heated, and every remedy applied, without avail; in one hour from his first being seized, he was no more. This quick death, added to the horrid land wind, gave me a very unfavourable opinion of the East Indies.

Captain Waddell, with a considerateness peculiar to him, and in a most engaging manner had, a few days previous to our arrival, separately invited each of his passengers to reside with him until we could deliver our letters, and have sufficience time to settle ourselves; and the morning we got into the roads he offered to take me on shore in his boat, observing he knew from my punctuality I should not keep him waiting, which he was sure the others would, and he therefore should not ask any other as he wanted to land as speedily as possible. I thankfully accepted his offer, and may without vanity add he did me justice in alluding to my punctuality, as through life I always made it a point correctly to keep every appointment whether of business or pleasure, never letting any person lose his time on my account. Immediately after breakfast, therefore, I left the *Plassey* with Captain Waddell, in a *masulah* boat, which are constructed expressly for passing the surf that breaks violently along the whole coast in three separate and distinct waves, the first bursting upon the shore, the second from one hundred to one hundred and fifty yards further out, and the third, or outer, nearly at the same distance from the second. The effect of this surf, and the numerous accidents that happen from it, is generally the topic of conversation the first fortnight of a voyage out; so that, although I was in some measure prepared for it, the tremendous roaring and foaming of the sea made my heart palpitate rather quicker than in common.

The boats are formed of broad planks, literally sewed together with the twisted fibres of bark from the coconut tree, the bottom flat, the sides straight up to a certain height, and then inclining inwards to the upper edge; both ends are alike except that at the stern there is a small platform upon which the person that steers stands. A boat thus constructed must necessarily leak greatly; one man is therefore stationed for the sole purpose of baling the water out; and, to prevent newcomers, especially women, from seeing the quantity of water constantly pouring in by the seams at her bottom, a weed, something like heath furze, is laid there more than a foot deep. They are about sixteen feet long, seven wide, and five deep, quite open, with a single board across for a seat at regular distances; are rowed by eight or ten, two sitting upon each bench, the passengers on the one nearest the stern. We had in the *masulah* with us a figure which I supposed to be a female dressed in white muslin coming close round the throat, the body also close, but continued into a kind of petticoat hanging loose and large to the feet. This I learnt was the Captain's *dubash*, a native man acting as general steward who provides every household article as well as of merchandise, and engages all inferior servants. In our way to the shore, he informed Captain Waddell that two large ships we saw at an anchor were the *Pigot*, Captain Richardson, and the *Hector*, Captain Williams (two of our Downs fleet) that came in the preceding day. We afterwards, upon comparing log books, ascertained that the *Plassey* was the first round the Cape by eighteen days, but the above-named two ships, and three others, having, instead of going the Mozambique Channel as we did, proceeded the outer passage, that is, ran down their easting in a high southern latitude, when they met with such strong westerly gales as to drive them two hundred and twenty odd miles every four-and-twenty hours for many successive days, whilst we, who were between Madagascar and the mainland, experienced light winds and calms, and thus outstretched us; such is the chance in navigating.

To return to the *masulah* boat. Notwithstanding the *dubash* and the rowers assured us the surf was very moderate that morning, I thought it the most terrific thing I had ever beheld; nor was my alarm at all lessened by observing, as we approached it, that Captain Waddell threw aside a large boat cloak which he had thrown over his own and my shoulders to protect us both from the spray of the sea and intense heat of the sun, and also took off his gloves. Upon my asking the reason of his so doing, he replied, "I don't know that there is any immediate danger, but it is as well to be prepared for the worst." (I had often heard he was an excellent swimmer.) Three or four strange-looking things now came close to our boat, which I understood were called *catamarans*, consisting of nothing more than two or three large trees, the trunk part only strongly lashed together, upon which sat two men nearly in a state of nature, as indeed were those of the *masulah* boat, having no sort of covering but a small piece of rag not entirely hiding their members, tied with a string round the middle. A very awkward exhibition this for modest girls on their first arrival. Use, however, soon reconciles them to such sights.

The *catamarans* accompany the *masulah* boats through the surf, and when an accident happens endeavour to pick up the unfortunate passengers. The men belonging to them are perpetually washed off by the violence of the sea but, being like fishes in the water, easily regain their seats upon the logs. It is curious to see how well they manage these unwieldly machines, and the rate at which they paddle them along. Upon coming to the edge of the outer surf, the man at the stern of our boat, steering with a long oar, began to stamp his feet and roar like a Bedlamite, the rowers joining in the hideous yell, pulling with all their might, all together frequently crying, "Yalee! Yalee! Yalee!" Before I knew where we had got to, I was astonished to see a pro-digious curling white foam following within a foot of our boat's stern, about which I found the people were perfectly indifferent; and Captain Waddell informed me that was the outer surf which we had safely passed. In like manner we went in with the second and third, reaching the beach with scarce a sprinkling, and we heard from many by-standers that the surf was uncommonly low. The *catamaran* people followed us, begging money for attending us, which I gave them with pleasure, heartily rejoiced at being clear of Madras surf. Upon jumping out of the boat I sunk up to my ankle in a burning sand, the effect of which I never can forget.

Upon the captain's landing he was saluted with nine guns from the fort, according to custom in those days. We were then conducted by the *dubash* to a very handsome house in Fort St. George, which had been taken by Captain Richardson for himself and our commander, pursuant to an agreement between them previous to leaving England. Here at one o'clock we set down to an admirable good dinner, and were vastly comfortable, Captain Waddell promising to introduce me to Governor Bourchier the following morning, for whom I had several letters; as I likewise had to General Joseph Smith, the Commander-in-Chief, Sir Robert Fletcher, Mr. Du Pre, first in Council, Mr. Ardley, Mr. Dawson (both also Members of Council), and many other gentlemen high in the service. With Mr. Dawson I expected to reside, he having married Miss Charlton, who, as well as a brother of hers, Francis Charlton, had been fitted out and sent to India entirely at my father's cost. Mrs. Dawson died about six months prior to my arrival at Madras to the great grief of her disconsolate husband. These Charltons were the children of a much valued friend of my father's who, dying in indigent circumstances, left a numerous family dependent upon the bounty of his friends.

The morning after our arrival when seated at the breakfast table, Captain Richardson came in from his ride, and addressing me, said:

"What! are you still here, young gentleman? Pray, why don't you go to the Fort Major who will provide you with quarters in the barracks, the proper place for you as a cadet."

"And pray," sharply retorted I, "who the devil are you that thus impertinently obtrude your opinion respecting what I ought to do? I take the liberty to tell you that I disclaim any right in you either to interrogate or to direct me, and desire none of your advice."

He looked surprised, but affected to laugh it off, saying I was a fine spirited boy and he must be better acquainted with me, offering his hand, which I coldly accepted, observing, I was not exactly the boy he seemed to take me for.

His first speech had stuck in my stomach, and I resolved not to eat another meal in the house of which he was in part the owner. Breakfast finished, we went to the Governor's residence, where I found my old friend and shipmate, Dick Bourchier, already snugly lodged. His uncle received me very graciously, and said I must dine there. From the Governor's I went to Mr. Dawson's, who, directly after reading my letters, showed me into a spacious and commodious chamber, which he said was exclusively mine, and I must in every respect consider myself as at home. He told me he would go with me to dinner, and take me in the evening to the Governor's Garden three miles out of town, it being the custom always to sup with the person at whose house you dine.

The dinner hour being one, the morning slipped away before I had delivered half my letters. A fine sharp young native, who spoke English, and followed me from the beach on my landing, still stuck close, as my servant. Him therefore I sent for my baggage, with a letter to Captain Waddell thanking him heartily for all his kindnesses to me; I concluded by declaring my determination never more to eat in a house where Captain Richardson was proprietor. At dinner I met my worthy commander, when he expressed much concern at my being so seriously offended by what Captain Richardson had said, assuring me he was a liberal-minded man and had no idea of hurting my feelings or being uncivil. I was nevertheless so prejudiced against him that I never would, although he condescended to make many advances to me afterwards, be more than a bowing acquaintance.

Having been at table nearly two hours, the Governor gave as a toast, "A Good Afternoon," the signal for breaking up. The company immediately arose and departed to take their afternoon's nap, a custom I did not adopt; instead of it, taking a walk to the Black Town, where Rogers, Dr. Gowdie, and other officers of the ship resided, and drank tea with them, after which I went home again and dressed for the evening. At half-past seven Mr. Dawson and I got into our palankeens to go to the Governor's Gardens, on the way passing through a large piece of water of such depth that for many yards it was up to the bearers' hips. When in the deepest part, one of them stumbled, and had very near rolled me out into the stream, which ran rapidly towards the sea.

Arriving at the house, I was much struck by the appearance of the entrance, beautifully illuminated, up an avenue of noble trees to the house. Precisely at nine we sat down to supper, all the commanders of the Indiamen being present, to whom the Governor gave an account of a tremendous hurricane that had occurred in the preceding month of November, in which recital he mentioned so many marvellous circumstances that in my own mind I pronounced him a most abominable liar. Subsequently, however, I had ocular demonstration that I was unjust in forming such an opinion, for I myself saw a ship's long boat which, when the storm arose, was lying on the beach, and by the force of the wind was blown near three miles inland, and there stopped by a plantation of palmira and coconut trees.

The next morning while I was dressing, a man opened my room door, and just popping his head in, said, with great quickness, "Governor send compliments, desire Master's company to dinner today," and, without waiting a moment, away he darted. This message was daily delivered, in a similar manner, during my stay at Madras.

Mr. Dawson now told me he would show me an Indian garden, and that thenceforward we should sleep every night at his country house. He accordingly drove me in his phaeton to Choultry Plain, an open space about three miles from Madras, where I found a dreary-looking habitation with only a few clumsy chairs and tables in it; so bare indeed was it of furniture that I could not disguise my astonishment; and this led the owner to tell me that during the war Hyder Aly's stragglers, or looties as they were called, committed such repeated depredations upon all the European habitations, even to the edge of the works of the Fort, that the proprietors removed everything valuable; and he added that it was upwards of a twelvemonth since he had ventured to sleep there, for which reason I must be satisfied with a couch, no beds being yet put up. We dined with Mr. Marriott, who lived within a quarter of a mile, who talked much of a melon he had for us after dinner, and which proved so watery and tasteless no one in England would have given twopence for a dozen such; but that fruit was then a great rarity at Madras. In the evening Mr. Dawson walked out to show me his boasted garden. After going over what I conceived to be a wild and uncultivated piece of ground, with scarcely a blade of grass or the least sign of vegetation, he suddenly stopped and asked me what I thought of a Madras garden; to which, in perfect simplicity, I answered, "I would tell him my opinion when I had seen one." This answer he replied to with, "When you see one, sir, why you are now in the middle of mine." The devil I am, thought I. Then what a precious country am I come to, if this is a specimen of a gentleman's garden! As there was no use in attempting to disguise my sentiments, I acknowledged that I considered the most barren part of Hounslow Heath far preferable.

At dusk we returned to Mr. Marriott's, where I was stuck down to pagoda (eight shillings) whist, and at ten o'clock walked home to our bare-walled, melancholy-looking chambers. Mine was a large hall, without a single article in it except a crazy old couch, upon which lay a miserably dirty-looking Chinese pillow as hard as the floor itself, and no bedding of any sort or kind. This was roughing it with a vengeance, and what I was not at all accustomed to. Sleep under such circumstances seemed entirely out of the question; for, as if a want of all the usual requisites was insufficient, the place was filled by myriads of mosquitoes of no small size. I, however, lay down in my clothes upon the rattan, where I tumbled about in a most uneasy state about hours, when I got up and walked up and down.

In another hour, I was surprised to hear Mr. Dawson moving. He soon entered my room, asking if I was ready to ride; to which, with evident surprise, I answered that it was the middle of the night. Mr. Dawson, with a smile, observed he had taken his usual allowance of sleep, four hours, and that he always was mounted before break of day. Of course, I made no further opposition, and away we went, taking a pleasant ride enough, the daylight appearing in half an hour after we left the house. On our way back, my nag, a handsome Arabian, and as Mr. Dawson assured me gentle as a lamb and free from every vice, gave a sudden and unexpected bounce sideways of several yards, an event I was wholly unprepared for. I, therefore, lost my seat and down I came in the middle of the road. Although not materially hurt, I was a good deal shaken, and vexed at my awkwardness; nor was that vexation lessened by seeing the melancholy-looking Dawson, with his cadaverous countenance, in so violent a fit of laughter that I thought he too would have fallen from his horse. Having indulged himself in this ill-timed mirth, he apologized thus: "I beg your pardon, Mr. Hickey, but there is to me something so superlatively ridiculous in a man's falling from his horse that I never see it without its exciting my risibility," and again he burst out laughing. I thought him an immensely stupid brute, but made no reply. The servants having caught my Arab, I once more mounted, resolved in future to be more attentive to the pranks of this gentle creature, without a vice.

Mr. Dawson and I had several conversations upon family matters, when he invariably expressed his surprise that my father should have sent me out as a cadet, especially to Madras, where the military line never could be an object for a gentleman; that the pay was too contemptible to afford the common necessaries of life, and particularly bad now a peace was made which barred all chance of promotion. This subject he so often dwelt upon that, tired of his prosing comments, I one day pettishly said:

"Since this is the case, and the prospect, according to your account, so forlorn a one for me, I think I had better return to Europe," though when I so said not an idea of the kind was in my contemplation.

Mr. Dawson immediately continued:

"Upon my word, I think it is the best measure you can adopt, and I advise you by all means to go home and let your father procure for you a writership in the civil service, which with his influence he can have no difficulty to accomplish; and then it may be in my power to serve you."

This language at once gave me a notion that I might, without incurring my father's displeasure, follow Mr. Dawson's recommendation.

I usually went every day into the Fort, and generally dined twice a week with the Governor, going to the Gardens to sleep, where, after the first night, I took care to supply myself with bedding and mosquito curtains. One day that I dined at Mr. Bourchier's, he congratulated me upon no longer being a cadet, a Commission of Ensign having passed the board both for me and his nephew, Richard, being the only two cadets of the season that would be promoted probably for three years to come. I thanked him, but said, "Mr. Dawson advised me to quit the army and get transferred to the civil service"; to which Mr. Bourchier observed he thought such a change desirable and well worthy the going home to obtain.

All agog at this approval from a quarter where I expected disapprobation, and delighted with the idea of leaving such an abominable place as Madras, I directly went to my friend Mr. Rider to communicate what had passed, and the resolution I had in consequence formed. Upon which, he (whom I had on our passage out made acquainted with my little history) in the kindest manner endeavoured to dissuade me from adopting so foolish and inconsiderate a measure, reminding me in nervous language of the immense expense my father had been put to in fitting me out, and the disappointment and mortification it must be to him to see me thus inconsiderately return. All this I felt myself; yet the idea of again seeing England drove poor prudence clear off; and the most Mr. Rider could effect was my promise that I would not hastily determine, or resign the service without mature consideration.

A week after the above conversation with Mr. Rider, he called upon me to say he clearly saw that I greatly disliked Madras, but he felt certain that I should be pleased with Bengal. He therefore wished me to apply to Mr. Bourchier to transfer me to that establishment, which he could easily do by giving me a recommendatory letter to Governor Verelst, or to General Richard Smith, the Commander-in-Chief. Such a change I had not the least objection to; on the contrary, I much liked the thoughts of it, and therefore forthwith posted away to the Government House and made my request in person. Whereupon Mr. Bourchier assured me it was utterly impossible, as he would soon convince me; and, calling for his private secretary, he desired him to bring the general letter, which he observed the *Plassey* had conveyed to India, and from which he read a paragraph stating that, as changes had frequently been made in the army from one Presidency to another, whereby great confusion and difficulties had arisen, the Court of Directors did most positively forbid and prohibit anything of that kind in future, upon any pretence whatsoever, and that no exchange of officers from one settlement to another should ever be permitted without an express order from the Court.

This regulation, carried out in the same ship in which I went, I conceived decisive. I, however, mentioned it to Rider, who persevered in urging me to go round to Bengal with him, where he was certain from his own personal influence he should be able to procure for me upon that establishment the same military rank I had obtained at

Madras. He then recommended me to ask Mr. Bourchier to let me retain the ensigncy and go to Bengal upon leave of absence; also to inform him that I made this application at his (Rider's) desire. I did so, but the Governor said it could not be done; that all he could do he would, which was not only to allow me to go to Bengal, but give me letters to some friends of his in that settlement who might be able to promote my views. He added that he thought it incumbent upon him to tell me, in his opinion, I was very wrong to leave Madras; that I ought to bear in recollection that, even if I succeeded in getting the same rank in the army of Bengal, I should always be liable to be recalled if the Court of Directors ever discovered the circumstance, and in such case they would, beyond a doubt, dismiss me from their service altogether. This possibility of a recall, even when I might have attained a rank of importance as an officer, seriously alarmed me; and upon further deliberation I resolved to return to England. Having communicated such my final determination to Mr. Dawson, he promised to write to my father and say I had so done in pursuance of his advice, and that he thought it the best step I could take.

Captain Waddell, having heard of my intention of returning to Europe, very kindly sent his purser, Mr. Jones, to me to say he should be happy to have the pleasure of my company on board the *Plassey*, and although he was bound to China first, I probably should not meet with any opportunity of reaching England earlier than his ship would be there. I therefore thankfully accepted his friendly offer; and, two days after I had done so, the Company's ship *Thames*, Captain Haggis, arrived in the roads from Bengal, on her way towards Europe. Such an opportunity I thought ought not to be lost, and I applied to the commander, a strange, rough sort of a tarpaulin, to ask his price, to which he answered he believed he might be able to spare me a small cabin in his steerage for three hundred guineas. Our treaty instantly ceased; and I made up my mind to take a peep at the Chinese.

The latter end of June, Captain Waddell told me I must prepare for departure, as he intended to sail in less than a week. I therefore went round to take leave of a numerous set of acquaintances I had made during my residence at Fort St. George, from many of whom I had received marks of great civility and kindness. The last time that I went to sleep at Mr. Dawson's garden, he told me he would, the next morning, show me a pretty place about ten miles to the northward, belonging to a friend of his, with whom we should spend the day and ride home in the cool of the evening, that I should eat as fine and high-flavoured oysters as ever I tasted in Europe. We accordingly mounted our horses before daybreak, and rode gently to the place, going the last four miles along the sand at the very edge of the sea, and enjoying a most refreshing breeze which blew upon us direct from the ocean.

Upon coming up to the door of the house, we dismounted, but not a soul appeared to receive us. Mr. Dawson, much surprised, conducted me into the hall, and loudly called, "Holloa, Boy, Boy!" the usual manner of summoning servants at Madras. After repeating this several times without any effect, he said to me, "This is very singular, nor can I account for it." He then proceeded to his friend's bedchamber, from whence I heard him exclaim, "Good God, poor Stone (or Stonehouse, I forget which) is dead"; and, again joining me, he told me he was lying upon the bed a corpse. After again calling in vain, we walked to a sort of lodge or farm belonging to the deceased, where we found several of the servants, who upon seeing us burst into violent lamentations. In a short time, one of them informed Mr. Dawson that his master's horse had been taken to the door, as usual, at daylight. The sun rising and he not coming out, his head man knocked at his room door; but, not receiving any answer, he opened it and entered, where he saw his master lying upon his bed, and approaching nearer, observed his mouth and eyes wide open; that, taking him by the hand, he found it clammy and cold, extremely terrified at which he ran out and called his fellow servants, who returned to the room with him; but, the moment they saw their master was dead, they all ran away to the place we found them in, where they had been shut up above an hour.

Instead, therefore, of the cheerful, pleasant day we had expected, Mr. Dawson was employed some hours arranging matters for the funeral. He sent a man on horseback for a doctor who lived about three miles off, and who came immediately. Upon examining the body, he said nothing could be done, that a change had actually taken place, from which he supposed he must have been seized with apoplexy soon after lying down. At three o'clock in the afternoon we set out on our return home, greatly shocked at the melancholy occurrence; at least, I was, for I certainly thought Mr. Dawson betrayed an indifference that did him no credit in my eyes, and treated this sudden death quite as a thing of course, and no importance.

Another extraordinary circumstance happened the ensuing day. I went into the Black Town for the purpose of visiting the *Plassey's* officers, where I found the house in the utmost confusion; and, seeing a number of persons in one of the rooms, I also entered, and saw they were gathered round a body weltering in blood upon the floor. Rogers, who was present, informed me it was our shipmate, old Forbes, who a few minutes before had cut his throat, and so effectually that he was already dead. He had been in a low and desponding way for a month, often grievously weeping and exclaiming what a miserable wretch he was, and that when the *Plassey* should sail from Madras he should be left destitute and without a single friend in the world. Upon our first arrival, he hired a small house in the Black Town, where he lived entirely by himself, until Gowdie and Rogers, seeing how unhappy the poor creature was, kindly received and fed him, whereupon he recovered his health and spirits; but, as the time approached when he must be deprived of their society, he again flagged, and fell into despondence, which led him to put an end to his life with a razor.

During my stay at Madras, a young gentleman came out from England very strongly recommended to Mr. Dawson, in consequence of which he resided in his house. His name Hall Plumer (brother to Sir Thomas Plumer, the present Solicitor-General, since appointed Vice-Chancellor of England); he was a writer upon the Madras establishment, and we became sworn friends. I shall say more of him hereafter.

On 6th July, Mr. Chisholme brought a remarkably fine-looking young man about eighteen years of age, whom he introduced by the name of Maclintock, saying he would be a fellow passenger of mine to China, where he was going for the recovery of his health. He had only been three years in India, unfortunately getting a venereal taint upwards of a year before I saw him. It had reduced him to so low a state, and brought on so many alarming symptoms, that the medical gentlemen advised his trying the effect of change of air and passing some months at Canton, where the winter was sharp and cold. Chisholme, who knew his connections, was much interested about him, and had asked Captain Waddell to give him a passage, a request that was granted in the handsomest manner, and half the round house allotted to his use. "Now," said Chisholme, "as you two are much alike in disposition, I think it would be a pleasant thing to both to be together, each of your apartments being sufficiently spacious to accommodate two. So, if you approve of my suggestion, do you, Hickey, go up to the round house, or let Maclintock come down to your half of the great cabin. I should conceive the latter the best." I readily acceded, and we agreed to swing our cots below. I had reason to be highly satisfied with my companion; for, during nine subsequent months that we were inseparable, I never once heard an angry or ill-natured word pass his lips. So placid and fine a tempered lad I never met with; he was also unusually accomplished and an excellent scholar.

On the 7th (July) I received notice that the ship would sail the following day; and Captain Waddell, with his accustomed kind attention, offered to take me off with him at one o'clock in the afternoon. But the same evening Chisholme and Maclintock called to say they intended going off soon after sunrise, at which time the surf never was so high as when the day was further advanced; and, Chisholme pressing me to join them, I consented and wrote a note to tell my commander. Before sunrise the next morning I was upon the beach, and saw a prodigious surf. The boat people, nevertheless, assured us there was not the least danger, and we embarked, taking the precaution to engage several of the largest *catamarans* to attend and stick close to us. We passed the first surf tolerably well, only getting a little spray of the sea over us. We then remained stationary at least half an hour before they attempted the second, though five or six times not a yard from the tremendous curl and break of the wave, which, to say the truth, occasioned me serious alarm; but I had the miserable consolation of seeing Chisholme still more frightened than myself; and he every moment called to the people of the *catamarans* to keep nearer to us, promising them, as well as our boat's crew, adequate compensation if they carried us safely through. Maclintock and I sat quite still without saying a word; but I am free to confess I was not sorry to hear Chisholme exhorting those about us to exert themselves and be careful. We then passed the second surf without receiving a drop of water, and in like manner the third.

We all three felt happy when we were fairly over it; and we had the satisfaction to see that our boat was better managed than two others that put off at the same time we did, both continuing beween the first and second surfs until long after we passed the outer one. Of course, we kept the promise Chisholme had made, and liberally rewarded the *masulah* and *catamaran* people. We reached the ship a little after eight o'clock in the morning. At two in the afternoon, our good captain came on board in the accommodation boat, as it is called, which belongs to government, and is always lent to persons of rank and consequence, sometimes, formerly to commanders of Indiamen, when they were treated with more attention and respect than of late. With the captain there came off a little weazen-faced elderly Armenian, who was going upon some mercantile business to China, and upon entering the ship seemed scared out of his wits. Immediately after our commander came on board, we got under way, as did five other of the ships bound to China, not one of which, except the *Triton*, could sail with the *Plassey*.

The fifth day we saw Pulo Penang, at the mouth of the Straits of Malacca, at that time uninhabited, but where the East India Company long since formed a colony, now in a flourishing state, having docks constructed in the harbour of sufficient dimensions to receive and repair ships of the line, and where several capital vessels have been built. Its name has been changed to Prince of Wales's Island. We ran through part of the Straits of Malacca with delightful weather and smooth water, in company with the *Triton*, for whom however we had daily been obliged to shorten sail several hours, until we reached the Dutch settlement of Malacca, where the two commanders agreed to

Thaïs by Sir Joshua Reynolds, believed to be a portrait of Emily Warren

By courtesy of the Waddesdon Bequest, Waddesdon Manor

Vauxhall Gardens in 1784. From a water colour by Thomas Rowlandson.

By courtesy of the Trustees of the British Museum

stop and fill their water casks, having left Madras rather short supplied with that requisite article, owing to the surf being high several days previous to our leaving it. We accordingly came to an anchor and immediately went on shore to a neat, pretty-looking town, in which we fixed our abode at a tavern close to the sea, the room in which we sat commanding a view of the roads and shipping. Captain Elphinstone joined our party, who, being a most gentlemanlike and pleasing man, proved a great acquisition. We likewise had his first officer, Mr. Parsloe, with us, a coxcomb of the superlative degree, who afforded us considerable entertainment from an extraordinary propensity to the marvellous, or, in plain terms, lying. Our table fare was very tolerable, the fish and poultry excellent, but marred from their cooking, everything swimming in oil; the fruits delicious, one especially so, the mangosteen, which I thought the most exquisite I ever tasted anywhere. The flavour, although sweet and rich, is extremely delicate, and any quantity of it might be eaten without risk of injuring the health. Captain Elphinstone was at them morning, noon, and night, the whole time lamenting he had so short a period to enjoy them, for it is impossible to keep them long; even on shore they spoil in twenty-four hours after being gathered.

When we were leaving the ship Rogers cautioned me respecting the women, saying, "Take care of yourself, Bill; the Malays are a dangerous and revengeful people, and you, who are by nature of an amorous disposition, will be looking after the girls, in which case, should any of the men discover you, certainly you will have one of their *creeses* up to the hilt in your guts." As he said this with great gravity, and I was utterly ignorant of the habits or prejudices of the people I was going amongst, I resolved to keep clear of all amours, and have as little as possible to do with the Malays. There being no bedchambers for guests at the tavern, sleeping apartments were engaged and prepared for us at other houses. Maclintock and I agreed to keep together; but were not able so to do from there not being a room with two beds in it.

After supper we retired to our respective chambers. Mine was a large one, level with the street, into which it looked, having a decent bed and furniture. Dismissing the servant who attended me to it, I examined the windows, which I found well secured by strong iron bars. I then locked the door inside, undressed and laid down, as I conceived, in perfect security. Notwithstanding the intense heat which instantly threw me into a profuse perspiration, the violent exercise I had taken in the day so fatigued me that I soon fell into a deep sleep, from which I was suddenly awakened by some person's shaking me. Greatly alarmed, I bounced up; nor was my terror diminished when I saw by the light of the moon that shone in the room a Malay man,

5+

almost naked, leaning over me at the bedside. I cried out, "Who is there? Who are you? What do you want?" to which he answered in broken English "Master caree (want) piccaninee girl? I catch bring here; Master not holloa, not frighten."

Much relieved at hearing such to be the object of his unwelcome visit, I quickly replied, "No, no, I thank you I am too much tired; not tonight." The fact is, the most modest female in existence might then have trusted herself with me, and no danger of molestation, fear having effectually banished everything like that. The man upon my repeated negative said, "Den me go, Master. Salaam, Master," and to my in-expressible astonishment instantly made his exit by jumping out at the window I imagined so well secured. The moment he was out, I rose to examine how this could have happened, and then discovered that one of the bars was without either nail or screw at the bottom, and altogether so loose that it could be pushed sufficiently on one side to admit a man to pass through. While I was busily employed about these bars, I heard a sort of stifled laugh near at hand in the street, upon which I began to suspect some trick. After watching near an hour without further noise or interruption, I laid down in my clothes —for I had dressed myself when the fellow disappeared—hoping to get a little rest; but all my endeavours were in vain. I therefore lay sweating until daylight, and then walked out into the town.

At breakfast I found from the whispering and laughing of the party that a plan had been adopted in order to frighten me, which object had certainly been accomplished. Mr. Parsloe, with a broad grin, hoped I had rested well, and had pleasant dreams. Whereupon Captain Elphinstone observed, "It is a pity, Hickey, you had not received these facetious gentlemen with the contents of a certain utensil in their faces, which their egregious folly so richly deserved." Rogers afterwards told me the scheme was suggested by Parsloe; but they had no notion that, in such a dreadful heat, I should so soon have got to sleep; for, had they, they would not have disturbed me. The Malay man they had employed was a servant at the tavern, and the very best pimp in the place, which qualification I benefited by the next night. Rogers, I learned (from himself) had taken the trouble of going with a carpenter in the afternoon, to take out the fastenings from the bar of the window for the man to enter at.

After spending four days very agreeably at Malacca, where we found much to see and entertain us, we returned to the *Plassey* and proceeded on our way to China, still accompanied by the *Triton*; but the additional water she had taken in so altered her sailing for the worse that, on the second day, we ran away and left her. Having cleared the Straits, our daily conversation was the probability of encountering a typhoon, or violent gale of wind so called, frequently happening in the China Seas towards the latter part of the year. Captain Waddell, in jocularity, used to desire me to keep a good look out of an evening; and, if the sun set, as seamen phrase it, angrily, casting a copper tint all over the sky, attended with a thick heavy atmosphere, we might expect a puff in a few hours. Four days after the captain had mentioned these symptoms to me, I was sure from his conversation with the officers at breakfast, and the orders he gave, that he expected bad weather. It was then blowing fresh, and by the hour of dinner the wind so increased that the topsails were close reefed. The sun that evening did set as he had described, the appearance being quite horrible; the thick and heavy clouds were of a dismal deep orange colour, and the sea became extremely agitated. The topgallant masts and yards were lowered upon deck and every preparation made for encountering a tempest. By eight in the evening it blew so tremendously that every sail was taken in, and we ran under bare poles. At nine, in an instant, the wind shifted almost to the opposite point. So sudden and violent was it that, had a single yard of canvas been out, the consequences might have been serious. As it was, they immediately hove to.

We lay tumbling about sadly, and had a dismal night, shipping heavy seas, which swept away everything they came against. The gale was accompanied by excessively vivid lightning and thunder as if the artillery of the world had all been discharged at once. This was the first storm I had ever been in; and greatly did the effects of it surprise me. The *Plassey* was one of the best sea boats that ever swam, behaving, as the seamen said, wonderfully well; yet the motion was so quick and violent that every timber and plank seemed to shake. All attempts to keep my legs being useless, I retired to my cot, which every moment struck the deck on one side or the other. Daylight made no favourable change. About eleven in the morning I got up, and being young and active I managed to get upon deck, where the grandeur of the scene, terrific as it was, greatly surprised me. I fastened myself with a rope upon the quarterdeck by the advice of the doctor, who had scarcely given it when, the ship, taking a deep and desperate lee lurch, he lost his hold, and away he flew like a shot to leeward, falling with great force against the ship's side, his head striking within two inches of the aftermost port out of which everybody upon deck thought he must have gone. He had a narrow escape from a watery grave, and was dreadfully bruised from the violence of the fall. Our cargo from Madras being cotton, the ship was so crank that she sometimes lay for half an hour at a time in a manner waterlogged, her gunwale being completely enveloped in the sea, so that I frequently thought she never would right again. The gale continued all the second day and night, but towards morning of the third moderated and soon after fell calm. The sea being enormously high and confused, she rolled and pitched to such a degree that the masts were every moment expected to go over her side. So serious a disaster fortunately for us did not happen; and, after several hours' terrible tumbling about in all directions, a fresh breeze and from the right quarter, sprang up; we made sail, which steadied the ship, and the following day saw the Grand Ladrones, a cluster of islands off the coast of China.

Severe as the storm had been, we did not start a rope yarn nor receive the slightest damage in any way. I never saw a creature so terrified as the poor devil of an Armenian. In the height of the gale, he frequently asked me what was to become of us, and what I would advise him to do. Vexed at his absurd question, and the childishness of his behaviour, I answered, "I recommend you to grin and bear it"— an expression used by sailors after a long continuance of bad weather. Not at all understanding my meaning, he soon after addressed Chisholme, requesting an explanation. Unluckily for him, Mr. Chisholme was out of temper and, damning his blood for a stupid old brute, bid him go to hell and f—— spiders, at same time giving him a push that drove him several yards; and down he fell flat on his back. He raised himself as well as he could, crawled to his cabin, and we saw no more of him until the ship was safe at an anchor. As we approached the land, the wind moderated, the weather became clear, and the sea subsided. In a few hours, a small vessel came alongside from which we got a Chinese pilot, who conducted the ship through the Bogue, a narrow channel or inlet from the ocean to the river, not near half a mile broad, with a fort upon each side, which as soon as we passed the river spread to a great width, and appeared covered with boats of different sizes.

Many of the smaller came close to the ship with a number of pretty-enough-featured girls, who immediately began chattering a strange kind of jargon; and they often cried out to the officers, "Hy yaw Massa, you come again. I washy washy for you last voyage; washy washy three piece, one man one catty; I washy washy your three piece." This I found implied bawdy, which they are fond of talking; though I also understood that these female orators are very rarely procurable, nor will any temptation of money induce them to enter the ship. They are washerwomen, receiving the linen from the ports, and returning them when ready in the same manner. Our sea pilot having taken the ship into Macao roads, we there anchored to wait the arrival of a river pilot, and were told we had no chance of one until the following day. I, therefore, after dinner went on shore to this miserable place, where there is a wretched ill-constructed fort belonging to the Portuguese, in which I saw a few sallow-faced, half-naked, and apparently half-starved creatures in old tattered coats that had once been blue, carrying muskets upon their shoulders, which, like the other accoutrements, were of a piece with their dress. These wretches were honoured with a title of soldiers. Not only the men, but everything around, bespoke the acme of poverty and misery. Satisfied with what I had seen, and nothing tempted by a printed board indicating the house upon which it was fixed to be "The British Hotel," where was to be found "elegant entertainment and comfortable lodging," I did not even take a look within, but walked as fast as my legs could carry me to the sea side, where Maclintock, as disgusted as myself with Macao, had procured a boat, in which we returned to our own really comfortable apartment on board the *Plassey*. Whilst on shore, we learnt that none of the other ships had yet entered the river, but that there were several direct from England then laying at Whampoa.

In the afternoon of the next day, having procured a pilot, we proceeded upwards, and in thirty hours were safely moored at Whampoa, having in the passage passed two bars, or banks of sand, having, when the tide was out, only seven feet upon them. We arrived at our moorings on 11th August, having been only thirty-three days from Madras, which was the shortest voyage that had then ever been made by an East Indiaman. We found at anchor five English ships, four Swedes, six French, four Danes, and three Dutch, all the foreigners being of the immense burthen of from twelve to fifteen hundred tons.

Whampoa is pleasantly situated, having two islands close to the ships, one called Deans, upon which each ship erects what is called a "bankshall," being a lightly constructed wooden building from sixty to one hundred feet in length, into which the upper masts, yards, spars, sails, rigging and stores are deposited, and, previous to being re-embarked, are all repaired and put into order. The other is called French Island, where the officers and sailors walk, or amuse themselves at different games for exercise and pastime. Upon French Island all the Europeans who die are buried. The morning after we reached Whampoa, which we got to at dusk, I was awakened at sunrise by the sound of music appearing to come from different directions, the effect being delightful. Looking out of the quarter gallery window, I saw that each of the foreign ships had an excellent band, consisting of every description of wind and martial instruments, the whole striking up the moment the sun appeared above the horizon, continuing to play for an hour, and the same in the evening, an hour previous to sunset. I never heard anything that pleased me more.

After breakfast, the captain's barge being made ready, with jack, ensign, and pennant flying, the crew all in clean white shirts and black caps, Captain Waddell, Mr. Maclintock, the Armenian, and myself got into it; and the men pulled away for Canton, distant from Whampoa about eighteen miles. The heat of the sun was intense; and

I felt much for the rowers. On the way two Chinese buildings were pointed out to us as *hoppo*, or custom-houses, at both which all boats, except those belonging to the commanders of European ships, which in compliment to their flag are exempted, are obliged to stop and undergo a strict search or examination by a petty mandarin, like our custom-house officers, to ascertain that there is nothing contraband on board. We were also shown, when nearly half way, a small inlet or creek called "Lob Lob Creek," from whence in *sampans* (the name of the country boats) came forth certain prostitutes, who, if required so to do, board the boats passing up or down, and thus satisfy the carnal appetites of the people belonging to the ships, this being the only spot where opportunities of that nature offer; for the magistrates of China are very rigid on that point, making it extremely difficult, indeed almost impossible, to procure a woman within the city or environs of Canton, or even on board the ships.

The females who ply at Lob Lob Creek are supposed so to do by stealth. I say "supposed," because the fact is that they pay a proportion of their earnings to the mandarin upon duty, who thereupon, like an upright administrator of justice, shuts his eyes and his ears to the breach of the law, those public officers being invariably corrupt. In fact, there is scarce any offence or crime, murder not excepted, that the perpetrator may not free himself from punishment for by paying a certain sum, according to the nature or degree of enormity of his offence. Money seems to be the idol they all worship.

9

CANTON AND BOB POTT

W<small>E</small> arrived at Canton about noon. The view of the city, as you approach it, is strikingly grand, and at the same time picturesque. The magnitude and novelty of the architecture must always surprise strangers. The scene upon the water is as busy a one as the Thames below London Bridge, with this difference, that instead of our square-rigged vessels of different dimensions, you there have junks, which, although in the middle of the fair weather season they navigate all along the coast of China and even to the Straits of Malacca, yet they never go out of sight of land, and for this plain reason—they are wholly ignorant of navigation and all its advantages. A junk is so constructed that one would be led to suppose the inventor's principal object had been to deter mankind from venturing upon salt water. Their shape lengthways is rather more than a semicircle, each end being many feet higher than the centre. At the stern there is a recess angular-wise several feet in depth, of no possible use, and looks as if it was intended to give every sea that strikes her abaft a fair chance of splitting the unwieldy machine in two.

Upon each bow is painted an enormous eye; and, if enquiry is made what they are for, the answer is, "Hi yaw, no have eyes, how can see?" They draw but little water, seldom more than five feet when loaded, have only one mast, with a slight bamboo, occasionally, used as a top-mast. Their sails are made of reeds, looking much like a mat, and answer the intended purpose very well, at least in the hands of China-men. In smooth water, and before the wind, they sail tolerably, but make sad work against an adverse wind or high sea. Being bigoted to everything that has been handed down from their ancestors, there is no prevailing upon them to attempt improvement in any way. If shown how deficient they are in many respects, and how greatly they might benefit by adopting European practice in arts and manufactures, they without hesitation admit our superiority with the utmost sang-froid, adding in favour of their own habits, "Truly this have China custom."

About half a mile above the city suburbs, in going from Whampoa, is a wharf, or embankment, regularly built of brick and mortar, extending more than half a mile in length, upon which wharf stands the different factories or place of residence of the supercargoes, each factory having the flag of its nation on a lofty ensign staff before it. At the time I was in China, they stood in the following order: first, the Dutch, then, the French, the English, the Swedes, and, last, the Danes. Each of these factories, besides admirable banqueting, or public, rooms for eating, etc., have attached to them sets of chambers, varying in size according to the establishment. The English being far more numerous than any other nation trading with China, their range of buildings is much the most extensive. Each supercargo has four handsome rooms; the public apartments are in front looking to the river; the others go inland to the depth of two or three hundred feet, in broad courts, having the sets of rooms on each side, every set having a distinct and separate entrance with a small garden, and every sort of convenience. Besides the factories which belong to the East India Company, there are also others, the property of Chinese, who let them to Europe and Country captains of ships, merchants and strangers whom business bring to Canton. For several years there has been an Imperial flag flying before a factory occupied by the Germans. The Americans (whom the Chinese distinguish by the expressive title of Second Chop Englishmen) have also a flag.

The number of supercargoes employed by the English East India Company in the year 1769 was twelve; but, when we arrived, there were only eleven resident, one being in Europe for recovery of his health. Those present were Messrs. Revell, Devisme, Torriano, Phipps, Wood, Harrison, Bevan, Rous, Raper, Blake, and Bradshaw. There were also two writers, Pigou and Rogers, who after five years' service become supercargoes. Upon our landing, Captain Waddell immediately conducted Mr. Maclintock and me to Mr. Revell's, the Chief Supercargo, who, after an exchange of compliments, took us to a handsome suite of rooms consisting of two spacious bedchambers with dressing-room adjoining each, two large sitting-rooms, and one for eating—the whole neatly furnished, and having a complete small library. Of these apartments he gave me the keys, saying they were for the exclusive use of Mr. Maclintock and myself during our stay in China. He also observed that, as it was customary for gentlemen to breakfast in their own chambers, every requisite would be amply supplied by the factory steward. He further informed us that all the supercargoes, and any guests that honoured them with their company, daily dined together in the great hall at two o'clock; but if at any time, from indisposition or choosing to be alone, we preferred dining in private, upon communicating such wish to the steward he would bring a bill of fare, and furnish whatever articles we ordered therefrom. After this gracious reception, he left us to repose or do as we thought proper until dinner. Maclintock and I sallied forth and were much entertained with the novelty of the scene. We entered several shops, and were soon surprised to find is was time to dress. In our way home I was at a loss which way to turn at the corner of a street, and my companion declared himself equally so; whereupon one of the most lovely boys I ever beheld, who had heard our doubts, came up with the utmost ease and familiarity, though perfect politeness, saying,

"I presume, gentlemen, you want to go to the Company's factory. If so, I shall have the pleasure to conduct you, as this gentleman," pointing to an elderly, stiff, and remarkably upright man, with a fan in his hand, "and I are going there."

We accepted the proffered civility of this charming youth, and thus commenced an acquaintance which ripened into as sincere a friendship as ever subsisted between two persons, and which continued uninterrupted for thirty years, ending only in his death. After walking a hundred yards, he wished his companion good morning, saying, "As we young folk shall move quicker than you like, we will leave you, but shall soon meet again." He then took hold of my arm and led the way. During our walk, he asked my name and that of my companion, which, having communicated to him, he jocularly said:

"The old quiz who just left us is Stephen Devisme, a devilish odd sort of a body, at present second supercargo, and will soon be chief, as Revell is going home this season. You'll like him well enough. I play all sorts of tricks with the old buck. Perhaps you have already heard of me, for I make myself conspicuous at Canton; but, lest you should not, I am Bob Pott. I command the *Cruttenden.*"

Observing I smiled at the latter part of his speech, he said:

"Aye, aye, you may laugh and think me a young hand to command an East Indiaman; but it's very true for all that."

Pott was at this period not quite fourteen and, as already observed, the most beautiful lad, every feature perfect, remarkably fair complexion, with a profusion of bright auburn hair hanging in natural ringlets about his head and face, most piercing eyes, and a figure of the exactest symmetry. There was a something altogether about him irresistibly attracting and engaging. Having shown us to our rooms, he said he would wait while we dressed, and then attend us to the dining hall. Upon our arrival there, he introduced us to Mr. Devisme and Mr. Wood (the only two gentlemen then in the room) with an ease and grace that would have become the most elegant courtier. Having letters from Madras friends to both Mr. Devisme and Mr. Wood, I took them from my pocket and delivered them. The two gentlemen thereupon requested I would command their services upon every occasion during my stay at Canton. In a few minutes, Pott

5*

observed another gentleman coming upstairs, when laying hold of my hand he drew me towards the door, saying in a low voice, "That is my chief mate." Then quitting me he went up to the stranger, took him by the arm and leading him up to me, made us shake hands, saying to the gentleman, "You must be friends with Mr. Hickey, for I have a great liking to him"; and, turning to me, he added, "This is Captain Baker of the *Cruttenden*, my ship," winking significantly. Captain Baker smiled and patting his protégé upon the head, said, "My dear Bob, there is no occasion for any new aid being called in for the purpose of completely spoiling an already sufficiently spoiled boy."

Whilst this was passing, Mr. Revell and the other supercargoes came in, with the commanders of the different Europe ships, also Mr. Carvalho, an elegant-looking man, who was supercargo to several large country ships then at Whampoa. Mr. Revell having introduced Maclintock and me to the whole party, we sat down, in number about thirty, to a capital dinner consisting of fish, flesh and fowl, all of the best, with a variety of well-dressed made dishes, being served up in two courses, followed by a superb dessert, the wines, claret, madeira, and hock, all excellent, and made as cold as ice. Mr. Devisme placed me next to him, and was attentive as possible. He briefly gave me some account of every person at table, in doing which I could perceive an inclination to be satirical. Having discussed the characters of the adults, he continued, "Young Pott is a boy of uncommon talents, but volatile to excess, and full of mischief as a monkey; and I am truly concerned to see every person in the factory, except myself, endeavouring to ruin him by every species of indulgence, and encouraging instead of checking his wild sallies and mischievous propensities. In short, sir, this place will undo him."

Notwithstanding this grave speech, I soon discovered he was one of the worst spoilers himself. He told me Pott was the son of the surgeon so well known for superior abilities in his profession, who having a numerous family of children, it became necessary to put them into different lines of life. Robert was intended for the sea, being his own choice, and was accordingly shipped as a "guinea-pig" (the name given to boys on their first voyage) on board the *Cruttenden*, so called after a brother of Mrs. Pott's, who was in the India Direction, and principal owner of that and other vessels of the Company's; of one of which he (Robert) was to have the command when competent to assume it. I afterwards heard that Captain Baker was a man who made his own interest the first object upon all occasions; and, being dependent upon Pott's family for his success in life, he felt the propriety of courting them in every way, and naturally enough thought he could not do so more effectually than by showing every possible attention to their young favourite, Robert, who, under that impression, was permitted to do whatever he pleased, the indulgencies being carried so far that the boy was not very wide of the truth in telling me he commanded the *Cruttenden*.

After setting near three hours at table, the company separated, Mr. Revell telling me we should assemble again to tea and coffee at seven. Mr. Harrison then asked me to join three or four friends in his room, to which I accompanied him, where I found Mr. Rous, Wood, Bradshaw, and Pott, already seated at a table with bottles and glasses; and all, except Pott, partook of some uncommon fine claret, Messrs. Harrison and Rous smoking cheroots. Here Bob (for so he insisted upon being called) placed himself close by me, expressing his joy in the most energetic terms at my having come amongst them, as I was the first reasonable creature he had seen since he came to China.

"Your chum," (continued he), "I cannot say so much of. To be sure he is a good-looking fellow; but then, there is something so cold, so damned repulsive and formal that he makes me sick, and I wonder how the devil you can endure one so every way unlike yourself."

I defended my friend as well as I could, telling Bob he greatly mistook the character of Maclintock, and upon better acquaintance he would like him; that he was by nature mild and gentle, but perhaps graver just now than usual from being in bad health and in the midst of strangers. I also said that, as he had been pleased so hastily to form a favourable opinion of me, and the reverse of Maclintock, I apprehend he might shortly see occasion to change his sentiments in both respects, of course to my disadvantage. He here interrupted me with:

"No, no. I am clear I am right. I am an admirable physiognomist, and never was deceived by a countenance in my life. You and I shall be staunch friends to the end of our lives. However, I shall be glad to see occasion to admit that I am wrong respecting Maclintock; and rest assured that, if I do, I have candour enough to allow it. Everybody says I am a wild and giddy chap; but I trust you will never find me obstinately persist in an error, especially as in the present case, where I had much rather find myself wrong than right." He certainly prophesied truly as to ourselves; we did remain unalterable and fast friends till his death terminated it.

At seven in the evening we returned to the hall and drank coffee and tea, after which some went to cards, some to billiards, whilst others walked up and down, or sat chatting on a terrace which projected from the hall and went several feet over the river, being supported by large piles; the situation was cool and refreshing. At ten supper was announced, from which every person retired when he thought proper to his bed. Maclintock and I had Chinese servants appointed to wait upon us, who we found in attendance at our rooms with candles, slippers and all the etceteras of the night. Next day, having finished our breakfast, Maclintock and I went to Mr. Devisme's who, after showing us a very choice collection of curiosities of his own, conducted us to the different manufactures to inspect the progress thereof. On our way he informed us that no Europeans whatsoever were ever allowed to pass the Gates of the City, a circumstance, as he said, little to be regretted, because in fact there was nothing in Canton worth seeing, whereas in the suburbs, where we were allowed free egress and regress, there was much deserving the attention of strangers. We were then shown the different processes used in finishing the chinaware. In one long gallery we found upwards of an hundred persons at work in sketching or finishing the various ornaments upon each particular piece of the ware, some parts being executed by men of a very advanced age, and others by children even so young as six or seven years.

An express now arrived from Whampoa with the agreeable news of the *Triton*, and other Madras ships, being arrived. Several of them, especially the *Hector* and *Nottingham*, suffered severely in the typhoon we had encountered; the *Hector* lost all three topmasts and materially damaged her cotton. The *Nottingham* was thrown upon her beam ends, and lay waterlogged so long that the men had axes in their hands to cut away the lower masts as the only chance of saving her, when she luckily righted. The following day I met my shipmate, Denil Court, who told me that, not liking Madras a bit better than I did, he had availed himself of an opportunity of leaving it by accepting the situation of surgeon to the *Ashburnham*, her doctor being so ill he was obliged to stay on shore.

The fifth day we dined with Mr. Carvalho, who entertained us sumptuously, having an excellent band of music playing during our meal. He had two pleasant young men in his family, with both of whom I lived much for several years after. One was Mr. Grady, who acquired a large fortune in Bengal and died in England many years ago; the other was Mr. Richard Sullivan, afterwards appointed to the Company's civil service at Madras, where he also became rich, returned to England and there held a post of emolument under Government. He was created a baronet and died a few years back. At Mr. Carvalho's I spent several of the happiest days of my life.

Bob Pott passed most of his time in our rooms, generally coming before I was up in a morning. He breakfasted with us; and, if he took it into his head that Maclintock was too long at the meal, or drank too much tea, he without the least ceremony overset the table. The first time he practised this, I was very angry at such a quantity of handsome China being thus mischievously demolished, and expressed my displeasure thereat, which only excited the mirth of young pickle. "Why, zounds!" said he, "you surely forget where you are. I never suffer the servants to have the trouble of removing a tea equipage, always throwing the whole apparatus out of the window or downstairs. They easily procure another batch from the steward's warehouse."

Doctor Court was a constant source of amusement to us. He had a mode of entertainment he was extremely partial to, which he denominated "hunting"; and we, in our morning excursions, sometimes met him "in full cry," when he always entreated we would join the chase. His sport was this. The Chinese are the best pickpockets in the world; and, although a European may not with impunity strike one of them, yet, should he detect a rogue in the very act of thieving, he is allowed to belabour the offender as much, and as long, as he pleases. Court, with all his eccentricities, possessed a great share of good sense and, although he affected the look and manners of an idiot to answer some private purpose, never in material points betrayed a deficiency of understanding.

The Chinese considered him to be absolutely mad, an idea that he encouraged with a view to annoy and torment them by various tricks, with the less risk to himself, as they never thought of complaining of a madman. He, therefore, used to tie one end of his handkerchief fast to the buttonhole of an under-flap he had to his coat pockets, leaving the other end hanging carelessly, as it were by accident, out of his pocket, and thus, with a vacant stare, stalk negligently up and down the most public and frequented streets of the suburbs. The light-fingered gentry, attracted by the appearance of the handkerchief, soon followed, making a snatch at the hoped-for prize. The instant Court felt the jerk, or attempt, he suddenly turned upon the thief whom he began to thrash with a stout but pliant bamboo he carried in his hand for the purpose. The fellows upon this usually took to their heels, Court pursuing, every now and then as he came within reach, taking a lick at him; and thus he would "chase" until out of breath and tired, or that the pickpocket darted into some narrow passage or house for shelter, to the infinite entertainment of the spectators.

His common address when he entered our rooms was, "Come, my worthies, (a favourite word of his) here's a charming day for hunting, *allons donc!*" He was perpetually playing some tricks upon the Chinamen, whereby he plagued them exceedingly, so that many of the principal shopkeepers set people to watch when the mad doctor was coming, and upon receiving notice of his approach barricaded their doors against him.

In the middle of September, Pott, being tired by the sameness of Canton, proposed a trip to Whampoa for variety, and the next day he and I embarked in a large sampan consisting of three spacious rooms, the steward of the factory having sent on board ample provisions in victuals and wines. On stopping at the first *hoppo* house and, according to custom, opening my trunk for examination, the mandarin took up a red morocco case containing combs and a pair of scissors, saying, "Cumshaw." This I did not understand; but Bob told me the fellow asked the case as a present, and he began abusing him for so doing, calling him a "Qui si," (son of a bitch), "Qui so," (cuckold), "Ladrone," (thief), and all the approbrious names he had learnt. This Chinaman showed evident marks of surprise at so young a boy's dealing out abuse so liberally, became exceedingly angry, and called to the people of his boat alongside with much apparent wrath and gesticulation, Pott only increasing his abuse thereat; but, as the combs were of trifling value, I thought it better to end the dispute by giving them to the mandarin, who accepted them with a profusion of thanks and went off in high glee, saying "Chin chin" as he departed, which is the common salutation. Bob was very angry with me for giving them, saying he would much rather have kicked the scoundrel than made him a present. At the second *hoppo* I got off for a marble wash ball.

When we were off Lob Lob Creek one of the boatmen, opening the cabin door, peeped in and said, "Master, Caree Lob Lob?" to which Bob directly answered, "Yes," holding up two of his fingers. In five minutes a little open boat came paddling towards us, and two very pretty girls jumped in at our window. Bob retired with one to the after cabin, leaving me with the other. We had been a very short time together when the same man opened the door again, quickly crying out, "Chop Chop Lob Lob, mandarin dee come." Regardless of him or his words, which I did not understand, I continued the business I was engaged upon; which when finished I called to Bob, who desired me to come in, and I found him and his companion sitting very quietly together. Having dismissed our Lob Lob ladies, we continued our voyage to Whampoa, and went on board the *Cruttenden*, where we were very hospitably received and entertained by the second officer, then in command. Early the following morning we went to the *Plassey*, where Rogers insisted upon our spending the day. Mentioning to him the circumstance that had occurred on our passage down and my astonishment at such a stripling as Bob thinking of a woman, he observed that in all probability we should both have cause to remember Lob Lob Creek for some time to come, there being no more than six women to satisfy the lusts of a fleet of five-and-twenty ships, the consequence of which had already shown itself, a number of their junior officers being diseased.

I was seriously alarmed at learning this, far more on Pott's account than my own, feeling really hurt that such a mere child (forward as he was) should get contaminated in my company, for which blame would deservedly attach to me as having led him astray. Upon expressing my concern and apprehensions to Robert, he requested me not to make myself uneasy about him, for that young and inexperienced as I might consider him, and as he comparatively certainly was, he knew better than to have any connection with Lob Lob Creek women, whom he always had and should continue to leave for the use of his elders! After spending three very merry days at Whampoa, we returned to Canton, where Maclintock gave me a card of invitation to two different entertainments on following days, at the country house of one of the Hong merchants named Pankeequa. These fêtes were given on 1st and 2nd October, the first of them being a dinner, dressed and served *à la mode Anglaise*, the Chinamen on that occasion using, and awkwardly enough, knives and forks, and in every respect conforming to the European fashion. The best wines of all sorts were amply supplied. In the evening a play was performed, the subject warlike, where most capital fighting was exhibited, with better dancing and music than I could have expected. In one of the scenes an English naval officer, in full uniform and fierce cocked hat, was introduced, who strutted across the stage, saying "Maskee can do! God damn!" whereupon a loud and universal laugh ensued, the Chinese, quite in an ecstasy, crying out "Truly have muchee like Englishman."

The second day, on the contrary, everything was Chinese, all the European guests eating, or endeavouring to eat, with chopsticks, no knives or forks being at table. The entertainment was splendid, the victuals superiorly good, the Chinese loving high dishes and keeping the best of cooks. At night brilliant fireworks (in which they also excel) were let off in a garden magnificently lighted by coloured lamps, which we viewed from a temporary building erected for the occasion and wherein there was exhibited sleight-of-hand tricks, tight- and slack-rope dancing, followed by one of the cleverest pantomimes I ever saw. This continued until a late hour, when we returned in company with several of the supercargoes to our factory, much gratified with the liberality and taste displayed by our Chinese host.

Court often proposed to us to take a view of the interior of the city, and at last we consented to attend him. Rogers and Dr. Gowdie agreeing to join the party, we set out early in the morning, at once discovering when we were out of our limits by the inhabitants of the houses coming to their doors to stare at us, the children following, hooting and calling out "Fanqui, Qui, si," and other epithets of reproach, some of them pelting us with bricks and stones. Thus we reached the gates of the city, where the guard stationed there attempted to arrest our progress; but our eccentric pilot, Court, shoving one away on each side, and sputtering a parcel of gibberish, pushed by, we all following. Upon entering the city, in addition to the former accompaniments of hooting, pelting and staring, out of every house we passed issued two, three or more dogs, all of which followed us, barking for a certain distance from their respective homes. Having walked through the city without seeing a single object of any kind that could in any way compensate for the ill-treatment we received, we continued our traverse about a mile into the country, when we returned, encountering the same pelting and insults we had before, and in an increased degree, dirt and filth of every kind being cast at us. Let no stranger, therefore, ever think of forcing his way into Canton in the expectation of his curiosity being gratified by handsome buildings, or in any respect whatever; for, like us, he will meet with nothing but insult and disappointment.

The 1st November being Mr. Wood's birthday, Pott insisted upon celebrating it in his (Mr. Wood's) own apartments, and ordered the steward to prepare and send there a dinner for six. He would not tell even me who were to be the party. At the appointed hour we met—it consisted of Mr. Wood, a nephew and namesake of his, who was fifth mate of one of the Indiamen, Joe Revell, a young friend of Pott's, sixth mate of the *Cruttenden*, Pott and myself. Pott presided, and when the cloth was removed, declared himself despotic as toastmaster. Mr. Wood upon this occasion furnished some very choice old Malmsey madeira, which we set to at, Mr. Wood, who was in but indifferent health, being on that account left at liberty to do as he pleased. The rest were ordered to fill bumpers to every toast. Between each glass a song was sung. Thus we continued till near eight in the evening, by which Bob became speechless and, in a very few minutes after, fell under the table quite insensible. The other three lads, being little better, were led off by servants.

Having seen Bob put to bed, I went to my own room, with my recollection perfectly about me, but extremely sick from having swallowed so enormous a quantity as I had of a rich, luscious wine. I, nevertheless, slept soundly until near ten o'clock the next morning, at which I awoke with so excruciating a headache I could not stir, the pain if possible being increased by Bob's just then entering my room hallooing at a prodigious rate, until he perceived that I looked ill, when he instantly desisted. I was then seized with a vomiting, which continued with scarce any intermission for three hours, and I actually thought would have killed me. I remained two days so ill that poor Bob was very uneasy, nor would cease importuning me until I agreed to see Dr. Gordon. That gentleman gave me some medicine that afforded me relief. He desired me to keep quiet a couple of days more, which I did, my young friend never leaving me. On the third morning I felt tolerably well and that day joined the usual party at dinner. On the 8th the wind changed, blowing fresh from the north, which produced an alteration I could not have believed had I not felt it. From a really oppressive degree of heat, it suddenly became so cold that we were all shivering with cloth coats on, and at dinner found a cheerful blazing fire most acceptable and comfortable. From that day there was a constant keen wind, with beautifully clear weather, enabling us to take as much exercise as we chose without risk of endangering our health, which was far from being the case during the heats.

From the nature of the place, as already described, Canton afforded little variety, except for the first few days, after which there was nothing but repetition of the same round; yet time flew rapidly away, and the period fixed for our leaving China was rapidly approaching. The *Cruttenden* and two other ships were to sail on 5th December. Bob Pott was so sincerely attached to me that, for several days previous thereto, he entirely lost his spirits at the thoughts of our parting. On the morning of the 2nd of the month, he came, soon after daylight, to my bedside to say he had a great favour to ask which I must promise to grant. I answered there was nothing in my power I would not readily do to gratify or oblige him; and so in truth I would; for, had the charming boy been my nearest and dearest relation, I could not have felt more attached than I was to him. He appeared delighted at my answer, and after a pause, looking wistfully in my face, and with some hesitation he said what he wanted was that I should leave the *Plassey* and go home with him in the *Cruttenden*. This request, so wholly unexpected and unlooked for, surprised and in some measure vexed me; for, although I should have been happy at being with him, I felt it would be as ungrateful as improper in me, after Captain Waddell's repeated kindnesses to me, thus to quit his ship; and, even had my respect for him not operated, Captain Baker was not exactly a man to my liking. Though always polite to me, there was an obsequiousness, a fawning manner, mixed with much Scotch pride, that rendered him contemptible in my eyes.

I stated my objections, touching upon the awkwardness (was no other impediment in the way) of forcing myself upon Captain Baker unasked. But the little monkey was prepared for this, and exultingly replied, "My dearest Hickey, never waste a thought upon such a wretch, a beastly swab as Baker, who will be proud of and flattered by the arrangement"; and he took out of his pocket a letter from Captain Baker to me, couched in the most friendly language, after many high-flown compliments adding that, if I would do him the honour to proceed to England on his ship, half the round house, or the whole of the great cabin, would be at my service, and he should endeavour to make everything as agreeable to me as possible during the voyage. This letter showed how much he yielded to keeping the favourable opinion of his guinea-pig, that he might thereby preserve his interest with the family; for one of his failings was a love of money, and that to so powerful a degree as to make him guilty of twenty shabby actions that deservedly brought him into disgrace with all the gentlemen of Canton.

Finding he must fail in having me for a shipmate, Pott then solicited me to accompany him to Whampoa and at least one day on their way from thence, which I willingly acquiesced in, consoling him by the probability of our overtaking him before he left St. Helena, from the superiority of the *Plassey's* sailing. Early on 5th December 1769, Pott and I left Canton; and, in an hour after we reached the *Crutten- den*, they got under way, dropping down close to the first bar, where the pilot brought to for the night. At supper another guinea-pig of Captain Baker's seemed disposed to ridicule Bob's melancholy, which made the latter rally and, at least, affect something like cheerfulness. Turning to me, he said, "Do you see this sneaking reptile, who, though twice my size, like a dastard as he is, suffers me to correct his insolence by manual chastisement, which I have often been obliged to do, and unless he ceases his present insolent and vacant grin, shall give you occular demonstration of by drubbing him heartily." The other lad immediately assumed a very grave look; and Bob continued, "The fellow's name is Wakeman. He is intended for a seaman, but I much doubt whether even the brilliant talents of my able commander there" —pointing ludicrously to Captain Baker who was at the table—"will ever be able to make him one."

Captain Baker angrily said:

"Pott, your impertinence is unbounded. It would be well for you to take a leaf out of Wakeman's book, who is in every point above you."

Bob, with a loud laugh, replied:

"Take a leaf out of that fellow's book! Damn me, if the whole book, with his contemptible body and bones into the bargain, is worth a single copper"—the lowest coin of China.

Captain Baker shook his head, saying, "I blush for you, sir."

"Aye," retorted Bob, "like a blue dog. But spare your blushes on my account. Your dirty lambkin there"—pointing to Wakeman—"needs them all."

I remained on board the *Cruttenden* until after dinner of the follow- ing day, the 6th, when I got into my sampan, slept on board the *Plassey* that night, and next day returned to Canton. I missed my lively com- panion exceedingly, as did everybody who knew the lively and volatile boy.

On the 15th Captain Waddell informed Maclintock and me he would convey us on board the following day in his barge. We there- fore spent that morning in taking leave of our foreign acquaintances, especially Mr. Chambers, the chief Swedish supercargo, also the Dutch chief, both of whom had behaved with the utmost politeness to us. After breakfast of the 16th, having offered our acknowledgments to all the English gentlemen, most of whom accompanied us down to the waterside, we embarked; whereupon they cheered us, we and our boat's crew returning the compliment. Thus I left Canton where I had spent four months very happily, having been received with a hospitality and kindness nothing could exceed. We reached the *Plassey* to dinner, (the anchors being then apeak) and dropped down the river until dark, when we anchored for the night. At daybreak of the 17th we weighed, running down at a great rate. In the evening being off Macao, the pilot left us. We then hove to until the next morning, when we ran out to sea. We experienced fine weather the whole run to the latitude of the Cape of Good Hope, amusing ourselves by fishing, firing at sharks, and all the usual pastimes practised on board ship in order to beguile the time. Off the Cape we had a smart adverse puff from the north-west, luckily only of twenty-four hours' duration. On 20th February 1770 at daybreak we made the Island of St. Helena, and at the same time a strange sail appeared upon our starboard beam, standing also for the island. At noon we spoke her being our old companion, the *Hampshire*. This was an extraordinary circumstance considering the difference of the two ships' voyages, she having been to Bombay and Bengal, we to Madras and China. At two in the afternoon we were well in with the land, which presents a most barren and wretched appearance. Both ships then hove to, each sending in a boat to announce the vessel's name and other particulars respecting them.

This little speck of land in the midst of an immense ocean is in the latitude, nearly, of sixteen degrees south, and longitude about six degrees west of Greenwich, it lying in the strength of the south-east trade wind. Captain Waddell sent on shore to take lodgings for himself, Maclintock, and me, which having procured, we landed, and went to take possession of them at the house of a Mr. Greentree. There we found very commodious and comfortable apartments, fitted up in the style of English houses. The morning after our arrival we went to visit Mr. Skottowe, Governor of the island, and Mr. Corneille, the Lieutenant Governor, the latter appearing to be a well-mannered, accomplished gentleman. In the morning of the 23rd (of February) the *Cruttenden* came in. I went on board the moment she anchored, and found my young favourite in fine health and spirits. Having prepared a trunk of clothes, I took him on shore with me to Mr. Greentree's, where he remained, delighted at once more being with me, and continued my guest and constant companion during my stay upon the island. We passed our mornings riding about the country on horseback, and the rest of the day in convivial parties, with dances every evening, an amusement the damsels of St. Helena are very fond of.

The 6th March being appointed for the two ships' sailing, the passengers of both were invited to dine that day with Mr. Corneille, there to meet and take leave of the Governor. As I had been informed we were not to sail until the following morning, I did not go on board until after midnight, staying so late at the particular request of Pott. I certainly never left a place in which I had resided a fortnight with so little regret as I did St. Helena. The comforts it affords are few indeed; scarce any fruit, bad bread, and no fresh butter. Yet the charges made for every article of life were enormously high. Pott accompanied me on board, and slept upon a couch in our cabin. At daybreak we got under way, and he bid me adieu, promising to call in St. Albans Street within twelve hours after he should reach London.

On the 11th we made the island of Ascension, famous for the fineness of the turtle caught there. The two commanders had agreed to stop one night for a supply of that rich and esteemed food. The island shows not the least sign of vegetation, being entirely covered with a kind of pumice stone, evidently of a volcanic quality. After leaving the island of Ascension nothing worthy recording happened until 11th April, when we sounded, expecting to find the British bottom, but were disappointed. A fresh south-west wind was then blowing, which at one in the afternoon suddenly shifted to north and by east, attended with sleet and snow. By three it increased to a hard gale. The weather having been dark and gloomy, we had not seen the sun the four preceding days so as to get an observation; but by the dead reckoning we were in the latitude of Ushant, and of course had not the Channel sufficiently open to stand in with so scant and strong a wind. We therefore lay to under a balanced mizzen. The *Hampshire*, upon seeing this, came as close to us as she dare venture in such a high sea, and Captain Smith hailed; but the wind roared so loud all his attempts to make us hear what he said were ineffectual; and soon after, to the great surprise of our navigators, we saw the *Hampshire* set her main and fore topsails close-reefed, with a reefed fore sail, and under that sail close-hauled stand in for the Channel, an example Captain Waddell did not think it prudent to follow. We afterwards heard that although they succeeded, and thereby avoided a week of extreme bad weather, they had done so at an immense and unjustifiable risk.

As the gale increased the sea became extremely high and confused, occasioning the ship to labour prodigiously. During four nights the motion was so violent, and the strokes the sea almost every minute gave the ship so terrific, I got no sleep. On the fifth, nature being nearly exhausted, I had fallen into a doze as I lay upon my cot, from which I was suddenly roused by, as I firmly believed, the ship's going to pieces. I heard a dreadful crash, and found my cot jammed, immoveably fixed, by what I had no doubt was the planks of her deck fallen in, some of which lay across me with a ponderous weight I could scarce breathe under. Expecting a rush of water every moment to overwhelm me, I lay gasping; when the ship, taking a deep roll the contrary way, relieved me of my load. Wondering what all this could mean, and still imagining death to be inevitable, I was agreeably surprised at seeing our cabin door open, and Chisholme, with a candle and lantern in his hand, calling out, "Well, my lads, how fare you in this confusion? What do you think of the last dip? Hang me, if I did not think she was over."

This was a most welcome sound to me, who supposed the ship had gone to pieces. Chisholme, coming close to my bed, suddenly exclaimed, "Zounds! what's the matter? What's the meaning of all this?" and away he darted, returning in a few seconds with Gowdie (the surgeon), and two or three people with lights, when my alarm was renewed by perceiving my shirt and bedclothes covered with blood. I knew not from whence it proceeded; but the doctor soon discovered the sanguinary stream issued from my head. He immediately cut off the hair, of which I had then an immense quantity; and, while examining the wound with his instruments as well as the dreadful motion would allow, he asked me whether I felt at all sick at the stomach. I answered, as the fact was, "exceedingly so"; and as I had often heard sickness was one of the symptoms of a fractured skull, I concluded mine was shattered. Gowdie having summoned his assistant, they together probed the wound, and at the end of half an hour, which circumstanced as I was appeared an age, he comforted me by saying, "Thank God, the skull is safe, but you have a desperate wound and have lost so much blood as must weaken you to a great degree, and will require your being kept very quiet."

Quiet and the then state of the ship appeared to me to be perfectly incompatible; he, however, dressed my head, and made the servants put clean clothes upon the bed and myself, and, making me swallow two pills, bid me lie still. Prejudiced as I was against the possibility of rest, I nevertheless within an hour went into a sleep so profound I knew of nothing that occurred for the following twenty-four hours, at the end of which I awoke refreshed, but with a dreadful headache. The doctor being summoned told me not to mind the headache, which proceeded from the large quantity of opium he had given me, and which had so well answered the purpose that all risk was over, and a few hours, with strong coffee drank frequently, would relieve me, all which was verified; and I had the satisfaction to hear the gale had broke up.

Maclintock and I had two-thirds of the starboard side of the great cabin. The remainder, except a passage to the quarter gallery, was converted into a sail room. Between the beams and the deck of that part so used for keeping sails in, there was stowed planks of rose-wood, each plank of an enormous weight, which Captain Waddell was taking to England as part of his private trade. These planks were supposed to have been immoveably fixed in, being secured by strong battens nailed across them from one beam to the other. The ship, however, laboured in so extraordinary a manner, at times being quite down upon her broadside, that the rose-wood forced off the cleets, slipping through into our cabin, passing over Mr. Maclintock whose cot was hung close to the bulkhead, without touching him, and going directly across mine, in doing which one of them came in contact with my unfortunate skull. The wonderful part of the story was that it did not beat my head to atoms. The doctor and his mate, having taken off the dressing and examined the wound, pronounced it to be doing as well as could be hoped for or expected. Having taken a basin of weak chicken broth, in a few hours the doctor gave me another opium pill, which secured me a good night's sleep, and the next morning I felt quite a different body. Gowdie told me when he first saw the wound he had no doubt but that the skull was badly fractured. I rather think it was slightly injured, because, for years afterwards, if I caught the slightest cold, that part of my head became so exceedingly tender and susceptible I could not bear a comb to touch it, which was the only inconvenience I ever experienced from the accident.

Two days after this mishap, the wind veered round to the westward and enabled us to stand for the Channel. The 18th we struck soundings in seventy fathoms, and the following morning had the pleasure to see a fine English cutter of one hundred and fifty tons burden within a quarter of a mile of us, from which a man came in a small boat on board the *Plassey*. He was of a Herculean form, with a healthy ruby face. From his dress and appearance I should not have supposed he possessed ten pounds in the world. Captain Waddell conducted him into the round house, where the following short dialogue ensued:

STRANGER: "Well, Captain, how is tea?"

CAPTAIN: "Twenty pounds."

STRANGER: "No, that won't do; eighteen—a great number of China ships this season."

CAPTAIN: "Very well, you know best."

STRANGER: "How many chests?"

CAPTAIN: "Sixty odd."

STRANGER: "Come, bear a hand then and get them into the cutter."

By this I found our new visitor was a smuggler. The foregoing was all that passed in completing the sale and purchase of so large a quantity of tea. In the same laconic manner he bought the stock of the different officers.

While the tea was hoisting out of the gun room and other places it had been stowed in, Captain Waddell asked the smuggler whether there was any public news, to which he at first answered:

"No, none that I know of"; but immediately after, as if recollecting himself, he added, "Oh yes, I forgot. Wilkes is made King."

"Wilkes made King!" exclaimed everyone present. "What can you mean?"

"Damn me if I understand much of these things," replied the man, "but they told me the mob took him out of prison and made him King —that's all I know."

A thick haze that had prevailed all the morning just then cleared away, and we saw the land (the Lizard) not more than four leagues distant. The cutter at the same time hailed to inform their chief they saw the *Albert* (custom-house schooner) to the southward.

"Do you, by God," replied he, and taking a spying glass from one of the officers, looked through it in the direction pointed out, directly saying, "Aye, aye, sure enough there she comes and under a cloud of canvas." Turning to Captain Waddell, he continued, "Come, Captain, you must haul off the land another league or so, and then let him fetch us with all my heart, and kiss my a——e."

Captain Waddell appearing to hesitate as to complying, the man hastily said,

"He can seize me at this distance from our coast. If, therefore, you don't stand further off, I must leave you."

Captain Waddell then desired the officer of the watch to brace the yards and keep the ship up a couple of points, which being done, in an hour and a half the smuggler said:

"Now, Captain, let them come and be damned, you may keep your course again."

The schooner was then within two miles, and in another hour came dashing by close to us in a noble style, and hove to upon our weather bow, when a most capital exchange of naval blackguardism took place between the smuggler's crew and the schooner, continuing a full hour; but, as the *Plassey* was then beyond the stated limits, they could not molest the cutter, and remained only to have the mortification of seeing a large quantity of goods transferred from the ship to her. At length they sheered off, when the smuggler observed:

"The fellow that commands her is one of the damnedest scoundrels that lives, and the only rascal amongst them that I cannot deal with, though I have bid roundly too." (I do not remember the name of this extraordinary revenue officer, or I would mention it, as, I am afraid, a rare instance of integrity in his line.)

Captain Waddell asked the smuggler whether he had recently sustained any loss by the Government vessels, to which he answered:

"No, nothing material this long time. I had a seizure of between five and six hundred pounds ten days ago, but nothing of importance for a twelvemonth"; by which it was evident he considered five or six hundred pounds no object.

The tea being all removed to the cutter, pen, ink, and paper was produced; the smuggler, sitting down at a table in the round house, calculated the amount due for his purchase; which Captain Waddell admitting correct, he took from his pocket-book a cheque, which filled up for twelve hundred and twenty-four pounds he signed and delivered it to the captain. I observed it was drawn upon Walpole and Company, Bankers in Lombard Street, and was astonished to see Captain Waddell with the utmost composure deposit it in his escritoire. The smuggler then being asked whether he chose a glass of wine or would stay dinner, he answered he could not afford to lose a minute; so must be off; but would take a *drap* of brandy. The liquor being brought, he chucked off a bumper, the servant directly filling a second. "That's right, my good fellow," said he, "always wet both eyes." He swallowed the second and returned to his cutter. The moment he departed, I asked Captain Waddell whether he felt secure in a draft for so large a sum by such a man as that; to which he answered, "Perfectly, and wish it was for ten times as much; it would be duly paid. These people always deal with the strictest honour. If they did not, their business would cease." For what he purchased from the officers he paid in guineas, to the amount of upwards of eight hundred.

LONDON REGAINED

O N 20th April 1770 we arrived off Dover, from whence a pilot came and took charge of the ship. In his boat Maclintock and I went on shore to proceed by land to London. Our voyage from China to England, including the stay at St. Helena, and notwithstanding the week we lay to in the chops of the Channel in bad weather, was performed in four months and four days, then the shortest that ever had been made by an Indiaman.

We dined and slept at the Ship Inn at Dover, and the next morning set off in a post-chaise-and-four for London, where we arrived at six the same evening. I ordered the chaise to my old place of resort, Malby's, ordered supper and sent for Brent, who within an hour had me in her arms, appearing rejoiced, although surprised, to see me thus early returned. This was a tantalizing scene to my friend Maclintock, then in the prime of life and full vigour of health; but he had already suffered so much and so long from an unlucky connection that he determined his future amours should be conducted with the utmost caution, and to avoid all promiscuous intercourse with the other sex. Great, therefore, as was the temptation at seeing a smart girl fondling with me, he prudently resisted. After supper with us and drinking a few glasses of wine, he retired to the Hummums (where no women were ever admitted) to sleep.

When we thus reached London I had twenty-seven guineas in my pocket, and felt no inclination to leave Malby's while any of it remained. The two first days I did not stir from the house, Maclintock eating and spending most of his time with us. The third morning, for the sake of a little variety, I sallied forth cap-à-pie in my Madras regimentals, intending to accompany Brent to Westminster Abbey, and to take a coach at the first stand we came to. Going along the Piazza chatting to Brent, who had hold of my arm, I suddenly and directly saw before me, and coming towards us, my father! Not doubting but he recognised me, I instantly slipped away from Brent, intending to address him as if that moment arrived; but, when close to him, I saw his mouth going at a great rate, talking to himself and deeply wrapped in his own thoughts. I therefore marched by without further notice. Brent, frightened out of her wits, insisted upon instantly going back to Malby's, and avoiding all further risk of discovery. We accordingly did so.

At dinner, Maclintock said he had that day been told that the Ombres Chinois was an entertainment worth seeing, and he intended going to it in the evening; upon which I determined to accompany him. At six o'clock, he, Brent and myself got into a hackney coach and proceeded to Panton Street, where the exhibition was. We found the room nearly full, and with difficulty procured seats. About an hour after we had been there, Brent eagerly laid hold of my arm, and, pointing to a gentleman who sat on the same row only four from us, said "My God, there is your brother!" I leaned forward, and sure enough there was Joseph, looking very attentively at us; but, as he did not seem disposed to speak or take the least notice of me, I concluded he was indignant at the foolish and unprofitable voyage I had made, and would not acknowledge me. I therefore resolved to let him sulk on. Brent pressed me to leave the place, which I peremptorily refused to do; and we sat out the entertainment. However, as I took it for granted my brother would mention his having seen me, I thought it prudent no longer to absent myself, and next morning I went to St. Albans Street, where I was received by my dearest father more graciously than I had any right to expect.

He told me they had for several days been in expectation of seeing me, Mr. Charlton having informed them of my return by the *Plassey*, which ship's arrival they had seen announced in the newspapers. By this it appeared that my brother Joseph had not betrayed me, for which I felt obliged and grateful. I, however, discovered soon after that I had given him credit for what he did not deserve, and that he actually did not recognize me at the Ombres Chinois. He told me himself he was looking at Brent, with whom he observed an officer; but he had no more idea of its being me than the Emperor of China. To account for my being so long in getting home, I had recourse to falsehood, telling my father that I had come round in the ship to Gravesend to save the expense of travelling. For such a deviation from veracity I ought to blush; but, alas, that was only one of many occasions I had to be ashamed of myself.

Mr. Charlton, to whom at St. Helena I had related what his brother-in-law, Mr. Dawson, had said relative to my coming to India as a cadet, had prepared my father for my return, and good-naturedly attempted to exculpate me, under such circumstances, from blame. The day after my arrival in St. Albans Street, my father addressed me very gravely and truly, representing the enormous expense incurred in equipping me for the East Indies, the whole of which was wantonly thrown away by my hasty and inconsiderate abandonment of the provision made for me in the army. He further said it appeared to him that I had only visited Asia for the purpose of showing myself there as an English nabob. He then desired to know what line of life I intended to pursue for my future subsistence; to which question I answered my wish was a situation in the civil service at Bengal. But such a nomination my father seriously assured me it was not in his power to obtain; that he would exert all his interest to get me exchanged from the Madras army to that of Bengal; which, should he not succeed in, he saw nothing left for me but to return forthwith to Fort St. George, as he could not, in justice to the rest of his family, allow me to relinquish the commission, the attainment of which had cost him so large a sum of money.

The next day, he went amongst his India friends in the City, and on his return told me that Sir George Colebrooke, Mr. Sulivan, and every person he had spoken to on the subject were much offended by the step I had taken and advised my going back to Madras, as a transfer to any other of the settlements would not be permitted. My father also said my ill-judged return became the more serious and unlucky from three great friends of his, Messrs. Vansittart, Scrafton, and Ford, having sailed for India a few months before in the *Aurora* frigate, as supervisors general of all the Company's oriental possessions, of course, with unlimited powers, all three of whom had faithfully promised to provide for me; that having absurdly deprived myself of such an opportunity of being essentially served was most unfortunate, and all I had for it was to endeavour to regain my station at Madras before the supervisors left it; that all the Company's ships of the season had already sailed, but he understood one of His Majesty's vessels would be sent off with dispatches within a month, respecting which he would make further inquiries. I could not feel otherwise than vexed at having lost so extraordinary an advantage as the patronage of the supervisors. Subsequently, however, it turned out that the hopes of benefiting by their means would never have been realized. The *Aurora* made a rapid and fine passage to the Good Hope, where they stopped for a supply of fresh provisions and water, being uncommonly crowded with passengers. She left the Cape in as high order in every respect as any ship that ever put to sea, and never was heard of more, although vessels were sent in every direction in search of her. The general opinion, therefore, was that she must have been destroyed by fire. Upwards of four hundred persons perished in her.

My father observed to me that, as seven or eight months must elapse before any of the Company's ships would sail, it was incumbent on me to employ myself usefully for that period, and not think of lounging about in dissipation and indolence. He also insisted upon my laying aside my military dress until I had a right to resume it, and recommended me to endeavour to acquire some knowledge of the laws of my country, which in every situation of life would be useful, employing some hours daily in the study of military tactics. I accordingly laid aside my cockade and red coat and once more took my seat at a desk.

At the latter end of the month (April), the *Cruttenden* arrived, when Bob Pott called upon me and I introduced him to all my family, who were much pleased with him and made him stay dinner. The next morning, he came again, taking me to his father's house in Lincoln's Inn Fields, where I was very kindly received by Mr. and Mrs. Pott, and several of their daughters, as well as an elder and younger brother of Robert's. I dined with them, and in the evening accompanied Robert to Drury Lane Theatre to see Garrick's famous pageant of the Stratford Jubilee, then in the height of its very long run; it had been got up at prodigious expense, in commemoration of the rare talents of our celebrated dramatic author, Shakespeare. Scarce a day passed without Bob and me meeting; I frequently dined at his father's, where I always received a hearty welcome from the whole family, especially Mr. Pott senior. But, early in June, I thought I perceived a change in his and others of the family's behaviour towards me, which daily became more evident.

I often enquired of Robert if he knew the reason of this alteration; when he answered he only guessed the cause, but should ascertain it to a certainty soon, and the moment he did so would inform me. A week afterwards, he called to tell me it was that despicable scoundrel, Baker, who had been prejudicing his father by a thousand misrepresentations and falsehoods, recommending my acquaintance with him (Robert) should be dropped, as I was introducing him to improper company, and should be the ruin of him. Enraged at such baseness in Baker, who, whenever I met him, seemed happy to see me, and paid me a number of compliments, I waited upon Robert's father, to whom I represented how greatly I felt the alteration in his manners towards me lately, desiring to be informed of the occasion. This he evaded, assuring me he was not conscious of any alteration in his conduct. I expressed my surprise at hearing him gravely assert what he must feel conscious was not the fact, adding that I had discovered the calumniator in Captain Baker, whom I should call to account for his infamous and malignant slander of me. Mr. Pott endeavoured to dissuade me from resenting what had passed, respecting which I begged to judge for myself, and went immediately to Captain Baker's lodgings attended by Robert's elder brother, who accompanied me, at Robert's and my desire, to witness what should pass. We found him at home. I directly charged him with his duplicity and baseness in unjustly traducing my character. He looked very silly, stammered out some incoherent words and, finally, positively denied ever having uttered a syllable to my prejudice; nor had he any cause for so doing. I then asked him whether he had not vilified me to Mr. Pott senior, advising him to insist upon his son Robert's dropping my acquaintance, assigning reasons for such advice highly prejudicial to my character.

The despicable wretch at once said, on his honour he had not, that he merely gave his opinion, in consequence of Robert's natural volatility, the less he was allowed to be abroad and in company the better. I remarked that I must despise the man who could give his honour to a deliberate lie, which, coarse as the term was, I verily believed to be the case with him; but, as he chose now to deny the fact, it only remained for me to caution him never in future to mention my name with disrespect, as, if he did, and it came to my knowledge, I should treat him as he deserved. We then left him without any salutation, Mr. Pott junior, observing to me he had never seen so despicable a fellow as Baker, and he should relate to his father most minutely the whole of the extraordinary scene he had just witnessed. This he faithfully did, and the next day I received a very kind note from Mrs. Pott requesting me to dine in Lincoln's Inn Fields, where I went, receiving a cordial welcome and hearty shake of the hand by Mr. Pott; but not a word passed respecting Baker; nor did I think it necessary to broach the disagreeable subject, knowing the unfair suspicion to be done away.

In May (1770) my much esteemed friend, Maclintock, took leave of me, and embarked for India, having been little more than a month in England; but he was an uncommonly prudent young man and anxious to get back to his duty. With real grief I afterwards learnt that, two days after landing in excellent health at Madras, he was attacked by one of the violent fevers of that inhospitable climate which in four-and-twenty hours terminated his valuable life. A more amiable and accomplished young man never existed.

In the spring my father and three sisters went to a house he had taken at Richmond. I then, for the first time since my return, made enquiries after my favourite Fanny Hartford, who I found had married a gentleman of fortune that resided entirely in the country, and to the present day I have never heard more of her. I now renewed my acquaintance with many of my former companions, male and female, and frequented the same houses as previous to my visiting India; but, not having similar resources as then, I was often hard run for cash, which drove me to various stratagems for raising the wind and enabling me nightly to attend some place of public amusement. I became a regular attendant at the Euphrates lodge of Bucks, also at the Battersea Red House meetings, the latter as much for the sake of the fair one I have already spoken of under the designation of "Silver Tail," as for the exercise of field tennis. I introduced Bob Pott, at his earnest request, to Tethrington, who declared him to be the finest lad he had ever met with, and became greatly attached to him. In December 1770, Pott again went to India in the *Cruttenden* with Captain Baker, as fifth mate!

Notwithstanding I generally spent the evening at some public place, I was diligent and attentive to business throughout the day, which brought forth some compliments from my father, who observed, if I persevered, it was not yet too late to make myself a proficient in the law, and, should I prefer so doing to continuing in the military line, he had not any objection. He, however, desired me to consider well ere I resolved, and not to pursue the law unless I felt confident of myself, and that I should not fall into similar errors as formerly. As usual, I deceived myself, thinking I possessed more resolution and fortitude than was in my nature. At the expiration of a month, I told my father I had maturely thought upon the subject, was convinced I could now control my passions, resist temptation, and act in every respect as prudence dictated. I therefore determined to stick to the desk. He answered, "Be it so, William, with all my heart; and I hope and trust I never shall have another occasion to upbraid you on the score of disappointing me."

During the winter of 1770, and the whole of 1771, I read a good deal, and attended the duties of an attorney's office with tolerable regularity, though I continued to frequent public places, especially Ranelagh, which of all others was most to my liking. In those days, people went there well dressed, the men always in swords; and, though I had resigned my cockade, I retained the use of side arms. I dropped most of my Wetherby acquaintances, taking in their stead a set of more respectability, amongst whom were Messrs. Prescott, Byde, and Lowry, all three sons of eminent bankers; also Robert Mitford, brother to the Captain of the *Northumberland* Indiaman (their father was immensely rich, though he still continued the business of a woollen draper in Cornhill); Farrer, a barrister, who afterwards acquired a rapid and large fortune as an advocate of the Supreme Court at Calcutta; and several other young men whose incomes were so large as to enable them to live at great expense. Here was the rock upon which I split, absurdly endeavouring to do as they did, without reflecting that my allowances were very inadequate.

In the winter of 1771, a set of wild young men made their appearance, who, from the profligacy of their manners and their outrageous conduct in the theatres, taverns and coffee houses in the vicinity of Covent Garden, created general indignation and alarm, actually driving away many sedate persons from their customary amusement in an evening. They were distinguished under the title of Mohawks, and as such severely attacked by the public newspapers, which, instead of checking, seemed to stimulate their excesses. They consisted of only four in number, their Chief, Rhoan Hamilton (afterwards known as an Irish rebel by the name of Hamilton Rhoan, having taken what had been his Christian for a surname). This gentleman, when he first came forward in the character of Mohawk, was in the prime of life, a remarkably fine figure upwards of six feet high, and perfectly well made. He, being a man of fortune, was the principal hero. The second in command was Mr. Hayter, whose father was an opulent merchant and bank director; the third, a Mr. Osborne, a young American who had come to England to study law; and the last, Mr. Frederick, a handsome lad without a guinea, said to be a son, or grandson, of the much talked of and unfortunate Theodore, King of Corsica. He had dubbed himself with the convenient travelling title of Captain; but no one knew from what corps he derived that rank.

This quartet were in a constant state of inebriety, daily committing the most wanton outrages upon unoffending individuals who unfortunately fell in their way. It fell to my lot to witness much of their insolent proceedings, for at the time they commenced them I belonged to two different clubs, one at the Shakespear, the other at the Piazza coffee house; at the quitting of which I generally fell in with those formidable fellows, and, being brim-full of wine, I invariably attacked them, reprobating their scandalous behaviour, and delivering my opinion thereon in unqualified terms of disapprobation, so much so that the bystanders have often been astonished that they did not instantly assail me. They sometimes did violently threaten; notwithstanding which, I persevered in reprobating their conduct and abusing them whenever we met, becoming so determined an opponent that I was soon distinguished by the, at least, less dishonourable title of, "The Anti-Mohawk," under which I had some high-flown compliments paid me by the sober old dons of the coffee houses annoyed by their enormities. These gentry did not always act together, sometimes separating and even singly insulting the quiet and well-disposed; but at a certain hour of the night they always met, usually at Lovejoy's, laying their plans of mischief for the ensuing day.

The following instance of brutality I was, in part, an eye-witness of. I was waiting in the Piazza coffee room for some friends with whom I had promised to go to the play, when Hamilton came in very drunk, according to custom. After talking to me a few minutes (for I was acquainted with all the four Mohawks) he walked to the bar, there asking Dennis, the master of the house, who was above. Dennis replied:

"None of your friends, sir."

"I understood," said Hamilton, "there were a party in the blue room."

"No, sir," answered Dennis, "a single gentleman, whom I do not know, is there waiting for three others whom he expects."

"Aye," said Hamilton, "then, damme if I don't go and take a peep at your stranger"; and up he walked, Dennis following.

The latter soon returned, entreating I would go up and endeavour to get Mr. Hamilton away; for he was apprehensive of mischief. I accordingly ascended. Upon entering the room, I saw Hamilton standing in a boxing attitude, whilst a genteel-looking young man of very slight form, and apparently in bad health, was striking at him without effect, as he met every intended blow, before it could reach him, with a severe stroke from himself under the assailant's arm. I directly stepped between them, saying to Hamilton:

"Is this a proof of your valour? Such a Herculean fellow as you are to attack such a man as this! For shame, for shame, Hamilton, you deserve to be scouted from the society of gentlemen."

Instead of any expression of anger at this address, he immediately answered:

"By God, it is very true, Hickey! I am ashamed of myself"; and, turning to the gentleman, he continued: "And, sir, I beg you ten thousand pardons. I have behaved scandalously, and will make every concession you demand. Can you forgive me? Again I beg your pardon."

In the moment of this conciliatory speech, in came Frederick, who instantly exclaimed: "What's this I hear? Zounds! Hamilton, do you beg any man's pardon!" Hamilton, in the moment, replied:

"No, by God, not to anyone breathing"; and turning to the stranger, he added, "I have beat you, and I'm damned glad of it. You are a damned scoundrel. However, if you wish for it I'll give you satisfaction whenever you please. Hickey knows me; everybody knows Hamilton, you scoundrel."

Upon this most extraordinary change of conduct, brought about by that despicable adventurer, Frederick, I felt extremely angry, and told Frederick he was an infamous bully that deserved to be kicked downstairs. He half drew his sword, when he was seized by Dennis and several gentlemen whom the noise had brought up from the coffee room, and forcibly carried down; when, both he and Hamilton becoming extremely riotous and violent, the gentlemen in the coffee room insisted upon the watch being called, or a constable. With considerable difficulty the two heroes were carried off to the round house, and there lodged for the night.

The stranger returned me his sincere thanks for my interference. He told me his name was Hare; that he came to the Piazza to meet some friends with whom he was to sup; that when Mr. Hamilton

The Promenade at Carlisle
House, about 1781. Chalk
drawing by John Raphael
Smith.

*By courtesy of the Victoria and
Albert Museum*

Joseph Hickey, the younger, the diarist's elder brother, 1778. Pastel by Thomas Hickey.

By courtesy of L. G. Duke, Esqre.

(whom he did not know) came into the room he was writing a letter. Hamilton, approaching the table without speaking, took up the ink-stand, which he was carrying off; when he (Hare) said, "Sir, I am using that ink; you must not take it away." Whereupon Hamilton turned round, seized the half-written letter from the table and tore it to pieces; that he (Hare), amazed at such an act, asked what he could mean. "Mean," retorted Hamilton, "I mean to give you a damned good licking"; and he accompanied this threat by putting his clenched fist close to his (Hare's) face; that he (Hare), fired with indignation at such brutality, and nothing doubting but that the assailant would strike him, he made a blow at Hamilton, which he met, striking the arm of Hare underneath, and so continued to do until he (Hare) was no longer able to raise his arm from his side, as already mentioned.

Mr. Hare then took off his coat and, turning up his shirt sleeves, the flesh of the right arm appeared black and dreadfully bruised from the wrist to the shoulder, which he said was attended with acute pain. He begged I would attend the following morning before the magistrate to relate such part of the transaction as I had seen; which I did at Sir John Fielding's, who, upon taking the deposition of Mr. Hare, mine, and Dennis's (the latter being summoned), compelled the two, Hamilton and Frederick, to give ample security to appear to any indictment or prosecution Mr. Hare might prefer against them or either of them, he (Hare) being required to enter into a recognizance to prosecute the culprits at the then next sessions.

Mr. Hare's feelings as a gentleman were by no means satisfied with the above measures; the hour, therefore, that he recovered the use of his arm, he sent a challenge to Hamilton, which was accepted without hesitation, personal spirit being one of the few qualities Mr. Hamilton possessed. They met, with each a second, when Hamilton received the fire of his antagonist, immediately discharging his own pistol in the air, desiring Hare to fire again if he chose it. Hare urged him to return his fire, saying it was no compensation for the uncommon ill-treatment he had received to stand a single shot, and that a refusal to return his fire, of course, made it impossible for him to proceed. Hamilton persisted in refusing to attempt taking the life of a man he had already so grossly and so unprovokedly insulted and maltreated, for which, since he became sober and conscious of his ill-behaviour, he felt the utmost distress and concern.

This apology, so full and unasked for, was by both the seconds con-sidreed as sufficient to satisfy the wounded honour of Mr. Hare. The latter gentleman, therefore, yielded to this opinion, and was about to quit the ground, when Hamilton, addressing him, said he was so ashamed of himself on account of what had passed that there was no reparation within his power he would not readily consent to, even to

6+

the insertion of an apology in the public newspapers. This offer was as handsomely refused by Mr. Hare, who professed himself entirely satisfied with the last declaration of Mr. Hamilton. They then parted with mutual civilities. What a lamentable thing that a man with such proper and becoming sentiments as Hamilton expressed at this meeting should ever have been guilty of the atrocious excesses and violence he was, not only before, but subsequent to, the above transaction! The fact is, his dissolute companions kept him in a constant state of intoxication, whereby they found they could manage him as they pleased, besides supplying themselves from his purse with cash, a scarce article with two of his associates, Frederick and Osborne. Mr. Hare, being upon the eve of departure for the East Indies, embarked prior to the commencement of the sessions, whereby the offenders escaped prosecution and the consequent punishment they so much deserved.

In the spring of 1772, my friend, Pott, returned from his second voyage to China. He immediately called upon me, grown an elegant figure, retaining all his beauty, and was soon pronounced by the women to be the handsomest young man in London. He told me Baker was an infamous scoundrel, and he had again proved him to be a despicable poltroon also, having submitted to his (Pott's) spitting in his face, which he actually had done a few days before he left the *Cruttenden*. "And thus," added he, "ends my career as mate of an Indiaman, for never more will I set my foot on board ship in that capacity." Upon which I asked what he intended to do in future. His reply was, "Curse me, if I know, William, not having yet given it a thought. The old boy (his father) must carve out something dashing for me."

About a week after his return, I received an invitation to dine in Lincoln's Inn Fields, when the father complained to me in strong terms of Robert's conduct, observing that what might have been forgiven in him as a mere boy became inexcusable at a more mature age. He said he had scrupulously enquired into all the circumstances of his last voyage, in every point of which he found Robert in the wrong, and that his behaviour to his commander had been most improper and disrespectful, in some instances scarcely short of mutiny. Mr. Pott also told me that Robert's conduct outward bound had been so inconsiderate that, after several unavailing remonstrances, Captain Baker had been under the necessity of breaking him, but upon their arrival in China, at the intercession of the supercargoes, had reinstated him, promising to bury in oblivion all that had passed to that period, notwithstanding which, his (Robert's) conduct on the homeward passage was more outrageous than ever. At this unfavourable representation of his conduct Robert only laughed, which put his father into a great rage, and he swore that he might starve for him if he chose to abandon the line chalked out for him. Then, addressing me, he said:

"Is this behaviour to be endured? This favourite of yours, Mr. Hickey, will certainly drive me mad. Here have I been making an interest to bring him forward in the service and procure for him the command of a ship, which he might have after one voyage more; and the bastard has the impudence to tell me he will not upon any terms go such voyage!"

"Nor will I, sir," (said Robert, interrupting his father). "There is not a single gentleman amongst them, nor shall anything make me mix or have to do with such a set of low blackguards."

During the summer, Robert and I were constantly together, making frequent excursions round the vicinity of London. I generally dined once a week with his family. Mr. Pott at last told me that, as he found Bob so obstinately determined to abandon the sea altogether, he must try what he could do to procure for him the appointment of a writer. Bob by this time had become quite a London rake, passing much of his time with the most admired and fashionable whores. He displayed peculiar taste in dress, though carried to excess in point of fashion, soon becoming the envy of all the young men of his day. I was one morning walking arm in arm with him in St. James's Park, his dress then being a white coat, cut in the extremity of *ton*, lined with a garter-blue satin, edged with ermine, and ornamented with rich silver frogs; waistcoat and breeches of the same blue satin, trimmed with silver twist à la hussar, and ermine edges. In our walk we met young Horneck, then Bob's counterpart both as to person and age, who had just become an ensign in the Guards. Horneck, struck with the figure and appearance of my companion, when abreast of us stopped and stared rather rudely. Whereupon Pott, turning towards him, said to me, "Look, William! there is a coxcomb that cannot bear a competitor, jealous as the Devil and envious too!" accompanying his remark by a peculiarly provoking laugh that was natural to him. Horneck coloured deeply, seemed mortified, but said not a word and went on his way.

The life I now led was by far too dissipated, and occasioned very frequent remonstrances from my father, who tried a variety of means to keep me at home. As he knew I was fond of drawing, he most kindly and considerately engaged a very ingenious man, Mr. Thomas Malton, to attend me twice a week and give me instructions therein, as well as in geometry and perspective. This Mr. Malton had been for several years a cabinet maker, having a large shop in the Strand; but, as nature had blessed him with an extraordinary mechanical genius, he was constantly engaged in experiments upon different subjects therein, employing every leisure hour in attaining a proficiency in the different branches of mathematics and natural philosophy. So powerfully did this inclination operate, as his knowledge increased, that he at length relinquished his trade, giving himself up entirely to his favourite studies. In less than a year after he had so done, he delivered a course of lectures upon geometry, in which he showed such talents and ingenuity as gained him not only the applause, but the support and patronage, of some of the most learned and able men of those days, which proved of importance; for he left off business with only about two thousand pounds, having then a wife and six children, three boys and three girls. Of this family I shall have occasion to speak again, as I became an inmate of their house.

Towards the close of the year Pott told me his father had procured for him a writership on the Bengal Establishment, but that he should not go out for a twelvemonth at soonest. Being sincerely attached to him, I was happy to hear he had succeeded in his object, though I regretted the consequent loss of his society. In the month of December, my father, by way of recreation, took me with him to Bath. I therefore took leave of Pott and the rest of my London associates for a few weeks, and on the 10th my father, Mr. William Cane, and Mr. William Burke, set off in a post-coach. We slept at Malborough, reaching Bath the next day to dinner. Here I passed six weeks very agreeably. Two days after our arrival I met, at the Pump Room, James Grant, with whom I made several pleasant excursions about the country on horseback, thus varying our scenes of amusement. The day after my return to town, Joseph Pott, the next brother to Robert, whom I had frequently called upon, and tipped at Eton School, came to St. Albans Street, and to my inexpressible surprise informed me that Robert had departed for Calcutta, being then at Portsmouth on board the *Houghton*, Captain Smith, wind-bound; that this measure was resolved on and everything arranged previous to my going to Bath, but kept secret from me to avoid the pain of a formal parting, which Robert said he could not support and thought it better for both to keep clear of.

I continued, but in an increased degree every month, to attend to my different club meetings, drank to excess, and in drunkenness often fell in with the Mohawks, whom I always vehemently opposed, notwithstanding which I escaped personal ill-treatment from them, to the surprise of all who witnessed the abuse I gave them. A new source of expense now sprang up; rowing ceased to be the fashion. Every young man that could afford it, and many that could not, got sailing boats. Of the latter description I certainly was; nevertheless I must have one, commencing with an open skiff carrying only a single sprit sail; but by degrees I rose to a half-decked vessel with boom and gaff mainsail, foresail and jib, furnished by my old Westminster friend, Dicky Roberts of Lambeth. In this boat I used to cruise in Chelsea Reach when blowing hard, so much so that the people on shore often stood watching me, expecting every moment to see me upset. Indeed, I sometimes could not help thinking that I presumed somewhat too much upon Mr. Hudson of Twickenham's prediction that clearly I was not born to be drowned. If I may be allowed to praise myself, I undoubtedly manoeuvred my little vessel with considerable skill and gained the approbation of all the watermen. The only assistance I required was one boy, to stand by the jib and foresheets when working to windward. So fond did I become of sailing that I went in a post-chaise to Folkestone, in the blustering and bleak month of March, for the express purpose of returning in a herring cutter, during which voyage we encountered a severe gale of wind from the eastward with hail and snow, the sea every instant making a complete breach over us. I could not help thinking it rather a singular thing to go in search of such weather by way of pleasure. The cold was so intense that I was obliged to have frequent recourse to the gin bottle. These sea parties soon made me hold the Chelsea Reach sailing in contempt.

About this period my friend, William Cane, commenced sailor, having caused a handsome cutter of twenty tons to be built for him by Cleverly, the Quaker, of Gravesend. With him (Cane) I often went, as I also did with Colonel Charles Cooper of the Guards (a natural son of Lord Holland's) who had a famous vessel which he called the *Porpus*. He lived in an excellent house about a mile distant from Tilbury Fort, having a charming woman for his wife. In this family I spent many happy days, and here I often met Mr. James Bigger of the East India house, who was as much attached to sailing as any of us. In the same neighbourhood resided General Desaguliers and Alderman Kirkham, who had both large vessels; but, accommodation and ease having been made the first object, they could not sail with Cane or Cooper's cutters; the latter from being fuller in the bows always beat Cane in a high sea, of which he became so jealous that he ordered Cleverly to build another of such construction as to outsail the *Porpus*; and the Quaker correctly executed the order, for we never fell in with a vessel at all near the same size that we did not beat hollow. Of this cutter I shall have occasion to say more hereafter.

Robert Mitford, whom I have already mentioned as one of the party that often met at the Shakespear and other houses in Covent Garden, was a near relation of the Mr. Boodle who, from having squandered away a handsome fortune, was reduced to the necessity of accepting the management of one of the fashionable gaming houses in Pall Mall which bore his name, being called "Boodle's"; and to this Mr. Boodle I was introduced by Mitford, after which introduction I spent many a jovial night at his house. At the time my acquaintance with him commenced, he was nearly sixty years of age, and, notwithstanding he had lived very freely, had still a good constitution, and was of a remarkably cheerful disposition. He was never happy unless he had a parcel of young people about him. I made one of upwards of a dozen who usually supped twice a week in Pall Mall, where he gave us as much champagne, burgundy and claret as we chose, the table being covered with every rarity in the way of eating. Nothing delighted him more than sitting out the boys, as he called us. Indeed, his head was so strong that he generally succeeded in so doing; and when he perceived his young guests began to flag, or become drowsy, he would get up, lock the door of the room, and putting the key in his pocket, strike up the song of " 'Tis not yet day" etc. His companionable qualities were extraordinary; and I certainly have passed more happy and jovial nights in his back parlour in Pall Mall than in any other house in London.

At the meeting of the Irish parliament this year, an absentee tax was proposed; that is, to make all persons who resided out of Ireland, but drew their fortune from thence, pay four or five per cent upon the amount so drawn. This measure, although a popular one in Ireland, was strenuously opposed by many men of rank and consequence in England, amongst whom the principal leaders were the Duke of Devonshire, Marquis of Rockingham, Earl of Besborough, Earl of Upper Ossory, Lord Milton, and several opulent commoners. These noblemen and gentlemen, who all received large incomes from Irish estates, united their abilities and influence in opposition to the passing of the act. They met at the Marquis of Rockingham's in Grosvenor Square to consult upon, and adopt, those measures most likely to be effective. Through the recommendation of Mr. Edmund Burke, I was employed at Lord Rockingham's upon this occasion upwards of a month, attending daily from nine in the morning until ten, eleven, or twelve at night.

My chief business was copying circular letters, and assisting in making them up, sealing, and directing. I sat at the same table with the Marquis, who I found to be a most affable and pleasing-mannered man. During such my attendance in Grosvenor Square I had thrice the honour of dining with the before-named noblemen and others who constituted the committee. The other days, my dinner was served for me in a small chamber adjoining the drawing-room in which I wrote. One of the days that I dined with the Marquis, I was much pleased with some delicious ale which his lordship said had been brewed at Wentworth (his seat in Yorkshire) upwards of twenty-five years before. It was soo soft and grateful to my palate that I was induced to take a second glass; upon which Mr. William Burke, who sat next to me, cautioned me to mind what I was about, the liquor I was so approving of being infinitely stronger than brandy and more likely to intoxicate. Undoubtedly, after drinking the second glass, I felt my head rather light and giddy.

Early in the year 1774, the outrages committed by the Mohawk quartet became so gross and frequent as at last to attract the notice and interference of the police magistrates, who, in consequence, set some of their myrmidons upon the watch. Those underling ministers of justice soon discovered the objects of their attention engaged in a violent riot in the playhouse of Covent Garden, where they had insulted and beat several persons. Whereupon they seized and carried them bodily off to the watch house, positively refusing bail. In the morning they were taken before the sitting justice in Bow Street, where the different parties aggrieved appeared against them, especially a gentleman who swore to Hamilton's having, without any provocation, spit in his face. Several were bound by recognizances to prosecute, and the Mohawks were all held to bail in very large sums. Hamilton, finding himself thus seriously attacked, deemed it prudent to decamp, thereby forfeiting his recognizances. He, however, had honour enough, previous to his departure, to indemnify the different tradesmen who, upon his credit, had become bail for himself and colleagues. He took up his residence in Paris. Mr. Hayter senior, ashamed of the behaviour of his son, whom he had made many ineffectual attempts to reclaim, upon the last public complaint did stand forward to bail him, which having done, he instantly sent him off to Holland with a view to put an end to the vile set he had associated himself with. Osborne, upon losing the advantage of Hamilton's purse, found himself alike bankrupt in character and fortune. He, therefore, embarked for his native shores of America, persuading Frederick to accompany him and try his fortune on the other side of the Atlantic. The latter there entered as a volunteer in one of the King's regiments, in which situation he behaved so well as shortly to obtain a commission, within a twelve-month from which time he was killed in one of the hard-fought battles of which so many occurred in that country. Thus ended the career of four young men who for a period of three years continued in one uninterrupted course of folly, intemperance and riot, to the utter disgrace of themselves, and of the police of the capital, which was either so relaxed, or so corrupt as to permit their course of iniquity to proceed uninterrupted.

By this time, I had, with my usual want of resolution, once more yielded to temptation, and fallen into all my old bad habits. Woman, dear, lovely woman, I never could resist. There was scarce one of any celebrity upon town, but what I was acquainted with. In a certain set of them, amongst whom were Sally Hudson, Clara Hayward, Mrs. Sturges, Mrs. Latour, the two Larkins, Vis-à-vis Townsend—so called from keeping a dashing carriage of that description—Lucy Wells, Kit Frederick, Cleveland, and many others, it was an established rule that, whenever any one of their frail sisters was laid hold of for debt, for them to collect together a party of volatile young men to join them in a party, and spend the days of confinement with the individual attacked. A famous bailiff named Willis generally contrived to get the writs that were issued against those unfortunate women directed to him. He kept a lock-up house in Great Earle Street, Soho; and, although by profession a tailor, he had fitted it up most elegantly as a tavern. Here we assembled, feeding upon every luxury procurable by money, and drinking the most expensive French wines.

An inevitable consequence of such a course of life to me was that I got rid of much more cash than my allowances afforded, and therefore incurred considerable debts. While my sword, watch, or any valuable article of dress remained in my possession, transferring the same to a pawnbroker secured me three or four guineas upon emergency. When all those sources were exhausted, I had recourse to my former disgraceful practice, expending upon my own extravagancies and follies large sums of money intended to pay counsel's fees, and other matters of business. Willis never scrupled letting any woman whom he arrested leave his house at pleasure to go to the theatres, opera, or any other public place they chose, until the writ was returnable; and in no one instance did he ever suffer thereby. If the person arrested failed in her exertions to raise the amount due amongst her own immediate friends, we who frequented the house made up the deficiency by subscription. The dissipated kind of life I had again fallen into could not escape the penetrating eyes of my father. He over and over again cautioned me, bidding me recollect all that had already occurred, and take care how I acted; but all in vain; and another important crisis of my life was now fast approaching.

II

A NEW DISGRACE

I N the month of August, Mr. Farrer one evening surprised us all at the Shakespear very much by telling us he should depart for the East Indies in a few days; for, having been informed from authority that a new court was upon the eve of being established in Bengal, under the direction of four judges to be nominated by His Majesty, in which court he understood there would be a great opening for the exercise of talents and industry at the Bar, he was determined to go out and try what he could do for himself as an advocate. He accordingly took his leave of us that night; shortly after which, an Act of Parliament was brought in and passed, whereby Warren Hastings, Esq., then Governor of Bengal, was appointed Governor-General of India, General Sir John Clavering, Colonel Monson, and Philip Francis, Esq., members of the Supreme Council, those four gentlemen constituting the Government.

By the same act, the Supreme Court of Judicature was formed, Sir Elijah Impey being appointed Chief Justice, Stephen Caesar Lemaitre, Robert Chambers, and John Hyde, Esquires, puisne Justices, the above-named Supreme Council and judges departing for India in the month of September (1774) on board of two old Indiamen, which were engaged and fitted up for the express purpose of conveying them to Asia. Mr. Farrer reached Calcutta some time before them, announcing himself as the avant courier of His Majesty's new court, in which he was to be the leading advocate. The consequence of this well-concerted plan was that he forthwith received retainers to an incredible amount, every native of rank or wealth being anxious to secure to himself the advantage of the new lawyer's surprising abilities! I myself heard Farrer dcelare that, previous to the arrival of the judges, he had received in hard cash upwards of five thousand pounds as retainers alone! In September 1775 the Supreme Council and judges reached Calcutta, and on 22nd October the court opened, Mr. Farrer being then admitted an advocate thereof; and, as he was the only regular-bred English lawyer belonging to it, and possessed more than ordinary talents, his most sanguine hopes were soon realized by his acquiring a noble fortune.

Towards the end of the year° the lamentable contest with America commenced, which, as everybody knows, concluded by their total estrangement from the mother country; and, to descend from great things to small, just at this time one of my boon companions, Gilly Mahon, an Irish adventurer who lived by his wits, went off with Miss Russell, a smart dashing girl of good family, being related to the Earls of Shelburne and Kerry. The personal accomplishments of the lady were not what caught Gilly, but the more substantial merit of two thousand guineas, which she had at her own disposal, besides a prospect of future pecuniary advantages. She had five brothers, all fashionable young men of high ton, every one of whom vowed vengeance against Gilly for seducing a sister of theirs; nor would Mahon, who was as bold as a lion, have hesitated to meet them all in turn had he been called upon, which he was not, the prudent relatives upon second thoughts resolving to leave the inconsiderate girl to her fate.

Gilly and his fair friend went over to Paris, where they resided several months, until, growing tired of each other, they had to part, he assuring her he would fulfil his promise by marrying her whenever she required him to go through that ceremony. With these liberal sentiments of each other, they both returned to London, Gilly resuming his former avocation, the lady embarking in splendid prostitution, in which capacity she soon reached the top of the ton, and was distinguished by the title of "The Bird of Paradise." There was a trifling circumstance that the hero had not thought necessary to impart to his innamorata, which was neither more nor less than that, when he went off with Miss Russell, he had a wife living, of which fact Miss Russell was soon appraised by one of her brothers; but it made not the slightest alteration in her attachment. About four months after their return from Paris, the good-natured spouse removed herself out of the way, by dying, whereupon the Bird sent to Mahon to say that, as he could now with propriety take a wife, she should like to have a right to bear his name, and sometimes perhaps make him liable for a milliner's bill. He making no objection, they were without further loss of time joined together in holy wedlock. They, however, never afterwards lived together, though apparently very civil to each other when they met in public, as they frequently did. She certainly was a lively little creature and an admirable companion, with whom I have spent very many cheerful days. She bore Mahon one child, a fine boy.

The repeated examples that occurred before my face of the sad consequences attending unjustifiable expense and dissipation had, un-

° The War of Independence, of course, is usually considered to have begun with the famous skirmish at Lexington in April 1775.

fortunately, no more than a momentary effect upon me. I transgressed, repented, and transgressed again, thus continuing an endless course of folly. During the last two years, I had never been entirely free from venereal taints, sometimes extremely ill and constantly using that powerful medicine mercury; nor did I ever give myself fair play—in the worst stages of the disorder, if I could move at all, frequenting my nocturnal haunts, sitting up whole nights committing every degree of folly and excess. Mr. Hayes, the surgeon who attended me, frequently remonstrated, observing that death and destruction must inevitably be the consequence of the life I led; and never shall I forget a speech he once made me. I had, as was often the case, by inattention, late hour and intoxication, whilst using mercury, thrown myself into a salivation; my head suddenly swelled to an enormous size; my tongue and mouth became so inflamed I could take no other nourishment than liquids; in which forlorn state he found me; when, instead of the pity and condolence I expected, he, in a great rage, swore he had a strong inclination to leave me to die as I richly deserved. His passion having vented itself, he with more temper said, "Indeed, indeed, William, you are playing the devil with a very fine constitution, for which folly, should you ever reach the age of forty, which I think impossible, your unfortunate body and bones will pay most severely." He proved a false prophet as to the length of my life; but I have often, when agonized with spasm and pain, thought of his prediction.

In March (1775) Mr. Perryn of the Chancery Bar (afterwards made a Baron of the Exchequer) wrote to my father to say he had a large payment to make in a few days, and therefore wished to receive what was due from the office. My father, much surprised, answered he was not aware of his office owing anything, the fees having always accompanied the papers sent. Mr. Perryn replied I was the person who had left the papers and best knew what had become of the cash. Being referred to upon this occasion, I had not a word to say. This unpleasant discovery naturally led my father to enquire how matters stood with other legal friends, the result of which proved equally to my discredit. My father found I had involved him to a considerable extent with Mr. Maddocks, Mr. Bearcroft, Mr. Ley, and Master Flett. No wonder, after all that had before occurred, this should have irritated him beyond measure.

Having ascertained the extent of the evil, he, with a degree of coolness that cut me to the soul, said, in the presence of all the clerks, "I now see, fatally see, that you are incorrigible. I have done with you for ever. From this hour I abandon you to your fate, which must be a deplorable one. It is a cruel circumstance that your infamy is likely to fix a stigma upon me and my family. We must endeavour to console ourselves under a consciousness that we do not deserve it. Go, base and vile young man, leave the house, never more to enter!" He then led me by the arm to the street, shutting the door upon me. Could I blame a parent whom I had so repeatedly, so grievously offended? Certainly not; nor did I. Conscience, that silent yet powerful monitor, told me I deserved every ill that could befall an undutiful, a perjured wretch, who thus ungratefully repaid the unbounded affection and kindness of as fond and indulgent a parent as ever child was blessed with.

What a sad reflection it is that I am compelled to record such accumulated, such repeated disgraceful actions of myself! My only consolation is that, although my follies (not to use a harsher term) were so numerous and so often repeated, yet my honoured father lived long enough to see an end of them, and most heartily and affectionately to congratulate me upon my having at last steadily settled in a fair, industrious, and honourable line of life, universally esteemed and respected in the society amongst whom I resided. Thank God that such has been the case and that I have not, in addition to my other offences, to answer for the truly heavy one of breaking a much-loved father's heart! Still, however, my wild oats were not all sown until long after the period just above mentioned; and I must yet record some further instances of a sad want of prudence in myself.

I left St. Albans Street, the place of my birth, and where I had been brought up with every possible indulgence and kindness by the most affectionate parents, with feelings I cannot attempt to describe. At times I could not help indulging a hope that my father (whose partiality towards me I knew so well and had so greatly presumed upon) would in some measure relent; but, upon a recollection of the heinousness of my offences, the fond idea vanished as soon as formed. What then was to become of me? An outcast! Bankrupt alike in character, fame, and fortune! Lost in gloomy meditation, I wandered about the town until a late hour in the evening, when I entered Lowe's Hotel in Henrietta Street, Covent Garden, went to bed, and there passed as wretched and miserable a night as ever unfortunate or guilty man did. I arose at eight in the morning, paid half a crown for my bed, out of two guineas and a half which I had in my pocket when I left home, and with a heavy heart, almost to suffocation, walked to Young Slaughters coffee house in St. Martin's Lane. Misery and distress was so strongly depicted in my countenance that, upon my entering the room and throwing myself on a seat in the most retired part, Preston, who kept the house, instantly came up to me and, kindly taking me by the hand, in the most feeling manner, said, "Good God, my dear Mr. Hickey, what ails you, what is the matter? You look dreadful. Can I do anything for you?"

This soothing address proved too much for me; I could not restrain my tears, and sobbed aloud, with a sensation in my throat like choking. From the early hour there was no one in the room but the people belonging to the house. Mrs. Preston and a very pretty barmaid seemed as much interested about me as Preston, and united their endeavours in persuading me to go upstairs and lie down. I, therefore, took the friendly advice, Preston himself attending me. When alone with him, I told him I was ruined, and with agony related what had occurred without attempting palliation. The benevolent man exerted himself to console me, insisting upon my remaining with him until some plan could be adopted for my future support. He then left me to take that repose my harassed frame stood so much in need of. I slept four hours, which relieved me greatly; and I firmly believe the humane and generous treatment I experienced from Preston and his family saved my life. His conduct was the more handsome and liberal because I, at that time, owed him more than thirty pounds for articles furnished me in the coffee and club rooms.

In the afternoon, Preston offered, though personally unknown, to go and speak to my father on my behalf; which I would not allow, from a conviction in my own mind that it could not avail. I afterwards learned that, notwithstanding my prohibition, the worthy creature actually did go to St. Albans Street, and there pathetically stated the alarming situation in which I had entered his house, and how extremely agitated and ill I still continued. At the Coffee House I remained six days wholly unnoticed, and concluded I was for ever abandoned. The seventh evening, as I was sitting, contemplating the melancholy prospect that presented itself in every point of view, my young friend Arthur Forrest* entered. He immediately took a seat by me, saying he had just heard from my family the unpleasant occurrence, and directly set out in search of me. He lamented that he could not give me any hopes of my father's relenting, who seemed to be offended past forgiveness, and had most seriously and positively forbid anyone ever to mention my name before him. Forrest, however, recommended my addressing him by letter, to which I objected from really and truly being utterly at a loss what to say.

After staying two hours he left me, promising to call again the following day. He did so, and renewed his wish that I would write with so much earnestness that, after repeated refusals on my part, I yielded, and did write to my father, acknowledging my base ingratitude, and the infamy of my whole life; that I had not a shadow of defence to offer; neither did I ask or expect ever to be admitted to his

---

* Son of Mrs. Forrest, "the most extraordinary woman in respect of eccentricities that perhaps ever lived," whose strange story we have been obliged to omit from the present edition of Hickey's Memoirs. Arthur, "a charming boy," in the author's affections "almost rivalled my early favourite, Pott."

presence again, my sole object in writing being to bid him an eternal adieu, and once more, with a heart overflowing with gratitude, to thank him for his unbounded affection and generosity, bestowed, as it had been, upon an ill-fated, worthless object. This letter Arthur Forrest undertook to deliver; three days after which, he again called, and after some conversation asked whether I should like to go and lodge and board at Mr. Malton's, who had taught me perspective and geometry, until some line of life could be settled. I answered that I was ready to go anywhere, or do anything my friends, if any I had left, deemed proper. He then engaged to arrange all matters for my removal; and the next day I went to my former instructor's, who had a neat, new house at Chelsea, exactly opposite the avenue leading up to Ranelagh. His family then consisted of himself, at that time about forty-five years of age, his wife, nearly the same, and remarkably well-looking, a shrewd, sensible woman, a daughter, Ann, just turned of sixteen, with a sweet and interesting countenance. Their eldest son, Thomas, had, when an infant, broken his leg, which was obliged to be amputated. He, of course, had a wooden one, which he used with wonderful dexterity and agility, running up and down stairs with considerable more rapidity than I could. He was a year younger than his sister, Ann; he inherited the extraordinary genius of his father, and was at that time one of the best draughtsmen in England. He has since established his reputation by several works of uncommon merit.

There were besides four younger children, two boys and two girls. I felt some surprise at so sedate and regular a family admitting as an inmate such a description of person as myself. The old folks received me with the utmost complacency and respect. Mr. Malton told me that my father had settled everything respecting my stay at his house, but had desired I might not be informed thereof. This was indeed a gratifying piece of intelligence to me, as it convinced me my revered father still thought of me and my welfare. The style of life I had now entered upon was as unlike what I had been long used to as could be. Here all was regularity, decency, and decorum. The provisions for the table, although humble, were always good, clean, and admirably well-dressed, consisting of a joint of meat, with plenty of excellent vegetables, followed by a pie or a pudding. We met at breakfast precisely at eight, dined at one, drank tea at five, and supped at half-past eight, retiring to our respective bedchambers rather before ten. Mine was the front room up two pair of stairs. The children soon became wonderfully attached to me, the elegant Ann too much so for both our comforts!

The first month glided away imperceptibly. During the mornings I amused myself by drawing and renewing my perspective, the evenings partly in reading, and partly playing cards with the family. I never wished to leave the house; the urbanity of manners of the master and mistress, and the sprightly playfulness of the little ones, rendered me happier than I had ever before felt; but I fear I ought in candour to add, as a material ingredient of this temporary felicity, the constant presence and society of the pleasing Ann. Her parents, without guile themselves and innocent as their own infants, knew not what suspicion was; nor did such an idea as my attempting to injure them through their darling daughter enter (for some time at least) either of their heads. The confidence they placed in my honour was unbounded, never hesitating to leave their Ann and me together. For a long time I withstood temptations almost irresistible, for which I gave myself more credit than I probably deserved. Towards the end of April, Ranelagh opened. Unfortunately, one of the few families the Maltons kept up an acquaintance with was that of the person who had charge of the property, and resided in the mansion house (part of the premises). His name has escaped my recollection; he was a well-informed, gentlemanlike-mannered man, who had formerly been engaged in an extensive line of commerce; but, being unlucky in some considerable speculations, he failed.

This gentleman or his wife called almost daily at Mr. Malton's, and he seemed sensible of the civility of my manner towards him, always courting my conversation. As he early discovered Ranelagh to be a favourite amusement of mine, and that I had been a regular and con- stant frequenter of it, he very politely presented me with a silver ticket, which he observed would not only give me admittance to the evening entertainments, but whenever I chose it in the daytime also, where it would amuse me to walk in the rotunda or gardens. Of this privilege I availed myself frequently, spending several hours of a morning roving about the gardens or rowing upon the canal, after which I entered the room, and amused myself in playing the few tunes I knew upon a very fine harpsichord that stood in the orchestra. In these rambles Ann Malton often accompanied me; and, although I was utterly ignorant of music, playing what I did entirely by ear, she always expressed herself pleased in my performance and was unwilling to let me quit the instrument. And now commenced our mutual danger. In these our solitary rambles, I at first contented myself with occa- sionally snatching a kiss from her delicious ruby lips, a freedom never strongly opposed and soon, on the contrary, met on her part with the utmost ardour.

Such an intercourse could not continue without imminent risk of her falling a sacrifice. The liberties she allowed me to take with her person increased; and I was more than once upon the point of accom- plishing the grand object, when her terror lest we should be discovered by some of the servants alone prevented it, and she proposed during the next moonlight nights to admit me to her bed. In this manner passed another fortnight when, being from habit more unguarded than formerly in my behaviour towards Ann, her mother's watchful eye took the alarm. She communicated her suspicions to her husband, who thereupon became more observant of our conduct. In a few days he cautioned me to be upon my guard, saying: "I have too much confidence in your honour, Mr. Hickey, to suppose you could deliberately lay a plan of seduction, or attempt to interrupt the harmony of my little family by an unsuccessful attack upon the chastity of my innocent child; for such I trust it would prove, were you so base as to make it. But I can perceive a growing familiarity between you and her, which, circumstanced as you respectively are, is imprudent and ought to be checked; otherwise you may fall into a fatal error before you are aware of your danger. Be upon your guard then, sir, I beseech you, and feel for a fond father and mother whose happiness or misery depend upon the conduct of their darling children."

This mild and sensible address had its due effect; and I resolved that nothing should induce me to dishonour his daughter. But, alas, nothing short of flight could have secured an adherence to my virtuous determination. The object of my admiration and lust daily and hourly before my eyes, and now unhappily become as willing as myself to transgress, courting instead of discouraging me—what was to be expected from a young pair so situated? She fixed upon a certain night for the fulfilment of what we both so ardently longed for. I then slept in a back room up two pairs of stairs, the father and mother with the three youngest children upon the middle floor, the elder boys in the kitchen, and Ann in the back parlour. Upon hearing the Ranelagh clock strike eleven, which was the hour agreed upon, I left my bed and, with a palpitating heart, crept downstairs. Ann had promised to leave the door ajar; but her mother (as I afterwards learnt) having occasion to go down for something after they had retired for the night, had shut it, the circumstance of finding it open creating a suspicion in her mind that all was not right, an idea of the careful parent that prevented me from the commission of a crime I have often since felt happy that I had not to add to the already sufficiently long catalogue of my offences.

Slowly and cautiously I turned the handle of the lock. The door opened, but in doing so creaked. I paused, anxiously listening for some seconds; when everything remaining quiet, I advanced, approached the bed and got into it, but had scarcely encircled the object I sought within my arms and our panting bosoms met, when, oh dreadful sound! I heard the door upon the middle floor open violently and, ere I had time to jump out of bed and reach the passage, the father stood before me, dressed, with a lighted candle in his hand. Never can I forget the pang I endured at that moment. In a tremulous voice, and greatly agitated, he said, "Base and unworthy young man, how can you face me after thus attempting to injure me in the tenderest point by depriving my unhappy child of her only inheritance, a good name, for ever? Within these few minutes have I been defending you against what I verily thought to be the caluminous suspicions of my poor wife, who it seems was better acquainted with your degenerate nature than I was. Did not my eyes behold you, as they now do, in this disgraceful and infamous situation, I could not have believed you capable of so profligate, so barbarous and inhuman an act." His distress prevented further utterance, and he burst into tears. In this awkward state the mother and maidservant made their appearance, the former observing to me "Oh, fye, fye, you ought to sink into the earth, if it would receive such a libertine. However, you had better, sir, now return to your apartment, and spare yourself the trouble of any similar attempts, as be assured I shall effectually guard my unfortunate daughter."

Like a detected thief I skulked upstairs, with feelings of sorrow and contrition impossible to describe. Certain it was I derived no small degree of consolation from the reflection that I had, although in so disgraceful a way, avoided ruining an innocent girl. The following morning at the usual hour I was summoned to breakfast, but declined going down; whereupon the servant brought the tea equipage to my room. From her I heard that Mrs. Malton, upon finding Ann's door open, had called her into her own chamber, where she had immediately mentioned the circumstance, observing that I meditated ill. Mr. Malton blamed her for the unjust suspicion; she, nevertheless, persisted, declaring that she would listen during the night and she desired her (the servant) not to undress herself. Thus all eager attention, cautious and softly as my movements were, they heard every one, heard me get out of bed, and every step as I descended; but, concluding I should pause on the creaking of the door, Mr. Malton allowed time for me to recover myself to make detection more secure. She further told me they continued up all night, and the moment daylight appeared her master went out towards London, taking his daughter with him.

From that day I have never beheld the pretty and gentle Ann Malton. I, however, had the satisfaction, several years after the above occurrence, to hear that she was married to a man of property and was very happy. At the dinner hour, being again summoned, I went down to the front parlour where the family were assembled at table, and I took my seat. For some minutes no one spoke, when the eldest son, Thomas, who did not seem to view the matter in so serious a manner as his parents, several times addressed questions to me, until his mother pettishly bid him hold his chattering tongue. Dinner being over, the younger children came in, all, as was their custom, directly clinging to my chair and caressing me; whereupon the mother rose taking them away with her. Mr. Malton then desired his son also to leave the room as he had private business to speak upon. Thomas retiring, the father addressed me to the following effect:

"After what happened last night, you must be aware, sir, that your absence from my family, whose peace you have disturbed and whose happiness it was your aim to destroy, is indispensable; to effect which I this morning called at your father's to announce to him the occasion that required it; but, finding him indisposed and out of spirits, I forebore to increase his illness, which I knew a communication of your misconduct would have done. The good gentleman expressed his satisfaction on the favourable report I had a week before made of your regularity and propriety of demeanour. 'If,' said he, 'my dear boy would always pursue the dictates of his naturally generous disposition, he would never err; but, unhappily, he possesses little fortitude, and yields to every temptation that presents itself. In England he cannot remain. A friend of mine has suggested a plan which I have thoughts of carrying into execution; but it cannot be effected for a fortnight or three weeks. Let him therefore pursue his studies under your instruction and good example until everything is finally arranged for his departure from hence.'

"Now, sir," continued Mr. Malton, "scandalous and unfeeling as your conduct has been to me and mine, still I should be sorry to be an impediment to your reconciliation with an offended father and to your future prospects; I therefore closed my lips on the subject of the injury you have done me, although my visit in St. Albans Street was for the sole purpose of communicating it and immediately getting rid of you. Here therefore you may remain until summoned by your father; but it would be as untrue as absurd in me to say that I can ever again esteem or respect you."

Having concluded this address, he left me. The following morning, upon entering the parlour to breakfast, I found Mr. Malton and his wife dissolved in tears, Mrs. Malton weeping bitterly. As I concluded myself to be the cause of this distress, I instantly declared my determination not an hour longer to obtrude myself upon them, and taking up my hat was actually going out of the house never to return, when Thomas came up to assure me I was not the cause of his father and mother's present grief, which arose from an account they had just received of the untimely death of their old and intimate friend, the housekeeper of Ranelagh, whom I have already mentioned, who had put a period to his life. Having left his bed in the middle of the night, he dressed and immediately walked into the garden, where he threw himself into the canal. One of the watchmen heard a splash of the water, but imagining it arose from the fish jumping he took no notice. In the morning, however, upon hearing that his master was missing, he mentioned the circumstance, and the canal being forthwith dragged the body was found. This unhappy gentleman's death by his own hands shocked me extremely. Though but a recent acquaintance, I had a great respect for him, was indebted to him for many acts of civility and kindness, and passed many happy and profitable hours in his society and converse.

Time now dragged heavily on when at home; for, having lost the gentle, fascinating Ann, Mr. Malton and his wife constantly eyeing me with cold and forbidding looks and scarcely ever speaking, I almost daily went over to the Red House from which I was a very short distance, and there consoled myself in the more cheerful company of Mrs. Lowry (alias Silver Tail), the daughter of Burt, the landlord. About a fortnight after the breach with the Maltons, the maidservant one morning followed me, on my going out, to say she had the night before heard from Nancy, who lived at a relation of her mother's at Islington and, as she greatly longed for an interview, would meet me any time I would appoint at the Crown public house in that town. For once in my life, at least, I did resist temptation, desiring the maid to say, "from my heart I wished her (Ann) well and happy; that, was I to obey the summons, I could not answer for myself; and, having so narrowly escaped the critical and dangerous situation we had been involved in, and as I was upon the eve of returning to the East Indies, it would be prudent to forgo the gratification of seeing each other." The servant seemed quite delighted at this determination, giving me due credit for the forbearance.

In the beginning of July, my father sent a messenger to desire I would go home the next day. I accordingly went to St. Albans Street, when my father, without recurring to former faults, or any upbraidings, to my infinite surprise told me that Mr. Burke had recommended my going to the West Indies to practice the law in the island of Jamaica, where all of that profession prospered exceedingly with only common attention and industry; that both Mr. Burke and his brother, Richard, had connections there who would, for their sakes, exert themselves to promote my interest and success should I prove commonly deserving. He also said, as I had served my full clerkship, at least in point of time, it would be advisable for me to procure my admission to the Roll of Attorneys of the Court of King's Bench previous to my departure.

He then desired me to return to Mr. Malton's to take leave of that respectable family, to whom I was under great obligations, and come home again the following morning. The leave-taking was a ceremony I would rather have dispensed with; but, as that could not be, I put the best face on, and in the evening informed Mr. Malton I was going to the West and not, as I had expected, the East Indies, to prepare for which I should leave his house on the morrow. He congratulated me upon the bright prospect opening to my view, adding that he sincerely wished me well. On bidding adieu to the children and their mother, the latter shook me with apparent cordiality by the hand, saying "God bless and protect you, sir, and grant that you may in a reasonable time return to your own country a rich and, what is better, a good man," with a very strong emphasis upon "good." And so ended all chance of my resuming a red coat in the service of the East India Company, or ever more mounting a cockade and military sword.

Upon reaching the house of my nativity, I took possession of my old chamber; three days after which, my father took me to Mr. Justice Yate's, one of the judges of the Court of King's Bench, who, being a friend of long standing, had offered the necessary certificate etc. for my admission. He received us at his residence in Spring Garden with the utmost politeness, insisting upon our partaking of his breakfast. After conversing for half an hour upon the common news of the day, he apologized for dismissing us, as he was obliged to go to Westminster earlier than usual to sit for the Lord Chief Justice. My father then asked when it would be convenient for him to receive me for the purpose of examination as to my being equal to the practice of an attorney. The judge thereupon, addressing me with complacency and gentleness, said, "Do me the favour to come and breakfast with me at eight o'clock tomorrow morning, and I will take care everything shall be ready. In the interim send your deed, or articles, to my clerk that he may take names, dates, and other particulars from them."

At the time appointed I attended; and in a terrible fright I was at the ordeal I imagined I had to pass through, and the probable loss I might be at in answering some of the many questions I understood would be put to me upon points of practice. Being conducted into his parlour where the breakfast things were all arranged, in five minutes the judge entered. We sat down, and he recommended his French rolls and muffins as of the best sort; but so predominant were my fears about the dreaded examination that I had no inclination to eat. Breakfast being over, he asked me how I liked the law, how long I had been out of my clerkship, and two or three other questions equally unimportant, when a servant entered to announce the carriage being at the door; whereupon he desired his clerk to be called, upon whose appearance he enquired whether Mr. Hickey's certificate was ready.

The clerk having it and other papers in his hand, the judge took it from him, and after perusal subscribed his name, and then said, "Now, Mr. Hickey, if you will be so good as to accompany me to Westminster Hall, I will get you sworn, and the business concluded." I accordingly

stepped into his coach which conveyed us to Westminster, and immediately going into court, where he had taken his seat upon the bench,
the proper officer was asked whether he had the roll, and, answering
in the affirmative, my certificate was delivered to him and read, as
was also an affidavit of my master, Mr. Bailey's. This being done the
judge ordered the oaths to be administered to me; after which, and
my subscribing my name to each, I was entered upon the roll as an
attorney, and making a respectful bow to the Bench and Bar, I retired,
most agreeably relieved from my apprehensions respecting the various
interrogatories I had expected would be put to me on the subject of
my qualifications.

The following day, my father gave me a letter, which he desired I
would myself deliver to Messrs. Nesbitt's, eminent merchants, in
Bishopsgate Street, the purport of it being to request they would procure for me a passage to the West Indies in one of their ships. I found
Mr. Arnold Nesbitt in the counting house, who, after reading the letter,
assured me both himself and brother should feel pleasure at all times
in complying with any desire of Mr. Hickey's. He said they should
dispatch four ships within the ensuing two months, and he would
advise my proceeding by the *New Shoreham*, a very fine ship, and
commanded by a respectable and worthy man. "I presume," added
Mr. Nesbitt, "your father knows that the passage money, and all those
sort of matters, must be arranged with the commander previous to the
ship's departure, as we owners never interfere about passengers, what
they pay being a perquisite of the captains." He then wrote an answer
to my father's letter, and desiring me to call again upon him that day
week, when he would introduce me to the captain, I took leave.

On the day appointed, I again went to Bishopsgate Street, when Mr.
Nesbitt gave me a letter to Captain Paul Surman, commander of the
ship *New Shoreham*, whom I found at the Jamaica Coffee House. He
appeared to be a plain, good-tempered man; a strong brogue plainly
marked his native country was Ireland. He told me he had not yet any
passengers, that I might therefore take my choice of the cabins; but
he had no doubt plenty would apply before his departure. He also
informed me that I should see most of the West India islands, as he
was to stop at different places to deliver goods he had on freight; that
the passage money to be paid previous to embarking was thirty
guineas, for which he should supply a table during the voyage. He
advised me to go on board the ship then laying off Rotherhithe, and
fix upon a cabin. This I did the following day, finding her a very fine
vessel, between three and four hundred tons burden, elegantly fitted
up, and lined throughout the after part with mahogany. I took possession of the cabin adjoining the principal one, into which it opened,
having a large scuttle which afforded abundant light.

My father forthwith paid the passage money, and fitted me out with his usual liberality. My esteemed and invariable friend, Mr. Edmund Burke, procured for me letters of introduction and recommendation to Sir Basil Keith, the Governor of Jamaica, Mr. Webley, the Chief Justice, Mr. Harrison, the Attorney-General, Messrs. Welch, Brownrigg, and Baker, barristers, the last being well known under the name of "Billy Baker"; also to Messrs. Lyon and Ridge, attorneys, besides several gentlemen, planters in different parts of the island. My father likewise furnished me with letters to some of his own friends, amongst whom were Mr. Robert Richards and Captain Stair Douglas of the navy.

On 1st September, 1775, I once more took leave of my family, and set out from St. Albans Street for Gravesend, where Captain Surman said all his passengers would go on board, as he did not intend to anchor in the Downs if the wind proved fair for proceeding down-Channel. In consequence of this recommendation, I went on board at Gravesend, where I found there was only one other passenger, Mr. Theophilus Byers, a sedate young Caledonian, going out as a clerk to a mercantile house in the island of Grenada. On 2nd September we unmoored, with rather a scant wind from the eastward, and very little of it, which made three days pass ere we reached Margate Roads. We had scarcely anchored there when the wind veered round to the westward, which carried us round the north foreland, and we worked into the Downs, anchoring there amidst a fleet of near four hundred sail, chiefly consisting of transports laden with naval and military stores, variety of provisions, livestock of sheep and hogs, intended for the British troops serving in America, the war with our colonies in that quarter then having broken out. Upon our ship's being moored, I went on shore, taking up my residence at the Hoop and Griffin Inn, which house Captain Surman had recommended as being, in every respect, far superior to the Three Kings. This character it certainly deserved, but still I found it bad enough; indeed all the inns of Deal are wretched in comparison to those of every part of the Kentish road.

We had only been twenty-four hours in the Downs, when a light air from the northward tempted the fleet to weigh; seeing which I went off to the *New Shoreham*, and found her just making sail. The whole fleet then stood down-Channel. The following morning the wind increased considerably, and before dark blew a gale, so that Captain Surman was afraid to venture carrying sail, and we lay to. At daylight, not more than ten ships were in sight out of the great number that had left the Downs with us; and, of those few, three had signals of distress flying. Before noon we discovered the French coast directly to leeward, it by that time blowing extremely hard. As an old cutter sailor, I knew our situation to be critical and dangerous, and saw evidently our commander was seriously alarmed, declaring the necessity of setting some sail as our only chance of clearing the land, and he gave orders accordingly; but so weakly were we manned, our crew consisting of no more than twenty-two, of whom half were landsmen, that some hours elapsed before we could effect close reefing and setting the topsails. The gale continuing with unabated violence, we made little headway, driving bodily to leeward. The sea ran dreadfully high, making the vessel labour and strain greatly. In this alarming situation we remained three days and nights; on the fourth morning, being the 9th of the month, the French coast was seen trenching away as far forward as the lee bow; and at the same time the main topsail sheet giving way, the sail in a few seconds blew to pieces; whereupon Captain Surman exclaimed, it was all over with us, and within three hours we must be on shore.

He was himself as perfect a seaman as ever walked a deck; nor were his officers inferior in knowledge of their duty. These three persons, aided by the boatswain, whose name was Jerry Griffin, performed wonders by their extraordinary exertions and spirited example. A reefed mainsail was set, which happily stood, proving of more service than the topsail had been, so that we evidently made less leeway. Griffin, the above-mentioned boatswain, was an uncommonly athletic and powerful man, upwards of six feet two inches high, of almost Herculean form, yet active as a deer. I early discovered him to be a strange and uncommon character. I shall have occasion hereafter, more than once, to state some of his peculiar oddities and out-of-the-way expressions. At daylight the land was still visible, though as far distant as the preceding day, that is, about four leagues.

At noon, in a severe gust, the mainsail and fore topsail both gave way in the same instant, the former blowing to atoms; but the latter, being a new sail, was saved, and soon reset. Towards night, in a very hard squall, the wind suddenly shifted to the south-west; whereupon Captain Surman determined to bear away for the Downs, in order to repair the serious damages sustained in the storm, particularly the longboat, which a tremendous sea that broke on board had stove. When running before the wind, she rolled so deep that almost everything fetched way, and a dismal night I passed. My spirits were, however exhilarated at, just as the day broke, hearing the anchor let go; when leaving my cabin I went upon deck and had the satisfaction to see the clouds dispersed and that it was a fine morning. As the sun rose, the wind moderated and the sea decreased. My fellow passenger, Mr. Byers, who had been so tortured by sea-sickness as to render him indifferent to all that was going on, now made his appearance, pale as death. I congratulated him upon our escape from shipwreck on the French coast, adding, "I suppose you will go on shore at Deal?" To which with some surprise, he answered, "Dear me, sir, do you think of doing so? I should be very glad could I venture." I replied, "Venture! Why not, what's the risk? I am determined to go by the first boat that arrives." "Then, so will I," said Byers.

Captain Surman, who had heard this conversation, addressing me, said, "Indeed, Mr. Hickey, it will, in my opinion, be very imprudent in either of you to leave the ship. From the present appearance of the weather, I have little doubt but the first breeze that comes (for it was then nearly calm) will be from the eastward, in which case I shall be away before you will be able to reach the ship, so far out as we lie." I replied that I was obliged to him for his prudent advice, which I was conscious was given from friendly motives; but that I was so exhausted from want of sleep and anxiety, that let the consequence be what it might, on shore I would go, if anly for a few hours. A boat just then running by, the man at the helm called out, "Does anyone want to go on shore, hoa?" I immediately answered, yes, and they came alongside, when putting a few shirts, etc., into a portmanteau, I asked Mr. Byers if he was ready; but the wary Scotch lad had been so deeply impressed by what the captain said, he was afraid to venture, and declined leaving the ship; I therefore departed alone.

At this time, (about half-past seven in the morning) there was scarce a cloud to be seen, a light air blowing from the south-south-west, which, while we were running towards Deal, freshened, and the boatmen observed to each other, it looked as if another gale was brewing. In about an hour we reached the beach, and a few minutes more placed me before a fire in a comfortable room looking towards the sea, and a good breakfast upon tbale, in the Hoop and Griffin; of which having partaken heartily, and thereby feeling greatly recruited, I sallied forth to make my observations. There were then upwards of a hundred ships of the fleet that had sailed with us at anchor in the Downs; and by noon upwards of seventy more came in, most of them having sustained damages, some materially, by loss of topmasts or lower yards. The pilots conjectured that, upon the shift of wind to the westward, the remainder had made a push for Portsmouth, or possibly some might be at anchor upon the flats off Dungeness. The weather continued clear and beautifully fine until one o'clock, when I went into the house to dinner, and whilst at my meal, a dismal alteration took place; the clouds suddenly collected; it became squally, looking, as seafaring people phrase it, "exceedingly dirty." By three it blew strong, with severe gusts, and at times rain. I, nevertheless, walked out to the waterside to collect the different opinions, and found all agreed a tempest was approaching; and they were right.

Before five it blew an absolute hurricane; the ships in every direction were seen driving from their anchors, although the masts and yards were lowered, as well as every other possible precaution taken. An immensely high and short sea arose, which occasioned so heavy a surf that not a boat would venture to encounter it, or go to the assistance of many vessels that were making signals of distress. Some, in the commencement of the gale, did attempt it, but, being swamped, discouraged the rest. In spite of wind and rain, I remained at the sea-side, and seeing the pilot that brought us from the river, I asked his opinion about the *New Shoreham*. He told me, hard as it blew, he did not think it was yet at the worst. "However," continued he, "your vessel is in the very best berth in the Downs, and I'll be damned if she wags while a ship's tackle holds, except the men-of-war," one of which, the *Arethusa* frigate, she lay close to. Scarce were those words out of his mouth when it appeared to me that the *New Shoreham* moved; and I said "Surely she now is drifting." The pilot, taking his glass, exclaimed, "By God she is, and will certainly be foul of the frigate, or compel them to cut." We, however, perceived that she passed without touching. The wind now veered about between south and west, accompanied by loud peals of thunder and at times heavy rain. By half-past five, nine ships that had parted from their anchors drove on shore between Deal and Sandwich, a distance of only eight miles; others having drifted foul of each other, were obliged to cut away rigging and masts to prevent the dire alternative of going to the bottom together; two were seen actually to founder. A more horrid spectacle I never beheld; yet so interested did I feel on account of the unhappy people on board the different vessels, that neither, wet, cold nor want of rest could induce me to quit the beach whilst a ray of light remained. At seven in the evening, no object being any longer discernible, I returned to my inn, where I drank tea.

While at table, hearing the people in the kitchen talk to someone just landed, I went out and found it was a pilot who left the *Arethusa* at half-past six to endeavour to procure another spare anchor. He told me he left only ten ships at anchor, four of which were men-of-war. Upon my enquiring whether he knew anything of the *New Shoreham*, he answered, she, with the rest, had drifted towards the North Sea, where, in all probability, every one of them would be lost upon some of the many shoals they must run upon. At eight o'clock I followed the advice of the hostess by drinking some excellent hot punch, and going directly afterwards to bed, where, although anxiety for the sufferings of the many poor drowning wretches kept me awake some time, fatigue at last got the better, and I fell into a profound and deep sleep, which continued uninterrupted for full twelve hours.

Upon entering the room where breakfast was laid out for me, and going to the window, a sad scene of desolation and ruin presented itself to my view. Of the numerous fleet that but twenty-four hours before had been proudly riding at anchor in the Downs, no more than eight now remained; and three of those were totally dismasted. The *Arethusa* alone was in the spot where she had brought to, all the others having drifted several miles; but she was one of the finest frigates in the navy, with a noble ship's crew. The weather, though not quite so bad as the preceding day, still continued very boisterous; but the clouds had dispersed and there was no rain.

Having breakfasted, I walked towards Sandwich. The beach was covered with pieces of wreck, dead bodies of the unfortunate persons that had perished, and hundreds of sheep and hogs from the Government transports. To describe the dreadful scene that presented itself is impossible; suffice to say, it was horrible in the extreme. I entered the town of Sandwich, enquiring of several seafaring people if they knew anything of the *New Shoreham*, but could gain no tidings of her further than that a West Indiaman was seen the evening before driving past Ramsgate, close in with the land, and a signal of distress out, made in vain, as the weather was too violent for any boat to attempt going off to the numerous ships that drove by, all with the same signals of distress flying.

BOUND FOR JAMAICA

AFTER being upon my legs from ten o'clock until past four, I returned to the inn much fatigued; but a good dinner recruited me. Whilst ruminating upon what I should do, and determining, if I heard nothing of my ship in the course of the following day, to return to London, it occurred to me that my St. George's Fields acquaintance of 10th May 1768, (Mr. Baker) was an inhabitant of Deal; and, the landlord of the Hoop and Griffin telling me he had seen him pass on horseback about two hours before, I immediately went to his house, where enquiring for him, the servant showed me into a parlour, and I found Mr. Baker with two London friends who were upon a visit to him, sitting over their bottle. He instantly recognized me, and received me with infinite kindness. Upon my telling him I had been two days at Deal, he upbraided me for not having sooner called. After a few glasses of wine, he conducted me into another room, where Mrs. Baker was preparing tea. She was a well-looking, smart woman, with two fine boys, her sons, leaning upon her chair, (both of whom, I believe, afterwards became post-captains in the navy).

During the 13th, ten more ships entered the Downs from the westward, supposed to be transports, all being in a shattered condition and bearing signals of distress. At three in the afternoon we returned to Deal, and after spending the rest of the day very agreeably at Mr. Baker's, I went to my inn to sleep. Upon rising the next morning, the 14th, I rejoiced to see the gale had abated, although it still blew strong. All the large boats were employed carrying off anchors, cables and other stores to the ships. In the forenoon, I mounted one of Mr. Baker's horses, when he, myself, and his two London guests rode to Margate, distant sixteen miles, where we also received dismal accounts of the mischief done during the hurricane. On our return to dinner, a boatman called at Mr. Baker's to let him know the *New Shoreham* was safe, and then working into the Downs, which she reached by four o'clock, and once more anchored. In the evening, the wind died away, it becoming almost calm. At midnight, I went to bed and at four in the morning, hearing a great bustle amongst the boats, I rose, dressed myself and going into the front room saw a black bank towards the horizon, in the east. Descending to the bar, I found a number of lodgers calling for their bills, as the wind was again fair. I did the same, and having by a little after five discharged it and got my portmanteau ready, I sallied forth, a boatman immediately announcing a fine breeze from the north-east, and asking if I wanted to go off. I answered "Yes, I did, to the *New Shoreham*." "She lies the very outermost ship," replied the extortioner. "However, I'll put you on board for ten guineas." Alarmed at the exorbitancy of the demand, which, by the by, exceeded my whole remaining stock of cash, I remonstrated, expressing a hope that he would take half the sum. This he absolutely refused, saying, "I'll be damned if I do, or if you find a boatman upon this beach who will take you on board for five guineas. It is now blowing fresh and will increase." In this dilemma, I began to apprehend I must lose my passage, and in great fright ran down to Mr. Baker's, who I had heard say he should rise at five to go out with the hounds. I met him just mounting his horse, when mentioning what had just happened and the state of my finances, he instantly said, "Oh never fear, Hickey, I'll be bound for it I get you off, and in one of the best boats too; or, if I am disappointed, you shall have my own." He then sent a servant to call a pilot of his acquaintance, who within five minutes made his appearance; when Mr. Baker said, "Charles, here is a most particular friend of mine who is going to the West Indies in the *New Shoreham*, and, not being very flush of cash, you must get him on board that ship for a guinea." "Lord love your honour, to be sure I will," said Charles, "for nothing, and with all my soul. They are now launching the *Lovely Susan* (his boat's name) to go off to the commodore with fresh beef, so your friend is kindly welcome to a passage." Then turning to me, he continued, "So step along, my master, we have no time to lose." This was delightful language to my ears, and cordially thanking Mr. Baker for all his attentions, I bid him adieu; but he insisted upon seeing me embark, sent a man for my portmanteau, and did not quit the shore until I was seated in the stern sheets of the *Lovely Susan*, and fairly through the surf.

A little before seven I was alongside the *New Shoreham*, completely drenched from the spray of the sea every instant breaking over us. I presented the boatmen with a couple of guineas, which greatly pleased them, they not expecting a sixpence, their master having ordered them to take me off without any charge whatever. I found the *New Shoreham* with her anchor apeak and, within a quarter of an hour after I reached her, running seven knots an hour, right before the wind. Thus I did but just save my distance.

Captain Surman congratulated me on having. although contrary to his advice, gone on shore, thereby avoiding the misery and distress they had encountered. He said that, when he perceived the ship began to drive with three anchors ahead, he gave everything up, and would not have given a single sixpence for vessel and cargo. He further told me they had driven so close to the *Arethusa* that their yard-arms touched, he being obliged, in order to prevent falling on board her, to cut from two of the anchors he was dragging, and within an hour afterwards the third cable snapped close to her bows. Mr. Byers lamented that he had not followed my example by going on shore at Deal. He said what I beheld from the land could give no idea of the actual horror of the scene, the wind roaring with such superlative force it became quite impossible to hear each other's voices; the ship every instant nearly overwhelmed by the seas that broke over her, so much so that all on board expected to go to the bottom; that they saw several vessels actually do so, close to them, whilst others, driving foul, tore away masts, yards, and rigging, involving both in complicated ruin. He said he was certain nothing enabled him to bear the terrors of the last three days but the immense quantities of gin he swallowed, which ran down his throat like the simple element water, not creating the least sensation in his stomach, or passing into it, like spirits. And this was the more extraordinary from Mr. Byer's never having thentofore drank anything stronger than small beer, his customary beverage being water.

We ran down-Channel in what, had we not been right before the wind, would have been deemed a hard gale. During the first three days, we had many ships in sight; the fourth morning we were, by reckoning, several leagues to the westward of Scilly, the weather becoming from thick and hazy to bright clear sunshine. We ran on, entirely alone. By this time I had quite got the better of sea-sickness, and was able to walk the deck, which gave me an opportunity of observing the ignorance of the crew. There were only three that could take the helm at all, and those yawed the ship about sadly; nor did they seem conversant with a single point of seamanship; so very deficient were they in every respect that I often wondered at the ship's ever reaching the West Indies. Happily for us the weather continued generally fine, having nothing more than a few squalls, in some of which we were compelled to carry more sail than prudence could authorize, from no other reason than inability to take it in quick enough.

Our table was very differently provided from what I had been used to in the *Plassey*; but in this Captain Surman was not to blame, for he had an abundant stock of poultry, sheep, and hogs, at the time we first sailed out of the Downs, the greater part of which was lost in the gale; and he had afterwards no opportunity of procuring a sufficient supply, all he could obtain being two or three dozen of fowls and a few ducks which were received while the ship was weighing anchor the last time. The salt provisions were excellent of their kind, and Mr. Scott, the chief mate, being a capital fisherman, the table was almost daily furnished with an albacore, boneta, or dolphin, and not unfrequently with all three, which he struck with a gig. Either of these fish, especially the dolphin, when dressed in the American manner, that is, cut in slices, with layers of pork and vegetables, and well stewed, is admirably good, and might meet the approbation of a fat Common Council man of the City of London. We had plenty of port wine and lisbon, which, with uninterrupted good humour, made the hours glide rapidly away. Our mess consisted of five: the captain, chief and second mates, Mr. Byers and myself, and I can confidently affirm nothing like an angry word passed in the little party during the voyage, which was made in the usual time, the Island of Barbados being seen early in the morning of 18th October.

When within three miles, this land presents to the eye one of the richest views that can be, one side being covered with the most luxuriant verdure, handsome buildings belonging to the planters, and windmills innumerable, the canes being ground by that machine. It did not appear to me that there was a single foot of uncultivated land upon the whole island. The *New Shoreham*'s first destination was Grenada; but Captain Surman, wishing to gain information, ran close in to Bridgetown, the capital of Barbados, and there hove to. A boat, with only caffres in her, having fruit to sell, came off, and we purchased pines, oranges, plaintains, guavas, star apples, etc., all of which were highly acceptable. These people, upon hearing we were bound to Grenada, said, "Oh, Grenada all gone, no Grenada now." This inducing further enquiry, we learnt that the chief town called St. George's, had recently been entirely destroyed by fire. After stopping an hour, we again made sail, passing St. Vincent's and two other small islands.

After the common run, we saw Grenada, the appearance of which was very unlike that of Barbados, being entirely covered by forests of wood, and not a sign of cultivation or habitation, until rounding a point of land, the ruins of the town were seen; and sad havoc the conflagration had made. In the valley not a single house was left standing, and only a few upon the rising ground. A government canoe that came alongside directed Captain Surman to stand on, and bring his ship to an anchor in the carenage situate on the south end of the island. Here we found a neat litle town, consisting of about fifty houses, all constructed of wood, whereas those of the capital were of masonry, mostly stone There is a strong fort standing upon an eminence, garrisoned, when we were there, by two regiments of infantry, one of them Highlanders, and two companies of Artillery. The carenage is separated from St. George's by a lofty hill. The accident of the fire had happened a fortnight previous to our arrival, having commenced at ten o'clock at night in a large store, or magazine, in which unfortunately were a number of casks of rosin, pitch and tar, which burnt with irresistible fury. The town, which had occupied an extent of nearly two miles along the sea-side, was in twenty-four hours reduced to a pile of ruins and ashes. There was only one tavern in the place, to which I accompanied Captain Surman as soon as the ship was moored, and got a tolerable dinner.

Mr. Richard Burke, who was Collector of the Customs for this island, had given me a letter to Mr. Irwin, an intimate friend of his; enquiring for which gentleman, I was told he had that minute entered the house, and being shown to the room where he was, I delivered my letter, which procured me the warmest possible reception, he expressing the greatest regard for Mr. Burk, about whom he made many earnest enquiries. Mr. Irwin was a gentlemanlike man, advanced in years, and an old inhabitant of Grenada. His residence being in the carenage, he had not suffered from the late disaster. In the evening he took me to his house, insisting upon my living with him during my stay. His mansion was entirely of wood, a melancholy dirty concern, but pleasantly situated, being within five yards of the sea, and commanding the circuit of the bay, in which three ships and a number of small craft were at anchor. He told me that four-fifths of the houses in the town were his property.

Having sent to the tavern to request Captain Surman's company, he gave us a bottle of admirable madeira. After a cheerful evening, and good supper, Captain Surman went on board his ship to sleep, and I was shown to a large, dark, shocking-looking chamber, the contents of which forcibly brought to my mind the first night I passed at Mr. Dawson's Garden, near Madras, in the year 1769. The thing upon which it was intended I should rest, dignified with the improper title of *bed*, was a crazy old wooden frame, with planks at the bottom, upon which was laid a kind of rug, not of sufficient substance to preserve my bones from the hardness of the boards. The rest of the furniture was of a similar description. I, who had never before been lodged in so wretched a place—for it was infinitely worse than Mr. Dawson's, which was at least airy and open—was struck with surprise and disgust upon entering it. Mr. Irwin seemed unconscious of its demerits and, having himself shown me into the dog-hole, cordially shook me by the hand, wishing me a good night, a wish I felt utterly impossible to be accomplished!

Low in spirits, I sat myself down, contemplating the misery that surrounded me, and, dreadfully bit and stung by insects, watched until the few inches of candle left with me burnt out. My ruminations were then continued in the dark, until, beginning to think daylight would never arrive, I determined to endeavour to get into the open air. I began groping about the room, but for the life of me could not find the door; tumbling over different things half a dozen times, I was completely lost, so that at last in absolute despair I sat myself down upon the floor, where a host of fleas in addition to the other annoyances assailed me. The heat, too, was intense, keeping me in profuse perspiration. A more miserable night I never passed. Truly rejoiced was I when the first ray of light appeared through the small casement. The instant I could discern the door I issued forth from my den, walking about the town for an hour when I saw a boat coming from the *New Shoreham* in which was Captain Surman, who the moment he saw the woeful plight I was in, said, "I was afraid such would be the case and had thoughts of advising you to go with me and sleep in your own cabin, but was afraid of giving Mr. Irwin offence. I see you have not had your clothes off; you had better therefore step into the boat, go to the ship, and lie down for a couple of hours." I accordingly did so, slept soundly, and got up refreshed; when I cleaned myself and returned to Mr. Irwin, who seemed amazed at my account of the way in which I had passed the night, declaring he did not know there was an insect in the house, as they never molested him. He ordered breakfast for me, and I made a hearty meal, enjoying the new bread and fresh butter.

The sixth day after our arrival, hearing that Mr. Byers was ill at the tavern, I called, and found him, as I conceived, very seriously indisposed, having a considerable degree of fever. I recommended his sending for medical assistance; but he would not listen to such advice, saying nothing material ailed him, and that a double dose of sea-water (of which he had daily drank two pints during the voyage from England) would set him to rights. Eight hours after I left him, he breathed his last! This very sudden death of my young shipmate greatly increased the insuperable dislike I had taken to Grenada, and made me anxious to leave it; but of doing so Captain Surman gave me no hopes for ten days, as he had a large quantity of heavy ironwork to deliver which Messrs. Nesbitt's agent was not ready to receive, having no secure place in which he could deposit it.

Being invited one day to dine with an officer of the garrison, he was attending me from the Fort to the sea-side between eleven and twelve at night, an Irish gentleman of the name of Todd also being with us. It was extremely dark, and as we approached a sentinel, who was conversing in his native language (Erse) with some person we could not see, Mr. Todd whispered us to stop. After listening a few minutes, he told us the man was speaking in terms that, if published, might cost him his life; "but," added he, "as my sentiments accord with his, I will merely caution him." Approaching the sentinel, who was a Highlander conversing with a comrade not upon duty, he asked the names of both men, which they readily gave. He then addressed them thus: "My lads, I distinctly heard what you just now said, and were it communicated to the Lieutenant Governor, or to your commanding officer, would place you both in a very disagreeable situation. But be not alarmed; I have no intention of that kind. Be more upon your guard henceforward, and do not pronounce yourselves safe from discovery because you converse in Erse, of which language I do not understand a word, but its similarity to Irish, which I am acquainted with, enabled me to give you this caution." The soldiers thanked Mr. Todd for his conduct towards them. During the remainder of our walk Mr. Todd communicated to us the purport of the conversation he had stopped us to listen to, which was nearly as follows:

SENTINEL: "So I hear our lads are under orders for America to harass and destroy the brave fellows for opposing tyranny and slavery."

COMRADE: "Yes, so I hear, and that our Regiment is to be sent from here as soon as ever there are ships to take them."

SENTINEL: "I don't like the job; sending Englishmen to cut Englishmen's throats, and that only for defending their lives and properties, is not fair."

COMRADE: "I believe most of the Regiment are sorry for going."

SENTINEL: "Why then, let them do as I daresay you and I shall—take the fair side."

The day after the foregoing extraordinary circumstance, I was taken ill, being attacked by violent headache and vomiting. Medicine, being immediately administered, relieved but did not cure me, the doctor declaring I had lurking symptoms of fever. This made me still more anxious to leave the island, which Mr. Irwin seeing, he offered me a passage in a small schooner of his that would sail the following day for Antigua, where I might stay until the *New Shoreham*, which was to stop there, should take me up again. This offer I gladly accepted upon Captain Surman's approval and assurance that he would touch at Antigua, and carry me on to Jamaica. That night I went on board the schooner, a dirty vessel, abounding with vermin. I, however, felt happy in the idea of getting away from Grenada, the only place I ever left, after no matter how short a residence, without a particle of regret. Mr. Irwin favoured me with a letter to his correspondent at Antigua, who in consequence thereof received me into his house, and where in a very agreeable family named Mathison, I spent ten pleasant days, having quite recovered my health during the short voyage. In the evening of the tenth day the *New Shoreham* arrived; and the next

7+

night we sailed from Antigua, having two gentlemen of that island who requested a passage to Jamaica.

The day after we left Antigua, the weather being delightfully fine, I was walking the quarterdeck with Mr. Scott, the chief mate, the people being down below at dinner, when Mr. Scott observing the flying boom of the lower studding sail had got foul of a fluke of the anchor, he went forward himself to clear it, in doing which he missed his hold of a rope, and fell overboard. As I saw the accident, I told the man at the helm to heave the ship to, and opened the cabin door to call the captain, who came out at the moment the sails were backing, which occasioned the ship to lay down so much, I thought she must overset. Every soul was instantly upon deck; the topsails were lowered and she righted. The boatswain exerted himself amazingly; a boat was quickly out, into which he and four men got, rowing in the direction in which Mr. Scott had fallen, the sea being so high we saw nothing of him. Captain Surman, looking out with his spying glass, soon called out, to our great joy, that they had got him; and in about half an hour more the boat was alongside. The body, for he was apparently dead, was immediately hoisted in, the boatswain saying he was in the act of sinking just as they reached him, although he was an excellent swimmer. Probably he had exhausted his strength by too great exertion at first.

The means practised in those days for recovery of drowned persons were then resorted to, one of which was bleeding (which has since been ascertained to be very prejudicial). The arm being tied up, Captain Surman paused, from an apprehension, as he had never blooded any person, that he might open an artery instead of a vein, a scruple of conscience that struck me as ill-timed and absurd; and I could not help expressing my opinion, remarking that, if left alone, clearly death, if it had not already taken effect, must be the consequence, and all risks ought therefore to be run. An incision was therefore made, but no blood followed. The other means, such as friction, the application of salt and strong volatiles, were continued two hours, without the smallest symptom of returning animation. At the end of that time the blood suddenly spouted out from the arm copiously for a few seconds, then as suddenly stopped; in ten minutes after which, the limbs became stiff, the colour of the skin changed, and life had evidently fled for ever. In the evening the corpse was committed to the deep.

The day after Mr. Scott's death we made St. Domingo, or, as it was then more generally called, Hispaniola, along which we ran, the next land that appeared being our destination, Jamaica, an island then considered as one of the most unhealthy in the West Indies, or in the world. This had often been the topic during the voyage, Captain Surman relating many anecdotes respecting it, and saying that several of his best friends had been carried off after only an hour's illness. With respect to himself, he observed, he had no reason to complain, as during his numerous visits to that place he had always been blessed with uninterrupted good health.

On 27th November 1775, we anchored within a cable's length of the shore, at the town of Kingston, the capital seaport of the island, where Captain Surman took me on shore, conducting me to a famous lodging-house situate in the High Street, kept and admirably well-managed by an elderly widow lady. Here he recommended to fix my board, there being an excellent ordinary daily at two o'clock, at which I might dine or not as I pleased. I accordingly engaged a handsome bed-chamber with a small dressing-room adjoining. At a little before two the captain accompanied me to an immense hall where a table was laid for thirty, having silver forks and spoons before each plate, beautifully white cloth and napkins, with every other correspondent requisite. I was introduced to several gentlemen as they entered. Precisely at two o'clock twenty-five of us sat down to a plentifully supplied board, having turtle in a variety of ways, the wines, madeira, hock, and port, little of the latter being drunk.

I was surprised to see the rooms precisely like those in England, windows sashed, glazed, and no larger than in Europe: the heat, consequently, was intense, even to oppression, as may be conceived in such a description of apartment, with a load of hot victuals upon the table, and twenty-five guests besides servants. So profuse a perspiration for two hours I never underwent. The attendants were black: a man named George, two young lads, and two females, Eve and Cataline. Unluckily for me Eve was stationed at the back of my chair. I say unluckily, because the noxious exhalation from her body outdid all the offensive smells that ever met a nose. Although I certainly profess no particular delicacy of stomach, it actually was so horrid it made me sick, and with difficulty I could keep in my seat. I was obliged to fortify myself with several glasses of madeira ere I could touch a morsel of victuals. No other person seemed to be at all annoyed by the dreadful effluvia. Such is the force of habit!

Our first call, in the evening, was at the most celebrated tavern in the place which Captain Surman told me was kept by a strange, eccentric fellow named Baggs, brother to the sporting and well-known Major Baggs. He had, on a former residence, in ten years acquired a fortune of upwards of twenty-five thousand pounds as proprietor of a tavern in Kingston, with which sum in his pocket he returned to England, where he burst forth upon the public in all the splendour of dress, equipage, and establishment. His object seemed to be to outshine in folly and dissipation all the puppies of the day; and he succeeded so completely that, at the end of four years, he had not a single guinea left. Whereupon, with the utmost composure, he prepared to embark once more for Jamaica, saying he was able to make a second fortune as he had done the first, and left it not in the power of any man in Great Britain to say he had acted dishonourably, or owed a shilling to gentle or simple. At the time of my arrival at Jamaica, this Mr. Baggs had been eight months returned, after having squandered away his fortune, and had resumed his occupation with extraordinary success, being in a fair way of making as rapid and large a fortune as before.

My conductor and I entered an elegant hall, brilliantly lighted with wax candles, several waiters being busily employed attending the guests in different rooms. Enquiring of a servant if Mr. Baggs was at home, he answered, "Yes, over the way," pointing to a door on the opposite side of the street. Thither we went, and found the person we sought, with three gentlemen, just rising from the dinner table. Mr. Baggs and his friends received Captain Surman very cordially, he being well known to them all. Upon my being introduced, Mr. Baggs asked whether I was related to Mr. Hickey of St. Albans Street; being told I was his son, come to settle upon the island in the profession of the law, he expressed much pleasure at seeing me, saying how happy he should be to assist me and promote my views by every means within his power, "and give me leave to add, sir," said he, "I possess some little interest and influence upon this island."

The morning after our visit to Baggs, Captain Surman took me in his *kittareen***** to the Chief Justice's, to Mr. Harrison, Mr. Welch, Mr. Baker and others, for whom I had letters, as well as to several of his own friends, of which he had many. We finished a busy morning by calling upon Mr. Robert Richards, who resided a short distance from my lodgings. He received me with a hearty welcome, but observed "a son of Joe Hickey's and a protégé of the Burkes' ought to have been with him the moment he set foot on shore." "However," continued he, "as you have taken a lodging for a month, and I am going away soon, you may as well retain it. At the same time, that shall be quite optional." And taking me to three neat rooms upon the second floor, he said, "These are exclusively yours, use them as you please. You will find everything you want. Today you and Captain Surman must dine me, and you will meet some of the principal men of the place." As Captain Surman had told me he was sure Mr. Richards would wish us to dine with him, he had declined the various invitations we received during our morning visits, and we accepted Mr. Richards's.

The following day Mr. Richards took me to Messrs. Lyon & Ridge, eminent attorneys, and old friends of both Mr. Edmund and Richard Burke, from whom I had letters to them; in fact, I fully expected to

* A one-horse chaise.

be received into their office as a prelude to my admission to practice in the Court. What then was my mortification and disappointment upon their immediately declaring the absolute impossibility of my having a chance of being put upon the roll of attorneys for several years to come; nor did they think I should be able to procure any employment worth acceptance, or such as ought to induce me to wait an opening; that at that time every attorney's office was overstocked with articled clerks, all of whom were waiting in hopes of admission upon the expiration of their indentures. The judges, finding the practitioners multiply so fast, had made a rule, intended for the benefit of the profession in general, by which the number was limited, so that it was impossible to be admitted except when a vacancy occurred. Of this Mr. Richards, who had himself been at the Bar, and filled the high office of Attorney-General, expressed some fear when he first read the letters I delivered to him; and, that fear being realized by what Messrs. Lyon & Ridge said, those three gentlemen coincided in thinking there was nothing to encourage my remaining at Jamaica. Messrs. Lyon & Ridge, nevertheless, observed that, if I preferred waiting until I could be admitted, they would readily give me a seat at one of their desks. Upon this, I begged a day to consider of their offer. On my way home, I asked Mr. Richards whether he thought I ought to accept or not. He answered, "certainly not"; for that the highest salary they could give me would not half defray my unavoidable expenses, and that I should be obliged to draw upon my father for at least one hundred pounds a year. He desired, before I gave a decisive answer, that I would consult Mr. Welch, as he would Mr. Paxton, Mr. Coleberne, and some others of the Court. This being done, they all concurred in advising my return to England.

Thus ended my Jamaica expectations; and, although in this instance I could attach no blame to myself, I felt greatly distressed at again disappointing my father; nor could I venture a conjecture of what was to be my future lot. I had been obliged to take twenty pounds from Mr. Irwin to defray my expenses at Grenada; and, where I now was, money would be required every month. Mr. Richards, the morning after my determination to return, observed I must want cash while at Jamaica. He therefore desired I would at my leisure draw for one hundred pounds, which amount he presented me with. My conscience smote me for thus trespassing upon the indulgent kindness of a fond father. Yet what could I do? I had no other human creature to draw upon.

[*Deciding that his presence was no longer necessary at Kingston, Hickey set out to explore the island. He found much there to interest and delight him. Among his other acquaintances, an "elegant-looking young man" named Bonynge became the writer's sworn friend, intro-*

ducing him to his eccentric father, described as the "most outré and extraordinary old quiz that ever lived," who entertained them on his estate at Bushy Park. Hickey was much impressed by the natural beauties of Jamaica. Visiting the sugar estates of the interior, he observed the humanity of some English slave-owners and the affection and gratitude that their slaves showed, but was horrified elsewhere to see a slave-girl being brutally flogged. The "scoundrel overseer" responsible, having been knocked down by Hickey, was sent to Kingston under military escort. Hickey left Jamaica early on 17th April 1776 aboard Captain Surman's ship the New Shoreham. *Before he sailed, he had received a letter from Joseph Hickey senior in London, "positively prohibiting me from returning" and stating that "should I, in defiance of his strict injunctions to the contrary, quit Jamaica . . . I might provide for myself, as he would having nothing more to say or do with or about me."*]

I left Jamaica with considerable regret; for, independent of its being the finest country I ever beheld, the extraordinary civilities and acts of kindness I experienced from many of its inhabitants claimed my warmest gratitude. The climate agreed with me perfectly. During a residence of near five months I lived extremely free in point of wine, and kept late hours, exposed myself to the heats and damps and all the sudden changes prevalent there, yet never had the slightest attack of fever, or any malady whatever beyond headache, which pain I was subject to in every climate. I am therefore bound to speak well of Jamaica.

When off the island of Cuba, I expressed a wish to see the famous fortress at the Havannah, against which our navy and army had been so successful several years before, whereupon Captain Surman goodnaturedly hauled in for the land, and ran so near that several shots were fired at us from the different batteries we passed; fortunately none struck us, though within a few yards of doing so.

Having entered the Gulf of Florida, we experienced a current so rapid as to set us from fifty to seventy-five miles to the northward every twenty-four hours, which appeared the more extraordinary as the wind blew strong from the north, thereby raising a high, short, and disagreeable sea, which tumbled us about sadly. We had scarcely cleared the Gulf when a violent storm arose, in the commencement of which we saw at a distance the two ships that had run from us off the west end of Jamaica. The gale increased so much at night we were obliged to lay to under bare poles, and blowing dead onshore began to be under some apprehensions. At daylight the other two ships, that had been to leeward, had made so much better weather of it than we did that they were four miles to windward of us. This increased our alarms. The third morning the ship suddenly sprung so dangerous a leak as to make it necessary to keep the pumps constantly going; and even then the water gained so fast that Captain Surman told us there was no alternative or chance of preservation but by bearing up and endeavouring to make the port of Charles Town in South Carolina, which, by reckoning, was directly under our lee.

We accordingly set our foresail, running for the land, which we saw close to us at three in the afternoon, before sunset got a pilot on board, and by dark came to an anchor off the town. Several armed boats came alongside, the officers from which told us our ship would certainly be made a prize of, as war was declared and they had many frigates out. Captain Surman, upon hearing this, immediately addressed a memorial to the Governor, stating that an act of providence had sent him into port for the preservation of the lives of those on board; he therefore trusted he should be allowed to refit and depart. This document Captain Surman read to me for my opinion previous to sending it, observing at the same time I must make up my mind to becoming a prisoner, as he was convinced no advantage would arise from his statement, the Americans in general, especially those of the southern provinces, being the basest and most unprincipled people under the sun. Upon this occasion, however, he did them injustice, the answer to his memorial being extremely liberal. It stated that Americans warred not with providence; that, the elements having forced the *New Shoreham* into their harbour, they scorned to increase our misfortune by using a right they were entitled to; and therefore every relief and assistance within their power should be afforded, and permission to depart when repaired to a distance of twenty leagues from their coast without molestation.

In consequence of this handsome determination, carpenters and other artificers were sent on board, the leak found and stopped. In three days she was reported fit to proceed, and an order was forthwith sent on board for us to put to sea within twelve hours, a pilot attending to conduct us out. Neither Captain Dobbins* nor myself was permitted to go on shore during our short stay; but we daily received an ample supply of fresh provisions, fruits, vegetables and bread from the town. Having passed the bar, we stood away with a fine fresh breeze.

Before we had been a week at sea the leak broke out afresh, not much to the credit of the Carolina workmen; and, bad weather coming on, it increased so quickly as to keep one pump at work night and day. Being attended with rain made it extremely disagreeable, from the necessity of keeping everything close shut, by which the steam from the sugar in the hold turned every article in our cabins the colour of lead, causing, too, a most offensive smell. Notwithstanding which

* A fellow passenger, on his way home after more than sixteen years' military service in the West Indies.

state of the ship, a branch of an Arabian jessamine, that was tied up
to the deck between the beams in the great cabin, continued blossom-
ing and bursting into beautiful flower the whole voyage, and arrived
at London in the most perfect vigour and condition. This is a very
extraordinary plant, the produce of Jamaica for many years back but
said to have come originally from Arabia. Its height, when full-grown,
is from forty to fifty feet, with a great spread of branches. The flower,
which is a bright red, is uncommonly rich, yielding a strong aromatic
scent, and is in full beauty before a single leaf makes its appearance.
It is a hardy plant: the piece I am speaking of I saw Captain Surman
tear off the tree, chuck it into the boat, and send it off to the ship just
as if it had been to burn, without the least care or attention; nor was
anything done to it during the passage; yet no part of it seemed at all
dry or decayed.

Captain Dobbins, who was a strong, robust man, proved a useful
hand at the pump, where every soul on board, including even the
commander, took his spell in turn, except that we passengers were not
summoned to it during the night. It continued to blow hard, but fortunately from the north-west, which was nearly right aft. Not a day
passed without something giving way, such as tacks, sheets, halliards,
or braces, which made the demand for cordage so frequent that at last
we had not a single fathom left. On the banks of Newfoundland the
weather was horridly bad, and notwithstanding a severe gale of wind,
there was so thick a fog we could not see the length of the ship. This
I was told is peculiar to that part of the world.

On 12th June, at daylight, a large fleet was seen right ahead, lying
to, which as we approached were ascertained to be men-of-war and
transports. At eight, one of the frigates spoke us, saying they were
bound to America with troops and stores, had been eight days from
Cork, five of which they had laid to in the same gale that was then
blowing. They also gave us the bearings of Cape Clear, distant, as
they supposed, forty-five leagues. As this corresponded exactly with
our ship's reckoning, Captain Surman stood on with confidence, knowing that one hundred and thirty-five miles would allow us a fair run
for thirty hours. It had always been a practice of his, when wind and
weather permitted, to run up mid-channel until abreast of the Isle of
Wight, which was the first land he made unless he happened to see
Guernsey, which he told us we most likely should have a view of by
noon the following day.

From the time of Mr. Scott's death, as already stated, Jerry Griffin,
the boatswain, had taken the command of a watch in his stead. The
night of the day on which the frigate spoke us, he relieved the second
mate at midnight, when he observed to him there was a great change
in the sea, which was become much smoother although the wind had

not decreased; he therefore supposed we must be well up-channel. This the mate did not think possible. Jerry commenced his usual walk, keeping a good look out. We were then running before the wind under double-reefed topsails, the topgallant masts and yards being down upon deck. He soon observed a black object upon the horizon, which at first he imagined to be a cloud; but, seeing it stationary, he then supposed it a ship. In about an hour it had so much increased in size that he became alarmed and called the mate, who could not discern anything. But, as the men upon deck all saw it and pronounced it land, he went to the captain's cabin and awakened him, telling him we were near some land; whereupon Captain Surman jumped up, and so did I, having heard him called. The moment the captain got upon deck he cried out, "Zounds! it is the Island of Guernsey. Here's the Gaskett lights within half a mile of us, and we shall certainly be upon the rocks." All hands were instantly summoned, the yards braced up, and the ship brought upon a wind. In less than an hour the day broke, when to our surprise and terror we beheld the black and terrific stony sides of Guernsey, with a most tremendous sea breaking over the rocks almost around us, some of them being within a few hundred yards. I thought nothing could save us. Providence, however, preserved us from destruction and we cleared every danger, passing so close to one set of breakers that I could have jumped upon them. It was a truly terrific and awful scene. By five in the morning we were well out to sea again, and the wind fell considerably. We therefore once more stood our course up-channel. By noon it became quite moderate and turned to a beautiful summer day; at sunset we saw the Isle of Wight and a number of ships standing in different directions; at daylight of the 14th saw the south foreland, and at half-past five anchored in the Downs, a fine clear day, not a cloud appearing.

Captain Dobbins having proposed that we should travel together to London, we took leave of our good-tempered commander, went on shore, and I once more entered the Hoop and Griffin Inn, where I ordered breakfast. At eleven we got into a post-chaise, and between four and five reached Rochester, putting up at the Crown, where Dobbins proposed staying the night. We made dinner and supper in one, walked to Chatham in the evening, and the next morning proceeded to London. As black was a cheap and good travelling dress, I had put on a suit of mourning. Having no intention of going to my father's after the letter I received from him at Jamaica until I had first felt my way a little, I advised Captain Dobbins, instead of going to a noisy inn, as he had intended, to let me introduce him to Lowe's Hotel, as far preferable in every respect. He agreed, and we there dined together, after which he went in search of his agent, and I to take a sly peep at St. Albans Street. Calling at Davies's mineral water warehouse, which was only three doors from my father's, I was informed that all my family were in town, and that an account had just arrived of the death of my brother Henry at Madras, whose loss I sincerely deplored.

Not knowing what was to become of me, or how I should act, it after much cogitation occurred to me that I had better consult my steady and attached friend, William Cane, Esq., upon the subject. I therefore immediately bent my steps to his house in Berners Street, but found he was at a country house at Erith, in Kent. The following day, with a clean shirt in my pocket, I set out for Erith, intending to walk the road until some return chaise should overtake me. Thus I marched to Shooter's Hill, when I reflected that, should Mr. Cane's house be full of company, my going there uninvited and unexpected might not be prudent. I therefore resolved to alter my plan by going to Gravesend, and from thence to address a letter to my friend stating the disagreeable situation I was in, and asking his advice. I stopped at Dartford, where I dined, drank a bottle of port, which gave me new vigour, and then continued my pedestrian journey, reaching Gravesend at seven in the evening. This was the longest walk I had ever taken, being full five-and-twenty miles, and I felt fatigued by it.

The next morning I wrote and sent my letter, and in the evening received the kindest answer, desiring me directly to come to his house, where a cordial welcome awaited me, that he would talk over the state of my affairs and see what plan would be best to adopt in future. To Erith I accordingly went, the family then consisting of Mr. and Mrs. Cane, Mrs. Johnston, her mother, and one child, a beautiful boy of four years old. The house, although upon a small scale, was neat and convenient, delightfully situated upon the edge of the Thames, down to which his garden went, his famous cutter, which I have already spoken of, lying at moorings within a few yards of his steps, forming a very pretty object. Mr. Cane's establishment was rather splendid than otherwise. He had an excellent town house in Berners Street, six male servants within doors—that is, his own man, two in livery, coachman, postilion, and groom, besides which there were two gardeners, a helper in the stable, and four hands in the cutter. He had five beautiful carriage horses, with three for the saddle, a coach, post-chaise, and phaeton. Being somewhat of an epicure, his table was always well furnished, and he took special care to have the best of wines.

At Erith I was surrounded with every elegance, and treated with respect and kindness by each individual of the family. We spent the first day very cheerfully, Mr. Cane forbidding anything relative to business. The next day he told me that, from the disposition he understood my father to be in respecting me, I must not expect much, or that he would even see me, adding, "But don't be cast down by what I have said. We shall be able to strike out something for you without his assistance; upon which point we shall have sufficient time and opportunities to consult together during a voyage I am going upon in a few days with some friends—and which party you shall join." He then ordered his phaeton, and I accompanied him therein to London, ordered my trunk from Lowe's Hotel to Berners Street, and after purchasing a supply of ready-made linen from Blunt's warehouse at Charing Cross, returned in the same carriage to Erith.

ENGLISH INTERLUDE

O N the 20th (of June) the company that were to go upon the cruise assembled at Mr. Cane's, consisting of Lord George Gordon (who afterwards engaged so much of the public attention and was the primary cause of the dreadful riots of 1780)—he was then a gay, volatile, and elegant young man, of the most affable and engaging manners; George Dempster, Esq., a member of Parliament and Secretary to the Order of the Thistle, the badge of which he wore suspended to a broad green silk ribbon round his neck; Sir Charles Bingham, afterwards created Earl of Lucan; Mr. Stephenson, who had made a large fortune in the East India Company's service at Bombay; Mr. Cane and myself, making six in number. The gentlemen above specified were all men of superior talents; and being of exactly the same political way of thinking, condemning the folly and injustice of the Government in endeavouring to dragoon the Americans into unconditional submission, we were in no danger of arguments or difference of opinion upon that head. Upon Mrs. Cane and her mother leaving the table after dinner, our host desired each guest to fill a bumper of champagne, which being complied with he gave, "Success to the Americans," a toast that was applauded by all present with enthusiasm, and which we daily did due honour to during the time we were out.

At night we went on board the *Henrietta*, the cutter being so named in compliment to Mrs. Cane, where we retired to our respective cots. Before break of day the crew got under weigh (having four additional hands, besides a channel pilot, for the voyage), standing down the river with a fine breeze at north-west. At seven we passed Gravesend. It having been previously resolved to keep early hours, we assembled to breakfast precisely at eight o'clock, dined at two and supped at nine.

In the evening we entered Margate Pier, where we landed, attended the Rooms, supped, and returned on board to sleep, the people directly warping out and bending their course towards Boulogne, off which port we found ourselves upon rising in the morning. The tide being out, we came to an anchor, stepping into our yawl to row on shore; but, when within thirty yards of the harbour, she grounded. A dozen flat-bottomed boats then approached, from whence issued a parcel of Amazonian fish women, with their petticoats rolled close up, their whole thighs being bare. These masculine creatures seized hold of us, lifting us, whether we would or not, out of the yawl and carrying us in their arms to the land, a smart contest, in which several of them lay sprawling in the sea, taking place who should secure the prey. One of our party, Mr. Stephenson, struck by the appearance of a fine, plump, naked thigh, wanted to ascertain whether the feel would correspond with the looks of the flesh, and put down his hand for that purpose; but the very instant that he did so the two women that had hold of him let go, and plumped him flat upon his back in the water, to the great entertainment of us all, who thought he deserved the ducking for his folly.

Upon reaching terra firma, we immediately proceeded to the houses of Messrs. Meriton and Smith, eminent English wine merchants, who carried on a prodigious trade in that town. Mr. Smith, who was well acquainted with Mr. Cane and Mr. Dempster, received us with true hospitality. After having sacrificed freely at the shrine of Bacchus, Lord George Gordon proposed a dash off to Paris for a couple of days, which being agreed to, three *voitures* were sent for, to be at the door at daybreak the next morning, when the whole party set off, and early on the third day entered the French capital, driving to a handsome hotel in Rue St. Sauveur.

The general appearance of the city by no means answered my expectation or the opinion I had formed of the far-famed Paris. It, however, certainly contains a number of magnificent public edifices. Mr. Cane and I went to visit Messieurs Panchaud, two brothers, who carried on the business of bankers, and with whom I had become acquainted at my father's in London, where they generally went once a year. They invited our party to dinner the next day, giving us a very cheerful "Faire Fête." We there met several of the *noblesse*, most of whom accompanied us to the opera in the evening. The following day we went to Versailles and saw the Royal Family at chapel.

Having made the most of our time and seen the rarities of Paris, we on the 28th (of June) commenced our journey back to Boulogne, arriving at Meriton and Smith's on 1st July, where we took another batch of his excellent wine, and prepared for sea, Mr. Cane sending on board the *Henrietta* a plentiful supply of champagne and claret, the hampers containing the same half filling the cabin. On the 2nd we sailed out of the harbour at high water with a fine fresh breeze from the south-west, which drove us on at a fine rate, bending our course across the Channel direct for Portsmouth.

We left Portsmouth the 18th, early in the morning, and on the 26th our party landed at Erith in high health and spirits, finding Mrs. Cane and family perfectly well. The same evening Lord George Gordon and the other gentlemen left us. The following day Mr. Cane took me to town, where he said business would detain him some days. Calling at the Jerusalem Coffee House, I there heard that my old friend and shipmate, Mr. Jacob Rider, was returned to England with an ample fortune, residing in Upper Harley Street. I immediately went in search of him, and found him in a capital good house, splendidly furnished. He introduced me to his wife, whom he had married in Bengal, by whom he had one child, a fine little girl then four years of age. He received me with the most affectionate regard, said he had lately made many enquiries about me in St. Albans Street, and was sorry to see I was in disgrace with my father, who seemed greatly offended with me. "However," added he, "I and the rest of your numerous friends and well-wishers must exert our influence to bring about a reconciliation; and that once effected, away with you to Bengal as fast as you can, where in the new Court established at Calcutta I am certain you will succeed, nature having intended you for the profession of the law."

Upon my return to Berners Street, I told Mr. Cane what Rider had said; and he was of the same opinion, promising me he would directly apply to all his India connections respecting the obtaining leave for me to go out as an attorney. The next day he took me to visit Mr. Gregory, who had resided for many years in India, where he had acquired an immense fortune, and was then a Director, with whom he was upon the most intimate terms. This gentleman readily promised to give his interest towards promoting the object I had in view, observing that I ought not to think of going out until the spring, which would not only secure me a good passage, but make me arrive at Calcutta in the most pleasant and healthy season of the year. Having ascertained that my father was gone to Bath, I called in St. Albans Street to see my sisters, from whom I grieved to learn that he continued inexorable respecting me, and was resolved to interest himself no further about me.

After passing a week in town, I returned with Mr. Cane to the elegant and tranquil scenes of his retreat at Erith, where everything was so comfortable and so pleasing as to make time glide away imperceptibly. Our mornings were spent in either sailing, riding on horseback, or driving in my host's phaeton to visit the numerous friends he had in the neighbourhood. In the latter end of the month of July, a relation of Mr. Cane's, Mr. Peter Wybrants, a fine young man, came over from Dublin for the purpose of being entered at the Temple, being intended for the Bar. This young gentleman had chambers of his own but spent much of his time in Mr. Cane's family, who were all sincerely attached to him. He therefore joined us on a party to Margate, where Mrs. Cane had been directed to go for the benefit of sea bathing.

On the 31st, Mrs. Cane (who never ventured upon the water) with her mother, Mrs. Johnson, departed for London, and from thence proceeded the following day by land to Margate. In the afternoon of the same day, Mr. Cane, Mr. Wybrants, and myself embarked in the *Congress*,* with a fresh south-west wind, reaching the place of our destination almost in the same moment that the ladies did. We immediately went to an excellent house that Mr. Cane had, by letter, engaged in Cecil Square, close to the new Rooms. After three days' sojourn Mr. Cane, Mr. Wybrants, Mr. Stephenson (whom I have already spoken of) and myself, set out on an expedition to Boulogne and down Channel. As we did not intend to remain many hours at Boulogne, instead of entering the harbour we came to an anchor outside the bar and went on shore in the boat, dined at Meriton and Smith's, returning at night to the *Congress* with an ample supply of wines for the voyage.

We immediately made sail, steering direct for Beachy Head, intending to visit Brighthelmstone and stay there some days. During our passage across the Channel it came on to blow strong from the southwest, a high sea arose, which made Mr. Stephenson so violently sick we apprehended his bursting a blood vessel. After a most boisterous night, we the following day made the English coast, and soon saw Beachy Head, distant about seven leagues, at which time it blew so hard we could scarcely carry a close-reefed mainsail and storm jib, the sea making a fair breach over us every moment, the pilot assuring us it would become much worse when off the pitch of the Head; upon hearing which, Mr. Stephenson begged most earnestly that he might be put on shore, he cared not where; for, if he were obliged to remain on board another night, he was sure he would die. Mr. Cane thereupon directed the pilot to stand close inshore in hopes of meeting with some fishing boat. We accordingly did run for the land, and the pilot soon informed us we were off the little village of Eastbourne. A small boat coming alongside, the people belonging to her said the gale would certainly increase, which induced Mr. Cane to resolve to stop a few hours to wait the result of the weather. Our whole party got into the boat and were landed through a tremendous surf which completely drenched us.

Eastbourne, since become a fashionable place of resort, was then only an insignificant fishing town consisting of about eight or ten scattered houses. The boatmen conducted us to the only public house

* During their expedition to France, Mr. Cane and his friends had re-christened his cutter the *Congress* as an indication of their pro-American sympathies.

in the village, a miserable-looking dwelling from the outside as I ever beheld, where from its appearance we expected neither victuals, drink or any sort of comfortable refreshment. Upon entering, however, we were shown into a very clean room where the landlady in five minutes made a cheerful and blazing fire. Whilst employed drying our clothes, Mr. Cane made enquiries whether we could have anything to eat. The hostess replied, if we could put up with fish and poultry, she could supply us; but she had no butcher's meat remaining. Being told we should be content with whatever she could produce, she promised to do her best, and in half an hour we sat down to a beautifully white tablecloth, and she brought in as fine a dish of fish as ever was seen at Billingsgate, with excellent lobster and oyster sauces. This was fol- lowed by a pair of tender, well-dressed chickens, and we finished an ample repast with good old Cheshire cheese. Concluding no wine was procurable in such a house, we washed down our food with tolerable ale; but one of the gentlemen asking if they ever sold wine of any sort, the landlady answered, "Yes, sometimes; but she could not expect such gentry as we would be able to drink it." A bottle was thereupon ordered, not with any intention of drinking it, but merely for the benefit of the mistress of the mansion, who had furnished us with so admirable a meal. A bottle being opened, I poured out a glass, which smelling, I found to be claret, and tasting, pronounced it very fair wine. Mr. Cane thereupon took some, which he instantly declared to be as high-flavoured claret as any in his own cellar. The consequence was a liberal potation, each of us drinking full two bottles. Another matter of surprise awaited us; for, upon calling for a bill, the landlady made a demand of eighteen pence apiece, amounting to six shilling. "Six shillings, my good lady," said Mr. Cane, "is indeed a most moderate demand; but you must tell us what we are to pay for drink as well as eating." "Oh, dear gentlemen," replied the woman, "I can make no charge for that. You are heartily welcome to the wine, and I'm glad you were able to drink it. The case is, my poor boys now and then run over to Guernsey on little matters of business and generally bring home with them a few dozen of wine which I seldom find occasion to use, and as it costs me nothing you are heartily welcome, and much good may you do with it."

By a few more questions we ascertained that her "poor boys" were neither more nor less than professed smugglers. With considerable difficulty we prevailed upon her to accept a guinea for as excellent a repast as ever four hungry fellows sat down to, and then began to talk of returning on board the *Congress* to proceed on to Brighthelmstone. Mr. Stephenson thereupon declared that nothing should induce him ever to set foot on board a ship or vessel of any kind again; and, as it still continued to blow hard, he advised the whole party to send to

Lewes for chaises and go across by land to Brighthelmstone, leaving the *Congress* to the management of her crew to convey her round by sea; orders to which effect were in consequence forthwith given to Johnson.

Having procured carriages from the nearest town, we reached Brighthelmstone in the course of two hours and a half. Here we anxiously looked out for the *Congress* that we might change our clothes, having nothing with us except what was on our backs. The morning, however, appeared without any tidings of the cutter. We were therefore under the necessity of sending to a slop shop and each purchasing a shirt, etc. After passing another anxious day at the principal inn, and still hearing nothing of the *Congress*, the south-west gale continuing with unabated force, Mr. Cane determined to return to Eastbourne in search of her.

After breakfast the second morning, Cane, Wybrants, myself and Tyger (an immense-sized Newfoundland dog of Mr. Cane's) stepped into a post-chaise with four excellent horses, and set off for Eastbourne, where upon our arrival we learnt that the cutter had been seen about six o'clock that morning running by to the eastward, apparently in distress, having no jib boom and the mainsail lowered down; that, while a boat was preparing to go off to her assistance, she hoisted her cross-jack and topsail and run up-channel before the wind at a great rate. Upon receiving this information we continued our journey along the coast, hoping she would stop at the first secure place. The wind was extremely high and blew in such violent gusts that at times we thought chaise, horses, and all would be driven bodily to leeward. The wind was from the sea; otherwise I should have felt very uncomfortable in running along the tops of exceedingly high hills and within a few feet of the edge of perpendicular precipices of many score fathoms deep.

After stopping at every town and fishing village on our route without getting any intelligence respecting the *Congress*, we late in the evening reached Dover, where we supped and slept. Early the following morning we walked down to the pier, when the master of one of the Custom House schooners said he had observed a cutter of the description we mentioned pass the evening before, at an immense rate, and stand round the foreland into the Downs. We thereupon continued our journey to Margate, where we found the *Congress* very quietly lying at anchor.

Johnson laid the whole blame upon the pilot, who he spoke of as being frightened out of his wits when off Beachy Head from the sea breaking heavily on board every two or three minutes; so much so that he (the pilot) insisted upon bearing away to prevent her foundering, notwithstanding he (Johnson) strongly objected, stating the neces sity of getting to Brighthelmstone, as he knew neither his master or friends had a change of linen with them. The pilot, however, said he alone was responsible for the safety of the cutter, and bear up he would and did.

As we were fatigued by our hurried journey along the coast of Hampshire, Sussex and Kent, we complied with the wish of Mrs. Cane and her mother by staying at home the whole evening, determining to play a family rubber at whist, take an early supper, and retire to bed by ten o'clock. After playing one rubber, I became so drowsy that I requested Mr. Wybrants to take my place at the card table, which he did; and I seated myself by the fireside, where I fell into a profound sleep, from which I awoke in the tortures of the damned, bouncing up and screeching with a dreadful pain in the right foot. The whole party seemed to enjoy my distress, laughing immoderately until the severity of the pain occasioned me to faint. All then were in the utmost distress on my account. Upon recovering myself, I entreated my boot might be cut off, which Mr. Wybrants instantly effected, and my foot was discovered to be in a dreadful state of inflammation. Oil and a variety of remedies recommended by the ladies were applied, but without procuring me the least relief. A surgeon was thereupon sent for, upon whose appearance I first learnt the cause of my sufferings arose from a severe burn. Mr. Cane not at all aware of the mischief he was about to do, observing me sitting cross-legged and fast asleep, twisted a piece of paper, which he dipped in the wax of the candle, and lighting one end, lay it upon the top of my foot. I had on a pair of thick wax leather boots, and so deep and profound was my sleep that the entire paper was consumed before the anguish awakened me. So grievously had it operated that the upper part of the leather was burnt to a cinder. The surgeon, having examined and dressed my foot, ordered me to bed, there to remain until he saw me again. He then told Mr. Cane that he was apprehensive from the situation and appearance of the wound some of the large vessels were so materially hurt that I might be a cripple for life, upon hearing which my friend Cane was beyond measure distressed. He instantly dispatched an express to London to summon Mr. Robin Adair to come and attend me; but that gentleman happening to be at Bristol at the time, Mr. John Hunter, who had undertaken to act for him during his absence, instantly left town and came to me. After meeting the Margate surgeon and inspecting my foot, he at once declared no ill consequence would arise, and that a few days' quiet, keeping my leg in a horizontal position, and frequently applying an embrocation which he ordered, would completely cure the hurt. And so it proved; in a week I was perfectly recovered, but during that period I was kept upon chicken broth and not allowed a drop of wine lest fever should ensue. The whole family had attended me with the utmost assiduity and kindest attention, Mr. Cane or Mr. Wybrants being constantly in my room, reading or contriving some means to amuse me. The ladies, too, generally passed a couple of hours daily in my chamber. Mr. Cane was much hurt at the suffering he had occasioned me, declaring every hour his concern, adding that it would for the remainder of his life prevent his ever using, or permitting where he could prevent it, any practical jokes of the same kind.

On the 11th I was so perfectly recovered as to be able to take a hard day's sail with Mr. Cane; and he then said, if the wind continued in the same quarter and equally fresh, he would the next day run over to Boulogne. Returning at six o'clock, completely drenched from the sea's breaking over us every five minutes, we took a larger allowance than usual of claret, I having as usual previously dispatched a bottle of champagne. After receiving three or four different summonses to coffee, we about ten o'clock went upstairs to the ladies. I had my recollection perfectly, but felt that I was very drunk and could scarcely stand. I, however, accomplished the getting to the drawing-room, where I seated myself as quickly as possible. The heat of the fire brought on a sickness of my stomach which made it necessary for me to retreat rather precipitately. Having cleared my overcharged stomach, I felt relieved but became so giddy I thought it prudent to follow the advice of the housekeeper, and instead of returning to the family went to bed, where I immediately fell into a profound sleep from which I did not awake until I perceived the sun shining brightly into my room, and looking at my watch found it was past nine. As we were to have started at five in the morning, I bounced out of bed, dressing myself with the utmost dispatch, went out to enquire the reason I had not been called. Meeting Mr. Cane's valet, I asked the cause of his master's not having risen to embark for France; upon which he said, "Is it possible, sir, you did not hear the confusion we were in for three hours last night? My master fell downstairs, and we all thought he was killed. My mistress was from fright thrown into hysterics, and screamed so violently I should have thought it must have awakened the soundest sleeper. In half an hour the house was filled with physicians and surgeons. The first report was that my poor master was dead, but I had soon the consolation to hear the surgeon reply, 'It may be so, but I'll answer for it he is only dead drunk.'"

Luckily, he sustained no material injury in his fall, which was head-long down a flight of twenty steps. His escape was extraordinary, he being a very heavy man. After I left the drawing-room, I understood, he got up to give some orders relative to our intended excursion the following morning, and in descending the stairs his foot slipped and he fell to the bottom, miserably bruised but without any fracture. His spirit urged him to appear at the dinner hour, when it was evident he suffered much, though he affected to laugh it off, thereby highly offending old Mrs. Johnson, who said he ought, instead of attempting to turn the accident into ridicule, to express his grateful thanks to a beneficent providence for preserving his life.

Mr. Cane, notwithstanding the remonstrances of his wife and her mother, and his being really scarce able to move, resolved to set off the following morning for Boulogne. Mrs. Cane begged me to exert my influence to prevent his going, observing how unfit he was to undertake such a jaunt; besides which he had engaged a large party to dine with him in Berners Street on the 17th, and it was then the 14th. I accordingly said all I could to dissuade him from going, but in vain; and at six in the morning of the 15th we sailed from Margate pier with a fresh breeze at south-west, which, although as dead a wind as could blow against us, and with an immense high sea, we nevertheless worked down to Boulogne by three o'clock in the afternoon, and by half-past four were housed with Mr. Smith in his comfortable parlour.

We found him just going to the dinner table, accompanied by two gentlemen, Captain Gamage, Commander of the *Belmont* East India-man, who was a cousin of his (Mr. Smith's) and come over to spend a month with him, and a Major Stuart, whose family (Scotch) had all been sincerely attached to their royal namesake, and his ancestors had followed the unfortunate monarch's fortunes. This Major Stuart had been born in France, and from his infancy employed in the military line, being honoured with the *Cordon bleu*, or Order of the Holy Ghost. He was, at the time I am speaking of, a fine-looking old man, apparently about sixty-five. This triumvirate we joined, partaking of a most excellent dinner. Champagne and burgundy were quaffed very liberally except by Mr. Cane and myself, we having previously most wisely determined to be upon our guard and to avoid excess. We therefore resisted all the solicitations and all the jibes of our companions, resolutely persisting in our refusal to touch either of the above-mentioned wines; but, as neither of us apprehended any danger from generous claret, we took a fair quantity of that. At eight in the evening, Johnson entered the room to say it was high water and the sooner we were on board the better. Mr. Cane had upon our arrival mentioned he was come to pass only three or four hours. He, therefore, rose to depart. Mr. Smith opposed our leaving him so soon; but, upon Mr. Cane's saying he must do so, having a large party of noblemen and gentlemen to dine with him in London the next day but one, he made no further objection, merely saying, "I am so sorry I must lose you so soon; but your reason for going is of such a nature as to make it incumbent on me to yield, and I shall therefore only require you to take the landlord's bottle at parting." To this no objection could be made; for, as the party consisted of five, a couple of glasses each would do the business. In that notion, however, we literally "reckoned with-out our host." In a few minutes his servant entered with such an enormous decanter as I never before beheld, full of claret. Cane bounced up, protesting he neither could nor would stay to encounter such an unreasonable quantity of wine. Mr. Smith declared we were in honour bound to drink "the landlord's bottle."

After much argument we set to and, in less than two hours emptied it, he admitting that it held rather more than ten quarts. My stomach revolted two or three times; but, by eating olives, I kept the wine down until our task was finished, when we rose from table and, taking leave of our companions, staggered to the pier, and got safely on board the *Congress*. By twelve o'clock at night we had, as we hoped, got fairly out of the harbour and over the flats, when she suddenly took the ground, becoming fixed and immovable. Here we remained till five in the morning of the 16th, when, the flood-tide having made, she once more floated and we commenced our voyage. I thereupon retired to my cot; but the motion of the cutter was so violent it set the wine aworking and I became dreadfully sick, continuing so the whole pas-sage across the Channel. We ran at an immense rate, so that by ten o'clock we were rounding the North Foreland where the water became smoother and I was enabled to get some sleep. This quite restored me, and I awoke at two in the afternoon a new man. Going upon deck, I had the pleasure to find we were past the Nore, running up the river at the rate of twelve knots an hour. By five we landed at Gravesend, got into a chaise-and-four, and before seven were seated in the delight-ful parlour at Erith.

The following day my friend Cane took me to Mr. Roberts's, an East India Director, to whom Mr. Gregory had spoken about me, and who in consequence thereof promised to obtain leave from the Court for me to proceed to Bengal in one of their ships. He received me with the utmost politeness, assuring me he should exert his interest in my behalf, and, observing there would not be another Court for near a fortnight to come, desired I would call again upon him about that time.

In the evening Mr. Cane returned to Erith, but I remained in Lon-don, being engaged to dine with my old *Plassey* shipmate, Mr. Jacob Rider, who had been some time returned from India, where I was most hospitably entertained. He told me he had spoken to General Richard Smith, Mr. Leicester, and other of his India connections, from all of whom he should get very powerful and useful recommendations for me. Upon breaking up at Mr. Rider's, I went to the Bedford Coffee House, where meeting Major Nugent, Jack Tethrington, and some others of the old set, they made me promise to dine with them the next day at the Shakespear. I accordingly did so, and there once more fell in with the choice female spirits, Pris Vincent, Newton, Sally Hudston, Kit Frederick, etc. The two first-named sung a number of delightful songs, and proved themselves in as fine voice as I had left them before my India voyage. The women all expressed great satisfaction at thus unexpectedly meeting me. This convivial party brought to my recollection many former scenes of dissipation which, though highly gratifying at the time, ultimately occasioned me acute suffering and remorse.

On the 20th, I returned to Erith, where I found Peter Wybrants just arrived before me. The following day we all went to dine with Mr. Wheatly, where we met General Desaguliers and a pleasant party of both sexes. The General, who had a fine yacht, proposed to Mr. Cane to take a sail towards Margate the next day, half the ladies present to go with him and half in the *Congress*. This being forthwith consented to, everything was arranged. At nine in the morning the company all assembled at Mr. Cane's to breakfast, from whence we embarked, running down to Northfleet where General Desagulier's yacht joined us, and his proportion of the ladies went on board his vessel.

The day proved unfavourable, being rough and boisterous. The general's boat had no chance with Mr. Cane's, the *Congress* going three feet to her one. After running about twenty miles below the Nore, we hauled our wind, the flood-tide having made. The wind was so strong we were obliged to treble-reef our mainsail, and even then she lay along very deep. When off Sheerness a Custom House shallop came off, which running past us very fast made Mr. Cane angry, and he desired his men to let out a reef, hoping thereby to keep way with them. He also desired the jib might be changed for a larger; but, aware of the influence of the latter, which is a very operative and pressing sail upon a cutter, he had most particularly directed that one man should stand by the sheet to let it fly in an instant should it be necessary. Mr. Cane was himself at the helm, and I had the mainsheet in my hand ready to ease off upon emergency. In a few minutes after our increased canvas was spread, we were summoned below, dinner being on table; but Mr. Cane, observing to me there was the appearance of a hard squall coming, said "We will remain upon deck, William, until the puff has passed by."

We then kept way with the shallop, which was upon our weather bow; the yacht we had run by as if she had been at an anchor, leaving her fast astern; when the squall suddenly took us, and a tremendous one it proved. Down we went, so low as to have five planks of her deck under water. I thought it all over and that she never would rise again. She lay completely waterlogged. The people of the shallop hove to, calling out to us to cut away the sheet or halliard of the jib. The general's yacht had ranged up close to us, and were in the act of hoisting out their boat to pick us up, thinking she must inevitably sink, when Johnson contrived by great exertion to crawl forward to the bitts, and taking out his knife cut the jib sheet, whereupon she instantly righted. This mischief arose from the fellow, who had been stationed at the jib, quitting it to clear a rope which he saw entangled in the lee shrouds; and, whilst so doing, the squall came on, immersing him so deeply in the water it required all his strength to prevent being washed away.

The ladies, who had just taken their seats at the dinner table in the cabin, were, together with plates, dishes, and every movable article, promiscuously dashed over to the lee side of the apartment, where they lay scrambling one over the other, intermixed with fowls, ham, collared meats and various viands, enjoying the fun, totally unconscious of danger, and concluding what had occurred was quite a matter of course upon a sailing party. Under which impression all would have passed over, had it not been for the stupidity of one of the company, Captain Read, of the Navy, who went into the cabin expressing his surprise at finding them so merry; "for," said he, "five minutes ago I would not have given twopence for the chance of our escape, which has been miraculous; nor was I ever in all my sea expeditions so near perishing."

Upon hearing this, the women began to scream, fall into hysterics, and betray all the usual symptoms of fright. The consequence to one of them, Miss Robinson, a lovely girl of eighteen, had nearly proved fatal. She had such a succession of fits from the alarm that her life was despaired of; nor did she recover it for many months afterwards. Mr. Cane, and indeed all of us, were astonished at the folly of Read; and Cane was particularly pointed and severe in his remarks upon his conduct. This squall subsequently caused many a laugh on board the *Congress*; for during a twelvemonth after it, if any of the glass or crockery proved deficient and Mr. Cane enquired what had become of the same, the answer invariably given was, "Oh, sir, that was broke in the great squall," although probably the subject of enquiry had been seen in use the preceding day. At six in the evening we landed, the ladies one and all protesting no consideration should ever induce them again to go upon the water.

A few days before Christmas, Mr. Roberts, with a number of Indians and others, dined with Mr. Cane, when that gentleman (Mr. Roberts) informed me he had obtained the permission of his brother Directors for my going out to Bengal, and that, if I would call at the Secretary's office within the course of a week, and make use of his name, Mr. Mitchel would do all that was requisite on my behalf.

On 2nd January 1777, I went to Mr. Mitchel, who told me the necessary documents should all be prepared for me by the 6th, on which day I found they were so; but I was not a little surprised at receiving amongst them Free Merchant's Indentures, because I had heard that it was nearly as difficult to obtain that mode of getting to India as the appointment of a writer. Mr. Gregory advised me to try to be on board the *Duke of Portland*, and gave me a letter of introduction to her commander, Captain Sutton, who behaved with the greatest civility, but expressed his concern at the impossibility of taking me in his ship, the whole accommodation being engaged for Mr. Wheler, a member of the Supreme Council. He, however, suggested the probability of my getting a berth in the *Sea-horse* which would sail at the same time, and kindly offered to speak to Captain Arthur, the commander, to receive me; and he requested I would meet him the following morning at the Jerusalem coffee house, where both he and Captain Arthur would be at noon. I accordingly observed the appointment and was introduced to Captain Arthur, who lamented his ship's being so crowded he could not give me a cabin to myself; but, if I would submit to be with three other gentlemen, I might have a passage in the *Sea-horse*. Circumstanced as I was, I without further hesitation settled the business. Captain Arthur's purser thereupon told me I must forthwith send one hundred guineas for a seat at the captain's table, which was double what I had paid to Captain Waddell in the year 1768.

A few days after I had engaged my passage, Mr. Howorth, a barrister and man of eminent talents, called upon me to introduce a brother of his, Humphrey Howorth, who was going out to India as an assistant surgeon in the service of the Company, and wished to be in the same ship with me, a wish I could have no objection to; but I told Mr. Howorth I was afraid he would find a difficulty in procuring a passage for his brother in the *Sea-horse* from her being already much crowded with passengers. To this he replied that Captain Arthur was a particular friend of his and would submit to any inconvenience to oblige him. He then asked me to dine with him on a future day, and he would get the captain to meet me.

At the appointed day I went, and was made acquainted with his brother, in whom I recognized a constant frequenter of the different billiard tables and tennis courts, to whom I had lost many sixpences. I had never heard his name, and considered him to be one of the numerous herd of pettifogging little sharpers who were constantly upon the look-out in the hope of fleecing some novice or unwary young man; nor do I believe I was much mistaken in forming such an opinion of Mr. Humphrey Howorth at the time I so used to meet him. He was my senior in years. Upon entering the room in the Temple where we dined, Mr. Howorth told me his friend Captain Arthur had consented to take his brother out to Bengal, and that his ship would probably sail early in April. The requisite cash for fitting me out and paying the passage was furnished by my steady friend Mr. Cane, without whose aid I know not what I should have done.*

Towards the end of the month (January 1777), I was attacked with the same sort of sore throat I had suffered under in the preceding autumn. I could not suppose there was anything venereal in it after what Mr. Howard† had said, and therefore treated it as arising from cold. As it did not yield at all, I became uneasy, mentioning the circumstance to Mr. Cane, who thereupon immediately took me to Mr. Adair's. That gentleman, upon inspecting, declared in the whole course of his practice he had never seen so virulent a case, adding he was astonished how I had contrived to swallow any nourishment, the entire mouth and throat being covered with the most dreadful ulcers, which from their appearance must have arisen from an old pox. I related all that had passed from the Velno's Syrup at Paris to Mr. Howard's last assertion of my being perfectly cured. As to the syrup, Mr. Adair observed the consequences that had followed were inevitable; it had merely checked the disease, leaving it to make the more dire ravage upon my constitution; but the conduct and inattention of Mr. Howard on the occasion struck him as altogether unaccountable. Mr. Cane then told him that, as I was upon the eve of departing for the East Indies, no time was to be lost; and Mr. Adair engaged to restore me to good health as ever, to effect which I must go through the very unpleasant process of salivation, and, of course, confine myself closely to my chamber.

As I could not with propriety go through a course of mercury at Mr. Cane's house, I took lodgings directly opposite my father's in St. Albans Street, which I was induced to do that I might have the use of his kitchen, of servants, etc., in supplying me with the requisite broths and other articles I should want during my confinement. I took possession of my new abode on 1st February, commencing the horrible ceremony of rubbing in the same evening. Being very susceptible of that powerful medicine mercury, I began seriously to feel its influence on the third day; and on the sixth my mouth became very sore and inflamed. A month of complete misery and pain ensued. My friends were all very kind, endeavouring by every means in their power to beguile my hours of anguish. My sisters and brother also came sometimes to see me; Mr. Cane and Mr. Wybrants never missed a day, the latter usually sitting two or three hours. With the latter occasionally came a Mr. William Burroughs, a distant relation of Mr. Cane's and then at the Temple preparing himself for the Bar. I derived the greatest

* Eleven years later, William Cane, who had meanwhile ruined himself and fled the country, was still hoping for repayment. Hickey, however, eventually discharged his debt, and the two old friends exchanged some amicable letters.

† Mr. Howard, Chief Surgeon to the Middlesex Hospital, had given a reassuring opinion on Hickey's malady, for which he had already been treated abroad.

advantage from the situation of my lodgings, especially when upon recovery, by being supplied with poultry, wines, and various good things from my father's. Mr. Adair had been uncommonly attentive during my confinement; and, as his professional skill was of the very first rate, I felt confident in a perfect cure. On 10th March, he pronounced me fit to embark for any part of the world; but he recommended me to use the warm bath and drink plentifully of sarsaparilla for a fortnight.

I therefore went to Nerot's famous baths in King Street, St. James's Square, where my career had nearly terminated. The effects of the mercury had reduced me extremely, and the heat of the bath brought on a fainting fit in a few minutes after I got in. The waiter in attendance had just then gone into another room for something he wanted. He was greatly terrified on his return to find me entirely under water, apparently dead. He roared out for assistance, which instantly arriving, I was taken from the bath, and by the application of strong volatiles soon recovered. Had the man remained absent a short time longer, probably there would have been an end of me. He got a severe rebuke for quitting the bath at all.

The first day of my emancipation I paid my respects to Captain Arthur, who told me himself and the other commanders were to take leave of the Court of Directors on the following Wednesday. He then advised me to be at Portsmouth by the 30th of the month. Whilst with him, Mr. Howorth came in, and we agreed to proceed together on that day (the 30th).

On the 14th (March) I returned to Mr. Cane's, who desired me not to engage myself for the following day, as he should have a pleasant party at his house at dinner and wished me to be present. I accordingly refused Mr. Rider and another friend who asked me; and, being detained late at the India House, the company had assembled, and before I could change my dress had sat down to table. Upon entering the room, I was agreeably surprised to see amongst the guests my father, who rose and received me with the utmost affection. Messrs. Edmund and Richard Burke were also present, who both kindly promised to give me letters to different friends of theirs in India.

The day after this dinner I had the supreme felicity once more openly to enter my father's house. He behaved with his accustomed goodness, only remarking that, as my own judgment must bespeak the necessity of a steady and decorous conduct in future, he would not distress me by a word more upon the subject of what had passed. He then presented me with fifty pounds, adding, too, his blessing and ardent prayers for my success. The crariage being prepared, he took me to Mr. Wedderburn, afterwards created Lord Loughborough and finally Earl of Rosslyn, who gave me a letter to Sir Robert Chambers,

one of the judges of the Supreme Court of Bengal. Our next visit was
to Sir George Colebrooke, then to Mr. Dunning, afterwards Lord
Ashburton, Mr. Dempster, Mr. Maclean, Mr. Potter, a Welsh judge,
and several others whose names I do not now recollect who all gave
me letters. My father wrote to Sir Elijah Impey, the Chief Justice,
with whom he had for many years been upon a familiar footing, also
to Mr. Macpherson, a member of the Supreme Council. Mr. Cane likewise procured many letters for me addressed to persons of the highest
rank in Bengal; the two Mr. Burkes wrote to Mr. Francis who had
received favours of importance from them, and they therefore had a
claim upon him; in short, I believe there never was a man better
recommended than myself. On 30th March I took leave of my invaluable friend, Mr. Cane, and his family, and of many others from
whom I had received numberless acts of kindness and civility. On the
31st I embraced my revered and indulgent father, as I verily believed
for the last time of my life, little imagining I should ever more behold
him or one of my relations; but all my wild oats were not yet sowed
nor my follies at an end.

After an affectionate adieu to my sisters and brother, Mr. Howorth
and I stepped into a post-chaise and, at four o'clock in the afternoon,
arrived at the George Inn at Portsmouth, where we found Captain
Arthur, his wife, and two of her sisters, the Miss Berties, who were
going out to India in the *Sea-horse* in search of husbands. Mrs. Arthur
was a fine, showy woman, dressed in the highest style of fashion, the
sisters rather plain in features but well accomplished. We immediately
went through the ceremony of introduction to the whole party, and
soon became familiar and pleasant.

On 1st April Mr. Wheler, with his lady and family, arrived at the
same inn where Howorth and myself were lodged. Mr. Wheler's party
consisted of himself, Mrs. Wheler, Miss Durnford (who, upon the
death of the above-named Mrs. Wheler, a few months after reaching
Bengal, supplied her place, the widower endeavouring to console himself for his domestic loss in her arms), Captain Richard Chichely
Plowden (now a Director of the East India Company) and his wife,
Mr. Markham, eldest son of the Archbishop of York, Mr. William
Harding, Mr. John Buller, and Mr. John Melville, the four last-named
being writers appointed to Bengal.

The wind remaining fixed at south-west, with fine clear weather, we
spent the time very agreeably in excursions round the neighbourhood
during the mornings, returned to Portsmouth to dinner, finishing our
evenings with the merry dance, in which the ladies of the *York* Indiaman joining us made a set of a dozen couples. In this manner three
weeks slipped rapidly away. On the 30th, whilst taking our wine after
dinner, it was announced that the wind had gone to the eastward,

whereupon preparations were immediately made for our embarkation. Several passengers went off to their respective ships that evening. Early the next morning, Captain Sutton of the *Duke of Portland* gave Mr. Howorth and myself a passage off in his pinnace, together with Mrs. Wheler and her company. Exactly at noon the three Indiamen, that is, the *Duke of Portland, York,* and *Sea-horse,* got under way. At two o'clock we sat down to an excellent dinner, our party consisting of Captain David Arthur, commander of the ship; the two Miss Berties; a nephew of the captain's (a fine boy of about fourteen going his first voyage as a guinea-pig); Lieutenant Colonel Henry Watson, Chief Engineer in Bengal; Major Lewis Mestayer of the same Corps; Captain James Dickson of the Infantry; Mr. Jacob Blaquiere, superintendent of piece goods; a son of his of thirteen, William Coats Blaquiere, a remarkably smart, clever lad; Mr. Richard Tilghman, a barrister of the Supreme Court; Mr. Robert Morse, the same; Mr. George Dallas (now a baronet), Mr. John Martin Playdell, and Mr. John Guichard Booth, all three writers for Bengal; Mr. Cleveland, an assistant surgeon; my friend, Mr. Humphrey Howorth, also an assistant surgeon, and myself; Mr. George Simson, chief mate; Mr. Henry Warre, second; Mr. James Laird, surgeon of the ship; Mr. John Wingrove, purser; and a Mr. John Cressy, being engaged in the service of Colonel Watson as head conductor of his intended works in Bengal.

This Cressy was an extraordinary creature; notwithstanding his being a superior mathematician and able mechanic, he was so deficient in point of education as to be unequal to penning a letter upon the most common subject, other than in the lowest language, void of everything like grammar. The foregoing list made the number of the captain's table twenty-two. The third mate's name was George Curtis (now an Elder Brother of the Trinity House), the fourth, Archibald Anderson. At Mr. Curtis's mess were Mr. MacCullock, now a lieutenant colonel on the Bengal Establishment; Mr. Frederick Maitland Arnott, an uncommon fine young man, going out as a cadet; Mr. James Agg, a modest and ingenious man, so superior to Cressy in address and manners as to cause great surprise to us all that Colonel Watson, in whose employ he also was, should have placed him at the third mate's mess, while the other vulgar fellow had a seat at the captain's table.

SECOND VOYAGE TO THE EAST

W E left Portsmouth on 1st May 1777, and had a pleasant run down-channel. In the Bay of Biscay we experienced some boisterous weather, as frequently occurs in that part of the Atlantic Ocean; fortunately the wind was fair, driving us on at an immense rate. We ate in the round house, where Captain Arthur and his nephew slept in swinging cots. Mr. Cressy's cot was hung in the cuddy, but taken down and stowed away every morning at seven o'clock, in order to leave a free passage to the round house, where we assembled to breakfast a little before eight. The Miss Berties' cabin was on the starboard side of the great cabin, with a private staircase from thence by which they ascended to the round house, thus entirely avoiding the steerage.

Having during both my former voyages been dreadfully ill with sea-sickness, I expected to undergo the same suffering upon this, but was agreeably disappointed, not having the slightest degree of it. Far otherwise was it with Howorth and Booth, who were excessively ill; Booth, in particular, during the first month scarcely ever left his bed. The outset of the voyage promised the utmost harmony and good humour. After being a few days at sea, Captain Arthur one day after dinner, and when the juniors of the party had left the table, proposed that we should keep "Saturday night" as a sort of jubilee evening, for which purpose claret should be drank and the merry song go round until the end of the first watch or midnight; that, as his pecuniary circumstances would not allow of his giving this weekly wine, he proposed our taking it in rotation alphabetically, he commencing. This was readily agreed to; and, after some discussion, the quantity of claret for the evening was settled at eighteen bottles.

The first Saturday went off inimitably well. We sat till twelve, having a number of capital songs by Messrs. Morse, Playdell, Mestayer, and Blaquiere senior, all of whom were proficient in music and admirable singers of catches and glees. Every person at table was obliged to contribute one song each night; and bad enough some of the performances undoubtedly were, though received with complacency and applause. After spending three following Saturday nights with the utmost conviviality and good humour, I observed to Captain Arthur that some of the gentlemen thought the quantity of wine too small and therefore wished an increase of six bottles more. Captain Arthur without the least demur agreed, adding that he would make a proposal at our next meeting that two dozen instead of eighteen bottles of claret should be allowed. He accordingly did make the motion in due season, which I seconded; when, oh, dire event! upon counting votes we were left in a minority, Captain Arthur, Colonel Watson, Major Mestayer, Howorth and myself voting for the increase, all the others against it. From this circumstance arose the dissensions and ill-temper that afterwards burst forth, producing some very unpleasant events. Captain Arthur was highly offended at being thus outvoted, and, as I conceived, not without reason. He observed that it was an indelicacy towards him, if not an absolute insult; for, as commander of the ship, it would be no more than common candour to allow him to be the judge of what was proper or otherwise respecting the internal management thereof; nor could it fairly be presumed he would sanction excess or immorality of any kind at his own table, which the majority of his passengers had by their votes plainly insinuated.

Much warmth of argument hereupon took place, which I, though unsuccessfully, endeavoured to turn off with jocularity, Captain Arthur, by nature haughty and tenacious of his powers as commander, being seriously mortified and offended, expressing over and over again his sentiments in angry terms. The party, in consequence, broke up immediately after supper without any singing and in ill-humour, Captain Arthur declaring there should be no more keeping of Saturday night. The following morning I spoke to him on the subject, observing that, as the next Saturday would be my turn to preside, I hoped he would let it go on as usual, and I trusted good humour might be restored. He was pleased to be very civil upon the occasion, paying me many compliments upon my general demeanour towards him when contrasted to that of some other of his passengers, readily consented to let my night take place, at which he would attend, but persisted in his resolution not to do so at any more. He, however, added that the round house should be at the service of the gentlemen every Saturday if they chose to meet there.

The following Saturday I exerted myself to restore harmony, which I soon found impracticable. Captain Arthur continued sulky and sullen; the two Miss Berties, taking their cue from him, became shy and reserved. Under the flimsy pretext of having colds, they refused to sing, retiring to their own private apartment as soon as the cloth was removed from table. Notwithstanding the vote, I had provided two dozen of claret. Some of our opponents having, as I suppose, counted the bottles as they were opened, refused to touch a drop beyond the eighteenth. This increased the commander's ire, who made some strong remarks upon the occasion; and the party broke up soon after eleven in a bad temper. The next Saturday to mine was Howorth's, on which night Captain Arthur and the ladies retired the moment supper was over. This offended Colonel Watson, who made some severe observations upon the captain's behaviour. The latter retorted with acrimony; and war was declared from that moment. Instead of the pleasantry and good humour that had prevailed for six weeks, we had nothing but peevishness, grumbling, and frequently extremely harsh and rude speeches interchanged.

This disagreeable change induced some of us to meet below, either in one of the officers' cabins, or in that of Mr. Dallas, who, although himself a milk-sop, very willingly offered his apartment; and this was the more liberal on his part, as we returned his civility and kindness by committing all sorts of depredations and irregularities, he being, like my friend Douglas of the *Plassey*, a man of taste. His cabin was fitted up in an elegant style, a perfect cabinet, ornamented with a handsome China paper, variety of pictures, and a large mirror, the whole of which we in some way or other deranged. These meetings in the steerage put a stop to the card parties in the cuddy, for some time at least, until Captain Arthur could form a set of his own; nor could he always collect his four, our jolly set being so attractive that we often seduced one of them, and neither of the ladies played whist. As we drank freely, we were frequently half-seas-over by supper, were consequently frolicsome and noisy, which offended our commander, producing cutting remarks at which I invariably laughed, turning what he said into ridicule; not so Colonel Watson, who always retorted with acrimony. Thus querulously we continued until drawing near the Cape of Good Hope; when something like better temper appeared from hearing we were to stop at that delightful part of the world.

On 13th July, Captain Sutton of the *Duke of Portland* spoke us to say he intended putting in, and hoped the *Sea-horse* would do the same. Captain Arthur replied he had no objection, provided the *York* accompanied. We then ran close to that ship. Upon putting the question, Captain Blanshard answered that, having abundance of water and stock on board, he should run on; but, as we must at any rate separate in a few days, his intention being to go the inner passage as the shortest to Bombay, his standing-on could make no difference to the other ships.

On the 15th, soon after daylight, we saw a large ship in the southeast, it then blowing strong from the south-west. We could just distinguish her colours to be English; she was therefore pronounced to be the Company's ship *Bridgewater*, bound to Bencoolen. At noon the same day, we made the land, at two in the afternoon were well in with the Table Mountain, and at six in the evening anchored in False Bay. We instantly were regaled with the most delicious fruits. The next morning the passengers went on shore to the house of Mr. Brandt, the Dutch Chief of this place, who, like most of his countrymen, had no objection to exchange his poultry and other articles of provender, together with execrable stuff he called wines, for British guineas. Upon landing, we sent off a messenger to the Cape Town to bring us a sufficient number of carriages to convey us thither.

In the morning of the 19th, we commenced our little journey in open caravans something resembling an English waggon, some in a miserable kind of phaeton, and some on horseback. The caravans, which, by the by, they thought proper to call coaches, were drawn by eight horses, wretched-looking, half-starved animals. Two persons sat on the box, one holding the reins and guiding the horses, the other carrying a tremendous long whip which he smacked loudly, and managed with considerable dexterity. After passing over a rocky, abominable road, the ladies complaining of the dreadful jolting, we in four hours reached the half-way house, where Mr. Wheler and his party had arrived a few minutes before. There being but one room, he invited us to join his mess, which all the *Sea-horse* passengers did, eating heartily of new-laid eggs and excellent bacon, though badly dressed. This dish, with cheese, made the whole of our fare. They gave us some stuff under the name of Constantia which, to my palate, was more like treacle-and-water than a rich and generous wine. Keen appetites, however, reconciled us to the poverty of the meal.

Our horses being reported ready, we renewed our journey, in little more than three hours arriving at the end of it. The approach to the Cape Town is extremely beautiful and romantic. In one direction is Table Bay, where during the summer months, which are the reverse of ours, the ships anchor. To the southward and eastward is a long range of stupendous mountains, amongst the nearest of which is the Table Land, so called from the top of it, for many miles in extent, being quite flat and, when seen from a distance, appearing like a table.

We took up our abode in different lodging-houses where we could find apartments. Colonel Watson, Major Mestayer, Captain Dickson, Dallas, Booth, Howorth, Arnott, Cressy, Agg and myself were in the same house, and, as we were informed, the best in the town. It was kept by Mrs. Vanrenen, a respectable and opulent widow lady. She had two daughters grown up, rather well-looking, and three younger by several years. We slept in double-bedded rooms, my companion being Mr. Arnott, to whom during the voyage I became greatly attached. He was a fine young man, in figure quite equal to Bob Pott.

Miss Hickey, one of the author's sisters, by Sir Joshua Reynolds.

By courtesy of Mrs. Harris Jonas, New York

Whampoa Pagoda, Canton. Drawn and engraved by Thomas and William Daniell.

By courtesy of the India Office Library

Soon after we left England, he told me he was a natural son of the Honourable Frederick Maitland, a post-captain in the Navy and son to the Earl of Lauderdale, by a native woman of Jamaica, on which island he (Arnott) was born.

We spent our time pleasantly enough, visiting and admiring the curiosities of that part of the continent of Africa. In the mornings and evenings, we walked in the Company's Gardens, which are well stored with curious plants, the choicest fruits and vegetables; there is also the finest menagerie in the world, in which are collected the most extra-ordinary animals and birds of every quarter of the globe. During the heat of the day we played at billiards or other games within doors. In the evening, we visited or went to the public entertainments, and generally had a dance previous to retiring to rest. Colonel Gordon, the second in command at the Cape, was very civil, showing us everything that was worth seeing. This gentleman's ancestors were Scotch; but his father, as well as himself, was born in Holland, and had from infancy been in the Dutch military service. He was a very accomplished man, an excellent classical as well as general scholar, spoke English and, indeed, all the languages of Europe fluently. Here we also met with another ingenious young man, Mr. Paterson, a great botanist, who had for several years been employed by that strange and eccentric woman, Lady Strathmore, to go into the interior of Africa for the purpose of collecting rare plants and natural curiosities of every description. Mr. Paterson published an account of his different excursions, a work that gained him some credit.

After a fortnight spent very agreeably at the Cape Town, we returned to False Bay to be ready to re-embark. On 5th August we were summoned on board our respective ships, and by three in the afternoon were fairly out at sea. To our great surprise, we found that the *Duke of Portland*, for whom between England and the Cape we were obliged to shorten sail every four hours, now out-ran us. As it was presumed this change must have arisen from the stowage of water, etc., taken in at the Cape, Captain Arthur immediately began to make various experiments and changes in the trim of the ship. Still, however, she beat us. Imagining, therefore, that they should shorten their passage by parting company, they availed themselves of blowing weather that commenced the day after we quitted the Cape, and a dark night, to get away from the *Sea-horse*. This manoeuvre of the *Duke of Portland*'s did not answer; for, in spite of her improved style of sailing, we arrived in the river Hooghly fourteen days before her.

I flattered myself that the stop at the Cape, and my shipmates mixing in general society, would have restored harmony and good humour upon our again coming together on board the *Sea-horse*; but I was grievously disappointed. Captain Arthur seemed more sullen and

8+

petulant than before, scarcely speaking to anyone except the ladies, Messrs. Tilghman, Blaquiere senior, and Dallas, all of whom he considered as decidedly of his party. This gave great offence to Colonel Watson, who daily made some cutting and severe remarks upon the insolent and presumptuous behaviour of commanders on board their ships, a set of people who, notwithstanding their impertinent airs, were no more than common stage-coachmen. The blockhead Cressy, too, with a view to please his patron, at times said rude and coarse things, rather at, than to, the captain, which the latter very wisely treated with the utmost contempt, thereby depriving the speaker of his object. When we had been at sea a week, Colonel Watson proposed, instead of setting in the round house after dinner, we should, upon the cloths being removed, adjourn to his, or some other, cabin and there take a few glasses of claret comfortably by ourselves; for which we had provided, whilst at the Cape, by purchasing three chests of that wine and one of hock. We had also laid in a stock of hams, tongues, sausages, herrings, etc., etc. The proposal was directly agreed to by Messrs. Mestayer, Dickson, Morse, Cleveland, Howorth, and myself, forming a party of seven, added to which we daily invited Mr. Laird, the officer not upon duty, and one of the young gentlemen. The consequence of this secession was that we generally drank too much; at least, Mestayer, who was a jovial soul, Howorth and myself did so, sitting at our bottle until summoned to supper, and often declining going to the round house at all at night, contenting ourselves with salaman gundy and other good things of our own. Sometimes, when in tip-top spirits from too large a dose of the juice of the grape, I used to go up and annoy the grave whist-players by my noise and rattling nonsense; so much so that Captain Arthur at last observed that my good humour was far more troublesome and vexatious than the crabbed moroseness and haughty reserve of Colonel Watson and others of his set.

In this manner we went on until we reached the mouth of the Bay of Bengal, about 8th October, which being too late in the season to venture upon the coast of Coromandel, where we should otherwise have stopped for a few hours, we stood down on the eastern side of the bay, had an admirable good run for seven days, and then made the land, which was entered in the log book as the island of Cheduba; upon seeing which entry Colonel Watson said it was not Cheduba but one of the islands on the coast of Arracan, considerably more to the northward. Lunar observations were not then come into general use, and none were ever taken on board the *Sea-horse*. Colonel Watson, amongst his many accomplishments, was a perfect algebraist, thereby correcting his watch to such a nicety as to render it to all intents and purposes a complete timepiece. By his account thus kept, he made the ship more to the northward and eastward than the reckonings of any of the officers; and during the voyage he had always been found right, especially with respect to the Cape of Good Hope, which we made within half an hour of the time he said we should, although by the ship's reckoning we were near three hundred miles from it.

The weather in the bay had been thick, with frequent squalls and much rain for six days successively, during which we had no observation. At dinner the day the land had been seen, Colonel Watson said aloud the island was not Cheduba, but one at least a degree and a half more to the eastward and northward. Of this remark Captain Arthur took no sort of notice; whereupon the colonel, addressing himself to Mr. Simpson, said, "I take upon myself, though no seaman, to assert that, if you stand on the same course you are now going, and at the same rate, by two o'clock in the morning you will run the ship ashore, and that very near the place where the *Falmouth* Indiaman was wrecked owing to a similar mistake, and every soul on board perished." Mr. Simson replied he thought we were further down the bay than the ship's reckoning gave; and Colonel Watson added he was clear the fact was so, and equally certain that we were at that moment upon soundings, probably in fifty or sixty fathoms. Captain Arthur, bursting with rage, looked as red as a turkey cock, puffing and blowing with more than usual violence; but he uttered not a syllable.

We continued standing on the same course, running seven knots an hour under topsails and foresail, not feeling quite comfortable at what the colonel had said, having, too, a dark night of twelve hours fast approaching and a strong gale blowing. At dusk, all hands were called to reef topsails, when most of the passengers, also Captain Arthur, were upon the quarterdeck. Colonel Watson asked the second officer, Mr. Warre, whether he had ascertained what depth of water we had; to which Mr. Warre answered, "No, sir, the captain does not consider it necessary." Colonel Watson replied aloud, "Good God! what madness or infatuation is this! Is it to be endured that a man should thus wantonly court danger and risk the lives of all on board, and to do so from sheer obstinacy?" The captain still continued silent. At eight o'clock, when the first watch was called, Mr. Simson went in to the round house to Captain Arthur, to say he thought they had better heave a cast of the lead; but the captain forbid it, observing it would be a pity to lose the time sounding would require, especially as there was no sort of occasion for it.

At eleven I turned in, and notwithstanding I felt uneasy at our precarious state, I soon fell asleep; from which I was suddenly aroused by a tremendous noise in the steerage. I jumped out of my cot and went into the steerage, where I met Mr. Booth, who had not been in bed. He immediately told me it was all over with us, that we were surrounded by rocks and no possibility of escaping. He then violently threw open the door of Messrs. Tilghman and Morse's cabin, crying out that in a few moments we must be all drowned, and desiring them to get up and help to save the ship. Mr. Tilghman, raising his head from the pillow, enquired what was the matter. "Matter!" answered Booth, "why, we are in three fathoms water, and the moment the ship strikes she must inevitably go to pieces." "That's not pleasant intelligence," said Tilghman, and directly laid himself down again in his cot. We went from thence into Mr. Cleveland's cabin, where we found him in great agitation, Mr. Blaquiere and Dickson being with him. Mr. Cleveland proposed that we should go upon deck to see if we could be of any use; but to that I objected, observing that we might increase the confusion by being in the way of the seamen, but could render them no aid and had better remain where we were. We therefore did so. It was then just three o'clock in the morning, the ship upon a wind, carrying a press of sail which made her lay down very deep. In about an hour, Dr. Laird came down with the glad tidings that we were rather deepening our water, the danger consequently decreasing; and, in another hour, Mr. Simson assured us we should do very well, having run into thirty fathoms. From him we learned the following particulars: that Captain Arthur had remained upon deck until twelve o'clock, during which time he (Simson) had repeatedly expressed his wish to sound as a matter of prudence; but the captain, notwithstanding he was evidently uneasy, resisted it, saying, "Tomorrow morning at daybreak will be early enough," and then retired to the round house; that, at midnight, when Mr. Warre, the second mate, came upon deck to take charge of the watch, he (Simson) observed to him that he felt convinced Colonel Watson was right as to the situation of the ship, and he therefore requested Mr. Warre would have everything ready for a cast of the lead and keep a sharp look out. The weather happily had become much clearer, though it still blew strong. We continued running right before it under double-reefed topsails. Mr. Warre, upon Mr. Simson's leaving him, immediately made the people pass the line forward, stationing men in each of the chains with coils ready to heave at a moment's notice. A little before two in the morning, Colonel Watson went out of his cabin and, whilst walking the quarterdeck with Mr. Warre, said he thought there was an evident change in the water, it having become smoother. He therefore had no doubt we had shoaled materially. Mr. Warre, being of the same opinion, had resolved to heave the lead without saying anything to the captain, and was in the act of ordering it, when a man from the bowsprit end cried out "Breakers right ahead and close aboard." In the same moment the leadsman hove the lead; and, finding it directly take the ground, he, in his fright, called out, "There's only three fathom." The utmost confusion and dismay ensued. Captain Arthur ran out of his cabin almost frantic, crying like a child that he was ruined past redemption and had sacrificed his own life, as well as that of all on board. In the most abject and pusillanimous manner he besought the crew and officers to exert themselves, if possible, to save the ship. In his fright he ordered and counter-ordered in the same breath, and was in such consternation he knew not what he said or did.

Mr. Simson, seeing him so incapable, advised his going to his cabin. Mr. Warre had, upon the first alarm, ordered the man at the wheel to put the helm up, braced the yards sharp up, and hauled his wind, heaving the lead as fast as it could be carried forward. The second cast we had ten fathoms, the third only seven, the fourth ten again, then several casts between seven and twelve fathoms; after which it suddenly deepened to twenty-five fathoms, when the risk was supposed to be over; yet so irregular was the bottom that, after having run at least a mile in twenty-five fathom, we had two casts with no more than seven fathom. At daylight, the mainland of Aracan was distinctly seen from deck, with breakers extending a great way out, over which the sea broke with immense fury. Our escape certainly was almost miraculous. Colonel Watson behaved with much moderation and propriety on the occasion; nor did he ever allude to the circumstance afterwards when Captain Arthur was present, a delicacy and forbearance our commander was scarcely deserving of; for his ignorance and obstinate stupidity had nearly cost us our lives.

On the 30th, a light breeze from the south-west luckily sprang up, which carried us into Balasore Roads, where we came to an anchor. At daylight of the 31st, we had the pleasure to see two schooners standing towards us with the Company's colours flying, from which they were known to be pilot vessels. By eight o'clock, one of them put a pilot on board of us, who took charge of the ship, immediately getting her under way, and stood for the river. In about an hour the wind failed; and, as the ebb tide began to make, we again brought to. We remained at anchor until four in the morning of 1st November, when we once more made sail, at noon anchored off the island of Sangor. Soon after having so done, a Bengal boat called a *paunceway* came alongside, which Colonel Watson engaged to convey him to Calcutta.

At two in the afternoon, the colonel, with his assistants, Cressy and Agg, Major Mestayer, Mr. Morse and myself, took our final leave of the *Sea-horse*. This mode of travelling did not exactly meet our approbation, *paunceways* being so constructed that you have not room to sit upright under the roof, or covering of mat to protect those within from sun or rain; nor is there any place to let your legs hang down in, passengers sitting upon a platform like tailors on their shopboard. The novelty of the thing, however, and every mile we went bringing us nearer to our destination, reconciled us to the uneasy position. We proceeded in high glee. The boat was rowed by six black fellows, who were not sparing of their labour; so that we went at a good rate, and by six in the evening arrived off Culpee, where the Indiamen and other ships of heavy burden then lay. Here we stopped to let the people rest and to wait for the next flood. Going a quarter of a mile up a creek, we landed at a poor shabby house, called a *tavern*, the appearance of which both internal and external gave us newcomers a very un-favourable idea of a Bengal house of entertainment. It was, in every respect, uncomfortable and beastly dirty. It was the colonel's intention that the party should sleep here; but not a single bed could be obtained.

In about an hour and a half after our arrival, we had served up some very excellent fish, tolerable fowls, with plenty of eggs and bacon, and what was a prodigious luxury to me who had been so long without it, capitally good bread. Claret and madeira we had plenty of in the boat; so that altogether we made a hearty meal. Having satisfied our appetites, we fixed upon a billiard table as our resting place, the colonel, Major Mestayer, and myself taking our respective stations at full length upon it. Sleep was, however, entirely out of the question from the myriads of mosquitoes that assailed us. At the end of three hours' misery, I arose and walked about the room, surprised at the hideous yells of jackals innumerable. Towards daybreak, the trouble-some insects quitted the apartment for the open air. I then lay down upon three chairs and, being exhausted from want of rest, fell into a sound sleep which continued upwards of two hours, and refreshed me wonderfully.

At eight I arose and did ample justice to the hot rolls, tea and coffee. At ten, the tide suiting, we re-embarked in our unaccommodating vessel, taking with us a plentiful supply of cold fowls and other articles of food. Colonel Watson said he hoped we should reach his house by dark; but, owing to the wind coming to the north and impeding our progress, we were disappointed. Finding this to be the case and our boat's crew quite tired from a severe day's work, it was decided that we should stop to let them refresh themselves at a small village called Woolburreah, where we all landed, Colonel Watson undertaking to procure curry and rice for us; for which purpose he began to speak Moors to the natives, which excited our mirth. We laughed heartily, not only at the language so new to our ears, but at the whole scene that presented itself and the many grotesque figures that appeared amongst the spectators. The colonel (absurdly as I conceived) took offence at our merriment, pettishly observing that, if we chose to laugh at his exertions to get us a hot meal, we might try for ourselves and see what we should make of it. We assured him very truly that our laugh was not at him but at the ludicrous figures and postures the black people put themselves into, and which was so entirely new to us.

Our apology was well received; he renewed his cookery, soon placing before us some smoking hot curries of fish and fowl, which we devoured voraciously, pronouncing them delicious, though I cannot say that I much admired them; nor did I ever become fond of Hindustani cookery. Having washed down our food with claret, we resumed our stations in the *paunceway*, rolling ourselves up in boat cloaks, and thus made it out for the night tolerably well. Between two and three in the morning, the flood tide making, we got under way; at daybreak we all mounted upon the chopper of the boat, at five came in sight of Garden Reach, where I was greatly pleased by a rich and magnificent view of a number of splendid houses, the residence of gentlemen of the highest rank in the Company's service who, with their families, usually left Calcutta in the hot season to enjoy the cooler and more refreshing air of these pleasant situations. Some of the occupants resided there throughout the year, going to town in the morning to transact their business and returning to the country in an evening. The verdure throughout on every side was beautiful beyond imagination, the whole of the landscape being more luxuriant than I had any expectation of seeing in the burning climate of Bengal.

In less than an hour we were at the upper part of the Reach, where we went on shore to Colonel Watson's, the beauty of which my powers of description are utterly inadequate to do justice to. The mansion was within a few yards of the edge of the river, upon an elevation, or bank, full thirty feet above the level of the water, commanding a noble view of Garden Reach with all its palaces downward, and upward Fort William, with the magnificent city of Calcutta, a sheet of water more than nine miles in extent, nearly two in breadth, covered with innumerable ships of different sizes. Colonel Watson had, within a brick wall, at least four hundred begahs* of land, which the East India Company had executed a grant of to him to construct docks, both wet and dry, building ships and establishing a complete dockyard. An immense range of buildings were already erected, intended for black-smiths, carpenters, sailmakers, and all the different artificers employed in a dockyard. There were also another range of handsome, well-constructed warehouses, in which were deposited naval stores of every description, working tools of all sorts, besides anchors, cables, cordage and canvas. Timber to a great value lay upon the premises in every direction; in short, there never was in any part of the world so stupendous and expensive undertaking, attempted to be carried into effect by a single individual, as this of Colonel Watson's. Yet, extensive and prodigious at it was, he would beyond a doubt have effected his object

* A begah equals about one-third of an acre.

had not a party started up to oppose and thwart him, which ultimately succeeded in the base plan, thereby stopping a work that would have done honour to the British name in Asia.

At the time I accompanied him to India, he had expended in the purchase-money, in preparations for executing this stupendous work, and collecting all kinds of stores, no less a sum than one hundred and eighty thousand pounds, an incredible amount for a private person to risk upon any speculation. Colonel Watson, whilst at Portsmouth, showed me such civility; in the course of the voyage our intimacy increased; and he observed he had little doubt but he should have it in his power to push me forward in my profession by introducing me to some of the most opulent and respectable natives. He also desired that, upon our arrival in Bengal, I would make his house my home until I could establish myself to my own satisfaction. I was highly pleased in viewing the extensive works, which the colonel took us over, explaining every part and particular. A European manager of his also attended, of whom the colonel enquired what news there was in Calcutta. The man answered he knew of none, but, recollecting himself, added, "Oh, I forgot to tell you we have lost two of our great people, General Clavering, the Commander-in-Chief, who has recently died, and Judge Le Maistre of the Supreme Court, who departed this life only the day before your arrival. I suppose you must have heard the minute guns which were fired for his funeral at sunrise this morning," said he, "from the ramparts of Fort William." The death of the judge was likely to be of importance to Mr. Morse and myself, both of us having letters of recommendation to him.

Previous to our arrival, Mr. Morse and I had agreed to keep house together; and he undertook to look out for a suitable habitation. At eleven o'clock in the forenoon, I was agreeably surprised by seeing my young friend and companion, Robert Pott, driving up the avenue in a very jemmy equipage. Our joy at meeting was sincere and reciprocal. He said he had an excellent apartment fitted up and ready for my sole use, which I must forthwith take possession of, and for that purpose accompany him in his phaeton into Calcutta; but this Colonel Watson, who overheard him, said could not be; nor would he part with me. He said he should be glad to see him (Pott) at all times at the docks, where he might have as much of my company as he pleased. He then invited him to dinner that day, which he accepted, observing that he must go back to town to tell Daniel Barwell, his chum, to entertain a large party that were engaged to dine with them. He insisted upon my accompanying him to Calcutta, which I did, finding it a pleasant ride of nearly four miles.

Although it was called the cold weather, the sun appeared to me to have prodigious influence, and to strike hotter than I ever felt it in

England at any season. Pott drove me to his residence, a noble mansion belonging to Richard Barwell, Esq., a member of the Supreme Council, who lent it to his younger brother, Daniel Barwell, and three friends, being Pott, Mr. Cator, and Mr. Gosling. I was immediately introduced by Pott in the most affectionate manner to the other inmates; after which he conducted me into very spacious rooms, elegantly furnished, and having some valuable paintings in them. They consisted of three chambers opening into each other. Pott told me these were exclusively appropriated to my use. In one, where a bed was preparing for me, Pott took from a writing desk a bundle of letters, all under one envelope, addressed to me. These he had prepared in the event of his not being upon the spot when I arrived, to ensure me a kind and hospitable reception from several of his friends. He, in these letters, spoke of me as the dearest friend he had in the world.

As one o'clock was at the time the general hour of dining, I was obliged to remind Robert and hasten him. Having fleet horses, we went back at a great rate, but found the colonel waiting for us. The next day Colonel Watson took me to the Government House to introduce me to Mr. Hastings, the Governor-General, General Stibbert, the Commander-in-Chief, and Mr. Barwell. When at the house of the latter, he observed to me in a whisper that the owner was an infamous scoundrel; that he felt a strong inclination, instead of paying him the compliment of a visit, to tell his opinion of him; "however, I suspect he is aware of the sentiments I entertain respecting him, and that I visit the public station he fills, not the individual." Mr. Francis, the other member of the Supreme Board, was then absent, being upon a visit at Chinsurah.

Pott, who always complained if I addressed him by any other title than of "Bob," having presented me with a buggy horse, I every morning drove into Calcutta directly after breakfast. Bob introduced me in the kindest manner to Judge Hyde and his family, saying to him with his usual familiar style, "My dear friend William must be taken care of; so pray mind you give him your support and interest whenever necessary," and turning to Mrs. Hyde (then a very lovely woman) he continued, "and the more civilities and attentions you show to the friend of my heart, whom I sincerely love, the more I shall love you, my charming Mrs. Hyde." To do this couple justice, they did invariably treat me with every possible degree of kind and hospitable attention.

Bob Pott likewise introduced me to Sir Elijah Impey, the Chief Justice, and to Mr. Chambers, afterwards Sir Robert, at both of which houses I was always treated most kindly. Sir Robert Chambers made a point of my spending every Saturday and Sunday with him at his house about two miles from town. His family then consisted of Lady Chambers, at that time a beautiful creature not more than eighteen

8*

years of age, two lovely children, a boy and a girl, Mrs. Chambers, mother of Sir Robert, a worthy and cheerful old lady, Mr. William Johnson, and Mr. William Smoult, both attorneys, who went out in the same ship with the judges, and under the immediate protection of Sir Robert. Mr. Johnson, at the time I arrived, was Clerk of the Crown and one of the Sworn Clerks in Equity; Mr. Smoult was Sealer and Clerk to Sir Robert. These two young men are now both dead.

A few days after my arrival in Calcutta, Mr. Morse called to say he had been informed by several persons, competent to judge of the measure, that it would be bad policy for us to live together; for that the natives, prone to mean suspicion, would conclude, when we acted on different sides as counsel and attorney, that the interest of our respective clients would be sacrificed to our private attachment to each other. Our intended junction as housekeepers was therefore given up and relinquished. This, however, made not the least alteration in our friendship or regard for each other, which continued unabated during our mutual residence in Bengal.

On 12th November, Sir Elijah Impey desired I would attend in Court the following morning, and I should be entered upon the roll. I accordingly did so, took the usual oaths and became Solicitor, Attorney, and Proctor of the Supreme Court, the latter branch being particularly productive, from the fees being nearly double in ecclesiastical business. My shipmates, Messrs. Tilgham and Morse, were the same morning admitted at advocates.

In consequence of my numerous acquaintances, I had many invitations to large dinner parties, which often led me into excess, it being the custom in those days to drink freely. Having landed in Bengal with my blood in a ferment from the intemperance committed on board ship, the evil was not lessened by daily superabundant potations of champagne and claret, the serious effects of which I began to experience by severe headaches and other feverish symptoms. On the 13th (November) I had been in town, and was returning to Colonel Watson's in my buggy about one o'clock, when I met Mr. Justice Hyde in his palankeen, who stopped me to say I was guilty of great imprudence by daily exposing myself to the sun, thereby running the risk of laying myself up with a fever. He, therefore, recommended me to have recourse to medicine forthwith. I promised to follow his advice; but, being engaged on the next day to a famous tavern dinner to be given by Captain William Palmer, I could not prevail upon myself to forgo the pleasure of joining the convivial set. I, therefore, went to the Harmonic, though suffering under an excruciating headache and pain in my back. My illness increased so much that, before dinner was half over, I was obliged to leave the table and house.

Pott, observing I turned very pale, followed me out, insisting on attending me home to his house instead of going to Colonel Watson's, a desire I willingly complied with, as I was, upon moving, seized with a violent sickness at my stomach. Being conveyed to Pott's, I was directly put to bed, my friend Bob only leaving me to procure the attendance of the doctors. He speedily returned, bringing with him James Laird and his elder brother, John Laird, then high in the Company's service and eminent in his profession. I soon perceived from the language of the latter that he was alarmed about me. Notwithstanding various medicines were resorted to, nothing would stop the vomiting, which continued the whole night, I expecting every moment to be my last. Towards morning, a delirium came on; and for four days I was not conscious of anything that passed. Upon recovering my senses, I seemed to awake as if from a horrid dream, accompanied with sensations of agonies so complicated I cannot describe. I found my beloved friend Pott, with several servants, standing by my bedside, he with a countenance expressive of the deepest sorrow; nor did he appear gratified at my knowing him, the reason of which, as I afterwards learnt, was that the physicians had told him it was all over with me, not the smallest probability of recovery remaining, but that most likely the delirium would cease a few minutes before death. He therefore concluded the fatal time was arrived. A blister that entirely covered my breast annoyed me greatly, especially one corner that was loose. I asked for a pair of scissors to cut it off. This induced Pott to suppose me again wandering; and I was astonished at his saying, "No, no, my dear William, you shall have no scissors I assure you."

I then explained what I wanted them for; when he instantly sent off for the doctors. Within half an hour I was surrounded by seven of them: that is, Dr. A. Campbell, Stark, Robertson, two Lairds, and my shipmates Cleveland and Howorth. They all looked very dismal, and I saw clearly they expected my dissolution; yet I never gave myself up, nor felt any particular dread at the thoughts of dying. I continued in this hopeless state ten days, the doctors in the morning thinking it impossible for me to survive until night, and the same from night to morning. In this forlorn condition I was allowed to drink as much claret as I pleased, and delicious it was to my palate; equally grateful and refreshing were oranges which were given me several times a day. In the height of the fever I had frequently been lifted out of bed and put into the warm bath, though without deriving any benefit until the 30th (November) about noon, when, just as they were taking me out of the bath, a rash suddenly appeared over my whole body, attended with a profuse perspiration. Dr. Campbell, who happened to be present, ordered the attendants instantly to cover me with shawls, observing the crisis was arrived and an hour would decide the business. He sat down by the side of my bed to wait the issue, and soon told

Pott he had hopes of saving me. A new medicine that was prescribed acted most favourably, so much so that, at a consultation of the doctors in the evening, I was pronounced in a fair way for recovery.

The following day, being 1st December, I had a slight return of fever, which soon yielded to medicine; and from that time I gradually came about, though I continued so weak I could scarcely turn myself as I lay on the bed, nor had I the least degree of appetite. The doctors teased me to eat, but obey I could not until about the 7th of the month, when I fancied I should like a little dry toast, which being prepared and brought I, with difficulty, swallowed a morsel, soon after which Dr. Stark arrived. His first question was, "Had I eat anything?" Upon my replying "Yes, some dry toast," he said, "Well, I am glad you have begun at last, though I had rather you had eat anything else; dry toast is not wholesome." In an hour after he left me, Doctor Campbell called, who likewise enquired as to eating, and being told what I had done, said, "I am glad to hear it; you cannot eat a better thing. Take it frequently and as much of it as you please!" So much for the difference of doctors' opinions! I, however, have no doubt but Doctor Campbell was right. The toast certainly did me good. I continued improving in health, but so slowly that it was the 17th before I could stir a step without assistance. Doctor Campbell said that in all his practice he had never seen a person recover from such a state as I was in. I certainly owed my life to the unusual exertions and attendance of the physicians, united to the indefatigable attention of Pott and his servants. On the 24th by Doctor Campbell's orders, being completely enveloped in shawls, I was put into a palankeen and once more conveyed to Colonel Watson's house at the docks, where, from the change of air, I recovered rapidly. In three days, my appetite became so keen there was no satisfying me. On 1st January 1778, the only traces of my illness were a very pale face and thin, emaciated body.

15

THE CALCUTTA ATTORNEY

SOON after my return to Colonel Watson's, he told me that my shipmate Cleveland had more than once expressed a wish that we should join and live together in a very good house he had taken, which, from its vicinity to the Court House, would suit me admirably. To this proposal I readily agreed, and, as soon as I had sufficient strength to go to Calcutta, called upon him. I found the house delightfully situated upon the esplanade, open to the southward and eastward, and commanding an extensive view both up and down the river, to which it was close. It belonged to Mrs. Ogden, the widow of a pilot then recently dead, who had left her this house with other property. The only reasonable objection that could be made was its being *cutcha* —that is, built with mud instead of mortar. Formerly the greater part of the buildings in Bengal were of that description, whereas there is now hardly one to be seen throughout Calcutta, being replaced by well-constructed solid masonry. For this house we agreed to pay three hundred sicca rupees, or thirty-seven pounds ten shillings, a month. Pott exclaimed upon entering it at the unfurnished state of it, and undertook to get it put into a proper condition for us, which he did, but at an expense of nearly one thousand pounds.

On 6th January we became joint householders. The following day, being that on which the term commenced, Sir Elijah Impey, Chief Justice, Sir Robert Chambers, the officers of the court, barristers and attornies, assembled at nine o'clock in the morning at the house of Mr. Justice Hyde, who always gave them a breakfast the first of every term and sessions, the whole body afterwards proceeding in a line to the Court, attended by the Sheriff, Under-Sheriff, his servants and constables. At the door of the Court House, one of the Supreme Council joined the procession and took his seat upon the bench, which was then considered a proper compliment to His Majesty's Justices. For many years back that ceremony has ceased to be observed. I had no want of clients, within a week after I commenced business, having twelve actions and three equity suits to prosecute or defend. The difference in the practice from that pursued in Westminster Hall at first puzzled me a little; but, the advocates and attorneys showing the utmost readiness to give me information and assistance, I soon made myself master of the forms.

Being invited to dine with Sir Elijah Impey after the Court broke up, I dressed and went there, where I met many of the principal gentlemen of the settlement, being introduced to those I was not already acquainted with, and passed a cheerful, pleasant day. On the 8th I went to Mr. Francis's public breakfast, it being the custom in those days for the Governor-General and Members of the Council to receive visits of compliments or strangers for introduction at breakfast, each having one morning a week for the purpose. Mr. Tilghman, who was related to Mr. Francis, and resided at his house, seeing me enter, immediately rose from the table at which he, with about thirty others, were sitting, and conducted me to Mr. Francis at the head of it, to whom I delivered my letters, which, to my great surprise, he directly opened and read. He had, however, previously pointed to a chair near him, on which I sat down.

Having perused the first letter he opened, he looked me full in the face and burst into a hoarse laugh, for which in a few seconds he apologized by observing that it struck him as superlatively ridiculous for Mr. Burke to imagine he could be of the smallest use to an attorney (placing a strong emphasis on the last word). I felt extremely mortified at his impertinent manner, especially before so large a company; and I believe my countenance showed that I was offended, for he suddenly altered his behaviour and made a great many civil speeches. He requested I would do him the honour to dine with him, lamented the very severe indisposition I had undergone, adding, if I would follow his advice, he would answer for it I never should be troubled with bile, his preventative being a glass of cold water as soon as I awoke in the morning, and another on retiring to rest at night. This, he said, a physician of eminence in London had recommended; and he had found it answer most completely.

At dinner I met Mr. Shee (now Sir George, a Baronet), Sir John D'Oyley, Mr. Peter Moore, Mr. Leonard Collins, Mr. Edward Hay, Mr. George Hatch, Mr. Richard Johnson, and Mr. John Haldane, with all of whom I became very intimate and lived in habits of great kindness. I lament to say the five last-named have been dead for several years. During dinner, Mr. Francis, speaking to a gentleman near him, said, "When do you expect to get away, Captain Newte?" and was answered, "I hope, sir, by this day month." Mr. Francis then addressing Pott, who sat next to me, asked him, "Are you ready to embark, Pott?" Robert replied, "I have not yet thought of a single article, but can provide myself fully in one week." This was the first I had heard of Pott's having any intention to leave India, and truly concerned was I at thus learning I was soon to be deprived of the society of my much-esteemed friend. Upon my upbraiding him for not telling me, he said he had daily meant to do so, but could not bring himself to speak upon a subject the very thought of which made him miserable; but family circumstances made his presence in England indispensable.

A succession of large and formal dinners followed Mr. Francis's, beginning with the Governor-General, Mr. Wheler, General Stibbert, Mr. Barwell, and in fact all the *Burra Sahibs* (great men) of Calcutta. The first really pleasant party I was at, after my illness, was given by Daniel Barwell, who, as I have before observed, kept house with Pott and others. The most highly dressed and splendid hookah was prepared for me. I tried, but did not like it, which being perceived by my friend Robert, he laughed at me, recommending me to funk away and I should accomplish the matter without choking myself. As, after several trials, I still found it disagreeable, I with much gravity requested to know whether it was indispensably necessary that I should become a smoker, which was answered with equal gravity, "Undoubtedly it is, for you might as well be out of the world as out of the fashion. Here everybody uses a hookah, and it is impossible to get on without." Mr. Gosling, less volatile and flighty than the rest of the party, immediately said, "Don't mind these rattling young men, Mr. Hickey, there is no sort of occasion for your doing what is unpleasant; and, although hookahs are in pretty general use, there are several gentlemen that never smoke them." I directly dismissed the hookah, never after tasting one. Often since have I rejoiced that I did not happen to like it, as I have seen the want of it, from servants misunderstanding where they were ordered to attend their masters, or some other accident, a source of absolute misery, and have frequently heard men declare they would much rather be deprived of their dinner than their hookah.

In this party I first saw the barbarous custom of pelleting each other with little balls of bread, made like pills, across the table, which was even practised by the fair sex. Some people could discharge them with such force as to cause considerable pain when struck in the face. Mr. Daniel Barwell was such a proficient that he could, at the distance of three or four yards, snuff a candle, and that several times successively. This strange trick, fitter for savages than polished society, produced many quarrels, and at last entirely ceased from the following occurrence. A Captain Morrison had repeatedly expressed his abhorrence of pelleting, and that, if any person struck him with one, he should consider it intended as an insult and resent it accordingly. In a few minutes after he had so said, he received a smart blow in the face from one, which, although discharged from a hand below the table, he saw by the motion of the arm from whence it came, and that the pelleter was a very recent acquaintance. He therefore without the least hesitation took up a dish that stood before him and contained a leg of mutton, which he discharged with all his strength at the offender, and with such well-directed aim that it took place upon the head, knocking him off his chair and giving a severe cut upon the temple. This produced a duel in which the unfortunate pelleter was shot through the body, lay upon his bed many months, and never perfectly recovered. This put a complete stop to the absurd practice.

Having partaken of several entertainments given at the Tavern by Captain Sutton and other gentlemen, I thought it incumbent upon me to return the compliment and accordingly bespoke the handsomest dinner that could be provided, for forty, at the Harmonic Tavern. On the day appointed, thirty-nine sat down to table, all of whom did ample justice to the feast, drank freely, some of my guests remaining till three in the morning, when they staggered home well pleased with their fare, and declaring I was an admirable host.

At the time I arrived in Bengal, everybody dressed splendidly, being covered with lace, spangles and foil. I, who always had a tendency to be a beau, gave into the fashion with much goodwill, no person appearing in richer suits of velvet and lace than myself. I kept a handsome phaeton and beautiful pair of horses, and also had two noble Arabian saddle horses, my whole establishment being of the best and most expensive kind. I was soon distinguished in Calcutta by the title of "the Gentleman Attorney," in contra-distinction to the blackguard practitioners, of which description I am sorry to say there were several. In fact, with the exception of Messrs. Tolfrey and Nailor, Foxcroft, Johnson, Jarrett (who was Solicitor to the Company) and Smoult, I never met any attorneys in the company I kept, which always was the best. Once a week I had a party to dine with me, when we kept it up merrily; but my chum, Cleveland, was not to be led astray by bad example.

Notwithstanding I lived so dissipated a life in point of drinking and late hours, no man laboured harder. I was always at my desk before seven in the morning and, with the break of half an hour for breakfast, never ceased work until dinner; after which, unless upon emergencies, I never took pen in hand. I had sufficient business to occupy myself and three native clerks. Money consequently came in fast, so that I never bestowed a thought about the price of an article. Whatever I wanted was ordered home; I made it a rule, however, to discharge every demand upon me the 1st of each month.

In the middle of February, my friend, Bob Pott, took leave of me and embarked in the *Ceres*, and towards the end of the same month Mr. Daniel Barwell also departed with Captain Rogers. In the *Ceres*, Mr. Jarrett, Attorney to the Company, also embarked for Europe, whereupon Mr. Nailor, through the interest of Sir Elijah Impey, succeeded to that lucrative appointment. My friend Colonel Watson now began his docks and erected two large windmills, being the first that had ever been built in Bengal exciting much astonishment amongst the natives. The two mills were exactly alike, being one hundred and fourteen feet in height, consisting of five stories of floors, the upper ones for grinding grain of every description, the ground floor to saw timber by circular saws worked by the wind, an ingenious invention then recently found out. It was one of my principal daily amusements to observe the progress of these works. The surprise of the native artificers was great beyond belief, when told that the operation of the wind on the sails at the outside would affect every floor, grinding flour or grain of some sort upon each. Indeed, they pronounced such an event utterly impossible.

Upon the first trial when the flyers were fixed, it was set in motion at a time when there were upwards of one hundred workmen employed on the upper floors, who seeing the immense timber in motion, and the whole fabric considerably agitated, were greatly alarmed, conceiving nothing short of magic could have produced so extraordinary an effect. In their fright, their first object was to escape from the building, and in their endeavours to effect that object they tumbled heels over head down the different flights of stairs. Such was their anxiety to get clear of what they considered the enchanted spot that several were seriously hurt. Altogether the scene was most strange; "*Wah Wah*," (an exclamation of surprise) was heard from all quarters!

I have already observed that Colonel Watson was not upon good terms with Mr. Barwell; and, conceiving he could carry on his scheme without his aid or assistance in Council, he paid him no sort of attention. This Barwell, who was a proud man, and tenacious of the public situation he held, highly resented, and malignantly determined in consequence to throw every possible impediment in the way. He got hold of an opulent native named Gocul Gosaul, who resided close to the colonel's works and claimed part of the land whereupon the docks were constructing. When the grant of land was first made by Government to Campbell,* he was directed, upon ousting the natives from their different spots of ground, to make each an adequate compensation or to give them an equivalent in ground elsewhere; but the natives of India, high and low, being superstitiously attached to the spot in which they were born and brought up, no consideration whatever will induce them to relinquish it; and this was strongly proved

* The scheme had originally been launched by Major Archibald Campbell, then Chief Engineer in Bengal, whose interest Watson had purchased at the beginning of the year 1777.

upon this occasion. Colonel Campbell could bring them to no terms. Miserable as the huts they resided in were, they were content, and peremptorily refused to leave them.

Force was therefore resorted to; the colonel sent a party of sepoys, who turned the wretched creatures out of their habitations and then levelled them with the earth. The persons thus treated went in a body to the Council House, where, with their usual noise, they cried out for justice. Colonel Campbell was thereupon asked the reason of such violence; to which he replied that he had always been ready to execute the orders of Government, had offered the proprietors five times the value of their land and buildings, or to give them a far greater quantity of ground in the neighbourhood; but that the parties complaining were so unreasonable as to refuse any terms, whereby the progress of the public works were impeded. Government then named four respectable gentlemen to determine upon the fair value of the spots of ground in question, which, when done, the proprietors should be compelled to accept. These gentlemen accordingly met many times during a period of ten months, when their opinions differed so widely as to the quantum of compensation that nothing decisive was ever done, nor any report made by them. The inhabitants, however, were effectually excluded from their land, and a high brick wall built round the whole space; immense ranges of workshops and godowns for stores were also erected.

Besides those expensive buildings, Mr. Watson, who had then joined Campbell in the undertaking, built a range of barracks sufficiently spacious to accommodate three hundred persons, part of their scheme being to purchase slaves at Mozambique and Madagascar to carry on the laborious part of their undertaking. Messrs. Campbell and Watson, who had already sunk a large sum, and aware how much more it would take to complete so stupendous a work, were, of course, extremely anxious to secure themselves against any future obstructions by native claimants or otherwise; and, after much consultation with their friends, it was deemed prudent for one or both of them to return to England there to solicit a legal grant of the land required from the Company. Colonel Campbell accordingly sailed for Europe, and in a few months was followed by his colleague, who, soon after his arrival in London, purchased Campbell's share in the concern, and so became sole proprietor of the premises. The Court of Directors entered upon the matter with great zeal, conceiving the plan when executed would prove of the utmost advantage, not only to the East India Company but to the British nation at large. They therefore gave it every encouragement in their power; a regular grant of the land to Colonel Watson was prepared by the Company's Law Officers, besides which Colonel Watson was allowed a certain tonnage in each of their ships of the season, free of all charge, to transport his marine and other stores to India. Possessed of this deed, which he conceived impossible to shake or at all to affect, he took his passage for Bengal on board the *Sea-horse* in 1777, being then appointed Chief Engineer.

Gocul Gosaul, of whom I have already spoken, a man of opulence, was one of those who had been dispossessed of a certain quantity of land, for which he had refused to receive any compensation, it being taken from him against his will. This Gocul Gosaul, upon the colonel's arrival, paid him a visit, at which time I was present, and was much struck by the elegance of his address and manners. In the best language he complimented the colonel upon his return to Bengal, expressing the gratification it gave him to see him and to hear that he was authorized to carry into effect an undertaking that must do honour to India. During this interview, not an allusion was made to his parcel of land, or anything like a complaint; so further otherwise, he was profuse in his offers of aiding the prosecution of the work by every means in his power, observing that he would readily advance, at any time, three or four lacs of rupees to promote the object in view. Yet this very Gocul Gosaul was the man that, a few months subsequent to these voluntary offers and civil declarations, became the colonel's first and serious opponent.

In this, however, he was encouraged by Mr. Barwell, at whose instigation he made a formal demand of the piece of ground of which he had been dispossessed; in answer to which application the colonel referred him to the Govenor-General and Council. Gocul Gosaul replied he had nothing to do with Government; that Colonel Watson had tortuously ousted him from his property and, if it was not forthwith restored, he should commence a prosecution against him in the Supreme Court by way of ejectment for the recovery thereof. Colonel Watson, alarmed at the threat, desired to see him; he repeatedly promised to call, but did not. The colonel, therefore, determined to go to his house, and did so, I, at his particular desire, accompanying him. Gocul Gosaul seemed much distressed, made a thousand apologies, and pleaded indisposition in excuse for not having waited upon the colonel according to his promise. His confusion was increased by the colonel's coolly saying, "Illness did not prevent you doing as you ought to have done. You very well know you acted under the orders of a member of Government, Mr. Barwell."

After remaining silent some minutes and looking extremely awkward, he observed Mr. Barwell was a great man and his protector; he was therefore bound to act in obedience to his wishes. The colonel, in a rage, said he (Gocul Gosaul) and his protector Barwell were a pair of infamous rascals, and instantly walked out of the house; three days after which an action was commenced; whereupon Colonel Watson went to Mr. Hastings, the Governor-General, to Mr. Francis, and Mr. Wheler, to inform them thereof, when they all reprobated the conduct of Mr. Barwell, to whom Mr. Hastings said he would speak privately upon the business and endeavour to stop the proceedings. He did accordingly speak to the gentleman, who was mean enough to deny his having at all interfered or influenced Gocul Gosaul in what he had done. Thus circumstanced, Colonel Watson had nothing left but to defend himself as well as he could. The land claimed by Gocul Gosaul was of the utmost importance, being a narrow slip of footpath to the waterside by which Gocul Gosaul and his family had formerly gone to the river to perform their daily ablutions. According to his pointing out his claim, it went directly through the centre of the newly finished windmill, interfering also with both the projected wet and dry docks. In short, if he succeeded in establishing his right to the land, it completely did away the possibility of carrying the proposed plan into execution.

The attorney employed by Gocul Gosaul was Mr. North Nailor, then the Company's Solicitor, and acting likewise for Mr. Barwell in all legal business he had to do, by which gentleman he had been recommended to Gocul Gosaul. The colonel having requested me to act on his part, I entered an appearance. I also desired to see the grant from the Company, which upon reading I found to be so strong in the colonel's favour that I immediately advised my client to apply to Government to act in the defence, they being bound to support their own acts. Colonel Watson accordingly did so; when the question was referred to Sir John Day, their Advocate-General, who without hesitation decided in the colonel's favour.

Gocul Gosaul, upon finding the matter thus seriously taken up by the Government, became greatly alarmed, apprehending that, should he persist in his demand, he might incur the displeasure of the Governor-General, a circumstance in those days of much importance. Having expressed his fears to Mr. Barwell, that artful man encouraged him to go on, reminding him that the chief object of the British Legislature in constituting a Supreme Court in Bengal was to efface from men's minds a too-prevalent idea that Europeans holding the most elevated rank might with impunity harass and oppress the natives of every description; that the duty of the judges was to prevent such oppression, or to punish the offenders when legally brought before them, to promote which object a pauper establishment of law officers were appointed and paid by Government, to act for those who could not afford to apply for redress from their own private funds. Gocul Gosaul, however, notwithstanding the encouragement Mr. Barwell gave him, proceeded in the action with extreme reluctance.

In a few months, the cause came to a hearing, when Mr. Barwell was subpoenaed as a witness, and underwent a long examination, in which, in the most positive terms, he swore that he had not in any manner directly or indirectly interfered in the subject-matter in dispute; nor had he ever advised or encouraged Gocul Gosaul to commence, or having commenced, to proceed in the prosecution. A crowded court heard these asseverations with astonishment; and few indeed were the number of the auditors who believed what he said. The trial commenced at nine in the morning, and did not finish until eight at night; when, Gocul Gosaul having sufficiently proved his right to a certain portion of the land from which he had been forcibly ejected, Sir Elijah Impey pronounced judgment in a very eloquent speech, in which he feelingly lamented the agitation of such a question as was then before him, pretty plainly saying he thought the Government ought, from every motive, to have prevented it. He then commented in severe language upon the conduct of, as well as the evidence given by, Mr. Barwell, a member of the Government. He observed that, painful as his duty was, it must be performed; and, notwithstanding himself and his brethren upon the Bench were sensible of the national loss in anything occurring to stop so magnificent and noble an undertaking, yet the law must take its course; all private feelings, all personal consideration must yield to the settled and established law of the land; that there must be a judgment for the lessor of the plaintiff for the quantity of ground he had established a right to. Thus a complete stop was put to the further progress of an undertaking that, if completed, would have been of the utmost national importance.

Mr. Cleveland and I continued joint housekeepers until the middle of April (1778); when, feeling ashamed at his contributing one-half of the house expenses, especially the serious article of wine, of which he scarcely ever took more than two glasses daily, nor rarely invited anyone to dinner, whilst I with my frequent parties were taking large potations, I determined upon dissolving our partnership, and took a house for myself which was then finishing, and I was to enter upon on 1st May. The one Mr. Cleveland and I inhabited was, as I have already observed, constructed of mud instead of *chunam*. The sun striking upon the southern front made it intensely hot; to correct which I sent for a native builder, directing him to put up a matted verandah. My landlady, Mrs. Ogden, hearing this, came to me in the utmost alarm, expressing her fears that I should throw the house down, the walls not being sufficiently strong to bear a verandah. Having purchased all the requisite materials, I did not like to give up my plan, though staggered by what she said. I, however, consulted Mr. Lyon, who pointed out some precautions, the adoption of which he thought would do away all risk. Pursuant to Mr. Lyon's hints, I built my verandah and found it of infinite advantage.

The months of March, April, and May in Bengal is the season for violent and sudden tempests called north-westers. Though tremendous in their appearance and effect, they are expected with pleasure from rendering the air cool and delightful. The Saturdays and Sundays that I did not go to Sir Robert Chambers's, I generally spent at Captain Thornhill's, the Master Attendant, who had a magnificent country house upon the bank of the river at Cosspore, four miles above Calcutta, where he received and entertained his numerous friends with the greatest degree of hospitality and good humour. Towards the end of April, whilst I was at this gay mansion, there came on one of the most severe north-westers that had been experienced for many years. It commenced about six o'clock in the evening, blowing for upwards of an hour an absolute hurricane, and, as was often the case, after so doing from the north-west suddenly shifted to the opposite point, north-east, returning with even increased force. As my house stood openly exposed to the north-east, I felt exceedingly uneasy about my newly erected verandah, expecting every instant to receive an account that the whole fabric was level with the earth. A little before twelve, I got into my phaeton and drove to town in as great a funk as ever I entered Westminster School knowing I was to be flogged. Upon turning the corner of a street close to which my house stood, I had the consolation to perceive at least that the body of the building still stood. Driving up to the door, however, I found my famous verandah entirely down and demolished, the wreck of it laying in the courtyard; yet I felt happy that it had not brought the crazy old building along with it.

I have already stated the strange reception I met with from Mr. Francis when I presented Mr. Burke's letter of introduction of me to him. Now it so happened that this pompous gentleman, who had so pointedly ridiculed the idea "of his ever having it in his power to be of use to an attorney," was under the necessity of bestowing a considerable part of his fortune upon the members of a profession he seemed disposed to treat so contemptuously; and this arose from the following circumstance. A gentleman in the Company's civil service, named George Francis Grand, had married a pretty little French girl, to whom Mr. Francis attached himself, and was supposed soon to have accomplished all he wished. He at least, by his conduct, laid himself open to be attacked by law. This occurred a few months after my arrival in Bengal; and Mr. Grand did me the honour to select me from the corps of attorneys to act on his behalf; but, upon his calling at my office for the purpose of giving instructions for commencing the action, I declined undertaking it, not from any particular attachment to Mr. Francis, but from motives of delicacy towards my respected friend Mr. Burke, who had introduced me to him. Mr. Grand did not consider my reason sufficient to justify my refusal to act, and continued to press me upon the subject; so that I had no other means of getting rid of his importunities than by leaving Calcutta.

The same morning that I did so, Mr. Grand once more went to my office, where meeting a fine lad, Mr. Stackhouse Tolfrey, then a clerk of mine, he persuaded that young man to commence the action; which having done he directly announced it to me by letter, apologizing for taking such a step without my special orders, but pleaded the earnest solicitations of my friend Mr. Grand. Though exceedingly vexed, I could not be angry with Tolfrey, conscious he had acted from the best motives. I, however, went to town and discontinued the action as having been commenced in my name without my authority. From the Prothonotary's office I proceeded to Mr. Grand's to express my displeasure at his having urged young Tolfrey to issue a writ contrary to my orders. He was very humble, made many apologies, paid me a number of compliments, and again entreated I would act as his attorney, which I, of course, again refused. He, thereupon, applied to another attorney, by whom the action was commenced. Mr. Francis, upon being served with a copy of the writ, brought it to me, requesting I would defend on his part; but which I also refused, declaring I would have nothing to do on either side.

In the then ensuing term, the cause came on for trial, wherein Mr. Shee, (now Sir George) cut an awkward figure, the Chief Justice observing that his behaviour had been as reprehensible as it was derogatory to the character of a gentleman. The only material facts proved against Mr. Francis were his frequent visits at the house when Mr. Grand, the master, was from home; his being discovered, disguised in black, with a ladder upon his shoulder, which he was seen to place against the wall of Mr. Grand's house; and his being discovered at night in Mrs. Grand's bedchamber by the servants. Yet upon that evidence, slight and unsatisfactory as it no doubt was, the plaintiff obtained a judgment. The defence was most ably conducted by Mr. Tilghman, who insisted upon the impossibility of the plaintiff's succeeding upon such evidence; and he quoted a variety of modern cases in support of his opinion.

As the judges differed, each gave his separate opinion, Mr. Hyde, as junior, commencing, who commented upon the evidence, observing that, though slight, it satisfied a judgment for the plaintiff. Sir Robert Chambers spoke next; he said he had very maturely read over and weighed the depositions and sincerely lamented he was compelled to differ from his learned brethren, by declaring he thought the plaintiff had totally failed to make out his case and must be nonsuited; in support of which opinion he cited many late cases wherein the law had been clearly laid down by the ablest civilians of the present day, men who were equally an honour and an ornament to the British Bench.

Sir Elijah Impey was evidently surprised and vexed at the depth of learning displayed by Sir Robert upon the occasion. He petulantly observed that he was not prepared to comment upon such a mass of learning in ecclesiastical law as had been, he thought unnecessarily and inapplicably, introduced by his brother Chambers, not a particle of which applied to the present case. He entirely concurred in opinion with Mr. Justice Hyde that the evidence entitled the plaintiff to a judgment, and that such judgment should be fifty thousand rupees! Mr. Hyde, in a low voice, said "Siccas." "Aye, Siccas, Brother Hyde,"* added the Chief. This produced a roar of mirth from the auditors, at which Sir Elijah was greatly offended.

Within a week after the trial, Mr. Tilghman presented to the Court a petition of appeal to His Majesty in Council against the judgment so given and, in the speech upon moving that the said petition be filed, quoted the same cases Sir Robert had done; whereupon the Chief Justice angrily observed, "This is precisely the language and construction of the law used by Sir Robert Chambers on Saturday last." "True, my Lord," replied Mr. Tilghman, "and I am proud at having such respectable authority for using it today." At the moment he said this, he received a note which I, who was setting next to him, saw was Mr. Francis's handwriting, consisting of only three lines. What the contents were I know not; but upon perusal Mr. Tilghman directly requested leave to withdraw the notion he had just before made, which being granted, no more was ever heard about appealing. Various conjectures were made thereon; but the prevailing opinion was that Mr. Grand, who was embarrassed in his circumstances, had proposed a composition and consented to take a part of the damages to put an end to the discussion; to which Mr. Francis readily acceded, thereby preventing the matters being brought forward in England to his disgrace as a married man. Soon after the decision of the cause the fair lady quitted India and went to Paris, where the famous Talleyrand saw her, was captivated by her beauty, and married her.†

It being the general custom of Bengal in those days to drink freely and to assemble in numerous parties at each other's houses, I, who had always been disposed to conviviality, soon rendered myself conspicuous, and by the splendour of my entertainments gained the reputation of being the best host in Calcutta. The dining hour being one o'clock, it was customary after that meal, and about sunset, to take an airing, driving to the racecourse, where the carriages all drew up and a general chat took place. I had one day given a dinner to a large party, one of whom was an Irishman, Captain Richard Heffernan, as benevolent and good a creature as ever breathed, but quite a *Paddy*!

---

* The sicca rupee was then valued at two and sixpence.
† She did not, however, marry Talleyrand until the year 1802.

I had filled them all so full of wine that, by seven in the evening, they had all slunk off except Heffernan; and he positively refused to swallow another drop. I therefore proposed giving him a little exercise; to which he consenting, I ordered my phaeton, and off we set as hard as a pair of high-mettled horses could go. By the time we had been out half an hour, it became quite dark, a matter of indifference to me whose head was overcharged with claret; and on I dashed pell-mell. My companion soon remarked, from the violent jolts of the carriage, that the way was cursed rough; and, at last, he asked whether I was sure I was in the right road; for so great a sea had got up he conceived it would be prudent either to shorten sail or bear up. I was obliged to confess I did not know where we had got to, and scarcely had I made that confession when away we went, phaeton, horses and all, into a hole twelve or fourteen feet deep which, as I afterwards ascertained, for eight months out of the twelve was filled with water, but at the time of our tumble was quite dry.

Stunned by the violence of the fall, we lay for some moments insensible; when, somewhat recovering, I endeavoured to extricate myself from the pit in which, amidst an almost inpenetrable darkness, we were enveloped. Whilst groping about, my companion, with his strong native accent, remarked, "Upon my conscience, this is a scurvy sort of a hole you have pop't me into, and the devil a chance do I perceive of getting clear of it." In a few minutes, I had scrambled up the side and reached the level. Having assisted my friend to do the same, I advised him to sit quietly there, while I went to a light I saw at a distance to procure assistance and ascertain where we had got to, and the state of my horses, both of whom I feared were killed. I, therefore, ran with all my speed towards the light, which having, as I conceived, nearly reached, my progress was interrupted by going heels over head into a deep ditch, the shock of which second fall totally unhinged me, seeming to dislocate every bone in my body. Fortunately some natives were passing near the spot at the time, who, hearing my groans, came up, and finding me incapable of personal exertion, said they would go to the hospital, close to which we were, and procure aid. They accordingly did so, and within a quarter of an hour a number of servants with palanquins and lights came to me, and I was conducted to the apartments of the head surgeon.

Upon my representing to him the situation I had left my friend in, and that of my horses and carriage, he sent off in search of them; and in about an hour I had the pleasure to see Heffernan with my favourite horses, both having escaped without serious injury. For myself, I was miserably bruised, yet, all circumstances considered, escaped wonderfully. The greatest injury my friend Heffernan sustained was alarm from the first pitch we had into the hole, from which he had no other hurt than a slight sprain of one ankle. He, however, declared that in future he would cautiously avoid putting himself under charge of a drunken pilot. My phaeton and the horses' harness were totally demolished.

On 10th May, 1778, I went into my new house, which belonged to Thomas Motte, Esq., then a respectable, and considered a very opulent, man. On 1st June, I invited a large party to dinner. Among the guests was my said landlord, Mr. Motte, whom I found a pleasant, well-informed man, also Mr. Shore (now Lord Teignmouth), Mr. Purling, Mr. Montgomery and his brother who commanded the *Bessborough* Indiaman, Mr. Kneller, Colonel Watson, Major Mestayer, and some other of my *Sea-horse* companions. I had likewise Captain John Durand, with whom I had been at school at Streatham. Although not then quite twenty-one years of age, he had the command of the *Northington*, one of the Company's ships. The morning had been very threatening, it blowing hard; by the time we sat down at table, it increased to a violent gale with incessant heavy rain. So heavily it poured down that not one of my party chose to encounter it, and we therefore continued drinking until morning. Some of my guests being then convinced it was the setting in of the rains, and might not cease for days, in spite of its fury set out for their own houses; but three remained with me until the morning of the 4th, when it suddenly cleared up, leaving the town completely deluged.

At that period, the King's birthday was celebrated with much pomp, the Governor-General always giving a dinner to the gentlemen of the Settlement, and a ball and supper to the ladies at night; at which entertainments everybody, *malgré* the extreme heat, appeared in full dress, with bags and swords. I made up for the occasion a coat of pea-green, lined with white silk and richly ornamented with a spangled and foiled lace, waistcoat and breeches decorated in like manner, being also of white silk. All the company appearing in splendid apparel made a very handsome show. The Governor-General presided at the dinner table. Upon the cloth being removed, he gave as first toast "The King," then "The Queen and Royal Family," "The East India Company," "The Army and Navy," "The Commander-in-Chief," "Success to the British arms in India," each toast being followed by a salute of twenty-one guns from cannon drawn up for the purpose in front of the Court House.

Notwithstanding I lived much in the best society, passing every evening in parties, my mornings were dedicated to hard work at my desk, from which cash accumulated rapidly. In the month of August, Mr. Cressy, also one of my *Sea-horse* shipmates, got into a dispute which occasioned infinite trouble to him. Two Bengali carpenters in the employ of Colonel Watson, being detected in purloining a quantity of tools and other things, were carried before Cressy as the Chief Superintendant, whereupon he, imprudently taking the law into his own hands, forthwith ordered the aggressors to be tied up and severely flogged, and then confined them in a godown for two days. The moment these men were released, they found their way to an attorney, who addressed a letter to Cressy saying, if he did not make ample compensation to the injured persons, actions would be commenced against him for assaults and false imprisonment. Cressy, instead of endeavouring to settle or conciliate, treated the application with contempt, setting the humble instrument of the law at defiance. Two actions were, in consequence, immediately set on foot, the damages in each being laid at five thousand sicca rupees. Writs of summons being served upon Cressy, a consultation was held at Colonel Watson's, who wished the actions to be defended in the usual manner; but this Cressy would not hear of, declaring he wanted no assistance and would plead for himself; that, being born and bred in Great Britain and then residing in a British settlement, he should insist upon his birthright, trial by jury. In vain did I endeavour to convince him that the court was established under the authority of Parliament, which empowered the judges, in all civil cases, to act also as jurors. He insisted that was contrary to the constitution and he would oppose it to his latest breath. Colonel Watson, finding him thus obstinate, requested I would point out the requisite steps to be taken. I accordingly did direct him how to enter an appearance with the Prothonotary and to obtain a copy of the plaint or declaration. I also drew a plea of the general issue, not guilty, substituting instead of the customary conclusion, "And of this he puts himself *upon the Court*," "And of this he puts himself *upon the Country*." In doing this, I informed Cressy that, unless the plaintiff's attorney was an egregious blockhead, it could answer no purpose, for that the process so worded must be considered as no plea, and the cause would be set down *ex parte*. Cressy still persevered; and the plaintiff's attorney neglecting to avail himself of the advantage he might have taken, filed a demurrer to the plea, which in due course being set down for hearing, Cressy determined to argue it in person, bestowing his whole time in preparing an address to the bench upon the occasion, for which purpose he ransacked a variety of authorities and writers upon the liberty of the subject, Magna Charta, etc.

A day being appointed for the argument of the demurrer, the court by eight o'clock in the morning was crowded by the British inhabitants of Calcutta, both civil and military; but the Chief Justice, being indisposed, could not attend. The discussion was therefore postponed. This happened in the middle of the Mahomedan festival of the Mohurrem, during which the lowest orders of Mussulman, by swallowing large quantities of an intoxicating drug called bang, work themselves up to a state of absolute madness and commit great excess. Their zeal was increased that year by the Nabob Sydaat Ali being in Calcutta. Soon after Sir Robert Chambers and Mr. Justice Hyde had taken their seats upon the bench and the common routine of business was entered upon, a prodigious mob assembled directly under the windows, when the beating of tom-toms (a small sort of drum in use all over Hindustan), and the shrill squeaking of their trumpets, made such a horrible din the counsellors could not possibly make themselves heard by the judges. Sir Robert therefore directed the constables in attendance to go down and disperse the people. In a few minutes, one of these constables, whose name was Roop, an old German, ran into court in great agitation, without his wig, crying out that he had been violently assailed by the mob who had severely beat him, carried off his hat and wig; and, upon his showing his staff of office, requiring peace in His Majesty's name, two English sailors, who were amongst the crowd, seized his said staff, swearing if that was the b——r's authority they would ram it up his a——e, and actually carried it off in triumph. Sir Robert Chambers, upon hearing this account, observed, "Mr. Constable, you need not be so very particular in your description."

The tumult, instead of subsiding, seeming greatly to increase, the Under-Sheriff was ordered to interfere and do his duty by forthwith dispersing the mob, which by that time had increased to several thousands, showing strong symptoms of riot. The moment Mr. Harry Stark (the Under-Sheriff) made his appearance in the street, the leaders of the band seized him, broke his wand, and were carrying him bodily away, when he was rescued by some of the Nabob's servants who happened to know him; but for which he would probably have been murdered. The mob then attacked and maltreated the bearers and hircarrahs* that were in attendance, waiting for their masters, demolishing every palankeen they could lay hands on. Another party assailed the Court House, discharging showers of brickbats through the windows, which were soon demolished, the bricks flying through the Court Room in all directions, for unluckily there was abundant ammunition from a part of the building being under repair.

In about half an hour after the first grand attack had been thus made, an alarm was given that the mob armed with *tulwars* (scimitars) had forced the sentries, and were in a vast body rushing up the principal staircase. A general panic prevailed, the spectators running in all directions to seek shelter. I was one who went with the stream seeking safety at the top of the Court House, where was also Mr. William Chambers, brother of Sir Robert, a gentleman well acquainted with the dispositions of the natives, and who seemed particularly uneasy at the situation we were in, declaring our lives were in imminent danger,

* Running footmen.

and that most likely every European would be put to death. I own I felt considerable alarm at finding matters becoming so serious; but the champion for the privilege of a Briton (Cressy), upon hearing Mr. Chambers's speech, very spiritedly said, "If such be the case, let us act like Englishmen and not run from a parcel of vagabond Indians. Let us resolutely face them and, at least, sell our lives dearly"; at the same time seizing a pike from the hands of one of the sheriff's peons who happened to stand near him, he continued, "Now, let all who feel like me follow my example," and he boldly descended the staircase, followed by many who were encouraged by his behaviour.

The event justified Cressy's spirit; the mob instantly retreated, and a party of Invalids from the old Fort arriving at that critical moment, the rioters went off after letting fly one terrible shower of bricks, Major Sturgeon, which was literally the name of the officer who commanded the Invalids, receiving a blow on his head which set the blood streaming down his face; in which condition he entered the court, desiring the judges to rest assured that he and his *brave fellows* would shed the last drop of their blood in defence of their Lordships! This part of the scene was most truly ridiculous, the more so from there being present nearly a hundred officers all with their swords on, who had been drawn to the Court House in the hopes of entertainment from hearing Cressy abuse the judges, but who seemed quite planet-struck when the riot commenced, and more frightened than any other of the spectators! The mob, although they left the front of the Court House, still seemed disposed to mischief, until a large body of Europeans, marching from Fort William, effectually dispersed them.

In this attack, I was one amongst many other sufferers, having a palankeen which cost me three hundred rupees totally demolished. The infuriate Mussulmen also broke down several of the gates to the entrance of a range called the Writer's Buildings, demolishing the windows, lamps, and everything that came within their power, pelting and beating every European they met with. So uncommon and extraordinary a breach of the peace occurring in the British capital of India, and upon the court itself, occasioned universal astonishment all over the provinces. A common opinion prevailed that Sydaat Ali had encouraged and promoted the riot, with a view to a general massacre of the Europeans; which coming to the Nabob's knowledge, he instantly published and distributed throughout Calcutta a strong and energetic disclaimer of his being directly or indirectly privy to the intentions of the mob or having anything to do with them; on the contrary, that himself and all his attendants had done their utmost to pacify the rioters and to quell the disturbance. He concluded a well-drawn address by offering a reward of five thousand rupees to any person or persons who would discover the principals, or any of those who had

either directly or indirectly promoted or encouraged the riot. In consequence of this outrageous tumult, Government issued an order that
thenceforward no religious processions should be allowed to pass
through the town of Calcutta during the celebration of the Mohurrem,
which order has from that time been strictly adhered to.

16

ON LEAVE FROM INDIA

CRESSY'S demurrer coming on for argument in a few days after the above extraordinary occurrences, the Court Room was once more crowded with auditors at an early hour. The business being called on, Cressy acquitted himself better than I thought possible, reading his document with much propriety and emphasis. The Chief Justice, who was prepared to hear something out of the usual line, sat with patience a great part of the time; but his natural irascibility operating at last, he completely lost his temper, interrupting Cressy every half minute, calling him a conceited, impudent blockhead, fool, madman, the weak instrument and tool of a man who ought to have known better than to encourage such absurdity and presumption, vehemently adding, "You obstinate fool! you are wilfully running your head against a stone wall, and must inevitably dash out your brains"; whereupon Mr. Justice Hyde drily remarked, "I defy him to do that for brains he has none; the fellow's an idiot."

Cressy having finished, a loud and general clapping of hands ensued, at which Sir Elijah was extremely offended, repeatedly roaring out like an angry schoolmaster, "Silence! Silence, I say"; which at last being obtained, he expressed his sentiments in indignant terms at the indecency of plaudits in a court of justice, and that any person guilty of such unwarrantable conduct was liable to commitment to prison. Order being restored, the counsel for the plaintiff in the action rose to address the court on behalf of his client, when the Chief Justice stopped him, saying there was no occasion to give himself the trouble of answering such offensive stuff, such trash, as had just disgraced the court; and again he very severely alluded to Colonel Watson as the instigator. He then took blame to himself for having allowed the time of the judges to be wasted in listening to such a farrago of nonsense and impudence as had been delivered by the defendant; "for," continued he, "although the plaintiff's attorney inadvertently demurred to the plea, instead of setting down the cause *ex parte*, as he should have done, still the judges, upon reading the record, ought to have rectified

the inadvertency and not have heard a syllable upon the occasion";
that, late as it was, he should then proceed to give judgment just as in
an *ex parte* case, and give a judgment for the plaintiff with four hundred sicca rupees damages and costs!

The other action against Cressy was not tried, his counsel advising
him to let a judgment go for the same damages as in the one determined, reserving a right of appeal. The agitation of this question
created a great interest not only in Bengal, but all over the Company's
provinces, Cressy receiving the most flattering and complimentary
addresses from every direction as the staunch supporter of the rights
and privileges of Englishmen. He was pronounced the Wilkes of India.
A subscription was instantly set on foot, by which a large sum was
raised and presented to him to reimburse him the expense and trouble
he had been put to. Colonel Watson was extremely desirous of appealing from the judgment of the court, a measure I could not sanction
because I saw no chance of success. I, therefore, said as much to the
gentlemen of the committee, but recommended their being governed,
not by what I said, but by the opinions of the counsel concerned in
the cause. To this they acceded; I therefore drew a case, stating every
circumstance candidly and fairly, of which Colonel Watson approved.
One copy was submitted to Mr. Newman, another to Mr. Lawrence,
and a third to Mr. Tilghman, who all in the most decided language
said no appeal could possibly succeed under such circumstances; nor
did they believe a lawyer could be found who would affix his name to
a petition of appeal in such a case.

Colonel Watson, notwithstanding this opinion, resolved the matter
should not drop. He therefore got together a few leading men, to
whom he proposed calling a meeting of the British inhabitants of
Calcutta, to deliberate on the steps most proper to be taken in order
to bring the question before the Legislature of Great Britain. A summons was issued; and, in January 1779, a very numerous assembly met
at the Theatre, at which a petition to Parliament was unanimously
voted, praying a repeal of the act under which the Court was constituted, and that British subjects might in India, as they were in all
other parts of His Majesty's Dominions, be allowed a trial by jury! A
committee was chosen to prepare such petition, and to do all that was
requisite to promote the success of the same.

Early in February 1779, the committee had prepared the petition to
His Majesty and to the Parliament of Great Britain, praying that
the act under which the Supreme Court was established might be
amended, especially by granting His Majesty's subjects resident within
the provinces of Bengal, Behar and Orissa, their right of trial by jury in
all cases, civil as well as criminal. A meeting of the British inhabitants
was then convened to hear this petition read, which was unanimously

St. John's Church, Calcutta. Coloured engraving by Thomas Daniell, 1788.

By courtesy of the India Office Library

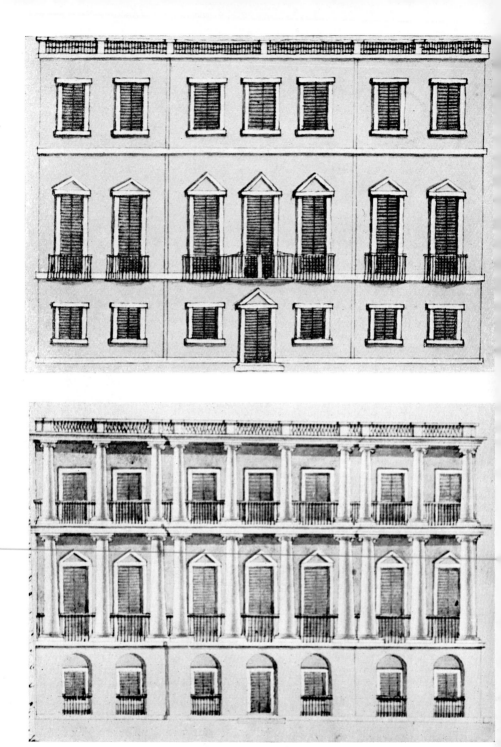

Hickey's own drawings of his house in Calcutta, before and after his
addition of a veranda.

approved and pronounced an eloquent and masterly performance. A further large sum was next raised by subscription to defray the expenses of carrying the object into effect. And now I first communicated to my friend Colonel Watson my wish to go to Europe for a couple of years, and to be the bearer of the petition, etc. He gave the most decided opinion against my taking what he called so inconsiderate and imprudent a step, observing that I was in the fair and high road to fortune, universally respected, living in the first society, in short, *"with the ball at my foot"*; to relinquish which unnecessarily seemed to him to be absolute insanity. Notwithstanding I felt the truth and full force of the colonel's remarks, yet, the idea of revisiting old haunts having once got into my giddy brain, I had neither prudence nor fortitude enough to resist.

Colonel Watson finding me obstinately regardless of what he and all my real friends urged, and that nothing could dissuade me from the voyage, he most kindly endeavoured to render the trip as beneficial to me as possible. He, at the next meeting of the committee, mentioned my sudden determination to leave India, and proposed that the petition should be delivered into my charge to convey it to Europe; that my expenses should be paid, and a further sum of two hundred pounds be allowed me annually for two years after my arrival in London; all which was agreed to by the committee, every member expressing himself happy at having an opportunity to comply with my wishes, though they lamented my thus early leaving Bengal. At a subsequent meeting, it was resolved that the allowance should be increased to four instead of two hundred pounds, and that I should be fully reimbursed the expenses of my voyage home.

In March 1779, I applied to Captain Arthur Gore, of the *Nassau*, for accommodation in his ship, which, together with the *Southampton*, Captain Lenox, were shortly to sail. These two ships, as I have already observed, had been assisting in Sir Edward Vernon's fleet for upwards of a twelvemonth. Captain Gore told me the whole of his round house and great cabin were already disposed of, but that I might have a spacious cabin on the larboard side of the cuddy for five thousand sicca rupees. I, therefore, closed the business at once by consenting to take that accommodation upon the terms proposed. Mentioning this to Colonel Watson, he said he would make the committee forthwith advance me ten thousand rupees to pay Gore and other port charges during my voyage; but I said I had already more cash than was necessary for those purposes and should prefer receiving the whole amount in England. The colonel still urging me to take a part at least, I drew upon the committee for the sum I was to pay Captain Gore; and lucky would it have been for me had I taken all that was offered.

The time of my departure fast approaching, I desired my banyan

9+

Durgachuru Muckerjee to prepare his accounts for settlement, which he promised, but neglected, to perform. My debts were soon ascertained. I having made it a rule to pay everything I owed at the end of each month, except my tailor, to whom I imagined I might be indebted from fifteen hundred to two thousand rupees, but to my utter astonishment received a bill for near five thousand. Certainly I had a great wardrobe of rich clothes. Having got intimation that I must embark, I again pressed my banyan for his accounts, but in vain; I could not procure them. I called to take leave of Sir Robert Chambers and Mr. Justice Hyde, both of whom were very civil and kind. Sir Elijah Impey had spoken with so much anger against me for the assistance I had afforded in the petition that I did not choose to pay him the compliment of a visit.

The 10th April being fixed for our departure, Mr. Lacam offered me the use of a very commodious yacht of his to convey me to the ship, then lying at the Barrabulla; and, Mr. Lacam being thoroughly acquainted with that difficult and dangerous channel, I thought it prudent to accept his offer. As I always shunned the ceremony of leave-taking, I left Calcutta privately on the 15th, having that morning received my final instructions and dispatches from the committee, and went down to Mr. Lacam's house, where I remained three days. In the evening of the 17th, Captain Gore, accompanied by Major Webber, called at Mr. Lacam's; when the Major, who lived within half a mile, invited Mr. Lacam and me to take an early dinner with him the following day, as we were to embark at four o'clock. The Major also communicated to me a plan he had formed for alarming a Captain Bentley of the Bengal army, who was going to Europe in the *Nassau*. This Bentley I had heard spoken of as little removed from an idiot, though he had intellect enough to scrape together two lacs of rupees, which sum occasioned him infinite anxiety. By nature suspicious, he had conceived no bills could be secure; he, therefore, determined to take the amount he possessed with him in cash, which was accordingly deposited in eight strong wooden boxes, and the freight paid for them. This treasure was sent off from Calcutta in a pilot schooner of the Company's.

Major Webber having asked Captain Bentley to join the dining party at his house, the hoax was to be there carried into effect. Being assembled on the 18th at Major Webber's, we at one o'clock sat down to dinner. In the middle of the meal, a gentleman came in, who almost immediately told us a melancholy event had occurred in the wreck of the *Warren Hastings* pilot schooner, which in going to Kedgeree had struck upon a sand, instantly overset, and was totally lost, every soul on board perishing; that in an hour not a vestige of her remained; and that the loss was the more serious from her having the packets for the two Indiamen on board.

Captain Bentley, upon hearing this, turned extremely pale, and with the utmost agitation said his money was on board her. Captain Gore said it was unlucky, but that he could not be a material sufferer as no doubt the property was insured; to which Bentley, in an agony, replied, "Oh no, sir, not a rupee of it. I am undone, ruined, undone for ever," and he burst into tears. Major Webber, who was a humane and benevolent man, was distressed beyond measure when he saw the serious effect of his joke, and instantly said he had no doubt but that the boxes of rupees would be recovered, and he would directly send a man on horseback to Calcutta to ascertain the particulars. Bentley continuing in a state of torpid despair, the Major in a few minutes left the room, and returning immediately said a messenger had arrived to say the account of the loss of the vessel was a mistake, it being a pariah sloop in company to which the accident had happened. Captain Bentley was then congratulated; but the fright had deprived him of the little sense he possessed and he could not rally, sitting weeping like a child.

Upon rising to go on board our vessel, I found Captain Bentley had no conveyance but a *paunceway*, a sort of boat very unequal to go down the river at that season. I therefore offered him a passage in Mr. Lacam's sloop, which he thankfully accepted. At five, we got under way with a strong gale from the south, which was in our teeth. Two miles below Mr. Lacam's resided Mr. Playdell, the father of my shipmate, who, with a large party that had dined with him, came to the waterside upon our passing and gave us three cheers, which we returned. That evening we anchored off Budge Budge, where I landed to shake Major Mestayer by the hand.

On the 19th it blew hard; the vessel we were in, nevertheless, made considerable progress, being admirably found and well manned. That day we worked down to Kedgeree, there waiting for the ebb tide. During the night, the wind increased and we tumbled about dreadfully. The *Southampton* that night lost three anchors. On the 22nd, after a boisterous and very unpleasant passage, we got on board the *Nassau*, then laying in a wild and open sea, surrounded by sands over which the surf broke tremendously in every direction. She was eight miles distant from the nearest land. The first man I beheld on going up the *Nassau*'s side was my old *New Shoreham* shipmate, Jerry Griffin, who I found was boatswain, and with whom I renewed my acquaintance.

The 23rd, the wind being less violent, the sea was not so high; and we got a little to rights. At slack water Mr. Stephen Bayard, a civil servant of the Company's, came on board to dispatch the ship. Upon entering the round house with his hat on, Captain Gore, with much hauteur, asked him if he knew where he was, to which Bayard coolly said, "Yes, on board the *Nassau* East Indiaman." Gore in a violent rage observed, "This is my apartment; and, did you possess the common civility due from one gentleman to another, you would not have entered it covered." This speech not producing the desired effect, Captain Gore added, "I advise your quitting this cabin; otherwise I shall certainly take off your hat for you in a way not the most gentle"; upon which Mr. Bayard made a precipitate retreat to the quarterdeck, immediately commencing upon the duty that had brought him on board; which having finished he left the ship without taking any further notice of Captain Gore. But, the moment his boat pushed from alongside, he stood up and called out in a loud voice, "Depend upon it, Mr. Irish Skipper, if ever I meet with you on shore I will reward your insolence of today as it deserves, by a kicking." This brutal speech put Captain Gore into a great rage; and it was with difficulty we prevented him from following Bayard to chastise him.

The 24th, 25th and 26th, it blew so hard the pilots dare not move the ships, though we expected our cables would part every moment, the strain upon them being so immense. In the afternoon of the 26th, I was sitting in the round house with Captain Gore, talking of the horrid weather, when Captain Bentley entered without ceremony. Captain Gore looked surprised, but politely pointed to a chair that was securely lashed. Bentley seemed agitated, as I supposed from alarm at the situation we were in; he, however, soon explained the cause by the following speech: "Captain Gore, you have made a laughing stock of me and treated me basely; I therefore hope, sir, as a gentleman you have insulted you will *favour* me with satisfaction."

Captain Gore, looking more wild than usual, raising both hands to his hair, a common motion of his when in a passion, and turning to me hastily said, "Zounds! sir, did you ever hear anything like this," and without waiting for my answer, said to Bentley, "What the devil do you mean? Do you imagine me to be as great an idiot as yourself?" "No, sir," simply replied Bentley, "but as I saw you behave so properly to Mr. Bayard, I was in hopes you would not refuse me satisfaction." "Satisfaction!" echoed Gore, "why zounds! man, do you expect me to leave my ship here, in the midst of sands and dangers in a gale of wind, to go the devil knows where to fight you?" "No, sir," again mildly said Bentley, "if you please we can settle it here." This drove the captain almost frantic, he violently exclaiming, "God damn your blood for an ass and fool! Get out! Get out, you stupid scoundrel, or I'll break every bone in your damned carcase and throw you over the balcony." Poor Bentley, seeing Captain Gore in such a rage, retired with all speed. After such a scene, I concluded the military hero would have remained in his cabin until we reached Madras, and there have called Gore out; instead of which he made his appearance, taking his seat at the supper table as usual and behaving to Captain Gore just as if nothing had happened.

On the 19th, the wind being less boisterous, we worked down a narrow channel about eight miles. The 30th, being still more moderate, we made a better progress. Whilst at anchor this day, another schooner joined us, from which a sircar° from Durgachuru Muckerjee's came, presenting me with a bond ready filled up for the penal sum of ten thousand sicca rupees, which he claimed as the amount due upon balance of account. Although satisfied I did not owe him two thousand, yet was I absurd enough to execute the proffered bond and deliver the same to the sircar, who went off well pleased with the success of his mission.

In the *Nassau* we had only three passengers—myself, Bentley and Lieutenant Grand of the Artillery, a young man going to sea for his health; he was brother to the husband of Mr. Francis's fair friend. Being, though young in years, a man of observation, he at once discovered Bentley to be a sort of body capable of being made an advantage of, and laid himself out to derive that advantage. Bentley was fond of cards, conceiving himself a superior player of piquet, an idea that Grand encouraged. They had frequent contests at the game for many hours together, in the early part of the contest Bentley generally rising a winner by three or four games. As we approached our destination, fortune changed, and the artilleryman was a gainer of near five thousand rupees by the contest! The fact was he could, and ought to, have given Bentley at least twenty points.

The officers of the *Nassau* were Mr. William Greer, chief mate, an absolute sot, who kept himself in a state of constant intoxication, as might well be the case from his grog, as he termed it, being always three parts spirit. The second was Mr. John Pascal Larkins, a worthy man and admirable seaman; Joseph Clarkson, the third, and John Rogers, the fourth; John Smith, surgeon; William Darling, purser. From the time the ship left her moorings at Culpee, Mr. Greer had been confined to his cabin under the plea of indisposition, which Captain Gore asserted was a mere pretence to avoid doing the duty of his station, an opinion that was strengthened by Mr. Larkins's declaring the same; and he was not a man to be biassed by prejudice or misrepresentation. Smith, the surgeon, was an absolute maniac, uncommonly able in his profession, but his general conduct so eccentric as to justify my having pronounced him a maniac. The nickname by which he was generally designated was "Quicksilver Jack."

We had horrid weather for several days after the pilot left us, an

° A Hindu upper servant.

uninterrupted gale, with tremendous squalls and incessant rain, accompanied by such peals of thunder and vivid flashes of lightning as are rarely seen or heard. During one of the most boisterous nights (by a little fair management with the man at the helm) we most happily parted from the *Southampton.* At daylight, she was not to be seen. Every measure was thereupon adopted to rejoin her; or perhaps I should be nearer the truth in introducing the word *not* before "to rejoin her." Be that as it may, we saw no more of her between Bengal and Madras.

We made the Andaman Islands during exceeding tempestuous weather, not a day passing without our carrying away tacks, sheets, or haul-yards, splitting sails every hour, and altogether being most uncomfortable. During the month of May we only had one observation. On 1st June, Captain Gore told me he despaired of ever reaching Madras, and said he must proceed to Malacca to refit and replenish; in the necessity of which all his officers agreeing, we bore up two points, standing direct for the Straits; but four-and-twenty hours afterwards the wind became somewhat more favourable, which induced a renewal of the endeavours to gain our destined port of Madras. About eleven o'clock in the morning of the 4th, the sun broke forth with great brightness, notwithstanding the tempest still raged with unabated fury. This afforded us the important advantage of an observation, whereby we clearly ascertained our latitude. The same afternoon, we distinctly saw the northern point of Sumatra and some small islands that lay off it. We also made the Nicobars, of which we had a clear and distinct view, thus ascertaining that the Sombrere Channel was fairly open to us, and nothing to obstruct our passage through it. We consequently stood boldly on, all in high spirits in spite of the bad weather, and resolved to do honour to the festival of His Majesty's birthday at our supper.

As the night approached, the gale increased so much that we could scarcely bear close-reefed topsails with the wind upon the beam. This did not prevent our filling some bumpers to George the Third's health, and being very merry. It drawing towards midnight, we were beginning to talk of retiring to our cots when Mr. Larkins sent a quartermaster to request Captain Gore would come upon deck, a summons that created some alarms amongst us, which was not a little increased by hearing a general uproar immediately afterwards and the people all in confusion. Upon going under the awning, I found land had been discovered close to us, extending from the lee bow to abaft the beam. Captain Gore, panic-struck, knew not what he was about, giving orders and counter-orders in the same breath, and crying out to put the ship about. In the midst of the bustle, Mr. Greer crawled from his cabin, desiring that an anchor might be let go, whereupon Mr. Larkins exclaimed, "An anchor, Mr. Greer! In the name of God, what can be expected from an anchor in such a sea as we are now encountering? Our only chance of escape is by making sail and endeavouring to clear the land that has so unexpectedly come in our way."

Every person on board competent to judge felt the force of what Mr. Larkins said; and all were equally ready to testify to the extraordinary skill and exertions of the boatswain, Jerry Griffin, who, when the men hesitated to perform a requisite duty from the risk attending it, himself set them an example, going out to the weather yard-arm of the main topsail, and succeeding in handing the sail, the whole time using the most extraordinary and out-of-the-way expressions. A reef was forthwith let out of each of the topsails, the courses reefed and set, and the ship hauled close to the wind; and this she bore admirably, though we had before thought too much sail was set, and something was giving way every half-hour. We perceptibly passed the land rapidly, which, when the nearest to us, appeared towering above the mast-heads and that we must inevitably be upon it. The night was uncommonly dark, with a tremendous sea running, rendering our situation truly alarming, indeed absolutely desperate. Upon my leaving the cabin, the other gentlemen followed, when Larkins entreated me to return, as we might be in the way and could be of no use. We, therefore, retired to the round house, soon after which Captain Bentley entered with a candle and lantern in his hand. Quite at a loss to account for this, I asked him the meaning of it; when, with his usual simplicity, he answered, "As I hear we are likely to go on shore, I should like to see where to land." This strange speech struck all present most forcibly, Darling, the purser, gravely observing, "I believe, Captain Bentley, your light will not prove of any use; for, in such a sea as is now running, if the ship once strikes, a few moments will decide our fate by consigning us all to watery graves."

In two hours we had cleared the land sufficiently to consider the danger over, and congratulated each other upon our miraculous escape. At four in the morning, the day dawned, showing us the land that had caused our danger within a short distance upon our lee quarter; but, as we had no ground with sixty fathoms of line, and all clear ahead, we had no further apprehensions. It is a most extraordinary circumstance that in a passage so much frequented as that of the Sombrere Channel was, and had been for a great number of years, by all ships bound from Madras to China, there should be almost in the middle of it an island totally unknown, or, at least, unnoticed in the charts of those seas; yet such indubitably was the fact. Having escaped this danger, our next dread was that, in crossing the bay, the current would drive us so far to the northward we should not be able to make Madras. Luckily, the wind proved favourable, so that we made the coast within three leagues of our port; off which place we anchored on 11th June, having been six weeks on the passage, then considered a fair period against the monsoon and when scarcely any of our ships were copper-bottomed.

Upon landing, I found Mr. Hall Plumer waiting to receive me, who immediately conveyed me to his house in the fort, where I had a couple of spacious and handsome apartments allotted to my use. Having dined with my friend, we got into his phaeton and drove to Choultry Plain, where he likewise had a delightful country residence, and where he generally slept, in the neighbourhood whereof he was building a magnificent mansion, the superintendance of which was his principal amusement early in the morning, previous to going to town, and again in the evening upon his return. He, at that time, had the contract for completing the works, particularly an entire newly constructed sea-line, presenting a truly formidable battery of the heaviest guns. Two days after my arrival at Madras, I called upon Captain Gore, who told me he had just received the unpleasant information that the foremast was discovered to be so badly sprung as to be wholly unfit to stand, and he feared there would be extreme difficulty in procuring a new one at Madras.

The months of June and July having elapsed without any tidings of the *Southampton*, people began to be apprehensive for her safety. Early in August, the *Nassau*'s foremast, being fished and made as complete as possible, was sent off and again put in its proper place. Sir Thomas Rumbold* told me he every week expected a large fleet from Europe under Sir Edward Hughes, and that if they arrived in time we should have Sir Edward Vernon in the *Ripon* to convoy us. On the 5th, Captain Gore invited me to dinner to meet my fellow passengers that were to be. I accordingly went and found Mr. George Smith, his wife and three lovely children, who were to occupy the round house, and Colonel Flint and his wife, as worthy a pair as ever lived. These, with the sagacious Bentley and the ship's officers, then on shore, made the party.

Every day now increased the alarms about the *Southampton*. Accounts arrived of the French naval commandant Trou Jolie having, with his squadron, left the Bay and sailed for the Mauritius, where it was said another officer waited to relieve him. All hopes of ever seeing the *Southampton* were over, when, early in the morning of 20th August, a large ship was seen to the northward, working up alongshore. From her appearance hopes were entertained that it might be a long-given-up ship; and so it proved. In the afternoon, the *Southampton* came to an anchor in the roads. Captain Lenox landed immediately, myself and Captain Gore going directly to congratulate him upon his arrival. He

* Governor of Madras.

appeared much surprised when told the *Nassau* had been ten weeks at Madras.

The day after the *Southampton* arrived, Captains Gore and Lenox each received an official letter from the Secretary to inform them they must respectively receive on board their ships eleven French officers and seventy private soldiers of the garrison of Pondicherry,* and convey them to England pursuant to an article of the capitulation; that the officers, being upon parole, were to be treated with respect and consideration merely as passengers. I happened to be with Captain Gore when he received this document, and never beheld a man in a greater rage than he was; he swore he would not take a man of them, desiring his purser to answer the government letter to that effect. The steady Darling, however, knew better than to do so. I had now reason to rejoice that I had fixed myself in the cuddy, thereby avoiding such a numerous addition to the residents between decks.

On 29th October, the French officers and privates embarked; when a new source of vexation arose to Captain Gore from one of the officers having a wife, for whom no provision had been made. Colonel Flint had half the great cabin, and Captain Bentley the remainder, except a common passage taken off to the quarter gallery, a corner of which passage Captain Gore was obliged to partition off for the lady to sleep in, being so small there was literally room only for the cot and herself to stand in.

In the morning of the 30th, I embarked. I found Captain Gore in a violent rage from the quarterdeck's being covered, and the passage blocked up by trunks, chests, bandboxes, and packages of every description, belonging to Mrs. Smith, who, he swore, had sent on board one hundred and twenty different parcels; and, to increase his perplexity, the French officers had made a formal complaint that they had no place to sleep in. To a man naturally irritable, this accumulation of untoward circumstances was a severe trial. Perceiving how much he was annoyed, I strove to console him, though rather unsuccessfully; for he continued to curse and swear outrageously at the unreasonable and shameful quantity of baggage with which the Smiths had encumbered the ship, declaring that in case bad weather came up, which might be expected every hour, the whole must, and would be, thrown overboard. In the midst of the bustle, Mr. Smith and his family came alongside in the Government boat, Captain Gore instantly attacking poor Mr. Smith with uncommon vehemence, for whom I felt great compassion, the poor man being before sufficiently tormented in attending to the complaints of his wife and children. Mrs. Smith was quite as furious as Captain Gore, whom she honoured with the epithets of "brute," "sea-monster," and "savage," vowing she would not stay on

---

* Pondicherry had been captured by the British for the second time in 1778.

ʊ*

board the *Nassau*. "As to you, George," said she, turning to her husband, "you may do as you please, stay or go, I care not; but, for myself, proceed in this abominable pigsty I will not." Mrs. Smith's intemperate behaviour quite silenced Captain Gore; and Mr. Larkins just coming forward and endeavouring to pacify the lady, succeeded. Good humour was restored; and Larkins engaged that, in a couple of hours, everything should be completely arranged to her perfect satisfaction. Whilst so employed, Captain Marlow entered, who seeing us so hard at work directly ordered up his boat's crew, a fine, active set of fellows, who soon cleeted and lashed everything in a capital style.

Captain Gore spoke not a word of French; nor did one of the passengers except myself. He therefore requested me to tell the officers they must excuse for a few days the confused state of the ship, after which everything should be arranged for their comfort and convenience. No men could behave better than they did, all of them expressing their readiness to submit to sleep upon their chests, or on the deck, until the ship was put to rights. They were remarkably quiet and good-humoured. Two of them, Colonel Rousselle and Major St. Paul, spoke a little English.

At two in the afternoon, Colonel and Mrs. Flint came on board; at five, the admiral made the signal to unmoor by loosing his fore topsail and firing a gun. Towards sunset, the horizon became exceedingly black, and there were strong indications of an approaching gale from the north-east. It fell dead calm, which was considered as a bad symptom; of course, we could not stir. At nine at night a torrent of rain poured down, which continued the greater part of the night, when the weather cleared up. At daybreak, just as I had fallen into a doze, after laying awake from the moment I went to bed, I was roused by the discharging of a gun, when jumping up and looking out I had the pleasure to see a beautiful morning with a pleasant breeze from the northward, and the fleet getting under way; at sunrise the fort saluted the admiral, which his ship returned. We made sail, soon losing sight of Madras, and had a capital run that day.

On 2nd November we entered Trincomalee, one of the most capacious and best harbours in the world, then belonging to Holland. The face of the country in every direction was beautifully romantic; the houses, with the exception of two or three, execrable. Joe Revell, being greatly attached to the Smith family, accompanied them to spend the time we were to pass at Ceylon in their society, and a prodigious acquisition he was from his uncommon flow of spirits and convivial qualities. As he spoke German fluently, he was of material use in procuring many things for us we otherwise should not have had. Through his interference a miserable residence was obtained for Mr. Smith on shore, also a room for me in the fort, but so dreadfully hot, and so tormented was I by mosquitoes in it, that I only tried it for one night, after which I always went on board the *Nassau* to sleep.

The day but one after that on which we anchored at Trincomalee the monsoon shifted, with a severe gale of wind, incessant heavy rain for six-and-thirty hours, and tremendous thunder and lightning. I remained the whole time on board and had reason to rejoice at being so well sheltered; for, upon landing when the weather cleared up, I found the Smiths, with Colonel and Mrs. Flint, to whom they had given a room, in woeful plight, their apartments being deluged, the rain pouring in through apertures innumerable, so that they had not a dry spot in the house, nor a single change of clothes to put on, all being completely soaked. During two entire nights they had been obliged to sit up, the children having thereby all got severe colds.

This grievance being forgot, we amused ourselves by fishing, hunting *guanas*, and making short excursions on the borders of most beautiful groves, also rowing about various inlets and small bays where we found innumerable *guanas*, an animal of the lizard kind but very much larger; they make a rich soup; many people think it even superior to turtle. The Dutch eat the flesh too; but that I never could bring myself to do. We got plenty of wild hog, with which the island abounds; a high-flavoured, delicious meat.

The frequent heavy showers of rain that fell made it very disagreeable, especially to the French officers and soldiers shut up between decks in a confined, close part of the ship, the heat oppressive, and wholly debarring them from all exercise. Day after day passed without bringing any intelligence respecting Sir Edward Hughes, which made Captain Gore miserable, from his dread that, if we were obliged to sail without convoy, the Frenchmen, who doubled our number, would murder us all and run away with the ship to France. This idea struck me with being as unjust as it was illiberal. The officers were elegant gentlemen, and, I firmly believe, men of the strictest honour, the privates, orderly, quiet, and well-behaved as could be; besides which they were not going to Europe as prisoners, but were, by an article of the capitulation, to be sent to England on parole, to be treated the same as any other passengers during the voyage, and on the ship's arrival at home to be dispatched for France at the expense of government. Captain Gore, however, was of a very different opinion to me; nor did he seem disposed to change it, always appearing uneasy at seeing the officers walking the deck in their uniforms and swords, which they daily did. To such a length did Gore carry his fears that it came to the knowledge of the French officers, who thereupon sent for me to their berth to express their surprise and mortification at Captain Gore's doing them such injustice, by suspecting them of conduct derogatory to their characters as officers and gentlemen. I could only endeavour to console them by assuring them the idea was confined to the captain alone, and advising them to take no notice whatever to it, by which I was convinced his ridiculous fears would subside. They, with the utmost good nature, promised to follow my advice.

No hopes remaining of Sir Edward Hughes's arrival, Sir Edward Vernon gave orders for the departure of the two ships, and on 30th November we sailed with moderate and pleasing weather. Scarce had we cleared the land ere symptoms of that horrible disease, the scurvy, made its appearance, a circumstance that increased Captain Gore's fears respecting the Frenchmen. The fourth day after we left Ceylon, he told me he must take the French officers' side-arms from them for the safety of the ship; that he intended therefore civilly to ask them to deliver the same into his custody until they reached England, when he would restore them. I without hesitation gave it as my decided opinion he would be very wrong to require such a sacrifice, Colonel Flint and Mr. Smith coinciding with me, telling Captain Gore nothing could justify an act of that sort. His fears, however, predominated, and he sent Mr. Darling, his purser, with a message to the French officers, requesting they would deliver up their swords and fire-arms, to remain in his custody during the voyage. After a strong remonstrance against such a requisition, the officers, who had appeared upon deck to express their sentiments, finding what they said had no effect upon Captain Gore, retired for about five minutes, when they reappeared, dressed in full regimentals, with their swords on, Colonel Rousselle again expressing his hope that Captain Gore would not enforce his order. Upon finding he was determined to do so, Colonel Rousselle went to the gangway and threw his sword overboard. His example was followed by the whole party except one, a lieutenant in the army, of most interesting appearance, who said he felt the unmerited insult so wantonly offered by the commander of the ship as sensibly as his brother officers possibly could; but having no subsistence independent of his profession, and his sword having been the last gift of a much-valued parent, then no more, he could not bring himself to throw it away as his comrades had very properly done. He then very gracefully presented his sword to Colonel Flint, entreating he would compassionate his acute feelings and retain the gift of a revered parent until the ungenerous suspicions of Captain Gore were done away, and he thereby be entitled to demand the restoration of it. Colonel Flint accepted the sword in a neat and most appropriate speech, lamenting the mistaken caution of Captain Gore requiring such a sacrifice of feelings, assuring the French officers that not only himself, but every English passenger on board the *Nassau*, entertained the highest respect for them. Captain Gore felt ashamed of his suspicions, yet had not candour enough to admit that he did so.

After being at sea three weeks, many of the crew were so seriously attacked by the scurvy as to be rendered incapable of doing duty, our distress being magnified by the weather's becoming very boisterous off the south end of Madagascar. We, however, proceeded until 15th January, at which time, being in the latitude of thirty-nine-and-a-half south in order to avoid the enemy's ships, a tremendous gale came on from the west-north-west, as adverse a wind as could blow; the ship was laid to under a balanced mizzen, tumbling about dreadfully. In three days, we lost six of the hands from the scurvy, all of whom died suddenly, three of them dropping to rise no more whilst at the helm. Within the following twelve days, our loss amounted to thirty-three, when we began really and truly to think we never should reach St. Helena, or any port. Captain Gore, terrified beyond measure at the forlorn state we were in, carried his weakness so far that at last he would not receive the sick list from the doctor, also forbidding any tolling of the bell as was customary previous to performing the funeral service upon a corpse being committed to the deep. He shut himself up in his cabin, from which he never stirred except to attend at meals.

In the height of the bad weather, it becoming necessary to hand the fore topsail (then close-reefed), the few men we had were so reduced and debilitated by illness that they remained two hours upon the yard in fruitless exertions and endeavours to do the duty they had been sent upon. This so enraged Jerry Griffin, the boatswain, that, after a volley of the most blasphemous oaths, he dropped upon his knees, raising his hands as if in an act of devotion, and prayed to the Almighty that there might not be living enough left in the ship to bury the dead. Soon after uttering this impious and horrid wish, he observed the poor creatures upon the yard were likely to succeed in furling the sail; he in the instant clapped his hands, exultingly crying out to the men aloft, "That's right, that's right. Well done, messmates, well done, my lads, my proper b——rs, as boys say at taw!" At this time I was under the awning with Colonel Flint, who said, "What can the boatswain mean? I never heard of such a term as taw in my life." To gratify the colonel, I asked Jerry for an explanation, when, scratching his head, he replied, "Damn me if I know exactly; but if you look in the dictionary I dare say you'll learn all about it." To *Johnson* we went, though without the least expectation of receiving any information, nor did we from thence, or from two other dictionaries when Mr. Smith observing that he had a very ancient dictionary in which he had often met with words unnoticed in more modern ones, we requested to see it, and upon its production were much surprised at finding the information sought for. After the explanation of "an unnatural crime, etc." followed these words, "Also a term used by boys in playing marbles." So that Jerry, in this instance, proved better versed in the English language than any of us were.

The following morning, Colonel Flint was talking to an invalid soldier whom he had often seen when serving with the army. As this man appeared to be free from scurvy, the colonel congratulated him upon preserving his health amidst such general and fatal disease, asking if he had used any particular means to avoid infection, when the fellow bluntly replied, "Grog, your honour, grog is your only. I'll be damned if scurvy, or any other malady, ever hurts me while I have plenty of grog, which possesses more virtues than all the contents of the doctor's medicine chest." During the conversation we were summoned to dinner, and accordingly went into the cuddy, where we were scarcely seated ere the doctor was called out; but, as that occurred daily, nothing was said by any present. In a few minutes he returned, to our inexpressible surprise and horror announcing the man whom Colonel Flint had just before been talking with was dead!—a shocking exit this, which occurred in many instances.

The great injustice Captain Gore had done our French officers and privates was now made manifest by their voluntarily coming forward and offering their assistance in working the ship; which from that hour they did with the utmost zeal, a few amongst them who had been seamen proving of the greatest use; and there is not a doubt but we owed our preservation entirely to them. Our companion, the *Southampton*, could give us no aid, the crew being all affected by scurvy though not of so fatal and disastrous a kind as ours. Smith (the surgeon) was grievously distressed at seeing the ravages made by the cruel distemper without having it in his power to prevent or alleviate the misfortune, though he made various experiments for that purpose. Wine, sugar, spruce, and every other anti-scorbutic procurable were abundantly supplied without material benefit. The three first men that died Smith opened, hoping to gain some information from the state of certain parts of the inside; but he was disappointed, all the vital parts appearing sound and healthy.

To return to our melancholy situation. A fine active lad about eighteen years of age, a midshipman, whose name was Smith, was amongst the earliest of those attacked by the scurvy. Being blessed with fine spirits and an uncommon share of fortitude, he resisted the fatal malady in an extraordinary manner, declaring he would not yield but would do his duty as long as he could stand. He kept his resolution, nor left the deck until he dropped, as was supposed, dead. Being conveyed to his cot and medicine administered, he rallied, though not sufficiently to be able to go upon deck again. We all felt extremely interested for this young man; the doctor's attentions, too, were unremitting. One symptom of the disorder was an extraordinary listlessness and disinclination to move. Being urged to exert himself, he repeatedly jumped out of his cot, but had not strength enough to support himself and generally fainted. Every comfort the ship afforded was given to him.

We had now only sixteen men who could do any duty of the ship's crew. Mr. Larkins therefore considered it high time to take some decisive step, and having spoken to Captain Gore privately without effect, he after dinner on 30th January, addressed him before us all, described the desperate state the ship was reduced to, being worked entirely by the French, no officer but himself and the fifth able to appear upon deck, the fresh provisions entirely exhausted, and only water for three weeks left; that under such circumstances they ought to make for the nearest port at all risks. Captain Gore, terrified at Larkins's speech, asked what he would advise; when Larkins instantly replied, "Make for the Cape as fast as possible." Captain Gore then directed him to speak the *Southampton* and say "our situation having become desperate, we must run for a port." Going as close as the sea would allow to our companion, the communication was made, when Captain Lenox said he thought it absolutely necessary for the preservation of both ships that we should go into the Cape. We accordingly stood direct for the land. The moment this measure was determined on, we went to inform the poor invalid Smith, who lay gasping in his cot, his death being expected every hour. He seemed much gratified by the intelligence, observing in a languid tone that, could he hold out to get a mouthful of fruit, he was sure he should survive.

The 1st February 1780, we struck soundings upon the Bank off Cape Lagullas, early the next morning saw the land; and, as it was then blowing very strong direct onshore, the two commanders determined to make for False Bay instead of rounding the Cape, as the most likely way to avoid any French cruisers. We accordingly (certainly at considerable risk) went close in under the land, running alongshore until four in the afternoon of the 2nd, at which hour we opened False Bay, stood directly in, and at six both ships came to an anchor. Our invalid, Smith, after we made the land, enquired every quarter of an hour with extreme earnestness when we should get in. About noon of the 2nd, he gave up all hopes, lay in the most melancholy state, uttering nothing but, "Oh, fruit, fruit, or I die." Soon after we anchored, a boat from the shore brought off a variety of fruits, vegetables, and refreshments. Everybody ran with the utmost anxiety to Smith's cot with fruit of all sorts. The doctor held a bunch of grapes to him, which the poor fellow (then speechless and entirely exhausted) by an effort raised to his lips, and with a deep groan expired. His death was sincerely lamented by all on board.

[*At the end of February 1780, there still seemed no prospect of the*

Nassau *setting sail again. Hickey, "having already been ten months from Bengal," then decided to continue his journey upon a Dutch ship, which landed him safely in Holland after a voyage of exactly three months. Here he visited Amsterdam, Haarlem, Leyden, Rotterdam, Delft and the Hague. At Helvoetsluys he caught the Harwich packet, reaching England at the end of June. His companion on this journey was his "little pet boy, Nabob," a young Indian page whom Hickey spoiled, but who presently turned out to be a disloyal and ungrateful servant.]*

17

EMILY WARREN

AT eight at night, we landed at Harwich. Mr. Wilkinson having given me a letter to a friend of his in the custom-house, who, he said, would have it in his power to expedite the clearance of my trunks, I sent a waiter with it from the Three Cups Inn, and my compliments, inviting him, if disengaged, to sup with me, as I proposed, if possible, proceeding to London by break of day. In less than half an hour he came. I found him a very gentlemanlike man; he thanked me for bringing the letter from Mr. Wilkinson, for whom he expressed a great regard. He said that, in consequence of my wish to go on, he had sent for one of the office searchers to come to the inn directly, which would prevent my detention until the office opened. Before supper was announced, this person came; whereupon I opened my large trunk, at the same time slipping three guineas into his hand. The man bowed low, and looking at the gentleman, the latter said, "Mr. Hickey tells me he has nothing but what is for his own use. Do not therefore disturb the packing." The man made another profound bow and, shutting the trunk, left the room. Thus, as matters turned out, had it been full of shawls and other India goods, the whole would have been safe; but, alarmed at what I had been told in Amsterdam, I had with me only one article I cared about. This was a Japanese cloak I had purchased for my father to travel in, being, although of great warmth, lighter than the thinnest cloth. It cost me two hundred and fifty dollars at the Cape of Good Hope.

At ten we sat down to supper, drank a couple of bottles of claret, which brought it to midnight, when my guest went to his own house, and I to bed until five in the morning; at which hour I dashed off in a chaise-and-four for Mistley Thorn, the first stage, from thence to Colchester, where I breakfasted, then to Witham, next to Ingatestone; at which place, Nabob complaining of hunger, I stopped that he might appease his craving and, not to be quite unemployed, I took a sandwich. From Ingatestone I went to Romford, and then to London, driving to the East India house in Leadenhall Street, in order to deliver a small packet addressed to the Court of Directors which I brought from Captains Gore and Lenox. This I gave into the hands of the secretary at six o'clock in the evening of 30th June 1780. From the India house I proceeded to St. Albans Street, where I found my three sisters, my father being upon his annual summer excursion to Paris and my brother out of town.

As I had not dined, my sister Mary ordered a hot supper to be got ready as quickly as could be. A little before nine, Mr. Richard Burke, brother to the great Edmund Burke, came in and stayed to partake of the supper. Being an old admirer of Mrs. Sulivan, wife of Mr. Stephen Sulivan, both of whom I left in Bengal, he made particular enquiries about her, which brought forward many anecdotes and circumstances of former times. This and the bottle, to which we made frequent application, beguiled the time so that Mr. Burke, taking out his watch, exclaimed, "Zounds! I could not have believed it. Do you know it is past four o'clock." We, thereupon, parted and retired to rest.

After breakfast, taking a coach, I proceeded with the petition and documents to the chambers of Mr. Irvine in the Temple who, jointly with Mr. Touchet, was appointed agent for managing the business in parliament. Mr. Irvine was a solicitor of eminence, and Mr. Touchet brother to the gentleman in the Company's civil service in Bengal, and just called to the Bar. The latter gentleman being sent for, the packet was opened and the contents examined in my presence. After perusal of the papers, Mr. Irvine observed that, in their instructions from the committee, they were particularly directed to consult me in every stage of the business, and should therefore take care to give me timely notice of their proceedings.

Upon my return home, my sister informed me of the death of my favourite, Tom Forrest, having lost his life from a wound received on board Lord Rodney's ship at the first relief of Gibraltar, at which I was greatly concerned. From my sister I also learnt the horrors of the riots that had occurred three weeks prior to my arrival, which from their novelty and violence paralysed the inhabitants of the metropolis from one extremity to the other, and from the consequences of which they had not yet recovered.° I saw, upon entering the City, some of the effects, and large parties of military, both horse and foot, upon duty in different places, especially at the Bank and in St. Paul's Churchyard. These excesses commenced on 4th June, the King's birthday, continuing with unabated fury the 5th, 6th, and 7th.

The 2nd (of July) Mr. Touchet and Mr. Irvine paid me the compliment of a visit in St. Albans Street, as did Mr. Paxton of Buckingham Street, who, although I had never seen before, I instantly knew from

° The Gordon Riots of June 1780, instigated by the eccentric Lord George Gordon whom Hickey had met with William Cane in June 1776.

his likeness to his brother in Bengal, William, now Sir William Paxton, about whom he came to enquire. Mr. Archibald Paxton and I soon became intimate and were afterwards much together. Enquiring what was become of my old and sincere friend Mr. Cane, I had the mortification to hear he was completely ruined and, as the only means of avoiding being imprisoned by his creditors, had left England, settling with his family in the South of France. At Mrs. Touchet's I met a pleasant party of eight, among whom was Miss Touchet, a clever woman, also two fine lads, Westminsters, named Imhoff, being sons of Mrs. Hastings by her former husband. The old lady treated us most hospitably; her son, two other gentlemen, and myself, doing justice to her excellent burgundy and claret. We did not break up until twelve at night.

On returning home, I found a smart fellow in livery, waiting to deliver a letter, which he said his mistress had sent him with at seven in the evening, ordering him to wait for an answer, no matter how long it might be before he obtained one. It was from Emily Warren, saying she had that moment heard of my arrival and entreated I would immediately call upon her. Enclosed in hers was a letter from my friend Bob Pott, to whom I had written from Amsterdam, to announce being in that city on my way to England. This was an answer, lamenting his being under the necessity of leaving London for Portsmouth, where he was to embark for Bengal in a ship commanded by Captain Collett. He also gave a short account of all that had occurred during his sojourn in Great Britain, dwelling much upon his unbounded love for Emily who had lived with him a year and a half, and who would have accompanied him to India could he have procured a passage for her; which he could not by any means effect, although he even proposed, and Emily agreed to put on the disguise of boy's clothes, in which dress he attempted to pass her as his servant; but Captain Collett's penetration at once saw the deception, and he told Pott it could not be, as it would lose him the command of the ship and be his ruin. He was consequently compelled to leave her behind; that, thus circumstanced, he relied upon my friendship and regard for him to bring out his darling Emily with me, which, if I should fail in my endeavours to do by an English Indiaman, I might easily accomplish on board a French, Swedish, or Danish ship; that he was rendered miserable at being separated from her, nothing saving him from utter despair but the certainty he felt that I would not forsake him in his distress and sorrow.

He further said he had left her in a handsome, well-furnished house in Cork Street, the rent of which he had paid fifteen months in advance, besides abundantly stocking it with all sorts of wines, coals, candles, and every article of housekeeping sufficient for the same period, and likewise left her a carriage and a pair of beautiful horses, which he had himself driven in his phaeton. He concluded by entreating me to pass as much of my time as possible with his dearest girl, whom he had prepared to love me, which he was sure she would do for his sake; and he referred me to her for a thousand particulars respecting them both. I wrote a short answer merely to say I would be with her by eleven o'clock the next morning, and then retired to bed; from which I was roused before eight, my father's servant saying a lady in a carriage was waiting for me at the corner of Pall Mall, seeming extremely impatient, that he objected to disturbing me so soon; whereupon she eagerly said she must see me, putting half a guinea into his hand.

Hastily putting on my clothes, I went down the street, where I saw a dashing bright-yellow vis-à-vis, having Pott's arms emblazoned thereon, an elegant pair of bright bay horses, the coachman and footman in smart frocks of blue faced with yellow and trimmed with a broad silver lace. But what was all this outside show compared to the lovely creature within, looking more than mortal! Never did I behold so perfect a beauty. I had seen this divine woman in 1776, then an unripe and awkward girl, but with features of exquisite beauty. That experienced old matron Charlotte Hayes, who then kept a house of celebrity in King's Place, where I often visited, had just got hold of her as an advantageous prize; and I have frequently seen the little sylph, Emily, under the tuition of the ancient dame learning to walk, a qualification Madam Hayes considered of importance, and in which her pupil certainly excelled, Emily's movements and air being grace personified, and attracting universal admiration whenever she appeared abroad. Sir Joshua Reynolds, whom all the world allowed to be a competent judge, had painted her portrait many times and in different characters. He often declared every limb of hers perfect symmetry, and altogether he had never seen so faultless and finely formed a human figure.

Upon my approaching the carriage, I thought she would have leapt out of it into my arms. Accepting her proffered hand, she eagerly drew me towards her, saying, "Come in, come in, my dear fellow; for so you, who are such a favourite of my angel Robert's, ever must be." Stepping in the carriage, she almost devoured me with kisses, laughed, cried, and was nearly in hysterics, to the surprise and entertainment of several persons that were passing at the time. Recovering a little, she ordered the coachman to drive home. In vain did I remonstrate and say that, being just as I jumped out of bed, I must go and dress myself; besides, my sisters would wait breakfast. It did not signify; go with her I positively should; aye, and stay too! She said I might write, send, do anything except leave her, that she had several servants, all of whom should go wherever I required them; and, if they were not sufficient, she would hire chairmen; that if I wanted more sleep I might go to bed at her house and no one should disturb me.

In short, had I been disposed to resist the importunities of this angelic creature, which I undoubtedly was not, it would not have been in my power. To Cork Street we drove, where she conducted me into a parlour that was neatness itself. After kissing me again and again with the utmost ardour and affection, she asked whether I really wished for more rest; for, if I did, a bedchamber should be ready in five minutes. I assured her nothing could induce me to lay down but her accompanying me; at which she smiled, saying, "Oh, you sad man, would you treat your friend, whose wife I am, so basely," and, with more gravity, added, "*That* must not be yet, whatever we may do hereafter." She then took me over the house, which was as complete a one as ever I saw in every respect; after which she said, "Now, my friend, this house and *all* it contains (laying a strong emphasis upon the word *all*) carriages, servants, and everything are at your disposal. You must consider them, and make use of them, as your own; for such was our dear Bob's desire, and such is my earnest request."

At nine we sat down to breakfast. While at table, another letter arrived from Robert. She left the room for a few minutes, and upon her return, putting her arms round my neck, eagerly said, "Oh, my dear, dear friend, you must comply with our Robert's desire and take me to Portsmouth that I may once more embrace him ere he leaves England." She then put his letter into my hands. It was addressed to me as well as her, as he concluded I should be in London, begging and praying me to get into a chaise and run down with Emily, the wind being west and no appearance of a change. I was forced to yield; whereupon, with impetuosity, she rang for her servant whom she ordered to get four horses for the chaise and another for the groom. I then told her it was impossible for me to leave town that day, having business of importance to transact. Most unwillingly she at last consented to wait until the following morning, upon condition that I would send for my portmanteau and sleep at her house that night, that we might set off very early. Finding me solicitous to return home, she ordered her vis-à-vis to convey me, bidding the coachman obey me throughout the day; nor would she suffer me to go without her servant behind, observing it would be dangerous for the coachman to leave the box. Thus attended, therefore, I proceeded to St. Albans Street, where I found my brother just come to town.

Upon quitting Emily, she told me, although she had sent a letter to me with the signature of Warren, she had long dropped that name, assuming that of Pott. This appeared to me strange; nor could I then account for it. My brother, who saw me drive up to the door, after the usual congratulations and greetings, remarked I had lost no time in

making an acquaintance with Mrs. Pott. "And faith!" said he, "you
are in high luck to be already upon such terms with a woman many
of the fashionable young men would give their little fingers to procure
a bow or acknowledgment of acquaintance from."

Having dressed, paid by devoirs to my sisters and promised to dine
with them, I proceeded in my vis-à-vis to the India House, where Mr.
Holt received me with the same warmth as at his visit in St. Albans
Street. I had not called at half the places I intended when I saw it
was three o'clock. I therefore drove home and dismissed my carriage,
writing a note to thank Emily for the use of it, adding that I should
come to her house from the Haymarket Theatre, where I was to go at
night with my brother. As the hours were more reasonable in those
days than at present, I found dinner waiting for me, Mr. Richard
Burke senior and Mr. William Burke being the only guests. The latter
was preparing to return to India overland, he having been appointed
Agent for the Rajah of Travancore. After a cheerful meal and plentiful
dose of claret, I retired to my room to equip myself in one of my gay
India coats, being of scarlet with a rich spangled and foil lace, made
from one of Sir Thomas Rumbold's, and of which I was not a little
vain. Upon my return to the drawing-room, my dress was greatly
admired, my brother only remarking he thought it a little too gaudy.

Having taken coffee, we four men went to Foote's, getting seats in
the balcony, opposite which I soon descried one of my Streatham
chums in the junior Lovelace, then a cornet of Dragoons. Observing
him look at the box I was in, smile, and quit his seat to come round,
I concluded he recognized me as I had him, and, upon his entering the
box I was in, held out my hand. Then it was I found he did not
recollect me; whereupon I mentioned my name. He shook hands with
much warmth, expressing pleasure at the meeting. "But," said he, "I
had no idea of your being an acquaintance. Seeing so unusual a dress
brought me round to look nearer at the wearer of it, who I presumed
could be no other personage than the *Lord Mayor's Trumpeter!*" This
facetious speech raised a laugh against me from all who heard it, at
which I was not a little disconcerted. It, however, put me so much out
of conceit with my finery that I determined not only to get rid of it
immediately, but also of upwards of twenty coats, equally ornamented
and rich, that I had brought from Bengal.

Whilst engaged in conversation with Lovelace, Mr. Richard Burke
said, "Who can that beautiful woman in yonder side box be nodding
and making signs to? They seem to be directed this way." Scarcely
had he said so when the box door opened, and one of the fruit-women
whispered to me that Mrs. Pott desired I would come down to her, she
having a place kept for me. Casting my eyes across the house, I saw
the beauteous Emily in all the splendour of most fashionable dress,

looking like an angel, seated in the front row of the side box next but one to the stage, an elegant-looking woman being on one side of her and a handsome young man on the other. The moment she caught my eye, she beckoned, and made all sorts of signs for me to come to her, which I hesitated doing from a disinclination to exhibit my trumpeter's coat in so conspicuous a part of the theatre, and before a crowded audience; but Lovelace said aloud, "Why the devil don't you obey Emily's summons, Hickey? She certainly will be up here in five minutes if you do not go down to her." I therefore thought it prudent to comply and, wishing my party a goodnight, I descended, escorted by the fruit-woman, who desired a box-keeper to open the door of Mrs. Pott's box; upon entering which I observed there was no seat vacant, when the gentleman on her right hand, instantly rising, politely said, "This, sir, is your place," and in spite of my remonstrances relinquished it, slightly bowing as he passed out.

If I felt doubtful respecting my dress, I had still more reason to be abashed at Emily's reception. I thought she would have embraced me; taking hold of both my hands, she said, "Now I have once more got you by my side, I shall take good care not to part with you again." Her manner towards me drew the attention of the whole house upon us, which made me entreat her to be less ardent. At my gravity she laughed heartily, adding she was too happy to be considerate and could not help betraying her regard for her *bashful swain*! I told her what had occurred about my dress; to which she replied, "Lovelace is an impertinent coxcomb. It was sheer envy in him, who would give his ears for a similar coat. It is an elegant and becoming suit, and I'll venture to assert there is not a better-dressed man in the theatre. Your hair, too, is charming. Pray, who is your operator? Is it your own servant?" I told her it was dressed by one of Courtoy's men, an Italian named Frescini, that he was not about ten minutes about it, and had intimated a wish that I would take him as a servant. Emily recommended me to secure him forthwith as an absolute treasure, and I took her advice.

Enquiring who the handsome young man was that had so civilly resigned his seat for me, she told me it was the handsome Jack St. Leger, sworn friend and companion of the Prince of Wales. "But," added she, "he is lately returned from the West Indies with a dreadful fever, which has reduced him, poor fellow, most dreadfully, and he is by no means himself yet." She further told me that he was intimate with my father and sister, attending all the parties in St. Albans Street, and she was sure he would be a prodigious favourite of mine. She then lamented that she had not introduced us to each other. The play and farce being over, I accompanied Emily to Cork Street, where we supped; after which she showed me to a neat bedchamber, which she said was over her own, and saluting wished me a goodnight. I observed that this was tantalizing me with a vengeance; whereupon she gave me another hearty kiss saying "Tomorrow night I hope to have Robert in my arms; but when he, poor fellow, has quitted the Kingdom you will be next to my heart, *and then*!" She once more embraced me and ran out of the room.

As I always made a point of being punctual, I was up and equipped for the journey ten minutes before the time fixed for departure, when Emily tapped at my door and immediately entered. She looked, if possible, handsomer than ever, was most becomingly dressed in a green riding habit, trimmed with gold frogs. For the first time I was the assailer, seizing her in my arms and gluing my mouth to her enchanting lips; nor was she backward in meeting it. At a quarter before five, we were seated by each other in her own post-chaise, which had every convenience for travelling a carriage could, and was in every respect as elegantly finished as her vis-à-vis; both were the work of the then celebrated Hatchet of Long Acre. We had four excellent post-horses. Tearing away at a great rate, we reached Kingston, our first stage, in an hour and a quarter. Two grooms, a man of about thirty and a lad of sixteen, set off with us, the boy riding in advance to prepare fresh horses and the man continuing by the chaise to pay the turnpikes. When leaving Kingston, I observed it would not be possible for the servants to keep on at the rate we were going, as they must knock up from fatigue; to which she replied, "Not they indeed, were it ten times the distance. Eighteen months ago they followed me to Holyhead when I was going to Ireland with Warren, who, by the by, I did not treat well; for I left him, who was as liberal as man could be and *adored me*, to go to Robert whom *I adored* and still *do adore*!"

We got to Guildford by half-past seven, breakfasted, and at eight went on to Godalming, then to Liphook, and from thence to Petersfield. Whilst changing horses at the latter place, Emily alighted, and during her absence the landlord said, "A glorious wind, sir, for the fleet." I asked what fleet he meant, to which he replied, "The East and West India which sailed last night at ten o'clock." I directly mentioned this to Emily, who would not give credit to it. The landlord assured me an express had stopped at his house that morning at seven, going up to the India House with an account of the whole fleet being clear out at sea with a fine breeze at north-north-east. Still Emily would not believe what she hoped was not true; so on we went to Portsmouth, which we reached at two in the afternoon. The master of the George Inn coming to the door upon our driving up to it, Emily eagerly asked, "Are the India ships gone?" to which the host answered, "Yes, ma'am, they sailed last night."

Poor Emily burst into tears and I apprehended would have fainted.

I made them carry her into the house and lay her upon a bed. After a long fit of tears, I prevailed on her to drink some warm wine and lie still for a few hours. Like an infant, she cried herself to sleep as I thought; when I walked to the sea-side, leaving a female servant to watch by her bedside. Upon the beach I saw the two servants, amusing themselves amongst the boat people, apparently as much at their ease as if they had only taken a morning's airing in Hyde Park. I asked them if they were not tired, when the lad sharply answered, "Tired, sir, with what? We have only rode seventy-four miles." "Well, my fine fellow," said I, "and, if occasion required it, could you set off for London again today?" "Aye, surely, sir," said both in a breath. A waiter of the inn that moment came up to say the lady wanted me; whereupon I walked back to the George, at the door of which stood Emily's chaise with four horses to it, and saddle horses ready for the two servants.

Upon entering the house, I met Emily, who entreated me to leave Portsmouth immediately. In vain did I importune her to take some nourishment first. She peremptorily refused and got into the chaise. I then went to the bar to ask what was to pay, and was told the lady had already paid the bill and for the horses to Petersfield. I, therefore, took my seat by her and we drove off. I felt somewhat surprised that, though indifferent about herself, she had not showed more attention towards me, by at least asking whether I chose to eat or drink previous to leaving Portsmouth, as I had touched nothing since breakfast. I, however, kept my feelings on that score to myself, but remonstrated against her hasty return as likely to affect her health from over-fatigue and anxiety; upon which she assured me she often had travelled six-and-thirty hours without taking any food, and that she could not bring herself to stay at a place where she had received so bitter a disappointment. She told me she had not closed her eyes, and feigned sleep supposing I should then walk out; that the moment I was gone she rose, paid the trifle that was due, and ordered horses. Taking out my purse, I desired to know how much the expense amounted to so far, that I might reimburse her, an offer that greatly offended her, she saying that, when she urged me to sacrifice my time and my own plans to accompany her, she had no idea of taxing me also with the expense, nor would she hear of it.

Observing the post-boys drove immoderately fast, I was about to call them, which she begged I would not, being anxious to get back to London; and she said she had promised them a crown each if they went to Petersfield in two hours, which they did (notwithstanding some long and steep hills) in twenty minutes less than the time stipulated. We went at such a rate the servants with difficulty kept up.

Emily being very low-spirited, I endeavoured to engage her in conversation by asking why she had not gone to Portsmouth with Robert;

to which she replied, "I would have given the world to have done so; but one of his sisters, her husband and two children going with him made it impossible." They only left him the morning he wrote to beg she and I would come down. "And now (she added) pray let me ask you, my dear friend, whether you are of the chamaeleon kind and can live upon air," accompanying her question by pulling out a drawer below the seat, in which was a nice-looking roast chicken, cold tongue, sandwiches of ham and beef, a bottle of madeira, with glasses and all the etceteras. These things the kind girl had procured at the George the short time I was absent. Being really very hungry, I ate voraciously, but could not prevail upon her to touch anything except a breast of the fowl. At Guildford, while changing horses, I compelled her to drink a dish of strong coffee and take some toast with it, after which we continued our progress, arriving in Cork Street about twelve at night, having thus travelled a distance of one hundred and forty miles in nineteen hours.

I found a note from my brother, requesting me to come immediately home. Fearing something had happened to my father, I instantly walked to St. Albans Street, where I had the happiness to learn from the servant letters had arrived from him in Paris that morning, and he was perfectly well. I then went into the dining-room where a large party were sitting. After supper, my brother upbraiding me for not calling at home the whole day, I told him I had been to Portsmouth, upon which he said, "Come, come, Mr. Nabob, none of your travellers' stories, if you please." I assured him it was true, he persisting it could not be. "For," said he, "did not I see you last night at the Haymarket?" I said he certainly did, but nevertheless I had been at Portsmouth. All the company declared they had never heard of so quick a journey.

I now wrote to my father at Paris to announce my arrival and the business that brought me; upon the subject of which I embellished a little, taking special care also to assure him I came with ample funds for the time I should remain in England. I had just finished and dispatched my letter when Emily sent her vis-à-vis for my use; stepping into which I went to a tailor named Knill, to whom I had been recommended as a fit person to equip me *comme il faut*. He advised my having a dark green with gold binding, dark brown with the same, a plain blue and, for half dress, a *Bon de Paris* with gold frogs, all which he spoke of as being much worn and of the highest *ton*. I bespoke the four suits accordingly. My next calls were at Rymer's for boots, Wagner for hats, and Williams of Bond Street for leather breeches. In three days I was to come forth a proper "Bond Street lounger," a description of persons then just coming into vogue.

Having promised to dine in Cork Street, I drove there and found Nabob already housed and quite at home, Emily having taken a great liking to him. Indeed, he was a little pet with all the ladies, being an interesting-looking, handsome boy. I dressed him, too, very smart as a hussar. As a servant, he was not of the least use to me. There came to dine with Emily, Harriet Powell, an old flame of mine, who had been a contemporary of Emily's at Charlotte Hayes's, and they had continued uninterrupted friends thenceforward. Powell was in high keeping, and drove to the door in an elegant chariot of her own. The fourth of the party was a gentleman dressed in the very extremity of the fashion, having a valuable diamond ring upon one of his fingers. He also arrived in his own carriage, and was introduced to me by the name of "Mount." I afterwards found him to be the only son of the great stationer upon Tower Hill, under the firm of Mount and Page. His father, being immensely rich, allowed this young coxcomb to squander what he pleased. I soon discovered Mr. Mount was no small favourite of Emily's.

The dinner and wines being of the best, and Mr. Mount no flincher at the glass, by seven o'clock we had disposed of a tolerable quantity of champagne. We therefore adjourned to the playhouse, going in Harriet Powell's carriage, and returning in the same to supper. At a late hour we broke up, and I was preparing to go home, when Emily said she must speak to me. Mr. Mount at that moment drew her aside; when a whispering conversation took place between them. He seemed angry. In a few minutes she wished him goodnight, and coming up to me said, "I have so much to say to you we must not part yet." She then led me, not to the chamber I had before slept in, but her own, where I passed a night that many would have given thousands to do. I, however, that night experienced the truth of what I had heard said —that she was cold as ice, seeming totally void of feeling. I rose in the morning convinced in my own mind she had no passion for the male sex, and that, if left to follow her inclination, she would have preferred sleeping alone to have a bedfellow. In that respect, how unlike was she to my first little companion of Drury Lane or to Nanny Harris, Fanny Hartford, Clara Hayward, and twenty other of my old favourites! Yet to look upon her was to look upon perfection, as far as figure and features went.

Notwithstanding this account of her, which is a just and faithful one, I believe she was sincerely attached to Pott, loving him as much as she was capable of loving anyone. I also believe that her partiality to me rose entirely from her knowing the affectionate regard he entertained for me. Of a common failing of her sex she possessed a large portion —that is, love of admiration and flattery. She was, too, with all her personal accomplishments, vain, weak, extravagant, and ignorant. As to the latter, that is not extraordinary, her origin and her life considered. Charlotte Hayes met her in the streets of London when not quite twelve years of age, leading her father, a blind beggar, about, soliciting charity from every person that passed. Struck with the uncommon beauty of the child's countenance, she set her myrmidons to work and, without difficulty, soon got her into her clutches. The young beggar proved an apt scholar so far as walking and common address, the more substantial points being totally neglected. She could neither read nor write, though by no means deficient or awkward in conversation; nor do I recollect ever to have heard her make use of a vulgarism or a phrase that could mark her illiterateness. I had been acquainted with her some time before I discovered the deficiency. True, I often observed that, upon her receiving a letter or note in my presence, she always left the room. I had frequently written to and received answers from her, but never saw a book in her hand, or in the house.

At last, I asked the meaning of this, when she candidly declared her ignorance. Upon expressing my surprise thereat, she said she had never had time to attend to learning, nor been connected with any person sufficiently interested about her to induce the acquirements of reading and writing until she went to Bob Pott, who intended to have been her instructor himself on the passage to India; but unfortunately he failed in his endeavours to get her on board ship. This discovery, mortifying as it was to her vanity, was attended with some advantages, as instead of running upon every occasion to her cook, her long-established amanuensis and secretary, I often officiated in reading and answering her billet douxs; by which means I discovered her incontinence, and that attachment to her absent love was no bar to her amours. Somewhat hurt at my finding out this infirmity (which, by the by, I had from my first acquaintance suspected) she solemnly protested that, whilst living with her dearest Robert, she had never once gone astray or known another man, an assertion I very much doubted the truth of.

On the 6th (July) I was engaged to dine in St. Albans Street to meet my favourite Miss Cecilia Forrest, Mr. and Mrs. Broadhead, the Duke of Hamilton, Sir Watts Horton, and other tonish friends of my eldest sister's. Being my first meeting with Miss Forrest, she cried much from recollecting her brother Tom's attachment to me. In the evening, she presented me with a lock of his hair, observing it would be a melancholy memento of my deceased friend and companion. I immediately had the hair set in a pair of sleeve buttons with his cypher, and have worn them from that time to the present day.

At night, Major St. Leger came in, when my sister introduced me to him. Smiling, he observed, "Although not personally acquainted, we had met and spoke before," alluding to the playhouse scene with Emily. My brother could not endure this gentleman from his coxcombry and insolent hauteur, neither of which failings could I ever perceive. In dress, he was like every other young man of fashion, and so far from foolish pride that when, as frequently was the case, I have met him walking arm in arm with the Prince of Wales, he, notwithstanding the elevated rank of his companion, always saluted and spoke to me with the utmost good humour and affability.

The 8th, I dined again in Cork Street. At night, Emily conveyed me to Vauxhall, she having heard me say I was fond of that entertainment, meeting several acquaintances there of both sexes. We formed a large party at supper, having French horns and clarinets playing to us until near three in the morning and drinking burnt champagne the whole time. About that hour we drove home. The following morning, Emily took me in her carriage to view the various scenes of desolation and enormity committed by the rioters. Dreadful and shocking to behold they were. We first drove to the ruins of Langton's distillery in Holborn, then to that of the Fleet prison and Newgate, the Toll Houses on Blackfriars Bridge, proceeding to the King's Bench in St. George's Fields.

While looking on and expressing my surprise that such excesses could have been committed in the very heart of the metropolis, the coachman, who had witnessed some of the outrages, assured me that, at the commencement, none were engaged in it but a parcel of the most abandoned women, and boys of from ten to fifteen years old, and he was convinced twenty resolute men might have dispersed the whole; but everyone seemed helpless and inactive; from which, and the mob finding themselves unopposed, their numbers accumulated, being joined by pickpockets, housebreakers, and thieves of every description. He told me that, at midnight of 6th June, he counted no less than eleven dreadful conflagrations, all raging with the utmost fury at one and the same time. This most extraordinary event, which struck the inhabitants of London with horror and dismay, originated in the fanaticism, or perhaps it would be more candid and nearer the truth to say, in the insanity of Lord George Gordon, son to the Duke of Gordon, and with whom I was upon the excursion I have related, from Mr. Cane's to France, and other parts, in the year 1776, at which time he was a reasonable and elegant young man.

About the middle of the month, my father returned from Paris, when I had the happiness to see him looking quite as stout and well as when I left him 1777. Upon entering the drawing-room at my father's, my sisters began to laugh heartily, the cause of which was a visitor that had just called to see me, whom they thus described. Notwithstanding the weather's being unusually sultry and oppressive, he was completely enveloped from head to foot in shawls, appeared quite worn down by age and infirmity, dreadfully yellow complexion, more hideously ugly

than any human creature they had ever beheld, and so deaf they with
the utmost difficulty could make him hear a word. "Then," said I, "his
name must be Lacam," which they admitted, producing his card. I
certainly should have known him by the description, which was not in
the least exaggerated. I had, however, that morning been informed of
his arrival, and that he had come from Bengal in the same ship with
Mr. Francis, Mr. Harwood, and my respected friend Mr. Tilghman.

My father's servant further told me that Mr. Lacam had been
brought to the door in a sedan chair. One of the men knocking, the
old gentleman put his head out at the window and enquired if *young*
Mr. Hickey was at home. Being answered in the affirmative, he, with
the aid of the two chairmen, with considerable difficulty made shift to
hobble up five stone steps which led to the hall, where being seated,
he requested Mr. William Hickey might be called to him, as he was
incapable of going further. The servant thereupon observed "Mr.
William Hickey was not at home." "Then why the deuce did you say
he was?" replied Mr. Lacam, and began scolding and grumbling at a
great rate. The servant with much humility remarked, "The mistake
arose from his (Mr. Lacam's) enquiring for young Mr. Hickey, which
led him to suppose he wanted to see his master's eldest son, who was
at home." "No, Mr. Jackanapes," angrily retorted Mr. Lacam, "I wanted
no such thing, and if you had not been the most stupid fellow in the
world you would have known it." The Eastern invalid was not to be
pacified. His chairmen being summoned, lifted and carried him down
the steps in their arms, he scolding in a loud key all the time until
once more seated in his chair.

The novelty of the scene, with the grotesque appearance of the
principal figure in it, attracted a considerable mob round the street
door and chair, which tended to increase his wrath. Seeing by his card
that he lived in Cecil Street, I directly went to his house, and arrived
there before he had recovered from the fatigue of his unsuccessful
attempt to see me in St. Albans Street. I found him looking wretchedly
ill. He told me he had recently been at death's door, expecting daily
to die during the voyage from India; that, at the time the ship arrived
off Dover, his dissolution was hourly predicted; and he felt sure he
owed his existence to the extraordinary attention and unceasing kindness of Mr. Harwood, who, although he had been absent from England
twenty years, and must consequently be anxious to see his relations
and friends, had humanely sacrificed his own feelings to the distressed
state he (Lacam) was in, staying with him until he acquired strength
enough to travel, and when he had done so, conducted him by short
stages to London. Having pronounced a deserved panegyric upon Mr.
Harwood, he suddenly flew to his favourite subject, "New Harbour,"
going over a subject of soundings, winds, and tides, that I had listened

to before times out of number, concluding his representations by declaring that, should the Court of Directors hesitate to do him justice, he was determined to bring the business before Parliament and endeavour to obtain a proper remuneration for his losses and disappointments through the House of Commons; to which tribunal he would cheerfully submit the merit of his claims.

After tormenting me for an hour with this hackneyed subject, he asked whether Captain Henry Mordaunt,* of the Bengal military establishment, who came to Europe in the same ship with him, and who had been making earnest enquiries of me, had yet found me. Before I could answer the question, the very person was announced. He entered the room with his usual scowling countenance, but for a minute smiled and shook me by the hand with apparent cordiality. He then began damning the climate, the brutality of the common people, and the general stupidity of London, cursing his own folly for being such a blockhead, such an inveterate ass as to quit the paradise of Hindustan to visit the sink of everything despicable, by comparison, *England!* a country no man who had ever enjoyed the blessings and comforts of India could feel comfortable in. As I saw that his cynical discontent and snarling annoyed Mr. Lacam, I proposed a walk, to which Mordaunt agreed, and we set out to visit Mr. Francis in Upper Harley Street.

Upon getting to his house, we were shown into the drawing-room where Mrs. Francis, with two fine-looking girls, her daughters, were sitting. In a few minutes Mr. Francis came in and was very courteous, making some civil speeches to me. He, like Mordaunt, abused the climate as being far inferior to that of Bengal. This I thought extraordinary in him who had been so short a time abroad. He particularly complained of the closeness of the rooms in London, the oppressive heat of which he said almost suffocated him. He invited Mordaunt and myself to dinner, good-humouredly saying he wished me to come that day because Tilghman, whom he knew I had a regard for, was to be with him. I accepted the invitation and was rejoiced to see my shipmate looking remarkably well. At night, Tilghman, Mordaunt, and myself went to Vauxhall, on the way to which they gave me the particulars of a duel that took place a few months before in Bengal between Mr. Hastings, Governor-General, and Mr. Francis, which ended without bloodshed. It originated in party dissensions in Council, those gentlemen always violently opposing and abusing each other.†

Wherever I went into public, Mordaunt fastened upon and stuck

---

* This strange personage was an illegitimate elder brother of the Earl of Peterborough, having been born before their parents were married.

† Philip Francis, of course, was afterwards to take an active part in his old enemy's impeachment.

close to me, always grumbling and snarling, and always excessively disagreeable; yet I knew not how to shake him off without absolute rudeness. As his constant theme was complaints of the stupidity of England, wishing he had never come near so horrid a country but remained in India, I endeavoured to console him by observing that he would be better pleased, and in better humour, after he had made some acquaintances with both sexes, as at present he knew scarcely anybody. Besides, London was always thin of company and barren of amusement at that season of the year.

I likewise observed that the absence of his brother, Lord Peterborough, who was upon the Continent, was an unfortunate circumstance as, had he been upon the spot, he would have introduced him to his numerous friends. To these attempts of mine to put him in good humour, he sulkily damned London and everything appertaining to it, saying that it was impossible anything could ever make him change his opinion respecting it, and, was there a ship to sail the following day, he would gladly embark on her for Bengal, in preference to staying another hour in such a sink of gloom and dullness.

Not having seen Emily for two days, I went to dine there, and in the evening accompanied her to Colman's Theatre, where Mordaunt, spying me, was soon at my side; nor could I get rid of him the whole play. Indeed, when the entertainment was over he made a bold push to be invited to supper with us; which I was determined he should not be, and whispered Emily not to ask him. I at last prevailed on him to leave us, upon a promise that I would next day introduce him at a house of fashionable resort where he would find a choice of beautiful girls, and might pass his leisure hours agreeably. I accordingly called upon him at his mother's, Lady Peterborough, in Dean Street, Soho, from whence I took him first to Mrs. Weston's famous receptacle in Berkeley Row, where having introduced him to the "Lady Abbess and her Nuns," we next visited Mrs. Kelly and her bevy of beauties in Arlington Street. Here, even the cynical Mordaunt was obliged to confess the women were lovely, and he made some efforts to say civil things to the girls; but his common address and manner was so morose and so unpleasant that the Cyprian lasses soon distinguished him by the appellation of the "surly Nabob."

18

LONDON DIVERSIONS

I T now drawing towards the end of the month, London being both
hot and dull, my brother asked me to make an excursion with him
to one of the watering-places, to which I agreed, observing, however, it could not be until subsequent to the 28th, for which day I had
invited a party to dinner at the Royal Hotel in Pall Mall. We accordingly met there, fifteen in number, the company consisting of Major
Bourke, Mr. Touchet, Mr. Archibald Paxton, the snarler Mordaunt,
Mr. Strange, his brother, Sir Thomas Strange, afterwards Chief Justice
at Madras, Sir Thomas Rumbold, Mr. Elphinstone, the India Director,
Mr. Dallas, now Chief Justice of Chester, Mr. Holt, Mr. Wilberforce
Bird, Messrs. William and Richard Burke, my brother and myself. The
master of the house furnished an admirable dinner, and all the wines
were of the best; nor did we spare them, some of the set remaining at
the bottle until four in the morning. My brother and I had arranged
everything for going to Margate on the 29th; but the overdose of
champagne rendered me totally incapable of moving; I was half dead
with headache and sickness at the stomach. This dinner cost me rather
more than forty pounds.

On the 30th, being somewhat recovered from my debauch, we set
off after breakfast for Margate, which we reached the same evening,
driving to Mitchiner's, where we each got an excellent bedchamber
and a very good sitting-room, commanding a full view of the pier and
roads with the shipping passing up and down. After we had been there
a fortnight, Mr. William Burke arrived, in order to cross from thence
to Ostend, on his way to India overland. He was accompanied by Mr.
Richard Burke junior, who had come to see the last of his friend on
British ground. Hearing we were in the house, they joined us and we
agreed to mess together during Mr. Burke's stay, which would only be
until a packet sailed for the French coast.

Whilst we were sitting at the window in momentary expectation of
dinner's being announced, a smart landau, with four post-horses, drove
up to the door, which Mr. Burke immediately observed contained two

10+

lovely girls, with an old woman and a child of twelve or thirteen, having seen them changing horses at Canterbury. Upon their alighting, I saw it was my Arlington Street friend, Mrs. Kelly, and two of her nymphs. I therefore ran down to speak to them. Whilst so doing, Mr. Burke joined us; and, calling me aside, he desired I would ask them to dine with us—a desire that somewhat surprised me, as I imagined he would cautiously have avoided introducing such personages to his young friend Richard, at that time a steady, reserved lad. As, however, I felt that was no business of mine, I obeyed his wish and gave the invitation, which the old lady most graciously and willingly accepted. Upon joining us, she became very communicative, telling us she was on her way to Ostend to place her daughter (the youngest girl) in a convent there for education, and that the other two ladies had kindly consented to bear her company to France and back again. Upon enquiring of Mitchiner, we learned that an Ostend packet would sail at seven o'clock the following morning, that being the hour of high water. Mr. Burke and the ladies sent instantly to take a passage and secure the best cabins.

At, and after, dinner, our whole party made rather too free with the champagne, the effects of which were particularly conspicuous in my brother; for, the wine being in and the wits out, he was easily persuaded to escort the ladies across the Channel and back, a piece of gallantry I most positively refused to accede to, protesting a voyage of nearly eighteen months had quite satisfied me, and I certainly would have no more to do with salt water until returning to India. The girls, however, ceased not to importune me, declaring I must and should go, and that they would pull me out of bed and forcibly convey me on board. My brother was so beastly drunk that at ten o'clock we were obliged to have him carried to bed. He had previously made strong love to Miss Kelly, the girl of twelve years old; at which the mother was greatly enraged. My brother, regardless of her anger, continued his nonsense, swearing the young one's bosom had already too much swell for a nun, and that no canting hypocritical friar should have the fingering of those little plump globes (clapping his hand upon Miss's bosom). The mother was indignant at these insinuations, hiccupping out her entreaties that he would cease to use such indecent language and action before her innocent child. "Innocent," echoed my brother, "oh, very innocent to be sure; but she knows a thing or two. However, I'll take her to bed with me and ascertain how matters are." In his endeavour to lay hold of her, he fell upon the floor in a state of insensibility; and then it was we had him carried to his room. Mother Kelly became vociferously wrathful, bestowing some tolerably vulgar abuse upon us all. Rising from her chair, she staggered to her daughter, whom she seized rudely hold of, and made her exit.

It being past eleven, we retired to our respective chambers, I having previously settled with one of the full-blown beauties to join me, being the only two that paired off. Before five o'clock in the morning, the other frail sister bounced into my room, awakening me out of a sound sleep, crying out that I and my bedfellow must rise directly, the rest being nearly ready, and my brother quite so. I renewed my assurances that my movement should not extend beyond the pier head, to which I would go and see them set sail. I accordingly dressed and, going downstairs, found my friends over an early breakfast. My brother had no recollection of the engagement he had entered into the preceding night, but seemed not unwilling to fulfil it, until he found me resolved not to make one; whereupon he likewise declined, joining, however, in the general upbraidings of me for my ill-nature, though he afterwards expressed his satisfaction at my having prevented his taking the cruise.

Mr. Burke complained of the wine's having heated him. He appeared low and dejected, I believe solely from being so soon to part from his favourite Richard. At half-past seven, they cast off their fastenings to the shore; in a few minutes after which they were fairly out at sea, and in little more than an hour were hull down running at a great rate before a strong southerly wind. By noon my new acquaintances, Metcalfe, Anderson, and half a dozen fashionable coxcombs, were with my brother and myself, making earnest enquiries after the "divine girls" they understood had arrived the evening before, seeming grievously disappointed when told the objects of their visit were by that time half seas over, on their way to Ostend. I could not help giving Metcalfe a wipe for his lamentations, observing I should have thought he had enough to attend to at home. He at that time was the professed keeper of Mrs. Cuyler, a great jack whore, without pretensions to manners or beauty of face or person, and only an under-strapper upon the stage of one of the London theatres. With this woman, however, such as she was, Mr. Metcalfe appeared to be deeply enamoured, nightly exhibiting himself by her side in the front row of a balcony box.

In the middle of August a report became current that our outward-bound fleet of East and West Indiamen had fallen in with a squadron of French and Spanish ships of war, and that a great number were captured; but it gained no credit and after two or three days died away. On 4th September, my brother and I returned to London, where I had not been six hours before the snarler Mordaunt heard of my being in town and came to St. Albans Street, if possible more discontented than ever. The day after my return, I called upon Emily, who declared it was her intention to have set off for Margate the very next morning in search of me, as she began to think I was lost. She told me she had been supremely happy during three days that it was thought the

Indiamen were taken from a hope of seeing Robert, but the account proved unfounded.

The night I came to town there was to be a masquerade at Mrs. Cornelys's rooms in Soho Square; and Emily said I must go with her to it. I therefore sent for a domino, etc., and at ten o'clock she and I drove there. She was in a man's domino, with a smart hat and feather, and looked charmingly, her fine figure and graceful air attracting attention wherever she appeared. She promised me to go home early, as I was tired by my journey and little sleep the preceding night, and said that, to avoid being importuned to stay by any of her acquaintances, she would not unmask. Vanity, however, prevailed over her inclination to oblige me; for, finding herself followed and admired in every direction, she could not resist the taking off her mask to let the delighted beholders see that the face corresponded with the figure they had been pursuing from room to room. One mask in particular persevered in following her, and whenever opportunity offered by my talking to any friend, poured abundance of fulsome compliments into her ears.

I suspected from her manner she knew who it was, though for some time she assured me that she did not. Upon pressing her on that point, she said it was a fine boy of Robert's acquaintance, named Treves. This young man I knew something of, and had often observed that he bowed to Emily whenever he met her. He was a handsome lad of seventeen, a great admirer and follower of the most celebrated women of the town; but, his means being very slender, he was forced to content himself with the liberty of bowing to several of them, and seemed happy when his salutation was returned; which was always the case with Emily, she honouring him with a gracious and familiar nod, or kiss of the hand. Some years afterwards, this Treves became one of the most dashing bucks of the metropolis, and the constant companion of the Prince of Wales, His Royal Highness having long been intimate with his father, a man of convivial habits, singing an excellent song, and in every way calculated to please such a dissipated character as the Prince then was.

One of the first persons I saw at Carlisle House (the name Mrs. Cornelys's then went by) was my blackguard friend, Sam Rogers, who coming to me, said aloud, "Damn my eyes, Bill, but I'm glad I've met with you, for I wanted to tell you that my uncle has met with an idle b——r who has a ship just finished, which, as he has some pounds to fool away, he had rather not command, at least, had rather not leave England so soon as she must; an exchange has therefore taken place. She is to be the *Osterley* and I her commander, he taking what was to have been my ship next year; so stand by, my lad, to be at a launch in five or six weeks."

At the same place, I likewise met James Grant, who made me

promise to accompany him to Drayton the next day. I did so, and was there first made acquainted with his brother Peter. James had with him at Drayton a little woman whom he kept, and was fond of supposing he had debauched, though I believe he had not more done so than myself. She had a good voice, sung prettily, and knew something of music, but was in my estimation as errant a whore, both in principle and practice, as ever existed. She never was a favourite of mine. Her proper name was Brown, she being daughter to an advertising tailor of that name upon Ludgate Hill. She had at least the merit of constantly keeping the interest of her father in view by recommending all her keeper Mr. Grant's friends to employ him in his business. This cost me some pounds, as I was obliged to get three or four suits of clothes made by him, which were so badly executed I never could wear them, and they were altered to fit my little Bengally.

I had not been more than an hour at Drayton when Emily's lad (the junior groom) brought me a letter from her, enclosing one written by Robert as a prisoner at Madrid, in which he says that, after the fleet had been three weeks at sea in hourly expectation of making the island of Madeira, they saw four strange sail in different directions, two being upon the lee quarter and two to windward. In half an hour after seeing the above four, two others were discovered right ahead. A line-of-battle ship that was the convoy thereupon made the signal to prepare for action; in consequence of which a smart post-chaise, a curricle, and gig of his, also some handsome mahogany furniture stowed between decks, were, upon the above signal to clear ship, all thrown overboard. The man-of-war then hailed the different Indiamen to say he thought the strange vessels were detached frigates belonging to a fleet of the enemy, and, if so, more of them would soon appear, in which case he should hoist a Union flag at the main topgallant masthead; and, upon seeing that flying, every ship must do the best to escape, both East and West Indiamen.

Then they run on until an hour before sunset, when seeing the Union hoisted they dispersed, his ship carrying a press of sail all night, but at daybreak had the mortification to see two Spanish eighty-guns ships within two miles of them, to one of which they were soon afterwards compelled to strike. Robert (I think) stated that six East Indiamen and a great number of West Indiamen were captured, the enemy consisting of upwards of twenty sail of large ships, Spaniards and French; that the ship he was in being prize to a Spaniard, he was taken into Cadiz, where all the prisoners, male and female, were treated with the greatest respect and kindness, all being at liberty upon parole; that he availed himself of that opportunity to see more of so famous a part of Europe, and, having obtained permission, proceeded to Madrid, where he met with equal attention, especially from the donnas, who, if they had a fault, it was overwhelming him with love; that, as he found from the liberality of the people there was no want of cash, and that he could get as much as he thought proper for his bills upon England, he should be in no hurry to leave so inviting and charming a country, which he must in common justice pronounce a perfect Paradise! By Emily's letter (or rather her cook's) I could perceive she did not at all like the rapturous style in which Robert spoke of the Spanish ladies.

The 7th (of September) I returned to town, being engaged to dine with Major Metcalfe on the 8th at his house in Suffolk Street, Middlesex Hospital. At this party I met Lord Fielding, eldest son to the Earl of Denbigh; General Smith,* of whom I have before spoken, relative to cheese, at the island of St. Helena; the General's son, a fine young man in appearance, who had, I know not why, been nicknamed "Tippoo"; Mr. Devaynes, the India Director; Captain Douglas, who commanded the ship *Queen*, and some others whose names I do not recollect. We had a very jolly set; and, as I was in those days a great promoter of hilarity, I invited all that remained to a late hour at table, being those above specified, to dine with me that day week at the Royal Hotel in Pall Mall. This they agreed to do. I added to the number Mr. Paxton, the discontented Mordaunt, and my brother, who, when the day arrived, was so much indisposed that he was unwillingly obliged to give up the pleasure of joining us. We had, as usual, a hard batch at drinking and were very merry, keeping it up until an early hour of the morning.

My brother, who never shunned a jovial set himself, took it into his head to tax me with being the instigator of his committing excess. Under this idea, certainly an unjust one as to me, more than once, when we were engaged to great tavern parties, he said to me, "William, this must, from some of the names I see in the list, be a sad debauch, which in prudence we had better avoid. Let you and I therefore get out of the way of temptation, mount our horses, and ride gently to Richmond, Brentford Ait, or any other place within ten miles of London that you prefer, where we might take a quiet dinner, a pint of port each, and jog soberly home in the evening." To so steady a plan, which I really liked, I readily consented. The event, however, never answered; entirely the reverse. The first excursion of this kind that we made we dined upon the island off the town of Brentford, where there is a house famous for dressing pichcock't eels, and also for stewing the same fish, and got so completely intoxicated we were incapable of

* On the voyage home from Canton, Hickey had encountered General Smith and had taken offence at his "insolent superiority and superciliousness," which were ill-suited, he felt, to the son of a man who had "kept a little cheesemonger's shop in Jermyn Street. . . ."

mounting our horses and obliged to take a post-chaise to convey us to town.

In the latter end of September, I had dined with some convivial fellows at St. Albans Tavern, where, according to custom, I took my full proportion of wine. My companions proposing to adjourn to King's Place, a wonderful fit of prudence came across me. I declined, declaring as I was close to my home, I would for once resist temptation and go to bed. "Aye, no doubt of it," said one of the young men, "with Emily, to whom you are sneaking away." I assured him he was mistaken, as was the fact; for, Bob Pott being daily expected to arrive from Spain, I did not choose to run the risk of his coming suddenly upon us and catching me in the arms of his inconstant girl. I therefore actually proceeded to my father's, distant only four doors from the tavern. Upon going in, the servant told me my Aunt Boulton, her three daughters, Mr. and Mrs. Broadhead, and others whom he named were in the parlour, sitting after supper. I marched into the room and, having scarcely spoken to my aunt and cousins since my arrival from India, I made a number of complimentary, flourishing speeches to them, with which they seemed highly gratified, declaring that being tipsy made me vastly agreeable, a pretty broad insinuation that they did not consider me so when sober.

I found my elder sister, Mrs. Broadhead, and one or two more were going to a masquerade at the opera house; and, as they recommended my doing the same, instead of stupidly going to bed, I at once subscribed to that opinion. Upon my ringing the bell to desire a domino and mask might be sent for, my sister observed she could supply me with a suitable character for the state I was in," and, going up to her own apartment, soon returned with a complete dress of white linen, being the garments worn at a particular convent in Paris. My female friends could with difficulty equip me, from excessive laughter at my hiccupping violently the whole time they were employed about it. Having at last accomplished the business, I got into a chair and was conveyed to the Haymarket. The house was very full; but I soon spied out my sister and her party, to whom I was staggering up, when they darted off and most cautiously avoided me, conceiving it would not tend much to their credit to be acknowledged by a *drunken nun*! undoubtedly not a character often seen. Indeed, the novelty of it attracted universal admiration; I was the cause of much wit and fun. A crowd of both sexes followed me, some putting ridiculous questions, others affecting to be shocked at beholding one of the sisterhood in so unseemly and disgraceful a state, exhorting me to retire to my cell and do penance for my grievous transgression.

I reeled about, singing, talking sad nonsense, and jostling every person that came in my way, every now and then tumbling and unable to rise until assisted by the bystanders. These falls, the heat of the place, and a few glasses of champagne at last produced sickness; and I relieved my overcharged stomach by a very copious vomiting of claret and all the mixture I had that day poured down my throat. My white dress was soon in a very filthy condition; nor was the effluvia I emitted of the pleasantest nature; so far otherwise that my till then close followers were glad to retire to more respectful distance, leaving me upon the floor like a hog, rolling and wallowing in my own nastiness; from which degrading and beastly state I was relieved by Mordaunt, who with more consideration and kindness than was usual with him, upon discovering me to be the object of the mirth that had for some time prevailed, got three or four waiters together, who took me up bodily, carrying me out and placing me in a sedan in a state of absolute insensibility. Mordaunt walked by the side of the chair; nor did he quit me until safe in charge of my father's servants and of Frescini, who conveyed me to bed, where I slept for full twelve hours. Upon getting up and dressing myself, I felt all over bruises and aches, the occasion of which I knew nothing about, having no recollection of anything that had occurred the preceding night. Much ashamed of myself did I feel when made acquainted with the follies I had committed.

The 15th being the day of my dinner at the Royal Hotel, about one o'clock I went to take my usual ride in Hyde Park, where seeing Emily's vis-à-vis, I galloped across the grass for the purpose of speaking to her, when I had the pleasure to find my friend Robert in the carriage with her. He had reached town that morning, and expressed most unfeigned joy at our once more meeting. He insisted upon my dismounting and squeezing into the vis-à-vis, protesting he would not part with me for that day at least; but, upon my telling him how I was circumstanced, desiring Emily to give him up to me for a few hours, and she good-humouredly complying, he promised to join my party in Pall Mall, with everyone of whom he was acquainted. I endeavoured to prevail upon Emily to accompany him, which she would not hear of, observing one woman among such a party of riotous men would only be an offensive intruder; nor should she herself like it. I went to Cork Street with them, at Robert's request sending for Frescini and my clothes. At five o'clock Robert and I drove to St. Albans Street, where, after stopping to take in my brother, we proceeded to the hotel. I made a point of always asking my father to be of my parties, which he declined, observing his race was already run; that, though he believed no man ever lived more freely than he had done, both his age and his inclination concurred to make him now avoid excess. He therefore felt he should contribute nothing by his presence amongst such jolly fellows and desired to be excused.

We had, in the opinion of all but Robert, an excellent dinner, he alone pronouncing it execrable, saying, "Let me give you a dinner at Le Tellier's, and I'll show you how a table ought to be covered to deserve commendation." All readily consented to indulge him. Five days afterwards, we partook of his catering, when certainly there was a more showy and far more expensive but, as I thought, not a bit better dinner as to the materials than mine. General Smith, Mr. Devaynes, and a few other of the graver sort having departed, Robert called for pen, ink, and paper, and wrote down the following names: Mr. Roe Yoe (M.P. for Coventry), Lord Fielding, Wilberforce Bird (of Wood Street), Lord Peterborough, Smith (Tippoo), Henry Mordaunt, Joseph Bird, William (now Sir William) Curtis, James Curtis, his brother, Messrs. Marjoribanks and Lovelace senior of the Guards, Captain Belford of the Horse Guards, Harvey Combe (now one of the Members for the City of London), Lovelace junior, Tom Vaughan (the author), Arthur Shakespear, Captain Sutton, Young Horneck (of the Guards), William Hickey and Robert Pott. "And now," said he, "let these twenty dine together twice a week during the winter, each person ordering a dinner at which he is to preside, at whatever tavern he pleases within London or Westminster, and, when the whole list has gone through, finally to fix at whatever house a majority of the members should pronounce to have been found the best."

The rules or regulations proposed were simple and few in number; the charge per head for the dinner to be left entirely to the discretion of the master of the house; the dinner to consist of every article procurable, whether in or out of season; any member absenting himself from the meetings, no matter what the cause thereof, to forfeit one guinea for each and every time he was so absent. The president for the day to discharge the bill and to collect by himself, or his own servants, the proportion due from each member; the proprietor of the house to send in his bill by one o'clock of the day next after that of the dinner to the residence of the president.

This plan, being unanimously approved, was immediately adopted; and, Pott being requested to commence by taking the first chair, I attended him to his favourite place, Le Tellier's in Dover Street, to order the dinner. He told the landlord the nature of the meeting, concluding thus, "From the experience of your cookery, I have no doubt if you exert yourself we shall finally establish ourselves at your house; and it will, I conceive, be well worth your while to endeavour to attract as constant customers twenty gentlemen who are indifferent about the expense and, being lovers of the bottle, will consume a handsome allowance of wine, in which, as I understand, the chief advantage to you tavern keepers arises." The landlord assured Pott he would take special care to have the table supplied with the very best provisions

10*

and, with respect to wines of every sort, he could venture to defy all England to supply better than his cellars were stored with.

Several of the members being about to leave town for a few days, the first dinner was ordered for 2nd October, on which day seventeen of us met, the elder Curtis being prevented from attending by illness, Lord Peterborough and Horneck being both upon the Continent. The landlord kept his faith with us, every person present agreeing in opinion that a better dinner could not be, and that all the wines were fair, the claret particularly good. Upon this general approbation, Mordaunt proposed no further trials and that we should at once establish the club where we had commenced so well. This being put to the vote, a majority were for adhering to the original plan, though it was observed that in all probability several of the members would have the dinner at Le Tellier's. Lord Fielding, requesting leave to be the next president, said he intended to try Hunt, of the Star and Garter in Pall Mall, where, if he was not greatly mistaken, we should be as well treated in every respect as on that day. The fact is, any set of gentlemen, acting upon the principle we did, must be served in the best possible manner; nor could there be any material difference between the taverns of repute.

In the early part of the winter, a new species of evening's amusement became quite the rage under the name of "The Promenade." Mrs. Cornelys's truly magnificent suite of apartments upon the principal floor were opened every Sunday night at seven o'clock, for the reception of company. So much did it take that the first people of the kingdom attended it, as did also the whole beauty of the metropolis, from the Duchess of Devonshire down to the little milliner's apprentice from Cranbourn Alley. The crowd from eight to twelve was immense. When in town, I never failed attending at it. There I first was in company with Charlotte and Nancy Barry, two sisters then in high vogue and much sought after by the young sprigs of nobility. There was a something about the eldest, Charlotte, though she certainly could not be pronounced a beauty, that pleased me beyond any woman I had ever seen, and I looked at her with admiration. She had hold of the Earl of Tyrconnel's arm, while her sister Nancy was escorted by Mr. Van, a dashing ensign in the Guards, who stuck so close to their respective fair companions that I had no opportunity of becoming acquainted with them that night.

In the middle of October, Bob Pott proposed that Emily, he and I should run down to Bath for a fortnight, to which I had no other objection that the possibility of its interfering with the business of the Bengal petition, Parliament being prorogued to 1st November. I therefore went to the agents, Messrs. Irvine and Touchet, who said the House would only meet on the 1st to adjourn to a future day, and beyond a doubt no business would be done. Upon this assurance I made one of the Bath party, spending fourteen days very agreeably in that gay city.

My father, hearing me talking to my brother about another party I proposed having at the hotel in Pall Mall, expressed his surprise that I should unnecessarily incur a heavy expense by giving dinners at those extravagant houses when I might have the use of his, with that of his servants, which would save me two-thirds of the expense, and be at least as comfortable, if not more so, than a tavern or hotel. "In making this offer," continued my father, "do not imagine, young man, that I intend to supply your dissipated companions with my wines; at least, with claret and madeira you must furnish yourself." I gladly availed myself of my father's offer; for, independent of the comforts I knew would attend adopting it, my sister Mary had great taste in the arrangements of dinners, nor was old Molly Jones at all inferior. As to the wines, I could confidently rely upon Mr. Paxton. All I had to attend to was taking care that my parties never should clash with those of my sister, of which she generally had one a week, consisting of what in the language of the day were called "fine people," especially as to the men. The first party I had in St. Albans Street proved the justness of my father's remark; for it did not cost me near half of what I had been charged for a larger company at the hotel, and was beyond comparison better, my guests all declaring they never had seen a more elegant or a better dinner, nor better served in every respect.

Mr. Strange, from Madras, was one of the party I am now speaking of; he came dressed in a very gay suit of pea green, trimmed with gold lace. His head, or his stomach, not being so strong as some of ours who were in the daily habit of drinking freely, he became very sick, vomiting for some time as he sat and, finally falling from his chair, rolled about in the unpleasant stuff he had disgorged. Insensible, however, of his own situation, there he lay until I summoned the servants to his assistance, who, calling a sedan chair, carried him off like a log to it, and he was conveyed home. Three days afterwards I met him riding in Hyde Park, when he told me he had been so dreadfully ill from the debauch as to confine him to his room two days, and that morning was the first time of his being out since. "However," said he, "it has cured me of ever wearing fine clothes in a male party any more, especially at such as yours, Hickey."

The fact is, I always was ambitious of sitting out every man at the table where I presided; which by a little management I generally accomplished, eating sparingly of some one plain dish, avoiding malt liquor, and desiring the servants to take away my glass after a hob-nob the moment I put it down, by which means I was better enabled to do the duty of president when the cloth was removed; from which moment I never flinched, and contrived to send my guests away quite happy and contented. When, as was sometimes the case, I felt the wine disposed to revolt, chewing two or three French olives without swallowing the pulp would relieve and enable me to get down half a dozen more glasses. By these little fair manoeuvres I established the character of being a capital host.

The 9th being the Lord Mayor's day, I arrayed myself in my full suit of velvet. Alderman Woolridge called at my father's and conveyed me in his chariot to Guildhall at half-past four o'clock; about half an hour after which the procession arrived from Westminster. At six, we sat down to a profusion of turtle and venison, followed by all the etceteras of French cookery, with splendid dessert of pines, grapes, and other fruits. I was seated between Mrs. Healy, sister to Wilkes, and Lord Lewisham, eldest son of the Earl of Dartmouth. Mrs. Healy almost enveloped me in her immense hoop, but was vastly attentive to me, whom she perceived to be a stranger, ordering one of her servants to wait upon me, and naming to me the different persons who sat at the same table, amongst whom were most of the great officers of state, the Lord Chancellor, judges, and Master of the Rolls. The heat from the crowd assembled and immense number of lights was disagreeable to all, to many quite oppressive and distressing.

The Lord Mayor's table, at which I was, and nearly opposite his Lordship, was less so than other parts of the hall, from being considerably elevated above the rest. The wines were excellent, and the dinner the same, served, too, with as much regularity and decorum as if we had been in a private house; but far different was the scene in the body of the hall, where, in five minutes after the guests took their stations at the tables, the dishes were entirely cleared of their contents, twenty hands seizing the same joint or bird, and literally tearing it to pieces. A more determined scramble could not be; the roaring and noise was deafening and hideous, which increased as the liquor operated, bottles and glasses flying across from side to side without intermission. Such a bear garden altogether I never beheld, except my first visit to Wetherby's, which it brought very forcibly to my recollection.

This abominable and disgusting scene continued till near ten o'clock, when the Lord Mayor, Sheriffs, the nobility, etc., adjourned to the ball and card rooms, and the dancing commenced. Here the heat was no way inferior to that of th ehall, and the crowd so great there was scarce a possibility of moving. Rejoiced, therefore, was I upon Alderman Woolridge's saying he would take me home whenever I wished it; I eagerly answered, "This moment, if you please." He thereupon took me through some private apartments and down a flight of stairs to a door opening into a back lane where his carriage was ready, into which we stepped without the smallest difficulty or impediment, and were driven home. Completely exhausted, I retired to bed, perfectly satisfied with having once partaken of a Lord Mayor of London's feast.

The 17th November, I received notice from Messrs. Irvine and Touchet that the petition was to be presented to the House of Commons on the 23rd, upon which day they requested my attendance and my company to dine with them afterwards at the British Coffee-house. I accordingly went on the day appointed to Westminster, Mr. Burke taking me in his hand, by which I got a very good place in the gallery, and was much entertained for two hours listening to the different speakers. The petition, being received and read, was ordered to lie on the table, the member who presented it observing he should, on a subsequent day, move that a committee be appointed to take it into consideration and report thereon. From the House of Commons I went to the British, then kept by Mr. Anderson, who gave us a very good dinner and excellent claret.

In the regular course of business, the petition was referred to a committee, General Smith being the chairman of it. Amongst the other members were Mr. Burke, Sir Gilbert Elliot, now Lord Minto, Mr. Long, and (on account of his uncommon parsimony) the much-talked-of Mr. Elwes. From the time of their first meeting I was obliged to attend daily in the committee room, and I underwent a very long examination relative to the practice of the Supreme Court of Judicature, and the general line adopted by the judges thereof in their official capacities.

Parliament being to reassemble on the 8th, Pott and I returned to town that I might resume my attendance upon the committee, the chairman having desired me to do so.* A few nights after I came to town, being at the Opera House, I saw Mordaunt standing in Fop's Alley with his brother, Lord Peterborough. I thought he looked less surly than usual. He soon after came up and shook me by the hand with much cordiality. I congratulated him upon the favourable change, remarking that he was in better spirits than when I left London, and I conjectured was not in such a violent hurry as he had been to revisit Bengal, *the only part of the world fit for man to live with comfort in!* (his own language). Whereupon he hastily exclaimed, "Oh, damn the place, don't mention it. I should be devilish glad never to be obliged to see it again so long as I live." Upon reminding him of my having predicted that when his brother returned to England and introduced him to his numerous connections, he would be better pleased with London and everything attached to it, he admitted I was quite right; for he felt as happy and contented as man could be.

* Hickey and his friend had been passing a few days at the country house of the great nabob Mr. Barwell, a parvenu of vast wealth and overwhelming arrogance.

A curious circumstance now occurred. I had dined with a jovial set at Wilberforce Bird's in Wood Street, Cheapside, where we drank a large quantity of wine. Soon after midnight, the company breaking up, someone proposed finishing the night at Malby's. A hackney coach being sent for, six of us crammed ourselves into it—Bob Pott, Coombe, Shakespear, Lord Fielding, Vaughan and myself. We had got as far at Ludgate Hill on our way to Covent Garden, when Pott, thinking the coachman did not drive fast enough, damned his blood and bid him move on. Coachie made a gruff answer, which offended Master Bob, who thereupon poked at him through the front window with the hilt of his sword, a salutation John Bull not approving, he instantly returned the compliment by the butt end of his whip. Pott, in a violent rage, crept through the window and began pummelling the fellow with all his might. After a sharp but short conflict, they tumbled together off the box into the street. A mob collecting, the horses were stopped, and we all got out to the assistance of our associate. A kind of general engagement ensued, chiefly between us and the watchmen who had come to support the rights of the brother of the whip. The battle ended, as might be expected it would, by three of us—that is, Vaughan, Pott, and myself—being violently seized and dragged to the watch-house in Fleet Market, Lord Fielding, Shakespear, and Coombe having very prudently made good their retreat, thereby avoiding being taken prisoners by the enemy.

The constable of the night, a respectable-looking person, upon seeing three full-dressed men brought in, all abominably intoxicated, upon the coachman's making his complaint, with great good nature said, "Come, come, young gentlemen, this is, I perceive, a drunken frolic. You must therefore pay for your folly, and go quietly home to sleep off the effects of too much wine." While the constable was speaking, a good fat-looking body, who declared himself to be a peaceable citizen and pastrycook in Fleet Street, came up, the blood streaming from his nose, protesting against the unjustifiable conduct and violence of our party, who had assailed and maltreated him merely because he had stepped forward and exerted himself to rescue them out of the hands of an offending mob, rendered more angry by the appearance of, and story told by, the coachman, who certainly had sustained some injury in the affray. Although my head was by no means clear, I, nevertheless, felt the full force of the kind constable's very sensible advice, and putting my hand into my pocket was about to make a pecuniary recompense for our transgression, when Pott, who was in one of his wicked and facetious fits, and resolved to have some fun before he paid, cried out, "No! No! I protest against the doling out of cash. So, old Bollocks, (to the constable) proceed, sir, to do your duty. Observe, I am a profound lawyer, deeply read in the statutes since the establishment of Englishmen's pride and glory, *Magna Charta*. So stand by, my old cock, and let me see that I do not catch you tripping; for blood and zounds, if I do I'll circumfloborate you and all your base understrappers."

The constable looked with some symptoms of surprise at Pott, and, after hemming once or twice, said, "I think, young gentleman, that after the experience of thirty years I do pretty well know my duty. I will convince you that I do know it by clapping you for the remainder of the night into the black hole, young gentleman, do you see, and have no doubt but the air of that agreeable apartment will restore your senses." "Black hole!" repeated Pott. "Take care, old Dogberry, you are upon the edge of a precipice, into which if you fall, the devil himself will not be able to relieve you, though I can. Proceed, therefore, with caution. You talk of black holes without a trial! You are a pretty son-of-a-bitch of a judge. Come, proceed. Ascend your magisterial chair and take down depositions; otherwise you will be all at sea, and cast away upon the rocks of error and ignorance. Proceed, I say!"

"Very well! very well! young sir, I believe you may be right in this notion, and I will act conformably." While preparing to take his seat, Pott slipped behind him and occupied it, to the great entertainment of the bystanders. Again the black hole was alluded to; Bob therefore relinquished the chair, which the humble representative of justice immediately filled, and taking up his pen, prepared his book. Bob, in the meantime, got behind him and twirled his wig round, putting the back part in front. Again a burst of laughter broke forth, and again the black hole was threatened. The constable then demanded to know his name. "George," answered Pott. "That's not true," observed the constable, "for I just now heard that gentleman (pointing to me) call you Bob." "That gentleman," said Bob, "is too drunk to tell his own name, and I am sure cannot distinguish any other person's. So get on, most upright judge, you second Daniel."

"Well, sir," asked the constable, "who are you?" "A son of the King's," said Bob. The man stared, and in a hesitating voice said, "I do not exactly understand what you are at, young sir. I wish you would act like a reasonable creature." "Proceed, thou mirror of all that's just, or by the mighty Jupiter I'll jumble you to mincemeat." The constable, losing his temper at being made a laughing stock, ordered the door of the black hole to be opened; whereupon Vaughan with vast solemnity addressed him, saying, "I have hitherto, sir, been a quiet spectator of all that has passed and, although wrongfully brought and detained here as a prisoner, have not uttered a syllable; but, when I hear you talk of more rigorous confinement of my friend, I consider it right to caution you as to your proceedings, for which, if wrong, depend upon it you shall be made responsible. And give me leave further to inform you that I am the more competent to caution you as to your measures from myself having the honour to be in His Majesty's commission of the peace for the County of Middlesex. I, therefore, once more recommend you to take care what you are about." "I am sorry to hear you are yourself a magistrate, sir," said the constable; "because, if that be the case, you ought to know better than to commit a breach of the peace by kicking up a broil and riot in the streets at midnight. However, sir, that matter you shall settle before the sitting alderman in the morning."

Growing tired of the scene, I took one of the constables aside; to whom I observed I thought my young companion had sufficiently amused himself, and that I should be obliged to him if he would settle the business and let us get home. This he very good-naturedly undertook and, after talking apart with the coachman, returned saying the coachman at first demanded five guineas, but had finally consented to take two. The disinterested pastrycook declined receiving any pecuniary recompense, very considerately saying the personal injury he had sustained was trifling; and, although he at first felt much offended at the treatment he had received, he was now convinced it arose entirely from a drunken frolic, the gentlemen not intending or wishing to injure anyone. I, therefore, paid the coachman two guineas, gave two more to the people of the watch, and we departed, cheered by the hearty huzzas of all present, the spectators declaring we acted like gentlemen; that they were sure if the *fair one* (meaning Pott) was not a son of His Majesty's he must be nearly allied to the royal family from his likeness to them; but, at any rate, be he whom he might, he had that night proved he was a very comical, and certainly was a very fine-looking, handsome fellow.

In the beginning of February, Pott told me he had agreed for the whole of the round house and half the great cabin of the ship *Lord Mulgrave*, commanded by Captain Urmston, which ship would sail for India in six or seven weeks; that, in consideration of a large sum of money, the captain had consented to receive Emily on board; and they both (Emily and Pott) flattered themselves that I would join the party by occupying the half of the great cabin, which he (Pott) had taken in the hope that I would do so. To this I answered that it was impossible for me to leave England until something decisive was done respecting the petition I had brought home. Pott thereupon laughingly said, "Psha! nonsense, Bill, why don't you speak honestly and say, as the truth is, that your money not being yet expended you have no inclination to leave this paradise? Nor do I wonder at it. Emily's vanity made her think you would sacrifice much to have her society during the voyage, while I had too good an opinion of your taste to suppose you would quit England until compelled by dire necessity. I only lament that my finances will not allow of my waiting another year for you, as by that time I fancy your stock will be pretty well exhausted. However," continued he, "under these circumstances you must be with us as much as possible until our departure," a desire I had real satisfaction in agreeing to.

Being at a masquerade with Pott and Emily at Cornely's, I there again met with Charlotte Barry, hanging upon the arm of my cynical friend, Mordaunt, who, after introducing me, whispered that he had taken her into keeping. Pott being seized with a violent headache, Emily and he went home before twelve o'clock, whereupon I joined Mordaunt and his new favourite. He, being fond of running about the rooms to speak to every acquaintance he saw, frequently left Charlotte under my care; and we soon became mutually attached, so much so that, from that evening, our love ended only with the dear girl's life.

Our club continued to meet twice a week, ultimately fixing entirely at Le Tellier's, I believe more from name and centrical situation than any superior merit. The house I pitched upon and gave my dinner at, or rather presided, was the St. Albans where, though one or two general snarlers found fault with the dinner, all admitted the wines to be exquisitely good, the champagne especially. About once a month I gave a dinner at my father's, my friends always doing me the honour to say neither Le Tellier, The London, or any tavern in the metropolis could surpass me in the excellence of the viands and liquors.

We had another very sociable meeting occasionally. Twelve or fifteen of us, attended by some of the most fashionable women of the time, going to March's, the Windmill, at Salt Hill, where we spent three or four days together in all sorts of frolic and fancy. We usually went on Friday, staying till Tuesday, except that, on Sunday evening, Mordaunt, Charlotte Barry and myself would, after dinner, get into a post-chaise-and-four and dash up to Cornelys's promenade, where after strolling round the rooms, chatting to acquaintances, we returned in the same manner to Salt Hill to sleep, but generally found some of the party up, engaged at hazard; to which several were greatly addicted, especially Major George Russell, who about four years before had returned from Bengal with a fortune of upwards of forty thousand pounds, the whole of which he had squandered away or lost at the gaming table, at the period I became acquainted with him not having five hundred pounds left.

My Sunday night excursions from Salt Hill to Soho Square cost me a coat each time; for Mordaunt, like my friend Bob Pott, always falling fast asleep in a carriage, Charlotte and I, during his naps, kissed and fondled like a pair of turtle-doves; and, as the women then wore large quantities of pomatum and powder, and Charlotte having a profusion of hair, I was constantly covered with the latter, which when Mordaunt observed he would say to me in his usual rough snarl, "What the devil have you been about to make such a figure of your clothes?" To which Charlotte without hesitation replied, "I followed your bad example and went to sleep with my head upon his shoulder." "Did you by God," said Mordaunt, "the more fool he for permitting it. I'll be damned if you ever shall spoil my clothes so." "Never fear, there is not the least danger of my attempting it," contemptuously said Charlotte.

19

MORDAUNT AND CHARLOTTE
BARRY

Riding in Hyde Park, I there met my Fleet Market watch-house
companion, Thomas Vaughan, Esquire. After talking together
some time upon common topics, he said, "I frequently see you
in Suffolk Street visiting my opposite neighbour, Major Metcalfe; and
yet, although so near, and that you have often promised to give me an
opportunity of introducing you to Mrs. Vaughan and a houseful of
daughters, you have never done me the honour of calling." I made
some commonplace apology, and the subject dropped. After riding
some time, we left the park together, and his horses standing at
Fozard's, we dismounted and walked up Piccadilly, during which he
took out his watch, observing, "It is, I see, only three o'clock; suppose
therefore, as you will afterwards have ample time to dress for dinner,
that you come home with me now and let me make you acquainted
with my family." As I knew not how to parry this proposal, I went with
him. Upon getting to his house, we found the street door open. Mr.
Vaughan therefore desired me to follow him upstairs, where without
any announcing he opened the drawing-room door.

Upon entering the room, I found six very nice-looking girls at high
romps, and all in deshabille. The two eldest were just rising into
womanhood, extremely elegant figures. They appeared distressed beyond measure at a stranger's thus unexpectedly coming upon them,
exclaiming, "Fie, Papa, how could you bring a gentleman in without
affording us an opportunity of retiring." Nor did the father lessen their
embarrassment by saying in an audible whisper to me, "There they are,
Hickey, a complete half-dozen, all good-looking girls. Damn me if I
know what is to become of them, or how I shall be able to provide for
them as they grow up. I only hope they may not have to turn out
whores." The coarseness and brutality of the speech, coming from the
lips of a parent in the presence of his own children, shocked me as

much as it distressed the girls, one of whom, with great naïveté said, "Indeed, Papa, you make the gentleman blush both for you and us."

Mrs. Vaughan was not at home; but I had been introduced to her a few evenings before at a great party given by Mrs. Treves. She was an uncommonly clever woman and had written several things of extra-ordinary merit, which were published under the name and as the production of her husband, though he was in no way equal to com-posing one of the kind, being a weak, empty coxcomb. They were particularly attached to the drama, constant attendants upon the theatres, criticising in the public newspapers all new pieces and new actors. Mr. Sheridan was said to have had this couple in view when he wrote the characters of Mr. and Mrs. Dangle in his celebrated work of *The Critic*. Mrs. Vaughan brought her husband a fortune of ten thousand pounds. He held a sinecure place under government of about six hundred a year; but, being not only extravagant but a bad manager, he was always involved, finding it difficult to support with decency a numerous family; indeed, he would have proved wholly unequal to do so had he not received material aid from the writings of Mrs. Vaughan, which becoming fashionable were read by everybody, consequently had a great sale. Three of this gentleman's daughters, some years after my awkward visit, went to India where they all married, one to Sir George Leith, Baronet, then a captain in His Majesty's army, another to Colonel Mitchell of the Company's service, the third I do not recol-lect to whom. The mother has been dead a long time, and Vaughan himself, as I am informed, a prisoner in the King's Bench for debt.

Towards the end of February, the committee to whom the petition from Bengal had been referred made their first report to the House of Commons, which rendered any further attendance on my part unneces-sary, a circumstance I was not sorry for, having just received an inti-mation from Charlotte Barry that Mordaunt was making a party to go hunting and shooting in Oxfordshire, requesting that I would be one amongst them. This I could not do, having promised Emily and Pott to accompany them to Portsmouth and see them embark, an order to do which they were in daily expectation of receiving. From this promise, however, I was relieved by Robert's calling one morning upon me and saying as he, upon consideration, felt that such a jaunt upon such an occasion must be far from pleasant to me, and would undoubtedly be most distressing to him as well as to his dear girl, when we should come to the final leave-taking, a ceremony he knew we mutually abhorred, he thought it would be better to waive the Portsmouth engagement and proposed in lieu of it that I should go with them to Salt Hill, to which he must pay a visit in order to see his brother, Joseph Holden Pott, then at Eton School; that he and Emily would stay there until summoned away, and I, after passing one or more days, as I pleased, with them, might slip off *sans cérémonie* and proceed to join the Oxfordshire party.

Thus it was arranged and executed. After spending three days at March's, all low in spirits, I rose at break of day on the fourth morning, and leaving Pott and his lovely companion in bed, stepped into a post-chaise for Reading, on my way to Chapel House near Chipping Norton to join the sportsmen, and so avoided the formal adieus of my greatly esteemed friend Pott and his beautiful Emily. Upon my arrival at Chapel House, Charlotte greeted me with extraordinary warmth, while her jade of a sister Nancy Barry (as wicked a little devil as ever existed) cried out, "Now's your time, Hickey. That beast Mordaunt was called away this morning by his Earl of a brother, who is on a visit at Lord Hilsborough's, somewhere in this county, to whom he wants to introduce the Nabob, so that you will have a couple of days' enjoyment together; and I have no doubt you'll *make the most of them.*"

The males of the party had not yet returned from the chase. From the women I learnt that it consisted of Joe Bird, Harvey Coombe, Wilberforce Bird, Van, Lord Semple, Lord Fielding, and Ulysses Browne, the last named having just then quitted the Horse Guards, in which he was an old captain but obliged to quit from having lived rather too fast for his income. He had been appointed an ensign in the East India Company's service at the island of St. Helena, for which place he was shortly to embark, a melancholy reverse for a man of the world who had lived all his life in the society of the first people in the kingdom. By five o'clock, the chasseurs being all assembled at the inn, we sat down to dinner, were extraordinary merry, and kept it up until midnight, when we separated.

Notwithstanding the fair opportunity and the mutual regard for each other that had commenced between Charlotte and me, we had both our scruples of conscience, from her then living exclusively with Mordaunt, whose intimate friend I was considered to be. She also assured me she never had been unfaithful to any man with whom she lived; that from her soul she detested her present keeper, Mordaunt, and would get rid of him very soon; but, while under his immediate protection, she wished to act with propriety. Neither could I forget Emily's speech to me when in something of a similar situation. Extraordinary as it may seem, we therefore had forbearance enough to retire each to our own chamber; but where I had been scarce a minute when in bounced the volatile, and certainly very handsome, Nancy, saying, "I must have a word or two with you this way; so come along. I shall not detain you long." At first I began to suspect she meditated an attack upon me herself; but, recollecting her keeper, Van, was in the house, I was sure that could not be the case. However, I followed her to another bedchamber door, which finding fastened, she rapped at it, calling out, "Charlotte, Charlotte, I want you. Make haste."

The door being instantly unlocked and opened by Charlotte, who appeared half-undressed, I could not resist the temptation, and clasped her in my arms; whereupon Nancy exclaimed, "That's right, and as it should be; so now to bed as fast as you can. You are sincerely attached to each other, and it would be an unheard-of piece of absurdity to let slip the joys that now await you both. Do you suppose, Hickey, that if Mordaunt's and your situations were reversed, and that Charlotte belonged to you instead of him, that he would hesitate on account of honour or friendship? Not he, I'll be sworn; so not a word more, but to bed with ye." And, saying this, out she ran, pulling the door after her. Nancy's argument, bad as it was, and our critical situation was irresistible; so to bed we went. By seven o'clock the following morning, Nancy again entered our room, and throwing herself between us upon the bed, said, "Well, how did you pass the night? More to your mutual satisfaction, I fancy, than I have. Van, completely knocked up by his confounded hunting all day and then swilling a quantity of claret, fell asleep the moment his head touched the pillow, amusing me by his abominable snoring; nor did he open his eyes till roused by a servant half an hour ago; and now he is off again like a Bedlamite screeching and hallooing after another fox. Well, how do you like each other after this *trial of skill?*"

I was obliged to stop the wanton rogue's further prating by kisses, from which, disengaging herself, she got off the bed, and left the room, archly saying as she went out, "I know Charlotte will by and by thank me for this visit." At ten we breakfasted, then mounted our horses, Charlotte being one of the best horsewomen I ever saw. We took a long ride towards Birmingham, during which we were once very near falling in with the hounds and obliged to turn short, galloping off as fast as our steeds would carry us in order to get out of their track, my fair companion having no more relish for the sports of the field than myself. At Chapel House I spent four as pleasant days as ever I experienced, in the enjoyment of women, wine, and admirable society. When at table, the men often remarked that, although I shunned the chase, over the bottle I was as keen a sportsman as the best of them. On the fourth evening, Mordaunt returned; and, as he seemed more savage and looked surlier than ever, I bid the party adieu; ordering a chaise-and-four I set off for London, giving Captain Browne a passage.

Upon reaching St. Albans Street, I found a letter from Mr. Pott, Robert's father, most earnestly requesting to see me immediately upon a business in which his happiness was materially concerned, as well as the future welfare or irretrievable ruin of his son, my friend Robert.

This letter I was concerned to see dated the morning upon which I had left town. I, however, thought it right to wait upon him, and directly went to his house in Hanover Square, telling him I had only that hour received his letter. He was much distressed upon first seeing me, and expressed his grateful sense of my kind attention towards him. Almost in tears, he said that, knowing the great influence I possessed over that inconsiderate boy Robert, he had taken the liberty of sending for me to beg my interference and exertions to preserve him from absolute destruction by preventing his committing an act pregnant with every possible evil, but which he feared was then past remedy, adding in an agony, "For, do you know, Mr. Hickey, the unthinking boy has taken that infamous and notoriously abandoned woman, Emily, who has already involved him deeply as to pecuniary matters, with him to India, a step that must not only shut him out of all proper society, but prevent his being employed in any situation of respect or emolument. I have, nevertheless, the melancholy consolation of feeling that I have strictly performed my duty as a parent towards him, and done all in my power to save him from disgrace and ruin, and if I have failed in accomplishing an object I had so much at heart, no blame surely can be ascribed to me; his folly be upon his own head; *mais ses vues sont courtes.*"

I received the same day a long epistle from Robert, telling me that, after an ineffectual attempt to get to sea, they had returned, and still lay wind-bound at the Mother Bank (Portsmouth); that he was extremely uneasy at the detention, as the old Buck (meaning his father) was stirring heaven and earth to defeat his wish of keeping his dear woman with him. "Nay," adds he, "do you know, Bill, he has carried it so far as to apply to the Court of Directors, and the stupid soap-boilers in consequence directed their addle-pated Secretary to address a letter *upon the service* to Captain Urmston, admonishing him against so unpardonable a fault as permitting a common prostitute to find her way to India on board his ship. But it's all in vain, my dear Will, go she must and go she shall, by all the powers of heaven and hell. Poor Urmston is in a woeful panic, saying it may be the means of his losing the command of his ship, and the service altogether, but I know better. The worst the cheese-mongering varlets of Leadenhall Street can do is to mulct him a few hundred pounds, which I, of course, shall pay, and they may kiss my bum fiddle." He then again pressed me to join them, observing he had a noble cabin quite complete and ready to receive me, with a set of passengers I should like; that unluckily there was one female amongst them, which would make it necessary, from common delicacy, that Emily should confine herself to her own apartment, but which was immaterial, as she had the balcony to take exercise in. I, however, felt no inclination to avail myself of this friendly offer, having too many attachments to England to quit it until dire necessity should make me do so.

Two days after this, I believe about 6th March, taking my usual exercise on horseback in Hyde Park, Mordaunt rode up to tell me he had the evening before brought Mrs. Barry to town, apprehending her to be dangerously ill; that the physicians, however, consoled him by saying that was by no means the case, and although she might be confined for some time, would ultimately do very well; but that perfect quiet was indispensably necessary, and that nothing should disturb or agitate her for a week or ten days. "For my part, Hickey," continued Mordaunt, "I begin to suspect she is in love with you; she is so damned ill-natured and out of spirits except when you are present, and, when you are, she is all life. The hour you left us at the Chapel House she became as cross as the devil, and I could get no good out of her. Damn her! I won't talk any more about her, but leave her to her infernal apothecaries' bolusses, draughts, and dark chambers. How horridly stupid London is, nothing going forward worth notice! I wish you was not so wedded to it, and would dash off somewhere for a week or so."

I told him I was ready and willing, having no particular inducements just then in London. But where should we go to? "To Portsmouth," said Mordaunt, "I was told an hour ago that the Grand Channel Fleet are at anchor there, affording to the people on shore a glorious spectacle. Let's get into a chaise and be off directly." That, I told him, I could not do, being most particularly engaged for the rest of that day, but would accompany him on the following morning at as early an hour as he chose. He growled sadly at this *delay*, as he called it, pressing me to give up my engagements and set off; but, as I positively refused, it was settled that I should breakfast with him the next morning at eight o'clock at his mother's house in Dean Street, Soho, from whence we should start on our expedition.

Upon my arrival at Lady Peterborough's I saw standing at the door a smart travelling post-chaise, having the family coat of arms and coronet handsomely painted upon the panels. Having finished our breakfast, we stepped into the carriage and set off in high style. Upon enquiring how Mrs. Barry was that morning, he replied, "Oh, curse me if I know anything about her, as from the infernal doctor's prohibition I am not allowed to touch her. I slept last night at my mother's; nor have I seen her since I brought her to town and left her at her lodgings the night before last. I have no doubt, Hickey, but you could cure her much sooner than the whole college of medical men."

When Mordaunt and I left London the weather was, as it had been for a fortnight before, serene and beautifully fine; but before we had gone twenty miles it became dull and overcast; and when we reached

Petersfield there was every indication of a complete change. The Forty-second Regiment was marching into that town at the time we entered it, on their way to Portsmouth, where they were to embark for India. The officers had engaged almost all the horses in the place; and before we could procure four, without which Mordaunt would never stir, it became dusk and began to snow. I, therefore, proposed staying where we were comfortably housed until the next morning, to which my companion readily agreed. We ate our dinner and supper in one, drank a bottle of claret each and went to bed. Upon getting up the next morning, I saw the whole country covered by a thick body of snow, the sky overcast and dull. We met at breakfast, Mordaunt looking as gloomy as the weather. While taking our coffee, I remarked that, the object we set out upon being entirely defeated by the unfavourable change in the weather, I thought the most prudent thing we could do would be to bend our course back from whence we came. Whereupon Mordaunt angrily said I might do as I pleased but, as he left town for the purpose of going to Portsmouth, most assuredly he should proceed. "For what purpose?" asked I. "Do you conceive it possible to see the Fleet or, indeed, any object, at the distance of one hundred yards in such weather as the present?" "That may be," growled my chum. "By God I'll go on. I perfectly understand why you are in such haste to return; it is that you may ingratiate yourself," and he muttered something more to himself; though I could not distinguish what he said, I knew he alluded to Charlotte; but, having determined not to be put out of temper by his moroseness, I mildly replied he was mistaken, that I had proposed relinquishing the rest of the scheme we had set out upon merely from seeing so unfavourable a change in the weather. Nevertheless, if he thought it advisable to go on, I was ready to attend him. Without a word more he told the waiter, who had come into the room to take away the breakfast things, to bring the chaise to the door as soon as possible. In a few minutes, it was announced ready; we got in; but before we reached Portsmouth the snow recommenced, falling so fast and so thick that when we got out at the George Inn we literally could not distinguish the houses on the opposite side of the street.

As it began to freeze before we left Petersfield, the roads were so slippery the horses could not keep their feet, and we were full four hours going the stage to Portsmouth. Mordaunt, more sulky than ever, would not speak when I wished to consult him about dinner. I therefore desired the landlord to furnish the best his larder afforded. At five we sat down to an excellent dinner; a few glasses of madeira restoring my misanthropic companion to somewhat better temper, we chatted over a bottle until after coffee was served, then played piquet until bedtime. The next morning, the weather had not in the least mended. We, nevertheless, so far set the snow at defiance as to walk to the coffee-room upon the parade, from whence in clear weather there is a fine prospect of Spithead and the Isle of Wight; but, in the state we had it, we could not see twenty yards from the windows. Here we met a number of naval officers, and entered into conversation with several. We also had a very good match at billiards, thus beguiling the hours until towards four o'clock, when two smart young lieutenants accepted an invitation we gave them to partake of our dinner at the George. We gave as much madeira and claret as they could carry away, and at midnight they departed in high spirits, well pleased with their entertainment.

A second day and evening went off vastly well. The third morning a tremendous snow continued falling, with severe frost. We repeated our visit to the coffee-room and played billiards; but, there being a court martial that drew away all the officers, we could not procure a single guest to join us at dinner, so that the *Snarler* and I had a tête-à-tête. I perceived he was much out of humour from his determined silence during the meal, and his frequent application to the bottle. Having drunk our coffee, I called for cards, beating him seven games not at all all improving his manners. A little before eleven, I looked at my watch to see the hour; whereupon with great violence he dashed down his cards upon the table and, looking fiercely at me, the following dialogue ensued:

MORDAUNT: "Pray, may I venture, without giving offence, to ask how long you propose staying in this attracting town of Portsmouth?"

HICKEY: "I cannot consider that otherwise than an insulting question, and most extraordinary to come from you, Mordaunt. Had I put such a one to you, it would have been more appropriate and reasonable."

MORDAUNT: "For the soul of me, I can't see why. Be that as it may, and let your object in continuing at Portsmouth be ever so good, I am satisfied, quite satisfied, by God! I have had enough of Portsmouth, the enviable, delightful spot, and will leave it this instant."

HICKEY: "Not in such a night as this is I imagine; for that would be too wild a measure for even the very eccentric Captain Mordaunt to adopt."

MORDAUNT: "The eccentric Captain Mordaunt, however, certainly will not stay another hour in this infernal town, sir."

HICKEY: "Probably you are not aware that travelling in such tremendously bad weather as the present, and through such a hilly country, must be attended with considerable personal danger. That, I fancy, will influence you, Captain Mordaunt, though prudential motives may lose their effect."

MORDAUNT: "Again you are mistaken; no motives whatsoever shall keep me here"; and he pulled violently at the bell.

A waiter obeying the furious summons, he ordered a bill immediately, and four horses to be put to his carriage to take him the first stage to London. The man stared and looked frightened, but did not move; upon which Mordaunt began to curse and swear, and walking towards the waiter, he made a precipitate retreat. In a few seconds Bolton, the landlord, made his appearance, saying, "The waiter, gentlemen, tells me you propose setting off for London." I interrupted him to assure him *I* had no thoughts of that kind, not being absolutely insane. He bowed to me, and addressing Mordaunt proceeded to observe the weather was more dreadful than he ever had known it; so uncommonly bad that he should feel averse to sending his horses and post-boys abroad in it; that the roads, from the immense fall of snow and severity of the frost, must, he imagined, be rendered impassable, or, at any rate, exceedingly dangerous. If, however, his (Mordaunt's) determination was to commence his journey at so inclement a season, he could have no chance of succeeding except by Gosport, the Petersfield hill being impracticable to ascend in such weather.

Mordaunt answered it was a matter of indifference to him by what road they took him, but go he would. The landlord withdrawing to order the horses might be put to, I resumed the conversation with Mordaunt by saying, "Surely, Mordaunt, this is an excessive wild scheme of yours."

MORDAUNT: "I cannot help your thoughts; mine happen to be very opposite; and I know no reason why yours are to bind me."

HICKEY: "Yet anyone except a madman would agree as to the propriety of my advice upon this occasion. One advantage I shall derive from your obstinacy: it will prevent my ever going upon an expedition with a madman in future."

MORDAUNT: "You are becoming amazingly rude."

HICKEY: "If I am, your strange conduct, your want of temper, and absurdity, to use no harsher phrases, justifies me."

MORDAUNT: "I cannot conceive upon what principle of civility or good breeding I am bound to shut myself up in an inn at Portsmouth, when it is disagreeable to me to continue there."

HICKEY: "Give me leave to ask what brought us here but your unaccountable perverseness and obstinacy. Did I not, when at Petersfield, strongly remonstrate against continuing the journey from seeing so total a change in the weather had taken place, and observe to you that, the purpose for which we set out being so completely defeated, the best thing we could do would be to return to London? Did you not most pertinaciously and mulishly insist upon going on in spite of frost, snow, and all I could say to induce you to abandon your intention?"

MORDAUNT: "Perhaps I did persevere in wishing to accomplish my object; perhaps, too, the *mulishness* you speak of influenced me. Certain it is the same *mulishness*, and not knowing or feeling myself your slave, now determines me to pursue my own inclination, which leads me to leave Portsmouth. But surely that need not influence you."

HICKEY: "Most indisputably it shall not, nor will I make such an ass of myself as to stir from hence without at least the benefit of daylight."

MORDAUNT: "My resolution is unalterable."

HICKEY: "I am ready to give you full credit for possessing a greater degree of obstinacy than ever fell to the lot of one man. I shall, nevertheless, take the liberty of once more repeating that I should not have been here but to indulge your capricious whim; that nothing could be more disgusting to me than remaining here in your society three tedious days; yet, that having occurred, I do not see the necessity of beginning a journey at midnight in such dreadful weather as now prevails. We arrived here together; let us return like reasonable men together. Stay till the morning and I will accompany you."

MORDAUNT: "Damn me if I stay a single hour."

HICKEY: "Then go, and be damned."

At that moment, Bolton brought the bill and pronounced the chaise being at the door, but again very strongly recommended Mordaunt not to stir until daylight. His advice was thrown away. He then took from his purse a bank-note, which he threw upon the table, saying, "There's fifty pounds, which I suppose will defray my share." I told him he had better keep his money for the present; that, as we had agreed upon leaving London one of us should pay the whole expense and settle upon our return, and I had hitherto done so; I should continue it, and call for his half when I reached London. He, thereupon, pocketed his note, stalked down to his chaise, and I went to my bedchamber. I had not been more than ten minutes in bed when the door of my room was opened with a great bang, and in marched Mordaunt, damning and cursing all fortified towns. Enquiring what was the matter, he replied, "The damned gate is shut and I can't get out." To which I answered, "It is a lucky circumstance for you; so now for God's sake go quietly to bed, and after breakfast we will set off together."

He continued muttering to himself and walking up and down the room; upon which I, with some warmth, declared that, if he did not choose to sleep himself, he should no longer disturb my rest; and I was actually rising to compel him to retire, when the landlord once more appeared, saying, "Now, sir, if you are resolved upon proceeding there is an opportunity of doing so. A dispatch is this instant going off from the admiral, and, of course, the gate must be opened to let the express pass." Mordaunt upon hearing this, without saying a word to me, ran downstairs, and in a few minutes I heard the carriage drive off. At nine in the morning I ate a hearty breakfast, then getting into a post-chaise, taking Frescini inside with me, proceeded towards London. I found the roads more dreadfully bad than I expected, being one sheet of ice; so that I actually wondered how the poor animals of horses could draw the carriage and preserve their footing, although frost-shod.

Upon reaching the inn at Godalming, I enquired whether a single gentleman and servant had been there that day, to which the waiter replied the only person that had gone towards London was the Earl of Peterborough, who left the house about an hour before, on his way from Portsmouth, his Lordship seeming very much out of humour at the detention he had met with on the road from the severity of the weather, and the difficulty his servant had found in awaking the hostlers and post-boys at the different stages in the night, complaining of one house in particular, where he had been kept above two hours before the horses were changed, and that one of them had afterwards fallen twice, both times throwing the rider. By the man's styling this person my Lord and Earl of Peterborough, I presumed that, from the arms on the carriage, and possibly Mordaunt's hauteur, they concluded it was the peer himself within. Just as I drove up to the door of the White Lion, Mordaunt drove from it. As I did not feel any inclination to encounter the additional difficulties of travelling during a dark and tempestuous night, I determined to remain where I was. I accordingly slept at Cobham, finishing my most disagreeable excursion the following morning and arriving in London at one in the afternoon.

I directly went to Mrs. Barry's in Queen Ann Street, where I was rejoiced to find her perfectly recovered. Upon offering my congratulations, she laughingly said, "The fact is, I was sick of nothing but Mordaunt's shocking temper. Having had a violent quarrel with him, it brought on a slight hysteric, which left an excruciating headache; so to get rid of the brute, at least for a time, I coaxed the physician he, in a great fright, had sent for, to say I must be left entirely alone and quiet for some days as otherwise I might be seriously ill. I was, however, monstrously vexed when I discovered that you was gone with him to Portsmouth. Thank heaven my gentleman is now laid up, and we shall have a little comfort."

Not knowing what she meant by his being laid up, I asked an explanation; when she replied, "Have you not heard of his accident? Tearing along like a madman as he is, last night in the dark through Wandsworth, his post-boys came in contact with a stage-coach just turning from a stable-yard. Mordaunt's chaise was overset and almost demolished, himself and servant being severely bruised, and Mordaunt's ankle sprained. One of his postilions was taken up for dead. Mordaunt in a fainting state was carried into the house, where his impatience and apprehension that his leg was broken, and likewise that he had some internal injury, made him insist upon an immediate removal, which, notwithstanding the remonstrances of a Wandsworth apothecary, and the entreaties of the compassionate people that had witnessed the accident, he persevered in. A coach being prepared with pillows, he was lifted into it, attended by his own servant and the apothecary to support him, and thus was conveyed to his mother's in Dean Street, where he arrived about eight this morning. Lady Peterborough, frightened out of her wits, instantly sent off for Mr. Pott, and two or three other eminent surgeons. This account was brought to me by Richard Mordaunt's groom not above an hour ago."

And so ended his precious journey from Portsmouth. It is unnecessary to add that Charlotte and I enjoyed ourselves, and were perfectly happy during his confinement. Upon his recovery, he called upon me and made the handsomest apology possible for his very rude and intemperate behaviour, especially for so abruptly leaving me to come by myself from Portsmouth. However, he observed, for that part of his obstinacy and folly he had been sufficiently punished both in person and purse; for, independent of almost breaking his neck, he understood from the coachmaker that his brother's carriage had sustained such material injury it would cost about fifty pounds to put it to rights.

During this visit he showed me a letter he had received the preceding day from Mr. James Grant* offering to let him the house at Drayton for six months from 1st May, as he had expressed an earnest desire to have it, and requesting him to come down for a couple of days, when he would show the many conveniences of the premises, and settle the terms upon which he would let it. "And now, Hickey," said Mordaunt, "convince me that you pardon my late ill-behaviour by accompanying me and Charlotte to Drayton. She particularly desired I would request it as a favour in her name." The latter sentence determined me, and I promised to go with them. I think it was about 15th March that we three went to Grant's, continuing there three days. The bargain was concluded and the house, furnished, with the stock of liquors of every kind, was to become Mordaunt's at the time before mentioned.

The club broke up at the end of March. The two last months of its existence I had scarcely been once at it, my whole time being given up to my new favourite, Charlotte, in attending her to masquerades, theatres, The Pantheon, and every other public place that was open, to no one of which would she ever consent to go unless I made one; and, although Mordaunt was exceedingly jealous of her avowed partiality towards me, he often entreated me to let them have as much of

* This was the James Grant who had saved Hickey from drowning in the year 1769. He had now left the service of the East India Company to become a West India merchant in the City of London. His country house was "at the retired and pretty village of Drayton, between Uxbridge and Colnbrook."

my company as I could, observing Charlotte was not at all the same person when I was absent, being then dejected and so damned ill-tempered he could make nothing of her. "Nay," said he, "she had even gone so far as to tell me to my face that her object and intention is to give herself up entirely to you!" After a pause, in which I could perceive he had worked himself into a rage, he with extreme vehemence added, "but that, by God, she never shall do, to you or any other man breathing so long as I live." As I felt awkward upon the subject, I made no answer; and, besides, I had given my solemn promise to Charlotte that I would avoid quarrelling with Mordaunt, and leave the bringing about a separation entirely to her.

He, one morning, took me to look at a famous travelling-coach, building for his brother in Long Acre. In size it was nearly, if not full, as large as the Lord Mayor of London's state carriage. It accommodated three persons on each side with superabundant room. In the centre there drew up from the bottom by springs a table, sufficiently large to dine six persons comfortably; under the floor were all the requisite apparatus of saucepans, gridiron, etc., for cooking, likewise knives, forks, plates, dishes, and other articles of a sideboard. Beneath the seats, complete bedding for four persons was stowed, which, when wanted for use, were taken out and placed upon a frame, crossways, four capital beds being made ready in five minutes. In a projection from the back of the body of the carriage, and the same forward, was ample stowage for wines, and all sorts of liquors, handsome cut-glass bottles of various sizes being secured in fixed frames, so that no motion, short of an absolute upset, could injure or derange them. In short, this stupendous vehicle was a moving house, having in and about it every convenience appertaining to a mansion. It was finished, in point of workmanship and decorations, in the highest manner, the Peterborough arms and heraldic ornaments being painted in a style of taste, and with a delicacy that did the artist infinite credit.

The young Earl's object in building so uncommon a vehicle was to ensure for himself every common comfort when travelling upon the Continent, especially through Italy, where by woeful experience he knew the inns were execrable, abounding in dirt and filth, the beds swarming with bugs, fleas and vermin of every description. The greatest objection to this carriage was its extreme ponderosity, which when I first saw it struck me so forcibly that I asked the coachmaker whether he did not apprehend its extraordinary weight might prove so serious as to render it useless; to which the mechanic candidly replied, "Undoubtedly it will, sir. Its weight is an insuperable impediment to its ever being of any real use, much less that for which it was intended, for no number of horses that could be attached together in harness would ever be able to drag it along the dreadful roads of Italy,

Germany, and many parts of France; and so I have taken the liberty
of telling his Lordship over and over again since this carriage has been
in hand; and, although I am convinced his own good sense satisfied
him of the truth of what I said, he insisted upon my completing the
work. Such crowds of people came daily to look at it while it remained
in the front shop as greatly to impede and interrupt my workmen, the
evil increasing to such a degree that I was at last obliged to remove it
to this private warehouse, and refuse entrance to all persons applying
to see it."

While Mordaunt and I were engaged in this conversation with the
coachmaker, Lord Peterborough came in; and, upon his brother's
repeating to him the purport of what had just been said respecting the
carriage, he readily admitted the justness of the opinion, saying he had
no idea he should ever be able to use it in the way he intended.
"However, that don't much signify," said his Lordship, "and it certainly
has been a source of much amusement to me and my friends whilst
building. Besides, Henry," addressing Mordaunt, "if I am disappointed
of its uses, it will serve you and your sultanas admirably well in your
excursions about the country; and, as you will neither require the
bedding, nor any of the stores, when all those are taken out, the
draught will be easy enough for four horses; and I am convinced it
will prove a most comfortable carriage to travel in." Mordaunt replied,
"Very well, Peterborough, I certainly shall make the trial ere long."

One of my horses being reported to be slightly diseased, I walked
up to Fozard's Stable in Piccadilly to enquire about him. Asking for
Fozard, the people told me he was at the other yard, in Park Lane; I
therefore went there, and was informed he was at Mr. Van's, who lived
at the corner of the gateway of the stable yard. Whilst thinking I might
as well take that opportunity of calling upon Mr. Van, one of his
servants came up to say Mrs. Van sent her compliments and requested
to see me. I followed the man into the house, who showed me up to
the drawing-room where Nancy Barry was. She looked much out of
humour, said she was at the window and saw me turn into the stable
yard, and hoped I would excuse her having taken the liberty of sending for me. Being really surprised at an address so formal and so
unusual, I demanded the reason; when she cried violently, telling me
Van would certainly break her heart by the conduct he was pursuing.
"Would you believe it possible, Hickey," said she, "he is at this hour
(two o'clock) making a beast of himself and in such company too!
What would become of him, were it to be known by any of his brother
officers in the Guards; or how would they be astonished could they
behold him in his present state with his elegant and accomplished
guest? There have they been since a little before eleven, stuffing themselves with cold venison pasty and swilling champagne till they cannot

William Hickey in 1819, with his Indian servant and his dog, by
W. Thomas.

National Gallery of Ireland

Calcutta street scene, showing the Old Court House and Writers' Buildings. Coloured engraving by Thomas Daniell, 1786.

By courtesy of the India Office Library

articulate a word. Do, for God's sake, go in and try to shame Van out of thus degrading himself."

She then led me downstairs, and opening a parlour door pushed me in. I saw Van sitting at a breakfast table, apparently stupidly drunk, and opposite him Fozard, the stable keeper, in not much better condition. Upon my entrance, Van began to mutter something about purchasing horses, at the same time attempting to pour out a glass of champagne; but he did not put the mouth of the bottle within a foot of the glass, the wine running about the table. Fozard, on seeing me, presented his hand, as if to shake hands, roaring out, "Ha! Hickey, how are you? Come, join in tossing off some choice stuff here of Van's. I have not often met with better. Van is a damned good fellow, but he can't drink with me. I'd settle a dozen such wishy-washy chaps. Come, let's you and I have a few bumpers together." Offended at the freedom of this address from a person whom I had never used the smallest degree of familiarity with, or ever known out of the line of his business, in which he had always behaved with the utmost respect, I, without saying a word, instantly left the room, telling the fair Nancy that was no time to remonstrate with Van were I so disposed, he being by far in too inebriated a state to listen to reason, or understand a word that was said to him.

11+

LIFE WITH CHARLOTTE BARRY

O N 1st May, at the particular request of Mordaunt and the desire of Charlotte, expressed to me privately, I accompanied them from London to take possession of the house at Drayton. Mr. Grant waited there to receive and entertain us, leaving us the next morning. I continued there two days, when the sulkiness of Mordaunt became so offensive, from morning to night abusing Charlotte and scowling at me, declining everything like conversation, that I could no longer submit to it; and bidding her adieu, I mounted my horse and rode to town. In the evening of the same day, Mordaunt, in great agitation, came to me at my father's, begging and entreating that I would return with him to Drayton, Charlotte being suddenly seized with an illness of so alarming a nature he was quite miserable about her. I told him his conduct was so unbecoming towards her as a woman that I was astonished any consideration on earth could induce her to remain another day with him; that, as to myself, his behaviour had been so strange and so rude during my last visit, I should not voluntarily subject myself to a repetition of it. He must therefore excuse by declining any more being a guest of his.

He begged so hard, however, and expressed so much sorrow and contrition for the violence he had been guilty of, ascribing it to a natural infirmity which he was resolved to correct in future, that I relented and consented to return with him to Drayton. He then told me that James Grant and Mrs. Grant would be of our party, and all should be good humour and hilarity. The following morning, we four went down together in a post-coach. Although only a distance of sixteen miles, and notwithstanding all Mordaunt's fair promises, the devil burst forth from him twice or thrice during our short journey; for which Mrs. Grant, who possessed a great command of words and could, when she pleased, be excessively severe, rated him unmercifully. She concluded a most bitter lecture, declaring her astonishment that so mild and sweet a girl as Charlotte Barry was could ever have consented to be an inmate of the same house with him, or, having inadvertently done so, that she should continue to submit to the caprices and ill-humour of so insufferable a brute.

This attack from the lady was renewed after dinner at Drayton, when she repeated all she had said in the coach. This she was led to do from his short and surly answers to Charlotte, notwithstanding he had represented her as being dangerously ill. He stood the attack with apparent composure for some time, but at last flew into a terrible rage, calling Mrs. Grant a dirty little drab, an impudent and most abandoned strumpet; whereupon Grant jumped up from his chair and, putting his fist close to Mordaunt's face, told him his own house alone protected him from that chastisement he was disposed to give him, and which his insolence and vulgarity so richly deserved. Poor Charlotte, dreadfully frightened, was thrown into hysterics by the scene; and whilst I and the servants were attending to and using means to recover her, Grant took his lady by the hand, walked to the inn, where they got into a chaise, and went off to London. It was upwards of an hour before Charlotte recovered.

The moment she was herself, Mordaunt began to bewail the misery constantly attendant upon his yielding to the momentary impulses he felt; and, turning to me, he said, "Hickey, you can have no idea of my sufferings. My whole soul is wrapped up in that woman (pointing to Charlotte) who by her neglect and contemptuous treatment drives me almost mad, so that I know not what I say or do. I fear she loathes and detests me in return for adoring her, and her only pleasure is involving me in disputes and quarrels upon her account. Into what a dilemma has she now brought me? In my frenzy I have shamefully ill-treated James Grant, who has upon several occasions shown himself my zealous friend. I must and will pacify him. There is no submission, no apology that I will refuse to make." I reminded him that the state Charlotte was in was ill-calculated to bear further noise or alarms, and recommended his being more temperate. To this he acceded, saying he would leave me to console his dearest girl, while he followed and endeavoured to make his peace with Grant "and the damned bitch he was so fond of!" We soon after retired to our respective chambers, Charlotte pleading her illness in order to be left alone for the night, which Mordaunt, though ungraciously, was obliged to consent to. The following morning while Mordaunt and I were at breakfast—for Charlotte did not leave her room—he told me he was going to London to apologize to Grant, and persuade him to return to Drayton with him, requesting I would take care of Charlotte during his absence. He said he would, if possible, be back to dinner, but desired I would not wait beyond the usual hour. He then called for his horse and set off at full speed, followed by his groom.

The moment he was gone Charlotte joined me, and we hugged ourselves in the thoughts of enjoying a few hours uninterrupted by his brutality. Time passed rapidly away. The time of dinner coming without Mordaunt's appearing, we sat down together and had a comfortable meal. In the evening we strolled about the grounds, which were very pretty. Agreeably disappointed at his continued absence, we took our coffee, tea and, at ten o'clock, supper; I then goodnaturedly began to hope either that he had broken his neck, or Grant had blown out his brains. At eleven we determined to go to bed. My room was the next to Charlotte's; and, as all the servants were in my interest, they were ready enough to do everything to accommodate and please me. Upon Charlotte's retiring, the butler, with great civility, begged my pardon for what he was going to say; but, as he and his fellow servants were sensible of my goodness to them upon all occasions, and the same respecting their worthy mistress, they had desired him to assure me that their master should not take me by surprise; for, in case he arrived in the night, they would take care to keep him long enough at the gate, and make sufficient noise, to apprise me of his approach. Besides which, his lady's maid would sit up.

Thus secured against accident, I with confidence usurped the tyrant's place. We rose at an early hour in the morning, breakfasted at ten, the customary time, and after it mounted our horses, bending our course towards the Great Western Road. When about two miles on the London side of Colnbrook, we met Mordaunt, with Mr. and Mrs. Grant, going at a furious rate to Drayton. After exchanging a few words, they proceeded, and we turned back. Upon getting home, we learnt that Mordaunt, on his reaching town, had directly gone in search of Grant, but after running about for several hours without success, resolved to wait patiently at Mrs. Grant's for his coming, which he did at one in the morning; when Mordaunt, though with considerable difficulty, made his peace, getting him a consent to accompany him to Drayton again, at eleven o'clock in the morning; before which time Mordaunt was at their door with a post-chaise-and-four.

Soon after we got to Drayton, Mordaunt and Grant went to the stable to look at the horses, the two women and I strolling about the garden, when the character of the master of the house was very freely discussed, Mrs. Grant avowing that, although James had thought proper to forgive his unexampled impertinence, she was far from having done so, and was determined in some way or other to be revenged for the infamous epithet he had bestowed upon her.

Mordaunt, in addition to his various eccentricities, had several antipathies. Himself beyond a doubt in some measure insane, nothing occasioned him so much terror as encountering any unfortunate maniac. It, therefore, became an object with these two wicked and mischievous girls, wherever they were and Mordaunt one of the party, to bring into the room some person labouring under that heavy affliction, a female, if procurable, whom they taught suddenly and unexpectedly to seize Mordaunt round the neck and embrace him. From a trick of this sort I was once witness to, I actually thought he would have died from the fright he was thrown into. Another of his violent dislikes was to frogs, the sight of which animal would put him into a cold sweat, and the same with respect to cats. Great pains were therefore taken to put in his way frogs and cats. At dinner, the day the Grants returned, Mordaunt was in tolerable good humour until offended by the incessant mirth of the two women; at which he grew crabbed, asking what the devil they were giggling at. From their significant nods and signs to each other, I conjectured some mischief was on foot, though I knew not what, not having been let into the secret.

The meat being removed, pastry succeeded. Mrs. Grant, drawing a dish to her, said to Mordaunt who sat next to her, "Captain Mordaunt, will you allow me to help you to a bit of this tart?" He gruffly answered, "No, ma'am," to which she with a broad grin replied, "Dear! now that's very ill-natured, for you like cherry tart and always eat it, and these are, I understand, the first of the season." He then said he could help himself, pulling the dish from before her, and began to cut it. The moment he took off a piece of the upper crust, out jumped an immense large frog, followed by two or three of lesser size in succession, as fast as could be. Mordaunt instantly fell back in his chair as if he had been shot. Recovering, however, in a few moments, he seized a carving knife that lay before him; and, had not Grant, who sat on the other side of him, arrested his raised-up arm, I have not a doubt but he would have stabbed Mrs. Grant. His face was of a livid hue, and countenance horrible. Both women, excessively terrified, screeched and ran out of the room, the servants gathering up and carrying off the offensive animals.

It certainly was as malicious as imprudent a prank, near producing an awful consequence; yet I could scarcely pity the savage man who suffered so materially under it. Although he did Grant and me the justice to say he did not suspect either of us of being privy to the circumstance, we had the utmost difficulty in pacifying him; nor do I believe we should have succeeded, had not Charlotte come to our aid, and by her caresses soon brought him about. She certainly had great influence over him, and he was dotingly fond of her. He professed to have pardoned Mrs. Grant, but took infinite pains to discover which of the servants had assisted in the infamous trick (as he termed it). None of the domestics would betray the actual persons. Mordaunt was therefore reduced to vent his spleen upon a poor under-gardener, because he said the damned animals must have been supplied by him, notwithstanding his protestations of innocence; and he dismissed him from his service.

On the 18th, we all went to London, and the following day to Epsom races, in Lord Peterborough's famous coach, which I have already described, being the first exhibition of it upon the road. We got on inimitably well with six horses and three postilions. Mrs. Grant, Charlotte and myself sat on one side, Mordaunt and Grant on the other. We had previously engaged private lodgings at Epsom, or, rather, in the neighbourhood, being half a mile distant from the town, for the race week. Each day, upon making our appearance on the Downs, the novelty of our vehicle drew the attention of all bystanders, a mob constantly collecting round us, with open mouths staring at the extraordinary machine and criticising every part of it. It certainly was the easiest and most comfortable carriage I ever sat in. The races being finished, we left Epsom for London, Mordaunt's natural vile temper not being at all improved by being three hundred pounds minus by the week's speculation, and that entirely owing to his obstinacy and self-opinion, which made him back a particular horse, notwithstanding Grant, who knew much more of the matter than he did, told him that several of the knowing ones had cautioned him against laying upon the favourite, as he had not a chance of winning. He spurned at that advice, lost his money, and the sulk consequently increased.

Charlotte and I kept a man and a horse in full exercise galloping backwards and forwards between Drayton and London; for, whenever Mordaunt was likely to be absent six or eight hours, she instantly dispatched the man with a line to give me notice, in consequence of which I was with her as speedily as four horses could convey me.

Mordaunt having invited me one day to take a seat with him in a gig his brother had lent him, which like all the Earl's carriages was uncommonly elegant and, of course, bearing the arms, coronet, etc., I accepted the offer. We set off from Park Lane, and drove through Hyde Park. In turning out of the Park, one of the stage-coaches, with a number of outside passengers, huzzaing and hallooing, frightened our horse. He began to plunge and kick, finally running us against a post of a new Sunday turnpike then erecting, whereby both shafts of the gig were snapped short off and Mordaunt thrown out, but not materially hurt by the fall. He then sent his groom on to Kensington to procure a post-chaise to carry us on the rest of the way. The carriage arriving in a few minutes, the gig was given to the charge of the hostler with directions to take it to a coachmaker's to be repaired, and he (Mordaunt) would call for it on his return from the country. We then proceeded to Drayton without further disaster.

The following morning, Charlotte, Mordaunt, and myself, during our ride on horseback, met Sir George Metham, a debilitated but high-spirited old debauchee. He was quite of the *vieille cour*, elegant and well bred. In the years 1770–1773, I had often been upon drunken parties with him. He instantly recognized me and bowed; being also slightly acquainted with Mordaunt, he joined us. In the course of conversation discovering that we were at Drayton, he observed he was only a few miles distant from that place, having a cottage upon Coleshill, to which he requested our company at dinner the next day, and addressing me in particular, said, "You, Mr. Hickey, will find an old friend there, who I am sure will be very happy to see you." Mordaunt, with more suavity than was usual, said he would wait upon Sir George with pleasure, provided he would go home with us and spend the rest of the day at Drayton. This Sir George consented to do.

Upon our getting there, he dispatched his horses and servant to say he should dine out, and to order his carriage to take him home at night, observing he was too old to venture on horseback in the dark and with wine in his head. Sir George still enjoying the bottle, we drank freely, so much so that Mordaunt got extremely intoxicated, became dreadfully sick at the stomach, and we were obliged to send him off to bed, a circumstance of which I availed myself, thereby gaining a pleasant bedfellow instead of sleeping alone. Sir George remained with Charlotte and me until midnight, when he wished us goodnight and departed.

The next day Mordaunt was totally incapable of moving, and so ill that he begged I would escort Charlotte and make his apologies to Sir George. I accordingly did so. Upon our arrival at Coleshill, I was much gratified at being greeted by a very old female friend, Mrs. Carter, with whom I had thentofore been engaged in many a jovial scene, she, in those days, being known by the name of Bet Pye. She appeared equally happy at the renewal of our acquaintance, and talking over matters long past. Sir George had merely told her a gentleman she had formerly known was coming to dine with her. The rest of the party consisted of a young man, natural son of Sir George's, Lord Spencer Hamilton of the Guards, and an elderly gentleman of the neighbourhood whose name I have forgot. We had a delightful day in every respect. So gay and cheerful were we all that the hours fled imperceptibly, until Charlotte, casually looking at her watch, exclaimed with surprise, "Is it possible that my watch can be right? If it is, time has indeed flown upon wings, for it is past two." And so it undoubtedly was. I thereupon rang to order the carriage; but Sir George, like an old sportsman, insisted upon our taking the *Dukkin Dorreege* (I know not whether I spell it correctly: it means the parting glass, or glass at the door, in the Irish language), and he produced some burgundy, which, if not quite equal to Mr. Paxton's, was of very superior quality to what was generally met with.

At three we drove off and, having sixteen miles to go, it was near five ere we reached Drayton. We found Mordaunt, early as it was, already up, stalking up and down the walk under the wall of the garden, in high dudgeon at our long stay, the cause of which he asked with great acrimony. He then said he supposed *we had not slept in the carriage*, with peculiar sullenness. However, whether we had or not, madam would not have many hours of it then, as he had received a letter which made his presence in town necessary by eleven o'clock, where he should be detained upon business some days. Charlotte and I, who were in those days full of health and vigour, declared our readiness, if he wished it, to set off immediately, neither of us feeling a want of sleep. This put him into good humour. He condescended to say it was very kind in us, and, as he was anxious to see his lawyer, he would avail himself of it. Breakfast being ordered to be made ready as soon as possible, by a quarter-past six we got it, directly after which we got into a post-chaise and departed for London.

My brother and I went to dine with the useful, if not respectable, Madam Kelly, in Arlington Street, who upon my entrance saluted me with a volley of abuse for having introduced to her house so mean and despicable a wretch as the dirty dog calling himself "Captain Macintosh." She was then interrupted by other company coming, and I did not learn the occasion of her wrath. In the evening we attended three of her chickens, in the old beldam's coach, to Turnham Green, to drink tea at the Pack Horse, and treat the misses to a swing, there being a capital one fixed up in the garden. We had only been a few minutes engaged at the swing when into the garden walked Mordaunt, with my dear Charlotte hanging upon his arm. She looked very much displeased, and would scarcely deign to speak to me. After a very short stay they returned into the house, and I saw no more of them that evening; but, upon getting home some hours afterwards, I found a letter from Charlotte, wherein she in strong terms upbraided me for degrading myself so far as to appear at a public inn with such companions as she had seen, concluding with an earnest desire, if I valued her advice, to avoid all connection with such females as I had spent that day with, alluding to two remarkably fine girls, though certainly rather notorious, who were distinguished by the nicknames of the Duchess of Portland and Duchess of Devonshire, from a likeness they were respectively thought to bear to those elevated personages. Charlotte's caution, however, was not given without reason; for both the above-named women, being high in fashion, were consequently much visited, and from their promiscuous intercourse with a variety of men must have been in constant danger of venereal taints. I was, however, fortunate enough, during the whole time I remained in England, never to be affected by that baneful disease, although I took no particular care of myself, nor ever hesitated taking any woman that offered as a bedfellow at Kelly's, Weston's, or any other of the convenient and accommodating houses I frequented.

In June, Mordaunt made a party for Drayton, of which I was one; and he proposed our going down together, saying he had received information that his brother's gig was repaired; and, if I had no objection, we should ride to Kensington and there get into it, letting our servants lead the horses on. This mode was adopted accordingly. Upon getting to the house, the gig was brought out, appearing as complete as ever; when Mordaunt, whose address to inferiors was always peculiarly haughty, with his usual insolent manner demanded a bill, which not being quickly brought he began to curse and swear at the people of the house. At last the mistress, a fat, comely dame of about forty years, came to the door (for we had stood in the street while the carriage was getting ready), presenting the bill with a profusion of low courtesies, my-lording my companion at an unmerciful rate. Mordaunt, who was a strange composition of sordidness and prodigality, took it into his head that the charges were too high, and he at once pronounced the maker of the bill an infamous cheat.

"I assure you, my lord," said the hostess with the utmost humility, "it is what the coachmaker charged, who is a respectable and wealthy tradesman of the town, working for many noblemen; and, as I had no reason to suppose he would make an improper charge to you, my lord, or anyone else, I paid the sum, as my lord, your lordship may see by his own handwriting," producing the coachmaker's receipt. Still Mordaunt continued to swear it was a damned infamous imposition, notwithstanding I endeavoured to stop him, and strongly recommended his paying the bill. My interference, instead of producing the intended effect, rendered him outrageous. He swore it was a villainous contrivance, a conspiracy between the thief of a carpenter and people of the alehouse, and by God! he would not pay a sixpence until compelled by law. In spite of Mordaunt's intemperate language, the mistress of the house continued humble, though evidently hurt at his insinuation; she mildly replied, "Indeed, my lord, you do me injustice. I am incapable of such conduct as you tax me with, my lord." "By God, I don't think so," said Mordaunt, "for I look upon you to be a damned cheating old bitch."

This was too much for the old lady's philosophy to bear. Her already sufficiently inflamed countenance assumed a deeper tinge, and clapping her brawny arms akimbo, she strutted close up to Mordaunt, vociferating in his face, "Bitch! Bitch indeed! Not half so much of a bitch as your mother. You a lord indeed! Marry come up! a pretty lord. I doubt your being one tho'ff your carriage and equipage bespeaks it. Howsomever if you be a lord, it must be a bit of bastard

11*

business," and away she walked into her house, muttering as she went, "Bitch truly, the mother of an honest family to be called bitch by a dirty, sneaking, pitiful lord." Mordaunt, completely dumbfounded, hastily put the sum demanded into the hands of the hostler, and stepping into the gig, we drove off amidst the sneers and hootings of a mob that had collected from the landlady's complaints and exclamations. I felt really pleased at the well-deserved humiliation and mortification Mordaunt's supercilious behaviour had brought upon him, and had a vast inclination to laugh at him. I, however, contented myself with observing, "I think, Mordaunt, you must now admit that it would have been better had you taken my advice by paying what was demanded." He gave me one of his diabolical looks, but made no answer; nor did he utter a single word between Kensington and Drayton.

We found Mr. and Mrs. Grant, with Captain Macintosh,* just arrived before us; and soon after Sir George Metham and Mrs. Carter drove to the door. Mordaunt continuing in his sulky fit, I resolved to increase his mortification, and effectually did so by relating what had occurred at Kensington, which greatly entertained the party present. Sir George Metham in perfect innocence of heart asked, "What made the woman suppose you a peer, Mr. Mordaunt?" To which question Charlotte sarcastically replied, "Oh! his mild and sweet manners, added to the arms with supporters upon the carriage; besides his servants sport the Peterborough livery, having coronets too upon their pistol holsters and saddle flaps. Who could do otherwise than suppose him a *prince*?"

Before the hour of dinner Lord Semple, Captain Addington of the Dragoons, Van, and Nancy Barry all arrived. We consequently sat down a jovial party, doing due honour to Mordaunt's wines, which were all of the best. The next morning we all rose at six o'clock, in order to be present at Guildford races, for which place we set off, eight of us in Lord Peterborough's famous coach, Lord Semple and Captain Addington in a post-chaise. The races being concluded, we went to an inn to dine, and late at night all returned to sleep at Mordaunt's.

In the garden of his house there was a large sheet of water, with a punt in it. After breakfast Macintosh got into it, cast off the chain and was most awkwardly endeavouring to push it along. Observing that he knew nothing at all of the matter, I told him how to place the staff or boat-hook; whereupon the gentleman, who was superlatively vain, and conceited, and supposed he excelled in whatever he undertook, was much offended, superciliously saying, "I'm excessively obliged to you for your kind instructions, though upon this occasion I do not happen to stand in need of them." I replied, "Indeed Macintosh, you are

* Hickey had been acquainted with Macintosh in Bengal. More recently, he had met him in the company of James Grant.

egregiously mistaken. You undoubtedly do very much want instructions; you cannot manage a punt at all."

He then persevered in his awkward attempts to get on, never stirring from the head of the punt, consequently turning her completely round by every push of the staff. Although he had met my inclination to advise so ungraciously, I explained the mode of getting on in those sort of boats to be by putting the staff to the ground, standing at the time of doing so at the head and running to the stern, taking care to keep the staff as close as possible to the punt's side, with a slight pressure inward upon the edge or gunwale as you approach the stern; by which mode she would dart straight forward and never turn round unless you wished it, and that would be effected by continuing near the head. "That's all vastly fine," said Macintosh, "yet in spite of your wonderful prowess I'll either punt or row with you for a hundred guineas." "If," answered I, "you are as ignorant in the latter as you have already proved yourself to be in the former, I should be ashamed of entering into a contest with you. I presume it possible that you may be a first-rate seaman and navigator, but must persist in saying you know nothing of punting."

He then renewed his offer to either punt or row against me; whereupon I made the following proposal: that he should punt once up and down the piece of water, Mr. Grant to observe how long he was in performing it; which having been ascertained, I would go five times up and down in less time than he had done the once, the loser to pay the expense of a dinner for any number the winner chose, not exceeding fifty, the dinner to be given within a fortnight, at whatever house of entertainment the winner thought proper to fix upon, not at a greater distance than twenty-five miles from town, the charge for the dinner, per head, to be unlimited and at the discretion of the winner, who was to order it and every matter relative thereto.

To this proposal Macintosh eagerly cried out, "Done, done, with all my heart, and I'll bet you five hundred guineas to five that you pay for the dinner." This bullying offer I declined accepting, though confident I should win had I doubled the times I undertook to pass and repass, and so I told him. "Unless," added I, "you have been playing the knave by affecting ignorance of a thing you perfectly understand"; of which piece of roguery, by the by, I began to entertain some suspicion. He, however, soon relieved me from all apprehension on that score, and that there was no deceit upon this occasion. Stripping off his coat and waistcoat, he commenced his task; and never did I behold a person so incompetent to execute what he had undertaken, nor one half so awkward. He greatly increased the expenditure of time by his extreme hurry. Half a dozen times he was within an ace of tumbling overboard, twice losing his staff, which he never could have recovered had not one of the servants jumped into the water and, pulling it from the mud, swam with it to him, a proceeding the whole company present pronounced unfair, but to which I made no sort of objection, remarking that, had he chosen, he might have taken a dozen spare staves with him in the punt.

Having finished his curious performance, he landed, seeming well satisfied with what he had done. I then took my station, going to the end of the canal without the punt's being a foot out of a straight line the whole way. The moment Macintosh saw this, he called out that he admitted my superior skill and had lost his wager. I, however, completed the five times, which having done I made another proposal to him; that was, to scull against him in boats of equal dimensions from Dickey Roberts's at Lambeth to Gravesend and back, or from Roberts's to Twickenham and back, giving him a start of ten miles, for another dinner of the same description as the former, and one hundred guineas besides. I also admitted there was some degree of arrogance in this proposal because, although punting was no part of a seaman's duty, or ever practised by them, rowing certainly was; and I believed from the first admiral of England down to a cabin boy, there never was an instance of a person's not knowing how to row. This he would not accept, saying he would not pull either of the distances I had mentioned for a thousand guineas. He also candidly admitted he had no doubt but I should beat him hollow, and the punting match fully satisfied him. The dinner was then fixed for the 19th, I undertaking to give him a week's notice when I had pitched upon the house it should be prepared at.

Upon the Drayton party separating, I returned to London, where I consulted several of my gay companions respecting what country tavern would be most eligible. For my own part, I considered either the Castle or Star and Garter at Richmond as highly suitable, knowing, as I did, by experience the exorbitancy of the bills at both those fashionable houses. As I made no secret of its being my determination to sweat the Scotsman's pocket to the uttermost, because I had in various instances found him paltry and mean, a gentleman with whom I was only slightly acquainted, hearing this declaration, said, "If such be your object, Mr. Hickey, let me recommend you to employ Logon, of the Bull upon Shooter's Hill, which is out and out the most extravagant tavern in all England, where, however, you will be served in a princely style, and find every article of the very best. He has just now the best batch of champagne I ever tasted."

This representation of Master Logon and his house, by a connoisseur and bon vivant, determined me at once. Mordaunt accordingly drove me to Shooter's Hill. The only orders I gave were that he would provide the best dinner that could be served, with turtle (if procurable), venison, and game of every kind, for a party of fifty, ladies and gentle-men. Logon assured me I should be satisfied with his exertions, telling me too that his head cook was not to be surpassed in all Europe, "and as to apartments, sir, please to judge for yourself." He then conducted us into a noble room, magnificently furnished, which he said had been fitted up only three months before, and was intended for an assembly established by the principal families for twenty miles round the country. There were two spacious rooms adjoining the large one for cards, and a suite of supper rooms below.

Having finished my business, Mordaunt and I got into the carriage, and were driving off when stopped by Logon's voice, who said, "I don't know, sir, whether I shall be able to procure a turbot or not, none having yet been brought to market this season; and, should any come in between this and the 19th, they will from their scarcity be un-commonly high-priced; I do not therefore think it right to supply such articles unless particularly ordered so to do." I told him by all means to get a turbot, were he even obliged to send half-way over to Holland for it, and not to regard the price. "And pray remember," said I, "to let us have your best French wines, which if approved my friends will do complete justice to." "Depend upon it, sir," answered Logon, "Better wines than I now have in my cellars are not to be found within His Majesty's Dominions. I have a small quantity of delicious burgundy remaining, which I shall lay by for you. I am sure you will be pleased with it. I actually have not tasted its equal the last twenty years."

My next consideration was relative to guests, upon which point I consulted Mordaunt, desiring him to give me the names of some strong-headed persons, both male and female. I observed my intention was to invite twenty-five only, leaving the like number for Macintosh, as the loser, to select—a measure, although by no means incumbent on me to adopt, I thought right and liberal. "He invite twenty-five!" exclaimed Mordaunt. "The dirty dog is not acquainted with five gentlemen in the kingdom; and, if he were with five thousand, the devil a single person will he ask, in order to render the expense as light as possible!" Feeling the force of this remark, I resolved to guard against the operation of it by immediately addressing a letter to Macintosh, requesting he would furnish me with a list of the names of those persons he meant to invite, that we might not interfere with each other and ask the same friends. To this he replied he would comply with my wish in a day or two.

Mordaunt, thereupon, again observed Macintosh never would or meant to give such list, nor would he ask any human creature to the dinner; and, as the day was drawing near, I called at his lodgings, and without equivocation told him that, unless he furnished me with the names of *his* guests on the following morning, I undoubtedly should invite the full number myself. He assured me that he had sent invitations to many gentlemen, and waited their answers which he had not yet received. As I had not a doubt but in saying this he told an abominable falsehood, and that Mordaunt's strong opinion of him was well founded, I felt an inclination to treat him as he deserved; but still I could not bring myself to preclude him from the power of having some persons of the party who were attached to him, if any existed. Of women, I had invited Pris Vincent, Kit Frederick, the lovely Clara Hayward, Mrs. Tempest, Bet Wilkinson (the "Blasted"), each of whom could with composure carry off her three bottles; three of the girls from Mother Kelly's, and a like number from Weston's; Charlotte and Nancy Barry were of the party when the wager was laid and determined; and Mrs. Carter was to accompany Sir George Metham. The male friends upon whom I chiefly depended for proper support at the bottle were Joe Bird, Sir George Metham, Van, James Curtis, Lord Fielding, Vaughan, and half a dozen other equally steady fellows.

Counting my forces, I found I had altogether invited thirty-eight. The day previous to that fixed for the meeting, Mordaunt and I rode to Shooter's Hill, when Logon said everything was purchased to his own perfect satisfaction; that he had ordered some capital horns and clarinets to attend, as he knew ladies generally liked music during dinner. I told him he had done properly in securing a band for us. I called that day three different times at Macintosh's without finding him at home, and had not a doubt he gave orders to be denied to me. I, therefore, the last time I was at his lodgings, left a note to ask whether he intended presiding as my deputy, as, if not, I should provide myself with a vice-president to fill that place I thought it his duty as loser of the dinner to occupy. I further wrote, in unqualified language, that I should deem his silence as an intended and premeditated insult. Within an hour after reaching home, I received a very civil answer, begging to decline the chair of vice-president from consciousness of his inability to do justice to it, disclaiming the most distant idea of giving me offence, for whom he felt the most sincere respect and regard.

Upon this refusal of Macintosh's, I asked James Curtis to officiate; but he pleaded a severe clap, which totally incapacitated him from hard drinking. My next application was to Vincent, whom I had often seen preside at the table with a decorum that would have done honour to Chase Price, or any of the most celebrated toastmasters. She was very good-humoured upon the occasion, observed she was getting old and must begin to think of a reform; that, had it been in a select party of friends, she would have complied with pleasure, but in so large and promiscuous a set of men and women she had rather not, though she would do justice to the dinner as a humble individual.

Finding everybody I applied to thus shunning the deputy's chair, I had no alternative, and was compelled to request of my brother to take it. I knew him to be quite equal to support me with credit, provided he acted with caution during the time of dinner; but I also knew the danger there was of his drinking too much while the victuals remained in hobnobbing the women in champagne, thereby incapacitating himself for a long sitting afterwards, which was my great object. I, therefore, previous to sitting down, begged and entreated that he would be upon his guard and avoid drinking at dinner. This he faithfully promised; but, as I was aware his natural love of the fair sex and his gallantry would entirely overset his stock of prudence, I ordered Frescini to stand behind him and carry off his glass as often as he filled it.

On the 19th, the company was assembled; we sat down to a dinner that completely fulfilled all that Logon had said respecting it, and all his promises. A more elegant, or a better, I believe, never was seen, the wines exquisitely good; every person present declared they had never seen so splendid an entertainment. I early perceived that my brother was falling into the error I had taken such pains to guard against. Frescini's attempts to relieve him were fruitless, for he filled and chucked down the contents of his glass without a moment's pause. The consequence was that, before the cloth was removed, he became intolerably noisy and drunk. With extreme difficulty I made him put about four or five toasts after dinner, when some of the women, observing he could scarcely keep himself from falling out of his chair, proposed going into the open air as most likely to restore him, some of the party leading him out of the room; and, notwithstanding my remonstrances, more than half the company followed.

Among the earliest of the seceders was Captain Macintosh, who, the instant my brother abandoned his post, loudly called out that the business of the meeting was over. This I heard him say more than once, but at the time was not at all aware of what he meant by it. I did not, however, long remain in ignorance. Eight or nine of us remained steadily engaged over the bottle, when, calling for more wine, Logon brought a supply himself; which having placed upon the table, he in a whisper told me that Captain Macintosh had been at the bar, demanded a bill, which he waited the making of, paid the amount, and immediately afterwards set off for London in a post-chaise, several times repeating that from that moment nothing further was to be charged to him. I, thereupon, desired Logon to mention aloud what he had just communicated to me, which he did, with some embellishment, saying: Upon some of the ladies leaving the room to go into the garden, Captain Macintosh followed them downstairs, turning to the bar, at which he with extreme earnestness asked for a bill; that while it was preparing, more burgundy being rung for, he positively forbid its being charged to him; for, as the party had broken up, he was no longer responsible, and he (Logon) must look to Mr. Hickey for payment of any future charges; that, upon the bill's being delivered to him, he read every item, and seeing five guineas charged for musicians he, with great anger, insisted upon its being struck out, saying whoever ordered them might pay, for he would not; that a dinner he had lost and must defray the cost thereof; but, if any gentleman thought proper to engage five, or five thousand, instruments of music, it could not be supposed that he was to be saddled with the expense; that he complained much of the exorbitancy of the bill, especially of four-guineas-and-a-half charged for a turbot, and got into the chaise damning the house and every person belonging to it. So violent was he, and so indecent in his abuse, that the postilions, hostlers, and servants assembled round the door actually hooted as he drove away. Upon this statement of Logon's, Lord Fielding requested my permission to give a toast extra, and filling a bumper proposed "Damnation to all such dirty vagabonds as Macintosh"; which being drank, he was unanimously voted to be a mean and despicable fellow, unworthy the future notice of any gentleman.

A few days after the Shooter's Hill party, I called in Arlington Street, where I was instantly assailed by Mrs. Kelly and all her tribe, exclaiming against me for having introduced to the house such an errant pickpocket blackguard as Captain Macintosh who it seems bilked every girl in the family, run in debt to the old lady near one hundred pounds for suppers and wines; and she had, not an hour before my entering, received certain information of his having suddenly and secretly decamped for Copenhagen, without paying his lodgings, or the poor fellow that had acted as his servant from the time of his arrival from India. I afterwards learnt that he left England several thousand pounds in debt to tradespeople and others. It was fortunate for me that I had been very much upon my guard respecting this person; and, although it was true that I first introduced him to Madam Kelly's house, I, at the time of doing so, and subsequently, told her that I knew but little of his character, and that little did not tend much to his credit, for which reason I advised her to caution the girls of her family against trusting him, and that she herself had better require immediate payment for whatever he had. The old woman was, notwithstanding what I said, deceived by his plausible manners and his fine clothes.

Charlotte Barry and I now became almost inseparable, besides being very frequently at Mordaunt's at Drayton. If he left that place but for a single day either with Lord Peterborough or any of his lordship's friends, I received immediate notice thereof; and away I went to console my favourite and pass some hours in her society uninterrupted by the brutality and ill-temper of Mordaunt. For the sake of her company,

I gave occasional entertainments at Richmond and other places in the vicinity of London; and we constantly went twice a week to extravagant suppers at Vauxhall, which sort of life ran away with a great deal of my money.

In July (1781) I hired one of Roberts' eight-oared barges and a smaller boat to attend with horns and clarinets, having previously invited a party to dine with me at the Castle at Richmond. At ten in the morning, my darling Charlotte, her sister Nancy, Mrs. Grant, and a sweet pretty little girl of sixteen she brought, Mordaunt, Grant, Van, the junior Lovelace, and myself embarked at Whitehall stairs, and proceeded to Richmond. The plan we had arranged was, after having dined, etc., to take wine on board our boat and row gently down to Vauxhall and there sup. Mordaunt from the moment we started was more than usually sulky and cynical, so much so as to throw a considerable damp upon the spirits of the party. At dinner he got exceedingly drunk, without its at all mending his temper. At nine at night we re-embarked; and he was so troublesome I protested, if he did not cease, he should be turned out of the boat. At this he became outrageous; and I actually ordered the helmsman to go to the bank just below Brentford, where I bid three or four of the watermen bundle him out.

Finding me thus resolute, he said he would go without force, but that I should answer for my ill-treatment of him. When quitting the boat, he wanted to take Charlotte with him, which I would not permit. Again, he was outrageous; but I made the people push off, leaving him to vent his fury by himself. We proceeded to Vauxhall, had a cheerful supper, and were just preparing to depart when the ferocious gentleman made his appearance in the gardens. He had hired a carriage at Brentford, in which, on his way to town, he slept off the fumes of the wine. Finding himself tolerably sober, he drove to Vauxhall; but neither drunkenness nor sobriety made any difference in him. Invariably a brute, nothing coud change him. Without taking the least notice of anybody except Charlotte, he began upbraiding her violently for not accompanying him upon his leaving the boat, and laying hold of her arm was about to force her away; whereupon I once more interfered, observed she was my guest for the day, and, unless by her own desire, she should not leave the party. Mordaunt talked big, was very free with threats of what he would do; but, upon making Charlotte take hold of my arm and assuring her she might rely upon my protection against all personal violence, he left us, vowing vengeance upon me. After setting Charlotte down at her lodgings, where I offered to remain but she would not permit it, I went home to St. Albans Street.

CHARLOTTE BECOMES "MRS HICKEY"

I N August, Mordaunt's resources began to fail. His chief suppliers of cash had been his mother (Lady Peterborough) and Mrs. Brown, a widow of good fortune, sister to her Ladyship; but his applications to those ladies became so frequent and to such an extent, they were at last, though reluctantly, obliged to tell him they could no longer furnish cash to support him in his extravagances. Driven to great distress, he asked a loan of the Earl, without success, the noble peer being as hard-drove as himself for money. After failing in every quarter, he had the meanness to write me a begging letter; wherein, after stating the predicament he was reduced to, he besought me to assist him with a couple of hundred pounds, which if he did not obtain in two days he certainly should be arrested and conveyed to a spunging house.

Notwithstanding I very much disliked the man, I felt unwilling to refuse, and having the amount by me I immediately sent it to him; for which he expressed in person the highest degree of gratitude, and that he never should be unmindful of the kindness. He also made the most sacred promise to repay me within six weeks, a promise he failed to perform; nor did I receive a guinea from him until two years afterwards in India. This sum was of consequence to me, as at the time I advanced it I began to have some fears for myself, the style I lived in running away with the cash so fast that the sum I brought home with me was nearly exhausted; but, as I had resolved to return to India at the end of the year, I flattered myself the salary allowed by the Bengal committee would be sufficient to bear me through.

In September, Mordaunt took Charlotte to Brighton; and I consequently once more occupied my rooms at my father's in St. Albans Street. Returning from a tavern dinner about two o'clock in the morning, I found one of my sister's large and elegant parties just breaking up, and was then introduced to the Duke of Hamilton, Sir Watts

Horton, Mr. Loraine Smith, and Mr. Macpherson, the last of whom was upon the eve of going out to Bengal in the Supreme Council, afterwards becoming Governor-General and a baronet.

On Mordaunt's return from Brighton, Charlotte sent for me to say she was resolved to leave Mordaunt, and requested I would take her under my protection. This I, with pleasure, acceded to. She then begged I would say nothing about it until our return to Drayton, when she would communicate her intention to Mordaunt and come back to London with me. Upon our arrival at Drayton, he was, if possible, more surly than ever, continuing so the whole day. After supper, Charlotte abruptly told him she intended leaving him the next morning, and no longer to submit to his brutality. This made him outrageous. Seizing a knife from the table, he swore, with the most horrible oaths, that, rather than permit her to quit his house, he would bury it in her heart; and, from his action and manner, I really expected him to put his threat in execution. I, therefore, instantly placed myself between him and Charlotte, reminding him that even insanity would not prevent his being hanged should he commit murder. He abused me in the grossest terms, insisting upon my leaving his house.

Having armed myself with a poker, I set him at defiance, spoke my sentiments of him with great freedom, and told him I would not stir unless Mrs. Barry accompanied me. The perspiration ran down his face in streams from rage; and I actually thought he must have died with passion. At Charlotte's most earnest entreaty, I consented to leave the house that night, and wait at Uxbridge until I heard from her. I, accordingly, after cautioning him, declaring I would make him responsible to the law for any act of violence, left Drayton and went to an inn at Uxbridge. The next day about noon, just as I was dispatching a messenger to her with a letter, I received a note from her saying Lord Peterborough had called with another gentleman to take him to Windsor; that previous to going he had, with a drawn sword at her breast, compelled her to swear she would not leave the house during his absence; but that she could not consider a promise so obtained at all binding upon her, and therefore requested I would send a post-chaise for her.

Ordering one immediately, I went myself in it to Drayton, took her in and drove to London, carrying her at her own desire to her sister Nancy at Mr. Van's in Park Lane. After a short consultation with her sister, we three sallied forth (Van being upon duty at the Tower) in search of lodgings, as Charlotte was determined no more to enter those in Queen Ann Street, they having been taken by Mordaunt. After looking at several, we fixed upon an excellent first floor in Upper Seymour Street, Portman Square, where Charlotte and I, after getting her trunks from Queen Ann Street, took up our abode, and slept that night unmolested.

The next evening, being that on which Vauxhall closed, Charlotte and I drove there about nine o'clock. One of the persons we saw upon entering the gardens was Mordaunt, in company with Lord Peterborough, and a large party of young men of fashion. To our utter amazement, he took not the least notice of either of us during the whole time we continued there, which was until near one, when we returned home. Between three and four, I was awakened by loud and repeated knocking at the street door, and, before I could get on my clothes, one of the servants had opened the door; when I heard the voices of several persons, especially Mordaunt's and the servant's, the latter strongly remonstrating against their going upstairs. By Mordaunt's language I knew he was drunk. Charlotte, much terrified, entreated I would not go out of the room. As I, however, felt that would encourage the party, I instantly unlocked the bedchamber door, when I met Mordaunt, Lord Semple, and two other young men in the regimentals of the Guards upon the stairs.

Addressing the strangers, I desired to know the meaning of such outrage upon a gentleman's private apartments. Mordaunt instantly replied, "Oh damn him! never mind him; he has got my woman away from me and, by God, he shall now give her up!" Lord Semple interrupted him, saying, "For shame, Captain Mordaunt, you have deceived us and thereby led us to the commission of an unpardonable offence"; and, turning to me, his lordship made the handsomest apology for the intrusion of himself and two friends; which they had been led into from Captain Mordaunt's telling them the house belonged to a female friend of his who had plenty of girls with her. To this I observed, the more his lordship knew of Mr. Mordaunt the more occasion he would find to blush for him and to feel ashamed of his conduct. The three gentlemen then by main force compelled Mordaunt to go downstairs and leave the house, he cursing and swearing that he would put me to death. As whenever he committed excess, which was frequently the case, he always visited Seymour Street, making a noise and riot at the house door, I considered it necessary to put a stop to it, and therefore determined upon his next attack to get a constable to carry him before a magistrate.

A few nights after his violent attack in Seymour Street, Charlotte having asked Mr. and Mrs. Grant to dine with us, we four went to the opening for the season of Covent Garden Theatre. We had not been long seated in one of the green boxes when Mordaunt entered. Being more than half drunk, he was, as usual, exceedingly abusive, offensive, and troublesome; whereupon I, with the utmost composure, assured him that if he did not desist, and instantly leave the box, I would break every bone in his body. Grant, too, at the same time loudly execrating his behaviour, he retired; but, at the door of the box, he called out, "Hickey, although you have treated me scandalously ill, by God I cannot bear to see you the dupe of that double-faced Scotch pedlar, Jemmy Grant, who, after benefiting by your hospitality for upwards of a twelvemonth, has now ordered his servants to refuse you admittance whenever you called at his house; and, not content with this, he abuses you wherever he goes as a thoughtless, extravagant spendthrift." Neither Grant nor myself made any comment upon this speech at the time. It, however, struck me very forcibly; for I thought I had lately observed a change in Grant's manner towards me. It also brought to my recollection having called several times in Colman Street without ever finding Grant there, which had never before occurred.

Determined at once to ascertain whether there was any foundation for what Mordaunt had said at the playhouse or not, I went the following morning to Grant's. Upon knocking at the door, the servant, who knew me perfectly well, said his master was out. I remarked that Mr. Grant was not in the habit of leaving home so early; but that, as such was the case, and I wanted much to see him, I would wait his return, and I immediately opened the parlour door, where, to the utter confusion of Mr. James Grant, he and his brother were sitting quietly at their breakfast. Addressing Mr. Peter Grant, I apologized for my unseasonable intrusion, shortly giving my reason for it, adding that I was sorry to find there was but too much foundation for what Captain Mordaunt had said; and that his brother James had acted towards me with a duplicity and meanness inconsistent with the character of a gentleman. James Grant seemed confounded and quite at a loss how to act. After a very awkward pause, he, in a hesitating, ungracious manner, said: it was evident to everybody that knew me that I was living in a style it was impossible I could support; that he had been credibly informed I had already applied to several persons with whom I had only a slight acquaintance to borrow money from them; that his situation in life as a merchant, a West India agent, and citizen of London—of course, everything depending upon his moral character and conduct in life—made it extremely indecorous for him to be seen constantly in public places with a set of dissipated and extravagant young men; nor could he afford to advance to me, or any other who lived beyond their means, cash to support a system of inconsiderate folly; that for these reasons he was free to acknowledge he was desirous of dropping the intimacy that had subsisted between us, although he should never cease to entertain the most sincere regard for me as an old and esteemed friend.

Extremely mortified at such an avowal from a man who had been my constant companion, and, as Mordaunt truly observed, a partici-

MEMOIRS OF WILLIAM HICKEY

pator in all my absurd and ill-bestowed hospitality, I spoke my sentiments respecting his conduct, and what he had just declared, in pointed and contemptuous terms, and, lamenting that it had ever fallen to my lot to have any intercourse with so despicable a being as I considered him, walked out of his parlour and house. Finding his servant waiting in the passage, I said, "You have been under the necessity of telling several falsehoods lately; though relieved from anything of that sort in future on my account, I fear in the service of such a man as your master you will always be liable to similar culpability." The man civilly bowed, but made no answer.

This unhandsome behaviour of Grant's had the good effect of making me turn my thoughts to the actual state of my finances; upon examining which, I found I had only remaining in my banker's hands about two hundred pounds, and three hundred and fifty odd from the Bengal agents, the balance of salary due to me. Besides which, I had a claim upon them for the extra expense I had incurred by proceeding from the Cape of Good Hope in a Dutch ship, which measure I had adopted solely with a view to expedite the object they had sent me to Europe upon, which amounted to upwards of eight hundred pounds. These united sums I flattered myself would prove sufficient to send me and my darling Charlotte off to India in the month of December, the dear girl having declared that her very existence depended upon my consenting to take her out with me. I immediately wrote to the agents, saying that, as my further attendance upon the business of the petition was unnecessary, I requested they would settle my account, which I enclosed, as I proposed embarking for India by the first ship of the season.

After a lapse of several days, they wrote to me to say that, as the committee in Bengal had not furnished them with any instructions or authority to defray any charges relative to my voyage to Europe, and having a very small sum remaining in their hands, they could not venture to take upon themselves the paying me the eight hundred pounds I demanded, without a previous reference to Calcutta. This was a thunderstroke to me; for, having entered into no written engagement with the committee, nor having any possible means of enforcing payment from Messrs. Irving and Touchet, I felt myself remediless. I, therefore, told Charlotte my situation, and the absolute necessity there was for our retrenching every kind of expense forthwith. I can safely and conscientiously affirm that, from that day, the dear girl never expended an unnecessary guinea upon her own account, and, as far as lay in her power, prevented my incurring any expense that could be avoided.

Having, prior to my unpleasant explanation with Messrs. Irving and Touchet respecting money matters, engaged to go upon a party into

Oxfordshire with Van, Nancy Barry, Harvey Coombe and a few others, we in the month of October set out upon it, and, after spending ten days very cheerfully at Chapel House, and stopping at Oxford two days to visit the different colleges and see all the curiosities of that seat of learning, returned to London and began directly to make preparations for our departure to Bengal.

Upon going to the India House to make enquiries about a passage, and afterwards for the same purpose to the Jerusalem coffee house, I had the mortification to find that, as three of His Majesty's regiments were that season going out for the further security of the Company's possessions, the whole accommodation of their ships were exclusively kept for the officers belonging to those regiments, and that it would be impossible for me to obtain a passage. Notwithstanding this unfavourable circumstance, I deemed it right to make every effort and therefore applied to several commanders with whom I was acquainted, saying I would submit to any inconvenience to get out. All expressed their inclination to oblige me, but declared the impracticability of accommodating a lady. Captain Thomson of the *Calcutta*, with whom I had been intimate, said he had given up his own cabin to the major of one of the regiments for himself, wife, and daughter; that he understood the lady to be in so precarious a state of health as to make it doubtful whether she would be able to proceed on the voyage; and, if she did not, he promised me the apartment, observing that her going or not must be decided in ten days.

The morning after returning from Oxfordshire, taking a ride in Hyde Park with Charlotte, we there met Mordaunt, who directly turned his horse and followed me up and down as long as we stayed, but did not offer to speak. At night, we went to the play, where we again found Mordaunt; and, being intoxicated, he became violently noisy, abusing both Charlotte and me in the most blackguard manner. He at last became so troublesome that three or four gentlemen, offended by the interruption to their entertainment, forced him out of the box. We saw no more of him at the theatre; returning home, we supped and retired to rest. About three o'clock in the morning, I was roused from sleep by a tremendous noise at our room door, and I soon heard Mordaunt calling me by name, with all sorts of approbrious epithets.

I immediately opened the door that went into the drawing-room, which I had scarcely entered when he made a blow at me with a thick stick he had brought with him. Luckily, he missed my head which he aimed at, but severely bruised my shoulder and arm. I instantly grappled him, got him down and belaboured him with his own stick until he roared for mercy, screeching out "Murder! Murder!" This brought up the master of the house, who summoned the watch, and Mordaunt was carried off to the round house. I then learnt that he had made his servant ring the street-door bell until Frescini got up to see what was the matter. The fellow said he had brought a letter from Captain Thomson of the *Calcutta* Indiaman for me, which was of the utmost consequence and required an immediate answer. Frescini thereupon called up one of the maids to strike a light, which being done he opened the street door; when Mordaunt rushed in, knocked the poor Italian down flat in the passage and ran upstairs, followed by the maid with the light, she crying out "Thieves!"

In the morning, I went to the watch house and found he had procured bail and was gone home, but so maimed and hurt they were obliged to carry him in their arms to the sedan chair that conveyed him away. I heard nothing more about the gentleman for four days afterwards; when Captain Grey of the Dragoons called upon me, as he said, at the request of Captain Mordaunt, who was still confined to his chamber from the ill-treatment he had received from me, and for which he required me to name time, place and weapons, to give him satisfaction. I told Captain Grey I was ready to comply with his desire if, after hearing my statement, he, as a gentleman, would say I ought to do so. I then related all that had occurred on the night of his brutal attack upon me at my own lodgings; at which Captain Grey was quite confounded, declared I had done no more than such infamous conduct deserved, and that I should have been completely justified in the opinions of all mankind had I put him to death at the moment. He then expressed his sorrow at having given me the trouble of an explanation, which he had been led to by the gross and ungentlemanlike misrepresentation of Captain Mordaunt, whose acquaintance he should drop in consequence, after telling him the discovery he had made of his falsehood.

A week after this visit of Captain Grey's, Mr. Van called in Seymour Street to say that Mordaunt had suddenly disappeared, no person knowing whither he was gone to, though many, to their cost, knew he had left debts to a large amount unpaid. The general opinion seemed to be that he had got on board an American vessel; but, upon further enquiry, I discovered that he had gone as fast as four post-horses could convey him to Margate, at which place he hired a small smuggling cutter to carry him over to Ostend, where he engaged a passage to India in a Danish ship that had touched at that port for the purpose of receiving him and other English passengers. I am free to confess I felt happy at thus getting rid of a man who had been a great grievance to me, and who never failed to annoy me some way or other when his spirit was raised by excess in wine.

Captain Thomson now wrote me a letter, expressing his concern that it would not be in his power to give me and Mrs. Hickey (for Charlotte had dropped the name of Barry, and assumed mine) a passage to India, the Major he had before alluded to, with his family, having determined to embark on board the *Calcutta*. He very civilly assured me that, could he have anyhow contrived it, he should have felt much pleasure in having us as shipmates; but it was impracticable.

I now began to feel seriously alarmed lest I should lose the season altogether, and was thereby rendered very miserable. In the midst of my anxiety, I one day dined at Mr. Plumer senior's, where mentioning the extreme difficulty I found about a passage, and my apprehension that I should ultimately fail in procuring one, Mr. Plumer said under such circumstances he would advise me to go to Lisbon; from which place I might find frequent opportunities of proceeding to India in as fine ships as any in the world, and have spacious cabins. He further observed that he had many esteemed friends in Portugal to whom he would give me letters of introduction, and he was certain I should in every respect find it an eligible way of getting to India. I at once determined to adopt that mode. He likewise told me that the end of the year would be the proper time for me to proceed to Lisbon, the earliest Portuguese ships sailing between 15th and 31st January. Charlotte was delighted with this arrangement. We spent the short period we had to remain in London at gaily as possible, attending the theatres, and every other public place of entertainment.

Mr. Plumer gave me the warmest letters of recommendation to Messrs. Horne and Sill, Devisme and Penry, Sir John Hort, the Consul-General, and Messrs. Mayne and Company. From other friends I obtained letters to the Honourable Mr. Walpole, the British Ambassador; Mr. Pasley, Mr. Koster, and several other respectable mercantile houses at Lisbon. As I found Mr. Plumer in some of his letters had mentioned me as a married man, I told my Charlotte thenceforward we must pass everywhere for man and wife; and, having had most convincing proofs of her sincere attachment to me, of her uncommon sweetness of temper, and many estimable qualities, I proposed making her really so by going through the marriage ceremony. But this she peremptorily refused, observing that she was already as happy as woman could be; that, should she avail herself of my generous offer and I at any future period repent of what I had done, it undoubtedly would break her heart. She, therefore, begged that she might still depend upon my disinterested love, which she felt confident she never should by any act of hers deservedly forfeit. From that hour I considered myself as much her husband as the strictest forms and ceremonies of the Church could have made me.

Towards the end of the month of December 1782, upon another review of my private affairs, I found only a few pounds remained in my banker's hands. I, therefore, once more applied to the agents, Messrs. Irving and Touchet on the subject of my disbursements in getting home from the Cape of Good Hope; but I had no better success than on the former occasion. The agents, however, who admitted they thought me hardly dealt by, of their own accord offered to advance me the sum of one hundred pounds upon my own security; which they accordingly did, and I granted my promissory note for the repayment thereof within three months after my return to Calcutta. Although this one hundred pounds furnished me with the means of paying off several small demands, I well knew how inadequate it was to clearing me from all debts, and enabling me to prosecute my Lisbon scheme. I, therefore, stated my unpleasant situation to Mr. Thomas Plumer, son of the gentleman I have above mentioned, and brother to my Madras friend, Mr. Hall Plumer. This Mr. Thomas Plumer is now, and has been for upwards of four years, His Majesty's Solicitor-General. Upon receipt of my letter, he also advanced me one hundred pounds upon my bond, payable in Bengal.

Although the much-loved original was to accompany me to India, yet I was desirous of possessing a good portrait of my dearest Charlotte. She had presented me with one painted by Engleheart which I thought did not do her justice, besides being a stiff, formal picture. This made me wish to have one by Cosway, then in high reputation as an artist, and very deservedly so. I, therefore, called to ask if he could oblige me by taking a miniature likeness in the course of a few days, I being upon the eve of leaving England. He replied that he never had been so deeply engaged in business, or so much teased by persons pressing for their pictures as at that period; nevertheless, as he really wished to oblige me, and saw a peculiar character of countenance in Mrs. Barry of which he was sure he should succeed in making a superior picture, he would for once in his life act a deceitful part by shutting himself up and refusing admittance to anybody, under the plea of illness, until he had completed the work. He requested she would come and sit to him the following morning. I accordingly accompanied her, and was much amused by observing the progress of the picture, soon perceiving that he would make a beautiful thing of it. Frescini, who, since Charlotte and I came together, always dressed her hair, did so upon this occasion in the most fashionable and elegant style, so much so as to draw from Cosway the remark that he never had seen a finer head of hair.

After she had sat twice, we one morning upon our return from riding, called at Cosway's in Berkeley Row, not with any idea of her then sitting again, she being in her riding habit, but merely to see the progress he had made during the preceding day. The weather being uncommonly clear and fine for the time of year, we had taken so long a ride as to put her quite in a glow, and she looked remarkably well. Some of her curls having blown loose, she had taken off her hat and was standing before a glass arranging them, when Cosway entered the room. He gave a start of surprise, exclaiming, "Good God! what an alteration for the better! I declare, on my honour, I should not know you for the same woman. Come here, come along with me this moment, just as you are, no more dressed head, powder or pomatum! I never saw such a change, so now is the time to show you off to advantage." Then, presenting his hand, he led her into his painting-room, rubbed out the elegantly arranged hair and drew her exactly as she then sat before me, making, as he had truly predicted, one of the most beautiful pictures I ever beheld, the likeness being inimitable. After sitting full three hours, I saw evidently that he was greatly delighted with it himself. With some difficulty I prevailed upon him not to touch it any more, feeling satisfied it could not be improved and might be hurt by attempting at a higher finishing. I would willingly have carried it away at that time; but that he would not hear of, saying he must touch the drapery a little, besides which he was too proud of his performance not to be desirous of showing it to a few persons who were real connoisseurs. A week afterwards I received it from Cosway, and it has ever since been my inseparable companion.

It now became necessary that I should leave England. I therefore fixed upon 1st January 1782 for my departure for Falmouth, being to embark at that place for Lisbon, and arranged my matters accordingly. As no one of my family, except my brother, knew of the attachment that subsisted between Charlotte and me, and consequently could have no idea of my intending to take her out with me to India, I was the more solicitous to keep that secret, which required some management. After consulting with Charlotte, it was agreed that I should proceed to Exeter without her, but wait her joining me at that city. Being rather short of ready cash, an indispensable requisite for travelling, I was under the disagreeable necessity of leaving Mr. Cosway and a few creditors unpaid, my unsettled debts not exceeding altogether one hundred and fifty pounds, the whole of which I discharged, with interest, in a few months after I reached Calcutta.

As I always had a particular dislike to formal leave-taking (which I believe I have already observed), instead of waiting to breakfast in St. Albans Street the morning of the 2nd as I told my sisters I should do, I ordered a post-chaise at midnight of the 1st, into which I and Nabob got. Thus, at the time my family imagined me to be fast asleep in my own room, I was dashing away at the rate of nine miles an hour towards the western extremity of our sea-girt island. For stealing off in this manner I had, by letters, many severe reproaches from my sisters; but my father and brother admitted they thought me right in avoiding a distressing unpleasant scene, always better shunned than courted. Through life, at least since I became to a certain extent my own master, I have made it a rule to quit those persons I loved, when doomed to separate, without announcing the precise hour of departure.

Poor Frescini, who had no doubt but that he should accompany me to India, was thrown into sad grief upon my telling him it could not be. The fact was that, having received intimation of the enormous expense attending a residence in Lisbon, I was compelled to reduce my establishment, an additional servant being a matter of serious importance. Previous to my leaving London, however, I took him to old Captain Larkins, father of the then Commander of the *Warren Hastings*, and who had always been very kind to me; and this worthy man promised me to procure a passage for him on board one of the Company's ships the following autumn.

About nine o'clock in the morning of the 2nd I breakfasted at Whitchurch in Buckinghamshire, fifty-seven miles from London, proceeded that day to Bridport in Dorsetshire, where I slept, and the following morning arrived at Exeter, one hundred and seventy-three miles from the capital. I took up my abode at the new *hotel*—a term then little known in England, though now in general use, every little dirty coffeehouse in London being dignified with the name of *hotel*!

Whilst prosing over a newspaper without knowing a word I read, about eight o'clock in the evening my Charlotte arrived, greatly fatigued, not having taken any refreshment, or stopped but to change horses, the whole journey. She was attended by a favourite female servant who had lived with her three years. She was one of the most beautiful creatures I ever beheld, accomplished far beyond her station, and, as Charlotte assured me, strictly virtuous, of a delicate form, with a little constant cough that I thought bespoke consumption; and so it unfortunately proved. Had her life been spared she would, I am convinced, have been soon advantageously married in India. That night was one of the happiest of my life, having the quiet, undisputed possession of the woman I most adored, who had proved the warmth of her affection for me by sacrificing country and friends to bear me company to a burning and unhealthy climate.

Whilst sitting at breakfast with my amiable partner the next morning, I received a very polite note from Dean Carrington, saying he had the moment heard of Mrs. Hickey's arrival, and entreating her company also at dinner. Before I could write an answer, the Dean and his lady were announced, politely coming to visit us; and thus did my Charlotte, for the first time, appear in a character nature as well as education intended her for, and which during the remainder of her short life she filled with credit to herself and me, becoming the admiration of everyone who knew her for her sweetness of temper and elegantly easy manners.

At the hour appointed we went to the Dean's, who introduced us to three grown-up daughters, all good fine young women. They, as well as their mother, were delighted with Mrs. Hickey, and before they parted that night urged her most kindly to endeavour to prevail upon me to leave the hotel and reside with them during our stay. The Dean informed me that the post of that morning had brought intelligence of four packets having all sailed together from Falmouth in the afternoon of the 2nd, that it was therefore certain no other would be dispatched for six weeks to come; and, as Falmouth was at all times a very disagreeable place for a stranger to reside in, we had better remain for a month at least at Exeter, which he hoped to render pleasanter to us than the former town could be, as he was sure his wife and daughters would do everything in their power to make it so.

In consequence of what the Dean had told me, I determined to follow his advice by remaining where I was, but, in order to avoid all risk of disappointment, limited my stay to half the period he had mentioned, that is, three weeks. The Dean and his family showed us as much kindness as if we had been friends of long standing. Thus time glided away imperceptibly until the day of our departure arrived, to the mutual regret of all parties. On 24th January, a melancholy crying-scene took place between the ladies, from which I tore my Charlotte away, placing her in a post-coach-and-four, and we drove off.

I hoped and intended to reach Falmouth the same night, but found the roads so extremely rough and bad my progress was slow. The days being very short, I thought it most advisable to stop at St. Michael's, eighteen miles short of our destination. There we slept in the most wretched of hovels, though by the sign before the door announced to be *an inn*, and to afford *entertainment* for man and horse. Having no inducement to stay in so poverty-stricken a house, we left it early in the morning, by ten o'clock arriving at Falmouth. This is a corporate town, and I will be bold to say the most despicable one in His Majesty's dominions. The post-boys, being left to make their own selection, drove us to the King's Arms, which they asserted to be the best house in the place.

Mr. Holt of the India House having given me a letter to the Company's agent, in the afternoon of the day of my arrival, having ascertained where he lived, I went to deliver it. His name was Bell. Upon reading the letter I gave him, he expressed the highest respect and regard for Mr. Holt, to whom he said he lay under great personal obligation; that it would therefore afford him much satisfaction to show every attention to any friend of his, and he begged I would command his best services. Mr. Bell, being a married man, invited us to spend the following day with him, where we were handsomely entertained. The party were delighted with my Charlotte's singing, an accomplishment she excelled in, her voice being both sweet and melodious. At this dinner I met Captain Smith, an old post-Captain in the Royal Navy, distinguished by the nickname of "Boolwaggey" from a ridiculous song he frequently sung in which that word was often repeated, and with peculiar drollery. This gentleman, having publicly expressed his disapprobation of some measure adopted by the First Lord of the Admiralty, had, in consequence, been dismissed from a frigate which he commanded, and from that time (which was several years before I saw him) had remained out of employ, although universally allowed to be a gallant and experienced officer. He had settled himself at Falmouth on account of the cheapness of living for a regular inhabitant. At Mr. Bell's I was likewise introduced to Captain Todd, Commander of the *Hanover*, a Lisbon packet, which being next in rotation, we, of course, should embark in her. Captain Todd told me he had no doubt of sailing in ten days, or a fortnight at furthest.

On the 30th of the month, I was agreeably surprised at being addressed by a tall well-looking young man, who introduced himself to me as an old and intimate friend; but, as I had no recollection of him, he told me his name was Daniel Hoissard, and that we were school-fellows at Streatham. I then recognized him as one of my favourites at that academy, though grown quite out of my knowledge. He had just arrived from London, on his way to Lisbon, where he was established in business, being a junior partner in Paisley & Company's firm. On 10th February, having received notice that we should sail the next day, I immediately sent off our baggage to the *Hanover*. Early in the morning of the 11th, we embarked, Mr. Hoissard accompanying us. The wind dying away, it was night before we got clear of the harbour. About eight, a strong gale sprung up, which drove us at so quick a rate that at daylight in the morning of the 15th we made the Rock of Lisbon, passed over the bar at the entrance of the Tagus by noon, anchoring in a couple of hours afterwards close to the city.

Lisbon forms one of the grandest spectacles imaginable from the river, and must strike a stranger with astonishment by its grandeur. It stands upon seven different hills, constituting a sublime and romantic scene. Mr. Hoissard proved of material service to us by his local knowledge, procuring far superior accommodations for us than we should have been able to get for ourselves. Taking us on shore, he conducted us to a noble mansion standing upon the point of a lofty hill, called Buenos Ayres. It commanded a full view of the city itself, of the river and vessels innumerable sailing in every direction, with a distant view of the bar and ships out at sea. The house was kept by an old Irish widow named Williams; and admirably well calculated she was for the situation, filling it with equal advantage and credit to herself and satisfaction to her guests. I had a suite of spacious rooms leading from one to another, consisting of a capital dining-hall, a handsome apartment for breakfasting, a superb drawing-room to receive company in, besides two lesser ones, an excellent bedchamber with dressing-room and all other requisites, the servants' chambers being over ours and communicating thereto by a private staircase. Nothing could be more commodious or elegant than the whole of the establishment; but the expense was enormous and considerably increased by the necessity of keeping our own table, it not being customary for ladies to join the general mess.

Our fellow passengers in the packet were, a Portuguese gentleman, Mr. Hoissard, and a Miss Nancy Spottiswoode, a clever, intelligent girl, daughter or niece, I forget which, of an eminent attorney in London. Her father being apprehensive she had symptoms of decline, sent her off to a milder climate, which was recommended by the faculty as the most likely to prevent a serious attack.

On the 17th, Mr. Nathaniel Bateman, a member of the Board of Trade of Bengal, arrived. His object in visiting Portugal was, like mine, to obtain a passage from thence to the East. Having had a slight acquaintance with him in Calcutta in the year 1778, we now renewed it, and agreed if possible to proceed on board the same ship. Upon making enquiries upon the subject, we had the mortification to learn that no Indiamen would sail at the soonest in less than three months. Sad news for me whose cash ran very low. Being without remedy, I endeavoured to make the best of the matter, that Charlotte might not discover the cause of my uneasiness. We therefore spent our time gaily, the mornings in viewing the curiosities of the city, contemplating the numerous mementoes that still remained of the horrid devastation made by the fatal earthquake in 1755, and the remainder of the day in pleasant society. We also went upon parties formed by Mrs. Walpole, or Mrs. Warden, to the different royal palaces and principal noblemen's castles, especially those of Cintra, and other beautiful spots within twenty miles of the capital, these excursions being made in carriages, on horseback, and donkeys (asses), the latter animals being exclusively for the ladies' use.

In March, I was introduced to Mr. Luis Barretto, a man endowed by nature with extraordinary talents and elegant address, though under the unfavourable circumstance of an extremely dark skin, indeed nearly black. He was the descendant of a Portuguese race that had for upwards of a century been settled with much credit upon the coast of Malabar in the East Indies, and were all opulent. Mr. Luis Barretto was born under the British Government, being a native of Bombay, at which place he was brought up by his father. Being early initiated in trade, and being active and diligent in commercial pursuits, he, whilst yet a stripling, amassed considerable wealth, as had likewise an elder brother, Mr. Joseph Barretto, by similar means, with the highest reputation for integrity at Calcutta in Bengal, where he had established himself. The spirit of enterprise that had always predominated in Luis Barretto induced him to engage a speculation of vast magnitude. It was that of carrying on an exchange of produce from every part of Europe with India, through the medium of Portugal, and under the flag of that nation, then at peace with all the world. But, being well aware how jealous the French were, and the rigidness with which that rival of England scrutinized the traffic conducted by neutral powers, he determined to use every possible precaution in order to avoid either seizure or suspicion.

In the latter end of the year 1781, he purchased a ship called the *Hornby*, constructed and built at Bombay, under the immediate eye of the then Governor, who honoured it with his own name. A stronger or more complete vessel, in every respect, never was launched in any country in the world. Her burden was upwards of eleven hundred tons. When he made the purchase she was nearly new, having been off the stocks only a few months. Upon becoming the purchaser of this truly fine ship, Mr. Barretto wrote instructions to his agent in London to prove and send out for him to Lisbon, there to wait his arrival, a certain quantity of lead, iron, copper, canvas and cordage, sufficient to be a cargo for her; which it was his intention to transport from Lisbon to Goa, the principal settlement of the Portuguese upon the coast of Malabar, at which place he knew he could without difficulty dispose of it to British merchants, or, at any rate, under the sanction of the Government of Goa might proceed with it in his ship to Bombay.

In October 1781, he sailed from Bombay with a valuable cargo of piece goods, spices, and cotton, he himself acting as supercargo, bound to Lisbon, but stopping at Goa to obtain his port clearances, all of which in the most unqualified terms certified the ship and cargo to be the sole property of Luis Barretto, the supercargo of her. It is, however, certain that private reports made not only his brother Joseph, but Governor Hornby and Mr. Holmes, a gentleman high in the Company's civil service at Bombay, part-owners of the ship and equally so in the cargo. Whether or not such was the fact, it is not in my power to decide; nor is it material, as he reached Lisbon without anything occurring to bring that question under discussion, disposing of his Asiatic goods to great advantage. His simple and clear mode of transacting business was so new at Lisbon as to call forth the unasked approbation and panegyrics of the Portuguese merchants. Upon his arrival he was introduced to the Marquis of Pombal, then Prime Minister, son of the celebrated nobleman who so long and so ably guided the affairs of that nation.

With this nobleman he became a favourite, and was upon several occasions highly complimented by him. Although, as I have before

The manuscript of Hickey's memoirs, showing his sketch map of the unchartered island on which the *Nassau* was nearly wrecked in June 1779.

The original vellum-bound volume of the Memoirs of William Hickey, which measures 17×11 ins. and is $3\frac{1}{4}$ ins. thick.

Little Hall Barn, William Hickey's house at Beaconsfield in which the Memoirs were written.

said, he was indisputably a Portuguese by birth, and more than commonly dark in colour, he resolved to make what he deemed a certainty doubly sure by being naturalized at Lisbon, thereby becoming an ascertained subject of His Most Christian Majesty's. He also changed the name of his ship to that of the *Raynha de Portugal* in compliment to the Queen. As a still further precaution, he caused his ship to be registered in due form in the Admiralty Court and in all the different offices resorted to upon similar occasions. In short, every precaution was taken to substantiate the property in ship and cargo strictly Portuguese, consequently neutral and beyond the reach of attack by belligerent powers. Yet all proved in vain, as will appear hereafter.

Mr. Barretto one morning took me on board the *Raynha de Portugal*, and a most commodious and beautiful ship I found her. In this visit we were accompanied by a Mr. Moore, an English gentleman who had recently been at the head of the Company's marine at Bombay, in which situation he had established his character as a first-rate seaman. During our stay on board, the crew were busily engaged receiving cargo, consisting of lead, iron, and copper, and stowing the same in the hold. Mr. Moore upon observing the manner in which they were doing this, expressed his surprise and disapprobation thereat, saying it was extremely improper and dangerous; for, if all the dead weight was placed at the bottom of the ship, it would occasion her to roll dreadfully, and, in the event of her encountering bad weather, might lose her masts, if not produce more fatal accidents. Mr. Barretto, who was himself totally unacquainted with such matters, thereupon asked Mr. Moore how such evils were to be remedied, and was directly told, "By raising the weight a few feet from her bottom, by filling up the space below with solid blocks or logs of wood, to act as dunnage."

Mr. Barretto then explained to his captain the remarks Mr. Moore had just made, which appeared to him so reasonable that he wished the manner of stowing suggested by Mr. Moore might be adopted; but against the necessity of which the captain violently declaimed, angrily saying he had been too many years at sea not to know how to stow a cargo and did not believe it was in the power of any English seaman to teach him any part of his duty. This captain having been recommended to Mr. Barretto as a skilful navigator and perfect master of his profession, it is not to be wondered at that Mr. Barretto should feel so much due to those who had so recommended him as to give him credit for meriting it. He, therefore, took no further notice of Mr. Moore's remark, and the same mode of stowing was continued, between seven and eight hundred tons of dead weight being placed from her keel upwards, the sad effects of which we subsequently felt, and

12+

had nearly consigned us all to watery graves, as I shall by and by particularly state. After this visit to the ship, I spoke to Mr. Barretto respecting his letting me accommodation for myself, Mrs. Hickey, and two servants, to India, which he said I might have, but that he should not sail for at least three months to come.

WITH CHARLOTTE TO INDIA

I HAD now the misery to see the health of my darling Charlotte in a declining state, and that, too, without any apparent cause; having no particular malady, yet she gradually fell away, entirely lost her appetite and spirits, and felt it unpleasant to move even from one room to another. I consulted Dr. Hare, the principal physician of the British factory, who had the reputation of being very skilful in his profession. After attending her twice a day for some time, trying a variety of medicines though without advantage, he recommended me to change the air by taking her away from Lisbon. Mr. Devisme, who happened to be visiting me when Dr. Hare gave this advice, immediately offered a country house of his, about eighteen miles from the city, in, he said, as healthy a spot as any in Portugal. I accepted his polite offer. Two days after he sent us thither in one of his carriages, with a confidential servant who had orders to supply all our wants. We found it a romantic and beautiful situation, upon a small rise from the sea, from which it was not quite a mile distant. Charlotte was delighted with everything about it, finding material benefit in four-and-twenty hours. She continued mending so rapidly that in ten days her health was perfectly restored. We therefore returned to Lisbon.

On 2nd April, two English frigates came in from Gibraltar, the *Cerberus*, commanded by Captain Mann, and the *Apollo*, Captain Hamilton. In the latter I found a former playmate and brother Westminster, a son of the famous Lady Ann Hamilton. He expressed sincere joy at the meeting and renewal of our acquaintance. In the course of conversation I learnt that he had brought with him another esteemed friend of mine, Captain William Cuppage of the Royal Artillery, whom I had known from his early infancy as an élève and protégé of Mr. Burke's. Captains Hamilton and Mann, at well as Cuppage, were constantly with us, and with the addition of the lively Nancy Spottiswoode, who had perfectly recovered her health, we made a pleasant little party daily in our apartments, clouded only by my dear girl's again beginning to droop. The surgeon of the *Apollo*, a clever man, said he was convinced nothing would do her so much service as trip to sea, whereupon Captain Hamilton very kindly offered us his cabin if we would go to England. I had a great inclination to accept the offer; but she would not hear of it, apprehensive that it might interfere with the India voyage, upon which she knew my future welfare depended. In a fortnight afterwards, the two frigates sailed.

Mrs. Hickey continuing to decline, Dr. Hare told me confidentially he was convinced the climate of Lisbon was so hostile to her that she would fall a sacrifice if she remained there. He also said, from what he had already seen, he feared the heat of India would never suit her constitution. This was grievous information to me; but upon receiving it I, without hesitation, resolved that she would not accompany me to Bengal, and I broke to her the necessity there was for our separation. As I expected would be the case, she was at first extremely hurt, declaring my refusing to let her go with me would prove more fatal than any climate; that all she desired was to expire in my arms or under my protection. By argument and mild persuasion, I at last prevailed on her, and she consented to do whatever I required. For this acquiescence I was in a great measure obliged to the friendly interference of Doctor Hare, Mrs. Walpole, and other of our acquaintances at Lisbon, who all exerted themselves to convince Mrs. Hickey of the necessity there was for our separation, at least for a time. I immediately engaged a passage for her and her servant on board the *King George* packet, commanded by Captain Wauchope, who treated her during the voyage like a fond parent; nothing could exceed his kindness.

Upon our arrival at Lisbon one of our first visitors was Mr. Thomas Hickey,* a portrait painter with whom my family had been acquainted and done him some service in his profession; but I had never before seen or heard of him. He occupied four handsome rooms on the ground floor of Mrs. William's hotel. When Doctor Hare pronounced the necessity of my Charlotte's leaving me, I applied to my namesake to paint her picture for me in oil colours. He made a good likeness, though strongly marked with the melancholy depicted in her countenance at the time she sat, from the thoughts of parting. As she insisted upon having my portrait to take with her, I sat, he making an admirable representation of me. Having promised my sister to send her my portrait from India, I thought the meeting with Hickey afforded a good opportunity of being better than my word. I therefore got him to copy from Charlotte's another of myself and forwarded it also to my sister by her.

On 5th May I took a melancholy and, as I really feared, a last farewell of her I loved more than anything upon earth. To attempt to

* Author of two portraits reproduced in the present volume.

describe the parting would be as impossible as useless. We were in agonies, our mutual friends at last carrying her away in a state of insensibility. I then locked the room door and, sitting myself down at the window fronting the water, watched first the progress of the boat that was conveying my adored girl to the packet, next the packet itself under sail bearing her rapidly away from me. So deep was my grief, and so lost was I in despair, that I attended not to repeated knocks at my door and summonses to dinner. I had no inclination to eat; all appetite was gone with the packet, whose progress engaged my sole attention, until passing over the bar and hauling to the northward she disappeared altogether. I then surveyed with the deepest interest every inanimate object that had ever engaged my Charlotte's attention. Involuntarily, as it were, I threw myself upon the couch on which she used to recline, and not an article of the furniture but became invaluable to me. At a late hour of the night I retired to my desolate, gloomy bedchamber.

Oh! what a difference to what I had been used to feel on going to rest. What a wretched, sleepless night did I pass. At five in the morning I rose, fatigued, nay exhausted, with a dry skin and feverish heat that I conceived must produce a severe illness, but which was averted by the unremitting attentions of Doctor Hare, and the solacing exertions of a number of friends, especially Mr. Hoissard, who, in a manner, forced me abroad, taking me to Mr. Devisme's, Mr. Paisley's, and other houses. By slow degrees I became more reconciled to what was not to be remedied, but never enjoyed myself in society as thentofore. I derived the greatest consolation from passing two or three hours in a morning with Charlotte's favourite, Nancy Spottiswoode, until all of a sudden I thought I perceived a change in her reception, becoming formal, cold almost to rudeness, and anxious to leave me.

Unwilling, in spite of appearances, to believe this possible, I mentioned my fears and my surprise to Mrs. Walpole, who instantly exclaimed, "I wonder you have been so long discovering the baseness of the selfish, ungrateful hussy, who almost from the day of Mrs. Hickey's departure began to speak disrespectfully of her; for which I, who knew how kindly and generously she had been always treated by that absent friend, and the number of valuable presents she had received from her, upbraided her for her shameful ingratitude, her want of every honourable sentiment in endeavouring to injure the character of a person who had done nothing but load her with favours and kindnesses. The detestable, unfeeling little wretch is beneath your notice, and certainly never shall more enter my house."

Thunderstruck at what I heard, and at a loss to account for her acting such a part, I immediately went to her and asked what she could mean by it. She had the further meanness and audacity to assert she had never uttered a word to the prejudice of Mrs. Hickey, for whom she felt the utmost affection. I told her she was an infamous liar in addition to her other vices; and, cautioning her against exercising her malignant talents in future upon Mrs. Hickey lest I should make a severe example of her, I left her weeping, more I believe, from concern at being discovered in her infamy than from contrition for her fault. From that time I had done with the imp, never taking smallest notice when we met.

On 21st May, I had the supreme felicity of receiving a letter from my dearest girl, dated at Falmouth, where she reached after a pleasant passage in eight days. She assured me the voyage had restored her to health. She could, therefore, look out for the first ship that should sail for India and embark in it to join me, without whom she did not consider life worth holding.

At the end of the month, I finally settled with Mr. Barretto for a passage on board the *Raynha de Portugal* by taking the state room, a spacious and excellent apartment, opening into the great cabin, and having two ports and two large scuttles in it. Mr. Bateman also took a cabin in the steerage of the same ship. That gentleman and myself at Mr. Barretto's particular request made a written application to the Portuguese minister in the marine department for his permission to proceed to Goa on board that ship; and we received a ready and polite acquiescence also in writing. In a day or two afterwards, Mr. Barretto brought two young men to my rooms to introduce to me as fellow passengers, they having been recommended to his attentions by his valuable friend Mr. Holmes. One of them was Mr. Kemp, going out as a mere adventurer, the other, Mr. Brown, appointed a cadet in the Company's army on the Bombay establishment. Mr. Barretto, when he made these gentlemen known to me, said he should reject all other applications, being resolved not to take more passengers.

On 4th June, while dressing to dine at the ambassador's, it being our King's birthday, I observed a vessel running up the river from sea, with a Union Jack flying at her main topgallant masthead, by which I knew it to be a packet. I therefore set out for Mr. Walpole's in high spirits, hoping to get a letter from my darling. During dinner the dispatches were brought in, and with them a single letter. Mr. Walpole, looking at the direction, said to his lady, "This is for you, my dear," sending it round to her. Mrs. Walpole, after opening and reading it, made an apology for leaving her company for a few minutes and went out of the room. Upon her return, addressing the party, she said a much-esteemed friend of hers was just arrived from England in the packet, and she had been giving directions for a carriage to go immediately to the hotel and bring her to her.

Soon after this, the ladies left the table. After we had been at the bottle about an hour, a servant came to the back of my chair and, whispering me, said his mistress requested to speak to me. Astonished at such a summons, I followed the man out. At the bottom of the stairs, Mrs. Walpole's own female attendant received and conducted me up to her lady's dressing-room, opening the door of which what was my amazement and agitation at my loved Charlotte's rushing into my arms, bursting into tears, and the next moment insensible in a fainting fit! Mrs. Walpole, considerately aware of some distressing incident from the unexpected meeting, had been secretly watching us, and, upon seeing Mrs. Hickey faint, appeared with hartshorn and all the usual remedies administered in such cases. By the application of these medicines, she soon recovered and was restored to composure. She then briefly informed me that, after she left Lisbon, she had found herself so miserable that she resolved, no matter how fatal the consequences might prove to herself, once more to rejoin and accompany me to Bengal, adding these words that are indelibly fixed in my memory: "My dearest William, if I am doomed to die an early death, oh do, at least, I beseech you, let me have the consolation of knowing that I shall draw my last breath and heave my last sad sigh in your loved arms! Without you I cannot exist. Besides, my William, I can confidently assure you that my health is entirely restored. I am as well as ever I was in my life." I felt too happy, too much rejoiced at once more being able to press her in my bosom, to utter a syllable of reproach at her imprudent and inconsiderate return; for such it certainly was; and, although I kept my fears to myself, I could not but feel alarmed for her life.

After her recovery from the fainting fit, Mrs. Walpole left us alone for near an hour, when she again entered the room, kindly saying, "Come, come my friends, I have allowed your tête-à-tête to continue long enough. I shall now insist upon your both joining our party at supper and drinking a bumper of burgundy to the health of our gracious sovereign, after which we must all join in the merry dance." Taking a hand of each, she led us to the room in which the company were assembled. All showed the most pleasing attention to my dear girl; and after a gay, cheerful evening we returned to our hotel in the ambassador's chariot.

The following morning, Charlotte introduced me to Mr. and Mrs. Pawson who had come out in the packet with her, with a view to get a passage in a Portuguese Indiaman to Bengal, where they were going to reside with a brother of Mr. Pawson's who was in the Company's civil service there. She likewise introduced me to Mrs. Aldus and a wild Irish brother-in-law, the lady being on her way to Madeira where her husband was a merchant. I found my darling looking remarkably well; and she said she felt perfectly so, but expressed considerable anxiety and fears about her faithful servant, Harriet, whose cough was greatly increased, as was the languor and weakness; and she had a hectic flush in the cheeks, with a brilliancy of eye that I thought augured ill. Doctor Hare, whom I consulted, thought so too, but observed nothing could afford her so fair a chance of getting over the disease as a long voyage. He, however, acknowledged the chances of recovery were much against her. Upon mentioning to Mr. Barretto Mrs. Hickey's unexpected return, and that she and her servant would accompany me to India, he directly gave me a small additional cabin adjoining my own, for Harriet to sleep in, which would also answer the purpose of a dressing-room for Mrs. Hickey.

In the middle of June, Mr. Barretto gave me notice that we must embark on the 22nd, as he undoubtedly should sail at daylight of the 23rd. My expenses at Lisbon had been great. I was obliged to borrow eight hundred pounds, procured for me by Mr. Hoissard; for the repayment of which I granted bonds, bearing an interest of ten per cent, payable in Bengal. The last ten days of our residence at Lisbon were spent in a round of entertainment given by our hospitable friends. Mrs. Aldus and her brother-in-law had, principally through the intercession of myself and Mr. Bateman with Mr. Barretto, obtained a passage to Madeira in the *Raynha de Portugal*, Mr. Barretto's objection to receiving them solely arising from the possibility of his not touching at the island if the weather proved boisterous; but, the lady being willing to run that risk, and we offering them our table, he consented.

On the 22nd, having finally settled all my accounts, I sent Harriet, who continued in a declining state, with Nabob and our baggage, on board, Charlotte and myself going to dinner at the ambassador's, where we found most of the principal English inhabitants assembled to bid us adieu. We had a splendid meal, followed by a concert and ball in the evening, at which the beautiful Mrs. Walpole kindly gave me her hand as a partner; and, though dancing had never been a favourite amusement of mine, so accompanied it proved delightful, and I entered into the full spirit of it. From Mr. Walpole's, we went directly to the waterside, where his barge was in waiting to convey us to the ship. At two o'clock in the morning, we got on board and took possession of our own cabin, where, notwithstanding the greatness of the change, Charlotte and myself slept sound until awakened at seven in the morning by the padre and ship's crew chanting their matins at the altar, which was close to the bulkhead of our apartment. The sound was grand and awful, occasioning in us both very pleasing sensations. Some of the voices were remarkably melodious. We had these prayers four times in the course of each day. Mr. Bateman slept in a hanging cot in the great cabin, the bed being taken down and stowed away in the daytime. Messrs. Kemp and Brown had each small cabins in the steerage.

Upon rising and going upon deck, I saw an elegant-looking man walking up and down, who politely bowed to me, Mr. Barretto soon after telling me it was a French gentleman to whom he had given a passage at the particular request of the Marquis de Pombal. Upon entering into conversation with him, I found he had resided many years in the East Indies, having been an officer of rank in the military service of different native princes. He appeared to be perfectly acquainted with Asiatic politics, possessing a strong natural understanding which had been highly cultivated. Upon further acquaintance, I discovered he had encountered many grievous misfortunes, and had been cruelly treated by those who, if honour or conscience had bound them, must have acted very differently towards him. Various instances of the basest ingratitude had in some measure soured his temper, rendering him at times morose or peevish; nevertheless the scholar and well-bred man were always distinguishable in his conduct and behaviour. He was returning to Hindustan powerfully recommended by the Portuguese Government, and with a hope of obtaining restitution from some of those persons who had defrauded him of his just rights. I am sorry to say his name has totally escaped my recollection.

On Sunday, 23rd June 1782, we unmoored at ten o'clock in the morning, dropping down the Tagus until three in the afternoon; when, the flood tide coming in, and a fresh wind having been blowing all day direct from sea, we were compelled to bring to a few miles below the Castle of Belem; at five, the wind suddenly shifting and becoming favourable, we got up our anchor and made sail; at six, passed the bar, soon after which we took a last view of the magnificent capital of Portugal, a city I left with considerable regret, having been received and treated there with the utmost hospitality and kindness by many estimable persons—by some individuals with an affectionate regard I never can forget.

We stood out to sea in company with the *Expedition* packet, commanded by Captain Dashwood. This vessel was considered one of the fastest sailers in the service of the Government; it was therefore very gratifying to us on board the *Raynha de Portugal* to see that we rather had the heels of her. At dusk we had got a good offing; the *Expedition* then left us, bending her course towards England, while we stood to the south-west, at the rate of eight knots an hour. The 24th, we saw two strange sail standing to the southward; the 25th, a schooner to the east-north-east which hoisted Russian colours; the 26th, in the evening, we saw the island of Madeira, distant about fourteen leagues, at which we were to complete the cargo with wine; at eleven at night, we hove

12*

to. The wind blowing fresh had raised a high sea which made the ship roll and tumble about dreadfully; so that we passed a wretched night. This was our first sample of what we might expect in bad weather, convincing us of the probability of Mr. Moore's prediction being verified. At daylight of the 27th, we made sail; at six, passed the east end of the island and, at eight, anchored in the roads of Funchal. We found only three small vessels there; but, soon after we anchored, a large ship came in, having been only thirteen days on her passage from Portsmouth.

Mr. Aldus having asked us to reside at her home during our stay, we gladly accepted the obliging invitation. At ten o'clock, her husband came on board to whom she introduced us. We accompanied them on shore to an excellent house of Mr. Aldus's. After dinner, he took us to Mr. Murray's, the British Consul, to Mr. Murdoch's, Mr. Ashmuty's and two or three other gentlemen's of the island. Mr. Murray engaged us to pass the whole of the following day with him at his country seat about four miles distance, up a mountain immediately above the town. In the evening we visited two monasteries, purchasing from the recluses their ingenious productions; from whence we went to a neat theatre where a comedy was very tolerably performed. My poor Charlotte was sadly annoyed by lizards, an animal with which Madeira is overrun, and some of a larger kind than I ever saw in any other part of the world.

The 30th, Mr. Barretto informed us he had shipped two hundred and forty pipes of madeira, being the quantity he intended to take, and requested we would all be on board early the following morning, as he proposed proceeding to sea at noon. On 1st July after breakfast, bidding adieu to our hostess, her husband conveyed us on board our ship in a commodious boat of his own, constructed for encountering the surf, which is sometimes tremendously high at Madeira. When we embarked, it was so nearly calm the ship dared not get under way lest the swell of the sea should drive her upon the rocks; but about three in the afternoon, a fine breeze springing up from the land, we weighed anchor and made sail, running from the island rapidly. Charlotte and myself were in perfect health; her favourite maid, Harriet, benefited materially at Madeira from the climate, as well as from Mrs. Aldus's nursing. I endeavoured to persuade her to remain there, Mrs. Aldus kindly promising to take care of her until quite restored to health; but no arguments of mine or Mrs. Hickey's could induce her to forsake her mistress, whom, let the consequence be what it would, she was resolved to follow while life remained.

The pipes of wine received on board at Madeira not only impeded the ship's progress by making her too deep in the water, but greatly increased her motion; at times we rolled so dreadfully deep it was with the utmost difficulty we preserved our seats at meal times. Nothing material occurred until the 10th of the month, when it blew hard, with an immense sea, which occasioned the ship to roll so deep we were in momentary expectation of the masts going over her side. The wind being right aft, we ran in these twenty-four hours two hundred and thirty miles. During the rest of the month of July, the weather continued boisterous and unpleasant; an immense high sea made the motion so violent and quick it was impossible to walk the deck, with difficulty to keep one's feet at all. Not a day passed without some accident of splitting sails or carrying away of parts of the rigging.

Mrs. Hickey's servant, Harriet Hammersly, became so reduced and weak she was unable to rise from her bed, and was evidently dying, of which she seemed conscious herself, but was quite resigned and the most patient sufferer that could be, never uttering a complaint, or even a murmur. Her melancholy and desperate situation gave my dearest girl great affliction, being much attached to her. On 1st August we got the south-east trade, very fresh, which drove us at a great rate. On the 3rd, the gentle Harriet was suddenly seized with a succession of fainting fits, in one of which she breathed her last, expiring without the slightest struggle, or even a sigh. In the evening, her corpse was committed to the deep, the burial service being read by Mr. Bateman, the whole ship's crew with their priest attending with the utmost gravity and decorum. The body was enclosed in a plain, neat coffin made by the carpenters on board. This was a cruel blow upon Mrs. Hickey, who was so affected by the death of her favourite and faithful attendant that for several days I could not prevail on her to join us at table, or to leave her cabin. The loss was in every way irreparable.

On 1st September, our latitude by reckoning was thirty-five, sixteen south, dismal, dark, threatening sky, hard squalls, rain, with an immense sea running, which made the ship labour very much. The 5th, so heavy a sea ran we apprehended being pooped every minute. The ship laboured dreadfully, tumbling about so that we split the mainsail from the violent jerks, and soon after both main and foretop sails; after which we ran under the foresail alone. The 6th, 7th and 8th, it blew strong, with at times severe squalls, rain, and a sea that seemed disposed to overwhelm us. The motion was quite horrid. On the 9th, it blew still stronger, with uncommonly black sky, the same high seas running, but more confused, some of them striking the ship with great violence. In the evening, the gale increased, attended by severe squalls. At 8 p.m., Mrs. Hickey, Mr. Bateman, Kemp, Brown, Mr. Barretto and the priest, whom we had invited to supper, and myself, had just seated ourselves, the chairs being made fast to the table, and the latter, as we thought, so well secured that nothing could move it, when we heard a dreadful crash upon deck. In the same moment, too, the vessel took so desperate a lurch as to tear the table at which we were sitting from its lashings; and the whole party, chairs, dishes, plates, and all the etceteras, were dashed in one promiscuous heap against the lee side of the cabin. Providentially, none of us received any material personal injury.

Sad screaming and more noise prevailing upon deck, I went up to enquire the cause of it. The night was so dismally dark that to discover anything by the eye was utterly impossible; but I learnt from one of the midshipmen, a young friend of mine, that in a sudden gust of wind the fore-yard had snapped in two in the slings, the consequence of which was the foretop sail yard gave way, and both sails were blown into ribbons. During my stay upon deck, the main topmast, with all its rigging, went over the side, being immediately followed by the fore-top mast, the main tack at the same time breaking. These complicated misfortunes I heard of from the people; for seeing was entirely out of the question. The dreadful crash of falling masts, with the flapping of the split sails and melancholy cries of the people, struck a general panic throughout the ship; nothing but confusion and despair prevailed, increased not a little by a piercing cry from below that the pumps were choked and would not work.

A more truly terrific scene could not be; in fact, we expected nothing short of going to the bottom. The greater part of the crew, as I understand is always the case with Portuguese sailors at times of imminent danger, abandoned their duty to assemble round their priest, with whom they joined at the altar, screeching out supplicatory prayers to their patron saint Antonio, and all the other saints in the calendar, to have mercy upon them. A few, however, who possessed more firmness of mind, at the head of whom was the boatswain, never ceased to exert themselves with constancy and firmness. It was by some of them ascertained, upon examination, that the alarm relative to the pumps was without foundation, arising from the carpenter's fright being so great, upon finding the well full of water, that he forgot to pull out a stopper or plug, the omission of which prevented them from working. We, nevertheless, had still evils enough to render our situation very precarious. In less than one hour, the ship, from being in good order, became an absolute wreck. Not a sail was left to the yards, all three topmasts gone and lower rigging torn to pieces, a dismally dark, blowing night, with a tremendous sea, in a high southern latitude and tempestuous part of the ocean, an increasing leak, and the ship labouring in such a manner as to excite a reasonable apprehension of its becoming still worse, formed such a complication of evils as to make our bearing up against them a very doubtful matter.

The error about the pumps being rectified, they were both kept at work without intermission, affording us the consolation of finding they decreased the water. This had the further good effect of doing away with the panic that prevailed among three-fourths of the crew. Upon mustering the people, it was discovered two were missing, supposed to have been carried away by some of the heavy seas that broke over the deck. The miserable men lost were one of the mates to the boatswain and a common seaman. The voice of the former was distinguished in the height of the confusion, crying for assistance; but none could be afforded where everybody thought only of his own preservation. Two other seamen were carried overboard when the main topmast fell; but, fortunately keeping their hold of some of the ropes, they regained a footing in the ship, thus being almost miraculously saved from drowning.

The roaring of the wind and sea, our cabin quite wet, with the natural anxiety from our situation, put sleep entirely out of the question. During the first gust, nearly every article in the great cabin and mine fetched way; we had considerable difficulty in again securing them, being employed therein all the latter part of the night. At daybreak, I again went upon deck, where I beheld the forlorn state we were reduced to. It still blew strong, the appearance of the sky bearing as threatening an aspect as the preceding day, the wind at north-north-west, with a mountainous sea, the deck strewed with broken rigging, which, as well as bits of the torn sails, also hung about the lower masts, the only ones standing. Altogether, it made a wretched exhibition. Upon examination, they discovered that the mizzen mast was sprung, all hands busily employed clearing the wrecks of masts, yards, sails and cordage, which occupied them the whole day. There we lay in nearly the same spot, tumbling about like a log upon the water, one pump being constantly at work night and day. Fortunately, we were strongly manned in point of number, having one hundred and forty sailors. The next misfortune was finding both the caps of the main and foremast injured by the topmasts being wrenched when going, that of the foremast materially.

Towards evening, the weather moderated, which enabled the people, who were greatly fatigued, to get some rest and sleep. Early on the 11th, their labours were renewed with fresh vigour, the first thing being to get a mainsail set, and a topgallant sail for a foresail, which gave her a little way through the water, thereby lessening the violence of the motion. This day Mr. Barretto called a council of his officers to deliberate upon the most prudent measure to be adopted in our critical and dangerous situation; when, after mature consideration, they were unanimously of opinion the best thing we could do would be to steer for the Mauritius as the nearest port. This determination being communicated to the boatswain, he condemned it as highly imprudent, observing they might reach India almost as soon as Mauritius. Besides, the approach to the French islands at that time of the year was extremely dangerous; and, should we meet with one of the hurricanes so common in approaching the land, it must prove the loss of the ship in her disabled state, and, consequently, of every person on board.

This opinion had no weight with any one of the officers, who all treated it with vast contempt; but in a very different way did Mr. Barretto view it. He thought it founded in good sense and fair reasoning. I own what the boatswain said carried conviction to my mind. My Charlotte considered only what she had understood to be the nearest port, therefore earnestly wished for the Mauritius; and, as the boatswain was not one of her favourites, her dislike to him greatly increased by this advice of his. In vain I argued in his favour; she was sure he was a ferocious, horrid man. The fact is, that, though of stern countenance, he possessed a mild and benevolent disposition, blended with the utmost degree of fortitude in the execution of the duties of his perilous profession, of which merit we had subsequently undeniable proof. He proved our preserver by his zeal and example.

The 12th proved a day of wonderful progress in getting the ship into some sort of sailing trim. They got up an old sprung maintop mast, which, by reefing it above the injured part, answered tolerably. Before dusk a new sail was bent to a spare yard, and we began to move through the water four or five knots an hour. The 13th the weather again became very bad, with violent gusts of wind, rain, hail, thunder and lightning, all of the severest kind. A short, irregular sea made the motion of the ship very distressing, and considerably increased the leak; nor could anything be done in the repairs of rigging or making more sail. This squally, disagreeable weather continued four days. The carpenter, however, contrived during it to prepare a new foretop mast and to fish the mizzen mast; so that, on the 20th, we had once more a tolerable quantity of sail set. The captain and officers then began to come round to the boatswain's opinion, and admit that he was right in proposing to stand on for India, in preference to making for the French islands.

On 1st October, a large leak was discovered by the ship's steward in the bread room, about two feet under water, the sea pouring in with an immense rush. This being immediately stopped, sanguine hopes were entertained that we might do with one pump. We were, however, disappointed, not finding the least difference in the quantity of water every hour. The 7th, the wind became moderate and the sea much smoother. The 13th, an immense swell annoyed us, though without increase of wind. The ship rolled so dreadfully nothing could remain in its place, and we were most uncomfortable. The leak became more alarming, making fourteen inches of water an hour. The 21st the weather appearing settled, the dead lights were withdrawn and our cabin once more received the cheerful light of day.

On 1st November, at one in the morning, we were taken aback in a sudden squall of wind and rain. Soon afterwards, it fell almost calm, the sea remarkably smooth, heat intense. Mr. Kemp, whose cabin in the steerage was small and confined, not being able to sleep, arose from his cot and went to sit in the quarter gallery for the sake of air. Whilst looking out at the window, he saw something that appeared very like land upon the lee bow. Going immediately upon deck, he pointed it out to the officer of the watch, who was so satisfied of its actually being land he directly caused the yards to be braced up, hauled close upon a wind, and sent to awaken the captain and Mr. Barretto. At daylight we were close in with two small islands, very low, being nearly level with the water, and covered over with trees. The nearest to us was within a short mile, bearing south-east and by south, another somewhat larger about three miles off bearing south-east and by east. Upon referring to the charts, found they could be no other than the Cocos and Hog Islands, only a few leagues from the island of Sumatra! We were just eleven degrees to the eastward of the reckoning; which made them in the meridian of Ceylon, for which island, as our captain imagined, we were standing direct. Fortunate indeed were we in there being so little wind during the night; for, had the weather been such as we had experienced during the preceding month, the ship would inevitably have plumped on shore, no look-out being kept from supposing themselves such an immense distance as eleven degrees of longitude from land and not having the remotest idea of being upon the eastern coast. So much for Portuguese navigation and Portuguese reckonings!

The serious mistake as to the situation of the ship was a sad disappointment to us passengers, as we had flattered ourselves with the hope of reaching Colombo in a few days, whereas we might now be many weeks ere we got into port, all the directories stating light airs and calms of long duration being prevalent off the coast of Sumatra in the months of November and December. The 2nd, it was quite calm, and we were in terror lest it should continue. The 3rd, the same, with extreme sultry weather. On the 4th, our Captain was seized with a violent fever, supposed to have been brought on by anxiety of mind and fretting at finding himself so egregiously out in point of longitude. It soon affected his brain, and he became so outrageous it was necessary to tie him down in his bed, sentries constantly watching to see that he did not break loose. In his frenzy he threatened death and destruction to every person that approached him. The strength he showed was quite wonderful; for he was a very slight-made man. Three different times he freed himself from the straps that bound him, when it was quite as much as four powerful fellows could do to hold him.

The 6th we had light airs of wind, an appearance of strong current from great rippling of the water; calm in the night, the heat quite overcoming and oppressive. The 7th, a light air again. The 8th, light winds but squally; thunder and lightning. The 10th, instead of having the harbour of the Grand Nicobar open and we ready to anchor within it, as we fully expected, we had the mortification to learn that the current during the night had set us so violently to the westward that we were at least five leagues to leeward of the island we had the evening before been abreast of. The wind was baffling, sometimes being so favourable as to encourage the endeavour to work up to the harbour. Thus we continued the whole day. In the evening, we were once more well in with the land, when it again fell calm, the current proving as hostile as it had been the preceding night. In the morning we were at least seven leagues to leeward. Another day was lost in fruitless attempts to work up to windward; we gained not a mile. Mr. Barretto therefore resolved no longer to attempt getting into the Nicobar, but stand directly across the bay for Point de Galle or, if we failed making that, to put into Colombo, which was at the southern point of the island of Ceylon. Directions were accordingly given for that purpose to the chief mate, the captain being still confined to his cabin from weakness, though he had recovered his senses.

The moment I heard the order given, and found that the ship was put before the wind, I felt a presentiment of the evils that awaited us. At dinner that day, I observed it was highly probable we might encounter the breaking up of the monsoon, as we unfortunately were at the critical time when such a thing might be expected every hour, added to which it was near the change of moon. For delivering this opinion I was laughed at by all my messmates except Mrs. Hickey, who, having been in the habit of relying upon whatever I said, became alarmed and uneasy. Mr. Brown was particularly smart in his comments, called me a croaker, and added, "Suppose we have a storm, what matter? We have already experienced more than one; yet here we are still. And why not surmount half a dozen more?" This speech was greatly applauded by his friend Kemp, and by Mr. Bateman. I then showed Mr. Brown the accounts of the most remarkable hurricanes that occurred in those seas, as recorded in the East India Directory, and the dreadful consequences of some of them; at which he again scoffed, pronounced those records to be either fabrications or preposterously exaggerated, and he did not believe a word of them.

For six succeeding days after we bore away from the Nicobars, we had gloomy, threatening weather, sometimes blowing strong in squalls, then suddenly falling quite calm, remaining so only a few minutes, when a violent gust succeeded; heavy showers of rain fell, which was very acceptable, furnishing an abundant supply of water, of which all hands were greatly in want. At daylight on Sunday, 17th November, (a memorable day to me) finding as I lay in bed the motion of the ship particularly uneasy, I got up to look out; and never, to the last day of my existence, shall forget the shock I experienced at what I beheld. The horizon all round of a blackish purple, above which rolled great masses of cloud of a deep copper colour moving in every direction with uncommon rapidity; vivid lightning in every quarter, thunder awfully roaring at a distance, though evidently approaching us; a short irregular sea, breaking with a tremendous surf, as if blowing furiously hard though then but moderate; the wind, however, whistling shrill as a boatswain's pipe through the blocks and rigging. The scene altogether was such as to appal the bravest men on board.

Going upon deck, I found a dead silence prevailing; not a syllable uttered by anyone, all looking in stupid amazement. Not a single precaution was taken, no dead lights to the great cabin or quarter gallery windows, not even a topgallant yard down; on the contrary, they and every other sail was set, notwithstanding they reckoned themselves within a few leagues of Ceylon, for which they were standing direct; and all this strange neglect at a time when a British vessel would have struck everything that could be, and made all snug as possible, in order to be the better able to receive the shock that was so perceptibly coming upon us. In great tribulation I returned to my cabin, telling Mrs. Hickey to secure anything she was particularly anxious about and prepare herself to undergo severe trials. I had a small, strong mahogany escritoire in which I kept my letters, papers of consequence, and few trinkets and valuable articles I had. This I jammed in between two of the projecting knees in my cabin, in such a manner that, until the ship went to pieces, it could not be thrown out of its place. At seven, we each of us swallowed a dish of tea, being the last and only refreshment we had for many subsequent sorrowful hours.

A DREADFUL HURRICANE

Although all violent tempests are in a great measure alike, partaking of the same circumstances and consequences as those I have already had occasion to attempt a description of, yet this was so peculiarly dreadful, and uor escape with life so wonderful, that I am led to relate the melancholy particulars. At eight in the morning, it began to blow hard, torrents of rain pouring down, rendering it almost dark as night. Then was an order first given to take in topgallant sails and reef topsails. The order was too late; the instant the sails were lowered, they were blown to atoms, being torn from their respective yards in shreds. The sea suddenly increased to an inconceivable height, the wind roaring to such a degree that the officers upon deck could not make themselves heard by the crew with the largest speaking-trumpets. Between nine and ten, it blew an absolute hurricane, far surpassing what I had any idea of. As it veered all round the compass, so did the sea increase infinitely beyond imagination, one wave encountering another from every direction and, by their mutual force in thus meeting, ran up apparently to a sharp point, there breaking at a height that is actually incredible but to those who unhappily saw it. The entire ocean was in a foam white as soap-suds.

At a quarter to eleven, the foretop mast, yard, rigging and all went over the side, the noise of it being imperceptible amidst the roaring of wind and sea. In a few minutes, it was followed by the mizzen mast, which snapped like a walking stick about eight feet above the quarterdeck; part of the wreck of it unfortunately got foul of the rudder chains, and every moment struck the ship's bottom with excessive violence. At half-past eleven, the foremast went, being shivered into splinters quite down to the gundeck. The fall of it drew the main mast forward, whereby the levers upon which the pumps worked (as they do in all ships built in the East Indies) were totally destroyed, putting an end to our pumping. Before noon, the main mast and bowsprit both went at the same instant. Thus, in the short space of four hours, was this noble vessel reduced to such a state of distress as few have ever been in. Our situation seemed hopeless; not a creature on board but thought every minute would be the last of their lives. When the masts were gone, she immediately began to roll with unparalleled velocity from side to side, each gunwale, with half the quarterdeck, being emerged in water each roll, so that we every moment expected she would be bottom uppermost, or roll her sides out.

Thus buffetted about on the angry ocean, I told my poor Charlotte, whom I had secured in the best way I could, and was endeavouring to support, that all must soon be over, it being quite impossible that wood and iron could long sustain such extraordinary and terrific motion, and such were my real sentiments. The dear woman, with a composure and serenity that struck me most forcibly, mildly replied, "God's will be done; to that I bend with humble resignation, blessing a benevolent providence for permitting me, my dearest William, to expire with you, whose fate I am content to share. But oh! my dearest love, let us in the agonies of death be not separated," and she clasped me in her arms.

Mr. Bateman, at the commencement of the gale, had gone upon deck, from whence he dared not again venture to stir, but was obliged to lay himself down under the wheel and there remain. Mr. Kemp and Mr. Brown had lashed themselves to the gun-rings of the aftermost port in the great cabin to prevent their being dashed from side to side. Whilst thus situated, three out of the five stern windows, frames and all, suddenly burst inward from the mere force of the wind, the noise attending which was such that I conceived the last scene of the tragedy was arrived; but, awful as that moment was, the recollection of the way in which Mr. Brown had doubted the facts stated in the Directory, relative to the hurricanes at the breaking up of the monsoon, recurred so forcibly that I could not help saying to him, "Now, Mr. Brown, I think you can no longer entertain a belief that the accounts in the Directory are fabricated or exaggerated." He made me no answer, but, raising his hands clasped together, looked the very image of despair.

The ship was apparently full of water, and seemed to be so completely overwhelmed that we all thought she was fast settling downward. Nevertheless, the velocity and depth of her rolling abated nothing, tearing away every article that could be moved. Not a bureau, chest, or trunk but broke loose and were soon demolished, the contents, from the quickness and constant splashing from one side to the other of the ship, becoming a perfect paste, adhering to the deck between the beams, many inches in thickness, so as, near the sides, actually to fill up the space to the deck. Amongst the furniture destroyed was a large bureau, with a bookcase top, belonging to Mr. Barretto, in which were deposited the whole of his ship's papers and his own private ones, scarce a remnant of any one of which was saved. During the severity of the hurricane, about twenty noble fellows, such as would not have disgraced the British Navy, at the head of whom stood the boatswain, acted with the same determined spirit they had shown on 9th September, doing all that could be performed by men, while the rest of the crew gave themselves up to despair, clinging round their priest, and screeching out prayers for pardon and mercy in such dismal and frantic yells as was horrible to hear.

So eager were the miserable enthusiasts to embrace the image of Jesus Christ upon the Cross (which the priest held in his hand) in the instant of their dissolution that they, in their endeavours so to do, actually tore it to pieces. By two in the afternoon, every bulkhead between decks, except that of my cabin, had fallen from the violent labouring of the ship. The altar also being demolished, an end was thereby put to the functions of the despairing priest. The reason of my cabin standing when every other yielded was that, being the state room, it partook of the general strength of the vessel, being erected at the time of her building and as firmly fixed as her decks; but the folding door that opened into the great cabin was soon torn off its hinges and broken to pieces, exposing to our view the foaming surges through the stern windows of the great cabin. My darling girl sat like patience itself, though drenched to the skin, and covered with filth from the washings that burst into our cabin.

It is a remarkable circumstance that, upon the foremast's going and the confusion and panic that ensued, the captain, who had for so many days been confined in a delirium, and so reduced that he could not without assistance turn in his bed, being told what had happened, and that the ship was sinking, instantaneously recovered vigour both of body and mind sufficient to allow not only of his jumping from his cot but going upon deck, where he issued his orders with as much, or perhaps more precision and skill than he had done during any part of the voyage. The first order he gave was by every possible means to lighten the ship. The sea, indeed, had already done much towards it for us by carrying off the whole of the masts, yards, rigging, and everything that was upon the upper deck. An attempt was therefore made to throw the guns overboard; but only five were so, and those at the imminent risk of the lives of the men from the excessive motion.

An attempt was likewise made to start the madeira wine. The two first men that went into the hold for that purpose were immediately jammed in between two pipes and killed; after which, no other would try. After exerting himself in a wonderful manner, by one of the violent jerks from a tremendous sea breaking on board, the captain was thrown down with such force as to break his right arm and receive a severe contusion on his head, which rendered him insensible. The chief mate, an active, clever seaman, was early in the gale carried away by a sea, washed forward, but luckily brought up in the galley under the forecastle, where he remained covered with wounds and bruises. The second mate was not seen after eight o'clock; it was therefore concluded that he had been carried overboard and lost. It, however, did not turn out so. He, apprehending nothing could save the ship, had shut himself up in a small booby hutch, or cabin, just abaft the helm upon the upper deck, where he spent the day between the brandy bottle and prayer book. The third officer had throughout showed the utmost fortitude and energy, sinking at last completely overcome by fatigue, and remained secured by a rope on the spot where he fell.

One of the most active persons on board was the French passenger of whom I have before made mention. He betrayed equal skill and resolution, suggesting and helping to carry into effect several things that proved of material use. This unfortunate man was particularly forward in the endeavours to throw the guns overboard; in doing which, one of them grazed his shin, making a slight wound in appearance, the skin being a little broken, which neither he himself nor anyone else that saw it considered of consequence. It, however, caused his death, as I shall hereafter state.

Mr. Barretto, as I have already observed, was no seaman; he, however, much to his credit, resolved to set his people an example by exposing his person to the raging element. He therefore remained upon the quarterdeck, lashed to the side, endeavouring to cheer and encourage the few sailors that were ready to do all in their power to prevent the ship from foundering. Thus he remained until two in the afternoon, when he fainted away; whereupon the people cast off the rope with which he was secured, and were about to convey him between decks, when, at the moment, an enormous wave came over the stern, sweeping them all away. Two of the poor fellows were irrecoverably lost; and for some time everybody thought Mr. Barretto had shared the same fate. He was, however, found amongst part of the broken rigging upon the forecastle in a state of insensibility, from whence he was with extreme difficulty carried between decks. Thus hour after hour passed with us in utter despair; but still to our amazement we remained afloat, which seemed to us little short of a miracle for a ship in such a state as ours was, so tossed about at the mercy of such a sea as never was seen, so involved in ruin and desolation on every side, making too, as she did before the hurricane commenced, thirty inches of water every hour, and not a single stroke of pump after half-past eleven in the morning; nor could anybody account for her not going to the bottom but by supposing she actually rolled the water out of her as fast as it came in!

At six in the evening, the fury of the storm had somewhat abated, though not sufficiently to afford us a hope of ever seeing another day; our surprise only was at surviving from hour to hour without the least expectation of escaping finally from a watery grave. At eight at night, the gale had evidently subsided or, to use a seaman's language, it had broken up. This encouraged the few men who had throughout behaved themselves like heroes to further exertions. At the imminent risk of their lives, some of them went over the stern and ultimately succeeded in cutting away considerable quantities of the rigging, sails, and yards that got so entangled with the rudder and rudder-chains as totally to prevent the ship's steering; by which our danger of foundering from the overwhelming sea was greatly increased. They also afterwards accomplished the throwing overboard of fourteen more of her guns, besides much lumber from between decks, by which the ship was importantly benefited, the rolling being less rapid and not so deep. By midnight, the sea had gone down a great deal, and the people were enabled to keep their legs enough to rig out one pump and set it at work. This being kept constantly at work, the water did not gain upon us, which gave everybody fresh spirits; and, for the first time since the commencement of the tempest, we began to entertain a hope of preservation. At break of day, the clouds moved with great velocity but were light in comparison to what we had seen. It still blew very strong, and there was a large, confused sea; yet, when we thought of what it had been, it appeared as nothing; besides, it was hourly getting more moderate.

Upon going upon deck, oh, what a lamentable sight was there! The first object I saw was the boatswain and some of the seamen bringing Mr. Barretto aft in a hammock they had put him into. It was an arduous task from her still rolling very deep, and he so sore he cried out upon the least pressure, or anything touching him. They at last got him into the great cabin, in the centre of which they hung the hammock with him in it. By ten in the morning (of the 18th), a bright sun shone forth, the sea became less agitated, and we began to entertain confident hopes. But, to counteract this unexpected good fortune, I found my dearest Charlotte much indisposed and feverish; nor could that be wondered at considering what she had suffered, drenched in wet for such a length of time, and not having a single change of clothes, or an article of dress left, all being destroyed, as were mine also, in the common ruin.

Amidst such complicated and general distress, it was scarcely to be expected that any particular attention would be paid to a single individual, although that individual was a female; but, so great a favourite had my darling girl made herself throughout the ship by the peculiar gentleness and suavity of her manners, that, from the moment a chance of escape from drowning appeared, she became the first object and immediate care of, I may safely say, everybody on board. Before nine o'clock in the morning (of the 18th), the carpenter, with three men to assist him, were at work in our cabin; by noon they had repaired the bed and got the whole apartment into some sort of order, with a canvas to roll up as a substitute for a door, whereby she could once more be in private.

Whilst this was going forward, Mr. Bateman entered, having in his hand a tin pot of madeira wine, made hot, which he had contrived to get prepared, and, what I considered of still more consequence, a pair of blankets *only half wet*, which he had procured from the gunner. He advised me to make Mrs. Hickey directly swallow the wine and then lie down between the blankets and endeavour to get that rest she stood so much in need of. This advice was too prudent not to be adopted; but, with all my influence, I could not persuade her to touch the madeira until I took the half of it myself, when she cheerfully drank the remainder of the comfortable beverage, declaring it to be the most reviving and grateful draught she had ever tasted; nor can that be wondered at, when it is recollected that, added to all our other miseries, we had been from two o'clock in the afternoon of Saturday until Monday noon, a period of forty-six hours, without the least particle of nourishment passing our lips, except one wretched dish of tea on Sunday morning. Having swallowed the wine, I made her lie down between the blankets, where she fell into a profuse perspiration, soon dropped asleep for a couple of hours, and then awoke greatly refreshed.

Having thus contributed all in my power towards her relief, I joined in searching amongst the heap of rubbish in the great cabin for anything worth preserving. We soon collected from thence a parcel of six-and-thirty-shilling pieces, or half-Joes as they are called in Portugal, two watches and various bits of gold and silver ornaments and trinkets. After ransacking in a mass of dirt, so blended together it was difficult to separate for a long time, I got hold of a small tin case, much bruised but unbroken. This I took to Mr. Barretto as he lay in his hammock, who joyfully exclaimed it was the ship's papers. He requested I would carefully open it and, should they be wet, get them dried, as they were of the utmost importance to him. I directly set about it; but alas! they were totally useless, the ink being entirely effaced although written upon parchment, most of them separating into pieces in attempting to unfold them. The only one that was at all legible, and that only partially, was Mr. Barretto's Portuguese naturalization.

Having lent my aid for the service of my friends, I next thought of my own concerns, and accordingly went to look after my escritoire, which I found in the spot I had placed it, and so firmly wedged in I was obliged to have recourse to the carpenter to extricate it. Upon opening it and examining the contents, everything in the way of paper was completely destroyed except three letters that I had received after all the others, and put into a leather pocket-book. My watch had sustained no other injury than what arose from the salt water which ruined the works or, as the boys call it, "the guts." What I lamented above everything else, though of no intrinsic value, was the loss of a large book in which I had copied the journals of every voyage I had made, and the remarkable circumstances that had occurred. This was utterly destroyed, as well as my admission as an attorney of the Court of King's Bench and solicitor of the Court of Chancery which were in it.

The boatswain, upon going over the ship's side to examine her condition, found she was more than three feet lighter than when we sailed from the island of Madeira, this great difference arising from the loss of the masts, yards, sails, and rigging, also from the guns and other heavy things that were thrown overboard. In consequence of her being so much more buoyant, the leaks decreased to nineteen inches of water an hour, a quantity that was easily cleared by the pumps, the other being put in order as soon as the storm ceased. Thirteen of the crew lost their lives, the greater part of them, as was conjectured, being washed overboard. Besides the two persons killed by the pipes of wine, three other bodies were found in different places, two of them under the beams upon which the boats had been stowed, the third between the coppers and ship's side, a space of only a few inches wide. It was a shocking spectacle; being so jammed in by the working of the ship, the intestines were squeezed out and the head forced completely round, the face being towards the back. These miserable corpses were committed to the deep in the afternoon.

Nothing in the way of eating could be found except ship's provisions of salt beef and damaged rice, having been wetted by the sea water; yet, such as it was, we were glad to partake, making at least a plentiful meal. We were reduced to the necessity of eating with our fingers; for not a knife was to be found the first day. We afterwards procured two from the seamen. After our salt meat and rice, we took a good quantity of brandy and water, and at seven in the evening lay down upon our bed, both of us sleeping sound for several hours, and that, too, in spite of an eighteen-pounder which was fired every half hour through the night, as a signal of distress to any vessel that might chance to be within hearing. They had considerable difficulty in making the gun go off, the sea having found its way into the magazine, as it had into every part of the ship. I rose at five in the morning of the 19th much refreshed; my Charlotte was also better than I expected. It was a beautiful morning, little wind and the sea gone down. While looking out, I was very agreeably surprised at seeing Mr. Barretto come up, assisted by his servant. He complained of violent pains all over him, but he could not remain in the hammock; it was so intensely hot.

Every creature on board was busily and earnestly engaged in endeavouring to get some sail set upon her, so as to give her way through the water. Part of her cargo consisting of canvas and cordage, the after hatches were opened to get at them; for, circumstanced as we were, the underwriters could not with propriety object thereto, being for the preservation of both ship and cargo. The gunner happened to have two small spars which he had stowed away in the gunroom, as part of his own private trade. These were got out at the gunroom port, which was opened for the purpose. One of them was soon set up in the place of the foremast, the other lashed to the stump of the mizzen mast. In about five hours, two small square sails were roughly put together. The wind being at east-north-east, we set our canvas, standing direct for Ceylon, from which it was supposed we could not be far distant.

In the afternoon, I saw our French passenger, whose leg had been hurt by one of the guns when throwing it overboard in the hurricane, sitting upon the deck in the steerage, bathing the injured part with a mixture of vinegar and brandy, afterwards covering it with coarse brown paper made wet with the same composition. Observing a considerable degree of inflammation round the wound, I took the liberty, unasked, of advising him to consult the surgeon of the ship, as I had always understood it to be dangerous to neglect such things in a hot climate. He civilly thanked me for my solicitude on his account, but wholly declined applying to the surgeon, whom he considered an ignoramus in his profession, adding, "I am too old a campaigner, sir, and have been too often cut up and maimed in every part of my body, where no surgical aid was procurable, not to know how to treat myself in a much worse case than this. Be assured, sir, my recipe is better than any of the nonsense the faculty would apply. Brandy, vinegar, and brown paper do wonders." Whether it was that the bone itself was seriously injured, or his habit of body, from living long upon salt provisions, operated, the wound became daily worse, so much so that I predicted bad consequences.

Through the 19th, nothing material occurred. The morning of the 20th, I was awoke by the sound of boat's oars. Rising and looking out of the quarter gallery window, I had the pleasure to see a boat coming alongside and a large brig close to us. Going upon deck, I learnt that it was the *Governor Hermsfelt*, a Danish vessel bound from Serampore in Bengal to Anjingo. She had been drawn to us by our guns. They had not felt any of the hurricane, but from a dreadfully high and confused sea and threatening sky knew there must have been bad weather near them, and therefore bore up upon hearing a gun several times, concluding it came from some vessel in distress. She supplied us with some articles of the utmost consequence for navigating our ship; that is, three large spars and three lesser ones to make into yards, which proved of great use; also with an anchor and cable, of which we had only one, the rest having been cut away to ease the ship in the hurricane and the cables thrown overboard with other things to lighten her. Comforts she had none to bestow, having no livestock at all. She, however, sent us a small barrel of pickled pork and a bag of biscuit, the latter a great treat, although old and full of insects. They also gave us the bearings of the land according to their reckoning; but they had not seen any since Point Palmiras.

Upon consulting with the commander of this vessel, he advised Mr. Barretto not to go to the southward, but to steer for Trincomalee, which was nearly under our lee, and by much the nearest port; for, as the current now set to the northward, we should make a bad hand in such a crippled state by attempting to make for Point de Galle or Colombo. Having given us all the assistance in his power, he proceedde on his voyage. According to his account, we were nineteen leagues from the land, thrice the distance we supposed. The 21st continued moderate and fair. This day one of the large Danish spars was fixed as a main mast, the other as a bowsprit, the smaller being used as yards; and, having made two tolerable-sized sails, we ran forty miles during the twenty-four hours. The 22nd, the weather still fine, we ran forty-seven miles. If, therefore, the reckoning of the Danish captain had been correct, we ought to have seen the land.

The 23rd and 24th were nearly calm; on the latter day, the last cask of provisions was broached, and abominably bad it proved; for, the pickle having leaked out, the meat was become rotten. We had only four butts of rain water remaining, and they were so strongly impregnated with tar as to be scarce drinkable, making us all very sick. Thus situated, without a single shift of linen or any other article of clothing, it may easily be imagined how anxiously the land was looked for. In the night, the people on deck, observing a strong rippling on the water, they hove a cast of lead and were surprised to find we were in twelve fathoms; at daybreak of the 25th, we were close to the land, with breakers within a mile of us, which as the current was driving us towards very fast, we came to with the Danish anchor and cable. As the 26th was a dead calm, we remained fast, firing a gun every half hour. The morning of the 27th the same; but in the afternoon, a light breeze springing up from the south-east, we got under way and run alongshore. We saw smoke rising from two different places a little way inland; but not a living creature appeared, though within three miles of the beach. At sunset, an extreme heavy shower of rain furnished a reasonable supply of water, which we stood in great need of. The 28th was a mixture of calms and hard squalls.

On Saturday, the 30th, we had a charming breeze from the eastward and, at daylight, saw high land bearing north-west, which some of the people declared they knew from its form was near Trincomalee. By our latitude at noon we found it must be so, as we were in eight degrees thirty-nine minutes north. We therefore stood boldly into a bay that appeared open before us, and soon after discovered the entrance to the harbour, fired a gun every ten minutes, and made the best display we could of an ensign with the arms reversed, as signals of distress, though the appearance our ship made must have sufficiently indicated that. At one in the afternoon, we plainly discovered the French flag flying in a fort upon the summit of a hill. Mr. Barretto imagined this to be a deception on the part of the English, not thinking it possible they could have suffered so important a place to be wrested from them by an enemy; but at 3 p.m. we were convinced such was the case by a French and Dutch pilot coming on board and taking charge of the ship. They informed us that the place had been taken in the preceding month of September by Admiral Suffren,* the British garrison having surrendered upon the French troops landing.

Before we could get into the harbour it fell calm. We therefore let go the anchor; soon after which a French officer came on board, who expressed the utmost astonishment at the dreadful situation he saw the ship in, his attention being particularly drawn to the sort of paste I have already mentioned formed by the splashing from side to side, as the ship rolled, of the contents of chests, trunks, etcetera, and which had completely filled up the space between the beams on each side, gradually decreasing in quantity towards the centre of the cabin. He said he would immediately report the lamentable state we were in to the Chevalier Des Roys, the acting Governor, who he was certain would give us all the assistance in his power, and which our un-paralleled misfortunes so well entitled us to. He, however, observed that they were themselves very badly off with respect to fresh pro-visions, their only certain food being salted meat and rice. He likewise told us there was only one ship of war at present there, the *Consolante* frigate, and a Dutch Indiaman. The following morning, being Sunday, 1st December, our ill-fated *Raynha de Portugal* was warped into the harbour, which, as I have before observed, is one of the finest in the world, of extent enough to receive, secure from all danger, all the ships of war of Great Britain, being completely landlocked, with excellent anchorage and deep water close to the shore.

Mr. Barretto, although by no means recovered from the effects of his accident, the hour the ship was safely secured went on shore to pay his compliments to Mr. Des Roys. I availed myself of the oppor-tunity to write to the Governor, representing to him the uncomfortable

* Pierre André de Suffren de Saint-Tropez (1726–1788) had been sent to the aid of the American Colonists in 1779; after which he began his celebrated cruise to the East Indies.

state we were in on board, in want of even the common necessaries of life, both as to food and clothing, and that Mrs. Hickey was much indisposed; for all which reasons I requested we might be permitted to reside on shore. In a couple of hours, Mr. Barretto returned with a very gloomy countenance, telling me nothing was to be expected from Mr. Des Roys, who had received him with the utmost hauteur, and behaved insolently; that, so far from fulfilling the promise of the officer by affording us assistance, he said he entertained such strong suspicions respecting the ship's being English property, as well as the cargo, that he was determined to detain her until the arrival of "the General" (the title the French always gave Monsieur Suffren) or of General de Bussy, who was daily expected from France. After such bad success on his own business, he presented my letter, which the Governor seeing written in English threw upon his table; of course, I had no answer.

Whilst speaking to Mr. Barretto upon this inhuman conduct and telling him I would go in person and state my case to the savage chief, we saw two boats approaching from the frigate, one filled with sailors, the other with military men. The whole came on board and took possession of the ship, placing a sentry with his musket and bayonet fixed at each gangway, with orders not to allow any person whomsoever to pass without the sanction of the French officer on board. The seamen then unhung our rudder, which they towed on shore. My blood boiled with rage at this unworthy treatment; but complaints were of no avail. The French commanding officer on board was a very gentlemanlike young man, lieutenant in the Regiment of the Isle of France, his name L'Anglade. He was quite shocked at the situation in which he found Mrs. Hickey, without food, without clothing, or the common comfort of a female attendant.

After expressing his concern thereat in very feeling terms, he said something must and should be done for the poor lady's relief, it being a disgrace to Frenchmen to permit a female to remain an hour in so unbecoming a state; that the whole of the passengers ought also to be relieved. Asking for pen, ink, and paper, he sat down and wrote two letters, one to Monsieur Mallé, the captain of the *Consolante*, the other to Monsieur Chevillard de Montesson, the Port Captain, or, as the English would call him, Master Attendant. Having despatched these letters, he observed privately to me that Monsieur Des Roys was universally disliked on account of his unaccommodating temper and unsociable manners, but was known to be an officer of merit and one of the ablest engineers in the service, having been very instrumental in the capture of the place, for which Monsieur Suffren had rewarded him with the temporary government; that he had acted with such tyranny in the office as to leave himself without a single friend. This was bad news for us.

Captain Mallé, upon receipt of Monsier L'Anglade's letter, immediately got into his barge and came to our ship, bringing with him tea, coffee, sugar, chocolate, biscuits, liqueurs, and various other articles for the table, also some pieces of white cloth, which, though rather coarse, proved very acceptable. A capital meal was prepared, being the first we had seen for a fortnight, to which we did justice by eating very heartily. Whilst at this repast, Mr. Chevillard came alongside with a quantity of fruit, eggs, a few fowls, some fish, and what was more acceptable than all, a small loaf of excellent bread. Upon seeing the miserable state we were in, he was as indignant as Mr. L'Anglade had been, swearing he would go to Mr. Des Roys and in the name of the King call upon him to act more like one of his liberal nation. Nothing could be more attentive and kind than these three gentlemen, by whose benevolent care my darling girl's sufferings were greatly alleviated.

On the 2nd before ten o'clock in the morning, Mr. Chevillard was again with us to say he had been ungraciously received by the Governor, who at first peremptorily refused to allow any passenger to leave the ship until he had Mr. Suffren's sanction for it; but upon his (Chevillard's) remonstrating against such brutal treatment towards an unfortunate female stranger, he consented to let her land. "If, therefore," continued this good man, "you will put Mrs. Hickey under my care, she shall be treated like a daughter and receive every accommodation the miserable hovel I inhabit will admit of. I will, if you please, take her and her servant on shore immediately."

How was his surprise increased upon my telling him Mrs. Hickey's female attendant had died on board ship soon after we left Madeira, and that she had ever since been without a servant! He expressed his concern at what she had undergone in the most feeling language. Truly grateful for his good intentions, I said I would speak to Mrs. Hickey, but apprehended she would not consent to leave me, and so it proved; for, upon mentioning what Mr. Chevillard proposed, she declared she would rather die on board ship than go on shore without me. During Mr. Chevillard's visit the *Consolante*'s barge came alongside bringing ladies' shoes, stockings, with variety of different sorts of cloth and four tailors, who forthwith began to cut out and sew; so that by the following morning Mrs. Hickey was very comfortably rigged. They then set to making some shirts, etc., for me.

Not satisfied with these munificent acts, the generous Captain Mallé presented Mrs. Hickey with a trunk, which having seen deposited in her cabin, he instantly departed to avoid our grateful thanks. Upon opening the trunk, we found it contained two complete suits of woman's apparel which the considerate and kindhearted man had procured from Mrs. Vansenden, wife of the Dutch Chief, who being about

Mrs. Hickey's size her clothes answered admirably well without alteration. From this lady, as well as her husband, we afterwards received
innumerable instances of kindness. Not a day passed without Mr.
Chevillard's visiting us, always bringing some little matter that he
thought might prove acceptable, especially bread, of which very small
quantities was made, owing to a scarcity of flour. A few of the French
officers did all in their power to correct the ferocity of Mr. Des Roys,
all of them assuring us the restraint would cease the hour any line of
battleship came in, and that one was daily expected.

Amongst those who showed us the most marked attention was Captain Gautier, who had a company of grenadiers in the Regiment of
Pondicherry. He early became greatly attached to both Mrs. Hickey
and me, which he testified by various ways. He was indefatigable in
his endeavours to obtain Mr. Des Roys' leave to let us reside on shore,
and would have succeeded, had it not been from the violence of Mr.
Bateman, who addressed several intemperate and disrespectful letters
to Mr. Des Roys, which so offended that haughty man that he with-
drew his half-given consent. Captain Gautier in the first instance requested I would let him be my banker, an offer I availed myself of
with gratitude.

Captain Mallé, upon seeing Mrs. Hickey and myself clad more to
our satisfaction than when we arrived, made us promise to pass the
following day with him on board his frigate, observing at the time he
gave the invitation that, although he had not the power of controlling
Mr. Des Roys in what related to matters on shore, he could act inde-
pendently of him upon the water. The 10th was therefore spent very
agreeably on board the *Consolante*, where we met several military
gentlemen. The company, very considerately and like well-bred men,
avoided speaking upon politics before me and Mrs. Hickey; but while
walking the deck in the evening, I learnt from one of the junior lieutenants that there had been four hard-fought engagements between
Monsieur Suffren and Sir Edward Hughes's fleets, in every one of
which the English had been defeated; that Madras was, at the time he
was speaking, closely invested by a well-appointed, well-disciplined
French army; while, on the other hand, the miserable garrison pent up
within the walls of Fort St. George were daily dying in scores from
disease and famine; that they were in hourly expectation of hearing
the place had surrendered, and only waited the arrival of a reinforcement of men, then on its way from the Isle of France, under the command of that brave and experienced general, Monsieur de Bussy, to
extend their conquests to Bengal, there being no doubt but that in a
few months the English would be routed out of all their Eastern
possessions. This was a melancholy history for me; and from the fall
of Trincomalee, as well as Suffren's fleet appearing to ride triumphant

and unopposed in those seas, I really feared it was but too true, and that the British sun was near setting in the East!

One of the guests, who sat next to me at dinner, informed me that the Governor was rendered more inexorable than he otherwise would have been towards us by a very insolent letter that Mr. Bateman had addressed to him; wherein, after many rude things, he charged him in plain terms with showing an interested partiality in my favour, I being allowed to visit about, going when and where I pleased, whilst he was most unjustly kept a close prisoner on board a wreck of a filthy Portuguese ship. Surprised and irritated at this intelligence, on returning to the *Raynha de Portugal*, I asked Mr. Bateman whether what I had heard was true. He answered it was, impudently insinuating it was the charms of Mrs. Hickey (though perhaps unintentional on her part) that had occasioned such evident and unjust partiality to us. This was more than I could patiently submit to; a violent quarrel ensued in which I did not spare him, giving my opinion of his behaviour in the strongest language; from the best of friends we became inveterate enemies.

I thought it right, in consequence of what I had heard, to write to Mr. Des Roys to assure him I had never been out of my ship except the one day to dine on board the *Consolante*; to which letter I received an immediate and polite answer, lamenting that he had not the possibility of granting lodgings on shore to all the English passengers, and that he considered it cruel in Mr. Bateman to insult him because he so cautiously avoided partiality to any person.

The day after our entertainment on board the *Consolante*, Mrs. Hickey complained of violent headache, sickness at her stomach, with an acute pain in her back and limbs. I found, by the languor and quickness of her pulse, she had a considerable degree of fever. I therefore expressed my extreme uneasiness to Mr. L'Anglade, enquiring whether medical assistance was procurable. He answered they fortunately had a gentleman of the first-rate abilities, Mr. de Boissières, their surgeon-major, who had the Chief Superintendance of the hospital in which were a great number of sick and of badly wounded officers and private men; and he would write a note to request his immediate attendance. He accordingly did so; and, before noon, that gentleman came on board. He was a man of excellent address, with the appearance of a person of fashion. After seeing Mrs. Hickey, he told me her disorder was a bilious fever, then very prevalent, by which he had lost many people in the hospital; but, as he found no particularly bad symptom about her, and the disease was met at so early a stage, he trusted, and had little doubt, but he should be able to check its progress. He directly wrote a prescription, giving it to the surgeon of the *Consolante*. who was present, to make up. He stayed not only until Mrs. Hickey took it, but to see the effect, which having completely answered his wish he went on shore, saying he would return by five or six o'clock.

Upon his return in the evening, he appeared surprised and alarmed at the great increase of fever. He remained by her bedside the whole night, administering the medicines himself. Early in the morning he was obliged to attend some surgical operations at the hospital, but came to us again at eleven, bringing with him a Malay woman, one of Mrs. Vansenden's servants, to wait upon my poor invalid. This was a prodigious acquisition; for, although she spoke not a word of English, she perfectly understood attending a sick-chamber, was indefatigable in administering the different medicines to a minute as directed by the doctor, and in every other point attentive as the most assiduous European could have been. On the third morning, Mr. de Boissières told me he was under serious apprehensions; for, notwithstanding every medicine completely answered its object, still the fever did not yield in the least, preying so much upon the general system that she was visibly sinking; and, unless a favourable change took place before the following morning, of which he had scarce a hope, I must prepare for the worst. These were sad tidings, attached as I was to my revered companion. With an aching heart, I watched through another night without a glimmering of hope to cheer me. As long as her intellects remained perfect, she, in the most placid yet tender language, endeavoured to console me, assuring me she should do well, conjuring me not to fret and to take some rest. Although too evidently labouring under agonizing pain, she allowed no complaint, not even a sigh, to escape her, lest it should increase my misery.

Two more days passed in this manner, when she became delirious, whereupon Mr. de Boissières with great tenderness told me he feared a very few hours would finally close the scene. He, nevertheless, continued his exertions with the utmost assiduity and kindness. Anxious to watch any favourable moment that might offer, he directed the surgeon of the *Consolante* to attend the sick and wounded in the hospital, while he took his former station by my poor favourite's bedside, with his fingers upon her pulse administering restoratives as the vibrations fluttered through the day. In the evening. she lay in a state of torpidity. The doctor, however, said, as she still respired faintly, he would continue to apply stimulants as the forlorn hope. Every five or ten minutes, he poured a glass of red wine down her throat, so that by midnight she had swallowed a bottle and a half, then falling into a quiet slumber. Before morning she opened her eyes; when, looking earnestly towards me who was standing by her side, she feebly took hold of my hand and endeavoured, but in vain, to put it to her lips.

Mr. de Boissières having retired just before to get a little sleep, I instantly summoned him. The moment he saw and felt her pulse, he pronounced the crisis favourably past and that she was safe unless a relapse occurred, to avoid which she must be kept quite free from agitation or noise. The event confirmed his opinion; in four days, I had once more the supreme felicity to clasp my adored girl to my bosom, with no other remains of her disease than the languor and weakness consequent of so severe an attack in such a climate. To the very eminent abilities and unwearied attendance of Mr. de Boissières I certainly was indebted for the life of my Charlotte. This worthy and excellent man unfortunately took an active part in the abominable and bloody Revolution; to which he finally fell a sacrifice, being one of the many who fell under the stroke of the fatal and destructive guillotine in Paris.

By the 23rd, my dearest love being perfectly recovered, we again accepted an invitation of Captain Mallé's and dined on board the *Consolante*. The 24th, the Dutch Indiaman sailed with a cargo of rice for Cuddalore, which the French had also recently taken from us, aided by the native powers hostile to Great Britain, and where both garrison and inhabitants were in the utmost distress for food, the famine which raged along the coast of Coromandel having extended to that part of the country, making dreadful havoc among the wretched natives. On Christmas Day, signal was made from Osnaburgh Fort of the approach of two large ships; at ten in the morning, the *Vengeur*, a sixty-four, commanded by Captain Cuverville, and the *Pourvoyeuse*, a forty-four gun frigate, commanded by Captain Trommelin, anchored in the harbour, having left the remainder of Mr. Suffren's fleet at Acheen completing their stock of poultry and other necessaries.

Our steady and zealous friends of Trincomalee persisted in representing the harsh treatment the English passengers of the *Raynha de Portugal* had experienced from Mr. Des Roys, at which Mr. Cuverville seemed much hurt; as his rank in the Navy made him superior to Mr. Des Roys, he forthwith issued an order for our being allowed to go whithersoever we pleased, an order Monsieur Chevillard politely brought to us himself, conducting Mrs. Hickey and her Malay girl, who Mrs. Vansenden insisted should attend Mrs. Hickey while she remained at Trincomalee, myself and Nabob, in his own boat, to his house, if such a title could be applied to the wretched hovel. It had thentofore been the residence of a Dutch pilot, consisted of a hall, or centre apartment, having a small one at each corner, the walls quite bare, not even plastered, neither roof nor sides being watertight. Certainly, my poultry in Calcutta were far better lodged.

Such as it was, however, it was generously given. Two of the corner rooms were allotted to Mrs. Hickey and me. No such thing as gauze being procurable to make curtains of, and there being myriads of

13+

mosquitoes, some defence against the stings of those tormenting little insects was absolutely requisite. Our attentive host, therefore, caused two large English flags to be sewed together, which was fixed over our bed, answering the intended purpose but keeping us dreadfully hot. Although at the very edge of the sea, we scarcely ever got any fish, which I never could account for. Our richest dish at table was wild hog, a delicate, though high-flavoured, meat, of which we had great abundance. Captains Cuverville and Trommelin came to visit us as soon as their respective ships were moored. Both were men of family, the former about fifty years of age, the other quite young. Captain Cuverville was an uncommonly pleasing-mannered man, who soon became a favourite of Charlotte's, and not less so with me. Indeed, we should have been ungrateful had it been otherwise, as he always treated us with the most marked and polite attention.

On 1st January 1783, a large Dutch ship arrived from Malacca with a cargo of rice. On the 14th, the *Consolante* sailed for Point de Galle in order to bring back a similar cargo with the addition of some flour, she returning on 17th February accompanied by the *Apollo* frigate of thirty-six guns from Europe, having brought out a large quantity of marine stores for Suffren's fleet, also the *Naiade* frigate of twenty-six guns, likewise from France with dispatches for the French Admiral. On the 18th, the *Fortitude*, an English East Indiaman which had been captured in the Bay of Bengal by one of the French cruisers, came in, and the same evening arrived a large grab called the *Blake*, commanded by Captain Light, who afterwards became Governor of Prince of Wales's Island, or Pulo Penang. The *Blake* had been taken by an enemy's cruiser off the coast of Coromandel.

In the morning of the 20th, a signal was hoisted at Osnaburgh for an approaching fleet, and at eleven Admiral Suffren with his squadron entered the harbour, exhibiting a very grand spectacle. It consisted of the *Hero*, of seventy-four guns, on board of which his flag, as commander-in-chief, was flying, the *Hannibal*, a seventy-four, bearing the distinguishing flag of the Count de Bruyère, as second in command, the *Illustre*, seventy-four, with the broad pendant of the Count Adhemar, the *Ajax*, sixty-four, *Aristien*, sixty-four, *Sphynx*, sixty-four, *Flamand*, sixty-four, *Sevère*, sixty-four, the *Le Fin* frigate, thirty-two guns, the *Blandford*, an English East Indiaman (a prize), with two English brigs and two schooners, all captured at different times.

PRISONERS OF THE FRENCH

IMMEDIATELY after the fleet came to an anchor, I went off in Mr. Chevillard's boat to the *Hero* in order to pay my compliments to Mr. Suffren. Upon getting on board, I was shown into an apartment similar to what in our East Indiamen is called the cuddy, directly before the round house, where were already assembled several commanders and officers of the fleet, waiting for audience upon matters of duty. Upon my entering the cabin, an attendant asked my name, which giving he instantly went in to announce to the admiral, five minutes after which I was admitted to the after cabin where Mr. Suffren was sitting at a table, having a number of papers upon it which he appeared to be inspecting; his secretary, Mr. Launay, and other persons were writing at the same table. He received me with the most engaging attention and politeness, and, pointing to a chair, desired I would be seated until he finished some matters of business that required dispatch.

I apologized for my unseasonable intrusion, observing that, as I broke in upon him, I would take some other opportunity of paying my respects when he might be less occupied. With the utmost good humour, he said he should be at my service in a quarter of an hour and requested I would sit till then. Of course, I did so; and this afforded me an opportunity of observing his extraordinary dress and figure. In appearance, he looked much more like a little fat, vulgar English butcher than a Frenchman of consequence; in height, he was about five feet five inches, very corpulent, scarce any hair upon the crown of his head, the sides and back tolerably thick. Although quite grey, he wore neither powder nor pomatum, nor any curl, having a short cue of three or four inches tied with a piece of old spun yarn. He was in slippers, or, rather, a pair of old shoes, the straps being cut off, blue cloth breeches unbuttoned at the knees, cotton, or thread, stockings (none of the cleanest) hanging about his legs, no waistcoat or cravat, a coarse linen shirt, entirely wet with perspiration, open at the neck, the sleeves being rolled up above his elbows as if just going to wash his hands and arms. Indeed, I concluded in my own mind that he had

been broken in upon and interrupted whilst at his toilette, but afterwards ascertained that he always appeared as above described during
the morning.

Having quickly dispatched the business he was engaged in, he dismissed the gentlemen that had been employed upon it, when drawing
his chair close to mine, he apologized for having detained me so long.
He then made a number of enquiries relative to my situation in life,
the circumstances of my voyage from Europe, and so forth, observing
he believed the *Raynha de Portugal* must certainly be considered as
an undoubted seizable ship; nay, from Colonel Des Roys's statement
respecting her, which was one of the papers he had under consideration
when I entered, he conceived he must make a prize of her. I, thereupon, mentioned the manner in which myself and the other English
passengers had procured accommodation on board the ship at Lisbon,
and that we had so done under the perfect conviction that she was to
all intents and purposes a Portuguese.

To this he replied that, let the determination be what it might
respecting the ship and cargo, which he again said probably would be
a condemnation of both, it should not affect the British subjects on
board her; for, although he might, and perhaps ought, in strict justice,
in such case to consider and treat us as prisoners of war, he would not
treat us as such; on the contrary, he would give permission for us to
proceed to the places of our respective destinations by the earliest
opportunity that offered. He condescended also to express concern at
the situation Mrs. Hickey had been reduced to during the monsoon
gale, and how much his inclination led him to alleviate our sufferings
by every means within his power.

During my interview, several letters and messages were delivered to
him. Fearful, therefore, of trespassing I rose two or three times to
depart; but he each time made me resume my seat, saying he had yet
many things to enquire about. Our conversation then continued for
upwards of an hour, when the Count de Bruyère being announced, the
Admiral observed he must unwillingly break off our conference for
the present, as the Count came to speak upon official business. He
requested I would dine with him the following day, and come early,
as soon after twelve as I pleased, and we would have some further
conversation. He then wished me good morning, and I left the cabin.
In passing through the cuddy I saw, amongst a number of others, Mr.
Bateman, waiting in the hope of being introduced, but which I heard
he did not effect until two days after, to his extreme anger and
mortification.

At the commencement of my interview with Mr. Suffren, I spoke
English, having been informed he understood and spoke it a little.
He was, however, often at a loss for words to express what he wished

to say, at which he seemed rather impatient, saying in French, "Surely you understand something of French, which is in such general use in England." I answered that I understood it tolerably, but spoke it very badly. He replied he was certain we should do better with what I called my bad French than with the abominable, indeed unintelligible, English of his. From that time, we always conversed in his language; and he, like a true Frenchman, was pleased to pay me many compliments. His behaviour towards me was at all times exceedingly affable and pleasing.

In the afternoon, Mr. Barretto called to show me a letter he had written and intended sending to Mr. Suffren, wherein, after giving a circumstantial account of himself, of his ship, and the cargo on board, he begged to be honoured with a personal interview, when he had no doubt he should be able to satisfy his Excellency that no possible suspicion as to the neutrality of the vessel could remain upon his mind. This address, which struck me as being admirably well written, being sent to the admiral, an answer was immediately returned through the secretary, naming an early hour, the next morning but one, at which the admiral would receive him on board the *Hero*.

When I went on shore from my first visit to Mr. Suffren, I found several boats lying opposite Mr. Chevillard's house, all having poultry in them which had been sent from the *Hero* and other ships as more likely to thrive upon land than stuffed up thickly in coops on board. The whole of them had been laid in at Acheen, where fowls are uncommonly large and fine, the Malays being famous breeders. They were together in bundles of about a dozen, which being carried within the enclosure of Mr. Chevillard's premises, the strings with which each of their legs were tied was cut, and the bird set at liberty. The first use made of this was a general engagement, each fowl attacking his nearest neighbour with the utmost fury, thus fighting most desperately, sometimes changing antagonists, continuing the battle until so exhausted neither of the combatants had strength left to peck at each other, many of them actually falling down as if dying. It was a most ridiculous sight to see about a thousand pairs of fowls thus hostilely conducting themselves towards each other. The violence of the conflict was not entirely at an end for two days; on the third, however, profound peace prevailed; as if by general consent, they became reconciled, eating their rice and picking up the small gravel together with perfect amity.

The 21st, while sitting at breakfast, Mr. Launay called to say Mr. Suffren requested I would be on board by half-past eleven if not inconvenient, which I promised to attend to. Mr. Chevillard's house was now a constant scene of bustle and confusion, being crowded from morning to night with the officers and seamen on matters of business, a change far from agreeable to Mrs. Hickey and myself, both preferring the tranquillity and quiet we had thentofore enjoyed, with the society of half a dozen very worthy men. I had reason to think many of the persons made a pretence for coming, hoping to get a sight of the beautiful and accomplished Englishwoman; for under such description she had been represented. She could not stir from home without being overwhelmed with fulsome compliments.

At eleven I went off to the *Hero*, and was directly shown into the admiral's apartment, where I found him exactly in the same deshabille as on the preceding day. The conversation began by his telling me the *Raynha de Portugal* would be detained as a prize. He said he had fully investigated her case, in which he found so many strange and suspicious circumstances that he could not, without a dereliction of his duty, do otherwise than arrest her. I observed to th eadmiral that Mr. Barretto had requested me to accompany him on the morrow, at the time he was to be honoured with an audience respecting the rights he claimed as being neutral property, but that I had not accepted the call from an apprehension that he (Mr. Suffren) might deem it intrusive on my part; whereupon the admiral with great vivacity instantly answered, "Intrusive! by no means, Mr. Hickey! On the contrary, I am happy to hear that you are to be present, and I readily add my entreaties to those of Mr. Barretto that you will be so."

He then asked what was my opinion respecting his naval opponent, Sir Edward Hughes. "For," said he, "I have been very much astonished, Mr. Hickey, to hear several of your countrymen speak in cool, if not disrespectful, terms of that commander, whom I have always considered and found to be a brave, skilful, and in every respect a very able officer. It has been my fate to be opposed to him in three different, hard-contested battles, in every one of which Sir Edward Hughes, in my humble opinion, gave positive proofs that he possessed consummate skill and abilities, equal to any man's I have ever had to deal with in my profession. His manners and general conduct, too, has uniformly been that of a brave and gallant officer, blended with the mild and benevolent disposition of a truly philanthropic citizen of the world." And again he asked what were my sentiments respecting the English admiral.

I replied that I was by no means competent to give an opinion, being altogether unacquainted with his merits or demerits, but judging by the reports of the public prints his character with the people was that of being a diligent, zealous and gallant officer. "And such a character he surely is deserving of," said Mr. Suffren, "a braver man does not live. I, however, cannot but feel surprised that such a man as Sir Edward Hughes can submit to being controlled by a person every way to vastly inferior to him as is the Governor of Madras, Lord Macartney. You, Mr. Hickey, I presume, may have heard how much I have been blamed, nay stigmatized as deficient in humanity, for sending certain English prisoners to an ally of ours upon the coast of Coromandel. Now, sir, I should be glad to have your unbiassed sentiments upon the whole of this case.

"It stands thus: I left Europe with a strong and powerful squadron under my exclusive and sole orders, the objects of this expedition I was going upon being twofold: first, to prevent the British from getting possession of the Cape of Good Hope and, in the event of succeeding in that, then to proceed with all dispatch to the coast of Coromandel, there to land a body of men to aid the exertions of our zealous Asiatic ally, Hyder Ally. Having been hurried away from France without near sufficient water for my people, it became necessary to stop for a supply; for which purpose I intended to put into one of the Canary or Cape de Verde Islands. Unfortunately for me, I decided upon Port Praya Bay, as being the best to obtain a speedy supply of that article at. Upon running for the harbour, I was astonished and vexed to perceive a British fleet riding at anchor; vexed because I felt the probability that thus unexpectedly falling in with the enemy might seriously interfere with, if not totally derange, all my plans. My surprise was not a little increased when I saw a British commodore's distinguishing flag flying at the masthead of the innermost ship, with a number of pendants around him, a forest of masts of merchantmen lying unprotected and exposed towards the mouth of the harbour.

"Such a spectacle (as novel as unaccountable) struck me forcibly. I at once knew it must be the squadron of Commodore Johnston, who I was going out to counteract the measures of; but how to account for a seaman's taking such a berth as Mr. Johnston had, leaving his convoy liable to be partially cut off or destroyed, in any other manner than from a wish to take the utmost care of himself, I knew not. I therefore resolved, notwithstanding a great superiority of the British ships, immediately to bring them to action. I, for that purpose, made the *Hannibal's* signal to lead in, run close alongside the commodore and engage. This order the Count de Bruyère executed in a style that covered him with glory. I seconded him by attacking two of the enemy's line-of-battle ships. Had all my captains done their duty with the same ardour the *Hannibal* and *Hero* did, it would have proved a woeful day for England! Suffice it to say, very different was the case. Three of the commanders for ever disgraced themselves, involving therein the noble families to which they were allied. These poltroons hung back and never brought their ships within gunshot of the enemy. The consequence was, after a conflict unparalleled in history, in which the *Hannibal* and the *Hero* sustained a galling fire from the whole of the British line for two hours, both were so crippled, especially the *Hannibal*, which was reduced to an ungovernable hulk, having lost all her masts, that I was under the afflicting necessity of ordering my ships off, not, however, until we had treated the English commodore and his squadron so roughly that he permitted me, damaged as I was, to tow the shattered *Hannibal* from the midst of them.

"Having got clear out of the harbour, I resolved to proceed without loss of time to the Cape, to which place I was aware the British squadron were bound. Willing for form's sake to have the sanction of those who served under me, I forthwith summoned all commanders to attend a council of war on board the *Hero*, when communicating my future intentions, the Counts de Bruyère and Adhemar alone agreed to the propriety of such intentions, the rest pronouncing my object impracticable and unjustifiably wild and chimerical. Two of the dastardly captains in particular said they could not proceed, not having water for more than twenty days; besides which, the state of the *Hannibal* made it impossible to go on unless I proposed sacrificing that ship altogether.

"I replied that I had no such intention; so far from it, I looked with confidence to the future services and assistance of the *Hannibal*, her gallant captain and crew, to aid me in the effecting the important plans I had in view. I further declared that the *Hannibal* must and should be new rigged at sea; and, as to water, those ships that had the smallest quantity should receive a proportion from others that had more, and an equal partition take place. If the entire quantity in the fleet would not afford a quart per day for each man, they must content themselves with a pint, nay, with half a pint; for to the Cape I certainly would go with the utmost dispatch. Those who had proved themselves poltroons in the battle were the most violent opponents of my wishes; but I regarded them not. The *Illustre* took the *Hannibal* in tow; every carpenter of the fleet was employed making lower masts, and such was their zeal and industry, as well as that of every seaman, that in eight days, although in boisterous weather, upon a turbulent ocean, she was as completely new-masted and rigged as if in Brest or any other harbour. I thus accomplished my purpose, reached the Cape in safety, and thereby defeated the object of Mr. Johnston and his large force, compelling him to be content with capturing or destroying a few empty vessels he found at anchor in Saldanha Bay.

"I then proceeded to India, where I had the mortification to find that Pondicherry, our chief settlement upon the coast of Coromandel, was in the hands of the enemy, Trincomalee, where we are now conversing, the same; so that I had no port into which I could put for repairs, for provisions, or upon any account whatever nearer than Mauritius. Sir Edward Hughes, with his fleet of nine line-of-battle ships, all in the completest state and fully manned, lay off Madras; I had eleven, several of them exceedingly leaky and in want of stores, and so weak, from the sad number of hands we lost at Port Praya, I could scarcely manoeuvre my ships. I, nevertheless, determined to steer for and engage Sir Edward. I did so; and, although no vessel was taken on either side, I reduced the British squadron to such distress as to be incapable of committing further hostilities for some time. Had not three of my captains betrayed their base cowardice, I should have obtained a decisive victory. I treated those villains, those traitors to their sovereign and their country, as they deserved by dispatching them with ignominy and disgrace to France!

"After running over to Sumatra for a few days, refitting and watering there, I again went to sea, scouring the Bay of Bengal and Indian Seas in every direction, and taking so many prizes that my fleet for many weeks actually subsisted upon the provisions obtained from them. A number of prisoners consequently were on board my ships, who from the peculiarity of my situation became a serious evil, as I was at a loss how to feed them. As I knew the English had a number of French prisoners, I addressed a letter to Sir Edward Hughes, proposing an immediate exchange. An answer was given in the politest and most benevolent terms, highly respectful and pleasing to myself as an individual. Sir Edward, however, avowed his inability to accede to my well-intended proposal, much as he wished for humanity's sake that it should be carried into effect, but that the exchange of prisoners rested exclusively with Lord Macartney, the Governor of Madras, to whom he therefore begged leave to refer me.

"Upon receipt of this information, I, without an hour's delay, addressed Lord Macartney upon the subject. This arrogant lord deigned not to give any sort of answer. My prisoners increasing by further captures, I again wrote to his Lordship, and again was insulted by his insolent and rude silence. Distressed beyond measure, I addressed the British admiral from whom I directly received an answer that did honour to his feelings as a man, but still lamenting his want of power to promote my humane object. By this time the evil was become so great that I once more, in the most forcible language, depicted to Sir Edward Hughes the forlorn state I was reduced to, and that if a cartel was not forthwith established I should be under the disagreeable necessity of delivering up the prisoners to Tippoo Sultaun, the only asiatic prince in alliance with my country. Having been twice treated with contumely by Lord Macartney, I particularly desired no further reference might be made to him whom I considered deficient in common good manners, and who had behaved towards me with a rudeness and impertinence unprecedented between gentlemen.

"The British admiral, for the third time, lamented his want of power to treat for an exchange in most pathetic terms, entreating that I would not adopt the measure I threatened of sending my prisoners to Tippoo,

13*

as he feared such a step would be worse than condemning the unfortunate men to death. To this I replied that I had no alternative; that I was sincerely desirous to avoid doing what he so feelingly deprecated, and would therefore (seriously inconvenient and distressing as it was) wait three days more for a definitive and, I trusted, favourable answer ere I dispatched the poor people, whose fate I deplored as much as he could; and, if ultimately driven to the necessity of delivering them over to Tippoo Sultaun, I would use every precaution in my power to avert the melancholy event he seemed to apprehend by securing for them humane and liberal treatment. I was given to understand that the admiral submitted my various representations to Lord Macartney without any effect, and thus was compelled to send several hundred English seamen and soldiers to Tippoo Sultaun; but, previous to so doing, I exacted from that prince's agent the most sacred and positive assurances that they should be humanely treated and exchanged at the earliest opportunity. For this, on my part, unavoidable measure I have been stigmatized, abused in the grossest terms, as void of humanity or feeling, as a savage wretch that ought to be scouted from all society. My character was thus attempted to be blasted with every approbrious epithet attached to my name. And yet, with how little justice was all this done. For let me ask you, Mr. Hickey, as a candid, unprejudiced person, what could I do?

"I have already told you how peculiarly I was situated, without a single port to receive and assist me on either side of India; without any other native friendly prince than Tippoo Sultaun; in actual distress for want of provisions, fresh or salt; with between four and five hundred prisoners distributed through my fleet, and increasing my difficulties by what they necessarily consumed. I exerted my strenuous endeavours without intermission to effect an exchange, and on my part would have done it upon any terms, however unfavourable to the nation I had the honour to represent. But all these endeavours failed; I could no longer keep the prisoners on board my ships; I could not send them to the Mauritius, having neither transports or vessels fit to convey them; and, indeed, if I had, I was conscious it would only have been throwing the weight off my own shoulders to place it upon the Governor and inhabitants of Mauritius; for, both at that island and at Bourbon, the most dreadful scarcity prevailed; the people were almost starved. It would have been unreasonable in the extreme to suppose that I was to set at liberty near five hundred, the greater part able seamen; common justice to my sovereign forbade such a measure! What then remained for me but to do as I did, previously taking every precaution that prudence and foresight could suggest to secure to the said prisoners humane and proper treatment? If Tippoo Sultaun, or those serving under him, broke their faith in this particular, why am I to be so blamed, why is the whole odium to be thrown upon me? I cannot, I declare on my honour, I cannot see the least show of justice in such conduct."

In this manner did Mr. Suffren express himself to me; nor could I do otherwise than give him credit for the force of his argument; and, although the barbarity with which the unfortunate people were treated, many of whom were actually murdered, must ever be lamented, I am free to say I cannot see the justice of attempting to fix the odium entirely and exclusively upon Admiral Suffren! Upon this subject he always spoke with great warmth; and I could plainly perceive it preyed upon his mind; yet he invariably insisted the English did not treat him with their natural liberality upon the occasion.

He had but just concluded the above narrative when dinner was announced; whereupon he retired to his state room, from whence he, in five minutes, returned, dressed in a blue jacket of thin coast cloth, his short collar buttoned, with a black stock on. He had also pulled up his stockings, buttoned his breeches' knees, and put on shoes instead of slippers. He then conducted me down his private staircase into the cabin below, where about forty gentlemen were assembled, among whom were the Counts de Bruyère and Adhemar. Mr. Suffren seated me on his right hand, a place I made an attempt to give up to the Count de Bruyère, who positively refused; and Mr. Suffren said, "Come, come! I must have you next me on one side or the other." The table was tolerably supplied, and we had as fine bread as ever I saw on shore, the wines light, but well flavoured, a very coarse table-cloth, not over clean, the knives, forks, etc., rough in the extreme. The admiral ate voraciously, more than once remarking to me that the heat of the climate did not take away his appetite, "though," he added, "I have often, with a very keen one, been reduced to a musty biscuit, full of vermin, with a small bit of stinking salt pork, as my only sustenance during the twenty-four hours. However, sir, I make it a rule always to conform to the circumstances of the day, be they as they may, good or bad; a military man is ever liable to hard rubs and ought to be prepared to meet them with fortitude and resignation."

Just after we sat down to dinner, the arrival of the little *Hannibal* was announced. This was an English fifty-gun ship taken by Mr. Suffren on his way to India. On board this ship, at the time of her being captured, was my London friend, Major George Russell, who left England with Robert Pott and Emily; but, whilst laying at St. Helena, the *Hannibal* touched there; and Major Russell being intimate with her commander, he offered to take him on to Madras, by which he would in all probability save at least a month. The major, therefore, removed to the *Hannibal*, which off the Cape unluckily fell in with Suffren's squadron in the night and was taken. Being a good sailer, Mr.

Suffren in a few days dispatched her as an avant courier to announce his approach at Mauritius. While upon the voyage, she fell in with a Danish Indiaman bound to Tranquebar, and Major Russell, obtaining the French captain's leave, after giving his parole not to serve until exchanged, went on board the Dane; otherwise we should have met at Trincomalee.

With the little *Hannibal* there also came in the *Coventry*, an English frigate of thirty-two guns, which had been captured some time before by a French seventy-four. Captain Wolseley, who commanded her at the time, had been sent to Mauritius, but left that island in the little *Hannibal.* He immediately came on board the *Hero* and was very politely received by Mr. Suffren. After dinner, coffee was served and then the *chasse café,* or liqueurs, when the party broke up. As I was passing through the steerage, along the main deck, I beheld such a scene of filth and dirt as I could not have believed had I not seen; it had more the appearance of an abominable pigsty than the inside of a ship of the line bearing an admiral's flag; and this was very much the case with all the fleet except two, the *Vangeur* and *Flamand*, both of which were as neat and clean as any British ship of war.

After stopping a few minutes to speak to one of the officers, I went up to the quarterdeck where the admiral was. He told me he was going on shore to take his evening's walk, which he never failed doing when in port. I was rather surprised at not seeing any preparation making, and still more at an uncouth figure, covered with pitch and tar, coming up to him and without the least ceremony saying, "the boat is ready." This person I found was the boatswain. The admiral then wished me a good evening, saying, "I should have offered you a passage on shore in my boat, small as it is, but that I see Chevillard's smart pinnace coming for you." Although very corpulent and heavy, he went down the ship's side by a single common rope as quick and light as any midshipman could have done, without a man at the side; and, seating himself in the stern sheets of the jolly-boat, took the helm, pushed off; and four young lads rowed him ashore.

I could not help expressing my astonishment at the scene, where-upon I was informed the general never left the ship in any other manner, unless upon occasions of state or ceremony, when he reluctantly yielded to custom. The boatswain was his factotum; nor did he ever apply to any other person for anything he wanted himself. With all his exterior roughness, he possessed the insinuating and elegant address of a French man of fashion; and, as a proof of attention to the fair sex, he had, without saying a word to me, ordered into his jolly-boat some papers of chocolate, liqueurs, China sweetmeats, and Acheen fruits, especially the delicious mangosteen, of which, though extremely difficult to keep beyond a few days, he had contrived to preserve some dozens in high preservation. These little articles of real luxury in our situation he, in person, presented to Mrs. Hickey, paying her many handsome compliments at the same time. He had but just left Mr. Chevillard's house when I reached it.

The universal attention and respect with which I and my dear Charlotte were treated raised the envy and spleen of Mr. Bateman to so great a degree that he began to slander us both, circulating some anecdotes as having occurred at Lisbon, which he imagined would lower us in the opinions of the French gentlemen. This ill-temper was further increased at finding a quite contrary effect to what he intended; his illiberality and the motive was seen through and only added to his own disgrace. His behaviour, however, being communicated to me, I gave him my opinion upon such base conduct in very pointed terms.

At noon, Mr. Barretto called, and we embarked together for the *Hero*. Upon getting on board we were immediately conducted into the admiral's apartment. Mr. Barretto, after producing the only two documents saved from the general havoc made by the storm, related every particular relative to his ship that had occurred from the time of his arrival at Lisbon until his departure from thence and putting into Trincomalee in the utmost distress. He concluded his narrative with an earnest desire that Mr. Suffren would issue an order for the ship's release that he (Barretto) might get her refitted for sea and conclude a voyage that had already proved so unfortunate. Mr. Suffren heard him with the utmost patient attention, nor once interrupted him; but, when his story was finished, he thus addressed him: "Mr. Barretto, I have duly weighed and considered every circumstance you have mentioned with the strongest inclination to put a favourable construction upon your case and comply with your desire, were it possible; but the facts are so clear, the proofs so strong and damning, that I cannot do otherwise than retain the ship, and, as far as I am empowered, condemn her as a legal prize, subject, of course, to the further and future consideration of the High Court of Admiralty at Paris." Mr. Barretto, upon hearing this unexpected determination as to his property, said, "May I, sir, request to know what are those 'facts' and 'proofs,' as you are pleased to call them, and which you consider so clear and damning?"

"Most freely," replied Mr. Suffren, "and I will unequivocally state them. Your ship is of British construction, built in a British port, and sold, as alleged, to a subject of a neutral power, but, after the declaration of war between France and Great Britain, fitted out at Bombay; from whence she sailed for Lisbon, where you put on board a cargo, not of Portuguese merchandise, but consisting entirely of staple articles of England, such as lead, iron, copper, canvas, and other marine stores. Yourself born and bred under the British flag at Bombay, and so conscious of your being a subject of that nation that, though calling yourself a Portuguese, you deemed it requisite to obtain a naturalization at Lisbon. With your English cargo you depart from Lisbon for Madras, another English settlement."

Mr. Barretto here interrupted the admiral, saying, "You are mistaken, sir, in some of your assumed facts. There are no other marine or naval stores on board; the cargo, as specified by you, undoubtedly was manufactured in England; but I purchased the whole in the city of Lisbon from Portuguese merchants and out of their warehouses, as I surely had a right to do. Equally incorrect are you in asserting that I was bound to an English settlement. I was not, sir; Goa was the place of my destination, as my papers should distinctly have shown but for the act of providence, and their destruction deprives me of my written evidence."

Mr. Barretto here ceasing to speak, the admiral resumed, "This act of divine providence I sincerely lament, Mr. Barretto, and have no doubt that misfortune alone deprived you of the usual papers; but there is yet more. You have English passengers on board, and with one exception, no other. I must repeat, too, you was bound to Madras. Otherwise (unless going to Bengal) what business could you have off Hog Island upon the coast of Sumatra, that of Malabar being, as you pretend, your destination?"

Mr. Barretto again interrupted Mr. Suffren to declare upon his honour that, however strange it might appear, such was the truth, and he could only lament the superlative ignorance of his navigator. Mr. Suffren said, with more warmth of manner than he had yet shown, "Fie, sir, fie, I blush to hear you! Can you for a moment suppose it possible that there is a person to be found who knows anything of seamanship that can, or will, believe so wild a circumstance could occur, as that of a ship under the management and direction of Europeans, bound to Goa, upon the coast of Malabar, making the land off Sumatra? Indeed, indeed, Mr. Barretto, it is too absurd; the deception is too palpable!"

Mr. Barretto renewed his protestations that such was the fact, however incredible. Mr. Suffren continued, "Were further proofs required I have them within my power, Mr. Barretto, from the unbiassed mouth of one of your own officers, who has voluntarily assured me that both ship and cargo are exclusively and entirely English property." This the admiral had learnt from the cowardly scoundrel of a second mate, who, in consequence of Mr. Barretto's upbraiding him for abandoning his post and his duty in the hour of danger, declaring he would publish his base conduct in Portugal, had adopted that mode of revenge.

Mr. Suffren ended by expressing his deep concern that so heavy a loss was likely to fall upon him (Barretto) individually and was proceeding in a strain of commiseration when Mr. Barretto very abruptly stopped him, saying, "Don't, Mr. Suffren, give yourself the trouble of bestowing your pity upon me, as useless as it is void of all sincerity; nor need you take so roundabout a way to disguise the truth or in a fruitless attempt to gloss over your tyrannical and unjust treatment of me. I can, without hesitation, account for the motive that influences you to commit what I can consider in no other light than a direct and absolute robbery, and a positive breach and infringement of the law of nations. Thus, sir, stands the facts. You see my ship, torn to pieces as she is, still a noble vessel, capable of being easily converted into a powerful vessel of war; you know that she has an immensely valuable cargo on board, which you are desirous of laying hands upon, right or wrong. In short, you want both ship and cargo, and, having no means of purchasing or paying for either the one or the other, avail yourself of the strong arm of power cruelly and unjustly to deprive me of my property."

This speech, delivered with the utmost gravity and composure, I conceived would have highly irritated and offended the gallant admiral; instead of which, he betrayed not the slightest symptom of anger, but with a smile upon his countenance mildly replied, "From my soul I wish, Mr. Barretto, I wish that you may be able to establish what you say, because in that case you would obtain ample restitution from my Court." Here the conference broke up; we got into our boat to return on shore and, while on our way, had the mortification to see the Portuguese flag, which had till then been flying, hauled down, and a French one hoisted in its stead.*

The unfortunate Frenchman of whom I have already spoken, who received the injury upon his shin in helping to throw the guns overboard during the hurricane, continued his own remedy or mode of treating the wound for some time after we got into Trincomalee, daily applying brandy, vinegar and brown paper. At the time of Mr. Suffren's arrival, the sore had put on a very serious appearance; the flesh around it became greatly inflamed attended with much pain. As I saw him almost daily, and found it likely serious consequences might arise from further neglect, I strongly urged him to apply to Mr. de Boissières, the surgeon major, which he most obstinately refused to do. Towards the end of the month of January, Mr. Brown, my shipmate, told me he had just seen the Frenchman's leg and had no doubt a mortification would soon take place. I thereupon immediately went to Mr. de Boissières' quarters and mentioned the circumstance to him, who

---

* Returning to Europe as soon as he recovered his liberty, Barretto obtained a certificate from the Marquis de Pombal that his vessel was *bona fide* Portuguese and, thereupon, instituted a suit against Suffren in the Admiralty Court of Paris. This action failed; as did his subsequent attempt to extract eighty thousand pounds from certain English underwriters. Nevertheless, we are told, Barretto accumulated a second fortune and, several years afterwards, died a rich man.

instantly went to the Frenchman's room, who very unwillingly showed the wound; upon examining which, Mr. De Boissières at once pronounced it to be a fatal case; that nothing could preserve the man's life but amputation of the limb, and that without further loss of time, there being certain symptoms of gangrene. He, however, dressed the sore, saying he would call again with other surgeons. He accordingly did so in the evening with two of the medical gentlemen, who, upon taking off the bandage, declared a mortification had already commenced, and they prepared their instruments to perform amputation.

The poor man, upon being told this, at once, and in the most decided manner, refused to submit to the operation. Being informed death must ensue, he with the utmost composure said, "Be it so. Since I was fifteen years of age I have been a soldier of fortune, a wanderer over every quarter of the globe, enduring every degree of hardship and bodily suffering that ever man encountered. Such must still be my fate. What then should I do deprived of a limb? Far better for me to leave the world than live so mutilated and rendered incapable of following my profession." This absurd reasoning Mr. de Boissières met and answered with great good sense and judgment, but all in vain; the self-devoted victim resolutely adhered to his determination. The surgeons, with the most assiduous attention, continued to exert their skill to save life and limb, but without success. In two days the wretched man expired.

I have already mentioned the high estimation Mrs. Hickey was held in by the gentlemen of both army and navy, especially by the latter, she and I greatly preferring them to the military as assimilating more with our dispositions and possessing a degree of plain, straightforward integrity, more congenial to us than the perpetual ribaldry and offensive gasconade so prevalent in the French military officers. It may easily be imagined that, amongst so numerous a body, we found several disagreeable coxcombs. Some of these soon began to address anonymous love letters to my Charlotte, which I would have let pass with the silent contempt they deserved, had I not perceived they annoyed her so much as to affect her health; and she daily urged me to prevail upon the admiral to let us depart. I, therefore, addressed the following letter to Mr. Suffren:

"Sir,

Although I am exceedingly unwilling to trespass upon your time, which I am aware must be fully occupied in matters of importance, yet the happiness of a most deserving wife leads me, sir, to entreat your attention for a moment. Our situation here, from various causes, is become extremely irksome and unpleasant, added to which the precarious state of Mrs. Hickey's health makes us both anxious to reach our destination. Upon her account solely I went to Lisbon to procure a passage from thence to India in a Portuguese ship. After waiting in that capital five tedious months we unfortunately embarked on board the *Raynha de Portugal*. A wretched and most disastrous voyage terminated by putting into this place, where we have now been upwards of three months. Mr. Chevillard, our host, has uniformly treated us with a degree of politeness and hospitality I fear rarely equalled, certainly impossible to be surpassed. The nature of the post he fills has, since the arrival of your fleet, kept him employed abroad almost the entire day, and to a gentleman of your experience and knowledge of the world it is scarcely necessary to observe that during the absence of the master a house is by no means the same or so well regulated as when he is present. Mrs. Hickey flattered herself, sir, that upon your Excellency's arrival we should almost immediately have been sent to the coast of Coromandel. Every day drags heavily on, and the continued detention preys upon her spirits, her health being affected by the uncertainty as to when any opportunity may occur for our departure. Will you then, sir, with your usual humane attention, and for her gratification, inform me when you imagine it likely that an opportunity will present itself for our getting away, as it will be some alleviation to her misery to have a period ascertained for the termination of our distresses. Once more entreating your pardon for the liberty I have taken,

  I have the honour to remain,

    Your Excellency's most obedient and most humble servant,

              W. HICKEY."

To this letter I received a very handsome and condescending answer from Mr. De Launay, the admiral's secretary, written by the latter's special direction, in which he assured me the earliest opportunity that offered should be embraced, the admiral very sensibly feeling for the disagreeable situation Mrs. Hickey must necessarily be in, and which he was earnestly desirous to put an end to by enabling us to proceed to a British settlement.

25

EN ROUTE FOR CALCUTTA

O N the 8th the *Cleopatra*, of forty-four guns, came in, having left General de Bussy the preceding day. The morning of the 9th a fleet appeared in the offing; and at one in the afternoon the *Fendant*, of seventy-four guns, bearing General de Bussy's flag at the maintop gallant masthead, the *Hardi*, also a seventy-four, and the *Argonaut*, of sixty-four, with thirty-eight transports, having the German regiment of the Prince Le Marque and other Europeans to the amount of two thousand five hundred on board and three hundred Caffrees, came to an anchor in the harbour. I directly went off to the *Hero* for the purpose of requesting the admiral (who had desired I never would scruple applying to him in person when I saw occasion) to bear me and by misfortunes in recollection and to mention the situation I was in to General de Bussy.

I found Mr. Suffren oppressed by heat, sweltering under a heavy laced uniform suit of clothes, which, however, in no way affected his temper or his customary kind manner. He, in his usual polite terms, assured me he should take the earliest occasion of mentioning my peculiarly hard case to the Count de Bussy, upon whom the chief command of both navy and army devolved. He then good-humouredly began to talk of himself, facetiously observing that he felt like a hog in armour; for so long a period had elapsed since he had been obliged to dress otherways than in the lightest and thinnest clothing that he was really uncomfortable; but etiquette required his waiting upon the Commander-in-Chief properly equipped, even at the expense of his feelings.

At five o'clock the same afternoon, Mr. Chevillard received a note from Mr. Launay, wherein, after speaking of some official business, he added that, should Mr. Hickey be disengaged, the admiral wished to see him. I therefore went off directly; when he told me several ships would be dispatched to Cuddalore in a few days, and I had better apply to Monsieur le comte de Bussy for permission to embark on one of them. I accordingly, on the following morning, being the 10th of the month, proceeded to the *Fendant*, where, after waiting about half an hour, I was introduced to the comte, who upon being told the object of my visit, expressed his concern that I should have had the trouble of coming on board, especially as what I required rested entirely with Mr. Suffren, that general having the entire and sole management of everything relative to the marine.

From the *Fendant* I went to the *Hero*. I found the admiral reading some papers he had just received from Monsieur de Bussy, with which he appeared highly pleased. He put one of them into my hand, desiring me to peruse it. I found it to be a letter from Mr. de Bussy, written in very complimentary terms. After bestowing great panegyrics upon his conduct in the command of the fleet, he entreated that he would continue to exercise his own superior judgment in all matters respecting the ships without any reference to him, as nothing should induce him ever to interfere in any maritime points. The admiral then told me he thought the transports might be watered in a couple of days; after which they, with a part of his squadron, would sail for the coast; and, sending for Mr. Launay, he directed him to take particular care that Mrs. Hickey and I were accommodated in the best way circumstances would admit of.

The 11th, I dined by invitation on board the *Hero*, where the admiral gave an entertainment to Mr. de Bussy and his suite. Upon my entering the cabin, he very civilly enquired after Mrs. Hickey's health, congratulating us both upon the prospect there was of our being at last released from all our difficulties. He observed that a circumstance had occurred that morning which made it impossible for him to tell me the precise day the detachment would depart; but, as it would probably take place very suddenly, it would be prudent to hold ourselves in constant readiness. I assured him we were, and should continue, prepared to embark at the moment we should be summoned. The 12th I went round to the various gentlemen from whom we had received the utmost kindness and attention, to express my own and Mrs. Hickey's grateful sense of their goodness, for which we returned our heartfelt thanks, and took our leave of most of them for ever.

In the evening, many of the captains, with the Prince Le Marque and his staff, assembled at Mr. Chevillard's, where many unsuccessful efforts to be merry were made and, without actually knowing why, the party sunk into silence and dejection. Mrs. Hickey and myself were sincerely affected at the thoughts of parting with several friends who had treated us with unexampled liberality; and those of that description who were present seemed equally to lament the thoughts of a separation from us. We were at length relieved from this state of melancholy by the entrance of Captain Duchillon of the *Sphynx*, a lively, facetious man, whose common boast used to be that he knew not what sorrow was, and that he never allowed the caprices and changes of that fickle dame, Madam Fortune, to lower his spirits or cause him one moment's uneasiness. Observing the company were not so cheerful as he expected, and guessing at the cause, he good-humouredly said, "I think it is highly probable we shall speedily meet again with these our agreeable and deservedly esteemed English friends, as Madras you know, comrades, must soon be in our possession, I trust previous to their having quitted it. But, should that not be the case, it cannot be long ere we renew the intimacy with them in Bengal, where (addressing himself to me) your old friend, Monsieur Suffren, with Monsieur de Bussy, and a few thousand followers meditate paying their respects."

This facetious gasconade created a general laugh; and, though said in joke, I really, from all I had heard and seen, feared there was too much foundation for. After supper, upon the party's separating, Captain Duchillon saluted Mrs. Hickey, and with unaffected warmth wished her health and happiness. Then, shaking me cordially by the hand, he said, "Adieu, my respected, although lately acquired, friend; and let me request, as you will in a few days see Lord Macartney, to tell him that his old acquaintance Duchillon desired his best remembrances to him; and that, as he has already had the honour of conveying him from his government of Grenada in the West, so he hopes very shortly to convey him to France from his government in the East."

I promised the rattling captain that I would take the earliest opportunity of delivering his civil message to his Lordship. Just at the moment we were parting, three guns were fired from the admiral's ship and, soon after, four more, which I was informed were signals for certain ships to unmoor; a few minutes after which, I received a letter from Mr. Launay desiring me instantly to go on board the *Blake*, the commander of which had instructions to receive me and Mrs. Hickey. At eleven at night, we accordingly left Mr. Chevillard's house, that gentleman being so occupied in dispatching the squadron that I had no opportunity of thanking him in person for the extraordinary generosity and kindness with which he had entertained us. I was, therefore, reduced to the necessity of doing so by letter. Captain Wolseley insisted upon attending us to the *Blake*, where he assisted in arranging everything for us in our cabin. Our baggage did not give us much trouble, having only a few changes of linen, for which, as already observed, we were indebted to our disinterested friends' generosity at Trincomalee.

Early in the morning of 13th March 1783, we got under way, as did the *Hero*, bearing the admiral's flag, the *Fendant* with General de Bussy's, the *St. Michael*, *Artisien*, *Sphynx*, *Petit Hannibal*, *Cleopatra*,

Fortune, Bellona, Coventry, Naiade, and fourteen transports containing the whole of the European troops and stores. As Cuddalore was only a short distance from Ceylon, and nearly in the same meridian, I was surprised to find the fleet steering east-north-east. I afterwards learnt the reason of this was an apprehension of falling in with the British under Sir Edward Hughes, then supposed to be on their way from Bombay to Madras. Had the English admiral been lucky enough to have met the enemy, the whole squadron, with more than two thousand of the military, must inevitably have been captured. After standing off the greater part of the night, they altered their course to north. Early in the morning of the 15th, the fleet came to an anchor in Cuddalore Roads, where the weather being moderate, and little surf before three in the afternoon, the whole of the troops were landed.

Mr. Boissières having given me a letter of introduction to the French surgeon major, I went on shore in search of him, where I was told he resided about two miles from the fort inland. I therefore walked out to his house through a burning sun, and on the way passed the skirts of a camp of Tippoo's, where a number of ferocious-looking fellows eyed me in such a manner as to create considerable alarm in my mind. I, however, reached my destination in safety, where Mr. Panchemin received me very politely. After making me drink a large glass of negus, which I stood in need of, being greatly fatigued and exhausted, he procured a native carriage drawn by a pair of bullocks, in which he accompanied me back to Cuddalore for the purpose of taking Mrs. Hickey to his house. He insisted upon going on board the *Blake* with me, which he did, conveyed Mrs. Hickey on shore, and in the cool of the evening all three went out to his pleasant mansion, where a plentiful repast of well-dressed curry and pilau awaited us, to which we did ample justice. Our host showed us into a spacious bedchamber, but without window frames, all the woodwork having been torn out by Tippoo's people to light their fires and cook their victuals.

The following morning, upon conversing with Mr. Panchemin respecting the means of getting on to Madras, I had the mortification to hear it was impracticable for a European, particularly a female, to travel by land, the entire country being covered with banditti, called *looties*, who lived by plunder, sparing neither age nor sex, friend nor foe, and who would certainly, after robbing, put us to death, as they did to all those who were unlucky enough to meet them. Equally difficult was it to proceed by sea, not one of the French fleet intending to go further to the northward than Cuddalore, from whence they were all to return to Trincomalee. Thus circumstanced, I thought we should be under the disagreeable necessity of going back to our former station. On the 16th, I went to the fort of Cuddalore to pay my compliments to General de Bussy; but he was so deeply engaged in business

I could not see him. He, however, sent an aide-de-camp to apologize for not admitting me and to request I would dine with him. I accordingly went and was not a little surprised to meet there my shipmate, Mr. Bateman, of whom I took not the least notice. Upon enquiry, I found that Colonel Des Roys had interested himself on Bateman's behalf, and by a personal application to Mr. Suffren had obtained permission for him to leave Trincomalee upon any vessel in which he could get a passage; and he had prevailed upon the commander of the *Artisien* to receive him on board, an act of kindness that availed nothing; for, not being able to proceed to the coast, he was compelled to return with Mr. Suffren's squadron to Trincomalee.

The 18th, the *Coventry* brought into the roads a large ship under Prussian colours, which upon coming to an anchor was observed to lay with a great heel. The *Coventry* had detained her, upon finding from her journal or log book that she had been at Tranquebar, from which place she had taken several English officers on board and was proceeding with them to Madras. General de Bussy and Admiral Suffren conferred together respecting this vessel; after which, the admiral sent for me to tell me the Prussian was from Europe, and in his opinion under very suspicious circumstances, so much so that, were he to be governed by his own opinion and sentiments, he certainly would have kept her, at least until he had an opportunity of further investigation into her legality; but that General de Bussy, always disposed to more lenient measures than he was, and wishing to act with moderation, did not consider himself justified in detaining her, as eventually she might be pronounced neutral property, and he could not deem her having a few English passengers a cause for seizing her. Mr. Suffren then continued, "I am glad on your account, Mr. Hickey, that this has happened, as it will afford an opportunity for you to get to one of your settlements. Go, therefore, immediately on board and arrange matters for your departure, as I shall release her directly."

The boat I had gone off in leaking dreadfully, the men in her refused to take me to the Prussian, saying she lay so far out, where there was so much sea running, they should not be able to keep her afloat. I was consequently obliged to return on shore in search of another; which having procured, I put off and had nearly passed the surf when three seamen hailed, entreating with great earnestness that I would give them a cast to the *Hero*, being already beyond their time of absence and no other boat to be got. I felt myself under too many obligations to several of their countrymen not to comply with their request. I, therefore, instantly re-passed the surf and took them in. They were all stout, well-looking fellows, expressing their thanks in very complimentary terms. Whilst in the boat, I asked them some questions about the different sea-fights between their fleet and ours, and what they thought of their admiral, Monsieur Suffren; whereupon they all spoke together with great volubility, giving such a panegyrical character of Mr. Suffren as must have highly gratified his vanity had he heard it. They spoke of the different engagements as having all been hardly fought for by both parties, and that the two fleets had sustained a dreadful loss of men. "As you will admit," said they, "when told that, since the *Hero*'s arrival in the India seas, her entire crew have been thrice replaced, the whole having been so many times destroyed." One of the men then concluded the account by again declaring the general was the greatest hero upon earth, and ended with, *"Oui, ma foi, c'est un bougre déterminé."*

Having put these jolly tars on board their ship, I proceeded to the Prussian, which lay full two miles on the outside of all the ships except the *Coventry*. I found her upon a deep heel, but the contrary way to what I had observed in the morning; from which I supposed it was done purposely to scrape off the barnacles and clean her sides. I subsequently found that was not the case, but that this extraordinary inclining one way or the other arose from the peculiar construction of her bottom. She had been built by an enthusiastic schemer, who took it into his head that he could built a vessel of such a form as to outstrip every other, besides carrying more cargo than ships of the same burden usually did; and this strange machine was the production. She sailed remarkably well, but never was upright and, when it blew fresh, lay along so that everyone expected her every moment to upset altogether. Upon first putting to sea, the commander and officers were so alarmed at the novelty of her movements that they put into Portsmouth to endeavour to get the evil corrected. The ship was docked, when the builders saw the nature of the ship's frame must occasion her to lay along with little weight or pressure from wind; but they did not conceive any particular mischief or danger would arise from the ship's being so easily affected. The anxiety of the captain, from having so strange a ship, deprived him of his senses; so that, for some months previous to their coming into Cuddalore, as above related, he had been confined to his cabin raving mad, the chief officer assuming the command.

Upon my getting on board, a ferocious-looking man, with uncommon rough and hard features, rendered still more uncouth by a large scar across his face, in a fierce and angry voice and manner accosted me with, "Well, who are you, and what have you to say? Are we to be still detained?" I replied that Admiral Suffren had sent me to take a passage for myself and wife on that ship to Madras, or any English settlement. "Your wife," retorted the savage-looking man, "no, no, friend, that will never do, by God! No woman can come here, I'll be damned if she can." I thereupon observed that the lady in question

would submit to any inconveniences, having been inured to uncommon hardships and sufferings for several months, and that it was
an object of the utmost importance to us to get away from the French.
"I don't doubt it, by God," said the same person. "I believe everybody
must be anxious to get out of their clutches, but I'll be damned if you
can get in here." I then observed that I would willingly pay any sum
he demanded for my passage in his ship. "My ship!" said he. "You are
damnably mistaken in supposing I have anything to do with the
infernal tub, further than having the misfortune to be a passenger.
No! no! bad enough without that, by God."

I then requested to speak to the captain. "You won't gain much by
that," said he, "for he is stark, staring mad; so is his ship; and damn
me! but I believe so are we all, and you as well as any of us; or you
would never talk of bringing a female into such a ship as this." Again
I stated my peculiar situation; it was all in vain. Finding I could make
no impression upon this man, who was the only spokesman, I addressed
another gentleman who stood upon deck, who shrugged his shoulders
but made no answer. I was therefore compelled to leave the ship and
make for the shore. On the way, it struck me that I might as well let
Mr. Suffren know what had occurred; for which purpose I stopped
alongside the *Hero*, and, although then quite dark, I went on board,
and, as usual, was directly shown into the admiral's cabin. After
apologising for my unseasonable intrusion, I mentioned the ill-success
of my application for a passage, and the positive refusal I had received;
whereupon Mr. Suffren said, "I am sorry, Mr. Hickey, you have had
so much trouble in vain. I must then try what I can do, and hope I
shall have better success."

He then rang his bell. An attendant appearing, he ordered him to
send the officer upon duty. The lieutenant forthwith coming, he
directed him instantly to dispatch a boat to the *Coventry* frigate that
lay close to the Prussian, with orders that the latter should not upon
any account be permitted to stir until Mr. and Mrs. Hickey, their servant and baggage, were received and accommodated to their satisfaction on board. Having sent this concise but peremptory mandate, he
laughingly said to me, "I fancy, sir, that will do our business and we
shall get our object from Master Prussian; so good night! Let me hear
tomorrow what has been done." Before I was off my bed the following
morning, I received a letter signed "I. Nixon, Lieut.-Col. E.I. Company's Infantry," saying that, as I was the sole cause of their ship's
detention, he, on behalf of himself and others, earnestly requested that
myself and family would have the goodness to embark as soon as possible, the whole cabin being entirely at my disposal. To this pleasing
information I returned an answer that, the moment a boat could be
obtain d, we would go off.

At eight o'clock, we accordingly did so, my poor Charlotte being much frightened at the surf, which was high, though we passed safely through it. Mr. Suffren having desired I would let him know the result of his interference with the Prussian, I stopped at the *Hero* not only for that purpose but to offer my grateful thanks to the admiral for the many favours conferred upon me. He expressed his satisfaction at my having succeeded, asking when I proposed embarking. I replied that I was then on my way, Mrs. Hickey being in a boat alongside. "Is she so?" said the admiral. "I now heartily lament my ship has not been accustomed to receive the honour of visits from the fair sex, and therefore we are without the means of getting Mrs. Hickey on board, which I should have been happy to have done. But, this being the case, I must go to her to offer my compliments and make my adieus." As he was in his usual undress, he hastily called his servant, with whom he retired for a few minutes to his private apartment; from which he returned with a uniform coat on and fully equipped.

Notwithstanding the ship had considerable motion, rolling rather deep, he stepped down her side as nimbly as a midshipman could have done, wished Mrs. Hickey joy at the near approach of an end to her most unfortunate voyage, and was altogether exceedingly gracious and kind. He, with much gaiety of manner, observed that, as the present visit must necessarily be his last, he should for his own sake make it as long as possible. I, however, soon discovered there was a liberal reason for his saying this; for he had directed his steward to pack up a variety of things which, in about half an hour, were put into our boat; when, taking Mrs. Hickey by the hand, he requested she would do him the honour to accept a few articles of refreshment for the short voyage she still had to perform, and some other trifles which he offered in token of his respect and regard for his amiable prisoner. Then gallantly kissing the hand he held, he condescendingly shook me by the hand, and wishing us both a happy meeting with our connections and friends, jumped up the side of his ship with the same agility he had descended, and we pushed off.

In a few seconds, to my infinite surprise, I saw the *Hero* manned, her crew giving us three hearty cheers (no doubt by the admiral's desire) which we returned. This handsome compliment was also paid us by two other ships as we passed close to them, the *Sphynx* and *Cleopatra* frigate. At ten in the morning, we reached the Prussian, where we were received by the same rough personage I had encountered the preceding day, whom I found to be the Colonel Nixon that had written to me. Coming up to me, he offered his hand, saying, "I take it for granted you are very angry with me for the reception I gave you yesterday; but I was damnably out of humour and really thought this truly extraordinary vessel was not a proper conveyance for a female. Such as it is, however, we must do our best for this good lady who bears her own recommendation upon her intelligent countenance, and whose pardon I beg for my abrupt speeches of yesterday. Had she been present they could not have been made, for those mild and benign features would effectually have softened and silenced me."

After this gallant address, he took her by the hand and led her into the round house, saying, "This, madam, is your room. The only condition we are compelled to make is that you will allow the party to mess in it, there being no other cabin large enough to contain us; and I assure you eating is no small consideration here, occurring regularly five times every day." He next politely thanked me for the quickness with which I had come off to the ship. Two gentlemen just entering the cabin, the colonel begged leave to introduce two Portuguese shipmates. "Though perhaps," observed he, "as no further necessity remains for disguise, it may be as well to announce them under their proper titles. This therefore is Captain Hallam, of His Majesty's 102nd Regiment of Foot, and this Major Alcock of the Company's service. We three left the southern army together, embarking at Tranquebar for Madras. Upon being seized by the *Coventry* and forcibly taken into Cuddalore, we were apprehensive from the general character of Suffren that he would, at any rate, lay hands upon us, even if he allowed the ship to escape his clutches. I am too well and too generally known to attempt any deception; but my friends here, not being in a similar predicament, resolved to assume the situation of Portuguese merchants, under which description they hoped to escape imprisonment."

From these officers, I had the supreme felicity to learn that our prospects were not quite so forlorn as they had been represented by the French; that, although it was too true the whole of our possessions upon the coast of Coromandel, but more especially Madras and its neighbourhood, were suffering under the dreadful calamity of famine, yet the fortress itself was in the highest order, well-garrisoned, and fully prepared to resist any attack the enemy might think proper to make; that the Bengal treasury was very rich, the country in the most flourishing condition, and a powerful reinforcement of men and stores of every description at that time on its way from thence to Madras, under the command of the very popular and distinguished officer, General Sir Eyre Coote.

I found what Colonel Nixon had premised respecting the frequency of the meals on board the Prussian strictly true; it was a perpetual scene of eating and drinking. The colonel seemed to have the chief command. Indeed, he early told me such was the fact, the Company's agent at Tranquebar having freighted the vessel for Madras and named him the chief director.

In the evening, Mrs. Hickey and myself only being in the cabin, I proposed examining Mr. Suffren's presents. We accordingly opened the parcels which we found to contain some papers of chocolate, a variety of preserves, confectionery, fruits, savoy cakes, liqueurs, etc., a pair of beautiful shawls, six pieces of very fine worked muslin, four pieces of Vizagapatam long cloth, four rich kincobs, and six pieces of hand-kerchiefs. It was a magnificent present. Between the shawls was a note written by Mr. Launay, written, as he stated, by Mr. Suffren's desire, requesting Mrs. Hickey's acceptance of the articles that accompanied; and, to do away with any scruples she might feel, he was further directed to inform her that the whole was originally English property, having with large quantities of the same things fallen into the general's hands from a prize he had taken in the Bay of Bengal. Mr. Launay in a postscript added, "He deemed it a necessary precaution to obtain Mr. Suffren's pass for us in case we should on our progress to Bengal fall in with any French cruisers." This document I have preserved as a memorial of uncommon attention, in so elevated a character as Mr. Suffren undoubtedly was, to two insignificant and unknown foreigners.

Colonel Nixon who, under an affected misanthropy and general roughness, possessed as much sensibility, and as great a degree of benevolence towards the whole human race, with as warm a heart as any person living, behaved to Mrs. Hickey and me with the most engaging attention. He listened to the melancholy tale of her sufferings with sympathetic compassion and feeling. Before we had been twelve hours in his company, he gave me a pressing invitation to accept apart-ments in his house at Madras, assuring me his wife, with three fine girls, his daughters, would be happy to receive Mrs. Hickey and con-sole her for her late misfortunes by showing her every kindness in their power. He told me he had been absent from his family upwards of a twelvemonth, serving with the army first against Hyder Ally and, since his death against an equal tyrant, his son, Tippoo Sultaun, as he was pleased to style himself; that he had left the southern army only four-teen days before in company with Major Alcock and Captain Hallam.

On 21st March, at about ten o'clock in the morning, we came to an anchor in Madras Roads, when Colonel Nixon, Major Alcock, and Captain Hallam immediately went on shore. In little more than two hours, Colonel Nixon returned in the accommodation, or Government, boat, renewing in Mrs. Nixon's name the most pressing solicitation that we would take up our abode at her house. "However," added the colonel, "it is but fair in me to tell you that you are not likely to be in want should you still decline my wife's invitation, as I think I left half a dozen different persons waiting upon the beach for your landing, ready to seize upon you; so that, in the amicable contest, I fear we shall stand no chance. Some along, therefore, and we must endeavour to divide you among us as well as we can; but Popham protests you must and shall be his exclusive guests."

My dear girl, who at no period of her life bestowed much time at her toilet, was soon ready, when the worthy colonel superintended the getting her into the boat and escorted us on shore. The surf was high, but we got safely through it. On the beach stood Mr. Popham and Mr. Porcher, the latter after congratulating us upon our arrival said he was obliged reluctantly to yield us up to Mr. Popham, who claimed a prior right to him. Popham told me everything was ready for our reception at his house in the Black Town; and, stepping into his chariot, we were driven to it, Porcher having accepted his invitation to dinner.

Mr. Popham was always an extraordinary being. Blessed with superior talents, improved by a classical education, he fell a martyr to a speculative disposition and a strong inclination for gambling, the latter foible having so deeply involved him he could not remain in his native country. At the time I arrived at Madras he, by his abilities, had raised himself to the top of his profession, and had for many months been Attorney to the Company; which honourable and lucrative situation, added to his private practice, must very speedily have secured to him a handsome independent fortune, had he stuck to the law alone; instead of which, he had twenty wild schemes afoot at one and the same time, which prevented his attending to his business in court, so that every person who employed him had too much reason to complain of his shameful negligence. He had recently built an immense mansion for his own residence, one half of which only was finished when we went to it, the workmen being engaged in the other part.

Mr. Popham, having shown Mrs. Hickey to a suite of rooms delightfully situated up two pairs of stairs, commanding a very extensive and beautiful prospect in every direction, proposed introducing me to the Governor, Lord Macartney, a compliment he thought I ought to pay without delay. We accordingly immediately went to the Government House in the fort. Lord Macartney gave me a most gracious reception, after the customary salutations telling me that my father was an old friend of his; which I well knew, having often seen his Lordship, when Sir George Macartney, in St. Albans Street. I likewise recollected frequently to have heard my father say that, when Sir George was first appointed Ambassador to Russia, he was prevented from setting off for St. Petersburg by a want of money to discharge some pressing creditors, and that he (my father) had lent him five hundred pounds to enable him to discharge them, and that after several of his own connections had positively refused to assist him. My father had been a fellow collegian with him in the University of Dublin.

His Lordship made many enquiries respecting the state of the French fleet, all of which I answered to the best of my knowledge. After having so done, I, without in the least softening the matter, told him what Mr. Suffren had repeatedly said about him; at which he appeared greatly hurt, declaring the French commander most unjust in charging him with want of delicacy and politeness; for that he had invariably answered the application relative to an exchange of prisoners, although, from some peculiar circumstances, he had it not in his power to establish a cartel. I also delivered Captain Duchillon's message in the very words he spoke; at which his Lordship laughed heartily, observing that, were it his fate again to be in the situation he was when at Grenada, there was not an officer in the navy of France whom he would prefer sailing with to Captain Duchillon, whom he knew by experience to be an honourable and kind-hearted man, to whom he felt himself under high obligation for the greatest attention and civility whilst on board his ship on the passage from the West Indies.

After a conversation of nearly two hours, Lord Macartney remarked it was then the hour of dinner; he therefore hoped Mr. Popham and I would do him the favour to stay; which, of course, we did, Popham sending home to Mrs. Hickey to apologize for his absence the first day of her being his guest. We sat down to what seemed to me very indifferent fare for a Governor's table. Indeed, his Lordship, at the beginning of the meal, said the melancholy effects of the dreadful famine with which they had been afflicted, though lessened, had by no means ceased; that provisions were still scarce from the distress of the country people who used to bring poultry and other articles to market; and that, in such a time of dearth, he thought it right to be as frugal as possible.

The 2nd, in the morning, upon Mrs. Hickey and me descending to the breakfast room on the middle floor, we there saw a gentleman sitting at the window, having much more the appearance of a corpse than a living creature. I never beheld a person looking so ill, an absolute skeleton. Upon our entering the room, he made an effort to rise, but tottered from extreme weakness, which my darling girl perceiving was greatly distressed, kindly entreating he would keep his seat, and expressed her concern at seeing him so much indisposed. In a languid and feeble voice, he returned thanks, saying he was materially better than he had been. Mr. Popham coming in, introduced us to the invalid as Captain Isaac Humphreys, private secretary and aide-de-camp to Colonel Pearse. He had been long confined from a jungle fever (something like our ague) with which he had been attacked while in a forest on the march from Bengal, and had brought him to the brink of the grave. I afterwards became very intimate with this gentleman.

Breakfast being over, I went to call upon several of my former acquaintances, particularly Major Cotgrove, Mr. Perryn, Porcher, Torin, Sullivan, the Advocate-General, Dr. Lucas, and Captain Sydenham, the Fort Major. I likewise left my name at Sir John Burgoyne's. Upon returning home, I found the famous Mr. Paul Benfield sitting with Popham and Mrs. Hickey. He had left England many months subsequent to me, having been only eighty-one days from London to Madras, overland. He had done me the honour to visit me several times in St. Albans Street, he having quitted India soon after I did, and getting home long before me. I had also been invited to, and was present at, some grand entertainments he gave at his magnificent house in Portland Place, our intercourse continuing until he one morning, upon calling at my father's, found Mr. Edmund Burke there, who had then recently attacked him in Parliament as a notorious defaulter, who had embezzled large sums of his employer's money which came to his hands from official situations he filled, had basely and iniquitously robbed and plundered the Nabob of Arcot, and was in many respects the greatest delinquent that had ever left India. Benfield appeared extremely awkward and embarrassed, spoke not a word from the time of Mr. Burke's entrance, and in a few minutes made his retreat, from which time he never more called; and, if I accidentally met him in public, he always looked another way to avoid the necessity of a salutation, concluding, I presume, that the member of a family upon the intimate terms he observed mine were with a person who had avowed himself so hostile towards him as Mr. Burke was not a fit acquaintance for him.

I was therefore a good deal surprised at receiving so early a visit from him at Madras. He made a number of civil speeches, invited us in pressing terms to his house on Choultry Plain, offered us the use of his various equipages, and having learnt that Mrs. Hickey was fond of the exercise of riding on horseback, said he would send an Arab she would admire, that would carry her delightfully, being as docile an animal as any in Europe. He accordingly did send a most beautiful creature, also another for me. A European servant attended with them, who said his master had directed him to wait upon me every evening to receive my orders for the following day. Mrs. Hickey had this day a number of female visitors, amongst the first of whom was Mrs. Nixon, with two of her daughters, Lady Gordon, Mrs. Barclay, Mrs. Floyd, Mrs. Taner, Mrs. Latham, the lovely widow Maclellan, the Belle Johnston, etc., etc. The return of these and many other visits, with the numerous parties made for our entertainment, occupied several days.

The 24th, the *Medea* sailed on a look-out cruise. That day we spent very agreeably with Colonel Nixon's family, whom we found truly amiable. In the evening, the colonel said he must be absent for a few minutes in order to pay his respects to the Governor. He accordingly walked across the parade. After a very short absence, he returned. Upon entering the room where a large party were then assembled, he bellowed out for the servants to attend; upon whose appearance, he ordered them instantly to blow out all the candles except one. During this whimsical operation, Mrs. Nixon looked on with the utmost composure, without interfering; but, as soon as the candles were extinguished, addressing her husband, she mildly said, "Pray, my dear, what is the meaning of this odd freak?" To which he replied, "I have just been to the Government House, where there is not a single taper burning; and that being the case, by God! madam, you ought to consider yourself damned well off in having a pair of candles." "Oh! if that be all, my dear," said Mrs. Nixon, "let the candles be lighted again," which was instantly done. The colonel then gave us the following ludicrous account of the visit he had just been upon.

"I went up the great staircase without seeing a single domestic, or any person whatsoever; the hall was in the same deserted state, without light. I, therefore, gave one of my most powerful holloa's! (and he almost deafened us with the imitation). 'Is there a living soul in the place or not?' Whereupon a mean-looking little rascal, who I verily believe had been purloining the bread and butter, popped his head out of a door that looked like a pantry, with a coconut shell about one-fourth part full of oil, and a single wick. Upon the little fellow's nearer approach, I discovered him that contemptible wretch Green, a sort of understrapping *sub-sub* secretary of the Governor's. I enquired whether Lord Macartney was at home, adding that the question was superfluous from the state of the mansion. The despicable little animal answered his Lordship was out taking his evening's airing in a carriage; but he expected his Lordship home every moment. 'The devil you do!' said I, 'and give me leave to ask, is this the way the house is darkened to receive him?' 'Candles will be lighted when his Lordship comes in,' said the little maître d'hôtel. 'Oh ho! will they so,' says I, 'then damn my blood, but this is a good lesson for me who left about thirty wax candles blazing in my hall. They shall be extinguished directly, and for once I'll live like a lord! So good night, my little soupe maigre, water-gruel visage. Tell your master—oh zounds! I beg your pardon, Mr. Sec.; the Governor I ought to have said—that I, Colonel Nixon, have been here to pay my respects'; and, having had sufficient of the little *sub-sub*, I walked away!"

This day a signal was made from the flagstaff that a strange sail was standing for the roads from the southward. At first it was hoped she would prove one of the fleet of Indiamen from Europe, or, what was of equal consequence, one of Admiral Sir Edward Hughes's squadron from Bombay. Everybody with the most eager solicitude ran out of the fort to the Master Attendant's apartment upon the beach to mark the approach of the vessel, who continued standing in, with her topsails lowered down upon the caps, and without showing any colours until within a quarter of a mile of the surf, when she hoisted a French jack and commenced a brisk fire upon a large Dutch prize and two country ships, although all three were as close in as they could possibly lie. The prize master on board the Dutchman, by this time having recognized the stranger to be the *Coventry*, which had been taken by Suffren, and that she was preparing to board him, instantly let out his cables and let his ship drift through the outer surf and take the ground, in preference to allowing her to fall into the hands of the enemy.

To the inexpressible astonishment of many hundred spectators assembled on the ramparts and the beach, not a shot was fired from the fort, notwithstanding with unparalleled effrontery the enemy stood so near in that she undoubtedly might have been sunk by the battery of the sea line which bore full upon her, she having the impudence to heave to and lie in that state for above half an hour. Having thus driven our three ships on shore, she leisurely made sail to the northeast. After she had got an offing of about two miles, the fort began to pepper away at an immense rate both shot and shells without the least effect. Upon enquiring into the cause of this strange conduct, we were informed that the keys of the storerooms under the works, in which the ammunition was kept, had been mislaid and could nowhere be found for more than an hour. An unpardonable neglect somewhere, and hardly to be credited that such a disgraceful event could have occurred in a British fortress, and that too during the midst of active and severe war! Yet so it undoubtedly was. The civilians of Madras were exceedingly smart in their animadversions upon this occasion.

On the 31st, two large ships were seen in the south, which as soon as their signals were visible, proved to be the *Resolution* and *Royal Charlotte* from Bengal, Sir Eyre Coote's distinguishing flag, as Commander-in-Chief, flying at the topgallant masthead of the former. Everybody was delighted at this sight, not only on account of the advantages likely to arise from his taking the field in person, but from his being revered by the whole army both European and native, who had the greatest confidence in his skill and abilities as a general officer; besides which, the supply he brought with him of men, money, and military stores, all which were greatly wanted, was of the highest importance.

The first boat that came from the *Resolution* threw a damp upon the general joy that had prevailed on these two ships' safe arrival, by bringing the sad tidings that Sir Eyre Coote was dying, if not already dead. The principal medical gentlemen of the settlement were forthwith sent off to the *Resolution* to give their aid to the lamented officer. In the evening, Sir Eyre Coote was brought on shore in a state of determined apoplexy, in which unhappy state he remained, quite insensible, until the following morning, when he expired. We then learnt these particulars from Captain Mercer of the *Resolution*, who was universally considered to be as able a seaman and skilful a navigator as ever stepped a quarterdeck. This gentleman, being sensible of the danger that existed of his falling in with some of the enemy's cruisers, kept as far out at sea as he dared venture to do without risking the being driven off the coast altogether by the current. His intention was thus to keep out at sea until in the latitude of Madras, then immediately to haul in for the land.

In the morning of the 28th (March), he discovered two sail in the north-east quarter, courses down, in consequence of which he hauled more off the land. He, however, soon had the mortification to find the two strange sail had seen him and his consort, and were in full chase. By noon, they had gained considerably; soon after that hour, five more ships of force were seen in different directions, completely surrounding them. Being senior officer, he spoke his consort, giving him instructions how to act during the night. From the moment the strange ships hove in sight, Sir Eyre Coote showed so extraordinary a degree of anxiety and uneasiness of mind as to make Captain Mercer quite apprehensive it might affect his health. By evening of the day they saw them, the enemy were within two miles of the English ships; but, in the course of the night, Captain Mercer manoeuvred with such skill and so successfully that at daybreak of the 29th they had increased the distance to nearly nine miles, the French then standing the contrary way to the *Resolution* and *Royal Charlotte*.

They renewed the chase for the whole of the day; and by evening the *Cleopatra* was so near as to commence a fire upon the *Royal Charlotte* from her bow guns, none of which took effect. As soon as it was quite dark, the two ships stood due east for one hour, then suddenly took in every sail, thus remaining stationary and the enemy losing sight of them. In the morning of the 30th, they had the pleasure to find this scheme had completely answered, there being only one sail just discernible from the masthead bearing west. By reckoning they were now in the latitude of Madras, Captain Mercer therefore determined to let the ships continue without canvas, hoping so small an object as the bare masts might escape observation. Unfortunately, that was not the case, as two hours afterwards three of the French ships were standing for them. Sir Eyre Coote, who had never quitted the deck, and had little or no sleep for two nights, suddenly fell from the chair in which he was sitting in a fit. In an hour he so far recovered as to enquire, with much agitation, whether the enemy gained upon them, and whether Captain Mercer thought there was a chance of escaping.

Captain Mercer, observing him to be in so desponding a state,

14+

assured him he had not a doubt that they should reach Madras in safety, although, in fact, he had scarce a hope left of so doing. He then used all his influence to prevail upon the General to take some refreshment and lie down for a few hours to recruit nature. He, thereupon, consented to drink some mulled Madeira wine, but said attempting to sleep would be fruitless. The enemy gained considerably, but towards evening were still at a distance of four miles. Captain Mercer told Sir Eyre that, just before dark, he would stand to the northward, which he trusted would induce the French to imagine he meant to push for Bengal again, and that they would follow in that direction. He then hailed the *Royal Charlotte*, directing her commander to keep as close as possible upon his quarter, when quite dark to hand all his upper sails and haul in direct for the land.

The night favoured them, being extremely squally with hard rain. Sir Eyre Coote's agitation, if possible, increased; he every minute enquired if the ships were seen. About midnight, the man stationed at the bowsprit end to look out, suddenly called out that a large ship was running on board of them, whereupon Sir Eyre instantly fell into a fit of apoplexy, from which he never recovered. This alarm arose from the *Royal Charlotte*, whose tiller rope broke in a severe gust of wind, upon which she flew short round and very nearly fell aboard the *Resolution*.

In the afternoon of the day on which the General died, his funeral took place with great solemnity. The church, from a want of room in the fort, had during the famine, been entirely filled with bags of rice. It therefore became necessary to clear the principal aisle, at the end of which near the pulpit the grave was dug. The corpse was carried from the Admiralty House by eight European sergeants, the pall being borne by Lord Macartney and five of the principal gentlemen of the settlement. The church, being situated in a narrow and confined part of the fort, did not admit of the three volleys being fired; the dragoons which were appointed to fire them, therefore, upon the body's entering the church marched off to the parade for the purpose, and did so to quick time, the fifes playing "Nancy Dawson," an awkward change from the solemn ceremony and certainly ill-judged, notwithstanding in a military sense it might be strictly correct.

On 2nd April, Mrs. Hickey and I went to pass the day at Mrs. Barclay's garden house a few miles from Madras, where both she and Mr. Barclay, her husband, gave us a most pressing invitation to fix our abode altogether, which I promised to do in a week or ten days, as it would take that time to prepare a sufficient stock of apparel for Mrs. Hickey and myself. In going to their house, a truly melancholy spectacle met our sight, at which my dearest Charlotte was beyond measure affected, the whole road being strewed on both sides with the skulls

and bones of the innumerable poor creatures who had there laid themselves down and miserably perished from want of food, being on their
way from different parts of the country to Madras, in the hope of
obtaining relief there—a relief it was not, alas! in the power of the
British inhabitants to afford, from the thousands and tens of thousands
that daily flocked towards the presidency.

On the 4th, a large fleet made its appearance, whereupon the remaining British ships prepared for action. It, however, proved to be the
expected Indiamen from Europe, under convoy of the *Bristol* of fifty
guns, commanded by Captain Burney. Upon coming to an anchor, we
heard that they had not seen anything of the French, nor been at all
aware of their imminent danger. The same afternoon that the India
fleet just arrived, the *Sceptre*, Captain Alms, came into the roads,
bringing with him the *Naiade* French frigate, then under the temporary command of Monsieur Joyeuse. The *Sceptre*, being some miles
to the eastward of the fleet in coming round from Bombay, discovered
from her masthead a strange sail which evidently endeavoured to avoid
him. He, therefore, communicated this to the admiral by signal, asking
permission to chase, which was granted but with an order not to lose
sight of his own fleet. Captain Alms, however, finding he gained upon
the ship he was in pursuit of, ventured to trespass upon the order he
had received by continuing the chase. In six-and-thirty hours, he came
up with and captured her.

On the 5th, I had the pleasure to meet my *ci-devant* Trincomalee
acquaintance, Captain Joyeuse, at Lord Macartney's. He appeared
dejected and low-spirited at the *fortune de guerre*, observing to me
that through life he had been an unlucky dog, whom the fickle Dame
was perpetually at war with and pelting him in every direction. Soon
after his arrival at Madras, he informed me that Lord Macartney had
just agreed to an exchange of prisoners, and a cartel would in a few
days depart for Trincomalee, by which opportunity I might forward
anything I pleased to that place. I thereupon directed my *dubash* to
procure for me a variety of different articles as presents for Mrs.
Vansenden, Captain Gautier, Mr. Chevillard, the Chevalier de Salvert,
and others.

On the morning of the 6th, Mr. Popham and I went to the Government House to breakfast with Lord Macartney, where I was introduced to his chief and confidential secretary, Sir George Staunton, who
told me he was well known to all my family and made many kind
enquiries after my father and eldest sister, as likewise did another
gentleman present, who was a stranger to me. I found this was Mr.
Lascelles, who held a lucrative situation under the Governor and was
in his suite. There was at breakfast the same morning several of the
commanders of His Majesty's ships and some captains of East India-

men, among the latter Captain Rattray of the *Duke of Athol*. The breakfast being finished, the company were talking of the dreadful consequences of the late famine, when a report of a gun, as it was supposed to be, drew the general attention, Lord Macartney saying it appeared to him more like an explosion than a gun. The whole party rose and, going to the windows that looked towards the sea, saw a prodigious column of smoke ascending from the midst of the fleet.

Sir Richard Bickerton, who was present, expressed his fears that it was a ship blown up, whereupon Captain Rattray exclaimed, "Not a doubt but it is, and equally certain that it is my ship." This proved too true; it was the *Duke of Athol*! She had by some accident taken fire, the first intimation of which was the flames bursting from between decks. Signals of distress being made in consequence, a boatful of men with an officer was instantly dispatched from every ship to her assistance. As she lay in the centre of the fleet, the boats reached her in a few minutes, one of the earliest on board being the *Superb's*, with her first lieutenant in it, a very active and zealous old officer.

This gentleman was a remarkable instance of the unrelenting persecutions of fortune. From early infancy, his history was a series of unmerited disasters and afflictions. After suffering every mishap a seaman's life is liable to, he rose to the rank of first lieutenant. When he had served upwards of thirty years, he was three different times put into flagships with a view to promotion; but each time some untoward circumstance prevented it. Once he was wrecked and only twenty persons saved; another time his ship was burnt; and the third he was taken by a squadron of the enemy and lay two years in a French prison. This most unfortunate man lost his life in the *Duke of Athol* whilst exerting himself in endeavouring to extinguish the flames, he and three other lieutenants belonging to different ships, being blown up.

At Madras, I heard much of my friend Bob Pott, who, with his lovely favourite, Emily, had made a considerable stay there. The men universally declared they had never beheld so beautiful a creature as Emily; and even the women admitted her extraordinary beauty of face and person. I also learnt that she died immediately upon her arrival in Bengal.

26

THE DEATH OF CHARLOTTE

WHILE sitting one morning at the breakfast table, a strapping young Irishman, upwards of six feet high, dressed in a plain scarlet frock, was ushered into the room. With a most thunderous brogue and a peculiar vulgarity of manner, he enquired which of us was Stephen Popham, Esquire, of Castlebar. Mr. Popham saying he was, the following dialogue took place between them, which I have endeavoured to spell so as to express the pronunciation of the young Hibernian.

STRANGER: "There's a litter myself brought from Dublin for you, Muster Popham."

POPHAM (imitating his accent): "Auch! and did you so, my jewel? What! all the way from Dublin. And pray now, what may your name be?"

STRANGER: "By my faith but I thought you would have perceived that by the litter you have got in your hand; but, as I never had reason to be ashamed of my fader's name, it is Sternball!"

POPHAM: "I believe, sir, the writer of this litter has lately received a stern-ball."

STRANGER (rather sharply, and with hauteur): "Sir."

POPHAM: "I say, sir, I belave the writer has lately had a stern ball lodged in his body."

STRANGER: "Upon my conscience I don't exactly know what you main."

POPHAM: "I think, sir, the gentleman who gave you this litter was killed in a duel."

STRANGER (looking rather fiercely and putting on his hat): "Faith and you may belave me when I assure you he was alive when he gave me that litter."

POPHAM (apparently alarmed, with less incivility, and dropping the assumed brogue): "Yes, sir, so I presume; but from the latest accounts I have received from Ireland I understood Mr. Martin unfortunately lost his life in a duel."

STRANGER: "Why then, your understanding is none of the best, for I left him five months ago in health. Look you (stepping close up to him) I'm not quite clare but what you mane to be impartinent, so until I can ascertain that point and act accordingly, I'll take lave and so good mhorning, Mr. Stephen Popham." And off he walked.

Mr. Popham then, addressing me, said, "Did you ever see such a damned Irish yahoo as that?" To which I answered, "Upon my word, Popham, I sat during the whole of this truly extraordinary scene, anxiously hoping every moment that I should see the yahoo, as you are now pleased to call him, take you by the nose, or spit in your face, which your unjustifiable behaviour richly deserved." As I said this with considerable warmth, Mr. Popham observed that I made use of strong language, to which I replied, I certainly never before witnessed such wanton and uncalled for impertinence as he had betrayed to-wards an utter stranger, who, from having brought him a letter of introduction, was at least entitled to the treatment due from one gentleman to another. Nor could I help adding, I was free to acknow-ledge the stranger had shown much more command of temper and forbearance than I should have done under similar circumstances. Finding I was quite serious, Mr. Popham, according to his usual cus-tom in such cases, turned the matter off with a laugh, saying I was too kind-hearted to deal with impudent upstart Irishmen.

On the 20th, I received a very polite note from Mr. Robson, purser of the *Superb*, to say the admiral had directed him to inform me that the *Tortoise* store ship would be dispatched for Bengal, and that he had requested Captain Serocold, who commanded her, to give Mrs. Hickey and me a passage. I, thereupon, immediately went to town, where I had only been a few minutes when Mr. Robson brought Cap-tain Serocold, who in the kindest manner expressed the pleasure it would afford him to comply with the admiral's wishes; that the *Tortoise*'s great cabin, with everything on board, would be heartily at my service, and he should feel proud of the honour of Mrs. Hickey's company. He told me he expected to sail in five days, and should only have one other passenger, Mr. Henry Thomas Colebrooke, third son of Sir George Colebrooke's, and who was just appointed to the Com-pany's civil service.

The 24th, I dined at Lord Macartney's, previously leaving Mrs. Hickey at Lady Gordon's with a gay party. Having received notice from Captain Serocold that he should depart the next day but one, the 25th was therefore fully occupied by taking leave of our numerous friends. On the 26th, directly after breakfast, we were accompanied down to the beach by Mrs. Barclay, Lady Gordon, Mrs. Latham, Mrs. Garrow, and other female friends, and quite a host of gentlemen, who all remained at the sea-side until they saw us over the surfs, when they finally saluted by waving handkerchiefs and hats to us, and departed. Upon getting alongside the *Tortoise*, we were politely received by Captain Serocold, who conducted us into a neat and commodious cabin. We found the people heaving up the anchor, and in an hour after we were on board the ship was under way.

We had a tolerable passage from Madras, arriving in Balasore Roads on 2nd June; on which day there was a new moon, and we had the mortification to find there was no pilot. As the weather appeared unsettled and the clouds looked wild, after cruising about almost the whole day, Captain Serocold considered it prudent to come to an anchor, which we accordingly did in twenty fathoms of water. A heavy sea running, and the ship being light, we rolled and tumbled about dreadfully. The India Directory (a very valuable and excellent work) advises all commanders of ships who reach the roads at any time between the new and full moon of June, and do not find a pilot there, by no means to come to an anchor, but stand out to sea. Captain Serocold, however, being in hourly expectation of seeing a pilot schooner, deemed it more prudent to remain in the usual track of them. The 3rd and 4th it blew fresh with a high, short, and breaking sea. Every person on board became impatient and uneasy under this unexpected and disagreeable detention in so wild and dangerous a sea.

In the evening of the 4th, an old Bengallee serang, who had begged a passage from Madras, said he had often taken his own vessel of about sixty tons over the sands, being well acquainted with the channel from long experience, and that he was ready and willing to go in a boat to see for a pilot. Captain Serocold asked him if he could not conduct the ship in, to which he modestly replied that, although he thought he could, it might be considered presumptuous in him to attempt it; and, the ship being of so much consequence, even his alarms on that account might lead him into error; and he would not upon any account attempt it short of indispensable necessity. Captain Serocold, after considering what would be best, resolved to dispatch this man in a boat. He accordingly had a longboat rigged, put his boatswain and four of the men into her, desiring them to follow implicitly the directions of the serang, and dispatched them with the flood tide, the serang saying he hoped to be back the following morning with a pilot.

The 5th, the weather was dark and squally. In the morning, a large ship from sea passed us. Captain Serocold made the signal to speak her, which she either did not see or did not understand. After running about four miles further in than we were, she came to an anchor. We had fired a gun every half-hour during the nights from the time we had anchored. This night the newly arrived ship did the same. The 6th and 7th, there was a great deal of rain; at times most severe gusts of wind with dreadful thunder and lightning, and a high sea, then suddenly falling quite calm for a few minutes; a dismally black, threatening sky all round. Captain Serocold became extremely uneasy, not only on account of his ship, but for the safety of the people sent off in the longboat. The 8th, the strange sail was observed to fire several guns in quick succession; and Captain Serocold, looking through his glass, thought she had a signal of distress flying, though from her distance and the thickness of the weather he was not able to ascertain with certainty whether such was the case; but, as she continued firing guns, he said he would make an effort to get nearer to her if he could manage to weigh the anchor.

Every soul on board, passengers and all, turned to at the capstan, and hove with hearty good will, but in vain. We could not stir the anchor in the least and were obliged to desist. After dinner, the tide not running so strong, another attempt was made, but equally unsuccessful. Captain Serocold then determined to slip his cable, leaving a buoy over the anchor to point out its situation; which having done, we ran within a mile of her, when Captain Serocold observed she must be upon the very edge of a sand over which the sea broke dreadfully; and, being directly leeward with a strong gale blowing, he was afraid to venture any nearer. He, therefore, let go the sheet anchor; when we perceived the ship to be an East Indiaman, and in an extremely awkward situation; for had she driven one hundred yards her loss must have been inevitable. She made many signals to us for assistance, which it was out of our power to render; nor could any boat possibly get from her to us, from the set of the tides and point the wind was in.

In this truly unpleasant way we remained until the 10th, when, the wind shifting to the northward during a severe squall, our companion in distress got under way and stood close to us. Captain Serocold then hailed, mentioning the helpless situation we were in with respect to hands, and requesting they would sent twenty hands to assist in weighing our anchor, and that we should keep together until we fell in with a pilot. They immediately hoisted out a boat, sending her off with the people required. The third mate, who accompanied them, told us it was the Company's ship *Chesterfield*, commanded by Captain Bruce Boswell, last from Bombay. He also informed us she was so leaky as to keep two pumps constantly at work night and day; that they had only twenty-five Europeans on board, including officers, all the rest being Lascars, who are miserable wretches at best, and who were nearly worn out with the fatigue of pumping. Captain Boswell therefore hoped we would detain his men as little time as possible.

The *Chesterfield* people, having soon accomplished the business they came upon, returned to their ship, when we both made sail, going in search of the best bower from which we had slipped; but, after cruising about three hours without being able to find the buoy, we were under the necessity of giving up the hopes of recovering it. We then stood more to the eastward together, anxiously looking out for a pilot. As we now gave up the longboat's crew for lost, it was some consolation to us to have the *Chesterfield* near. Our situation certainly was very alarming, being in constant dread of bad weather from the season, the critical time of the moon, and threatening appearance of the sky all round.

Two more days we had to endure this scene of constant anxiety and suspense, but at daylight in the morning of the 13th had the satisfaction to see a pilot schooner approaching; and, as she neared us, Captain Serocold afforded us inexpressible pleasure by saying he saw his boatswain and people on board of her. At ten o'clock, a pilot came to the *Tortoise* and took charge, one of his mates at the same time going to the *Chesterfield*. Captain Serocold, although a remarkably mild, good-tempered man, was so offended at the shameful negligence he had experienced that I really thought he would have flogged the pilot, especially when the rascal impudently observed it was unreasonable to expect small vessels could cruise in the roads during such tempestuous weather. Captain Serocold, however, commanded himself so far as not to strike him, but assured him he would represent the matter to the admiral, which would cause him to be dismissed the service.

The boatswain said the old serang had taken the longboat up in a capital style, most correctly telling the depth of water there would be all the way; that, not finding any pilot off Ingelee, nor in the creek, into which they looked, they proceeded up the river, stopping at every place they thought it likely to hear of one, but none were to be met with; and thus they reached Calcutta, where, without losing a moment, they applied to the Master Attendant, who forthwith ordered a vessel to be dispatched. Four-and-twenty hours nevertheless elapsed ere she was ready. Off Fulta, on their way down the river, they run her upon a dangerous sand called the James and Mary, where she lay aground two entire days and nights, in the most imminent risk of oversetting every tide. The springs having commenced, the afternoon of the 11th she fortunately righted and once more got afloat. So careless, or so ignorant were the people on board that she again grounded a few miles below Kedgeree, remaining fast for six hours.

Captain Serocold, upon hearing so extraordinary an account of the pilot's conduct on his way down, sent for him upon the quarterdeck, and calling for the boatswain he directed that officer to have a rope reeved to the main yardarm with a running noose, which being immediately done, he turned to the pilot and said, "You have already, in my opinion, proved yourself a very worthless scoundrel. You see that rope that I just ordered to be rigged out. Now, by God! if you run my ship on shore between this and Culpee, the instant she takes the

14*

ground shall be the last of your life, for I'll certainly hang you at that yardarm!" The fellow looked very simple and, after a pause, said, "I hope, sir, there is no danger of any accident's happening. I shall take all the care in my power to prevent it."

At noon, we got under way to go once more in search of the anchor and cable we had slipped from, which the people of the pilot vessel soon discovered; when we directly stood for the mouth of the Hooghley river, in company with the *Chesterfield*, the sky continuing very black and lowering. At five in the afternoon, it fell quite calm, torrents of rain pouring down upon us; and in the night we had much thunder and lightning. The whole of the 14th it continued calm, which kept us fast at anchor. The 15th, we proceeded about twelve miles; the 16th, 17th, and 18th it blew strong from the north-west; we could not, therefore, stir, all the time pitching forecastle under. In the afternoon of the 19th, the weather cleared up and, the wind veering round to the southward, we got under way, at sunset saw the land near Ingelee; on the 21st, came to an anchor off Culpee (the place I passed a wretched night at on my first arrival at Bengal in the year 1777, with Colonel Watson, chief engineer). In approaching this dreary spot, I observed in the midst of the jungle a beautiful column, apparently of stone. Enquiring what this could be in so desolate and wild a place, I was informed the seafaring people had christened it "Pott's folly," though it ultimately proved of public utility, being of considerable advantage to the pilots when bringing ships in from sea, from its being a conspicuous landmark, always visible when no other object was so in blowing weather. I shall say something more of this column presently.

There being no means of getting Mrs. Hickey away, we were under the disagreeable necessity of remaining in the abominable hole three days; at the end of which time, by bribing high, I prevailed upon the mangee of a pinnace I found laying in the creek, awaiting the arrival of a gentleman hourly expected from Vizagapatam, to convey us up the river as far as Budge Budge, where my old *Sea-horse* shipmate, Major Mestayer, commanded, who I knew would give us a hearty welcome, as well as furnish the means of taking us on to Calcutta. We arrived at his quarters, an excellent and spacious house within the fort, on the 16th, where we experienced the most cordial reception. The following morning, he dispatched a servant with a letter from me to Robert Pott (to whom I had also written during my stay at Madras, requesting he would take a house, hire a set of servants, etc., etc.) to ascertain whether he had done anything for me. On the 28th, in consequence of my letter, he made his appearance in person, having come down in a beautiful and elegantly appointed boat of his own construction and building.

As I had in my letter from Madras informed him of the companion I had with me, and the footing she was upon, notwithstanding my repeated offers to make her my wife, he was prepared to receive her as an utter stranger; and, in spite of his disposition at all times to laugh, and his having been well acquainted with her in England, he conducted himself with the utmost propriety and decorum. He, with great ceremony, told her he rejoiced much at the introduction, be-speaking infinite pleasure in the acquaintance, adding that he had comfortable apartments, with everything suitable, prepared for us at his country house, to which he was ready immediately to escort us; but Major Mestayer would not hear of our leaving him until the 30th, on which morning, soon after breakfast, we embarked in the before-mentioned vessel, which in three hours transported us to Pott's residence, a noble mansion situated upon the bank of the river, five miles from Calcutta, the property of Mr. Stephenson, a gentleman at the top of the civil service. Here we landed on the said 30th June 1783, thus terminating as disastrous a voyage as ever unfortunate people made, of exactly eighteen months from the day I left London.

I found Pott's family consisted of himself, his first cousin, George Cruttenden, who came out with him as a cadet, and Mr. Thomas Trant, a cadet from Madras, likewise a shipmate. This gentleman, who was about thirty years of age, had been brought up in a merchant's counting-house in Ireland, and was conversant in all matters of business and account. During the voyage, Pott persuaded him to relinquish the army and to depend upon him for his future success in life. Upon their arrival in Bengal, he employed him as a sort of general steward, giving him the entire management and control over all his servants and domestic concerns. Mr. Trant informed me that Pott had at first suffered severely at the sudden and unexpected loss of his favourite Emily, but that the violence of his grief was not of long duration. At the time of my arrival in Bengal, he certainly appeared to be in excellent health and high spirits.

From Mr. Trant I also heard the following particulars of her death. Pott and she sailed from Madras in the month of May (1782) on board a ship belonging to, and commanded by, Mr. John Maclary, a very respectable and worthy man, Emily then being in perfect health. She was, however, greatly annoyed by what is called the prickly heat, a sort of rash or eruption upon the skin very prevalent in hot countries, especially in Asia. It is attended with a sharp pricking pain like the points of pins penetrating the body in every part, so that it is difficult to lie down in bed. It is, however, considered a sign of vigorous health. Newcomers are more subject to it than old residents, arising, as is supposed, from the superior richness or nicer susceptibility of the blood and general system. Drinking anything cold instantaneously and greatly increases it.

Emily, impatient under the torture of this teasing complaint and with an insatiable thirst upon her, had frequent recourse to draughts of extremely cold water (made so by art), mixed with milk. The ship they were on board of was to go quite up to Calcutta. Just as they were off Culpee, Emily, in quick succession, drank two large tumblers of the above-mentioned mixture, the last of which was scarcely down her throat when she complained of feeling excessively faint and ill; that her sight was failing, as she could not distinguish any object before her. The prickly heat was observed suddenly and entirely to disappear. She fell back upon the couch she was sitting on, and in a few minutes was a corpse. So rapid and so unexpected a proof of the uncertainty of life gave a great shock to every person on board, more especially to poor Pott, who was inconsolable, and outrageous in his grief. For several hours he would not be persuaded she had ceased to exist.

He, however, but too soon had unanswerable evidence such was the fact from the body's becoming black and putrid, emitting the most offensive smell. A coffin therefore being prepared with the utmost dispatch, the corpse was finally enclosed therein, placed in a boat astern of the vessel, with a very long painter or headfast, and thus was towed up to Calcutta, where it was interred in the burial ground of the town. Pott caused a magnificent mausoleum to be constructed over the grave by Mr. Tiretta, the Italian architect, at an expense of near three thousand pounds; and, not content with paying this compliment to her remains, he employed the same Tiretta to build the column I before mentioned, amongst herds of tigers at Culpee, because off that wild, jungly place she breathed her last, which column cost him another thousand pounds!

On 1st July, my former banyan, Durgachuru Muckerjee, came to pay his respects to me and express his surprise and concern at my returning without being appointed to the Company's civil service, a situation he did not seem disposed to believe so difficult to procure as, in fact, it was. He had provided a smart palankeen for me, likewise a complete set of bearers to carry it, besides various other necessary servants. The same morning, Mr. Stackhouse Tolfrey and several other of my former acquaintances came to visit me. Tolfrey gave me the mortifying intelligence of my name's having been struck off the Roll, so that I was no longer an attorney of the Supreme Court. The Chief Justice, Sir Elijah Impey, upon the arrival of Mr. and Mrs. Pawson in a Portuguese ship, having heard that I was at Lisbon on my way back to India, he forthwith caused written notices to be stuck up at all the customary places in Calcutta requiring all and every attorney who had suffered twelve months to elapse without doing any business in the line of their profession, within *fourteen days* from the date of such notice to appear in court and there assign their reason for not practising; and, in case of any attorneys not complying with that order and accounting satisfactorily for his ceasing to practise, their or his name or names would directly be struck off the Roll.

This extraordinary measure was evidently levelled at me, in revenge for my having been instrumental in forwarding the petition to parliament, soliciting for trial by jury in all civil as well as criminal cases, the prayer of which petition, had the legislature complied with to the extent demanded, would materially have abridged the power, and consequently the influence, of the judges. That Sir Elijah suffered private pique against me to affect his conduct there could be no doubt, no other attorney being in a similar predicament with myself; that is to say, having been a year without practising his profession. At the time the said notices were published, I was at Trincomalee, a prisoner with the French, quite ignorant of any such step having been taken. The fourteen days having passed and I not appearing, my name was thereupon erased from the Roll by the Clerk of the Crown under the direction of the judges.

As I considered this step a premeditated piece of malice, and had no doubt of the same sentiment being adhered to, I resolved at least to let the proud Chief Justice know what were my sentiments upon the occasion. I accordingly addressed a letter to him, wherein I, in most unqualified language, reprobated such illiberal behaviour as he had betrayed, concluding by expressing the most sovereign contempt for this great luminary of the law. This letter I read to Pott, who said it certainly was ill-calculated to conciliate; but, nevertheless, he had so high an opinion of the goodness of the Chief Justice's heart and of his (Pott's) influence over him that he would himself undertake the delivery of the hostile letter, adding at the same time that he would *wig* a lawyer for the farce of a fourteen days' notice for a man to appear who, for aught he knew to the contrary, might be some thousands of miles distant.

The following morning Pott presented me with a letter, the contents of which very much surprised me. It was, as my friend told me when he delivered it, from Sir Elijah Impey, whom he described as being in a damnable rage when first perusing mine to him, but that he soon laughed him into better temper. It was as follows:

"To Mr. Hickey.
Sir,
    The Court, some time since, on the petition of the practising attornies, stating the decline of the business of the Court, thought

proper to limit their number. To ascertain the number proposed and that it might not be prevented from being full by the names of persons standing on the record who had no further thoughts of practising, the Court framed the rule under which, as I suppose, your name was struck out, the Court esteeming absence for a long time without any cause for it known to the Court to be evidence of having no further thoughts of practising. You will see by this that what has happened to you could not proceed from any idea of your having given any cause for dismissal, but of your having voluntarily relinquished your profession. As that was not your case, and, on the contrary, you have returned with an intention to prosecute it, and more especially as you could have no knowledge of the rule until your arrival, I should esteem it severe and I may say unjust not to restore your name to the Roll. I will take on myself to say you will find no difficulty in it, and if you will call on me I will recommend to you what I think the proper mode of getting it done, as I wish to give you every assistance in obtaining what I think to be your right.

I am, sir,

Your very humble servant,

E. IMPEY."

In consequence of this advice coming from such high authority, Pott the following morning conveyed me in his carriage to Sir Elijah's at the Court House, where, during my absence in Europe, the Court had been moved to, it being a noble pile of building, close to the edge of the river at Chaund paul Ghaut, and in which Sir Elijah, with his family, resided.

Being shown into the study, the Chief Justice in a few minutes entered. I rose and bowed, to which salutation he made a slight return by a doubtful bend of his head; whereupon my friend Robert, who knew the former habits of intimacy I had been upon with the great man, burst into one of his laughs. The chief, offended thereat, angrily and haughtily said, "I cannot discover any cause for your boisterous and ill-timed mirth, Pott. Give me leave to ask what has occasioned it?" Pott made no answer, but continuing to laugh violently, Sir Elijah said peevishly, "Unless you can restrain your unseasonable mirth, sir, and conduct yourself more decorously, you had better leave the room." Then, turning to me, he said, "I am going into court directly; if you think proper, follow me there, sir." Pott, taking up his hat, and still laughing, went to the door, from whence he called out, "Good morning, Sir Elijah. While you are doing my friend Bill Hickey justice, I'll go and chat with Lady Impey, whom I hope to find in a somewhat better humour than you are," and he darted away.

I, according to the Chief Justice's advice, followed him into the courtroom. The moment he had taken his seat upon the bench he addressed the Bar and officers, saying, "That the judges being satisfied with the reasons assigned by Mr. William Hickey, lately an Attorney of the Court, for his absence, had consented to comply with his desire of being re-admitted. Let the usual oaths therefore be administered; after which, Mr. Clerk of the Crown, restore his name to the Roll of Attornies." This being immediately done, I once more became an Attorney upon Record.

I found but little alteration with respect to the members constituting the Supreme Court. The only one that had quitted the Bar was Mr. Charles Newman, the Company's senior counsel. This gentleman, having served his employers for several years with equal zeal and ability, felt so hurt that they should supersede him by sending out an Advocate-General that he immediately resigned his situation and, having acquired a very handsome fortune in his profession, embarked for Europe on board the unfortunate *Grosvenor*. This ship left Bengal at a period when lunar observations were little known or practised. By their common reckoning they were within a degree or two of the latitude of Cape Lagullas, though several hundred miles to the eastward of it. They therefore stood on for the land with the utmost confidence; as was thought, too, in perfect security; but in the middle of the night the ship ran on shore upon the continent of Africa, where she was totally lost. At break of day, they found themselves within two miles of the shore, the sea breaking so heavily over the wreck that all expected every moment to perish. Nevertheless, by the exertions of the crew, aided by the Caffre inhabitants of that part of the coast, the greater part, with all the passengers except two children and some native female servants, reached the shore in safety. They were, however, instantly made prisoners of and conveyed a great distance inland. During their long and fatiguing march, two of the common seamen made their escape, and after undergoing incredible hardships succeeded in reaching the Cape of Good Hope. The fate of the rest of the sufferers has never been ascertained, although several persons were sent in search of them, but without success. This unfortunate event occurred in the year 1780 or 1781.

On 7th July, Mr. Ley, second mate of the *Chesterfield* Indiaman, who had been in the same situation on board the *Lord Mulgrave* when Pott was passenger, came to his house, in which from that day he continued a settled inmate, shamefully abandoning his profession when in the prime and vigour of life, to become an indolent dependant and toad-eater to Pott, in which disgraceful situation he remained for several years; indeed, until Pott, from losing his office as Resident at the Nabob's Court at Moorshedabad, could no longer afford to maintain him in sloth and idleness.

On the 8th, being told a gentleman wished to speak to me in private, I went into an antechamber, where I found Captain Samuel Cox, who, after the usual congratulations upon my being once more an inhabitant of Calcutta, expressed great concern that his first visit should be of so unpleasant a nature, but that attachment of a very long standing made it incumbent on him to accept the disagreeable office. After premising this much, he said he had called on the behalf of Mr. Nathaniel Bateman, who so strongly felt the language I had held towards him when personally present, as well as the contemptuous and disrespectful manner in which I had often spoken of him to various French officers, naval and military, whilst we were both residing at Trincomalee, that it rendered it imperiously necessary for him to demand of me satisfaction. His (Captain Cox's) business therefore was to request I would name time, place and weapons, for the meeting, unless, as he sincerely hoped might be the case, I made so violent a proceeding unnecessary by apologizing for what had passed. I instantly observed that anything in the way of apology from me was wholly out of the question, as I really and truly thought the illiberal and unhandsome behaviour of Mr. Bateman deserved all I had said of him. It was thereupon arranged that we should meet the following morning at sunrise, at the back of Belvidere House, at Alypore, with pistols, each attended by a friend; that he (Captain Cox) should accompany Mr. Bateman.

Upon the departure of my unpleasant visitor, I informed Pott of all that had occurred, entreating he would go with me, which he instantly consented to, saying, "By God, Bill, you shall shoot the dirty little rascal through the head. I have a delicate pair of Wogden's that will do his business effectually." This 8th July was to be an eventful day to me; for, whilst sitting after breakfast in Pott's verandah towards the river, I received a letter from Mr. John Lewis Auriol, the person who had made me a present of little Nabob previous to my embarking for England; in which letter, after complimenting me upon my marriage and safe return to India, he enquired about the boy he "lent me" to act as a servant during the voyage, adding that if I had no further occasion for him he should be glad to receive him back, being at that time greatly in want of his services. As Nabob had clearly been an absolute and unconditional gift of Auriol's, I felt somewhat vexed at so unexpected and unjust a claim. I knew Auriol to be a niggardly, parsimonious fellow in all his pecuniary transactions; but I could not have thought him capable of such deliberate meanness. Nabob had never been the least use to me as a servant. He had, however, been treated by myself and the whole of my family with the utmost generosity and kindness, which he repaid with the basest ingratitude; yet still I conceived he was personally attached to me; for which reason, although I considered him undeserving further attention, I resolved not to give him up to so different a master as Mr. Auriol would prove, unless he himself voluntarily consented to the change, which I own I thought impossible.

Sending for him into the verandah, I mentioned the purport of the letter I held in my hand, asking him if he had any recollection of his former master, Mr. Auriol, to which he answered, "Yes, he remembered him very well." My next question was whether, during the four years he had lived with me, he had not been treated in the most kind and indulgent manner by me and by every one of my family in England. He coldly replied, "Yes." I then said, "Mr. Auriol now desires to have you back, claiming you as his exclusive property. This he, undoubtedly, has no right to do; nor shall he have you unless you should be desirous of changing masters. Now, therefore, what say you? Will you stay with Mrs. Hickey and me, or do you prefer going to Mr. John Auriol?" Without a moment's hesitation, and with an exulting smile, he answered he had rather go to Mr. Auriol! Mr. Pott had before him a folio volume of the encyclopedia into which he had just been looking. So enraged was he at the little wretch's extraordinary ingratitude that, uttering a great oath, he let fly the immense volume at the young culprit's head; but it luckily missed him. I ordered the unfeeling boy out of sight, telling him he might go to Mr. Auriol's with the servant who had just brought me the letter.

I had but just dismissed Mr. Nabob when Durgachuru Muckerjee came in. Immediately producing the bond I had executed to him upon my departure for England, he observed the principal and interest then due upon it amounted to upwards of eight thousand rupees; which sum he should be glad if I would forthwith pay, and also provide myself with another banyan, as he did not choose any longer to be in the service of an attorney. As at no period of my life was I disposed to submit to insolence from any description of person, but more especially from a native of Asia, I told Master Durgachuru he was an impertinent scoundrel, bidding him leave the house as quickly as possible; otherwise I should order my servants to kick him out. He followed my advice without a moment's pause, proceeding from Mr. Pott's to his attorney's, whom he instructed to issue a writ of *capias ad satisfaciendem* against me, in consequence of which I was obliged to borrow the amount and discharge his demand.

Before daybreak of the 9th, I gently left Mrs. Hickey in a profound sleep; and, dressing myself in the next chamber, Pott, whom I found up and dressed, and I stepped into his post-chaise, driving to the appointed ground at Belvidere, distant about three miles. Mr. Bateman and Captain Cox arrived almost at the same instant that we did. The ground being measured (twelve paces) by the seconds, it was, after a short discussion, determined that we should toss up for the first fire. Mr. Bateman won, discharged his pistol and missed. I then fired mine, but equally without effect; whereupon Mr. Bateman said it was then the time for him to declare, upon his honour as a gentleman, he never had used any disrespectful expression either of me or Mrs. Hickey, neither by writing nor parolly, and that I had been entirely misinformed relative thereto, his language of complaint having been confined to the injustice and illiberality with which he and the two other English gentlemen, Messrs. Kemp and Brown, were treated by the French at Trincomalee; and that he had never even introduced my name, or made any comparison as to our relative treatment. Upon this declaration, so seriously made and at so momentous a time, the seconds interfered, a reconciliation instantly took place, when I felt not the least reluctance to apologize for the improper language I had used, and which I was now convinced I had used under the mistaken impression upon my mind. The seconds were much pleased with our respective conduct; Mr. Bateman and I shook hands; and thus we parted perfectly reconciled.

The 12th my London hairdresser, Frescini, arrived and took up his abode at Pott's as one of my establishment. He came from Europe in one of the China ships to Madras, and from thence in a small country vessel. I agreed to pay him one hundred sicca rupees a month, with board and lodging; besides which I gave him permission to dress as many ladies as he could without interfering with his attendance upon me. The remainder of the month passed in receiving and paying visits. Every evening, Pott drove Mrs. Hickey and me in his phaeton to the racecourse, where it was then the fashion for the carriages to draw up round the stand, the gentlemen and ladies passing half an hour in lively conversation.

As many of my former native clients had applied to me on matters of business, I was obliged to go to town daily, Mr. Tolfrey having very obligingly accommodated me with an apartment in his house to receive them. He, however, strongly urged me to fix myself in Calcutta as speedily as possible, being convinced I was losing a great deal of money by residing out of town and not being accessible at all times to the natives who were desirous of consulting me professionally. In the middle of August, I succeeded in getting a capital house in a central part of the town, and not far distant from the courthouse, which was particularly desirable to me, who was obliged to attend there daily in the execution of my business as an attorney. It was the property of an old woman, a Mrs. Brightman, who let it to me at three hundred sicca rupees a month, I binding myself to pay at that rate of rent for one year certain.

THE DEATH OF CHARLOTTE

Towards the end of the same month, the *Crocodile* frigate, or rather, I believe, sloop of war, commanded by Captain Williamson, who several years afterwards disgraced himself in the famous action with the Dutch on the Dogger Bank, he at that time commanding the *Agincourt*, arrived at Calcutta, having on board passengers from Europe, Sir William and Lady Jones. Sir William was appointed to fill the vacant seat on the Bench occasioned by the death of Mr. Justice Le Maitre, which happened so far back as the month of November 1777. The second morning after Sir William's arrival, Sir Elijah Impey sent a written paper in circulation to every gentleman belonging to the court, inviting them to breakfast at his apartments the following day, and proceed in a body from thence for the purpose of being individually introduced to the new judge, previous to his being sworn into office. The advocates, officers, and attornies in consequence obeyed the summons; but, as I did not choose, after Sir Elijah's reception of me, as already stated, to partake of his coffee or tea, I joined the cavalcade on their way from the courthouse to Sir Robert Chambers's, and in my turn was made known to Sir William Jones, who, upon my name being mentioned, said he believed we had formerly been schoolfellows at Harrow. I replied it was not me, but two elder brothers of mine who were there in his time.

We now heard of another battle having been fought between the British and French fleets, off Cuddalore, the issue of which, notwithstanding the superior condition of Sir Edward Hughes's ships over those of the enemy, was in no way creditable to the English, the most that we could say being that it was a drawn battle. No ship was taken or destroyed on either side; but the conflict was most sanguinary. I was greatly concerned to hear that in this action my worthy and respected friend the Chevalier de Salvert lost his life, being cut in two by a cannon-ball on the quarter-deck of the *Flamand* whilst gallantly fighting his ship, and encouraging her crew to use their utmost exertions to ensure success. I truly grieved at his death, notwithstanding he died fighting against my country; but that was no fault of his; and I firmly believe a better man never lived. Such are the dire and lamentable consequences of war, the best men often being the most unfortunate.

A rumour prevailed in Calcutta that the *Crocodile* had brought out Sir Elijah Impey's recall, in order to answer certain charges of having been guilty of several acts incompatible with his public station of Chief Justice of the Supreme Court; which charges it was intended to bring forward as soon as he arrived in England. This rumour proved to be well-founded, as Sir Elijah took his passage and embarked in the month of January.

Having furnished my house very handsomely, at an expense of upwards of twelve thousand rupees, including plate, we, on 1st September, went into it and commenced regular house-keepers, my Charlotte undertaking to manage the interior business. Upon thus settling in town, it became necessary for her to go through a disagreeable and foolish ceremony in those times always practised by newcomers of the fair sex, and which was called "setting up"; that is, the mistress of the house being stuck up, full-dressed, in a chair at the head of the best room (the apartment brilliantly lighted), having a female friend placed on each side, thus to receive the ladies of the settlement, three gentlemen being selected for the purpose of introducing the respective visitors, male and female; for every lady that called was attended by at least two gentlemen. One of the three gentlemen, receiving the hand of the fair visitor at the door, led her up to the stranger, announcing her name, whereupon curtseys were exchanged, the visitor accepted a proffered seat amidst the numerous circle; where after remaining five, or at most ten minutes, she arose, the salutations were again exchanged and the party retired to make way for the quick successor, this moving scene continuing from seven o'clock in the evening until past eleven. The same occurred the two following evenings, to the dreadful annoyance of the poor woman condemned to go through so tiresome and unpleasant a process. A further inconvenience attended this practice, which was the necessity of returning every one of the visits thus made. As the society of Calcutta increased in number, "setting up" became less frequent, and about the year 1786 ceased altogether, persons from thenceforward selecting their acquaintances according to liking, as in Europe. .

Upon my return to Bengal, I found my Margate acquaintance, Metcalfe, with the rank of major in the army, and filling the post of military storekeeper, a situation in those days the most lucrative in the Company's service, which he had attained by most perseveringly courting the heads of the Government. Shortly after his last arrival in Calcutta, he married Mrs. Smith, widow of Major Smith of the Company's Infantry, who was brother to the far-famed General Richard Smith of cheese-mongering celebrity, of which I have already spoken upon meeting him at the Governor of St. Helena's table when on my way home in the beginning of the year 1770.

This fair dame (who is now Lady Metcalfe, her husband having purchased the title of baronet) had no one merit to recommend her, at least that I could discover, unless it was a great similarity in figure, in masculine vulgarity of manners, to his ci-devant favourite, that notorious jack whore, Mrs. Cuyler. But, having expressed these unfavourable sentiments of the lady, it is only common candour to admit that everyone did not see with my eyes; for Mr. William Pawson, an old civil servant of the Company's upon the Bengal establishment, was so deeply enamoured with her charms that, although she had not a single guinea in the world, he proposed marrying and settling a handsome sum upon her, an offer she spurned at with the utmost scorn. Notwithstanding which, the unhappy lover persevered in his endeavours to make her relent, renewing his attack three different times, all equally unsuccessful.

He was as worthy a creature as ever breathed, but clearly not the brightest genius. In proof of which I must state that I was once present with him in a large company, where matrimony was the topic under discussion. After much had been said pro and con upon the subject, Mrs. Smith, looking full in Mr. Pawson's face, with a marked and peculiar manner, and in a sharp, angry voice, said, "I certainly cannot tell who is destined to be my future husband; but this I can confidently affirm, that I never will become the wife of *a fool!*" Poor Mr. Pawson, who was on the next chair to the one I sat in, thereupon turned to me and, with the utmost simplicity, accompanied by a long-drawn sigh, said, *"That's me!"*

Upon settling in Calcutta, I soon got into considerable practice; and I had the gratification to find that I gave general satisfaction to my employers and was sometimes complimented by the adverse party for my candour and liberality. I kept, as I had always done wherever I resided, the first company of the place, upon all occasions treating my inferiors with civility and respectful attention in their lines, but ever discouraging any attempts towards familiarity; and thus I retained the good opinion of all ranks. It being necessary to keep a carriage for Mrs. Hickey, I purchased a neat London-built chariot, for which I paid three thousand sicca rupees, a phaeton for my own use at eighteen hundred, and three excellent draught horses which cost me seventeen hundred and fifty, then considered a very reasonable price. All these heavy purchases, with the addition of wines and other liquors, always the most serious article in India, involved me in debt to an amount of upwards of forty thousand sicca rupees; for the whole of which I was obliged to pay an interest of twelve per cent per annum, a debt so heavy as to prove a load about my neck for full twenty years afterwards.

I was scarcely settled in my house in Calcutta ere my dearest Charlotte's health began visibly to decline, although, to my daily remarks thereon and entreaties that she would take care of herself and let me consult a physician, she invariably desired I would not do so; for that nothing ailed her that could be attended with danger, and she was sure the approaching cool weather would entirely carry off the trifling complaint she had. Whilst at Pott's country house, she had been more than once attacked with sudden and violent pains in her breast, upon which occasions I procured the medical assistance of Dr. James Wilson, who resided in the neighbourhood; when he gave me the comfortable intelligence that nothing was to be apprehended, the attacks being altogether nervous; and he agreed with her in thinking the change of weather would entirely restore her. This made me less uneasy than I otherwise should have been. The seeds of a fatal disease were, nevertheless, then lurking about her, the progress of which was probably hastened by the uninterrupted course of entertainments she was engaged in, and the late hours she necessarily kept in consequence; for all my old acquaintances and many new ones were abundantly civil.

Early in the month of November, the subscription assemblies for the season commenced. Beaux without number proffered their services to escort Mrs. Hickey, whom I endeavoured to dissuade from going, from her indifferent state of health; but my entreaties and arguments were all thrown away. Nothing short of a positive command would, I saw, be observed; and so strong a measure I did not like to use. She assured me she felt considerably better and stronger than she had been, and was quite sure it would do her no harm. All the ladies of her acquaintance encouraged her to be at least present, even if she had fortitude enough to resist dancing, an amusement she was remarkably fond of, and which she excelled in. Indeed, they could not see any serious objection to her partaking of a couple of dances; but that I did take upon me peremptorily to forbid.

Before the month of November was over, Mrs. Hickey's health became evidently worse, although she would not confine herself to the house, nor admit that she was so ill as to require either particular care or the advice of physicians. But I, who anxiously watched, perceiving an almost daily increased weakness and languor, insisted upon her receiving Doctor James Stark, then the favourite practitioner of Calcutta; and I accordingly summoned him. After asking her a variety of questions, he wrote a prescription, recommending her continuing quiet at home and not to have any large parties for some days at least. All which conditions she reluctantly yielded to. During her confinement, as my business necessarily occupied much of my time, I was glad to find our friends exceedingly attentive, several ladies coming to sit with her a great part of the day. Bob Pott often called, contributing much to raise and keep up her spirits by his extraordinary cheerfulness and vivacity. Very early in December, we were deprived of his agreeable society by his being appointed Chief of the District of Burdwan, a place about sixty-five miles distant from Calcutta, then considered one of the most lucrative situations in the civil service, but which Robert notwithstanding affected to dislike, and to be offended with Mr. Hastings for giving him so insignificant and *paltry* an office, he loudly declaring the Governor-General ought to have turned out Sir John D'Oyley from the residency at the Nabob's Durbar at Moorshedabad and put him into it, he having been nominated thereto by the Court of Directors, a presumption and expectation of Pott's that certainly was unreasonable in the extreme.

Upon my return from England in the year 1783, again settling in Calcutta and resuming the practice of an attorney, I applied to those gentlemen that had been members of the committee for conducting the business of the petition to Parliament for trial by jury in civil case, to reimburse me the expenses I had incurred in conveying such petition to England, etc.; some of which gentlemen were well-disposed to comply with my demand, considering the same as just and reasonable. At the head of those feeling and declaring their opinion thus, stood my zealous advocate upon all occasions, Colonel Watson. But Colonel Pearse, who had then just returned from the coast of Coromandel, Mr. Shore and others, opposing it—not, as they declared, from any personal enmity towards me, but from conceiving they were not individually liable to be so called upon—the just intentions of Colonel Watson and those equally well-disposed were frustrated. Two of my warmest friends also were lost to me, Mr. Cottrell being dead and Mr. Higginson embarked for Europe. Thus situated, I was driven to the necessity for applying to the Supreme Court for redress. But, previous to so doing, I prepared and submitted my case to counsel, therein truly stating every particular relative to it, especially that of having not only given up my time and professional assistance entirely to the committee for more than two months prior to my sailing for England, but having likewise disbursed large sums of money in paying the Keeper of the Records and different officers of the Court for a great variety of copies of official documents which it had been deemed requisite to procure in the progress of the petition, and which, had I made out a bill for as an attorney, would have amounted to more than the sum I now demanded.

Upon this case I got an opinion most clearly and decidedly in my favour, saying I was indisputably entitled not only to a pecuniary remuneration for my personal attendance and services upon the committee as an attorney, but also a complete reimbursement of all sums of money I had expended for the advancement of the object in hand; but that, as I had no written instrument to show the nature of the contract subsisting between me and the committee, I must necessarily have recourse to a Bill in Equity against those persons who had employed me, the prayer of which bill must be to compel them to a specific performance of their parol agreement made with me. I accordingly prepared a Bill of Equity, laying the draft thereof before Mr. Brix, an experienced advocate of the Court, for his perusal and signature, who returned it the ensuing day without making the least alteration, accompanying it with a complimentary letter, wherein he was pleased to say it was by far the ablest and best-drawn pleading that ever had been laid before him, to which therefore he affixed his name with peculiar satisfaction, feeling convinced I could not fail of obtaining that redress the hardships of my case so eminently called for.°

Just at that time, my dearest Charlotte's situation became more critical. I observed her daily becoming weaker. With anxiety inexpressible, I summoned Doctors Stark and Wilson to meet at my house and consult upon her case. They did so. The result was their advising me immediately to take her upon the river for a few days and try what effect change of air might produce. I caused a large and commodious boat to be forthwith prepared. On 7th December, carefully conveying her on board, we proceeded to Budge Budge, where my valuable friend Major Mestayer received us into his hospitable mansion with all his accustomed and kind liberality. During the first four-and-twenty hours of being there, my dear woman became somewhat better, but then rapidly fell off and, expressing much solicitude to be at home, on the fifth morning we re-embarked and returned to Calcutta, where I landed her vastly weaker than when she left it and in every respect worse. Still neither of the medical gentlemen considered her as being in actual danger. While I was at Budge Budge, Mr. Morse had been appointed Sheriff, which office he was to enter upon the duties on the 20th. According to his promise, he nominated me his Deputy or Under-Sheriff; but I was so engaged in watching my darling, whom I saw gradually and fast sinking, that I could think of nothing else. She would not allow that she was at all worse, though compelled to admit she suffered greatly. All patience and resignation, she bore a painful disease with a degree of fortitude unexampled, never when I was present uttering a complaint or even a sigh, lest it should increase my unhappiness.

On the 19th, Doctor Stark, for the first time, told me he apprehended his patient in extreme danger; that so alarming a change for the worse had taken place in the preceding night he saw no hope left, and her death, even in a few hours, would not surprise him. This was horrible tidings; nor can I attempt to describe the grief with which it overwhelmed me. During the succeeding night I never for a moment quitted her bedside, though she repeatedly urged me, in the strongest manner her enfeebled state would admit, to retire and take some rest. Rest, alas, was wholly out of the question. The 20th, she continued nearly the same. On that day, I was under the indispensable necessity of going out to the gaol to receive charge of the prisoners, civil and criminal, examine the lists and state of the prison, etc., etc., with the

° The case was submitted to arbitration, and Hickey's claim was settled by the committee early in 1784.

ex-Sheriff. Oh! what a morning did I pass. I scarcely knew what I said or did, and was in a constant tremor from the momentary expectation of the fatal event being announced.

The assignments and various deeds to which I was a party being executed, Mr. Morse considerately insisted upon my going home instead of to the sheriff's office, and not to bestow a thought on business until Mrs. Hickey should be better. Alas! too sure did I feel that time would never arrive, for that I was doomed to the misery of losing her. Upon going home, I found her nothing worse. On entering the room, she languidly smiled, held out her emaciated hand, saying she was not in quite so great pain. I could perceive this was only said for the purpose of comforting me. Thus she continued four more days. In the morning of the 25th (a fatal Christmas Day to my happiness) after about three hours of perturbed, uneasy sleep, procured from large doses of laudanum, she awoke; when, seeing me hanging over her in an agony of grief, she cast a mournful look upon me, then raised her poor arms and, drawing me towards her, kissed me with her almost clay-cold lips—such a kiss as I never can forget!

The effect of it is indelibly engraved upon my memory, never to be effaced! In a faint and scarcely audible voice, she bid me be comforted and submit to the fiat of the Almighty, said she had dreamt she had been delivered of eleven children, the terror of which had awakened her; that she should soon be well and relieved from excruciating suffering. After a long pause, she again entreated that I would not repine at what was unavoidable, adding, "God bless you, my dearest William, God bless you! Oh, leave me, leave me!" and fainted. The physicians entered at that moment; when Doctor Wilson exclaimed, " 'Tis all over. She's gone." This was the last I saw of her. They forced me from the apartment and the house. She continued to breathe, but without any other sign of existence, until ten o'clock at night, when with a gentle sigh she expired! It is those only who have truly loved, and survived to mourn the loss of all they held dear upon earth, that can conceive the agonies I endured. My sorrow yielded not to the exhortations of numerous friends who, with the most humane intention, endeavoured to console me, bidding me reflect that she was released and happy! But such reflections had no power to conquer my regret or reconcile me to the sad event. On the contrary, they increased, they embittered, the severity of my pangs. In many instances did I verify the truth of the observation "that, when we first conceive we clasp pleasure to our breast, we in fact invite the stings of pain."

Upon obtaining the uninterrupted possession of my adored Charlotte, I thought of naught but supreme felicity, a felicity that proved of short duration, being checked almost every day of my life by an anxiety the most excruciating and distressing on her account. When the cruel hand of death seized upon her, then it was I felt, oh most keenly felt, the horror of my situation and the dismal loss I had sustained in being suddenly deprived of so much excellence. Safely may I say, I truly, fondly, loved her, loved her with an affection that every new day, if possible, strengthened. Our tastes were similar; our foundations of happiness depended upon each other; kindred feeling was the standard of both, and we were perfectly satisfied each with the other. Her funeral took place on the 26th, every respectful attention being showed to her memory. Her remains were followed to its last sad mansion by a host of friends of both sexes, who sincerely loved and respected her living, and truly mourned her dead.

FINIS